BELIZE

LEBAWIT LILY GIRMA

Contents

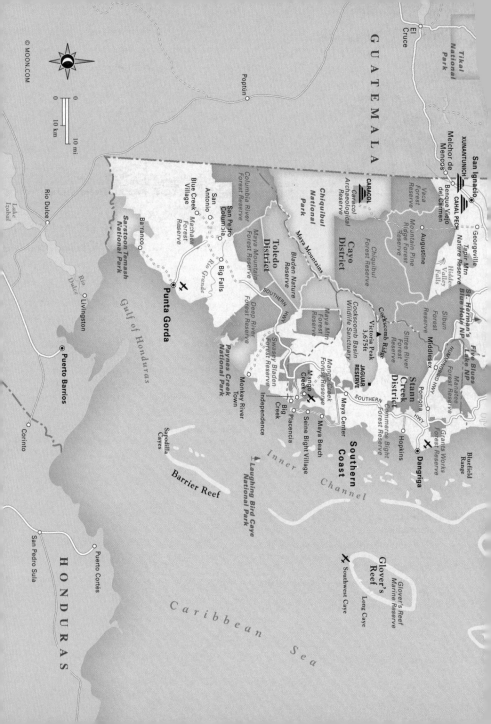

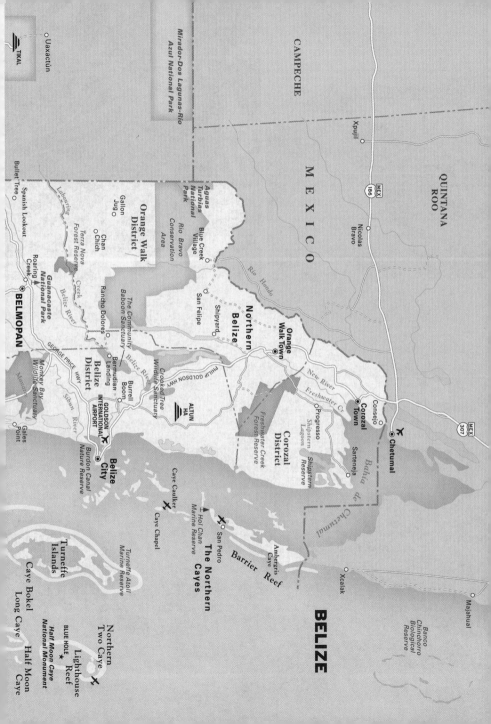

My first 10-day trip to Belize ended up lasting three weeks, courtesy of an extension and a stiff airline change fee. But I felt no remorse: This small country had surprised me with its mind-boggling diversity in both nature and culture.

"The Jewel," as Belizeans affectionately call their home, has a spectacular living reef—the second largest in the world—with premier diving and snorkeling. A handful of its 200 offshore islands offer the kind of seclusion and dreamlike surroundings that continue to provide both luxury and romance.

For those willing to explore deeper, the rewards are even richer. Virgin rainforests boast more than 30 percent protected land. The largest cave system and the tallest waterfall in Central America are here. Riverbanks are home to singing birds, giant iguanas, and roaming jaguars. Miles of turquoise Caribbean water and golden sand and a dazzling array of marinelife—from whale sharks to the rare seahorse—are the lures of the coast.

Clockwise from top left: dock in Caye Caulker; howler monkeys in the Toledo District; butterfly in the Cayo District; San Ignacio sunrise; scuba diver; waterfalls in Cristo Rey.

Beyond its natural wonders, Belize is an unexpected cultural and sensory feast. This is a Caribbean country at heart, with splashes of ancient Mayan, African, and European influences. That mélange underpins every aspect of life, from a cuisine of coconut rice and beans, tacos, and mashed plantains to annual celebrations of both Caribbean and Latin Carnivals.

In Belize, no two days are the same. Canoe down to the farmers market to sample fresh *pupusas*. Scour ancient Mayan ceremonial caves and cool off under waterfalls. Drink cashew wine from a Kriol vendor. Hike through rainforests filled with medicinal trees to the roar of howler monkeys. Laze around a beachfront village all day and dance barefoot to Garifuna drums at night.

A small country with a big heart, Belize will continue to surprise and teach you. That's the jewel you'll take home.

Clockwise from top left: Xunantunich Archaeological Site; Garifuna women on Hopkins Beach; sunset on The Split; waterfall in Cayo.

10 TOP
EXPERIENCES

1 **Dive and Snorkel:** The Belize Barrier Reef, the second longest in the world, is filled with over 300 species of fish and myriad opportunities for novice and expert divers and snorkelers. Explore the country's nine marine reserves—including **Half Moon Caye National Monument**—and three **coral atolls** (page 24).

2 **Caye Hop:** Belize's offshore plots range from vibrant, populated islands such as **Caye Caulker** (page 111) and **Ambergris Caye** (page 77) to isolated escapes such as **South Water Caye** (page 235) and diving-friendly favorites like the **Silk Cayes** (page 278).

3 **Feast on Belizean Cuisine:** Local dishes and drinks are a treat, whether **Kriol** (page 49), **Garifuna** (page 227), or **mestizo** (page 330).

4 **Experience Garifuna Culture:** Enjoy **Garifuna Settlement Day** (page 225) at dawn in Dangriga, or sign up for a **drumming** (page 239) or **culture class** (page 240) in Hopkins.

<<<

5 **Descend into the Underworld:** Venture inside **Actun Tunichil Muknal** (page 182) or **Barton Creek Cave** (page 192), fascinating chambers that once served as the Maya's underworld.

>>>

6 **Wander Mayan Archaeological Sites:** Belize is filled with magnificent reminders of its past at archaeological sites like **Altun Ha, Xunantunich,** and **Lamanai** (page 30).

<<<

7 **Hike through the Jungle:** Explore Belize's verdant terrain in areas such as the **Mountain Pine Ridge Forest Reserve** (page 197), **Mayflower Bocawina National Park** (page 254), and **Río Blanco National Park** (page 318).

>>>

8 **Watch Wildlife:** Choose your own animal adventure. Seek howler monkeys and iguanas at the **Community Baboon Sanctuary,** spot birds by boat at **Crooked Tree Wildlife Sanctuary,** or catch a glimpse of a jaguar at **Cockscomb Basin Wildlife Sanctuary** (page 26).

>>>

9 **Visit the Mayan Villages of Punta Gorda:** Experience a traditional homestay (page 300), or take a tour to see a day in the life of this ancient culture (page 292).

10 **Celebrate Independence:** Belize's month of independence overflows with cultural experiences, showcasing the country's unity and diversity in Belize City (page 46), San Pedro (page 93), and Orange Walk (page 329).

Planning Your Trip

Where to Go

Belize City

This stretch of coastline, islands, and swampy lowlands includes former capital **Belize City**, still the hub of Belizean city life and the heart of its colonial past. A few historic sights and events, such as **Carnival** (for Belizean Independence Day) and the **Museum of Belize**, make it worth a quick visit, even for a couple of hours. Whether or not you appreciate the city's unique grit and Caribbean texture, don't miss nearby attractions like **The Belize Zoo**, **Community Baboon Sanctuary** and surrounding Creole villages, **Crooked Tree Wildlife Sanctuary**, and **Altun Ha**.

The Northern Cayes

This group of islands is the most visited part of Belize. **Ambergris Caye** lures with swanky **beach resorts**, endless **bars**, and plentiful **restaurants**, and is the most tourist-heavy destination. **Caye Caulker**, just down the reef, offers a less dizzying pace with a palpable Caribbean vibe and opportunities for snorkeling at **The Split**, swimming with nurse sharks and rays at **Caye Caulker Marine Reserve**, or viewing manatees at **Swallow Caye Wildlife Sanctuary**. The northern atolls of the **Turneffe Islands** and **Lighthouse Reef** offer spectacular **wall diving**, beautiful beaches and birdlife, plus Jacques Cousteau's old favorite, the **Great Blue Hole**.

Belmopan and Cayo

Once the heart of the Mayan civilization,

Caye Caulker

population, with an Afro-Caribbean beat, cultural and outdoor activities, and a strategic location close to **Billy Barquedier National Park.** Just down the coast, tranquil **Hopkins** has long stretches of **beach** and plenty of dining and accommodation options, as well as a strong Garifuna vibe. Farther south, the **Placencia Peninsula** is the home of "barefoot perfect," 16-mile beaches and the low-key but touristy village of **Placencia.** The surrounding Stann Creek District offers some of the best hiking in Belize, including **Mayflower Bocawina National Park** in the Maya Mountains, through which five waterfalls cascade, and the world's only jaguar preserve at **Cockscomb Basin Wildlife Sanctuary,** a hiking haven. Off the coast of Dangriga, the Southern Cayes of **Tobacco Caye, South Water Caye,** and **Glover's Reef Atoll** offer spectacular diving and snorkeling, while **Laughing Bird Caye National Park,** off the coast near Placencia, is a World Heritage Site.

Punta Gorda and the Deep South

Forest and reef, river and ruins, caves and ridges—all await the small handful of visitors who get off the beaten path into the "deep south" of Belize. Whether you follow **Eladio Pop's Cacao Trail** through Punta Gorda or take a private drumming lesson at one of the Garifuna **drum schools,** find the opportunity to sign up with a **homestay program** in the Mayan villages, where you can immerse yourself in everyday life. The archaeological sites of **Lubaantun** and **Uxbenka** beg exploring, as do the beautiful waterfalls at **Río Blanco National Park** and **Blue Creek Cave.** Farther off the coast, **Sapodilla Cayes Marine Reserve** offers top-notch, uncrowded snorkeling and diving.

Northern Belize

Northern Belize is often skipped by travelers—unless they've heard about the gorgeous accommodations along the **New River,** lining the vast Mayan ruins of **Lamanai Archaeological Site,**

Belize's western interior offers a remarkable selection of outdoor activities. Explore the Mayan archaeological sites of **Xunantunich,** near **San Ignacio,** or **Caracol,** farther south. Wander the **Belize Botanic Gardens,** spelunk through **Actun Tunichil Muknal**—one of the world's most amazing caves—or overnight in a **jungle lodge** on the Macal River or in the **Mountain Pine Ridge,** where you can dip in several waterfalls. While the capital of **Belmopan** might not grab your attention, its surrounding countryside boasts the gorgeous **Banana Bank Lodge and Belize Horseback Adventure** and the beautiful **Hummingbird Highway,** snaking south through the district to some of the most beautiful parks, including **St. Herman's Blue Hole National Park,** and to iconic adventure lodge **Ian Anderson's Caves Branch.**

Southern Coast and Cayes

Dangriga is the center of Belize's **Garifuna**

or **Chan Chich Lodge,** a rainforest eco-lodge at the **Gallon Jug Estate,** where Belize's wildcats are often spotted. These are all set deep in the bush and as popular with birders and naturalists as they are with archaeologists and biologists. Aside from these draws are the hubs of **Orange Walk Town** and **Corozal.** Corozal is a great launching pad to nearby picturesque **Sarteneja,** home of Belize's traditional wooden sailboat building.

Before You Go

High and Low Seasons

High season is mid-December through May, a period many travel agents will tell you is the "dry season," in a vain effort to neatly contain Belize's weather patterns. In many years this is true, with sunny skies and green vegetation throughout the country during the North American winter. However, November can be dry and sunny, while December, January, and even February can play host to wet cold fronts that either blow right through or sit around for days. The weather has become more unpredictable each year, like most places in the world.

June, July, and August technically form the **rainy season**—which may mean just a quick afternoon shower or rain for days. This also means significantly discounted accommodations. August is most popular with European backpackers, while December and February are dominated by North Americans. Some tourism businesses shut down completely during the month of September and part of October, the peak of **hurricane season.**

Your best bet? Be prepared for clouds or sun at any time of year. A week of stormy weather may ruin a vacation planned solely around snorkeling, but it could also provide the perfect setting for exploring the rainforests or enjoying a hot tub in the Mountain Pine Ridge.

Tikatoo, the rescued jaguar, at the Banana Bank Lodge and Belize Horseback Adventure

- **Culture:** Visit Dangriga, Punta Gorda, and San Ignacio.

- **Diving and Snorkeling:** Visit the Northern Cayes and the Southern Coast.

- **A Honeymoon Spot:** Visit San Pedro in the Northern Cayes, book a jungle lodge in Cayo, or escape to Glover's Reef Atoll off the Southern Coast.

- **Adventure on a Budget:** Visit Caye Caulker, Cayo, or Hopkins.

- **A Family Vacation:** Visit Caye Caulker, Cayo, Burrell Boom, Crooked Tree Village, and Punta Gorda.

- **Wildlife:** Visit Crooked Tree Village, Cayo, the Southern Coast, or Orange Walk.

Passports and Visas

You must have a **passport** that is valid for the duration of your stay in Belize. You may be asked at the border (or airport immigration) to show a **return ticket** or ample money to leave the country. You do *not* need a visa if you are a citizen of a British Commonwealth country, Brazil, Belgium, Colombia, Denmark, Finland, Greece, Iceland, Italy, Japan, Liechtenstein, Luxembourg, Mexico, South Korea, Spain, Switzerland, Tunisia, Turkey, the United States, or Uruguay. Visitors for purposes other than tourism must obtain a **visa.**

Vaccinations

Technically, a certificate of vaccination against **yellow fever** is required for travelers older than one arriving from an affected area, though immigration officials rarely, if ever, ask to see one.

In general, your **routine vaccinations**—tetanus, diphtheria, measles, mumps, rubella, and polio—should be up to date. **Hepatitis A vaccine** is recommended for all travelers over age two and should be given at least two weeks (preferably four weeks or more) before departure. Hepatitis B vaccine is recommended for travelers who will have intimate contact with local residents or potentially need blood transfusions or injections while abroad, especially if visiting for more than six months. It is also recommended

for all health care personnel and volunteers. **Typhoid** and **rabies vaccines** are recommended for those headed for rural areas.

Transportation

The vast majority of travelers arrive in Belize by air at **Philip S. W. Goldson International Airport,** approximately 10 miles outside Belize City. From the airport, short domestic flight connections are available around the country. A few travelers fly into **Cancún** as a cheaper back door to Belize; once there, they board a bus or rent a car and head south through the Yucatán Peninsula to reach Belize or catch a bus and a boat over to the Northern Cayes. You can also fly Tropic Air from Cancún to Belize or Aeromexico from Mexico City to Belize.

Belize is small and extremely manageable, especially if you fly a **domestic airline** from tiny airstrip to tiny airstrip. You can also get around by **rental car, taxi,** or **bus,** which is most affordable. Another option is to let your resort or lodge arrange your airport transfer and pick a local tour company for your excursions.

Water taxis are another way to get around in Belize, especially to and from Ambergris Caye and Caye Caulker and the mainland; there are regular daily routes between Belize City and these islands.

The Best of Belize

A week provides just enough time to see a few of Belize's major destinations and get a taste for just how much more there is to discover. This trip includes plenty of self-guided activities, as well as some guided tours. One thing is certain: You won't run out of things to do and see!

Day 1

Arrive at the international airport just outside of Belize City. Hop on your connecting Tropic Air domestic puddle-jumper flight to laid-back **Caye Caulker**; stay camera-ready to capture the gorgeous views. After dropping off your bags at the hotel, schedule a snorkel trip to **Caye Caulker Marine Reserve** for the next day, then watch sunset at **The Split** and **Lazy Lizard Bar,** the island's social headquarters. Continue on with dinner alfresco at **Hibisca by Habanero**—pick the fresh catch of the day and relax on the outdoor veranda. Walk the sandy streets up to **I&I**

Reggae Bar for a drink on the rooftop and some island tunes, or head to **El Portal** at The Split for cocktails and dancing by the sea.

Day 2

Today you'll head out on a half-day morning **snorkel** trip to **Caye Caulker Marine Reserve's Shark Ray Alley.** Swim and snorkel alongside a dozen or more nurse sharks and stingrays, among other marinelife, and admire coral gardens. Back on the island, grab your things and catch the early afternoon water taxi to bustling **San Pedro.** Spend the rest of the day walking around San Pedro Town, with plenty of opportunities to shop, eat, swim, barhop, and be merry. Grab a romantic dinner at **Red Ginger** or Mayan specialties at **Elvi's Kitchen,** and end the night with drinks at the over-the-water **Palapa Bar and Grill.** If you're a night owl and it's the weekend, continue on to **Jaguar's Temple** nightclub.

Tobacco Caye

Flip-Flop Zones

With a coastline along the Caribbean Sea and more than a dozen offshore sandy islands, Belize has enough variety on and off the mainland to satisfy the most avid beachcomber. Though erosion has increased, as well as sargassum—you'll want to ask ahead what the beach status is where you're headed—there are still great places to enjoy a day of sun. The best stretches of beach are along Belize's east and south coasts and on the Southern Cayes. The following are the best sandy spots.

- **Half Moon Caye Wall:** On the southeast corner of Lighthouse Reef Atoll, crescent-shaped Half Moon Caye has a stunning beach dotted with palm trees and endless views of the Caribbean (page 140).

- **South Water Caye:** Easily reached from the coasts of Dangriga or Hopkins, this mile-long island remains one of the few spots in Belize where you can actually swim from beach to reef. The best stretch belongs to **Pelican Beach Resort** (page 235).

- **Hopkins Village:** On the eastern coast of Belize, this long stretch of beach is perfect for morning walks and jogs (page 242).

- **Placencia Village's Point:** The 16-mile-long Placencia Peninsula in southern Belize has been dubbed "barefoot perfect," but head to the Point for a lovely beach corner and clear water (page 260).

- **Silk Cayes Marine Reserve and Laughing Bird Caye National Park:** These protected marine reserves are ideal for sunning and swimming in glorious turquoise

life in Hopkins Village

Caribbean waters. Both are also popular snorkeling and dive spots (pages 278 and 280).

- **Ranguana Caye:** Gorgeous turquoise waters and fine white sands surround this private two-acre island just 18 miles from Placencia (page 281).

- **Sapodilla Cayes:** The remote Sapodilla Cayes' **Lime Caye** and **Hunting Caye** have beautiful turtle-nesting beaches (Oct.-Apr.). You'll likely be the only one burying your toes beneath the fine white sand (page 307).

Day 3

Catch the first water taxi to Belize City. Stash your bags at the water taxi terminal while you explore the **Swing Bridge,** the **Fort George** area, and the **Museum of Belize** for an hour. Transfer to the **Cayo District** by bus, shuttle, or car. As you travel along the George Price Highway, visit the **The Belize Zoo** or stop for a hike at **Guanacaste National Park,** near Belmopan. Overnight at a lodge in **Bullet Tree Falls,** or head to downtown **San Ignacio** and settle into your guesthouse or stay at **Cahal Pech Village** resort, with stunning views and access to nearby ruins. For more solitude, opt for **Black Rock Lodge,** one of the area's remote jungle lodges. Spend the evening strolling the mellow town, then grab food at **Crave House of Flavors** on West Street.

With nine protected marine reserves, Belize's claim to tourism fame is diving. Many visitors are eager to explore the wonders of the second-largest coral reef in the world. The Belize Barrier Reef stretches approximately 155 miles north to south and is its own underwater ecosystem, also including three atolls.

- **Hol Chan Marine Reserve:** Belize's most-visited marine site is worth a stop when staying on the Northern Cayes. Highlights include **Shark Ray Alley** and the **Coral Gardens** (page 79).

- **Turneffe Atoll:** This popular snorkel and dive destination is a protected marine reserve with two don't-miss dive sites: **The Elbow** (page 135) and **Gales Point** (page 137).

- **Lighthouse Reef:** Lighthouse Reef Atoll is among Belize's favorite diving destinations, home to the **Great Blue Hole** (page 138), **Half Moon Caye Wall** (page 140), and **Long Caye Aquarium** (page 140).

- **South Water Caye Marine Reserve:** Whether off **Tobacco Caye** or **South Water Caye,** there is plenty of marinelife to explore (page 231).

- **Glover's Reef Atoll:** Belize's southernmost atoll spans nearly 80 square miles and is home to fantastic marinelife (page 236).

- **Gladden Spit and Silk Cayes Marine**

snorkeling near the Northern Cayes

Reserve: Come for that elusive, once-a-year (Mar.-June) whale shark experience (page 278).

- **Sapodilla Cayes Marine Reserve:** Sapodilla Cayes are as remote and exclusive as it gets. Top spots include **Lime Caye Wall, Ragged Caye,** and **The Shipwreck,** a massive sunken ship surrounded by abundant marinelife (page 307).

Days 4-5

Rise early and visit the Mayan ruins of **Xunantunich,** on foot, by mountain bike, or on horseback. Or opt instead for a canoe trip up the **Macal River.** Depending on the water level, you might make it to the **Belize Botanic Gardens.** If you're more adventurous, spend the day on an exhilarating cave trip to **Actun Tunichil Muknal** in the Tapir Mountain Nature Reserve, or find "**the showers**" waterfalls in **Cristo Rey.**

The next day, venture past the Vaca Reservoir

on a **pontoon boat adventure,** or you could enjoy a ride along the **Mountain Pine Ridge** to the Mayan ruins of **Caracol.** Along the way, take a dip at **Río On Pools** or get more off the beaten path with a short hike to **Big Rock Falls,** where you can cool off in a jade pool. Stop at **Calico Jack's Village** for a unique zip-line experience or for a photo op at **Thousand Foot Falls,** one of the highest waterfalls in Central America.

Day 6

Inland or island? A couple of puddle-jumper

flights—or a drive down the Hummingbird Highway—will get you to **Dangriga**. Take an afternoon trip to **Cockscomb Basin Wildlife Sanctuary,** where you can hike through the rainforest past fresh jaguar tracks and chill in waterfalls under a green canopy. Overnight here for night walks or sunrise hikes. You could also end the night with dinner back in Dangriga at **Pelican Beach Resort** and head to town for cold beers and dominoes under a thatch cabana at **Wadani Shed.** Island lovers could instead hop on a boat and transfer to nearby **Tobacco Caye** or **South Water Caye** for diving and snorkeling along the pristine southern barrier reef and some blissful beach time. These islands are oh-so-stunning and romantic.

Day 7

Take a Tropic Air puddle-jumper flight back to Belize City, and start planning your return.

Extend Your Stay

From Dangriga, catch the first bus down to **Hopkins** and soak in some Garifuna culture, go beachcombing, and enjoy fine dining. Sign up for a drumming lesson at **Lebeha Drumming Center** or a half-day Garifuna culture and cooking class at **Palmento Grove Cultural & Fishing Lodge.** Bury your toes in the sand while enjoying a traditional Garifuna meal at **Laruni Hati Beyabu Diner,** or wine and dine at **Chef Rob's Gourmet Cafe.** Spend the next day fishing, lazing in a hammock, or bicycling through Hopkins to the nearby village of **Sittee River.**

For Adventure Junkies

With pristine coral reefs, epic mountains, and teeming rainforests, Belize is the ideal destination for outdoor adventure. Get your heart racing by exploring the largest cave system in Central America, more than 11 national parks, and numerous forest and marine reserves and wildlife sanctuaries.

Bag a Peak

Arrange a summit hike of **Victoria Peak,** the second-highest point in Belize at 3,675 feet, through the Audubon Society. The steep three-to four-day trek (30 miles round-trip, Feb.-May only) starts from **Cockscomb Basin Wildlife Sanctuary,** near Maya Centre. You'll be one of the few to reach the summit, where you can celebrate with a panoramic view of Belize's coastline.

Climb a Waterfall

Thrill seekers will love rappelling their way down **Mayflower Bocawina National Park**'s five stunning waterfalls of varying heights—from the "smaller" **Bocawina Falls,** at a height of 125 feet, to the 1,000-foot **Big Drop Falls.** If you only venture to one, make it **Antelope Falls.**

In the Toledo District, take a refreshing swim in the gorgeous waterfall pool at the **Río Blanco National Park**—after cliff diving from the top of the waterfall.

Belize's claim to fame is the second-largest barrier reef in the world, most of which is a designated UNESCO World Heritage Site, home to some of the top dive sites. **The Great Blue Hole** is the holy grail of diving. This circular sinkhole, with depths of more than 400 feet, is not for novices. Prepare to roam through caverns and around stalactites and, if you're lucky, hang out with nine-foot gray Caribbean reef sharks.

Go Underground

Spelunking in ancient Mayan caves is a must in Belize. **Actun Tunichil Muknal** tops the list, but there are numerous caves worth exploring. The **Waterfall Cave,** in the Cayo District, won't disappoint. Located at **Ian Anderson's Caves Branch Adventure Company and Jungle Lodge,** it's a long hike through a dry cave with low ceilings. The reward is a waterfall that topples over the rocks; the brave can climb up the

Filled with national parks and wildlife reserves, Belize is home to an estimated 145 mammal species, 139 reptile species, and at least 500 bird species.

- **Community Baboon Sanctuary:** Spot howler monkeys, birds, iguanas, and armadillos at this sanctuary in Bermudian Landing, less than an hour's drive from Belize City (page 62).

- **Belize Audubon Society:** In addition to managing Belize's protected areas and wildlife reserves, the society also runs top birding hot spots like **Crooked Tree Wildlife Sanctuary** (page 66) and **Half Moon Caye National Monument** (page 140).

- **The Belize Zoo:** Located outside Belize City, this delightful zoo is home to the country's native animals (page 70).

- **Caye Caulker Forest Reserve Estuary:** A short boat ride from the island, this portion of Caye Caulker's North Forest Reserve is a habitat of crocodiles—who lay and hatch their eggs here—birds, spiders, and iguanas (page 113).

- **Tropical Wings Nature Center:** Near San José de Succotz, this center has one of the highest numbers of butterfly species (page 188).

- **Green Hills Butterfly Ranch and Botanical Collections:** In the Cayo District, this butterfly breeding, education, and research center sits on Mountain Pine Ridge Road (page 193).

- **Cockscomb Basin Wildlife Sanctuary:** Increase your chance of an encounter with a jaguar, puma, margay, tapir, or ocelot with a hike or overnight stay (page 256).

Crooked Tree Wildlife Sanctuary is a birding hot spot.

- **Fallen Stones Butterfly Farm:** An exclusive visit here is for guests of Hickatee Cottages only (page 302).

- **Río Blanco National Park:** Beautiful butterflies and birds flutter away in Punta Gorda's pristine park (page 318).

- **Chan Chich Lodge:** On the Gallon Jug Estate, lodge guests list their numerous wildlife sightings on a community chalkboard (page 341).

rocks and jump down into the refreshing pool. While you're there, go for your next thrill: Ian Anderson's **Black Hole Drop,** an unforgettable full-day experience of rigorous hiking followed by rappelling 400-feet into the rainforest, landing at the entrance of a cave.

Cave tubing is as thrilling as it gets. This popular activity involves floating on a river in a large rubber inner tube as you pass through cavernous chambers and rainforest, dodging stalactites and rocks as a helmet lamp lights your way. The most exciting cave tubing experience is on the **Caves Branch River,** in the Cayo District, or on the **Mopan River.**

Cockscomb Basin Wildlife Sanctuary

Hike the Rainforest at Night

The thrill of a night rainforest hike is unlike any other. You haven't experienced the rainforest until you see it come alive in the dark of night, guided only by your flashlight. You can hike **Cockscomb Basin Wildlife Sanctuary**'s trails after dinner with Belize Audubon Society naturalists, where you might just spot a jaguar; or **Ian Anderson's Caves Branch Adventure Company and Jungle Lodge** and **Pook's Hill Lodge** offer nighttime hikes and tours, such as night canoeing on a lake or river—talk about an adrenaline rush!

Swing Through the Rainforest

In Cayo's **Mountain Pine Ridge,** the folks at **Calico Jack's Village** challenge you to go for *el columpio,* the jungle swing. Grab hold of a rope from the top of a re-created Maya pyramid and swing 200 feet up in the air into rainforest oblivion.

Belizean Roots

Belize is a cultural melting pot, where descendants of ancient civilizations and unique ethnic groups peacefully coexist. Immerse yourself in Belize's diverse population—which includes Kriol, Garinagu (the collective noun for Garifuna), Maya, mestizo, Mennonite, East Indian, Chinese, and even Lebanese—to get the most of local culture. Listen to Kriol, dance to African drums, sample Mayan corn tortillas, tour a Garifuna temple, or attend one of many carnival festivals.

Day 1

Arrive in **Belize City** and sample your first plate of stew chicken with rice and beans at **Deep Sea Marlin's Restaurant & Bar.** Gaze

Rhythms of Belize

Belize's annual bashes are the perfect way to glimpse Belizeans' celebratory spirit and get a taste of the music—more than six genres, each unique to a particular region and culture.

- **Summer Fiestas** (July): Towns celebrate their patron saints with giant fairs, games, concerts, and plenty of outdoor grills all set up inside the town stadium. Visit **Benque Viejo del Carmen's Benque Fiesta, Orange Walk's Fiestarama,** and **Ambergris Caye's Día de San Pedro.**

- **Deer Dance Festival** (Aug.): **San Antonio Village** showcases all things Maya. The highlight is a deer dance costume performance (an ancient ritual reenacting the hunting of a deer) set to traditional Mayan harps.

- **Pan Yaad** (Sept.): This lively steel pan concert is a treat, with up to five bands from around Belize performing in the heart of **Belize City.**

- **Carnival** (mid-Sept.): **Belize City** hosts a colorful Caribbean Carnival. Orange Walk Town's mestizo-themed **Orange Walk Carnival** is just as popular and held on September 21, Belize's Independence Day. **San Pedro** celebrates its carnival in February.

- **Garifuna Settlement Day** (Nov. 19): **Dangriga** turns into a massive street party on the eve of Garifuna Settlement Day. Don't miss the drumming and *punta* dancing at Wadani Shed. The merriment continues into the next

marching band performing at Fiestarama

day with the reenactment at sunrise and street parades.

- *Brokdong Bram* (Dec.): A traditional *brokdong bram* celebration takes place in the village of **Gales Point** and in **Burrell Boom** at Christmastime. *Brokdong* is a festive Creole genre blending various instruments, including drums, maracas, banjo, and even the jawbone of an ass.

over Haulover Creek as you listen to daily Kriol chatter drowning out the reggae music. Take a leisurely afternoon stroll to the **Government House and House of Culture** to soak in the colonial history, then cross the street to admire **St. John's Anglican Cathedral.** Catch a taxi to enjoy a quiet early evening alfresco at **Bird's Isle Restaurant** for fresh seafood and Creole specialties.

Day 2
Rise early and go for a Creole breakfast at **Black Orchid Resort** in **Burrell Boom,** a riverside lodge where you can listen to the monkeys howling above the Belize River. Continue on with a boat ride down this historic waterway; or you could catch a taxi ride to the **Community Baboon Sanctuary** in nearby Bermudian Landing, where you'll hike, learn about Kriol culture, and explore local villages. Grab some fresh cashew wine from a roadside vendor (but save the drinking for later). Pitch a tent at the Community Baboon Sanctuary, arrange a homestay with a local family, or head back to Black Orchid for the night.

Day 3

Travel south to **Dangriga** on the Southern Coast. Dangriga is the "culture capital of Belize," where a mere walk in town is indeed a cultural experience. Stop at **Y-Not Island** beach, where you might catch Garifuna drum makers at work, or simply stroll the waterfront. Grab a local lunch with views at **Pelican Beach Resort,** then head to **Wadani Recreation Centre** (known as "Wadani Shed") at sunset to throw back a Guinness and watch the locals play dominoes. Better yet, stay late to catch some live drumming if you're there in November. Before the day ends, schedule a next-day trip to **Sabal Farm,** the only cassava-making farm in the country.

Day 4

Start your morning at the **Gulisi Garifuna Museum** and take in some history on this Afro-Caribbean culture. Afterward, tour the **Marie Sharp's Store and Factory** and learn why her hot sauce bottles are on every tabletop and in every restaurant in Belize. Don't forget to sample her jams, too. Save the afternoon for your prearranged trip to nearby **Sabal Farm.**

Days 5-6

Catch a bus south and hop off at the village of **Maya Centre.** Julio Saqui can give you a guided tour of the **Maya Centre Maya Museum,** where you'll learn about Mayan culture through displays and live presentations. Walk or get a ride to **Nu'uk Che'il Cottages and Hmen Herbal Center,** run by Aurora Garcia Saqui, niece of the late illustrious Maya healer Elijio Panti. Tour the four-acre botanical garden and medicine trail, then overnight on-site or ask about a **village homestay.**

The next day, book a healing session or massage, attend a seminar on Mayan herbal medicine, or explore the nearby **Cockscomb Basin Wildlife Sanctuary**'s numerous trails and a handful of waterfalls.

Day 7

Hop on a bus north to sleepy **Hopkins** and take a well-deserved beach break. Hopkins's

making *hudut* in Hopkins

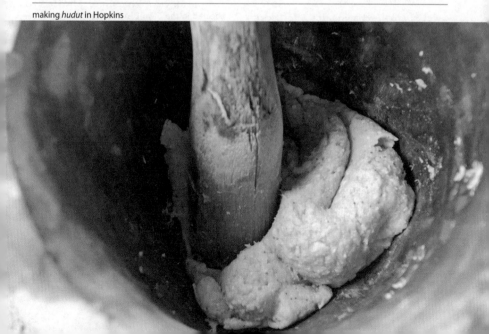

The Mundo Maya

It's estimated that at the height of the Classic Period, the area known as Belize was home to at least one million Maya. Today, Belize is home to 11 partly or fully excavated, protected Mayan archaeological sites. Each had an intricate role in Mayan history and architecture. The **Belize Institute of Archaeology** (NICH, www.nichbelize.org) manages all archaeological sites.

- **Altun Ha:** This ancient trading center, surrounded by rainforest and vines, is where the largest jade head carving in the Mayan world was discovered (page 60).

- **Caracol Archaeological Site:** Belize's largest and most impressive Mayan site sits deep in the Chiquibul Forest Reserve, with several pyramids, including the tallest countrywide, Canaa, reaching 136 feet above the plaza floor. It is believed that Caracol toppled neighboring Tikal and shut it down for more than a century (page 199).

- **Lamanai Archaeological Site:** Besides the impressive temples engraved with jaguar heads, the boat ride on the New River to Lamanai and the surrounding rainforest are ideal for birding and wildlife-watching (page 335).

- **Uxbenka Archaeological Site:** This is Belize's oldest Mayan city dating back over 2,000 years, where at least six carved stelae were found, including one dating from the Early Classic Period (page 317).

- **Marco Gonzalez Maya Site:** Ongoing

Xunantunich Archaeological Site

excavations at this site on Ambergris Caye turn up exciting discoveries each year (page 80).

- **Xunantunich Archaeological Site:** Located in the Cayo District, Xunantunich is easily one of the most scenic sites in Belize. This ancient ceremonial center has the second-tallest temple, El Castillo, at 135-feet high (page 188). Stop by the smaller **Cahal Pech Archaeological Site,** a 10-minute walk from downtown San Ignacio (page 163).

beaches are some of the best in the country—pick a spot along the thick, golden stretch and gaze out at the calm sea. If you see piles of sargassum, hop on a snorkel boat trip to the nearby cayes for clean beaches and turquoise waters. When you get hungry, find **Laruni Hati Beyabu Diner** and sample Marva's plate of *hudut*, a signature Garifuna dish, or go to **Tina's Kitchen,** another favorite. Claim your hammock or simply sit on your porch at **Coconut Row Guest House** for a relaxing overnight stay.

Extend Your Stay

Stay in Hopkins or immerse in the deep south? Grab breakfast at **Tina's Kitchen** (her fry jacks are also some of the best I've had in Belize); ask about her weekly Garifuna specialties. Experience a Garifuna culture day with **Palmento Grove Cultural & Fishing Lodge,**

Hopkins beachfront at Coconut Row Guest House

for a combination of kayaking, a cooking class in a traditional kitchen, and fishing. At night, go for some live Garifuna drumming on Tuesday at **Driftwood Beach Bar and Pizza Shack.** Hop over to neighboring **South Water Caye** on a snorkeling trip and marvel at the southern barrier reef's splendor. End the night in Hopkins by wining and dining at the talented **Chef Rob's Gourmet Cafe.** You could also head directly to Punta Gorda and experience a **Mayan village homestay,** or get a full Mayan culture experience day in Indian Creek Village—complete with cooking and cacao making—through **EcoTourism Belize.**

Belize City

Belize City is often a visitor's introduction to the country. While the views you catch exiting the airport may not match your image of an exotic destination, it isn't long before the landscape starts to live up to expectations.

The nation's most populated district packs a lot in its punch: the hustle and bustle of Belize City, lush mangroves and crocs of the Old Belize River, black howler monkeys of the Community Baboon Sanctuary, and Mayan archaeological site Altun Ha.

Although it hasn't been the capital since 1961, Belize City remains central to the life of Belizeans. While it may lack beaches and the pretty ocean views of the cayes, it has plenty to offer, giving a more complete view of the country's historical background. At the heart of the

Highlights

Look for ★ to find recommended sights, activities, dining, and lodging.

★ **Fort George:** Take a stroll through this breezy seaside neighborhood with its ramshackle colonial homes, old hotels, restaurants, and cafés (page 37).

★ **Museum of Belize:** Housed in the old prison, this museum has rotating exhibitions, an incredible stamp collection, and displays of Mayan history that make it worth a visit (page 40).

★ **Carnival:** Belize City is at its most festive in September, when Belizeans celebrate their independence from Great Britain. The Caribbean float parade is a highlight (page 46).

★ **Altun Ha:** Head north to this ancient Mayan trading center, the most extensively excavated—and the most visited—ruins in Belize (page 60).

★ **Community Baboon Sanctuary:** This ecotourism sanctuary offers an adventurous menu of wildlife hikes, nighttime canoe trips, and Creole culture (page 62).

★ **Crooked Tree Wildlife Sanctuary:** One hour north of Belize City is this wondrous habitat for hundreds of resident and migratory birds (page 66). After birding, explore new community experiences such as a botanical garden tour or a Kriol cooking class.

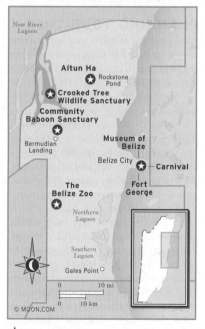

★ **The Belize Zoo:** See animals native to Belize housed in natural environments and learn of efforts to preserve the country's jaguars (page 70).

country's British colonial past, Belize City is the center of Creole culture and commerce, offering museums, art, markets, and authentic eateries. The rice-and-beans shacks, boisterous fish markets, men playing dominoes in the park, roadside drink stalls, and slow-paced surrounding villages give this district a distinctly Caribbean feel.

Thanks to the city's central coastal location, nowhere is too far, making Belize City a hub for exploring the country. Transportation options are plentiful—from water taxis to the Northern Cayes to buses and flights connecting other major jumping-off points. And if Belize City itself fails to appeal on first glance, its outskirts will surprise. A visit here means proximity to inland hiking and wildlife-watching—from crocs to howler monkeys or maybe even a jaguar—and a multitude of options for nearby escapes or adventures.

PLANNING YOUR TIME

An exploration of Belize City is a must for anyone interested in a bigger picture of the country—even if you have only a few hours between bus and boat connections. You can see the sights in one rushed day (or two relaxed ones) and get a sense of the true Caribbean, or "Kriol," spirit of this town. It's fairly easy to get to and from the main city sights on foot, but you could also sign up for a day tour. Favorite stops include the **Belize Museum, House of Culture,** busy Swing Bridge area leading to downtown **Albert Street** (with its lovely views of sailboats), and seaside **BTL Park,** with its gorgeous lawn and food kiosks. Although Belize City lacks the evolved dining scene of more touristed parts of the country, there are enough decent restaurants and authentic local eateries to get by, including the country's best Creole cuisine. Most of the sights are between Regent and Albert Streets or along the Philip Goldson Highway, and upscale hotels can be found in the historic Fort

George neighborhood, near the city center. Avoid walking or going anywhere outside of these areas.

If you have more time, you might explore the city's surroundings, which offer plenty of nature, wildlife, and history. Spend an afternoon at **The Belize Zoo**—enjoyed by adults and children—or the **Community Baboon Sanctuary,** both a mere hour away by car and easily reached by bus. Hop on a **river tour** for wildlife-spotting or hike the Mayan site of **Altun Ha.**

ORIENTATION

The old **Swing Bridge** spans Haulover Creek, connecting Belize City's Northside to its Southside, and it is the most distinct landmark in the city. North of the bridge and creek, **Queen Street** and **Front Street** are the crucial thoroughfares. On this side of the bridge, you'll find the **Ocean Ferry Water Taxi Terminal,** an important transportation and information hub. On Front Street, across from the water taxi, are the post office and the library, which has a quiet sitting room and Internet access. Walking east on Front Street toward the sea, you'll find several art galleries and shops before you come to the second water taxi terminal to the north cayes, the **San Pedro Belize Express,** and to the **Tourism Village,** the hopeful, Disneyesque name for the cruise ship passenger arrival area, its access closed to the outside world. The rest of the adjoining Fort George historic area is, in contrast, genuine and interesting to see. Some of the higher-end restaurants and best cafés are also here.

On the Swing Bridge's south end, **Regent Street** and **Albert Street** make a V-shaped split and are the core of the city's banking and shopping activity. There are a few old government buildings here too, as well as Battlefield (Central) Park and a couple of guesthouses. Southside has a seedier reputation than Northside (aside from downtown, don't go

---

Previous: black-collared hawk on Crooked Tree Lagoon; Fort George; Crooked Tree Village offers a glimpse of real Kriol life.

Belize District

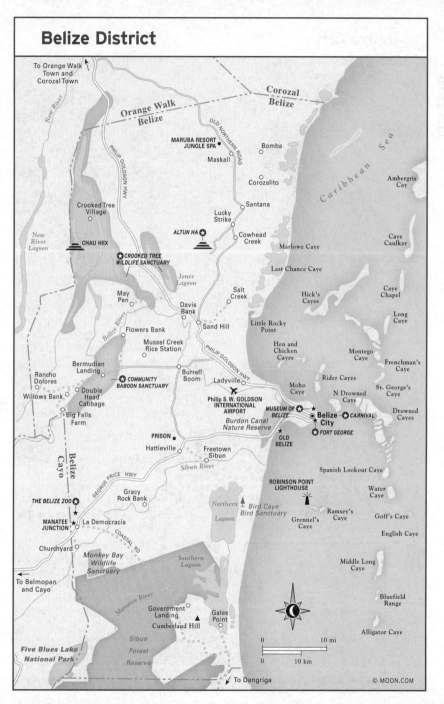

To Orange Walk Town and Corozal Town

New River

Orange Walk Belize

Corozal Belize

PHILIP GOLDSON HWY

OLD NORTHERN ROAD

MARUBA RESORT JUNGLE SPA

Maskall

Bomba

Corozalito

Santana

Lucky Strike

Caribbean Sea

Ambergris Cay

Cave Caulker

Crooked Tree Village

New River Lagoon

CHAU HIIX

ALTUN HA

Cowhead Creek

Marlowe Caye

CROOKED TREE WILDLIFE SANCTUARY

Jones Lagoon

Salt Creek

Last Chance Caye

Caye Chapel

May Pen

Davis Bank

Hick's Cayes

Long Caye

Belize River

Flowers Bank

Sand Hill

Little Rocky Point

Mussel Creek Rice Station

PHILIP GOLDSON HWY

Hen and Chicken Cayes

Montego Caye

Frenchman's Caye

Rancho Dolores

Bermudian Landing

Burrell Boom

Ladyville

Rider Cayes

St. George's Caye

Willows Bank

COMMUNITY BABOON SANCTUARY

Moho Caye

N Drowned Caye

Double Head Cabbage

Philip S. W. GOLDSON INTERNATIONAL AIRPORT

MUSEUM OF BELIZE

Belize City

CARNIVAL

Drowned Cayes

Big Falls Farm

Burdon Canal Nature Reserve

FORT GEORGE

Belize Cayo

PRISON

OLD BELIZE

Hattieville

Freetown Sibun

Sibun River

Spanish Lookout Caye

GEORGE PRICE HWY

Gracy Rock Bank

Northern Lagoon

Bird Caye Bird Sanctuary

ROBINSON POINT LIGHTHOUSE

Water Caye

THE BELIZE ZOO

MANATEE JUNCTION

La Democracia

COASTAL RD

Ramsey's Caye

Grennel's Caye

Goff's Caye

Churchyard

Monkey Bay Wildlife Sanctuary

Southern Lagoon

English Caye

To Belmopan and Cayo

Middle Long Caye

Manatee River

Government Landing

Cumberland Hill

Gales Point

Bluefield Range

Five Blues Lake National Park

Sibun Forest Reserve

Alligator Caye

0   10 mi

0   10 km

To Dangriga

© MOON.COM

Belize City

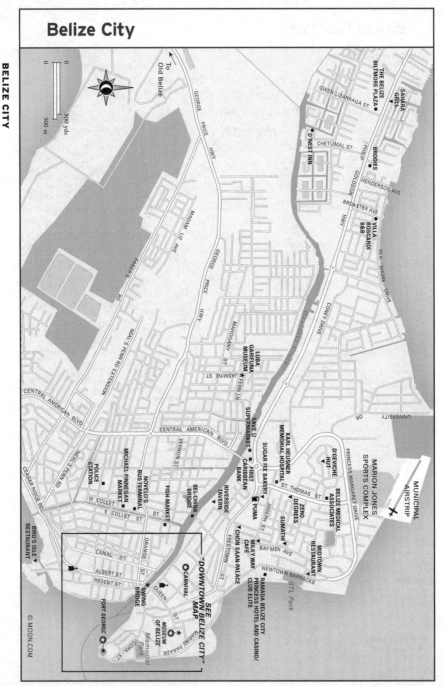

0
0
500 yds
500 m

To
Old Belize

THE BELIZE
BILTMORE PLAZA ●
SAHARA
GRILL ●
GWEN LIZARRAGA ST
BRODIES ●
CHETUMAL ST
D'NEST INN ●
PHILIP
GOLDSON
HENDERSON AVE
BROASTER AVE
VILLA
BOSCARDI
B&B ●
SEA SHORE DRIVE
GEORGE PRICE HWY
MADAM LIZ AVE
FABER'S RD
NEAL'S PENN RD EXTENSION
GEORGE PRICE HWY
CONEY DRIVE
MAHOGANY ST
LUBA
GARIFUNA
MUSEUM ★
JASMINE ST
FERN LN
CENTRAL AMERICAN BLVD
CENTRAL AMERICAN BLVD
UNIVERSITY DR
UNIVERSITY
MARION JONES
SPORTS COMPLEX
MUNICIPAL
AIRSTRIP
SAVE U
SUPERMARKET ■
SUGAR FIX BAKERY ●
FIRST
CARIBBEAN
BANK ■
KARL HEUSNER
MEMORIAL HOSPITAL ■
D'CEVICHE
HUT ▲
PRINCESS MARGARET DRIVE
BELIZE MEDICAL
ASSOCIATES ■
ST. THOMAS ST
ZERO
DEGREES ▲
JOSEPH ST
SUMATHI ▲
MIDTOWN
RESTAURANT ▲
BTL Park
VERNON ST
POLICE
STATION ■
MICHAEL FINNEGAN
MARKET ■
NOVELO'S
BUS TERMINAL ■
FISH MARKET ■
BEL-CHINA
BRIDGE
RIVERSIDE
TAVERN ▲
PUMA ●
CHON SAAN PALACE ▲
MILKY WAY
CAFE ▲
BAYMEN AVE
FREETOWN ST
NEWTOWN BARRACKS
RAMADA BELIZE CITY
PRINCESS HOTEL AND CASINO/
CLUB ELITE ●
NEAL'S PENN RD
CEASAR RIDGE RD
BIRD'S ISLE
RESTAURANT ▲
W COLLET ST
E COLLET ST
CANAL ST
ALBERT ST
REGENT ST
ORANGE ST
QUEEN ST
CARNIVAL ★
"DOWNTOWN
BELIZE CITY"
MAP
SEE
SWING
BRIDGE
FORT GEORGE ST
MUSEUM
OF BELIZE ★
MARINE PARADE
Memorial
Park
FORK ST

© MOON.COM

south), which is monitored more closely by the police. For a walking map of the city, stop by the **Belize Tourism Board** office (tel. 501/227-2420, www.travelbelize.org) on Regent Street; the map includes a great walking tour of the city's main sights.

Sights

A morning stroll through the weathered buildings of Belize City, starting in the Fort George Lighthouse area and walking toward the Swing Bridge, gives you a feel for this seaside population center. This is when people are rushing off to work, kids are spiffed up on their way to school, and folks are out doing their daily shopping. The streets are crammed with small shops, a stream of pedestrians, and lots of traffic. One thing Belize City isn't is boring.

★ FORT GEORGE

The **Fort George** area, a peninsula ringed by Marine Parade Boulevard and Fort Street, is one of the most pleasant in Belize City. Meander in the neighborhood and you'll pass some impressive homes and buildings, including a few charming old guesthouses. The Baron Bliss Memorial and Fort George Lighthouse stand guard over it all.

The sea breeze can be pleasant here, and you can glimpse cayes and ships offshore—don't miss your chance for a selfie beside the colorful Belize sign next to Fort George Lighthouse, the second of its kind in the city. Once you round the point, the road becomes Marine Parade and runs past the modern Radisson Fort George Hotel and **Memorial Park,** a grassy salute to the 40 Belizeans who lost their lives in World War I.

From the Radisson Fort George Marina, you'll get a good view of the harbor. Originally this was Fort George Island; the strait separating the island from the mainland (the site of today's Memorial Park) was filled in during the early 1920s. The entire area is easy to navigate on foot.

Baron Bliss Memorial

Henry Edward Ernest Victor Bliss, also known as the "Fourth Baron Bliss of the

Fort George area

Downtown Belize City

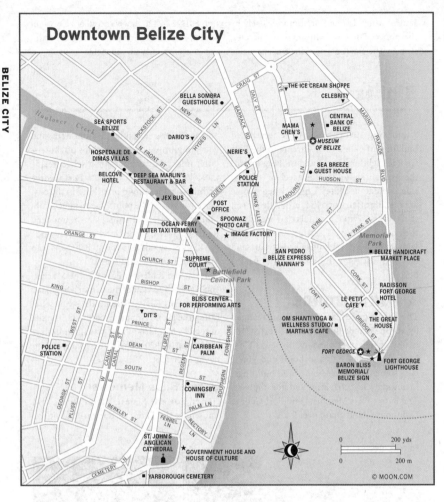

Former Kingdom of Portugal," was born in the county of Buckingham in England. He first sailed into the harbor of Belize in 1926, although he was too ill to go ashore because of food poisoning he had contracted while visiting Trinidad. Bliss spent several months aboard his yacht, the *Sea King,* in the harbor, fishing in Belizean waters. Although he never got well enough to go ashore, Bliss learned to love the country from the sea, and its habitués—people on fishing boats and officials in the harbor—all treated him with great respect and friendliness. On the days that he was only able to languish on deck, he made every effort to learn about the small country. He was apparently so impressed with what he learned and the people he met that before his death, he drew up a will that established a trust of nearly US$2 million for projects to benefit the people of Belize.

More than US$1 million in interest from the trust has been used for the erection of the Bliss Institute, the Bliss School of Nursing, and Bliss Promenade as well as contributions to the Belize City water supply, the Corozal

Your Best Day in Belize City

Even if you only stay one night, there's plenty to see and do in downtown Belize City for the day—including an introduction to the country's past colonial history, its Creole culture, and some of the tastiest Creole dishes in Belize. Just go with an open mind and take in this truly unique Central American city.

- Hop in a taxi and start your morning at the **Museum of Belize** (8 Gabourel Ln., tel. 501/223-4524, www.museumofbelize.org, 9am-4:30pm Tues.-Fri., 9am-4pm Sat., US$5)—with fascinating collections of Mayan artifacts, in addition to rotating exhibits. Next head to the **Belize House of Culture** (tel. 501/227-3050, www.nichbelize.org, 8:30am-5pm Mon.-Thurs., 8:30am-4:30pm Fri., US$5). This colonial building turned museum houses an interesting selection of period items, including silverware, glassware, and ancient utensils. Don't miss taking a stroll on the sprawling sea-facing lawn at the back of the building, where functions are often held. Cross the street and marvel at **St. John's Anglican Cathedral,** the oldest Anglican church in Central America.

- From there, walk back up Regent Street toward the city center to **Deep Sea Marlin's Restaurant & Bar** (Regent St. W., tel. 501/227-6995, 7am-9pm Mon.-Sat., US$4) for a Creole lunch of stew with rice and beans, river views, and local tunes.

- After your meal, stop for a refreshing cold beer and desserts at **Spoonaz Photo Cafe** (89 N. Front St., tel. 501/223-1043, spooners@btl.net, 6:30am-6:30pm Mon.-Thurs., 6:30am-8pm Fri.-Sat., 6:30am-3:30pm Sun., US$1-6) on its outdoor riverside deck, if you need it. Continue walking to the nearby historic **Fort George** area, where you can quickly view the **Fort George Lighthouse,** facing the Caribbean Sea. Join a yoga class steps away at **Om Shanti's** new waterfront studio.

- Just outside Belize City, you'll find plenty of nature and wildlife to explore. Visit **The Belize Zoo** (Mile 29, George Price Hwy., tel. 501/822-8000, www.belizezoo.org, 8:30am-4:30pm daily, US$15 adults, US$5 children)—an educational treat for all ages, where Belize's species are on display, including the tapir and all five wildcats. Continue on to the village of Burrell Boom for a hike at the **Community Baboon Sanctuary** (tel. 501/622-9624, cbsbelize@gmail.com, www.howlermonkeys.org/lodging, 8am-5pm daily, US$7), where you'll spend an hour hiking the rainforest and spotting birds and howler monkeys. Or arrange for a drive farther north to explore the picturesque birding hot spot **Crooked Tree Village,** one of Belize's authentic Creole villages.

- Back in the city, head for a seaside dinner at **Bird's Isle Restaurant** (90 Albert St., tel. 501/207-2179, 10am-midnight Mon.-Sat., US$5-13) for more local fare or end up at the **Radisson Fort George Hotel's Baymen's Tavern** bar for happy hour treats (5pm-10pm) and a live DJ on Fridays.

- Up for a late night? Shake your buns at **Sit & Sip** (162 Newtown Barracks, across BTL Park, tel. 501/223-2453, info@sitandsipbelize.com, 10pm-3am Thurs.-Sat.), where the millennial crowd parties to the latest international tunes.

EXTEND YOUR STAY

Got more time? Arrange for a stay at one of the surrounding riverside lodges, including **Belize River Lodge** (tel. 501/225-2002, U.S. tel. 888/275-4843, www.belizeriverlodge.com, 3-night package US$1,545) and **Black Orchid Resort** (2 Dawson Ln., U.S. tel. 501/225-9158, www.blackorchidresort.com, US$150-295). Get your host to arrange a boat ride down the **Old Belize River** and its spectacular giant mangrove cathedrals, and spend the day wildlife-spotting—from crocodiles to birds.

Town Board and Health Clinic, and land purchase for the building of Belmopan.

An avid yachtsman, Bliss stipulated that money be set aside for a regatta to be held in Belizean waters, now a focal point of the National Heroes and Benefactors' Day (formerly gala Baron Bliss Day) celebrations each March. The baron's white granite tomb is at the point of Fort George in Belize City, guarded by the Fort George Lighthouse and the occasional pair of late-night Belizean lovers.

Fort George Lighthouse

Towering over the coastline and facing Belize Harbor, the Fort George Lighthouse was built as part of the memorial for Baron Bliss, Belize's greatest benefactor. In fulfillment of his dying wish and financed with the generous proceeds he left the country, the tall structure was erected next to his tomb and memorial. While the public cannot enter the lighthouse, it remains an important historic landmark in Belize City and is easy to spot while touring the Fort George area. The views from here also make for a nice photo op.

★ MUSEUM OF BELIZE

Housed in the old city jail (Her Majesty's Prison was built in 1857 and served as the nation's only prison until the 1990s), the small but worthwhile Museum of Belize (8 Gabourel Ln., tel. 501/223-4524, www.museumofbelize.org, 9am-4:30pm Tues.-Fri., 9am-4pm Sat., US$5) includes historical artifacts, indigenous relics, and rotating displays on topics such as *Insects of Belize, Maya Jade,* and *Pirates of Belize.* Philatelists and bottle collectors will love the 150 years of stamps and bottles on display.

IMAGE FACTORY

A few doors up from the Swing Bridge, the Image Factory Art Foundation (91 N. Front St., tel. 501/223-4093, chokscatter@yahoo.com, www.imagefactorybelize.com, 9am-5pm Mon.-Fri., 9am-noon Sat.) is the official pulse of the Belizean art and literary scene. In addition to offering the best book selection in the country (both local authors and some foreign titles), there is gallery space for semi-regular art events, usually held on Friday evenings at happy hour. There's also a separate arts and crafts shop at the back filled with gorgeous Belizean paintings, sculptures, and other unique creations.

ST. JOHN'S ANGLICAN CATHEDRAL

The lovely old St. John's Anglican Cathedral (S. Albert St. at Regent St., 7am-6pm daily), across from the House of Culture, is one of the few typically British structures in the city. It is also the oldest Anglican church in Central America. In 1812, slaves helped erect this graceful piece of architecture, using bricks brought as ballast on sailing ships from Europe. Several Mosquito Coast kings from Nicaragua and Honduras were crowned in this cathedral with ultimate pomp and grandeur; the last was in 1815. The church is surrounded by well-kept green lawns and sits next to a lively schoolyard. It's usually okay to walk right in and quietly admire the impressive interior with its stained-glass windows, mahogany pews, and the antique organ. You can leave a little something in the donation box on your way out.

One block from the cathedral is the Yarborough Cemetery, the city's first burial ground, with the graves of Belizean citizens dating back to the 18th century, as well as some who died during World War II.

GOVERNMENT HOUSE AND HOUSE OF CULTURE

Opposite St. John's Cathedral, at the southern end of Regent Street and facing the Southern Foreshore, is the House of Culture museum in the old Government House (tel. 501/227-3050, www.nichbelize.org, 8:30am-5pm Mon.-Thurs., 8:30am-4:30pm Fri., US$5), which, before 1961's Hurricane Hattie and the

1: Museum of Belize; 2: Battlefield Central Park

ensuing construction of Belmopan, was the home and office of the governor-general, the official representative of Queen Elizabeth. (Today's governor-general can be found in Belmopan, at Belize House.) For a long time these grounds were used as a guesthouse for visiting VIPs and a venue for social functions. Queen Elizabeth and Prince Philip stayed here in 1994. The elegant wooden buildings (built 1812-1814) are said to be based on designs by acclaimed English architect Christopher Wren. Sprawling lawns and wind-brushed palms facing the sea surround Government House, making it ideal for the year-round outdoor functions, art events, and concerts that are still held here.

Wander through the wooden structure and enjoy the period furniture, silverware, and glassware collections, plus a selection of paintings and sculptures by modern Belizean artists. Stroll the grounds, on the water's edge, and enjoy the solitude. Also on-site is the headquarters of the National Kriol Council, with some Kriol language phrasebooks for sale.

LUBA GARIFUNA MUSEUM

Founded in 1999, even before the Museum of Belize, the **Luba Garifuna Museum** (4202 Fern Ln., tel. 501/202-4331, Luba_Garifuna@ yahoo.com, 8am-5pm daily and by appointment, US$5) is the first Garifuna museum in the country. Tucked off the beaten path in a residential area, the museum showcases Garifuna culture and history. You'll be surprised at the collection of arts and crafts, cooking utensils, photographs, and traditional clothing. Items have been gathered over a period of 30 years and are clearly

displayed, showcasing key rituals and ceremonies. If you're lucky, you'll meet Sebastian Cayetano, founder of the museum and co-founder of the National Garifuna Council and a well-respected teacher and resource on the Garinagu people of Belize.

The museum is off Jasmine Street, which is off Mahogany Street in the St. Martin's area. A guided tour (US$10) is also available, and the museum offers a cultural package (on request, US$200 for 10 people) for large groups, which includes a tour of the museum, food sampling, and a dance and drumming show.

OLD BELIZE

In addition to Cucumber Beach, a swimming lagoon, a zip line, a waterslide, and other water sports, **Old Belize** (Mile 5, George Price Hwy., tel. 501/222-4129, www.oldbelize. com, museum tour US$2.50, zip line US$20) also features the **Cultural and Historical Center** (10am-8:30pm daily), a 45-minute tour through 1,000 years of Belizean history—probably the only thing even slightly worth seeing if you venture here. It's kind of like a walk-through museum, but with various relics and simulations. Some of the displays from the former Maritime Museum are now housed here and include models of boats used in Belize as well as photos and bios of local anglers and boatbuilders. On cruise ship days (usually Tues. and Thurs.), a Belizean cabaret showcases the dances and songs of Belize's cultural groups. There's also a marina, a helipad, and an average restaurant (tel. 501/222-5588, 11am-10pm daily) that is mysteriously popular with well-off locals, perhaps due to the waterfront setting. It's five miles out of the city and, to be honest, not worth the trip if you're pressed for time.

Crime and the City

Like many Central American countries, Belize has its share of problems with drugs, gangs, and violent street crime. However, due to its extremely small population—70,000 inhabitants, compared to millions in most Central American capitals—Belize City's problems are nowhere near as severe as those of El Salvador, Honduras, and Guatemala's cities. Still, violent crime has increased in Belize City, particularly during 2018 and the start of 2019, mostly in the form of robberies at well-known establishments, including restaurants, as well as inner city shootings. Much of this violent gang culture is imported from the United States by deported Belizean youths.

Most—but not all—violent crime occurs in the Southside part of Belize City, many blocks away from the traditional walking paths of visitors, but occasional incidents have occurred throughout the city and in broad daylight. There is criticism that the government could be doing more to battle crime, including stiffer enforcement of the law. Be vigilant at all times, anywhere in the city.

For the most part, you'll be fine sticking to the sights, around which there's lots of pedestrian traffic and daytime activity. Most locals are friendly and helpful with directions or other questions. To be safe, use the same common sense you would in any city in the world:

- Before you venture out, have a clear idea of how to get where you're going and ask a local Belizean, like your hotel desk clerk or a restaurant waiter, whether your plan is reasonable.

- Don't walk around at night under any circumstances.

- Taxis are plentiful and inexpensive—use them. Generally, only those with green license plates should be considered. But most Belizeans have a personal taxi driver whom they know and trust; ask your hotel to call one they know for you, and ask for cost before you depart.

- Don't flash money, jewelry, or other temptations; if threatened with robbery, hand them over. Report all crimes to the local police and to your country's embassy.

Sports and Recreation

You'll find the best diving, fishing, and other water activities off the cayes, north to south. Aside from these, Belize City offers river and wildlife tours, as well as your classic city park or spa pampering, if you prefer to take it easy.

RIVER TOURS

Boat tours on the Old Belize River—which has stunning mangrove cathedrals and wildlife from birds to crocodiles—can be arranged through the area's locally run riverside lodges. Contact **Black Orchid Resort** (2 Dawson Ln., U.S. tel. 501/225-9158, www.blackorchidresort.com) or **Belize River Lodge** (tel. 501/225-2002, U.S. tel. 888/275-4843, www.belizeriverlodge.com, 3-night package US$1,545).

PARKS

A simple, enjoyable way to spend an afternoon or watch the sun go down in Belize City is to hang out "seaside" (as the locals call it) in one of the city parks. **BTL Park,** within walking distance of the Ramada Belize City Princess Hotel, is a favorite at sunset; grab a drink and a bite from a delightful international variety of food booths. There's Jamaican, Mexican, Honduran, vegan, and even Filipino, among others. Sit back on the benches while the breeze blows all along the seaside or take a stroll. There are also swings and a playground for kids. You're likely to spot lovers as well as families, who come here in the early evenings to stroll, wind down, jog, or just chat. Going seaside is popular on Sunday, with lots of families taking a breather from their long week.

Another popular seaside spot is across from Memorial Park and along the Marine Parade promenade. Avoid hanging out at either of the parks late at night.

On the south side and the city's central Albert Street, the historic **Battlefield Central Park**—once a meeting place for labor activists in the 1600s—sits at the mouth of the city's main shopping area and downtown businesses along Albert and Regent Streets. In this tiny yet bustling square are a couple of ice cream and snack kiosks, as well as card-playing locals and food vendors. There are a few benches, and it's safe to enjoy during the day. Across from the park is the Supreme Court building, decorated with a long veranda. An antiquated town clock is perched atop the white clapboard building.

DIVING AND SNORKELING

The Belize Barrier Reef is less than 30 minutes away and offers excellent wall dives and idyllic snorkeling. Turneffe Islands Atoll and Lighthouse Atoll are one and two hours away, respectively, by boat. These sites are perfect for anyone in the city on business or for travelers staying in Belize City. There are also manatee-encounter trips available as well as outings to Swallow Caye Marine Reserve.

Belize City has two dive shops. **Sea Sports Belize** (83 N. Front St., tel. 501/223-5505, www.seasportsbelize.com, US$160 for a 2-tank dive, US$95 for a snorkel tour, lunch included) is across from the post office, two buildings east of the Swing Bridge. Sea Sports has been in business 15 years and is a PADI 5-Star Instructor Development Center, offering equipment sales, scuba instruction, and daily dives and snorkeling at Hol Chan and Shark Ray Alley, fishing, and manatee-encounter trips. They use small boats and take groups of no more than eight people per guide. They can also arrange overnight packages with lodging at St. George's Caye, Belize's first capital.

Hugh Parkey's Dive Connection (tel. 501/223-4526 or cell tel. 501/670-6025, www.

belizediving.com, www.belizeadventurelodge.com, barrier reef dive US$105 pp, minimum 4 people; 2-tank dive at Turneffe US$150 pp, minimum 4 people, lunch and equipment included) is based at the Radisson Fort George Marina and offers all manner of trips and certification courses. Hugh Parkey's has the biggest day-trip boat fleet around and provides diving services for the cruise ships that call on Belize; they can arrange accommodations at nearby Spanish Lookout Caye.

BOATING AND SAILING

Ask at any of the tour companies, marinas, or dive shops to see what's available; there should be a decent range of charter opportunities, plus day trips and sunset cruises. Sailing and snorkeling trips to Caye Caulker (US$65) are offered, as well as sunset cruises to Ambergris Caye (US$35).

FISHING

Fantastic river, reef, flats, and deep-sea fishing is available from Belize City. You can fish for tarpon in the morning and bonefish in the afternoon. Deep-sea opportunities include mackerel, wahoo, kingfish, and billfish. Most lodges in the area can set up fishing trips; contact the **Belize River Lodge** (tel. 501/225-2002, U.S. tel. 888/275-4843, www.belizeriverlodge.com, 3-night package US$1,545) to start. You can also try **Sea Sports Belize** (83 N. Front St., tel. 501/223-5505, www.seasportsbelize.com, river fishing US$500 per stop, reef fishing US$600 per stop for up to 4 people), which runs professional custom sportfishing trips on rivers and to stunning sights offshore; prices include equipment, a guide, and lunch.

SPECTATOR SPORTS

The basketball court on Bird's Isle used to be packed to the gills during local championship games. Ask around to see if any games are coming up. Catch a soccer game (called "football" here) at the stadium at 3:30pm Sunday. There's loud, booming pregame music and lots of security. The stadium is across the street from the Ramada Belize City Princess Hotel on Barrack Road.

MASSAGE AND BODYWORK

Om Shanti (10 Fort St., www.omshantibelize.com, tel. 501/227-2247, 7am-8pm Mon.-Sat., 8am-3pm Sun., from US$75) is the newest spa addition to the city, perfectly located across the Caribbean Sea, in the heart of the Fort George neighborhood. Set in a historic building that was once the customs house, the menu of massages is extensive, including Epsom salts hot baths. There's a yoga studio on the first floor for more bodywork—inquire about weekly classes. Relax on the outdoor deck at the on-site vegan Martha's Café afterward, where fresh juices and lunches are served.

The Radisson Fort George Hotel offers spa services at the Nim Li Punit Spa (2 Marine Parade Blvd., tel. 501/223-3333, sam.rah@radisson.com). Or put yourself in the hands of Harold Zuniga (85 Amara Ave., tel. 501/604-5679, haroldzuniga@yahoo.com), a U.S.-trained physical therapist, masseur, and acupuncturist. If you're up for relaxation coupled with a day trip, tucked in the village of Maskall just 1.5 hours' drive from the city is the unique Belize Boutique Resort and Spa (formerly Maruba, Mile 40.5, Old Northern Hwy., tel. 501/225-5555, U.S. tel. 800/861-7001, www.belizeresortandspa.com, US$251-465). The offerings are numerous, but don't miss getting the Mood Mud Massage; you'll not only leave with baby-soft skin but also a memorable photo of your body covered in nothing but mud and . . . a hibiscus flower. You can also get manicures, pedicures, and facials.

Entertainment and Shopping

Belize City is even more alive during the September Celebrations, a month packed with events, music, dancing, and a full-blown carnival parade along Central American Boulevard growing larger and more popular every year.

Bliss Promenade skirts the waterfront and brings you to the towering Bliss Center for Performing Arts (Southern Foreshore, tel. 501/227-2110, www.nichbelize.org), which hosts social functions, seminars, arts festivals, and drama series throughout the year. It is also the location of a theater, a museum, and a library as well as the Institute of Creative Arts. Step in to grab a calendar of events.

NIGHTLIFE

Thursday is the biggest night for dancing in Belize City, followed by Friday, especially those that fall on a payday. Nightclubs come and go like hurricanes; keep your wits about you and ask where the latest safe place to party is. A once-popular nightspot for dancing,

Club Elite (Ramada Belize City Princess Hotel, Barrack Rd., tel. 501/223-2670, 10pm-4am Thurs.-Sat.) attracts a maturer clientele, offering bottle service and international DJs. Serious dancing usually doesn't get started until after 11pm, and the well-heeled crowd is of a wide age range. At Sit & Sip (162 Newtown Barracks, across BTL Park, tel. 501/223-2453, info@sitandsipbelize.com, 10pm-3am Thurs.-Sat.), you'll find millennials shaking their bodies to a range of soca, reggaeton, and other dance tunes in a dimly lit, spacious lounge and bar. Others relax to the tunes on the small outdoor terrace. Keep an eye on the weekly calendar for themed nights, including a Wednesday wine night with live local jazz. Security is tight here, and the location is ideally close to the Radisson.

Ask around to find out where the best happy hours are held—they often feature live music and free *bocas* (deep-fried something, probably). The bars at the Radisson Fort George Hotel (2 Marine Parade Blvd., tel. 501/223-3333), the **Biltmore** (Mile 3, Philip Goldson Hwy., tel. 501/223-2302), and **Ramada Belize City Princess Hotel and Casino** (Barrack Rd., tel. 501/223-2670) are popular and provide safe, contained venues—and some of the highest drink prices in the city. **Bird's Isle** (90 Albert St., past the House of Culture, tel. 501/207-6500), or "Island" as locals call it, is popular for karaoke on Thursday (5pm-1am). **Riverside Tavern** (2 Mapp St., tel. 501/223-5640), or just "Tavern," has plenty of bar fare and cocktails on Friday as well as other weekday happy hours.

FESTIVALS AND EVENTS

TOP EXPERIENCE

September Celebrations

For three weeks—from September 1 all the way through September 21 (Independence Day)—Belize City hops on one long party train to celebrate the country's freedom from Great Britain in 1981. Streets, lights, and bridges in the city are decked out in the national colors—red, blue, and white—and everyone is on a celebration high. It's quite the time to visit Belize City, particularly if you're a culture and history buff (not to mention the prices in low season are oh-so-right).

★ CARNIVAL

Belize's Caribbean spirit is on full display during the Caribbean-flavored Carnival (mid-Sept.). You'll see colorful floats, men and women in sexy, extravagant costumes, and trucks and massive speakers blasting either *punta* or soca music as the crowd and revelers hop and dance all along Central American Boulevard. The parade often starts on the south side of town around 2pm; be sure to arrange a taxi ride to and from the event and arrive about an hour early if you want to save a spot. After Carnival, the celebrations continue at BTL Park with an all-night outdoor concert, food and drink vendors, and plenty of seaside dancing.

PAAN YAAD

This lively seafront steel pan concert held at the House of Culture features the best bands from around Belize and makes for a night of Caribbean musical bliss, with the historical mansion serving as gorgeous backdrop combined with a Belizean buffet and drinks.

ST. GEORGE'S CAYE DAY

St. George's Caye Day (Sept. 10) commemorates the 1798 Battle of St. George's, when British forces repelled a Spanish invasion of Belize. The day begins around 10am with a ceremony full of pomp and circumstance at Memorial Park on Marine Parade Boulevard, just a few steps from the Radisson, where you'll glimpse the prime minister along with other important figures. A colorful citizens' parade follows around noon, with plenty of music and dancing, from the park all the way to Albert Street.

INDEPENDENCE DAY PARADE

Catch this parade (Sept. 21) celebrating Belize's independence from Great Britain. Similar to the St. George's Caye Day, Belize City holds its own with uniform parades, marching bands, floats, and children and adults all wearing the blue-red-white national colors and waving flags. The celebrations usually begin at Memorial Park around late morning and continue on throughout the afternoon and evening.

SIR BARRY'S BELIKIN BASH

Held at Memorial Park with live performances from the country's top artists, this free two-day outdoor concert (Sept.) commemorates the life of Sir Barry Bowen, the popular Belizean business magnate who created Belize's beer brewing empire and passed away tragically in 2010. There's plenty of dancing, food tents, and beer keg contests from 9pm until the wee hours of the morning. This is where you'll get acquainted with Belizean music and party spirit; watching the men and women competing in exaggerated "hip shaking" just to win free beer is highly entertaining.

Other Festivals and Events

The **Benefactors' Day Parade and Annual Boat Regatta** (Mar. 9) is a national holiday that both celebrates and commemorates the nation's largest benefactor, Sir Baron Bliss. Festivities are centered on an annual boat regatta and are usually followed by parties. The events and times can vary; consult your host or local papers for details on location and times.

The National Arts Festival (usually in Feb.), organized by the National Institute of Culture and History, was launched in 2012 to showcase local artistic talent in Belize—from painters to sculptors, tattoo artists, jewelers, and more. Booths and displays are located downtown along Albert Street, and there is a parade and live music stages at Battlefield Central Park. It's one big celebration of creativity. Contact the Institute of Creative Arts at the Bliss Center for Performing Arts (Southern Foreshore, tel. 501/227-2110, www.nichbelize.org) for a schedule of events.

SHOPPING

Gift shops, craft stalls, and street vendors line Front Street near Tourism Village as well as just south of the Swing Bridge. In the Fort George area, check out the **Belize Handicraft Market Place** (Memorial Park, 8am-5pm Mon.-Fri., 8am-4pm Sat.), near the Radisson.

Wine is increasingly in vogue in Belize. Once difficult to find, it's now fairly well stocked at the super-size **Brodie's** (Mile 2.5, Philip Goldson Hwy., tel. 501/223-5587, brodies@btl.net, 8am-9pm Mon.-Sat., 8am-2pm Sun.) and at **Premium Wines & Spirits** (166 Newtown Barracks, tel. 501/223-4984) or **Karl Menzies** (104 Barrack Rd., tel. 501/223-0896).

At the **Traveller's Liquors Heritage Center** (Mile 2.5, Philip Goldson Hwy., tel. 501/223-2855, www.onebarrelrum.com, 10am-6pm Mon.-Fri., bar until midnight Fri.-Sat.), Belize's premier rum producer offers a fun stop on your way in or out of town. The Heritage Center consists of a historical display, a selection of its many products at bargain prices, an open-air bar and restaurant, and most importantly, a tasting bar where you can sample all 27 varieties of Traveller's Liquors rum. Ask about the "vintage edition rum" to bring home some premium spirits.

A few stores have small but pertinent book selections featuring several shelves of Belizean and about-Belize books. The **Image Factory** (91 N. Front St., tel. 501/223-4093, www.imagefactorybelize.com, 9am-5pm Mon.-Fri., 9am-noon Sat.) has the best collection. **Angelus Press** (10 Queen St., tel. 501/223-5777, 7:30am-5:30pm Mon.-Fri., reduced hours Sat.-Sun.), on Queen Street right around the corner from the Image Factory, has a complete corner of books and maps behind all the office supplies and services.

Food

Belize City's upscale restaurant scene has yet to explode, but in its place you'll find a host of tasty, reasonably priced, and authentic Belizean food. Residents often grab a boxed meal on the way to work, home, or the next errand. Lunch is big, often consisting of stewed meat and rice and beans, seafood, soup, and other Creole and Latin specialties. Pastries and desserts are popular as well, and you'll find plenty of street vendors selling fast foods, snacks, fresh fruit juices, and more.

BELIZEAN

The city is packed with traditional Creole eateries and shacks doling out the best lunch in the city—better than seated restaurants. One long-standing local option is ★ **Dit's** (50 King St., tel. 501/227-3330, 8am-6pm Tues.-Sat., 8am-3pm Sun., US$4-6), a fifth-generation family-run Creole institution, serving freshly baked pastries—you must try the jam rolls—as well as pies and other traditional Creole desserts along with the wide menu of local specialties. It's always packed with Belizeans—a good sign.

Nerie's (Queen St. and Daly St., tel. 501/223-4028, www.neries.bz, 7:30am-10pm daily, US$5-9) was featured on the Travel Channel in a program about traditional Belizean fare, and while it's not as great as it used to be, it's a decent pick if you're in the area; order stew chicken, fish fillets, soups, and daily specials, including oxtail, jerk, and Garifuna *serre* (fish stewed in a broth of green banana and coconut milk and spiced with garlic, black pepper, and thyme).

A couple of streets from the Swing Bridge are the infamous meat pies at **Dario's** (33 Hyde's Ln., 5am-2pm Mon.-Sat., US$0.75), delicious hot, flaky pastries filled with meat or chicken. Go early if you want them fresh. **Pou's Meat Pies** (New Rd., 5am-2pm Mon.-Sat.) is also nearby; try both and decide who rules the city's meat pie district.

Adjacent to Atlantic Restaurant, the nameless **tin-roofed brown shack** (Mile 3, Philip Goldson Hwy., 11am-3pm Mon.-Fri., US$3.50-5) serves excellent dishes for a fantastic price. Order the chicken curry, or try the conch soup in season—the choices are endless. It also has fresh-squeezed juices and is convenient to guests staying at the various hotels in the area.

★ **Deep Sea Marlin's Restaurant & Bar** (Regent St. W., tel. 501/227-6995, 7am-9pm Mon.-Sat., US$4) is on Haulover Creek, next to the Belcove Hotel. It's a cheap and sometimes raucous fishing joint, with tasty Belizean and American staples and simple seating with breezy waterside views. The breakfast fry jacks are said to be out of this world.

Tropicolada Cocktail Hut (7 Fort St., tel. 501/223-1066, 11am-10pm Tues.-Sat., US$6-10), near Tourism Village, serves some of the best ceviche in Belize City as well as a wide range of Belizean and Central American dishes and pretty cocktails. Tropicolada closes earlier on Tuesday and later on karaoke Friday.

★ **Bird's Isle Restaurant** (90 Albert St., tel. 501/207-2179, 10am-midnight Mon.-Sat., US$5-13), or "Island" as the locals call it, has a long-standing reputation and an excellent waterfront location on a small islet to the south of downtown Belize City. Any taxi driver will know it, or just walk south past the Anglican church on Albert Street until you can't walk any farther. This is a casual affair in a gorgeous outdoor setting, with a spacious yard as well as indoor seating and a waterfront deck where you can watch the fish and birds glide by. Expect large portions of local comfort dishes, including stew beans, hamburgers, and sandwiches. Another option for authentic ambience and food on the way out of town is **Fu Wi Flavaz** (Mile 9, George Price Hwy., tel. 501/667-8509, 6:30am-3:30pm Mon.-Sat.,

Kriol Eats: *Wah Belly Full*

Stew meat served with coconut rice and beans is a typical Kriol dish.

The most authentic Belizean Kriol food you'll find is right here in the vicinity of Belize City, the heart of the Kriol or Caribbean culture. There's no way you could starve here between the coconut-based dishes, the meats, the multitude of baked treats, and the very affordable meals. Here's what you shouldn't miss.

- **Boil-up:** This isn't served as frequently, but when available, you should jump at the chance to taste this uniquely Caribbean stew mix of pig tail, fish, hard-boiled eggs, yams, plantains, sweet potato, and cassava—all *biled up* in a sauce of tomatoes, onions, and peppers.

- **Meat pies** are serious business—so much so that there's a constant debate on who makes the best: **Dario's** (33 Hyde's Ln., 5am-2pm Mon.-Sat.) or **Pou's Meat Pies** (New Rd., 5am-2pm Mon.-Sat.). Join the club and be your own judge.

- **Pastries and sweets** are a part of Kriol life. You'll find children selling their mothers' Creole bread, buns, and johnnycakes, often baked with coconut oil. Stop by **Dit's** (50 King St., tel. 501/227-3330, 8am-6pm Tues.-Sat., 8am-3pm Sun.) to sample traditional jam rolls, hot off the oven by noon, as well as bread pudding, coconut pie, or some "plastic" pudding, made with cassava.

- **Soup:** Of the more than a dozen Kriol soups you could sample, the best-known is beef soup (head to Bird's Isle on Tuesday for the best) and cow-foot soup.

- **Stew chicken** is the unofficial national dish of Belize. Often served family-style on Sunday, it's also sold throughout the week at various eateries. Along those same lines, you'll find stew beef on the menu and some sort of fry fish or fry chicken. These dishes are almost always served with a heap of coconut rice and beans (not to be confused with beans and rice, which is white rice and beans served separately) or plantains and coleslaw. For some of the best, head to **Deep Sea Marlin's Restaurant & Bar** (Regent St. W., tel. 501/227-6995, 7am-9pm Mon.-Sat.), by the Swing Bridge.

- **Wine:** Fermenting fruits, plants, and herbs is a tradition in the Belize River Valley. Locally made and potent (6-12 percent alcohol) but delicious wines are worth sampling, particularly the blackberry, cashew, or rice wines. These can be found in villages across the district.

7:30am-4:30pm Sun., from US$5), a family-run restaurant serving Belizean meals, including tasty barbecue, Creole shrimp, and fry jack breakfasts, among other options, in a large zinc-roof bamboo dining hut with open shutters, wooden seats, and fragrant with flower plants.

Garifuna food was sparse on the Belize City food scene until **Lerisi Garifunaduau** (4 Marine Parade Blvd., tel. 501/603-4289, 11am-4pm Tues.-Wed., 10am-9pm Thurs.-Sat., US$10) came along and opened its doors permanently, in a thatch-roof covered brown building steps from the sea. It's a great option for lunch, when a daily Garifuna specialty—usually *hudut*—is served on the seaside deck where the breeze blows against the beat of Garifuna music. Note that the evening menu only offers fried fish and other fast foods, but no Garifuna dishes. There's live drumming on Thursday, Friday, and Saturday evenings, and the occasional *punta* and *paranda* concerts. A couple of blocks past the Ramada Princess Hotel, **Thirstys Belize City** (164 Newton Barracks Rd., tel. 501/223-1677, thirstythursdaysbz@gmail.com, 3pm-2am Thurs.-Sat., US$8-15) is a popular pre-party joint with a savory menu, DJs, and breezy patio.

Over on Regent Street, close to the Belize Tourism Board, is the tiny shack and window service of **Caribbean Palm Fast Food** (11:30am-2pm Mon.-Fri., US$3-5), where Shawna and her mother dish out savory, super-cheap Creole lunches every day. Get here early—it's popular.

The chain **Wingz** (Mile 3.5, Philip Goldson Hwy., tel. 501/223-0048, 11am-10pm daily, US$5-20) is a popular pick for Belizeans, who flock to this open-air restaurant after work for a cold one and some wings—served with various flavored sauces, ranging from barbecue to jerk—or for a burger.

A nice neighborhood experience is a trip to the **D'Ceviche Hut** (5672 Vasquez Ave., tel. 501/223-6426, 11:30am-10pm Thurs.-Sat.,

US$11). The proprietor, Don Enrique, works for the fishing cooperative, and he doesn't mess around about freshness. There's no menu, just ceviche. As you take your seat, shout out "shrimp," "conch," or "mixed" (also lobster in season) and you'll get a large plate that feeds 3-4 people. It's fun, friendly, and very popular with locals. Arrange a taxi there and back so you don't have to negotiate the confusing streets in this neighborhood. Another solid pick is **CBL Ceviche** (270 Chetumal Blvd., Belama 2, tel. 501/629-4648, 1:30pm-10pm Thurs.-Sat., 3pm-9pm Sun., from US$5), serving shrimp ceviche, smoked pork *salpicón,* and homemade micheladas, among other drinks, from its small back patio.

CHINESE

There are more authentic Chinese restaurants in Belize City than you can imagine. They all make decent greasy dishes, but a few stand out, such as **Chon Saan Palace** (1 Kelly St., tel. 501/223-5447 or 501/223-7100, 11am-11:30pm Mon.-Sat., 11am-2:30pm and 5pm-11:30pm Sun., US$4-7, delivery optional). In addition to Chinese standards, there are many seafood and steak options.

Mama Chen's (7 Eve St., tel. 501/620-4257, 10am-6pm Mon.-Sat., US$4-6), on the corner of Eve and Queen Streets and close to the Belize Museum, is a good choice for vegetarians. Choose from veggie chow mein, spicy beef dumplings, crispy spring rolls, sushi, and bubble tea (the "bubbles" are sweet seaweed balls that are slurped up through a thick straw).

MIDDLE EASTERN

Belize City's small Lebanese community ensures that there are a few authentic Lebanese restaurants in town. You can't go wrong with **Sahara Grill** (Mile 3.5, Philip Goldson Hwy., Vista Plaza, tel. 501/203-3031 or 501/605-3785, 10am-3pm daily, US$4-15), right across from the Best Western Biltmore Hotel. It has a long menu of kebabs, hummus, and falafel, plus addictive shawarma wraps and gyros as well as *sheesha* water pipes.

1: Bird's Isle Restaurant; 2: Lerisi Garifunaduau

INDIAN

For East Indian curries and dal, ★ **Sumathi** (19 Baymen Ave., tel. 501/223-1172, 11am-11pm daily) is a solid choice, with both outdoor and indoor seating. It's got a great weekly lunch buffet (US$5), plus air-conditioning and a large Indian menu with plenty of vegetarian options. It also offers takeout and delivery anywhere in the city. The food is so good that expats from as far away as San Pedro or Punta Gorda order takeout via plane.

ITALIAN

Pepper's Pizza (4 St. Thomas St., tel. 501/223-5000, 10am-10pm daily, US$17) offers free delivery within city limits.

INTERNATIONAL

Belize's Belikin brewing family runs the ★ **Riverside Tavern** (2 Mapp St., tel. 501/223-5640, 11am-10pm Mon.-Thurs., closes later Fri.-Sat., US$15-35), an upscale sports bar whose massive "gourmet burger" (10-ounce patty US$9, super-size 16-ounce patty US$12.50), made of Belizean beef from the Bowens' Gallon Jug Estate, is one of the best in the country. The Cuban burger is also delicious, but the King Kong just sounds scary. Or try the coconut-crusted shrimp, other rich bar foods, pastas, and seafood options. There's beer on tap, and the very convivial atmosphere is popular at happy hour or for Thursday karaoke; it's a meeting place for Belize's who's who crowd. There's just one downside to this place: table service can be very slow.

★ **Midtown Restaurant and Bar** (168 Newtown Barrack, tel. 501/203-3000, 11am-11:30pm daily, US$10-25) has a cozy, casual chic interior, a short walk from the hotels and parks in the Newton Barracks area. The menu features a variety of options, from salads to steaks, lobster, shrimp curries, burgers, and pastas, among a myriad of tasty options, and the portions are large. It's a solid pick for a nice lunch or dinner out. Be sure to have a ride to and from this area.

Celebrity Restaurant and Bar (Volta Bldg., Marine Parade Blvd., tel. 501/223-7373, www.celebritybelize.com, 11am-10pm daily, US$9-20) is near the water, next to the national bank and museum. You enter through a dark, swanky lounge emerging into a bright restaurant with a huge variety of seafood, pasta, steaks, and salads. The best deal is Celebrity's takeout menu (US$5), the giant plate of fish-and-chips and the ceviche. They're also open for hearty breakfasts 8am-3pm Saturday and Sunday. Folks rightfully rave about the quesadillas and Budapest Chicken.

The **St. George's Restaurant** (Radisson Fort George Hotel, 2 Marine Parade Blvd., tel. 501/223-3333, 6:30am-10am, 11:30am-2pm, and 6:30pm-10pm daily, US$20) serves a grand buffet and has a standard menu of international fare and seafood. Outside around the bar, the **Stonegrill Restaurant** (10am-10pm daily, US$15-20) offers a fun, meat-sizzlin' meal inside or on the heavily vegetated outdoor patio. The burgers are surprisingly good.

CAFÉS

European in flavor is **Le Petit Café** (2 Marine Parade Blvd., tel. 501/223-3333, ext. 750, 6am-8pm daily, from US$1), attached to the Radisson Hotel in the Fort George area. It offers delicious baked-twice-daily Belizean and European pastries and cakes, ham-and-cheese croissants, hot panini, and possibly the best cup of freshly brewed coffee in town. It also makes excellent johnnycakes, plain or stuffed. The café now has Wi-Fi.

Dessert and ice cream junkies can also find their joy at **Zero Degrees** (18 St. Thomas Place, tel. 501/223-5132, zerodegreesicecream@yahoo.com, 9am-8pm Mon.-Thurs., 10am-9pm Fri.-Sat., 2pm-9pm Sun.), also serving ice cream cakes.

Over at **The Living Room** (The Northern Shops, Mile 1, Philip Goldson Hwy., tel. 501/223-4156, 9am-7pm Mon.-Sat., later weekend close, US$2-5), you can sip on gourmet coffee, chilled or hot (the macchiato is popular), and delicious teas (coconut among other flavors) inside a small and cozy space. Johnnycakes come in fresh in the morning, and the sweet-toothed can indulge in the treats of the day, whether cakes, muffins, lemon tarts, or tiramisu. In the evening, enjoy a cold glass of wine in the tapas lounge.

The health-conscious ★ **Martha's Café** (at Om Shanti, Harbour View House/Old Customs House, Fort St., tel. 501/227-2247, US$2-10) is a wonderful addition to the Fort George area, near the Radisson Hotel. Set on the top floor of a colonial building, there's ample seating indoor as well as on the seafront deck terrace. Sample an Om Shanti cold press juice (no water, no sugar added)—the ginger-pineapple-apple combo is deliciously refreshing. Lunch on a number of tasty picks—vegan tamales with a side salad, no bun vegan cheeseburgers, cucumber sandwiches, or garden veggie lasagna, among other healthy options. Be sure to sample Maratha's popular vegan carrot cake, or opt for the vegan ice cream.

The Ice Cream Shoppe (17 Eve St., next to Mama Chen's, tel. 501/223-1965, icecreambelize@gmail.com, 11am-7pm daily, closes later on weekends, US$5) is an ice cream parlor with diner-type booths just a few steps away from the Belize Museum. Try the delicious craboo flavor, made from the eponymous Belizean fruit.

A bit off the beaten path, **Sugar Fix Bakery** (8 Heusner Crescent, tel. 501/223-7640, sugarfixbelize@gmail.com, 6:45am-7pm Mon.-Fri., 6:45am-3pm Sat., from US$2.50) is a small and colorful shop tucked behind the Puma gas station serving up fresh-baked croissants and johnnycakes to go along with your coffee in the morning and Creole bun in the afternoon. They also offer delicious cheesecake—the best in the city—and other sweet treats. The calzones are excellent. There are three tables for those who aren't in a rush.

Spoonaz Photo Cafe (89 N. Front St., tel. 501/223-1043, spooners@btl.net, 6:30am-6:30pm Mon.-Thurs., 6:30am-8pm Fri.-Sat., 6:30am-3:30pm Sun., US$1-6) is conveniently located a stone's throw from the Swing Bridge, the water taxi terminals, and the city center. It's a tad pricey compared to local bakeries, but a much-needed trendy hangout spot downtown to cool off from a hot afternoon in the city with Belizean coffee, pastries, johnnycakes, and lunch specials—including local dishes or quiche. There's also an outdoor patio, away from street noise, and a waterfront bar with views of the Swing Bridge.

Hospedaje Dimas Villas (59 N. Front St., tel. 501/601-4510, 7am-5pm daily) has a casual local café, gift shop, guesthouse, and Internet hub. There's a comfortable little space with a back porch and dock over Haulover Creek, ideal for sunning or people-watching. Local dishes are available for lunch. There's an espresso bar in the Ocean Ferry Water Taxi Terminal while you wait for your boat, and at San Pedro Belize Express you don't want to miss **Hannah's,** with regular coffee and delicious johnnycakes and other local and sandwich menu items.

The Taiwanese-owned **Milky Way Café** (29 Baymen Ave., tel. 501/223-5185, 10:30am-9pm daily) is a favorite with locals, from adults to schoolchildren. It offers frozen cappuccinos, mochas, bubble milk tea (originally a Taiwanese specialty), and other coffee concoctions as well as delicious smoothies and Chinese food.

GROCERIES

Brodie's (Albert St. and Regent St., tel. 501/227-7070, 8am-6pm Mon.-Fri., closes earlier Sat.-Sun.) is a department store, supermarket, deli, drugstore, and more—a Belizean institution. You can also stock up on your way into or out of the north edge of town at **Save-U Supermarket** (San Cas Plaza, tel. 501/223-1291, 8am-9pm Mon.-Sat., 8am-2pm Sun.). This modern air-conditioned market sells everything any supermarket in the United States would carry, and it's reasonably priced, though not necessarily less than Brodie's.

Accommodations

All room rates are for double occupancy in the high season and may or may not include the 9 percent hotel tax. If you're traveling alone or May-November, expect discounts at some, but not all, of the following hotels.

UNDER US$25

Budget options in Belize City are getting smaller each year, particularly with the rise in city crime. While unofficial rooms and guesthouses have opened, do note that they are not licensed by the Belize Tourism Board, while the listings that follow are. On North Front Street, a short walk from the Swing Bridge, is the quiet family-run **Hospedaje Dimas Villas** (59 N. Front St., tel. 501/651-0839, smokinbalam2@yahoo.com, US$15 s, US$30 d) with four cozy and clean rooms, all airy with fans, two with private baths; all have access to a caged balcony over Haulover Creek at the back (with a small dock for sunning, if you choose) and a nice upper-floor balcony with street views as well as a nice downstairs café (meals from US$2). There's a gift shop, a pay phone, and Internet access on the ground floor. The guesthouse also offers weekly and monthly rates, bag storage (US$2 per bag per day), and a friendly atmosphere.

The Seaside Guest House (3 Prince St., tel. 501/227-8339, www.seasideguesthouse. org, US$20-55) is popular among the hard-core backpackers. The guesthouse is down a narrow, quiet alley off Regent Street, near the Belize Tourism Board. The couple of guest rooms are tiny, barely bigger than the beds, but the common spaces both upstairs and downstairs are good for meeting travelers from all over the world. Choose from shared bunk space or private guest rooms. There is hot water in the community bathroom, a breeze on the ocean-facing porch, and a friendly family-run atmosphere in this former Quaker house. Three cheap meals a day (US$3-5 each) are available, though there are plenty of outside eateries in this central area. If you know you're coming to town, make a reservation—the Seaside can sometimes fill up fast.

US$25-50

A better value is ★ **Bella Sombra Guesthouse** (Hyde Lane, 501/631-8989, US$35-50), with six spacious rooms and a location close to the water taxi and a block from Dario's meat pies and from the bus stop to Crooked Tree Village. Rooms are basic but clean, with private bath, TV, air-conditioning, and minifridge, as well as Wi-Fi. The exterior appearance may be confusing but don't let that deter you.

The **Belcove Hotel** (9 Regent St. W., tel. 501/227-3054, www.belcove.com, US$33-52), centrally located on the south bank of Haulover Creek just west of the Swing Bridge is well taken care of, clean, and bright. While there was a recent armed robbery here, it could happen anywhere so stay alert. There are 13 guest rooms on three floors; options include shared or private baths with fan or the works (air-conditioning and TV). The porch over the creek is fun to watch boats from, and cheap lively eats are right next door at Deep Sea Marlin's Restaurant & Bar. It's a great base for a walking tour of the city, and tour packages can keep you busy on the reef or at inland sights. The only downside is the slightly seedy two blocks on Regent Street between the hotel and the Swing Bridge; take a cab to and from the hotel door at night.

US$50-100

On the same street as the Belize Tourism Board and near the House of Culture, **Coningsby Inn** (76 Regent St., tel. 501/227-1566, www.coningsbyinn.com, US$50-60)

1: Villa Boscardi Bed & Breakfast; 2: view from a waterfront suite at the Ramada Belize City Princess Hotel and Casino

has 10 rooms with TV, private baths, air-conditioning, wireless Internet, and minibars. There's a second-story bar and restaurant with a front balcony; breakfast is US$6. Common-area carpets are run down, but guest rooms are clean and the staff is friendly.

Located in Buttonwood Bay, an upscale residential area just three miles north of downtown and seven miles south of the international airport, ★ **Villa Boscardi Bed & Breakfast** (6043 Manatee Dr., tel. 501/223-1691, www.villaboscardi.com, US$85 plus tax, includes breakfast) is an excellent value and a wonderful retreat from city noise. It's just a block away from the sea and from the prime minister's home and a 10-minute drive into the city. Owner Françoise, an interior decorator by training, takes pride in her villa, ensuring the spotless guest rooms convey the cozy at-home atmosphere of a bed-and-breakfast but a notch up. Guest rooms and suites are located inside the house or at the back of the property with garden views. A honeymoon suite is also available. Hot breakfast is included and served fresh daily, courtesy of the friendly housekeeper Anna. There's free Internet access and a common desktop and kitchen, and taxis are easy to come by as the guesthouse keeps a list of drivers handy. It's an ideal place to return to after a long day of activities. Shopping and several restaurants are within walking distance, including the delicious Saffron Bay Restaurant just a street behind on Seashore Drive.

In the same area as Villa Boscardi but a few blocks on the other side of the highway in the Belama neighborhood, **D'Nest Inn** (475 Cedar St., tel. 501/223-5416, www.dnestinn.com, US$82-92) is a two-story Caribbean-style bed-and-breakfast surrounded by an English garden. Gaby and Oty offer five comfortable guest rooms decorated with Belizean antiques, all equipped with private baths, air-conditioning, TVs, and wireless Internet. Multicourse breakfasts feature lots of fresh fruit and conversation with your hosts.

US$100-150

The six-floor **Ramada Belize City Princess Hotel and Casino** (Barrack Rd., tel. 501/223-2670, U.S. tel. 888/790-5264, www.ramada.com, US$120) has 170 concrete guest rooms, with slightly worn baths, and all with the same air-conditioning, cable TV, and breakfast. Overall, you'll find much better value elsewhere, particularly at the B&Bs mentioned above. But if you're looking for lots of on-site entertainment, the Princess Hotel houses Belize City's only cinema and bowling alley; there's also a pretty but shallow pool, a gift shop, a beauty salon, a conference room, bars, restaurants (the one over the dock has lovely views), and a tour desk. The on-site marina has docking facilities and water sports, and the popular casino (across the street) and Club Next disco are open midnight-4am daily.

After World War II, visiting English dignitaries came to Belize with plans for various agricultural projects, but they couldn't find a place to stay. As a result, the **Radisson Fort George Hotel** (2 Marine Parade Blvd., tel. 501/223-3333, U.S. tel. 800/333-3333, www.radisson.com/belizecitybz, US$139-174 plus tax) was built, and it remains the premier lodging in town. The Radisson's 102 nicely appointed full-service guest rooms sport all the amenities you'd expect, including outrageously priced minibars. This resort-style hotel has two swimming pools (for guests only), a poolside bar, the Stonegrill Restaurant (with delicious burgers), a lively indoor bar and deck at the Baymen's Tavern, and fine dining and a massive breakfast buffet in St. George's Dining Room. All the restaurants host special events and happy hours. Full catering facilities and banquet rooms are available. All kinds of tours, such as diving, caving, and golfing, are organized right out of the hotel. The Villa Wing across the street includes restrooms, a new business center, a gym, and an expansion of Le Petit Café, connecting it to the Villa Lobby with enlarged seating area and wireless Internet (for guests only).

Best Western Plus Belize Biltmore Plaza Hotel (Mile 3, Philip Goldson Hwy., tel. 501/223-2302, U.S. tel. 800/528-1234, www.belizebiltmore.com, US$140) is the local Best Western branch, three miles north of the city center (seven miles south of the international airport) on the Philip Goldson Highway. Recently upgraded, the Biltmore is popular with business travelers; its 75 mid-size guest rooms surround a garden, a pool, and a bar and have cable TV, phones, and modern baths. There's also Internet service, an excellent gift shop, an overpriced dining room (US$12-20) with mediocre international food, and a lounge. The hotel may be convenient for flights, but you'll need a car or taxi to get around.

US$150-200

★ **The Great House** (13 Cork St., tel. 501/223-3400, www.greathousebelize.com, US$183) is a charming colonial-style boutique hotel, built in 1927 and recently renovated to show off its 16 unique, spacious, and colorful guest rooms (there are no elevators, just stairs). Both tiled and hardwood floors offset the pastel walls and modern furniture; the guest rooms in back have more charm than the rest. Internet access is included in the room rates, as is a light continental breakfast at the best café in town, Le Petit, next door. Downstairs, you'll find a high-end real estate company, a business service center, a delightful wine bar, and the Smoky Mermaid restaurant, with a sushi bar extension.

Information and Services

VISITOR INFORMATION

The central office of the **Belize Tourism Board** (BTB, 64 Regent St., tel. 501/227-2420, U.S. tel. 800/624-0686, info@travelbelize.org, www.travelbelize.org) is in Southside, near the House of Culture. They have an excellent free first-timer's map with a suggested walking tour of the city. The **Belize Tourism Industry Association** (10 N. Park St., tel. 501/227-1144, www.btia.org, 8am-5pm Mon.-Thurs., shorter hours Fri.) can also answer many of your questions and provide lodging suggestions. The **Belize Hotel Association** (BHA, 13 Cork St., tel. 501/223-0669, www.belizehotels.org) is a nonprofit industry group representing some of the country's most respected resorts and lodges; the staff can help you decide where to stay.

BANKS

Most of the city's banking is clustered in one strip along Albert Street, just south of the Swing Bridge. This includes **Atlantic Bank** (tel. 501/227-1225), **Scotiabank** (tel. 501/227-7027), **First Caribbean International Bank** (tel. 501/227-7211), and **Belize Bank** (tel. 501/227-7132). Most banks have ATMs and keep the same hours (8am-1pm Mon.-Thurs., 8am-1pm and 3pm-6pm Fri.).

HEALTH AND EMERGENCIES

For **police, fire,** or **ambulance,** dial 90 or 911. Another ambulance service is **B.E.R.T.** (tel. 501/223-3292). **Belize Medical Associates** (5791 St. Thomas St., tel. 501/223-0302, bzmedasso@btl.net, www.belizemedical.com) is the main private hospital in Belize City. The fairly modern 25-bed facility provides 24-hour assistance and a wide range of specialties. Or try **Karl Heusner Memorial Hospital** (Princess Margaret Dr., tel. 501/223-1548, www.khmh.bz).

MEDIA AND COMMUNICATIONS

The main **post office** (150 N. Front St., tel. 501/227-2201, www.belizepostalservice.gov.bz, 8am-noon and 1pm-5pm Mon.-Thurs., 8am-4:30pm Fri.) is across from the Ocean Ferry Water Taxi Terminal. A second post office (corner of Dolphin St. and Raccoon St., tel. 501/227-1155, 8am-5pm Mon.-Fri.) is at Queens Square on the Southside.

As elsewhere in the country, an increasing number of hotels and guesthouses offer at least a single computer for guests or even wireless Internet access for your laptop. There are a few broadband Internet cafés in Belize City, though not as many as in San Ignacio or San Pedro.

The **Turton Library's Computer Center** (N. Front St., tel. 501/227-3401, 9am-7pm Mon.-Fri., 9am-1pm Sat.), tucked away in a narrow air-conditioned room above the library, has five speedy computers; they are the cheapest in town at US$1.25 per hour. **Angelus Press** (10 Queen St., tel. 501/223-5777, 7:30am-5:30pm Mon.-Fri., shorter hours Sat.-Sun.) has a few machines available for US$1.75 per hour. More expensive options are available in Tourism Village and in the business centers of fancier hotels.

Transportation

Most sights are relatively close together in Belize City, and you can walk from the Southside's House of Culture to the Belize Museum in about 30 leisurely minutes. This route is generally safe during the day, even more so if you are traveling in a group; I have walked it solo several times.

Check with the travel agencies in the main Ocean Ferry Water Taxi Terminal; they may be able to hold your backpacks for the day or arrange for longer storage (US$1 per hour, US$5 per day). The nearby **Hospedaje Dimas Villas** (59 N. Front St., US$2 per bag) offers storage for the day if you're passing through. Ask your guesthouse if you can leave a bag there as well.

GETTING THERE
Air
The **Municipal Airport** (TZA), called "Muni," is on the waterfront behind the Marion Jones Sports Complex, one mile from the city center. Two Belizean domestic airlines, **Tropic Air** (tel. 501/226-2012, U.S. tel. 800/422-3435, www.tropicair.com) and **Maya Island Air** (tel. 501/223-1140 or 501/223-1362, www.mayaislandair.com) provide steady service in and out of Belize City to outlying airports all over the country. It's cheaper to fly to local destinations from here.

From **Philip S. W. Goldson International Airport** (BZE, 10 miles west of town, tel. 501/225-2045, www.pgiabelize.com), it's a 20-minute taxi ride to downtown Belize City (US$25), less in the opposite direction. There are no other transportation alternatives unless a friend is picking you up.

Bus
Domestic bus service is handled almost entirely out of **Novelo's Terminal,** on West Canal Street at the western terminus of King Street. If you arrive by bus, it's about 10 blocks to walk downtown to the Swing Bridge. From Novelo's, cross the canal and stay on King Street until you reach Albert Street, then make a left. Continue three blocks to the Swing Bridge and water taxi terminal. You can also cross the street and take a right on Orange Street just one block up, then stay on Orange Street all the way to town; it's always busy with foot traffic. This walk is usually safe during the day, but should not be attempted at night. When in doubt, take a taxi, and have one referred if possible; a good rule of thumb is not to walk any streets that appear deserted. International bus service to Guatemala and Mexico and ferry service to Honduras are offered by a handful of companies with offices in the **Ocean Ferry Water Taxi Terminal** (north end of the Swing Bridge).

GETTING AROUND

Boat

The country's two water taxi companies have their terminals in the city, with an all-day schedule of departures and returns to the Northern Cayes. The islands are very close; Caye Caulker is a mere 45-minute ride, San Pedro is 1.5 hours away, and St. George's Caye is a 25-minute ride.

The **Ocean Ferry Water Taxi Terminal** (tel. 501/223-0033, www.oceanferrybelize. com) is at the north end of the Swing Bridge, with boats leaving 8am-5pm. Some boats are now equipped with free Wi-Fi.

San Pedro Belize Express (tel. 501/223-2225, www.belizewatertaxi.com, US$15-20 pp one-way) departs just a few blocks farther down, near the Tourism Village, 7:45am-5:30pm daily.

Verify first and last departures, as those tend to change seasonally. The trip is pleasant on calm sunny days when the boat isn't full, but otherwise be prepared to squeeze on, and it can be a cold and wet ride if the sky to the east is dark. A few of the boats are covered; others will pass out plastic tarps if it's really raining hard.

Taxi

To hail a taxi, look for the green license plates, but better yet, ask your hotel or guesthouse to call you one and keep the numbers or make arrangements with the driver for the duration of your stay. From the international airport to Belize City, the flat fare is US$25; from the municipal airstrip, expect to pay US$5 or less. The fare for one passenger carried between any two points within Belize City or any other district town is US$3-5. If you plan to make several stops, tell the cabbie in advance and ask what the total will be; this eliminates lots of misunderstandings, as taxis often charge by the stop. They can also be hired by the hour (about US$16-25). For longer trips to or from town, try **Rey's Taxi Service** (tel. 501/624-5537)—he can arrange rides anywhere in Belize, including airport pickups—or Kenneth Bennett of **KB Taxi Service** (tel. 501/634-2865) for in-city runs or prearranged long-distance drop-offs.

Tours

If you prefer to delegate the logistics of your trip, local travel agencies can book local and international transportation, tours, and accommodations across the country. **S&L Travel and Tours** (91 N. Front St., tel. 501/227-7593 or 501/227-5145, www.sltravelbelize.com, 8am-5pm Mon.-Fri.) is easy to find, next door to the Image Factory. Belizean owners Sarita and Lascelle Tillet run a first-class and very personable operation; they've been in business for more than 30 years. They can get as creative as you like, whether you want a custom vacation, a photo safari, a bird-watching adventure, or anything else you can imagine.

Got extra cash? Splurge on a helicopter tour over the Belize Barrier Reef and the magnificent Blue Hole with **Astrum Helicopters** (Mile 3.5, George Price Hwy., tel. 501/222-5100, U.S. tel. 888/278-7864, www.astrumhelicopters.com, US$1,200 for 4 people). Astrum also offers airport helicopter transfers to 22 of Belize's five-star resorts.

Along the Philip Goldson Highway

After escaping Belize City's traffic and passing the international airport, you'll cruise up the Philip Goldson Highway (formerly known as the Northern Highway) to Mayan sites, monkeys, and more.

★ ALTUN HA

Altun Ha (9am-5pm daily, US$5) is 34 miles north of Belize City and has become one of the more popular day trips for groups and individuals venturing from Belize City, Ambergris Caye, and Caye Caulker; it is the most visited archaeological site in Belize. A Mayan trading center as well as a religious ceremonial site, it is believed to have accommodated about 10,000 people. Archaeologists, working amid a Mayan community that has been living here for several centuries, have dated construction to about 1,500-2,000 years ago. It wasn't until the archaeologists arrived in 1964 that the old name, Rockstone Pond, was translated into the Mayan words *Altun Ha*.

A team led by Dr. David Pendergast of the Royal Ontario Museum began work in 1965 on the central part of the ancient city, where upward of 250 structures have been found in an area of about 1,000 square yards. So far, this is the most extensively excavated of all the Mayan sites in Belize. For a trading center, Altun Ha was strategically located— a few miles from Little Rocky Point on the Caribbean and a few miles from Moho Caye at the mouth of the Belize River, both believed to have been major centers for the large trading canoes that worked up and down the coasts of Guatemala, Honduras, Belize, Mexico's Yucatán, and all the way to Panama.

Altun Ha spans an area of about 25 square miles, most of which is covered by trees, vines, and rainforest. It was rebuilt several

times during the Pre-Classic, Classic, and Post-Classic Periods. The desecration of the structures leads scientists to believe that the site may have been abandoned because of violence.

A gift shop and restroom facilities are at the entrance. Local tour guides (US$10 per group per half hour) are available at the entrance. If you're coming to Altun Ha as part of a package, consider insisting that your tour provider use a local guide; this ensures that local communities benefit from the site.

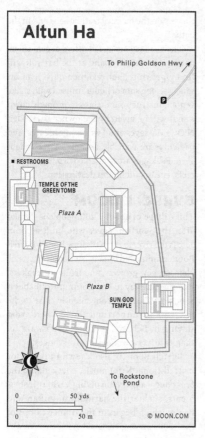

Altun Ha

To Philip Goldson Hwy

P

■ RESTROOMS

TEMPLE OF THE
GREEN TOMB

Plaza A

Plaza B

SUN GOD
TEMPLE

To Rockstone
Pond

0   50 yds
0   50 m   © MOON.COM

Rockstone Pond

Located near Plaza B, the reservoir, also known as **Rockstone Pond,** is fed by springs and rain runoff. It demonstrates the advanced knowledge of the Maya in just one of their many fields of expertise: engineering. Archaeologists say that an insignificant little stream ran through the rainforest for centuries. No doubt it had been a source of fresh water for the Maya—but maybe not enough. They diverted the creek and then began a major engineering project, digging and enlarging a deep, round hole that was then plastered with limestone cement. Once the cement dried and hardened, the stream was rerouted to its original course, and the newly built reservoir filled and overflowed at the east end, allowing the stream to continue on its age-old track. This made the area livable. Today, Rockstone Pond is surrounded by thick brush and alive with rainforest creatures, including tarpon, small fish, turtles, and other reptiles.

Sun God Temple

Structures includes palaces and temples concentrate around two main plazas. The tallest building is the **Sun God Temple,** rising 59 feet above the plaza floor. At Altun Ha, the bases of the structures are oval and terraced. The small temples on top have typical small rooms built with the Mayan trademark—the corbel arch.

Temple of the Green Tomb

Pendergast's team uncovered many valuable finds, such as unusual green obsidian blades, pearls, and more than 300 jade pieces—beads, earrings, and rings. Seven funeral chambers were discovered, including the **Temple of the Green Tomb,** rich with human remains and traditional funerary treasures. Mayan scholars believe the first man buried was someone of great importance; he was draped with jade beads, pearls, and shells.

Next to his right hand was the most exciting find—a solid jade head now referred to as **Kinich Ahau** (The Sun God). Kinich Ahau is, to date, the largest jade carving found at any Mayan site. The head weighs nine pounds and measures nearly six inches from base to crown. It is reportedly now housed far away in a museum in Canada. The two discoverers of the jade head some 40 years ago, Winston Herbert and William Leslie, still reside in Rockstone Pond and Lucky Strike villages. On November 29, 2006, they were honored by the National Institute of Culture and History for their find.

Transportation

To reach Altun Ha from the Philip Goldson Highway, continue past the Burrell Boom turnoff (to the Community Baboon Sanctuary) and drive on to about Mile 19, where the road forks; the right fork is the Old

Northern Highway, which leads to Altun Ha and Maskall Village. The entrance is 10.5 miles from the intersection. The road is in horrible condition and not getting any better with the increased traffic.

Altun Ha is close enough to Belize City that a taxi ride is your best bet (US$100 round-trip). Kenneth Bennett of **KB Taxi Service** (tel. 501/634-2865) is an excellent driver who will wait for up to 2.5 hours while you tour the site. You can also opt for a tour operator that specializes in these trips, such as Mr. Lascelle of **S&L Travel and Tours** (91 N. Front St., tel. 501/227-7593 or 501/227-5145, www.sltravelbelize.com).

Note that Altun Ha is a popular destination for cruise ship passengers (usually Tues. and Thurs.)—if you don't want to share your experience with busloads of tourists, check with the park before coming. In general, it's easy to avoid the crowds if you get here when the park first opens.

BELIZE BOUTIQUE RESORT AND SPA

By any standard, **Belize Boutique Resort and Spa** (formerly Maruba, Mile 40.5, Old Northern Hwy., Maskall Village, tel. 501/225-5555, U.S. tel. 800/861-7001, www.belizeresortandspa.com, US$251-465) is an interesting sight in the middle of the forest, located about a mile out of Maskall Village. Many visitors come just for the day; it's a popular stopover for Altun Ha explorers who decide to enjoy lunch and a mud mask (pick the Mood Mud Massage) before heading back to San Pedro, Belize City, or other nearby destinations. The resort's verdant landscaping is enhanced by intriguing focal points spread around the grounds: a tiny glass-decorated chapel, a *palapa*-covered stone chess table, and a pool that seems to spring from the rainforest, complete with waterfalls. The uniquely named guest rooms—Moon, Fertility, Mayan Loft, and Bondage, to name a few—continue the eclectic motif with carved masks, mosaic-tile floors, standing candles, concrete fountains, tiled tubs, screened windows, and fresh flowers on the massive feather beds and in the baths.

The **restaurant** often offers decent international fusion fare, and at the bar you will find viper rum ("for real men only"), an insanely strong shot of liquor infused with snake venom. Instructions on how to properly down a shot will be given by the owner-bartender, Nicky. Massages, mud wraps, manicures, and pedicures are available, as well as a free-weight gym. Packages are available with tours to the reefs, ruins, and inland destinations.

BURRELL BOOM

This village of about 1,200 people is named after the Scottish logger who built a boom across the river to catch his logs. Today, Burrell Boom is inhabited by subsistence farmers, anglers, cashew growers, and fruit winemakers. It is the gateway to the Community Baboon Sanctuary, but also conveniently close to the international airport and a good way to avoid staying in Belize City if you don't want to, thanks to a few wonderful river lodges.

Burrell Boom is also known in Belize for its traditional Kriol music, particularly, the *brokdong*—a genre involving various instruments, such as the harmonica, guitar, and banjo, which began in the timber camps of the 1800s among enslaved Africans. An annual festival, or *bram,* in December celebrates the *brokdong* with various Kriol musicians performing at Burrell Boom's Black Orchid Resort.

TOP EXPERIENCE

★ Community Baboon Sanctuary

The **Community Baboon Sanctuary** (CBS, tel. 501/622-9624, cbsbelize@gmail.com, www.howlermonkeys.org/lodging, 8am-5pm daily, US$7) is a nonprofit organization consisting of 220 members in seven local communities who have voluntarily

1: Altun Ha; 2: howler monkey at the Community Baboon Sanctuary

Saving the Baboon

One of the six species of howler monkeys in the world, the black howlers (*Alouatta caraya*) are the largest monkeys in the Americas. Robert Horwich of the University of Wisconsin-Milwaukee was the first zoologist to spend extended time in the howler's range, which covered southern Mexico, northeast Guatemala, and Belize. The results of his study were disturbing. In Mexico the monkeys were being hunted for food, and their habitat was fast disappearing. Conditions in Guatemala were only slightly better. Here, too, the monkeys were hunted by locals in the forests around Tikal, and as the forest habitat shrank, so too did the number of howler monkeys.

In the Belizean village of Bermudian Landing, however, the communities of monkeys were strong and healthy, the forest was intact, and the locals seemed genuinely fond of the noisy creatures. This was definitely the place to start talking about a wildlife reserve. Horwich, with the help of Jon Lyon, a botanist from the State University of New York, began a survey of the village in 1984. After many meetings with the town leaders, excitement grew about the idea of saving the "baboon." Homeowners agreed to leave the monkey's food trees—hog plums and sapodillas—and small strips of forest between cleared fields as aerial pathways for the primates, as well as 60 feet of forest along both sides of waterways.

An application was made to World Wildlife Fund USA in 1985 for funds to set up the reserve. Local landowners signed a voluntary management agreement set forth by Horwich and Lyon—and a sanctuary was born.

According to sanctuary manager Fallett Young, who died in 2009, there have been successful relocations of some of the thriving monkey troops around the country, including to the Cockscomb Basin Wildlife Sanctuary, where howlers hadn't been heard since they were decimated by yellow fever decades ago.

In the case of the Community Baboon Sanctuary, educating people about conservation and encouraging their fondness for nature were more successful than stringent hunting laws. The managers of the sanctuary are villagers who understand their neighbors; much of their time is spent with schoolchildren and adults in the villages concerned. Part of their education includes basic farming and sustained land-use techniques that eliminate the constant need to cut forest for new milpas (cornfields).

Another result is the unhindered growth of 100 species of trees, vines, and epiphytes. The animal life is thriving—anteaters, armadillos, iguanas, hicatee turtles, deer, coatis, amphibians, reptiles, and about 200 species of birds all live here.

A lively debate continues among traditional conservationists about allowing people to live within a wildlife preserve. However, Belize's grassroots conservation is proving that it can succeed.

agreed to manage their land in ways that will preserve their beloved "baboon" (the local term for the black howler monkey). Because of community-based efforts to preserve the creature, there are now 3,000 individual monkeys living freely in the forests and buffer zones between people's farms. Since 1998 the CBS Women's Conservation Group has overseen the organization and its members, with a female representative from each of the seven villages. More recently, the CBS member landowners received US$15,000 in microgrants to improve their small businesses and communities. CBS feels remote but is less than an hour's drive from Belize City, making it both a popular day trip and a destination for anyone who'd rather wake up to the throaty roars of Belizean howler monkeys than the bustle of Belize City.

There are enough trails, rivers, and guided tours to keep you busy here for a couple of days. All activities are arranged through the CBS Visitors Center in Bermudian Landing; group trips and guides from local hotels are also available. A basic nature walk is included with the entrance fee to the visitors center and museum (feel free to tip your guide), which is small but has very informative displays on a range of topics—from the history of CBS to the local Kriol culture and Belize's wildlife.

There are 1.5-hour and 3-hour **canoe tours** and a 2-hour **driving tour** of some of the different sanctuary villages. Those staying overnight should definitely take advantage of the nighttime trips, such as the 3.5-hour crocodile canoe trip up Mussell Creek and the 2-hour night hike into the surrounding forest. If you'd like to experience the local culture, request a **Kriol cultural package** (groups of 12 or more, US$15 pp), with food and dance performances.

If you're lucky, between February and August you might catch a village softball game or cricket match.

Food and Accommodations

A popular choice for adventurous travelers is the CBS's homestay program—you'll stay with a local family in primitive conditions, bathing with a bucket and talking with your host family in the evening. The **Women's Bed-and-Breakfast Group** (tel. 501/660-3545, www.howlermonkeys.org, US$42 pp, includes breakfast and dinner) has established a network of accommodations throughout the seven sanctuary villages, offering visitors a traditional Creole-style stay. Arrange your stay in one of these "bed-and-breakfasts" at least 24 hours in advance through the **CBS Visitors Center** (tel. 501/245-2009 or cell tel. 501/622-9624, www.howlermonkeys.org, 8am-5pm daily) at Bermudian Landing.

The **Black Orchid Resort** (2 Dawson Ln., U.S. tel. 866/437-1301, www.blackorchidresort.com, US$150-295) is a relaxed riverside resort within striking distance of a number of area attractions. Locals and guests rave about this place, which is a mere 11 miles from the international airport, but feels as remote as other upcountry rainforest lodges. Black Orchid's owner, Doug Thompson, is a native Belizean who lived in the United States for 36 years and is currently the president of the Belize Hotel Association. He also runs a tour company to whisk you around the region (and a free airport shuttle); or stay on the grounds and enjoy

the swimming pool, popular among locals on the weekends, or the shaded picnic tables, kayaks, and canoes. Sixteen spacious guest rooms are comfortable and have all the basic amenities, and there is an on-site restaurant and bar. Ask about the Jaguar Eco-house and three-bedroom villa for longer-term rental or for families.

Another excellent choice for anglers or ecotour seekers is the ★ **Belize River Lodge** (tel. 501/225-2002, U.S. tel. 888/275-4843, www.belizeriverlodge.com, 3-night package US$1,545), offering package stays only. A fishing lodge par excellence, it's run by a welcoming couple, Mike Heusner and Marguerite Miles, both of whom know their country inside out and have plenty of tales to share. There are eight cozy guest rooms with screened porches and gorgeous river views. Meals are shared family-style and often consist of delicious Belizean specialties. Mike sits on the board of the Audubon Society and is a great source of information on the country's wildlife and conservation efforts. You really don't have to be an angler to stay here, and the lodge is accessed via a short two-minute boat ride from Burrell Boom's banks. The lodge now also operates a sister resort on Long Caye, near Caye Chapel.

Campers can pitch a tent (US$5 pp) on the visitors center grounds or arrange for a meal (US$5) with a local family. There are privies and cold showers available. Next door, the **Howler Monkey Resort** (tel. 501/607-1571, www.howlermonkeyresort.bz, US$60-95, not including meals) has a selection of cabins, a screened restaurant, and a path to the river.

Transportation

Bermudian Landing is only 26 miles from Belize City, or about a 45-minute drive, and 22 miles from the Orange Walk District. From Belize City, drive north on the Philip Goldson Highway for 13 miles, then turn left toward Burrell Boom (notice a sign to turn left for the Black Orchid Resort). Follow signs to the Community Baboon Sanctuary Museum and Visitors Center, located across a soccer field.

Try not to get confused by the distracting private tour guide signs posted en masse just prior to the museum, and ignore any gestures for you to stop. This is not the official CBS site, and you won't be supporting the community by skipping CBS, who have very competent guides, know the history of the sanctuary, and work with the villages. Look for the CBS logo.

Two bus companies travel between Bermudian Landing and Belize City. In Belize City, McFadzean buses depart from the corner of Cemetery Road and Amara Avenue, and Russell buses leave from Euphrates Street and Cairo Street. Seven buses depart Belize City between noon and 9pm Monday-Friday; there's a shorter schedule on Saturday. There are no buses in either direction on Sunday. The bus takes about an hour. Four early morning buses leave Bermudian Landing 5:30am-7am, and there are two in the afternoon at 3:30pm and 4pm Monday-Saturday.

The sanctuary is close enough to the city or the international airport that you can consider a taxi or an escorted tour for a day trip. Negotiate taxi prices ahead of time. The Community Baboon Sanctuary can arrange airport transfers for reasonable prices.

SPANISH CREEK WILDLIFE SANCTUARY

Spanish Creek Wildlife Sanctuary is a 2,000-acre protected area rich in wildlife but short on infrastructure. It's near Rancho Dolores, due west along the Burrell Boom Road, beyond the Community Baboon Sanctuary, and accessible by bus from Belize City. For more information and to visit, contact the Rancho Dolores Environmental and Development Group (tel. 501/625-2837, www.belizeability.com).

CROOKED TREE

Crooked Tree is only a 33-mile drive from Belize City, or a little over an hour by bus. The island village and the wildlife sanctuary are primary destinations for serious birdwatchers. Other visitors will enjoy paddling in the water, hiking numerous trails, or reveling

at the annual cashew festival. Most visitors to the area can also enjoy the simple pleasure of mingling with the islanders, the majority of whom are of Kriol descent and were born and raised here. Walking through the village will reveal the simple farming and fishing community lifestyle they lead. Most villagers are related by blood or marriage, making it "one big family" in every sense of the phrase.

The Crooked Tree area itself is a network of inland lagoons, swamps, and waterways. The sanctuary also encompasses the freshwater lagoon that surrounds the area. The Crooked Tree Lagoon is up to a mile wide and more than 20 miles long. Along its banks lies the village of Crooked Tree, settled in the 1750s during the early days of the logwood era. This island, surrounded by fresh water, was once accessible only by boats traveling up the Belize River and Black Creek; the waterways were used to float the logs out to the sea. It wasn't until 1981 that the three-mile-long causeway leading into the village was built, bringing cars, buses, and other modern conveniences to the village.

Crooked Tree Village

The village is divided into three neighborhoods: Crooked Tree, Pine Ridge, and Stain, with a total population of about 1,000. Villagers operate farms, raise livestock, and have a small fishery. Visitors will find the village spread out on the island, with more cattle trails, half roads, and fence line than roads. There are a few well-grazed athletic fields, five churches, a small restaurant, a nurse-staffed clinic, and scores of stilted wooden houses, each with its own tank to catch rainwater. It's a tranquil community with children playing football and softball, biking around, racing horses, or whacking a ball around the cricket pitch.

TOP EXPERIENCE

★ Crooked Tree Wildlife Sanctuary

At the Crooked Tree Wildlife Sanctuary, 16,400 acres of waterways, logwood swamps, and lagoon provide habitat for a diverse array of hundreds of resident and migratory birds all year long.

The sanctuary was established by the Belize Audubon Society to protect its most famous inhabitant, the jabiru stork—the largest flying bird in the western hemisphere, with a wingspan of up to eight feet. Multitudes of other birds (285 species, at last count) find the sanctuary a safe resting spot during the dry season, with enormous food resources along the shorelines and in the trees. (During my visit, I saw beautiful vermillion flycatchers and a white ibis, among many others.) After a

rain, thousands of minuscule frogs, no more than an inch long, seem to drop from the sky; they're fair game for the agami heron, snowy egret, and great egret, quick hunters with long beaks. A fairly large bird, the snail kite uses its particular beak to hook meat out of the apple snails.

Two varieties of ducks—the black-bellied whistling duck and the Muscovy—nest in trees along the swamp. All five species of kingfishers live in the sanctuary, and you can see ospreys and black-collared hawks diving for their morning catch.

Black Creek, with its forests of large trees, provides homes to monkeys, Morelet's crocodiles, coatimundis, turtles, and iguanas. A profusion of wild ocher pokes up from the water, covered with millions of pale pink snail eggs. Grazing Brahma cattle wade into the shallows of the lagoon to munch on the *tum tum* (water lilies), a delicacy that keeps them fat and fit when the grasses turn brown in the dry season.

Although several organizations had a financial hand in founding the park, the **Belize Audubon Society** (tel. 501/223-5004, www. belizeaudubon.org) operates here with the assistance of the community and devoted volunteers. Note that visitor hunting and fishing are not permitted.

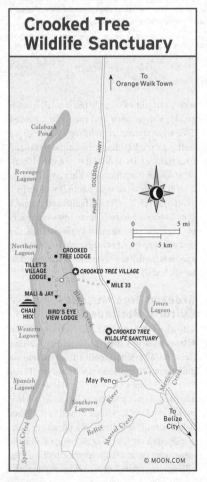

Crooked Tree Wildlife Sanctuary

To Orange Walk Town

Calabash Pond

Revenge Lagoon

PHILIP GOLDSON HWY

0   5 mi

0   5 km

Northern Lagoon

CROOKED TREE LODGE

TILLET'S VILLAGE LODGE

CROOKED TREE VILLAGE

MILE 33

MALI & JAY

CHAU HIIX

BIRD'S EYE VIEW LODGE

Black Creek

Jones Lagoon

CROOKED TREE WILDLIFE SANCTUARY

Western Lagoon

Spanish Lagoon

May Pen

Southern Lagoon

River

Mexico Creek

Belize

Mussel Creek

Spanish Creek

To Belize City

© MOON.COM

Crooked Tree Lagoon

The best way to experience **Crooked Tree Lagoon** is by boat, and there are all kinds available at each hotel. Contact your lodge or guesthouse, all of whom will have birding and tour guides on staff who will answer questions about the flora and fauna of the sanctuary. It's possible to explore the area in a rented canoe or kayak, motor through on a guided tour, or hike the system of boardwalks through lowland savanna and logwood forests; observation towers provide wide views across the lagoons. Birding is possible year-round, but peak times are February-April.

Annual Crooked Tree Cashew Festival

The namesake of this relaxed inland island village is the cashew tree, which grows prolifically throughout the area. The unique nut has always contributed to the community's economy, especially for its women, who have been able to secure additional income for their households by selling cashew products. The situation is even better today, as the products are more often sold directly to local consumers and travelers than to distributors in Belize City, as they were in the past.

To celebrate the bent branches and their heavy fruit, the people of Crooked Tree Village throw a big cashew harvest festival the second weekend in May. It's a fun hometown fair with regional arts, music, folklore, dance, and crafts. And, of course, it's a chance to sample delicious cashew wine, cashew jellies, stewed cashews—you get the picture.

Seek out the demonstrations showing how the cashew nut is processed; it's interesting stuff. The fruit, or the cashew "apple," is either red or yellow, with the seed hanging from the bottom of the apple. The meat of the apple can be stewed or made into jam or wine, while the seedpod is roasted in an open fire on the ground. Roasting the cashew stabilizes the highly acidic oil and at the same time makes the pod brittle enough to crack. The nut is partially cooked during this step in the processing. The seeds are then raked so they cool evenly and quickly.

The cashews are then cracked by hand, one at a time. Those who handle the nuts wear gloves, as the shell contains a highly irritating poison that for most people causes blisters and inflammation. Processing removes all the poison.

Crooked Tree Community Experiences

In 2018, visiting JICA volunteer Yoshi Wakabayashi spent a year in Crooked Tree to help create a series of cultural experiences aimed at attracting more visitors to this authentic Kriol village. Whether or not you're into birding, you now have opportunities to immerse in families' homes and learn about the village from its residents, via a handful of community and nature tours.

Sign up for **Mrs. Ava's Cooking Class** (tel. 501/660-5701, devon.gillett31@gmail.com, US$25 pp half-day, call ahead to arrange). Set in her home kitchen, Mrs. Ava welcomes you at 9am and shows you how to make the national dish, among other menu options—stewed chicken with rice and beans, with side potato salad—as well as Kriol bread pudding. She'll share lots of stories along the way, about growing up in the village and raising her sons, and you can tour her backyard farm, where pigs and turkeys roam. This hardworking entrepreneur will then let you share the meal you've prepared on her veranda.

Another highlight is the **Good News Garden Tour** (tel. 501/669-4541, US$20 pp)

with Evangeline Gillett, affectionately known as Ms. Vange, born and raised in Crooked Tree and a teacher by training. Ms. Vange is a walking encyclopedia on medicinal plants and fruit trees, and will share a ton of valuable information during the tour of her spacious garden, at the heart of which stands a beautiful, giant oak tree. You'll taste fruits, and discover over 60 plants and trees that grow organically over seven acres—the monkey apple fruit, the craboo, sorrel, and others—that are endemic and imported. Take bottles of her cashew preserves home.

Crooked Tree Museum and Cultural Heritage Center

Launched in June 2018, the **Crooked Tree Museum and Cultural Heritage Center** (tel. 501/637-8141, crookedtreemuseum@gmail.com, 10am-noon and 1pm-3pm Tues.-Sat., US$5 adults, US$1 children) is a welcome addition to the village, offering historical background on the village as well as the lower Belize River Watershed and Kriol culture. On display are a number of archaeological finds—some were uncovered underneath one of the village's churches—as well as items donated by residents, dated photographs, and cultural tools. It's well worth making a stop if you're in the village, whether pre- or post-birding.

For more information on the tours and prices, please visit www.visitcrookedtree.com, also a great resource on visiting the village. Note that there is still no ATM in the village.

Food and Accommodations

There are several accommodations options in low-key Crooked Tree as the area continues to gain popularity, starting with **Tillet's Village Lodge** (tel. 501/607-3871, www.tilletvillage. com, US$40-80). The famous Sam Tillet—renowned as one of the premier Belizean naturalists—died in 2007, but his family is carrying on the tradition. The lodge is in the middle of the village, not on the water, and the guest rooms are small and plain but clean and with private baths and tiled floors. Nature walks are US$15, and you can also go horseback riding or do a "jungle survival" trip.

As you approach the island on the causeway (on the shoreline off to the left), you'll see one of Crooked Tree's longest-running properties: **Bird's Eye View Lodge** (tel. 501/225-7027 or 501/203-2040, www.birdseyeviewbelize. com, US$65-150). The 20 guest rooms all have private baths and various comforts, even if slightly dated, including air-conditioning. Camping (US$10) is also available in the yard adjacent to the entrance. The rooftop bar and patio is a nice spot to take in the breeze and do some bird-spotting, even after your four-hour daybreak bird-watching boat cruise on the lagoon. Meals are US$12 for breakfast and lunch; dinner is US$15. Boat rentals, tours, and airport pickups can be arranged. Boat tours for up to three people cost about US$125; ask about village tours and cashew-making tours in season (Mar.-June).

On the shore of the lagoon north of the causeway, **Crooked Tree Lodge** (tel. 501/626-3820, www.crookedtreelodgebelize. com, US$40-60) is a small, well-landscaped, and quiet retreat of 11.5 acres with six stilted wooden cabanas with en suite baths, including a bigger one for families (sleeps up to 7,

US$120). Camping (US$10) is possible, and pets and children are welcome. Three daily meals are available at additional cost. Wide-ranging boat and birding tours can be set up with local guides. There is wireless Internet, a restaurant, and a small bar, all on the lagoon's edge.

The lagoon-front **Jacana Inn** (tel. 501/604-8025 or 501/620-9472, jacanainn@yahoo.com, US$50 d) has 13 ground-floor guest rooms with queen beds, minifridges, private baths with cold showers, fans, and Internet access. The building isn't much to look at, thanks to a second-floor extension left under construction, but being steps from the lagoon at this price is a highlight. There are bikes and canoes for rent as well as in-room meals on request.

Beck's Bed and Breakfast (tel. 501/633-3398, www.becksbedandbreakfast.com, US$90, includes breakfast) is a family-run, beautifully appointed guesthouse that now boasts the added perk of a swimming pool. There are three rooms, with plenty of shared relaxation lounge areas and terraces to enjoy the views and birds. There's Wi-Fi, cable TV, and other meals can be arranged.

In the village, the only place to dine out as of publication time is at **Mali & Jay's** (10am-9pm Mon.-Thurs., 10am-11pm Fri.-Sat., US$4-5), a clean and modern restaurant run by village native Maurice Gillett, who returned home after 30 years living in Oakland, California. Maurice is friendly and offers daily, tasty Belizean specialties. He grows his own vegetables and herbs, including peppers. Ask about his fresh fruit smoothies too.

Transportation

To reach Crooked Tree by car, drive north on the Philip Goldson Highway to Mile 33 and turn left. Continue until the dirt road turns into the three-mile-long earthen causeway that leads into Crooked Tree. You can also catch the **Jex Bus** (34 Regent St. W., tel. 501/663-3301 or 501/663-2740, US$2.25 one way) in downtown Belize City to Crooked Tree. The bus leaves promptly at 10:50am

Monday-Friday, arriving in Crooked Tree at 12:30pm; it is parked an hour prior to departure. You can also hop on any of the buses heading north from the main Novelo bus station to Corozal starting early in the morning; request a stop at the Crooked Tree junction and then get a ride from there into the village.

From Crooked Tree back into Belize City, the Jex buses depart mornings only at 5:25am Monday-Friday and 6:20am Monday-Saturday; verify the times before departure. Other options include catching an hourly bus back toward Belize City from the Crooked Tree junction on the highway, which is easy, or hire a taxi or local tour operator.

Along the George Price Highway

Driving west from Belize City, the George Price Highway (formerly the Western Highway) passes from wetlands to pine savanna, with the Maya Mountains draped across the horizon through your windshield. Most of this region is drained by the Sibun and Caves Branch Rivers, which empty out into a large lowland wetland before arriving at the sea. This central chunk of Belize is mostly wild, dotted by a handful of small villages, rainforest lodges, natural attractions, and parks. The most popular of these is the Belize Zoo.

The milepost markers between Belize City and San Ignacio will help you find your way around the countryside. If you're driving, you can match the markers as you go by setting your odometer to zero as you turn onto Cemetery Road at the western edge of Belize City.

The George Price Highway eventually leads to Belmopan, the smallest and most unassuming national capital in Central America.

FREETOWN SIBUN

Three miles south of Hattieville, as you make a left turn by the Hattieville Police Station (a yellow building), the small village of Freetown Sibun (community tel. 501/209-6006) has a population of less than 100, if that. People who had escaped enslavement founded the village back in the day, and its population used to peak around 2,000 during big logging runs. Today, you can find

campsites, canoe rentals, and hiking trails. Taxis to the village are plentiful from the traffic circle in Hattieville.

★ THE BELIZE ZOO

Established in 1983, the **Belize Zoo** (Mile 29, George Price Hwy., tel. 501/822-8000, www.belizezoo.org, 8:30am-4:30pm daily, US$15 adults, US$5 children) is set on 29 acres of

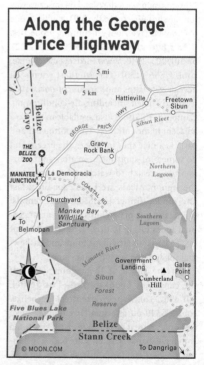

Along the George Price Highway

0   5 mi
0   5 km

Hattieville
Freetown Sibun
Sibun River
GEORGE PRICE HWY
Belize Cayo
THE BELIZE ZOO
Gracy Rock Bank
MANATEE JUNCTION
La Democracia
Northern Lagoon
COASTAL RD
Churchyard
To Belmopan
Monkey Bay Wildlife Sanctuary
Southern Lagoon
Manatee River
Government Landing
Gales Point
Sibun
Cumberland Hill
Forest
Five Blues Lake National Park
Reserve
Belize
Stann Creek
© MOON.COM
To Dangriga

tropical savanna and exhibits more than 125 animals, all native to Belize.

The zoo keeps only orphaned animals and those injured and rehabilitated, born in the zoo, and received as gifts from other zoos. The environment is as natural as possible, with thick native vegetation, and each animal lives in its own wildlife compound. Displays include Tapir Town; ask about Lucky Boy, a beautiful black jaguar the zoo helped rescue and rehabilitate.

In collaboration with the Panthera organization, the government of Belize, and the U.S. Fish and Wildlife Service, the Belize Zoo also runs the only problem **jaguar rehabilitation** program and in situ jaguar research program in the world. Problem jaguars, which prey on livestock and domestic animals, are trapped and brought to the zoo for behavior modification training—instead of a bullet. In difficult cases, the animals are transferred to zoos in the United States; the Milwaukee and Philadelphia zoos have received problem cats from Belize. The latest resident, Chiquibul, is a jaguar cub that joined in 2016 after being rescued from drowning inside the Chiquibul Forest. Chiqui is now an ambassador for her species and has a new home in the zoo to raise awareness about the threats, abuses, and environmental losses occurring in her former home.

In 2010, Hurricane Richard tore through the zoo, destroying many of the cages and structures. With superhuman efforts, the zoo staff and an army of volunteers participated in immediate reconstruction. In 2016, Hurricane Earl inflicted less damage, but the surrounding communities suffered greatly, and the zoo has been actively involved in helping them get back on their feet. Your visit to this special site will always go a long way.

The Belize Tropical Education Center

The Belize Tropical Education Center (tel. 501/832-2004, tec@belizezoo.org) across the street from the zoo was created to promote environmental education and scientific research. Meetings are held here for zoological news, reports, and educational seminars attended and given by people involved in zoology from around the world. The center is equipped with a classroom, a library, a kitchen and dining area, and dormitories that can accommodate as many as 30 people (US$30 pp, includes breakfast and dinner). Great nature trails weave through the 84-acre site, and bird-watchers can avail themselves of a bird-viewing deck. Also available are canoe trips, nocturnal zoo tours (a real treat), and natural history lectures. Cafeteria-style meals cooked for the zoo staff are available for purchase.

Transportation

The zoo is at Mile 29 on the George Price Highway. It is included in many day tours from Belize City and often as a stop during airport transfer to or from your lodge in the western or southern parts of Belize. Independent travelers can easily jump off the bus from Belize City or Cayo; bus fare from Belize City is US$1-2.

MANATEE JUNCTION

Driving west, note the junction with **Manatee Highway** to the left at about Mile 29. Look for a service station and motel of sorts on the southeast corner of the junction; its Petrofuel sign makes an especially good landmark at night, when it glows with bright colors. This improved dirt road, or "Coastal Highway," is the shortcut to Gales Point, Dangriga, and the Southern Highway. It's always a good idea to top off your tank, stock up on cold drinks, and ask for current road conditions here. Heavy rains can cause washouts on a lot of these "highways." This is a drive best done in daylight because of the picturesque views of rainforest, Mayan villages, and the Maya Mountains in the distance. Your best bet, however, is to drive the Hummingbird Highway to Dangriga and the south to avoid roughing up your car.

GALES POINT

This tiny, unique Creole settlement occupies a thin two-mile-long peninsula jutting north into the Southern Lagoon. Gales Point is 15 miles north of Dangriga or 25 miles southwest of Belize City, but getting here makes it feel farther. Depending on which accounts you read, the 400 or so modern inhabitants are descended from either logwood cutters or people who had escaped enslavement, known as "maroons," and settled here in the 1700s. Gales Point is a traditional Creole cultural stronghold. If you're lucky, your visit to Gales Point will coincide with the full moon, when the entire village often participates in a roaming call-and-response drumming and dance circle. In the weeks before Christmas, the frequency of *sambai* drumming events increases, reaching a crescendo on Christmas Day and December 26 with a unique village-wide music and dance celebration known as *brokdong bram*. Gales Point is also known for its homemade cashew wine.

The **Southern Lagoon,** which surrounds Gales Point on three sides, is part of an extensive estuary bordered by thick mangroves. Their tangled roots provide the perfect breeding grounds for sport fish, crabs, shrimp, lobsters, and a host of other marinelife. Rich beds of seagrass line the bottom of the lagoon and support a population of manatees. These gentle mammals are often seen basking on the surface of the water or coming up for air, which they must do about every four minutes. This is a popular place to observe the manatees, often spotted close to a warm spring-fed hole in the lagoon. Tours to see manatees can be arranged through any of the Gales Point accommodations; trips are also available to see birds and caves in the region and to go fishing.

In July 2008 Gales Point experienced the most devastating floods in its history, as the entire lagoon rose and covered much of the peninsula, a phenomenon that did not occur even during massive Hurricane Hattie in 1961. It has since recovered but remains just as remote and untouristed as ever.

Accommodations

There are some loose homestay programs and places to camp in the village; ask around the village for the latest information. **Gentle's Cool Spot** (tel. 501/668-0102 or 501/666-9847) is one local service that provides traditional *fiyah haat* (fire hearth) cooking plus a few stuffy clapboard guest rooms (US$18-28). Gentle's veranda is a favorite gathering place for locals, and Gentle also provides tours.

Manatee Lodge (tel. 501/532-2400 or 501/662-2154, U.S. tel. 877/462-6283, www.manateelodge.com, US$85) is at the very northern tip of the peninsula and caters to birders, sportfishers, and independent nature-loving travelers and families. The eight guest rooms have nice wood furnishings, private baths, 24-hour electricity, and a veranda with views of the surrounding lagoon and sunsets behind the Maya Mountains; rooms sleep up to four. The lodge offers access to a wildlife habitat completely different from the rest of Belize in the shallow brackish water and mangroves of the Southern Lagoon. The number of shorebirds and waterfowl is impressive, and to encourage guests to see local wildlife, the lodge provides each room with a canoe. Binoculars and bug repellent are a must. Children under age 6 stay free, and children ages 6-12 are half price. Moderately priced and delicious home-cooked Creole and continental meals are available; so are transfers and multiday packages.

Transportation

To get to Gales Point by car, either choose the Manatee Highway, also called the Coastal Highway, and expect rough muddy roads if it's raining, or take the Hummingbird Highway, which is about 25 miles longer but smoother (for most of the way, anyway). The most enjoyable—and expensive—way to reach Gales Point is the 90-minute boat ride from Belize City, which winds through bird-filled canals, rivers, and lagoons, and you may spot crocodiles, manatees, or dolphins. Manatee Lodge can arrange a boat transfer, but it is very expensive; it's worth it if you have a group. There used to be several weekly buses from Belize City, but they were not running regularly at last check; call Manatee Lodge for current schedules or possible rides. You could also reach out to Dangriga-based and Gales Point native Brother David of **CD's Transfer** (1163 3rd St., tel. 501/502-3489, cell tel. 501/602-3077, breddadavid@gmail.com) to negotiate a simple ride to and from Gales Point.

MONKEY BAY WILDLIFE SANCTUARY

Monkey Bay Wildlife Sanctuary (tel. 501/822-8032, www.monkeybaybelize.com) comprises tropical forest and riparian and savanna habitats stretching from the George Price Highway down to the Sibun River, which flows from the Maya Mountains through the coastal savanna on its path to the Caribbean Sea. The 3,300-acre wildlands of Monkey Bay include the natural habitat of nearly all the animals represented at the Belize Zoo, just east on the George Price Highway.

This is a fantastic retreat—for student groups, families, naturalists, and paddlers alike (though most of the sanctuary's business is with study-abroad and service groups). The sanctuary maintains field stations in the Mountain Pine Ridge and Tobacco Caye. The main campus is home to exotic mammal species, including tapirs, pumas, and jaguars, as well as Morelet's crocodiles. More than 250 species of birds have been recorded. The sanctuary borders the Sibun River biological corridor and contains documented remains of ancient Mayan settlements and ceremonial caves. A trail system carries you through it all; you can hike, rent a canoe, or hire a caving guide—this is serious spelunking country as well. One option is a three-night camping expedition, on which you'll hike to Five Blues Lake National Park. Another is a canoe trip on the Sibun River (US$35 pp), which you can combine with a caving expedition (US$50 pp).

You'll find two miles of trails and good swimming at the nearby Sibun River. With the government's 1992 declaration of the 2,250-acre Monkey Bay Wildlife Sanctuary across the river, there now exists a wildlands corridor between the sanctuary and the Manatee Forest Reserve to the south.

Food

There are a few notable restaurants clustered around Mile 31, right around where you first see the sleeping Mayan giant in the hills to the south (the hill formations in this area look like a person lying on their back). You'll first come to the popular **Cheers** (Mile 31.25, George Price Hwy., tel. 501/822-8014, www.cheersrestaurant.bz, 6am-8:30pm Mon.-Sat., 7am-7:15pm Sun., US$5-15), with its interesting collection of orchids, license plates, and T-shirts. Oh, and the food is excellent. Ask about its cabana accommodations.

A bit farther, just past the turnoff for Monkey Bay, is **Amigo's** (Mile 31.7, George Price Hwy., tel. 501/802-8000, adellalockwood@yahoo.com, 8am-9pm daily, US$5-9), another friendly, screened-in bar and restaurant with Belizean and continental food, from salads to burgers and more.

Accommodations

Some travelers find themselves intrigued enough by the goings-on at this environmental education center and tropical watershed research station that they opt to stay in one of Monkey Bay's primitively rustic guest rooms longer than they had planned. The accommodations share the grounds with a screened-in dining area and a barnlike library and study space (more than 500 titles are available for reference, with lots of local information).

Choose from a campground in a grove of pine trees with sturdy wooden tent platforms (US$10.90 pp), a private room or mountain-view cabin (US$32.70-55), or dormitories (US$22 pp); they all share common composting toilets and solar showers. You can also stay in one of the primitive wooden field station rooms in the central building (US$27). Including all the bunks in the dormitory, there are 50 beds here. Freshly prepared meals are available, as are a range of learning and adventure activities throughout Belize. There's a lovely backyard peppered with hammocks and a path leading to the river.

Monkey Bay offers various cultural learning programs that include homestays with Mayan and Creole communities at Maya Centre or Crooked Tree Village; it also has a curriculum of tropical watershed ecology field courses. Groups and individuals are welcome for internships and volunteer programs as well.

Transportation

Monkey Bay Wildlife Sanctuary is at Mile 31 on the George Price Highway; look for the entrance sign on the left side of the highway. The entrance is a stone's throw from Cheers restaurant.

The Northern Cayes

The Northern Cayes are Belize's greatest tourism draw: postcard-perfect islands, quick access to the Belize Barrier Reef, and lodging, restaurant, activity, and entertainment options to fit backpacker or celebrity budgets.

Close to Belize City and once the favorite hideout and playground of pirates, the Northern Cayes are ideal for adventurers short on getaway time. This cluster of islands provides excellent access to two of Belize's three atolls—Turneffe and Lighthouse Reef (including the iconic Great Blue Hole)—for world-class diving, snorkeling, and fishing. And that's not all: As the most tourist-ready region in all of Belize, the Northern Cayes host an estimated 70 percent of visitors for their first Belizean experience. This fusion of local culture with a constant

Highlights

Look for ★ to find recommended sights, activities, dining, and lodging.

★ **Hol Chan Marine Reserve:** The second-largest barrier reef in the world is less than a mile offshore from both Ambergris Caye and Caye Caulker. Spending a day here is akin to swimming in a giant aquarium (page 79).

★ **Bacalar Chico National Park and Marine Reserve:** This UNESCO World Heritage Site at the northern tip of Ambergris Caye boasts spectacular snorkeling and diving (page 80).

★ **The Split:** Caye Caulker's main swimming area draws visitors and locals alike who sun themselves on the wooden decks, snorkel, or dance at the on-site beach bar (page 113).

★ **Swallow Caye Wildlife Sanctuary:** This protected area is home to the endangered West Indian manatee (page 115).

★ **The Elbow:** Advanced divers visit this steep drop-off where swift currents collide, hoping to spot deepwater predatory fish as well as a wall of sponges (page 135).

★ **Half Moon Caye National Monument:** This beautiful crescent-shaped island on Lighthouse Reef Atoll is home to more than 4,000 red-footed boobies and 120 other bird species. It's also one of the best diving spots in Belize (page 140).

stream of international visitors makes for one lively scene.

Avid divers tend to stay on one of the atolls to minimize travel time to top dive sites; otherwise, it's a two-hour boat ride each way from Ambergris Caye or Caye Caulker. Ambergris, generally referred to as San Pedro, attracts those seeking constant activity—there is incessant hustle and bustle, not to mention pretty hotels and pools, chic lounges, fine dining, and plenty of bars and nightlife. Smaller Caye Caulker attracts the laid-back, off-the-beaten-path traveler, those who seek immersion in local island life, exploring sand-only streets on foot or bicycle (there are no cars here!). There's an amusing sibling rivalry between the two cayes—larger Ambergris Caye considers Caye Caulker slow and boring, while the smaller caye is content with the lack of noise, paved roads, and crowds. In reality, each has a varied slice of Belize to offer, excellent water sports, and island fun, and neither is a wasted visit.

PLANNING YOUR TIME

A common dilemma is whether to stay on Ambergris Caye or Caye Caulker, each unique in rhythm and scenery. The good news is that they are a mere 20-minute water taxi hop away from each other, with tours available from either base.

Ambergris Caye's foodie treasures and luxury accommodations attract travelers seeking both excellent diving and nonstop nightlife. San Pedro is considered the "trendy" part of Belize, with more resorts, bars, lounges, eateries, and general day-to-day activities than most of the country. There's a steady buzz here, and events take place year-round, attracting not only visitors but also Belizeans from the city seeking a quick, fun getaway. **Hol Chan Marine Reserve** is the most popular dive and snorkel site in Belize. Located on and around the northern tip of Ambergris Caye, **Bacalar Chico National Park and Marine Reserve** hosts an incredibly diverse array of wildlife and offers excellent snorkeling and diving.

Caye Caulker's slower yet rhythmic Caribbean vibe will appeal to the laid-back visitor while still offering excellent diving opportunities. **The Split** is the favorite go-to swimming and sunset rendezvous spot on the island. **Swallow Caye Wildlife Sanctuary,** at the north end of the Drowned Cayes, is a protected area with nearly 9,000 acres of sea and mangroves to explore.

Outside these two cayes are the upscale **Turneffe Islands,** with diving opportunities at **The Elbow** and **Lighthouse Reef Atoll,** home to the some of the best dive spots in the world—**Half Moon Caye** and **Long Caye.**

San Pedro and Ambergris Caye

TOP EXPERIENCE

Ambergris Caye is Belize's largest island, just south of the Mexican Yucatán mainland and stretching southward for 24 miles into Belizean waters. Ambergris (AM-bur-giss) is 35 miles east of Belize City and about 0.75 mile west of the Belize Barrier Reef. The island was formed by an accumulation of coral fragments and silt from the Río Hondo as it emptied from what is now northern Belize. The caye is made up of mangrove swamps, a dozen lagoons, a plateau, and a series of low sand ridges. The largest lagoon, fed by 15 creeks, is 2.5-mile-long **Laguna de San Pedro,** on the western side of the village.

San Pedro Town sits on a sand ridge at the southern end of the island, the only actual town on the island and the most-visited

---

Previous: Kayaking at sunset is popular on Caye Caulker; a sign welcoming you to The Split area; nurse sharks at Hol Chan Marine Reserve.

The Northern Cayes

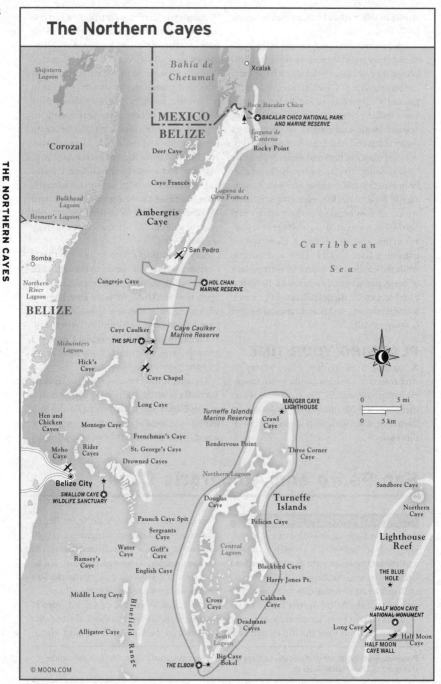

Shipstern Lagoon

Bahía de Chetumal

Xcalak

Boca Bacalar Chico

BACALAR CHICO NATIONAL PARK AND MARINE RESERVE

MEXICO

BELIZE

Corozal

Deer Caye

Laguna de Cantena

Rocky Point

Cayo Francés

Laguna de Cayo Francés

Bulkhead Lagoon

Bennett's Lagoon

Ambergris Caye

Caribbean

Sea

Bomba

San Pedro

Northern River Lagoon

BELIZE

Cangrejo Caye

HOL CHAN MARINE RESERVE

Midwinters Lagoon

Caye Caulker

THE SPLIT

Caye Caulker Marine Reserve

Hick's Caye

Caye Chapel

Long Caye

MAUGER CAYE LIGHTHOUSE

Turneffe Islands Marine Reserve

Crawl Caye

Hen and Chicken Cayes

Montego Caye

Frenchman's Caye

Rendezvous Point

Three Corner Caye

Moho Caye

Rider Cayes

St. George's Caye

Drowned Cayes

Northern Lagoon

Sandbore Caye

Belize City

SWALLOW CAYE WILDLIFE SANCTUARY

Douglas Caye

Turneffe Islands

Northern Caye

Paunch Caye Spit

Pelican Caye

Lighthouse Reef

Sergeants Caye

Water Caye

Goff's Caye

Central Lagoon

THE BLUE HOLE

Ramsey's Caye

English Caye

Blackbird Caye

Harry Jones Pt.

Middle Long Caye

Cross Caye

Calabash Caye

HALF MOON CAYE NATIONAL MONUMENT

Bluefield Range

Deadmans Cayes

Long Caye

Half Moon Caye

Alligator Caye

South Lagoon

HALF MOON CAYE WALL

THE ELBOW

Big Caye Bokel

0   5 mi

0   5 km

© MOON.COM

destination in Belize. It is chock-full of accommodations, restaurants, bars, golf carts, and services. San Pedro is also the most expensive part of Belize, with prices for some basic goods and foods double the mainland prices and sometimes even more than similar services and restaurants in the United States.

The town is increasingly more populated and traffic more intense as a result, as more expats move here and more businesses open, particularly with the new paved road north of the bridge, which has opened access to a previously remote area of the island.

ORIENTATION

Whether arriving by air or sea, your trip to Ambergris begins in San Pedro Town—the heart of the island's activity, where most of the restaurants, bars, nightlife, shopping, and hotels are clustered. Three streets run north-south and parallel the beach on the island's east side. Residents still refer to them by their historic names: **Front Street** (Barrier Reef Dr.), **Middle Street** (Pescador Dr.), and **Back Street** (Angel Coral St.). Another landmark is at the north end of town, where the San Pedro River flows through a navigable cut. This spot is often referred to as **"the cut"** or "the bridge," referring to the toll bridge that replaced the hand-drawn ferry. Past the bridge are some exclusive resorts, hotels, and lounges. You'll also hear the term "south of town," referring to the continually developing area south of the airstrip and south of San Pedro Town, accessed by Coconut Drive and starting past Ramon's Village Resort, where more upscale retreats can be found, along with some casual and lively outdoor bars.

SIGHTS
★ Hol Chan Marine Reserve

Once a traditional fishing ground back when San Pedro was a sleepy village of a few hundred people, **Hol Chan Marine Reserve** (www.holchanbelize.org, US$12.50 pp) is the most popular dive and snorkel site in Belize,

with tens of thousands of visitors each year. The site is four miles south of San Pedro and makes for an affordable morning or afternoon trip. In town a small visitors center on Caribeña Street has information on the reserve. Nearly all tour operators on Ambergris and Caye Caulker offer trips to the Hol Chan cut.

Once you visit, you'll quickly understand the popularity of the reserve—and why it is important to help preserve it. Established as a marine park in 1987, when fishing was banned, Hol Chan boasts an amazing diversity of species. The reserve focuses on creating a sustainable link between tourism and conservation, protecting the coral reef while allowing visitors to experience and learn about the marinelife living here.

On most trips to Hol Chan there will be an added stop at **Shark Ray Alley**—a nearby zone of the reserve where southern stingrays and six-foot-long nurse sharks have gathered over the years thanks to anglers who often cleaned their catch in this area. Used to getting their scraps of fish, the nurse sharks anticipate the boats and are used to humans—although it is best to keep a safe distance. The thrill of jumping in waters surrounded by these creatures is something to experience at least once.

Note that it is officially illegal to feed or touch the fish. Even if your guide tells you differently, and even if you see other groups caressing the nurse sharks and rays, this is against the reserve rules and regulations and against all normal protocol for interacting with wildlife—as it should be. That said, San Pedro anglers and tour guides have been feeding the animals in this spot every day for over 15 years, so some argue that an exception should be made or there is some educational benefit to interacting with the animals. Best to leave only bubbles, I say.

Snorkeling at Hol Chan usually ends with a stop at the **Coral Gardens,** where you'll explore vibrant reef formations at shallow depths of under 15 feet.

San Pedro House of Culture

Tucked a couple of streets back from the beachfront area of San Pedro, the **San Pedro House of Culture** (across from the Sports Stadium, Angel Coral St., tel. 501/226-5100, guillermo.paz@nichbelize.org, 8am-5pm Mon. and Fri. only, free) is small, but an encouraging effort at sharing more of Belize's and Ambergris's history with visitors—something that was otherwise lacking on the island. The showroom displays artifacts found at the Marco Gonzalez Maya Site and Garifuna instruments and utensils, as well as hosting rotating exhibits of interest to the San Pedro community. The one I experienced was an excellent Rastafari and Bob Marley exhibit celebrating the icon's 70th birthday. A volunteer is on hand to explain and guide you through if you need. There's no entry fee, but visitors are free to donate or tip as they see fit.

★ Bacalar Chico National Park and Marine Reserve

On and around the northern tip of Ambergris Caye, **Bacalar Chico National Park and Marine Reserve** hosts an incredibly diverse array of wildlife, offers excellent snorkeling and diving—with at least 187 species of fish—and is rich with history. The Bacalar Chico Canal is reputed to have been dug by Mayan traders between AD 700 and 900, creating Ambergris Caye by separating it from the Yucatán Peninsula. The reserve has a wide range of wildlife habitat; 194 species of birds have been sighted there. The landscape consists in part of sinkholes and cenotes created by the effects of weathering on the limestone bedrock of Ambergris Caye. On the eastern side of the reserve is **Rocky Point,** the only location in the Belize Barrier Reef Reserve System where the reef touches the shore. This is one of Belize's most important and prolific sea turtle-nesting sites, home to at least 10 threatened species. In 1997, Bacalar Chico—along with the Belize Barrier Reef Reserve System—was designated a World Heritage Site by UNESCO.

Bacalar Chico also contains at least nine archaeological sites: Mayan trading, fishing, and agricultural settlements that were inhabited from at least AD 300 to 900. A 10th site just outside the reserve boundary is regarded as especially important for its remaining wall network throughout the settlement and its potential to provide missing information about the transition from the Mayan Classic Period to modern times. The reserve also contains evidence of Spanish and English habitation during the colonial period, including several Spanish-period shipwrecks offshore.

A ranger station in the northwest area of the park has a **visitors center** (tel. 501/663-2865, greenreef@gmail.com) and displays of area history, including old glass bottles and Mayan relics found within the reserve. A picnic area offers a barbecue.

TRANSPORTATION

A couple of tour companies offer land and snorkel trips to Bacalar Chico out of San Pedro. Start with **Seaduced by Belize** (tel. 501/226-2254, www.seaducedbybelize.com, US$105 pp) and **Searious Adventures** (tel. 501/226-4202 or 501/226-4206, www.seariousadventures.com, US$90).

Marco Gonzalez Maya Site

Those looking for a little Mayan history right on the island can find it at the **Marco Gonzalez Maya Site** (www.marcogonzalezmayasite.com), just a 30-minute golf cart ride from San Pedro, at the south end of Ambergris Caye. Contact **Jan Brown** (tel. 501/662-2725, US$10 site, US$8 transportation), a passionate expat and the reserve's chairperson, for a private guided tour of this virgin site. Currently under study, it was inhabited by the Maya for 1,600 years.

While the site continues to be preserved, cleaned, and examined for what it will reveal of the history of the coastal Maya, it is literally a museum in the wild. A tour is an eco-adventure in itself, requiring careful navigation to avoid stepping on pieces of Mayan ceramics, with rainforest wildlife encounters along the way. Over the past few years,

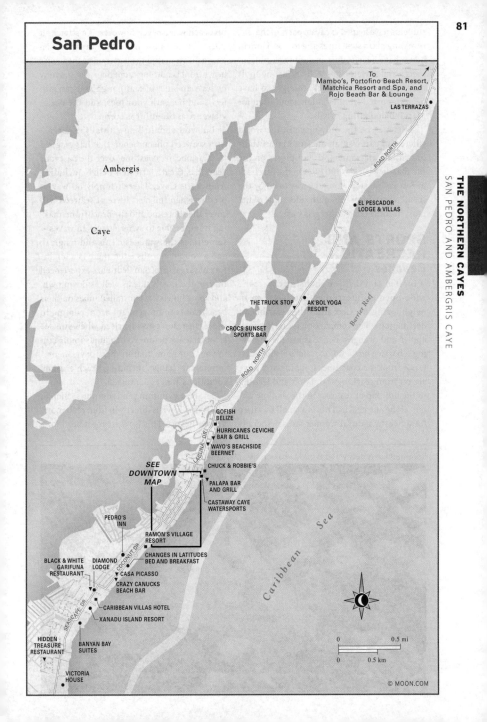

San Pedro

To Mambo's, Portofino Beach Resort,
Matchica Resort and Spa, and
Rojo Beach Bar & Lounge

LAS TERRAZAS

Ambergis

Caye

ROAD NORTH

EL PESCADOR
LODGE & VILLAS

Barrier Reef

THE TRUCK STOP

AK'BOL YOGA
RESORT

CROCS SUNSET
SPORTS BAR

ROAD NORTH

GOFISH
BELIZE

HURRICANES CEVICHE
BAR & GRILL

WAYO'S BEACHSIDE
BEERNET

LAGUNA DR.

CHUCK & ROBBIE'S

SEE
DOWNTOWN
MAP

PALAPA BAR
AND GRILL

CASTAWAY CAYE
WATERSPORTS

PEDRO'S
INN

Caribbean Sea

RAMON'S VILLAGE
RESORT

CHANGES IN LATITUDES
BED AND BREAKFAST

COCONUT DR.

BLACK & WHITE
GARIFUNA
RESTAURANT

DIAMOND
LODGE

CASA PICASSO

CRAZY CANUCKS
BEACH BAR

SEASCAPE DR.

CARIBBEAN VILLAS HOTEL

XANADU ISLAND RESORT

HIDDEN
TREASURE
RESTAURANT

BANYAN BAY
SUITES

VICTORIA
HOUSE

0   0.5 mi

0   0.5 km

© MOON.COM

students have helped excavate parts of the site, revealing plaza structures and tombs. Human bones have been found, including skull fragments and skeletons as well as cutting tools made out of volcanic rock, thought to have been imported from Honduras and used for Mayan bloodletting rituals.

This may be the only place in the world where you can visit an ancient Mayan trading city on an island and spot pieces on the site that date back to 100 BC. On the way back to San Pedro, stop along the way to enjoy the scenic views from the south side, some of the most beautiful on Ambergris Caye.

SPORTS AND RECREATION
Beaches

It is often said that you shouldn't expect the wide-open uninterrupted beaches seen in neighboring Mexico and other Caribbean destinations. The comparison is one between apples and oranges: Belize is unique in having a barrier reef, and one that's a short distance from the coastline, stopping any wave action from reaching the shores and leading to the buildup of seagrass in the shallow waters along the beach. This is a small sacrifice for a nearby natural wonder. To say there is

no beach whatsoever, however, is a stretch. It does require a little trekking away from San Pedro Town to find the better ones; the town's beachfront is nothing more than a long, sandy pedestrian sidewalk, although you can still feel sand beneath your toes, and the ocean views are as beautiful as ever.

But you should know this: the sargassum seaweed phenomenon that has plagued the Caribbean's coastlines over the past four years has greatly affected Belize, including Ambergris Caye. There's simply no way to predict when the next wave of seaweed will cover the shoreline and the beachfront, making it impossible to swim. It goes in waves—sometimes the water is clean and magical, and a couple months later, there is a big influx of sargassum. San Pedro has experienced this on the north side as well as downtown, and some hotels have installed tubes on their beachfronts to prevent any from coming to shore. Just don't be surprised when you see it. In fact, ask before you go, if it's important to you. But know that in these days of environmental change, including beach erosion, conditions aren't guaranteed.

The best swimming and sunning section in San Pedro Town is directly in front of Ramon's Village Resort. This is where most head for a

bone fragments discovered at the Marco Gonzalez Maya Site

swim and a snorkel. Numerous docks also give access where swimming might otherwise be difficult—but please beware of boat traffic, and make sure you are visible at all times, as there have been accidents in the past.

Beach enthusiasts have more choices just a short 15-30 minutes from town. A few of the hotels and bars on Ambergris Caye's north and south ends have wider, softer white-sand areas and better swimming entry points, although patches of seagrass are ever present.

One option is to head north of the bridge (by water taxi, bike, or cart, depending on how far you are going) and park yourself at one of the several beachfront bars or resorts—Palapa Bar is a great spot, as is Portofino resort, well worth the lengthier 30-minute boat ride with its boutique yet laid-back atmosphere, infinity pool, and calming views. Grab a meal or a cocktail and you can use the docks and dip your toes in that sand and clear water (don't venture far, please and watch for boats).

Secret Beach, north of the island and clearly no longer a secret, is lined with beach bars and lounge chairs and has a typical tourist atmosphere reminiscent of Mexico. If you're up for that, by all means head there, knowing it's slightly overrated (and avoid going on a bad weather day when you'll find seaweed all over the shoreline).

To the south, lovely stretches shaded by dozens of palm trees can be found by Victoria House, one of the nicest resorts on the island, or by Catamaran Beach Bar at Caribbean Villas. Start at any of these and hop your way along the beach.

Diving and Snorkeling

Almost every hotel on Ambergris either employs local dive shops or has its own on-site shop and dive masters. Most offer similar services: resort courses (from US$160), PADI or NAUI certification classes (US$450-470), snorkel trips to Hol Chan Marine Reserve, Bacalar Chico, Mexico Rocks, and other local areas. Some also offer night dives, and a few have nitrox capabilities. Local reef two-tank dives are about US$75-80 with all shops, plus rental fees and tax.

For beginner PADI diving courses, daily local reef dives or snorkel day trips, **Chuck and Robbie's** (Boca del Rio Dr., tel. 501/610-4424, www.ambergriscayediving.com, 2-tank dive US$80) are a favorite. They also offer nighttime dives at Hol Chan Marine Reserve. **Scuba School and Holiday Center** (dock across from Holiday Hotel, tel. 501/226-2886, www.scubaschoolbelize.com) is also popular for offering a more personalized instructor experience.

Snorkeling gear can be rented from **Ramon's Village Resort** (Ramon's Dive Shop pier, tel. 501/226-2071, U.S. tel. 800/624-4215, www.ramons.com, half-day US$5,

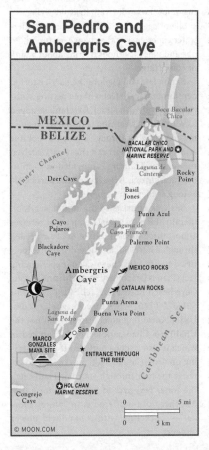

San Pedro and Ambergris Caye

Boca Bacalar Chico

MEXICO
BELIZE

BACALAR CHICO NATIONAL PARK AND MARINE RESERVE

Inner Channel

Deer Caye

Laguna de Cantena

Rocky Point

Basil Jones

Punta Azul

Cayo Pajaros

Laguna de Cayo Francés

Palermo Point

Blackadore Caye

Ambergris Caye

MEXICO ROCKS

CATALAN ROCKS

Punta Arena

Buena Vista Point

Laguna de San Pedro

San Pedro

Caribbean Sea

MARCO GONZALES MAYA SITE

ENTRANCE THROUGH THE REEF

HOL CHAN MARINE RESERVE

Congrejo Caye

0   5 mi

0   5 km

© MOON.COM

full-day US$10), and there is decent marinelife just at the end of its dock, specially created for those seeking to snorkel in town. If you decide to explore from another dock, beware of boat activity at all times, as there have been serious accidents. Snorkel trips to the Belize Barrier Reef are also available. Mexico Rocks, on the reef north of town, is a great place for snorkelers to see a huge variety of coral formations, as well as species like angelfish and butterfly fish.

TURNEFFE ATOLL, LIGHTHOUSE REEF, AND THE GREAT BLUE HOLE

Dive excursions to Lighthouse Reef Atoll, where the Great Blue Hole (for advanced divers only) is located, or to Turneffe Atoll are all-day affairs. Because of the distance and the cost of fuel, dive shops will usually have a minimum number of people (between 8 and 10) for a trip to go out; contact them ahead of time to see what's available. In high season, numbers are easily reached. Expect a 2.5-hour journey out to the atolls, departing around 5:30am (a couple of hours later for Turneffe trips) and returning at 5pm. It will be worthwhile: the waters in these parts are simply spectacular, as are the diving and snorkeling. Most dive shops have trips that go out to these areas.

Ultimately, what makes the difference is the experience of the instructor or dive master, the quality of the equipment, the specialty in dive sites, the size of the boat, and the size of the groups (an important factor if you want to avoid "cattle boats"). Prices are pretty standard around the island: three-tank dives to the Blue Hole are US$250-325 and to Turneffe US$235. Your dive shop will pick you up and drop you off at your resort dock, and lunch is included, as well as snacks and nonalcoholic beverages.

Dive shops with proven reputations for safety and service and that offer the most comfortable boats and regular dive excursions to the Great Blue Hole, Lighthouse Reef, and Turneffe Atoll include **Amigos del Mar** (Beachfront San Pedro, across from Lily's, tel. 501/226-2706, www.amigosdivebelize.com), with frequent trips to the Great Blue Hole (one local dive prerequisite; US$260 plus US$40 park fees), snorkeling (US$195 with three stops, plus park fees), and Turneffe Atoll (US$230); **Ecologic Divers** (beachfront, tel. 501/226-4118, www.ecologicdivers.com), another reliable shop taking no more than 12 divers at a time—as well as offering night dives, and private charters; and locally owned and operated **Scuba School and Holiday Center** (dock across from Holiday Hotel, tel. 501/226-2886, www.scubaschoolbelize.com), offering a more personalized experience.

Snuba and Sea Trek

To change it up a bit from regular snorkeling or for those who want to avoid diving, try snuba or sea trek. Both allow for an underwater experience and a chance for fun photo ops and videos without fretting about a tank or equalizing.

Snuba lets you explore the barrier reef at depths of up to 20 feet without getting scuba certified and without a heavy tank strapped to your back: Breathing is through a regulator, receiving air through a long 20-foot line attached to a support raft that floats safely at the surface. Training is provided in 15 minutes, and anyone over age eight can participate as long as they can swim.

Sea trek consists of hiking the seafloor, literally: Plop on a cool helmet that receives almost three times the amount of air needed through a hose. So far, the only outfitter certified to offer this new way of experiencing Hol Chan is **Discovery Expeditions** (Exotic Caye Beach Resort pier, tel. 501/671-2882 or 501/671-0746, www.discoverybelize.com, US$88, including hotel transfers but not the US$10 Hol Chan park fee) out of San Pedro, which is also a snuba outfitter. If you're staying on Caye Caulker, you may be able to arrange the tour through your hotel and catch the water taxi over to San Pedro for a day. Another option offered is to "power snorkel"—snorkeling with a handheld power scooter.

Boating and Sailing

Explore the Caribbean the way it's meant to be traveled: by sea. Old standby boats include the "old-school sailing trip" aboard the refurbished *Rum Punch II* (moored north of Cholo's Sports Bar, tel. 501/610-3240, US$75), operated by longtime resident and captain George Eiley, offering glass-bottom-boat snorkel tours, beach barbecues, and sunset charters.

The *Sirena Azul* (Blue Tang Inn, corner of Sandpiper St. and the sea, tel. 501/226-2326, U.S. tel. 866/881-1020, www.bluetanginn. com) is a 40-foot Belizean hardwood beauty operated out of the Blue Tang Inn. Made by a boatbuilding family in the northern village of Sarteneja, and with an added onboard engine and restroom, this sailboat is an experience worth the extra cost. Sunset sails (US$55 pp, drinks included; private charter US$440 for 1-6 people) are popular, although the boat also goes on snorkeling day trips.

Another popular and fancy cat for private rental or for sunset sails is *Seaduction,* operated by **Seaduced by Belize** (tel. 501/226-2254, www.seaducedbybelize.com). **Ecologic Divers** (beachfront, tel. 501/226-4118, www. ecologicdivers.com) offers sailing charters aboard its two 50-foot catamarans as well as sunset dinner cruises by the reef.

Xsite Belize Sailing (Tackle Box dock, tel. 501/610-0226, www.xsitebelizesailing. com, from US$45-200 pp) takes you island tubing, fishing, or snorkeling at Turneffe for the day, or sailing. **Lady Leslie** (tel. 501/600-8435, www.ladyslesliebelize.com, US$100) is a popular pick for day-trip catamaran sailing to Caye Caulker on a 38-foot catamaran, which includes a snorkel stop at Hol Chan and Shark Ray Alley first, lunch on Caye Caulker on your own, and a sunset trip back to San Pedro; as is **Tuff Enuff** (tel. 501/615-9762, www.tuffenuffbz.com, US$95).

For a more rustic and laid-back sail, spend the day with the Rubio brothers snorkeling, fishing, and drinking aboard *No Rush,* a quaint 36-foot catamaran that can be booked through **Unity Tours** (tel. 501/226-2326 or 501/600-5022, www.ambergriscaye.com/unitytours, full-day snorkel US$75 pp, half-day US$50 pp). **Reef Runners** (tel. 501/602-0858, www.ambergriscaye.com/reefrunner, full-day snorkel US$45 adults) has 24-foot-long glass-bottom boats for snorkel tours and fishing trips, and guides know these waters well. You can't miss the bright yellow boats docked beside the San Pedro Belize water taxi terminal.

A notch up is **Belize Sailing Vacations** (tel. 501/629-4642 or U.S. tel. 888/200-0370, www.belizesailingvacations.com, from US$1,395), providing luxury sailing charters with "the amenities of an all-inclusive luxury resort aboard your own private catamaran, tailored to your own personalized itinerary." This dream itinerary ranges from island-hopping to snorkeling and diving along the way or just relaxing on board. A popular choice is *Doris,* a 50-foot catamaran with four air-conditioned cabins, four baths, lounge areas, plasma TVs, and your very own chef on board (from US$1,700 for two).

Fishing

The area within the reef is a favorite for tarpon and bonefish. Outside the reef, the choice of big game is endless. Most hotels and dive shops will make arrangements for fishing, including a boat and a guide. Ask around the docks (and your hotel) for the best guides. Serious anglers should consider Abner Marin at **GoFish Belize** (Boca del Rio Dr., tel. 501/226-3121, www.gofishbelize.com, from US$350 half-day reef fishing), one of the most qualified and reputable guides around. Or try **Uprising Tours Fishing** (Barrier Reef Dr., tel. 501/662-7413, uprisingtour@yahoo.com), another sure bet with half- or full-day chartered fishing trips; ask about its lobster beach barbecue fishing trip.

Kayaking

Little wave action and regular trade winds make kayaking a great option off Belize's cayes. Ideal spots to navigate are on the south side of the island near Xanadu Island Resort

Catching the Big Three: The Grand Slam

Chasing tail in Belizean waters is on the dream list of anglers worldwide and has been for decades. Many also head here for a chance to achieve the grand slam: catching a tarpon, permit, and bonefish in one day. Doing so is no small feat—some spend as much as a week of daily excursions and even years attempting it. Those who succeed automatically gain a spot in a de facto exclusive group of top-rated anglers.

While visitors can conduct their own grand slam fly-fishing mission year-round in Belize, Ambergris Caye holds an annual catch-and-release sportfishing tournament and event known as the **Tres Pescados Slam Tournament.** It's the fly-fishing competition of all fishing competitions, with teams descending on San Pedro from other countries and parts of Belize to strive to catch the big three in just three days. Teams consist of one or two fly fishers and a Belize Tourism Board licensed guide. Held annually in the summer (usually August) since 2009, the competition is more intense than ever to win prestigious titles, including Top Guide, Top Female Angler, Best Men's and Women's Casting, and generous cash prizes.

The money raised by the tournament supports a worthwhile cause. Up to 15 teams and 40 anglers participated in the 2018 tournament, raising US$25,000 that went to benefit the Defend Cayo Rosario Campaign—to prevent building over-the-water structures in a protected section of Hol Chan Marine Reserve—and Yellow Dog Community and Conservation Foundation.

Nonfishing family members can have fun too, as the three-day event includes weekend-long games and activities, usually held at Central Park in San Pedro.

or Victoria House, with wider open space and less boat activity. The north end also offers quieter options for rowing in safety. Many hotels provide complimentary use of kayaks. If not, check with **Ramon's Village Resort** (US$15 per hour, US$35 per day). **Lisa's Kayaking** (Mile 1 north of the bridge, between Ak'bol and Truck Stop, tel. 501/601-4449, www.lisaskayaking.com, US$8 per day, US$40 per week) rents kayaks and also offers four- or eight-hour guided kayak tours around Ambergris Caye as well as on the Belize River.

Stand-Up Paddleboarding

BIG SUP (Boca Del Rio Dr., Chuck and Robbie's dock, tel. 501/602-4447, www.bigsupbelize.com, 8am-5pm daily, US$15 per hour, includes basic tips) has gorgeous stand-up paddleboards available for rent—including racing boards—and beginner classes and SUP tours to the reef. If you're into yoga, you'll want to show up at 1pm Tuesday for its popular weekly Yoga SUP class. Owners Derek

and Kelly Angele have been working on setting up the first Belize SUP Association. Just north of the bridge, **Lisa's Kayaking** (Mile 1 North, between Ak'bol and Truck Stop, tel. 501/601-4449, www.lisaskayaking.com) offers SUP (US$15 per hour) and double kayaks for rent (US$15 per hour or US$30/half-day).

Wind Sports

The latest wind sports are always the rage. It's not surprising, given the often ideal weather conditions. There's that "constant breeze in Belize" that locals love to brag about—the result of Caribbean trade winds hitting the islands November-July. Combine them with a nearby reef that creates flat waters, and voilà!

Ramon's Village Resort (www.ramons.com) has windsurfing or Hobie Cat catamaran lessons (US$45-70 for 2 hours) and equipment rentals (windsurfing US$20 per hour, Hobie Cat US$30 per hour). Its dock was destroyed by Hurricane Earl, but the boats and services are still in full swing.

A great way to relax and catch spectacular views of the island and reef, weather permitting, is to parasail with **Castaway Caye**

1: sailing along Caye Caulker; **2:** BIG SUP's weekly yoga on paddleboards

Watersports (Palapa Bar Dock, Boca del Rio Dr., tel. 501/671-3000, www.castawaycaye. com, US$99 single, US$179 double). Castaway also offers Jet Ski rentals (US$89 per half hour) and kayak rentals.

Birding and Wildlife-Watching

Although many people come here for the reef, Ambergris also offers some birding and nature tour opportunities.

Take a boat ride along the north of the island, where wildlife can be spotted along the beach and also in the lagoon on the back side, a peaceful, rarely visited part of Ambergris. Sightings may include egrets, great herons, and, if you're lucky, crocodiles. For customized routes and other island nature tours, check with any of the beachfront operators or with **Seaduced by Belize** (tel. 501/226-2254, www.seaducedbybelize.com).

Xanadu Island Resort has a lush marked nature trail at the back of the property; stop in at the front desk for directions.

Another potential bird-watching spot all the way south of the island is the **Marco Gonzalez Maya Site** (tel. 501/662-2725, www.marcogonzalezmayasite.com, US$10 site, US$8 transportation). Kill two birds with one stone (no pun intended) by visiting a Mayan site—the only one of its kind on Ambergris Caye.

Belize Food Tour and Cooking Classes

Hop on a "Savor Belize" evening food walk with **Belize Food Tours** (tel. 501/631-5923, www.belizefoodtours.com, US$72) and learn about the island's history and the basics of Belizean food in one fell swoop. Run by native San Pedranos whose family once owned a popular restaurant called Lily's, you'll taste some of the local favorite Mayan, Creole, and mestizo eats in Belize—from fry jacks to *garnaches, pupusas,* and fish—as well as discover the island's favorite restaurants. Portions are sufficient given the multiple stops. Drinks are also sampled, including juices and beers. The evening walk is leisurely and begins at

Elvi's Kitchen, continuing on to a variety of Kriol and mestizo restaurants as well as off-the-beaten-track spots, for a three-hour degustation at seven stops. There's also a lunch tour, and if you're more curious, sign up for **cooking classes** to learn how to make a few Belizean favorites right in Belize Food Tours' modern kitchen studio.

Inland Tours

While staying on Ambergris Caye provides plenty of entertainment and pretty sights, Belize's beautiful interior of rainforests, rivers teeming with wildlife, caves, and Mayan sites is not to be missed. Most tour operators in San Pedro offer full-day trips to the mainland, or they can easily be arranged through your hotel.

If you're looking to combine tours and save a few bucks, check out package deals and book them in advance. **Searious Adventures** (tel. 501/226-4202 or 501/226-4206, www. seariousadventures.com, US$150) offers interesting ones. If your schedule only allows one land tour, opt for the daylong safari along the New River—one of Belize's most beautiful bodies of water, filled with wildlife—which brings you to the Lamanai Archaeological Site (US$152 pp). Another option combines a cave tubing experience in Cayo with a trip to the Belize Zoo (US$169 pp). Both tours are offered daily mid-November-mid-April.

Massage and Bodywork

If your hotel lacks a proper gym and you'd rather pump iron than dive, the **Train Station** (tel. 501/226-4222) is 2.5 blocks south of the bridge. CrossFit is also established here, and you'll find a qualified center at **CrossFit San Pedro Town** (Sea Star St., tel. 501/670-5575, www.crossfitsanpedrotown.com, US$15 per class). In San Pedro, you'll find both scheduled yoga classes Tuesday, Thursday and Saturday mornings (8:45-9:45am, drop-in US$8) and private sessions (US$75 up to four persons) at **Sol Spa** (Phoenix Resort, tel. 501/226-2410, www.solspabelize. com, 9am-5pm daily), a small but cozy retreat offering a range of treatments and massages like Honeymoon Bliss, Solar Therapy, and Maya Abdominal Massage.

A short distance before reaching the bridge going north, for a more casual option and an authentic Caribbean setting, look for Shirlene Santino's **Just Relax Massage** (between Caye Casa and Wayo's Beach Bar, Boca del Rio Dr., tel. 501/666-3536, shirlenesantino@ yahoo.com, deep tissue US$40 per hour, house calls US$55) and her seaside massage chair and hut. Shirlene has special oils for any ailment, from sunburn to backaches. Call ahead for an appointment.

Jordana's Art of Touch Spa (Diamond Lodge, Coconut Dr., tel. 501/602-8424, spa@ diamondlodgebelize.com, 9am-5pm daily) is small and cozy, tucked inside a quiet, charming villa turned boutique hotel right in town yet away from the hustle of San Pedro. The masseuse I had was excellent and I nearly fell asleep. Other beauty services are available onsite, including facials, body wraps, manicure and pedicure, and waxing.

Farther up north is **Serenity Spa and Wellness Center** at Las Terrazas Resort (U.S. tel. 501/226-4249, www.lasterrazasresort. com), with the "Unbelizeable Facial" and other treatments.

Ak'bol Yoga Retreat (tel. 501/226-2073, www.akbol.com, 9am Mon.-Sat., 10am Sun., US$15 per hour) is one of the few places in Belize offering daily yoga classes (usually at 9am), popular among residents.

ENTERTAINMENT AND EVENTS

San Pedro boasts the most active nightlife in the country, whether your idea of fun is dancing up a storm, barhopping, dining to live music, or betting on chicken poop—it's all here. San Pedranos have a weeklong calendar of places to be. Wednesday and Saturday are the biggest nights out, and water taxis actually change their schedules to accommodate revelers. Front Street (Barrier Reef Drive) also closes off to traffic on the weekends starting at 6pm on Friday, Saturday, and Sunday from

Spindrift Hotel down to Pescador Drive. But other nights are popular as well, including Monday for live *punta* music and Thursday because of the Chicken Drop. In general, the hot spots don't get going until 11pm or midnight, with lots of warming up in various bars before the partying begins.

Nightlife
BARS AND LOUNGES
Diving or touring by day and partying by night form the standard San Pedro scene, although some really do barhop all day long. There are enough watering holes on the island for serious drinkers. Lately, more upscale lounges have found their way to the north and south of the island. Boca del Rio Drive is also lined with several bar options.

Starting in the center of town, the buzz-filled beachfront **Cholo's Sports Bar** (tel. 501/226-2406, 10am-midnight daily) is a modest but perfect local hangout and the heart of San Pedro's social scene. You'll find the cheapest drinks in town (US$1.50 for a rum and Coke) and plenty of people-watching from the outdoor tables, as it's close to the water taxis and dive shops. Ceviche is the only bar snack, but it's made fresh daily. Expect to see only men on the inside, sitting at the bar or playing pool.

A few stumbling steps from Cholo's on the roadside is **Lola's Pub** (Barrier Reef Dr., tel. 501/206-2120, 4pm-midnight weekdays, 11am-midnight Sat.-Sun.), a popular after-work or weekend hangout. Beautifully lit shelves house top-shelf liquor, and the bistro-like atmosphere is casual and friendly, with a couple of flat-screen TVs and music.

Farther down the beach is **Fido's Courtyard** (Barrier Reef Dr., tel. 501/226-3176, www.fidosbelize.com, 10am-midnight Mon.-Fri., 10am-2am Sat.-Sun.), the largest bar-restaurant complex in town, catering mostly to travelers with a live rock band (and sadly, no local Belizean music) almost every night in the high season and an all-day full menu that ranges from bar foods to dinner.

Place your bets at the weekly **Chicken**

Drop at 6pm Thursday in front of **Wahoo's Lounge** (Barrier Reef Dr., tel. 501/226-2002) and adjacent to **Caliente Restaurant** (tel. 501/226-2170, 11am-9:30pm Tues.-Sun.). A chicken is let loose on a numbered grid after revelers place bets on which number the chicken will choose to soil. The winner takes a cash prize, but not before cleaning up the poop. Warm up at Wahoo's bar with two-for-one rum punches and a DJ playing calypso and upbeat local sounds on the beach, or with Caliente's two-for-one happy hour (4pm-6pm daily) and delicious nachos.

The slightly more upscale **Caprice Bar Grill** (Holiday Hotel, Barrier Reef Dr., tel. 501/226-2014, holiday@btl.net, 9am-midnight Mon.-Sat., 11am-9pm Sun.), with interior and beachfront dock seating, is a decent choice for its popular half-price weekday happy hour (3pm-6pm Mon.-Fri.).

Hurricane's Ceviche Bar and Grill (Beachfront, Boca del Rio Dr., tel. 501/226-4124, 10am-10pm Tues.-Sat.. 1pm-10pm Sun.), set on a dock over the water, serves a variety of—you guessed it—ceviche. It has a very friendly barkeep, hammocks in the sea, and a narrow, hidden top deck for views of the water and the beach. The **Rehab Bar** (Barrier Reef Dr., no phone, daily), a small patio bar next

to the Jaguar's Temple disco, is a favorite for people-watching.

South of San Pedro, **Crazy Canucks Beach Bar** (beachfront, S. Coconut Dr., tel. 501/670-8001, 11am-midnight daily) has live music and dancing on Monday, Thursday, and Sunday afternoons. You'll find happy customers and meet interesting characters playing cards, horseshoes, dominoes, and other games. Also on Coconut Drive, directly across from Canucks, look for the **Roadkill Bar** (S. Coconut Dr., tel. 501/628-6882, 3:30pm-midnight daily), another popular open-air hangout with karaoke on Wednesday and a free beer with a shot of tequila for US$5 until 9pm. The "panty-ripper" cocktails are delicious.

A short distance before the north bridge is the lively **Wayo's Beachside Beernet** (Boca del Rio Dr., tel. 501/226-2035, 10am-midnight daily), a casual, colorful outdoor hangout ideal for drinks, a bite, and a swim all day long, or for nighttime fun with the occasional karaoke evening. Across from the bar, a *palapa* and a hammock are set even closer to the water. Owner "Wayo from Cayo" will even pick you up at night and give you a ride back if needed—ideal for solo female travelers.

A stone's throw away is **Sandy Toes**

Wayo's Beachside Beernet

Beach Bar & Grill (Boca del Rio Dr., tel. 501/624-1300, ish_lizbey@yahoo.com, 9am-midnight daily, US$3-5), a casual, wooden beach bar popular with locals and travelers, where there's never a dull moment, from the friendly owners to the frequent live music and Sunday barbecue specials. The food is decent—try the stuffed jalapeños and the ceviche.

After years of being north of San Pedro, the legendary Palapa Bar and Grill (beachfront, Boca del Rio Dr., tel. 501/226-3111, www.palapabarandgrill.com, 11am-about 11pm daily) moved beachfront in San Pedro Town, taking over the old Wet Willy's dock. And then, in August 2016, to everyone's dismay, the wooden bar was knocked down like a pack of cards by Hurricane Earl. Miraculously, it was rebuilt by December of the same year with the help of its many fans and supporters. It's still a must-stop while on Ambergris, whether for lunch, sunset, or a lazy evening of appetizers (US$4-6), barbecue, beer, and cocktails. For the full Palapa Bar experience, bring a bathing suit so you can swim and float in an anchored inner tube and have the bartender lower you down a bucket of beer and take up your empty ones, day or evening.

Rojo Beach Bar (North San Pedro, next to Matachica Resort, tel. 501/226-4012, www.azulbelize.com, noon-10pm Tues.-Sat., later bar close on weekends) is a trendy but casual waterfront spot with beds, a pool, fancy cocktails, and absolutely delicious food (kitchen closes at 9pm).

If a quieter, predinner glass of wine is more your beat, try the Friday night wine social at Wine de Vine (Coconut Dr., tel. 501/226-3430, www.winedevine.com, 4pm-8pm Fri.).

Legends Road House (north of the bridge, tel. 501/624-5231, 7pm-11pm Mon.-Sat.) is mostly notable for its live reggae jam on Tuesday, but may also host live music other nights of the week, as well as pool tables, darts, and cocktails outdoors. Take in the sunset with your cold beer and a lively crowd at Crocs Sunset Sports Bar (north of the bridge, Tres Cocos, www.crocsbar.com,

11am-10pm daily), perched over the lagoon. There are occasional live music nights; check ahead.

DANCING

Monday is "happening" at Crazy Canucks Beach Bar (beachfront, S. Coconut Dr., tel. 501/670-8001, 7:30pm-11pm Mon.) with a live reggae band. Get ready to throw back the cocktails, meet locals, and get jammin'. The band begins around 8pm.

You can dance to a live band on Wednesday (and just about any day of the week) at Fido's Courtyard (beachfront, tel. 501/226-3176), a popular beachfront restaurant and bar, and Saturday gets going when the bars close at midnight and everyone wanders across the street to Jaguar's Temple (tel. 501/226-4077, www.jaguarstempleclub.com, 9:30pm-4am Thurs.-Sat.), the most popular and decent nightclub in Belize. The two-story interior is complete with a large dance floor, two bars with spacious standing room, air-conditioning, and just the right amount of snazzy disco lighting. A newer addition is Club Inferno, located at backpacker favorite Pedro's Inn (Seagrape Dr., www.pedroshotel.com, no cover), on weekday nights and weekends with a live DJ—check social media for updates. After Jaguar's, the insatiable night owls often stumble over to Daddy Rocks Nightclub (tel. 501/607-2229, 10am-4am Thurs.-Sat., 11am-4am Sun.), just across the street in the park. It has a can't-miss-it flamboyant exterior (you'll have to see it to believe it). The music is more the reggae and dance hall type—with the occasional live band on Saturday—while Jaguar plays a mix of all genres, from house to reggae and Latin, and attracts more of a "cool" crowd, though as a visitor you'll dance at either one. The fun gets started around 11pm-midnight and can go until 4am and sometimes later.

Festivals and Events

San Pedro's festivals are scattered throughout the year. These celebrations bring even more

Your San Pedro Live Music Schedule

Music aficionados will find their fix in San Pedro. It has the most frequent, steady, weeklong schedule of musicians and bands you'll find anywhere in Belize, although other parts of the country tend to have more local sounds and less in Western genres. Overall, San Pedro's offerings reflect a mix that keeps visitors and locals happy on a year-round basis—from soothing Latin melodies over dinner to light rock, jazz, and blues bands catering to travelers and expats to local *punta* rock sounds for a taste of the Afro-influenced Garifuna side of Belize. And there's no extra cover charge! Up for it? Here's your weeklong itinerary.

- **Monday:** Start out at **Crazy Canucks Beach Bar** (beachfront, S. Coconut Dr., tel. 501/670-8001) for live reggae (8pm-11pm). The crowd is a mix of visitors, expats, and locals.

- **Tuesday:** Head to the live reggae jam (7pm-midnight) at popular **Legends Road House** (north of the bridge, tel. 501/624-5231). Ask about the other live music nights, including Saturday.

- **Wednesday:** Although nothing's set on this day, check out regular live music venues like **Palapa Bar and Grill** (beachfront, Boca del Rio Dr., tel. 501/226-3111, 11am-about 11pm Sun., US$4-6), **Dive Bar** (0.5 mile North Bridge, tel. 501/226-3365, 7am-midnight daily) for visiting and local artist performances with a view.

- **Thursday:** It's **Fido's Courtyard** (Barrier Reef Dr., tel. 501/226-2056, www.fidosbelize.com) for a beachfront setting. A regular lineup of light rock or jazz bands (6pm-close) fills this large indoor and outdoor space. While there isn't much "local" about Fido's, it's there if you need an option. Not to be missed is the local Belizean music at the **Chicken Drop** (6pm-midnight) just down from Fido's at **Wahoo's Lounge** (Barrier Reef Dr., tel. 501/226-2170, www.wahoo's loungebelize.com), playing a mix of calypso, reggae, *punta*, and more. It's possibly the closest you'll come to dancing barefoot to local music on San Pedro's "beach."

- **Friday:** Indulge in live reggae (7pm-9:30pm) at **Blue Water Grill** (on the beach, behind the SunBreeze Hotel, tel. 501/226-3347).

- **Saturday:** Start out with **Iguana Juan's Saturday Reggae Brunch** (corner of Angel Coral St. and Pelican St., from 11am), or you can rock and roll into the night (8pm-10pm) at **Wahoo's Lounge,** followed by a stop at **Pedro's Inferno** (Pedro's Inn, Seagrape Dr., www.pedroshotel.com) for a DJ club night.

- **Sunday:** Sunday is "Funday" in Belize. Businesses shut down except the bars and restaurants, and everyone relaxes, swims on the beach, drinks Belikins, listens to music, and breaks out the barbecue grills. Head to **Crazy Canucks Beach Bar** (noon-close) for barbecue, live music, and beachside games.

crowds, but experiencing them is a chance to witness the San Pedrano joie de vivre.

The **San Pedro Carnaval** (mid-Feb.) encompasses copious amounts of colorful paint splattered on the crowd, egg throwing, men dressed like women, and all-around Mardi Gras-type debauchery. The highlights of three days of partying include cultural dance performances on opening night as well as *comparsas*, street dance groups competing for prizes.

The two-day **Lagoon Reef Eco-** **Challenge Kayak Race** (tel. 501/226-2247, www.ecochallengebelize.com, June, registration US$200-500) attracts professional, amateur, and junior kayakers (over age 15) from around the world to compete in a 60-mile race around the entire island. The race begins south of Ambergris, passes by the lagoon side and through mangrove cayes on day one, and reaches the northern tip at Bacalar Chico for the night before continuing back down the island along the reef on the second day. The funds raised go toward promoting the connection between the island's lagoons and the reef—both an integral part of the island's ecosystem and vital to the livelihood of its inhabitants.

Lobsterfest (first week of June) is among the most anticipated events on the island. It celebrates the opening of the lobster season with weeklong bar crawl events—for which you can collect points and enter incredible trip giveaways—outdoor food festivals, and cook-offs and ends with a big Saturday night concert in Central Park.

San Pedro hosts the **Día de San Pedro** (end of June), a three-day festival in honor of Saint Peter, the island's patron saint. There are traditional dances, pageants, food vendors, and music showcasing the island's mixed Belizean, Mexican, and Mayan heritage. If you can only attend one day, come opening night.

The **Costa Maya Festival** (first weekend in Aug.) is considered among Belize's biggest festivals—perhaps in size, because it attracts guests and participants from the neighboring Maya Mundo in one vibrant celebration of heritage. It's worth checking out to sample all the food vendors.

SEPTEMBER CELEBRATIONS

The island celebrates **Independence Day** (Sept. 21) with the **Independence Day Parade.** San Pedro's parade rivals even the capital's, with carnival floats, costumes, marching bands, free rum and beer, beach after-parties, and children and adults dancing in the streets. It's an ideal time to visit, not least for the festivities and off-season prices.

SHOPPING

Gift shops abound in San Pedro, especially on Front and Middle Streets. They've got your postcards, beach apparel, towels, hats, T-shirts, hot sauces, and the usual knickknacks.

Arts and Crafts

Belizean Arts (Fido's Courtyard, tel. 501/226-2056, belize.belizeanarts@gmail.com, www.belizeanarts.com, 11am-7pm daily) sells art, jewelry, ceramics, and carvings by Central American and Belizean artists. The well-established shop has the largest selection of original paintings in Belize.

Inside **12 Belize** (Tarpon St., top floor of Vilma Linda Plaza, tel. 501/610-5272, 8am-4pm Mon.-Fri.), you'll find a gift shop featuring Belizean-only products, selected from artists all around the country. Whether it's coffee and cacao from Punta Gorda, handcrafted soaps from Caye Caulker, or woven purses from Maya Bags, you'll have access to the latest and greatest, made right here in Belize. Each product rack has a label on its creator, and staff are on hand to offer more information. Owner Laura Goldman launched the boutique after high demand from brides for made-in-Belize gift packages.

Belizean Melody Art Gallery (Barrier Reef Dr., tel. 501/631-7481, belizeanmelody@gmail.com, 11am-6pm Mon.-Wed., 11am-7pm Thurs.-Sat.) has carefully selected paintings, crafts, and unique handmade souvenirs, all guaranteed as made in Belize. San Pedro native, owner, and artist Melody Sanchez Wolfe is passionate about providing an outlet for the success of fellow Belizean talents, some as young as 18. Hand-painted shell magnets are just an example of some unique made-in-Belize souvenir items, and the gorgeous paintings aren't to be found anywhere else. Ask about Melody's Paint N Splash events hosted at her studio north of the bridge or other locations in town, where you can create and go home with your own piece of art.

Directly across the street is the new San Pedro branch of Belize's popular gift store, **Orange Gallery** (14 Barrier Reef Dr., tel. 501/824-3296, www.orangegifts.com, 9am-5:30pm Mon.-Fri., 9am-5pm Sat.-Sun.), carrying works by artists from the Cayo District, including jewelry and stainless steel knives.

Clothing and Jewelry

The small, established **Ambar** (Fido's Courtyard, tel. 501/226-2824, babethambar@

Downtown San Pedro

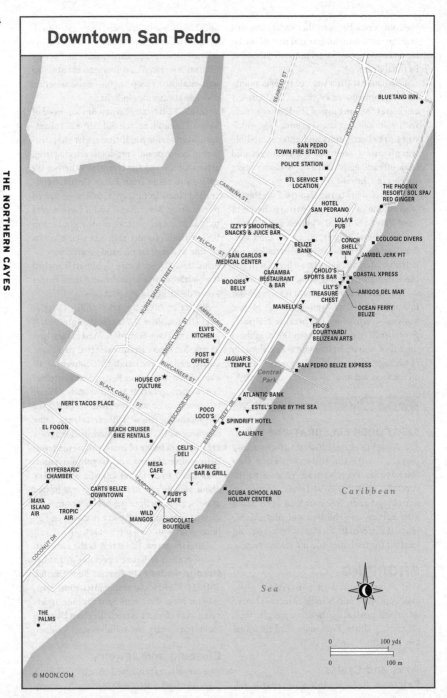

SEAWEED ST

PESCADOR DR

BLUE TANG INN

SAN PEDRO
TOWN FIRE STATION

POLICE STATION

BTL SERVICE
LOCATION

CARIBEÑA ST

THE PHOENIX
RESORT/ SOL SPA/
RED GINGER

HOTEL
SAN PEDRANO

LOLA'S
PUB

IZZY'S SMOOTHIES,
SNACKS & JUICE BAR

PELICAN ST

CONCH
SHELL
INN

ECOLOGIC DIVERS

SAN CARLOS
MEDICAL CENTER

BELIZE
BANK

JAMBEL JERK PIT

NURSE SHARK STREET

CARAMBA
RESTAURANT
& BAR

CHOLO'S
SPORTS BAR

COASTAL XPRESS

BOOGIES
BELLY

LILY'S
TREASURE
CHEST

AMIGOS DEL MAR

AMBERGRIS ST

MANELLY'S

OCEAN FERRY
BELIZE

ANGEL CORAL ST

ELVI'S
KITCHEN

FIDO'S
COURTYARD/
BELIZEAN ARTS

POST
OFFICE

BUCCANEER ST

JAGUAR'S
TEMPLE

Central
Park

SAN PEDRO BELIZE EXPRESS

BLACK CORAL
ST

HOUSE OF
CULTURE

PESCADOR DR

ATLANTIC BANK

NERI'S TACOS PLACE

POCO
LOCO'S

ESTEL'S DINE BY THE SEA

BARRIER REEF DR

EL FOGÓN

SPINDRIFT HOTEL

BEACH CRUISER
BIKE RENTALS

CALIENTE

CELI'S
DELI

HYPERBARIC
CHAMBER

MESA
CAFE

CAPRICE
BAR & GRILL

Caribbean

CARTS BELIZE
DOWNTOWN

TARPON ST

MAYA
ISLAND
AIR

TROPIC
AIR

RUBY'S
CAFE

SCUBA SCHOOL AND
HOLIDAY CENTER

WILD
MANGOS

CHOCOLATE
BOUTIQUE

COCONUT DR

Sea

THE
PALMS

0   100 yds

0   100 m

© MOON.COM

yahoo.fr, 10am-5pm daily) offers beautifully handcrafted jewelry—from anklets to necklaces and rings—made with a variety of imported stones, from resin amber to Mayan jade, onyx, and larimar, as well as silver. Owner Elizabeth moved from France over 20 years ago and is an experienced healer who is passionate about her store and loves to welcome newcomers into her creative space.

Gourmet Goodies

Two chocolate stores in town source their cacao from Punta Gorda's Cacao Growers Association. The **Chocolate Boutique** (Barrier Reef Dr., next to Wild Mangos, tel. 501/226-3015 or 501/610-4828, www.belizechocolatecompany.com, 10am-6:30pm Mon.-Sat.) has chocolate bars, truffles, and "kakaw" powder as well as chocochino and other delicious chocolate drinks. The cacao body oil and bars make great gifts.

For unique decadent gifts, the **Rum, Cigar & Coffee House** (Pescador Dr., 1 block from Elvi's Kitchen, tel. 501/226-2020, 9am-9pm daily) has a walk-in humidor with Cuban and Belizean cigars as well as its own San Pedro-made Jankunu rum cream creations (which are very tasty, I might add) and delicious freshly roasted Guatemalan Arabica coffee. The coffee is available for sale and sampling (US$1 per cup), and the shop has a couple of tables should you decide to savor it on-site.

Wine de Vine (Coconut Dr., tel. 501/226-3430, www.winedevine.com, 9am-8pm Mon.-Sat.) has the finest selection of imported wines in all of Belize, and a worldwide assortment of cheeses and meats. It offers free wine-tastings and also sells it by the glass.

FOOD

Dining out can be expensive in San Pedro, but there are cheap meals and snacks at many bakeries as well as the fast-food carts in the Central Park.

Belizean

Breakfast is serious business in San Pedro. You can smell the freshly baked bread and johnnycakes as you walk down Front Street.

★ **Ruby's Café** (Barrier Reef Dr., 4:45am-6pm Mon.-Sat.) and **Celi's Deli** (Barrier Reef Dr., tel. 501/226-0346, 6am-6pm daily) have been bustling every morning for decades with workers, visitors, and party animals eating breakfast at dawn and stocking up for day trips. Ruby's has the absolute best local pastries in town, from stuffed massive fry jacks to soft and crunchy johnnycakes and more, not to mention coffee—in short, you cannot visit San Pedro and not stop in at Ruby's. **Celi's,** second only to Ruby's, is popular for its plain or stuffed johnnycakes and sought-after meat pies that you can enjoy across the street on the Holiday Hotel's beachfront deli (owned by the same family).

For breakfast, longtimer **Island Torch Bar & Grill** (Laguna Dr., across from Tan Mart, 6am-10:30pm Tues.-Sun.) is a perennial favorite despite several relocations. Also nearby, when you're looking to grab a tasty breakfast plate or burrito and eat among locals, is **La Esquinita** (corner of Buccaneer St. and Pescador Dr., 6am-11am daily), perhaps one of the few remaining small mom-and-pop food spots in San Pedro, where you'll find dive instructors and guides fueling up before work. It's good, cheap, and only a block from Front Street. If you're staying near the airstrip, keep an eye open for **Boomers** (Coconut Dr., across from Paradice Ice Cream, tel. 501/226-2299, 6:30am-2pm Tues.-Sun.), with open-air picnic tables and a window where you can order johnnycakes, eggs, bagels, pancakes, and regular coffee; there's a menu board posted outside.

On the back of the island, a few local eateries offer the cheapest stew chicken, rice and beans, or burrito dishes on the island. The popular ★ **El Fogón** (2 Trigger Fish St., tel. 501/226-2121, www.elfogonbelize.com, 11am-3pm and 6:30pm-9pm Mon.-Sat., US$4-6) is an authentic family-style eatery with flavorful Creole and mestizo dishes home-cooked on an open-fire hearth and served in a small fenced, thatched-roof-shaded, sand-floored

1 Celi's Deli · EST. 1989 · OPEN DAILY 5:00 am – 5:00 pm

2

3 El Fogon "Authentic Belizean Cuisine" Opening Hours Mon. – Sat. Lunch – 11:30 – 3 PM Dinner 6:30 – 9 PM CLOSED ON SUNDAY

space. Tucked just a block north of the Tropic Air airstrip, it will not let you down. The restaurant recently started serving dinner (US$16-30), with plenty of grilled seafood choices and kebabs along with either rice or pasta and sides.

For fun beach-like ambience with sandy floors, picnic tables, and Latin music, ★ **Elvi's Kitchen** (Pescador Dr., tel. 501/226-2404, 11am-10pm Mon.-Sat., US$10-40) is a must among San Pedrano experiences. Doña Elvi's family-run restaurant serves the ultimate Belizean version of soul food—home-cooked, authentic cuisine with a kick. Don't miss the cheese-stuffed jalapeños, Mayan fish, or to-die-for coconut shrimp curry, among many other options. There's also a popular Mayan buffet on Friday night with live Mayan music (and if you must know, Elvi's makes some of the best margaritas in town).

A popular ceviche venue in town is the casual **Lily's Treasure Chest Restaurant** (beachside on Barrier Reef Dr., tel. 501/226-2650, 7am-9pm daily, US$9-17). It also serves affordable Belizean dishes and has a spacious outdoor patio.

Exactly one street back and parallel to El Fogón is **Neri's Taco Place** (Chicken St., 5:30am-11:30am and 5:30pm-9pm Mon.-Sat., 5:30am-noon Sun.), dishing out some of the best tacos (US$0.50 for 3) and cheap, delicious eats that you order at a small window. There are a couple of picnic tables outside, and it gets very crowded with locals on Sunday. It's off the beaten path but well worth finding.

Boogie's Belly (Pelican St., tel. 501/670-8080, 6:30am-11pm Mon.-Sat., from US$0.50) makes its own meat pies in-house, in addition to serving up a host of other local favorites including tacos, hot Creole buns, and johnnycakes. Breakfasts are popular—egg sandwiches, fry jacks, and even chicken with waffles. Some say the meat pies here are the best, but I prefer the ones that come in from Belize City. Boogie's still makes for a fun

breakfast spot, with sandy floors and plenty of local hustle and bustle.

On the beach side up front, ★ **Estel's Dine by the Sea** (on the beach behind Atlantic Bank, tel. 501/226-2019, 6am-4:30pm Wed.-Mon., US$12.50) is a relaxed, ideal breakfast spot. Besides the morning treats, Estel's is great on Sunday with barbecue lunch and live music.

My Secret Deli (Caribeña St., breakfast, lunch, and dinner daily, US$3-5) is a great place to get affordable and tasty local fare—stews, chicken fingers, soups, and other fast faves—in a town that's overrun with pricier restaurants. It offers outdoor seating and plenty of ambience.

Sample some Garifuna dishes while you're in town, at **Black & White Garifuna Restaurant** (off Seagrape Drive, just past Diamond Lodge, tel. 501/605-2895, noon-8pm daily)—daily menu includes *hudut, darasa*, and other local specialties.

Mexican and Latin

Right in the heart of the main drag, **Poco Loco's** (Barrier Reef Dr., tel. 501/632-6636, noon-9pm Mon.-Sat.,US$6-10) offers a modern outdoor food court with various windows serving menus ranging from tasty burgers, pastas, and chicken sandwiches at one to soups and salads at the other. There's limited seating, and prices are on par with sit-down restaurants.

Waruguma (Angel Coral St., tel. 501/633-0931, 11am-9:30pm daily, US$8-18) is rightly famous for its savory *pupusas* (available for lunch but grilled outdoors on the patio in the evenings starting at 5pm), megasize burritos, and other Salvadoran treats, all at a great price. So gigantic are the burritos that there's a wall of fame dedicated to those who have managed to finish one by themselves. Waruguma suffered from a block fire in 2016, but bounced back quickly at this location, now set a bit farther back from the street.

If you're searching for the best conch fritters on the island, along with fresh seafood in all sorts of combinations—grilled, blackened,

1: Celi's Deli; **2:** Boogie's Belly; **3:** El Fogón

steamed, Mexican, Creole, breaded, fried, you name it—stop at ★ **Caramba Restaurant and Bar** (Pescador Dr., tel. 501/226-4321, 11am-10pm Thurs.-Tues., US$5-15), with its lively and colorful indoor and outdoor bar and patio. The seafood here is tasty and plentiful, as is the meat—look out for the Bacon Macho Burger. Prepare your stomach, and make reservations for dinner, as the place gets packed.

Slightly higher-end yet still casual, **Caliente** (in the Spindrift Hotel, Barrier Reef Dr., tel. 501/226-2170, 6:30am-9:30pm Tues.-Sun.) offers Mexican cuisine and seafood on an open porch or in a waterfront dining room. It is famous for the good-for-hangovers lime soup (US$4.50) at lunch, generous seafood dinners (US$12-22), as well as tasty Mexican staples—try the beef nachos, a perfect snack on Thursday before the Chicken Drop next door at Wahoo's Lounge.

Mexican food lovers will enjoy the **Lone Star Grill & Cantina** (tel. 501/226-4666, noon-9pm Wed.-Mon., US$10-18), a very far trek south but well worth it both for the ambience and the tasty belly-filling dishes, including chimichangas, El Jefe burritos, chalupas, enchiladas, and more Mexican favorites. There are also "gringo favorites" of the burger-and-fries variety.

Inside the San Pedro Holiday Hotel the swank beachfront **Caprice Bar Grill** (Barrier Reef Dr., tel. 501/226-2014, 9am-midnight Mon.-Sat., 11am-9pm Sun., US$15-32) delivers Caribbean and Latin cuisine. The quesadillas are to die for, and the portions are large. The outdoor covered deck is ideal for the popular happy hour (3pm-6pm daily), with half-price mojitos, margaritas, and rum punch as well as US$2 beer specials.

For tasty Latin Caribbean cuisine, **Wild Mangos** (42 Barrier Reef Dr., sandwiched between Ruby's Hotel and the library on the beach, tel. 501/226-2859, noon-3pm and 6pm-9pm Mon.-Sat., US$12-20) serves amazing versions of local favorites (ceviche, fish tacos, quesadillas, burritos) prepared by one of Belize's most distinguished chefs, Amy Knox. You cannot go wrong here, with offerings such as Mango's Mongo Burrito, seafood specials, Amy's Chef Salad, and rum-glazed bacon shrimp.

International

Mesa Café (Tarpon St., tel. 501/226-3444, 8am-2pm Mon.-Fri., from US$5) serves delicious breakfasts (the coconut French toast is heaven), quiches, salads, sandwiches, burgers, and pies. It's at the entrance to the Vilma Linda Plaza, a peaceful oasis in the bustle of downtown; the tiled courtyard is filled with lush plants and a small fishpond.

Park yourself outdoors for lunch at ★ **The Truck Stop** (Mile 1 North, tel. 501/226-3663, truckstopbz@gmail.com, noon-9pm Wed.-Sun., US$4-10), Belize's first food park, with a collection of containers each dishing a range of international cuisine: Latin American as well as Southeast Asian—served on biodegradable plates—and even an ice cream truck. Grab one of the picnic tables or a barstool, or meander to the back to indulge lagoon-side on the dock. The spot has a fun island ambience and is a great place to meet fellow travelers if you're exploring solo. Don't miss out on the frozen coconut mojito. There's a swimming pool, movie nights, a monthly farmers market, a pig roast on Sunday at 1pm, and even an occasional *Amazing Race* contest.

For a nice Ambergris evening away from town, take a golf cart or water taxi to one of the restaurants north of the bridge. The cheapest and most casual places are Palapa Bar and Ak'Bol. Up north, just a 10-minute ride and complete with a pool, red couches, and sultry music, and with an ultra-tasty menu, is ★ **Rojo Beach Bar and Lounge** (tel. 501/226-4012, lunch and dinner Tues.-Sat., entrées from US$27). Rojo offers a Belizean-inspired menu with a sophisticated twist, including pizzas, and enticing cocktails—ask for the daily concoction or try the poison martini—in seductive yet casual surroundings. It has a thatched-hut bar and a prime beachfront spot.

Sunday Beach Barbecue

Estel's Dine by the Sea

Sunday is "Funday," as they say in San Pedro and in the rest of Belize. Businesses close, families lunch together after church, kids swim off the docks, and adults relax in the shade beside barbecue grills. Heaps of perfectly smoked chicken, lobster, and other meats come off the grill and are washed down with Belikins. The rest of the afternoon is spent fishing, competing in horseshoe tournaments, dancing to live music, or napping beside a palm tree. It's the cure for a week's hard work (or a Saturday night hangover).

Belizeans are masters of the barbecue, and this skill manifests itself most on the weekend. If you're not lucky enough to be invited to a local's outdoor food fest, there are a few options where visitors can get a taste of this Belizean tradition. Several beachfront establishments in San Pedro Town offer a Sunday barbecue special, complete with beachside seating, pools or docks, and live music. Some also throw in games for all-around good cheer.

You can't go wrong at **Estel's Dine by the Sea** (tel. 501/226-2019, 6am-close Sun., US$12.50), a family-run gem serving succulent barbecue ribs with your choice of pork, chicken, jerk wings, sausage, and generous sides. You'll see owner Charles Worthington outside at 6:30am, perfecting the meat on a massive grill. Get your outdoor patio table early (by noon) and sip a cold beverage while you listen to a soothing acoustic band play light rock tunes.

Sunday Funday at **Crazy Canucks Beach Bar** (beachfront, S. Coconut Dr., tel. 501/670-8001, US$5-10) is somewhat of an expat institution. The place attracts the largest crowd of all on Sunday afternoons and starts rolling later than most, at 3pm. It also has a live blues band, and you can try your hand at the horseshoe tournament.

To escape the Sunday action in town, the ever-lively **Palapa Bar and Grill** (beachfront, Boca del Rio Dr., tel. 501/226-3111, 11am-about 11pm Sun., US$4-6), is perfect almost any day, not just Sunday.

Another option is to head out on a special day's sail to a nearby caye for an island beach barbecue getaway Belizean-style. For more information, check with the **Rubio brothers** of **No Rush Sailing Tours** (tel. 501/600-5022, unity_tours@yahoo.com).

Barbecue

Besides the informal street barbecues, which offer the best-value food around, a rotating schedule ensures a beach cook-up nearly every night of the week. Your choice of chicken, ribs, or fish runs US$5-10. Also on Sunday, a host of beachfront eateries offer a special barbecue menu, coupled with live music; it's a sort of tradition in San Pedro.

On Friday, you'll see a steaming grill outside the **Lions Club** building (Barrier Reef Dr., across from Manelly's) for the weekly fundraising barbecue. Starting at 2pm, anyone is welcome to buy a plate or "boxed lunch" of grilled chicken with generous side servings (US$4.50). There's also a bar onsite. All the money made is pooled to help members who are in need or suffer a disaster. In case you were curious, Friday night is also bingo night, so popular among the locals that many negotiate their weekly work shifts around it.

It's often difficult to find authentic Jamaican jerk outside Jamaica, but ★ **Jambel Jerk Pit** (Barrier Reef Dr., beachside at SunBreeze Suites, tel. 501/226-3515, 7am-9pm daily, US$8-20) rises to the challenge, and its weekly Wednesday all-you-can-eat buffet with live music is a great value (6pm-9pm Wed., US$20 pp). The location, on a poolside and beachfront deck with umbrellas, is ideal.

Italian

Pizza is available for delivery or dining in at dozens of places on the island. **Pepperoni's Pizza** (Coconut Dr., tel. 501/226-4515, 5pm-10pm Tues.-Sun.) is the most popular for both quality and price—a large 16-inch specialty pie goes for US$20 and is served deep-dish style. **Pirates** (Pescador Dr., tel. 501/226-4663, 4-10pm daily, US$4-25) is also good and does slices in the evenings.

Adjacent to Pepperoni's is the casual **Ammore' Pasta da Donatello e Davide** (Coconut Dr., tel. 501/634-5641, www.ammorepasta.com, 6:30am-9pm Wed.-Mon., US$15-20) run by an Italian expat couple. My

dish was decent but overpriced for the setting and small portion.

Fine Dining

San Pedro has an ever-evolving selection of trendy restaurants offering international fare and flair; if you don't pay for such indulgence with an expanded waistline, you'll surely pay for it in cash. If you're *really* dining out—an appetizer, a couple of drinks, an entrée, and a dessert—expect to pay as much as you would in a U.S. city: US$40-80 per person, more if you like your wine. Remember that many upscale restaurants add tax and a service charge, and there's a fee for using a credit card, so bring enough cash. Reservations are recommended at all of the following restaurants, especially in the high season.

Of the finer restaurants, **Blue Water Grill** (on the beach, behind the SunBreeze Hotel, tel. 501/226-3347, 7am-9:30pm daily, entrées from US$19) is known to offer some of the best values and biggest portions. The menu has hints of Hawaiian and Southeast Asian cuisine; try the coconut shrimp stick with black-bean sweet-and-sour sauce. Sushi is offered on Tuesday and Thursday; there are dishes like snook with banana curry along with comfort plates like lasagna. And many swear by the lime tart.

★ **Red Ginger** (Phoenix Resort, Barrier Reef Dr., tel. 501/226-4623, www. redgingerbelize.com, 7:30am-10:30am, 11:30am-2:30pm, and 6pm-9:30pm daily, US$9-37), in the Phoenix Resort toward the north part of San Pedro, has an indoor air-conditioned dining room and trellised outdoor patio. The food here is divine. It specializes in local cuisine with an international twist—grouper ceviche with mango, empanadas with pork, and plantains with buffalo mozzarella and sautéed basil. There are homemade bagel sandwiches for breakfast, Indian chicken curry and Cajun gumbo for lunch, and appetizers, salads, pastas, seafood, and steaks, plus a delicious and filling five-course tasting menu (US$45) for dinner; there's a big wine list, half-price martinis on Saturday, and brunch on Saturday and Sunday. For live music, stop by on Wednesday or Sunday.

★ **Casa Picasso** (Sting Ray St., tel. 501/226-4443, www.casapicassobelize.com, 5:30pm-9:30pm Tues.-Sat., US$10-30) is one of the best fine dining experiences in San Pedro. The restaurant, a spacious yet cozy dining-room setting with art, drapes, and mood lighting, focuses on a farm-to-table experience with Belizean delights—think tapas like pan-fried crab cakes, pork belly in oyster sauce, potato ricotta gnocchi, salads, soups, or unique entrées such as the banana leaf-wrapped fish fillet or the filet mignon. Desserts aren't to be missed either. Enjoy a free shuttle pickup and return with your reservation if you're staying in town.

Hidden Treasure Restaurant (2715 Flamboyant Dr., Escalante area, south San Pedro, tel. 501/226-4111, www.hiddentreasurebelize.com, 5pm-9pm daily, US$15-22) is an intimate open-air restaurant, beautifully lit under a *palapa* roof. There's a long list of appetizers, lunches, dinner items, and desserts, from seafood bisque to Mayan-accented snapper and spare *buhurie* (Garifuna-spiced ribs).

Restaurant Palmilla (at Victoria House, 2 miles south of San Pedro, tel. 501/226-2067, 6:30am-2:30pm and 6pm-9pm daily, reservations encouraged, US$24-50) combines Mexico with Belize with fresh local produce, seafood, and meats, as well as soups. Start with crispy snapper cakes with chipotle beurre blanc, black beans, and roasted corn succotash; follow with black-bean or *chilapachole* (corn) soup; then savor main dishes like cashew-crusted grouper.

★ **Mambo's** (Matachica Beach Resort, tel. 501/223-0002, www.matachica.com, lunch and dinner daily) is pure indulgence, serving rich and artful heaps of snappers, scallops, shrimp, lobsters, and calamari—you can try them all in the amazing Deep Blue entrée (US$34). Appetizers, such as soy-glazed snapper carpaccio, are US$10-16; save room for the chocolate mousse.

Portofino Restaurant and Green

Parrot Beach Bar (tel. 501/226-5096, lunch and dinner daily, dinner entrées US$18-35) is six miles north of San Pedro, and staff will give you a complimentary boat ride to join them for dinner, although from no farther south than Fido's dock. Expect local cuisine with European flair, including spider crab-laced snapper and other creative seafood specials. Lunch is also excellent, with delicious chicken finger baskets and an enormous vegetarian selection (US$6-14), and they'll set up a romantic table on the end of the pier if you'd like.

Dessert

Go to **Manelly's** (Barrier Reef Dr., 11am-5pm daily) for homemade ice cream—it is known for its "coconut creation." Or sample the frozen custard at **DandE's Ice Cream** (Pescador Dr. 11am-5pm daily), where a couple from Pennsylvania dairy country turn out fresh flavors every day, including soursop, from a local fruit that makes for a tart Belizean treat. For pastries and sweet bites, from sausage rolls to apple turnovers, doughnuts, and cinnamon buns, ride down to **The Baker** (Coconut Dr., next to Marina's Supermarket, tel. 501/629-8030, 7:30am-5:30pm Mon.-Fri., 7:30am-2pm Sat.), where you can either sit as you eat or grab it and walk over to the beach to enjoy your treats. There's also freshly baked bread.

For fresh fruit drinks head to **Izzy's Smoothies, Snacks & Juice Bar** (corner of Pescador Dr. and Caribeña St., tel. 501/674-0233, izzy_sanpedro@yahoo.com, 7am-6pm Mon.-Sat., 8am-3pm Sun., US$2-7)—like a pineapple and coconut blend—or a lean green juice. A trek all the way south of San Pedro can be worthwhile for gourmet and iced coffee drinks at **Rum + Bean** (Mahogany Bay Village, Sea Grape Dr., tel. 501/236-5102, www.rumandbean.com, 7am-8pm daily, US$3-13), a cozy coffee shop that is now a favorite expat stop, also for its fast Wi-Fi. Have the butterscotch frappé, or wait for happy hour and go for one of the signature "craft cocktails with a soul"—like the One Barrel Mule.

Groceries

There are several medium-size supermarkets around San Pedro, all generally open 8:30am-9:30pm daily, though hours may vary. One of the cheapest is the locally owned **Marina's Market** (next to Xanadu Island Resort, Coconut Dr., tel. 501/226-3647). **The Greenhouse** (Pescador Dr., next to St. Francis Xavier Credit Union, tel. 501/226-2085) boasts the freshest produce and seafood, including cold cuts and unique grocery selections. **Caye Mart Supermarket** (north of Castillo's Hardware Store, tel. 501/226-3446, samirbelize@gmail.com) has wine selections as well as imported Carib and Presidente beer. **Island City** (beside Wine de Vine) is packed with all your favorite spirits. You can easily spot fresh fruit stands roadside around town.

ACCOMMODATIONS

Ambergris Caye has over 100 licensed hotels, mostly midrange and increasingly upscale resort lodging. The few places geared toward backpackers and extreme budget travelers are located either right in San Pedro Town or on the outskirts by the airstrip. Of course, what you give up in beach quality you get back in location: "In town" means being in the middle of the buzz of cafés, bars, boutiques, dive shops, dancing, and dining. And those in town can easily escape north or south for the day as well, for more exclusive restaurants and scenery.

If you're more into privacy, all the action is easily accessible from any resort on the island by boat, taxi, or golf cart. In downtown San Pedro, the word *beachfront* refers to the very narrow strip of sand that is used more as a pathway for pedestrians and boats than for lounging on sand. You can find plenty of space to sun yourself, but as you move farther from town, either to the north or south along the island, the beaches fronting the resorts become wider, softer, and more exclusive.

Keep in mind that rates across the board are subject to seasonal fluctuations, service charges, and government taxes. Always verify and ask about discounts before booking.

In addition to hotels and luxury lodges, there are many apartment and house rentals available around the island. To start, check the classifieds from the *San Pedro Sun* (www.sanpedrosun.com/classifieds). Another source for vacation homes is **Caye Management** (tel. 501/226-3077, www.cayemanagement.com), which has an office that's open daily on the north edge of town at Casa Coral.

Under US$25

A reliable option is **Ruby's Hotel** (tel. 501/226-2063, rubys@btl.net, US$21-44), with 23 basic, clean guest rooms in a well-maintained building right on the water in the heart of the village. Ruby's Café and pastry shop downstairs is excellent and a San Pedrano institution, and you can sit on your room's balcony or the common deck space with some fresh morning johnnycakes and watch the beach traffic below. Guest rooms have either a shared or private bath with a fan or air-conditioning.

Located in Boca del Rio, **Sandbar Beachfront Hostel** (7 Boca del Rio Dr., from US$20) is the only value-packed budget hostel in San Pedro, with solid bang for your buck considering its seafront location in town. It offers clean dorm rooms with bunk beds, A/C, and shared bathroom facilities. There's a bar and restaurant on site.

US$25-50

Right in town, the family-run ★ **Hotel San Pedrano** (Barrier Reef Dr., tel. 501/226-2054, sanpedrano@btl.net, US$35 with fan, US$45 with a/c) has six guest rooms, from single to triple, that make up the island's self-proclaimed "top of the low end." From the breezy upstairs veranda it's easy to eat a bite, read a book, or watch the street below. Each guest room has hot and cold water, a private bath, a ceiling fan, and optional air-conditioning. The amenities are basic, but the hotel is a stone's throw from all the action in town and steps from the water taxi pier.

The only budget option north of the bridge is the **Ak'bol Yoga Retreat** (tel.

501/226-2073, www.akbol.com), which has 30 guest rooms (US$35 s, US$50 d) in a long wooden building with a massive shared restroom-shower-locker room. The resort is on a narrow beach strip and has a yoga deck and an average restaurant on-site.

US$50-100

The charming pink-and-white beachfront ★ **Conch Shell Inn** (tel. 501/226-2062, conchshellinn@gmail.com, US$74-94), beside SunBreeze Suites, was the third hotel to open in the early days of tourism. Renovated in 2008 and well maintained, the five upstairs single and double guest rooms have great views, tiled floors, and kitchenettes with all the amenities; the cheaper downstairs rooms are steps from the sea. All guest rooms are beachfront, and there are portable air-conditioning units (US$10) available if needed. Daily maid service and a lovely private front courtyard with hammocks and beach chairs make this a great beach vacation spot in town.

★ **Pedro's Inn** (Seagrape Dr., off Coconut Dr., tel. 501/226-3825, www.pedroshotel.com, US$55-65) was once upon a time a youth hostel, with two rows of 14 wooden stalls, each with a bed, a ceiling fan, a locker, and access to shared bath facilities. It is good for anyone seeking a budget hotel—the rooms are above Pedro's Sports Bar and poker room, so you've got an on-site nightly social scene with a lively cast of characters and pizza available for delivery. Pedro's has two swimming pools with lounge chairs, a deck, and a shaded picnic area. It's back by the airstrip, a 10-minute walk from the town center or US$3.50 by taxi. Across the street, Pedro's has 32 standard hotel rooms (US$50-65) with air-conditioning, TVs, private baths, and fans, including 12 deluxe rooms with pool views (US$80). Guests of Pedro's now also have access to the beach at Caribbean Villas. There are also DJ club nights on the weekends.

A few steps away is the bright, well-kept **Spindrift Hotel** (Barrier Reef Dr., tel. 501/226-2174, spinhotel@btl.net, www.

spindriftbelize.com, US$54-150), a three-story building offering clean, spacious guest rooms with all the amenities, including Wi-Fi and balconies. There's a wonderful massive veranda overlooking the beach, and the hotel is sandwiched between Wahoo's Lounge, home of the Chicken Drop, and Caliente Restaurant. This is where I stayed my first time in San Pedro, and it was ideal.

On the north end of town, toward the bridge, **Hotel del Rio** (tel. 501/226-2286, www.hoteldelriobelize.com, US$70-170) is a quiet hotel on the beach that offers great value. Accommodations range from basic economy rooms with shared baths and cold water to bigger colorful casitas built of pimento palm, some with a king or two queen beds. There is also a larger villa (US$600 per week) in the back. Hammocks are available to enjoy in the private beachfront courtyard.

US$100-150

The central and cheerful **Holiday Hotel** (Barrier Reef Dr., tel. 501/226-2103, U.S. tel. 713/893-3825, www.sanpedroholiday.com, US$134-163), the island's first hotel and still under the original family's management, keeps getting better. The 16 clean, spacious guest rooms have air-conditioning and fans, private baths, and beachfront verandas. Lots of water sports and boats are available.

One of Belize's only dedicated yoga resorts, **Ak'bol** (1 mile north of the bridge, tel. 501/226-2073, www.akbol.com, US$145-165) has seven cabanas on the beach in a naturally landscaped garden, a small pool, and a shaded yoga garden within earshot of the sea. The cabanas have raised beds, local decor, a loft for the kids, unique conch-shell sinks, and private outdoor rainforest showers. There's an on-site beach bar, although the food is hit-or-miss and service can be slow. There are also daily yoga classes, which are popular with residents, and retreat packages.

South of San Pedro, a quaint and homey option is **Changes in Latitudes Bed and Breakfast** (36 Coconut Dr., next to Belize Yacht Club, tel. 501/226-2986, www.

Honeymooning on Ambergris Caye

Ambergris Caye is Belize's top honeymoon pick, not least for its numerous resorts, fine dining and entertainment options, and short distance to the Belize Barrier Reef. While San Pedro Town is the hub, the island is large enough that couples can choose to stay on the south or north end, secluded parts that are either a short walk to town (south) or a boat ride away (north) for added isolation. Whether spending the day in a hammock on an isolated beach stretch or exploring San Pedro Town's alley-size streets, there are choices to suit all couples.

Most resorts offer five- to seven-day packages, which often include all meals and one snorkel or day trip for two. Picking a resort will ultimately come down to the hotel setting, amenities, and type of getaway you seek. A few stand out from the pack and are a good place to start your research.

For a luxurious experience away from the noise but close enough to the action in town, the award-winning **Victoria House** (Coconut Dr., tel. 501/226-2067, U.S. tel. 800/247-5159, www. victoria-house.com, US$205-1,195) is a solid option with beachfront villas or *palapa*-roof casitas facing one of the best stretches near San Pedro, as well as numerous on-site amenities including two swimming pools. The Reef Romance package is chock-full of goodies, including massages for two, champagne, and a private candlelit dinner.

You'll hop on a 20-minute private boat ride from San Pedro to reach the Zen **Matachica Beach Resort** (tel. 501/226-5010, www.matachica.com, from US$275), on the island's northern side. Colorful thatched-roof cabanas with hammocks sit on a deserted, powdery-soft white-sand beach—a postcard-perfect greeting as you near the shoreline. An excellent on-site restaurant, water sports equipment, spa, and friendly staff make this an easy pick. Honeymoon packages include two-day trips, one to the reef and the other to the mainland's beautiful Lamanai Archaeological Site. Be sure to reserve a seafront cabana and wake early for sunrise views from your bed. A stretch remoter than Matachica is **X'Tan Ha Resort** (tel. 501/226-2846, U.S. tel. 844/360-1553, www.xtanha.com, from US$275), a delightful boutique resort with one-bedroom beachfront villas a couple of steps from a lovely white-sand stretch with shallow entry and plenty of umbrellas and chairs. The bar and restaurant are excellent, but the staff here truly stand out.

changesinlatitudesbelize.com, US$105), with six small and cozy guest rooms with air-conditioning, ceiling fans, private baths, and pool privileges at Exotic Caye Beach Resort a few doors down. The B&B is serious about the breakfast, made fresh daily and served in the outdoor common room, and there's a board updated daily with suggested activities and nightlife. The location is ideal, just a few steps from Ramon's Village Resort, the best swimming stretch in town. Use of bicycles is complimentary, as are outdoor lockers for drying wet clothes, and there's on-site security at night.

US$150-200

Inside an elegant three-story building of tropical colonial design, on the corner of Sandpiper Street and the sea, is the delightful

★ **Blue Tang Inn** (tel. 501/226-2326, U.S. tel. 866/881-1020, www.bluetanginn.com, US$165-265). The 14 tasteful guest rooms sport lots of warm, rich wood paneling and have kitchens, private baths, ceiling fans, and air-conditioning. The grounds are well kept, with a gated but beach-facing swimming pool by the entrance, and the rooftop balcony is breezy and pleasant, with a killer sunset view. It's a great pick for some boutique luxury right in town, ideal for couples or friends. Continental breakfast is served daily on the terrace facing the beach.

The **SunBreeze Hotel** (tel. 501/226-2191, U.S. tel. 800/688-0191, www.sunbreeze. net, US$188-248) is a full-service beachfront hotel with 43 guest rooms built around an open sand area and pool. Guest rooms have two queen beds, air-conditioning, tile floors, local artwork, private baths, and direct-dial phones; Front Street starts next door, and the entrance is yards from the airstrip. There's an on-site dive shop, a top-notch restaurant (Blue Water Grill), and many other services. The SunBreeze has some of the few fully wheelchair-accessible guest rooms in the country. It also rents suites at the other end of Front Street, on the beach across from the Belize Bank, at **SunBreeze Suites** (tel. 501/226-4675, U.S. tel. 800/820-1631, www.sunbreezesuites.com, US$199-225), which offers one-bedroom suites with full kitchens, guest queen sofa beds, and air-conditioning. The suites can sleep up to four adults per room; families and children are welcome. They have less of a standard hotel feel and are more akin to self-catering condos—and are cozier for it. There is a wonderful small Jamaican restaurant on-site called **Jambel Jerk Pit.**

Farther south is **Mata Rocks Resort** (tel. 501/226-2336, U.S. tel. 888/628-2757, www.matarocks.com, US$155-220), a small hotel tucked on the south end of Ambergris with six suites and 11 ocean-view guest rooms centered around a pool; the rooms, while not huge, have plenty of basic amenities, such as air-conditioning, cable TV, wireless Internet, bikes, transfers, and continental breakfast at the tiny on-site bar. The architecture is unusual—all white, clean, and Mediterranean. Don't forget your sunglasses if you stay here.

US$200-300

A short walk to town, the beautiful, luxurious oceanfront suites at ★ **The Palms** (tel. 501/226-3322, www.belizepalms.com, US$204-289), a boutique condominium resort on the beach next to Ramon's Village Resort, are in a shaded compound and an excellent value. Secluded yet centrally located, the resort has an idyllic small freshwater pool in a well-kept garden and 12 one- and two-bedroom ocean-view suites, executive suites, and a poolside casita. Amenities aren't spared, and the furnishings are wonderful. The Palms feels like your own luxurious vacation home

and an oasis in an otherwise bustling San Pedro. It's perfect for couples or friends seeking tranquility but wanting to remain close to restaurants, beach, and activities.

★ **Xanadu Island Resort** (tel. 501/226-2814, U.S. tel. 866/351-4752, www.xanaduislandresort.com, US$220-240) is one of my favorite accommodations in San Pedro, on the south side of town. It's ideal when there are no big families staying with small kids (the pool gets crowded). The resort is a cluster of luxury monolithic domes with thatched overlay roofs nestled in lush landscaping. There is a private nature walk and bird sanctuary. Nineteen suites are available with fully equipped kitchens, and there is a choice of studios and one-, two-, and three-bedroom units. The beachfront lofts are stunning, and the service is top-notch. There's a restaurant-bar next door at Caribbean Villas' **Amber Beach Bar** if you need coffee first thing in the morning and don't care to brew your own.

Diamond Lodge (2 Sea Grape Dr., tel. 501/226-4377, www.diamondlodgebelize.com, US$200-350) offers something different in San Pedro with this former private villa turned into a boutique hotel that feels like a friend's plush weekend home. There are 10 rooms on two levels, a pool big enough to have your own corner, and an on-site mini-spa, Jordana's Art of Touch. Breakfasts are the highlight, prepared by in-house Chef Patrick who hails from Corsica, France, and served dining room style across the state-of-the-art open kitchen. Rooms are intimately sized, decorated with Belizean art, and so comfortable you might end up holing up for the day, but you're also a short walk from a handful of cafés, pizzerias, Black & White Garifuna Restaurant, and the beach. The lodge hosts a weekly, five-course Chef Series the first Friday of every month, open to the public.

Ramon's Village Resort (Coconut Dr., tel. 501/226-2071, U.S. tel. 800/624-4215, www.ramons.com, US$210-475) is somewhat of an institution in San Pedro. So when a section of this full-service resort with 71 guest rooms was struck by yet another accidental and devastating fire in August 2013, the entire island came to the rescue. In just under four months of rebuilding, the resort has brand-new cabanas and a swimming pool. Standard seafront guest rooms run from US$210 and the presidential suite goes for US$475; the guest rooms are nice, although the "kitchenettes" are not much more than a sink and a microwave. The property's 500-foot beach is practically in San Pedro Town and has decent walk-in snorkeling. There's a restaurant and bar, as well as on-site dive gear, guides, and an inland tour operator. You can rent windsurfing boards, snorkel gear, and golf carts. Ramon's suffered damage to its dock and dive shop in 2016 with Hurricane Earl, but boats and water sports services are still operating just fine.

One of the island's top-class acts, ★ Victoria House (Coconut Dr., tel. 501/226-2067, U.S. tel. 800/247-5159, www.victoria-house.com, US$210-795) has a luxurious selection of suites and several multi-family mansion-like two- to five-bedroom villas set along one of the nicest stretches of beach south of town. Expect colonial architectural elegance on a well-manicured, tranquil piece of property about two miles south of San Pedro. The stucco and thatched casitas with tile floors are placed around several sleek infinity pools; you also get a full-service dive shop with private guides, the Admiral Nelson Bar, and one of the top-rated restaurants in the country (Restaurant Palmilla).

Banyan Bay Suites (Seagrape Dr., tel. 501/226-3739, U.S. tel. 866/352-1163, www.banyanbay.com, from US$275) is a luxury family resort with all the amenities in its 32 suites, including balconies and whirlpool tubs. Lots of activities and lessons for children are available; full dive trips and inland trips can be arranged. There's also an on-site dock restaurant, Rico's, and a wedding chapel at the tip of the dock. It's close to San Pedro Town, yet away from the noise and on a nice section of the beach.

A little more than four miles north of San Pedro, you'll fall in love with the über-stylish, exotic yet unpretentious ★ Matachica Beach Resort (tel. 501/226-5010, www.matachica.com, from US$275), with 26 spacious casitas, suites, and luxury villas clustered along a beautiful stretch of white sand, front and back. The casitas are named after fruits (mine was Cherry); each bears its own color and matching porch hammock and is styled with local art and a blend of African- and Asian-tinged decor. The resort offers a full range of amenities, a spa with two treatment rooms, an infinity pool with a jetted tub, plus a vast lounge—with a pool table and ample seating—that connects to Mambo's restaurant. There are no flat-screen TVs or phones, nor will you miss them—Matachica is all about Zen. Proximity to the reef, which is visible from the white sandy shores, makes it ideal for water sports, from paddleboarding to kayaking; all are complimentary, as are the private daily boat shuttles to town. The resort is ideal for an intimate wedding or a secluded couple's getaway. An exciting addition are the two one-bedroom luxury beachfront villas—Luna and Aqua—with soaking tubs and a spacious wooden outdoor deck outfitted with a whirlpool tub facing the sea.

Located 7.2 miles north of San Pedro, X'Tan Ha (tel. 501/226-2846, U.S. tel. 844/360-1553, www.xtanha.com, from US$135-275) is a delightful boutique resort with luxury one-bedroom beachfront villas, equipped with all the bells and whistles, including a full kitchen, air-conditioning, a living room with futons for extra sleep space, a dining room, and cozy elevated king beds. The beach is a lovely white stretch with shallow entry and plenty of umbrellas and chairs. The bar at X'Tan Ha is lively compared to most north-end resorts, with a couple of picnic tables in the water, and the on-site restaurant is excellent (the cheesy potato pancakes for breakfast sent me to heaven). X'Tan Ha is a favorite among couples seeking escape and low-key evenings.

Over US$300

The Phoenix Resort (Barrier Reef Dr., tel.

501/226-2083, U.S. tel. 877/822-5512, www.thephoenixbelize.com, US$425-675) raises luxury up a couple of notches in San Pedro. This large condo resort has 28 of the largest furnished suites on the island, with every amenity you can imagine both in and out of your room, including king beds, granite countertop kitchens, and even iPads. It has a pool, a restaurant, a gym, and a spa, all in a big walled compound toward the north of town on the beach side, and there is full concierge service for activities on and off the island (complimentary kayaks, paddleboards, and bicycles). It's *très* contemporary chic.

Portofino Beach Resort (North, tel. 501/226-5096, www.portofinobelize.com, from US$310, or US$2,299 3-night all-inclusive) is another long-standing luxury lodge right on the beach, but with a deep swimming pool, an excellent on-site restaurant (meal plan available), and friendly staff. It has 15 units, including two treetop suites and a honeymoon-VIP villa with full amenities. You can use the lodge's sporting equipment to play around all day—it's only a 15-minute kayak paddle to excellent snorkeling at Mexico Rocks.

Less than three miles north of San Pedro, the family-run **El Pescador Lodge & Villas** (tel. 501/226-2398, U.S. tel. 804/661-2259, www.elpescador.com, 3 nights US$1,480) was constructed in 1974 as one of the world's premier sportfishing lodges, and it has evolved into a modern, upscale eco-lodge resort. There are 13 newly rebuilt, gorgeous seafront double rooms in the original mahogany lodge—still cozy and with colorful paintings, for a luxurious feel—and private one-, two-, and three-bedroom villa accommodations, all of which are centered around three stunning saltwater and freshwater swimming pools and gorgeous palms. The villas can be locked off into smaller sections, and each is outfitted with a spacious seafront deck, a full kitchen with a sit-up bar, baths with gorgeous tiling, and Belizean-made hardwood floors. The resort offers more than fly-fishing trips, including smaller customized ecotours and diving with resident licensed dive master Alonzo Flota. Guests mingle over communal meals on the lovely large outdoor patio and at the on-site lounge, complete with a bar and a pool table, at the end of the day's activities. You'll find that anglers and their nonfishing families (there are spa services available, yoga classes nearby, cycling, and more) are repeat visitors, and many know each other from past years.

Las Terrazas (Mile 3.5, North Ambergris

Ramon's Village Resort beachfront

Caye, U.S. tel. 800/447-1553, www. lasterrazasresort.com, from US$430) is a slick affair of 39 fully equipped "residential townhomes" around a pool area and restaurant serving "Southwestern cuisine with Caribbean flair." This is a full-service luxury resort with many activities and packages.

The farthest out north, **Sapphire Beach Resort** (North Ambergris Caye, tel. 501/670-2480, www.sapphirebeachbelize. com, US$175-450) is the definition of a laid-back getaway—even slower than at X'Tan Ha, with ultra-spacious beach villas, small pools, and kayaks for guest use. The reef is a stone's throw, and you can anchor and relax there if you wish. The chef at the on-site El Zafiro Restaurant delights with his unique creations and presentation style—don't miss the lobster curry fettuccine. The sunset colors this far north of the island are spectacular.

INFORMATION AND SERVICES
Banks
There are plenty of banks in town. Belize, Scotiabank, Atlantic, and First Caribbean have international ATMs. There's also an ATM in the big supermarket just south of Ramon's Village Resort.

Health and Emergencies
Prescriptions and other medicines can be found at **R&L Pharmacy** (tel. 501/226-2890, open daily) by the airstrip, and there are plenty of smaller pharmacies around town. If you need medical attention, all hotels and resorts keep a list of doctors and transportation options to call in the middle of the night, including a helicopter to take you to the hospital in Belize City in the event of a major emergency. For other medical concerns, go to the **San Pedro PolyClinic II** (tel. 501/226-2536, 8am-noon and 2pm-5pm Mon.-Sat.), located behind Wine de Vine and the Island City Supermarket, facing the airstrip.

Dr. Daniel Gonzalez's **Ambergris Hope Clinic** (tel. 501/226-2660), next to Castillo's Hardware Store, is another option. For diving

emergencies, the island has two **hyperbaric chambers—one located behind the Tropic Air airstrip** (tel. 501/226-2851 or 501/226-3195), and the other at **Ambergris Hope Clinic** (Pescador Dr., tel. 501/226-2983 or 501/226-2660 after hours, 8am-9pm Mon.-Fri., Sat mornings); or call **Dr. Antonia Guerrero** (tel. 501/628-3828).

The **police department** (for emergencies tel. 911, south substation tel. 501/206-2022) and **fire department** (tel. 501/226-2372) are both in San Pedro Town near the big BTL antenna on Pescador Drive.

Media and Communications
Things change quickly in San Pedro, especially prices. Before your trip, you can take a look at Ambergris's two weekly papers, the *San Pedro Sun* (tel. 501/226-2070, www. sanpedrosun.com) and the online *Ambergris Today* (Pescador Dr., tel. 501/226-3462, www. ambergristoday.com), both solid resources. *Ambergris Today* includes comprehensive reviews of the latest and best establishments in town, including resorts, restaurants, and more.

The **post office** (Pescador Dr., 8am-4pm Mon.-Thurs., 8am-3:30pm Fri.) is next to Elvi's Kitchen. There are several Internet cafés in town, some with Wi-Fi and others with desktops—most are on Front Street. Try **Pelican Internet Cafe** (Barrier Reef Dr., tel. 501/206-2153, 7am-10pm Mon.-Sat., 8am-10pm Sun., US$5 per hour) a block north of Fido's, with wireless Internet access, coffee and alcoholic beverages, and air-conditioning. Otherwise, most businesses (restaurants, hotels) do provide Wi-Fi free with consumption.

TRANSPORTATION
Getting There
AIR
The 2,600-foot-long runway of **San Pedro Airport (SPR)** is practically in downtown San Pedro. Belize's two airlines, **Tropic Air** (tel. 501/226-2626, U.S. tel. 800/422-3435, www.tropicair.com) and **Maya Island Air** (tel. 501/223-1140 or 501/223-1362, www.

mayaislandair.com) fly more than a dozen daily flights between San Pedro, Caye Caulker, and Belize City—and another five to and from Corozal. Tropic Air is the most popular and the one I've always used. Tropic also flies to Mexico City. The flight from Belize City's international airport to San Pedro takes about 15 minutes and costs US$115 round-trip. Taking the water taxi is cheaper, although you'll need to catch a taxi from the international airport to get to the water taxi terminal.

BOAT

Two companies provide scheduled water taxi service between Belize City and the islands: **Ocean Ferry** (across from Cholo's Sports Bar, tel. 501/223-0033, www.oceanferrybelize.com) and the **San Pedro Belize Express Water Taxi** (close to Spindrift Hotel, tel. 501/223-2225, www.belizewatertaxi.com), with the latter offering more daily departures between Belize City and Ambergris Caye, a 75-minute ride that costs US$28 one-way, or Caye Caulker, a 45-minute ride costing US$18. Both sometimes carry free Wi-Fi on the boat.

In Belize City, the **Ocean Ferry** Water Taxi Terminal is on North Front Street next to the Swing Bridge, with boats leaving between 8am and 5:30pm daily. The **San Pedro Belize Express Water Taxi** departs from the Tourism Village in Belize City. Boats depart San Pedro from the pier across from the Central Park, 6am-4:30pm daily. Always check the schedule before making plans; usually there are extra boats on weekends and holidays.

Thunderbolt Water Taxi (tel. 501/610-4475, thunderboltwatertaxi@gmail.com, http://ambergriscaye.com/thunderbolt) runs a once-daily trip to Corozal from San Pedro at 3pm (US$22.50 one-way, US$42.50 round-trip), and from Corozal to San Pedro at 7am. The trip takes two hours in each direction. The departure pier in San Pedro is by the old football field; ask anyone to direct you to Thunderbolt. The newer **Isla Norte Ferry** (tel. 501/637-3757 or 501/610-4757, US$25 pp one-way) offers a daily run from San Pedro to **Sarteneja and Corozal Town,** departing at 3pm from San Pedro and arriving in Corozal at 4pm, and from Corozal to San Pedro, departing at 7am from the municipal pier and arriving in San Pedro at 8:30am.

Getting Around

Walking is feasible within the town of San Pedro; it's about a 10-minute stroll from the airstrip to the main strip. Once you start traveling between resorts to the south or north, however, you may want to go by bicycle, golf cart, taxi, or boat. At one time, cars were a rarity, but together with golf carts they are taking over the town streets and even the north side of Ambergris. Most of the electric golf carts have been replaced by gas-powered ones, and hundreds ply San Pedro's rutted roads. Cobbled streets mean less dust and fewer potholes downtown.

The toll bridge connecting San Pedro Town with Ambergris's north side is free for pedestrians. From 6am to 10pm, bicycles pay US$1 to cross, and golf carts pay US$5 round-trip.

BOAT

Usually the smoothest and quickest way to travel up and down Ambergris Caye, water taxi service is available from **Coastal Xpress** (tel. 501/226-2007, www.coastalxpress.com). Boats share a dock with Amigos del Mar dive shop, in front of Cholo's Sports Bar, departing for points north and south 5:30am-10:30pm daily, with special late-night schedules on big party nights (Wed.-Sat.). Daily scheduled runs are posted online. The fare, usually US$5-14 each way or US$25 for a day pass, depends on how far you are going. The farthest resort at press time is Blue Reef. Most restaurants will radio the ferry to arrange your ride back to San Pedro Town. Coastal Express also offers private charters starting at a minimum of three people.

TAXI

Minivan taxis (with green license plates) run north and south along the island at most

The Golf Carts of San Pedro

It's the most common dilemma when planning a stay on Ambergris: Do I really need a golf cart to get around? It can take a chunk out of your travel budget, so decide beforehand whether to stay in San Pedro Town or not. Carts are most useful for those staying at one of the many resorts south of San Pedro, especially if you plan on coming into town often to shop, eat, and explore, day or night. The road to the north end of Ambergris is currently being paved, but can get bumpy still, and it requires a toll (US$5 per day) to cross the north bridge. To explore farther north, you either have to hike or take the Coastal Xpress water taxi. If you're staying right in San Pedro, everything is pretty walkable, although a golf cart could be fun for a day's exploration.

Golf carts are common on Ambergris Caye.

Ambergris's carts all used to be electric, but now most companies have gas-powered carts. It'll set you back as much as renting an automobile on the mainland, but if you're staying south of town and have multiple passengers (a family, for example), it's probably worth it. Expect to pay around US$75 for 24 hours and at least US$310 for a week. Drivers must be age 17 and have a valid driver's license. You will likely be required to leave a security deposit in the form of your credit card imprint or cash.

In the high season, reserve a cart in advance. Most companies will deliver to your hotel or pick you up at the airstrip. Your choices begin with **Carts Belize** (across from Tropic Air terminal, tel. 501/226-4090, www.cartsbelize.com) and **Taskae Golf Cart Rentals** (Coconut Dr., tel. 501/226-4490, www.monchosbze.com), both close to the airstrip with relatively large fleets. Toward the north end of town, **Cholo's** (Jewfish St., in town, tel. 501/226-2406, www.choloscartrentals.com) is reliable and has a small fleet of carts. Another option is **La Isla Bonita** (north of town, tel. 501/226-3446), an extension of Caye Mart Supermarket; it's a family-run business offering reasonable cart prices. Be sure to check these companies' websites and social media pages for specials throughout the year.

When driving your cart, carry your valid driver's license and follow all normal traffic laws, including one-way street rules. Note that Front Street closes to all but pedestrian traffic on Friday, Saturday, and Sunday evenings from 6pm. Make sure you park on the correct side of the street (it alternates every few weeks; just do what the locals are doing). Be sure to pay attention to the map you are given, don't speed or terrorize pedestrians into a corner, beware of unexpected bicycle riders, and watch for schoolchildren and one-way streets. Last but not least, always lock your cart.

hours; just wave one down and climb in. Expect to pay about US$4-7 to travel between town and points south. Within town, you'll pay around US$4. There are several drivers that you (or your lodging's front desk) can call as well, including **Island Taxi** (tel. 501/226-3125) and **Amber Isle Taxi** (tel. 501/226-2041). But I highly recommend **Manuelito Contreras** (tel. 501/627-0177), one of the best on the island—you can call anytime day or night, and he also knows all the doctors in case of emergency.

BICYCLE

Many resorts have bicycles that their guests can use for free, and others have them for rent, as do a handful of outside shops. Try the new wheels at **Beach Cruiser Bike**

Rentals (Pescador Dr., tel. 501/607-1710, solenyancona@gmail.com, 9am-7pm Mon.-Fri., 9am-9pm Sat., 10am-5pm Sun., US$11/24 hours, US$47.50 per week), where you can also grab ice cream and smoothies. Up north, **Lisa's Kayaking** (Mile 1 north of the bridge, between Ak'bol and Truck Stop, tel. 501/601-4449, www.lisaskayaking.com, US$8 per day, US$40 per week) also rents beach cruiser bikes.

TOURS

Most resorts have their own tour desk to help you choose and schedule excursions. In town, you'll find plenty of independent tour companies as well. **Belize Tropical Tours** (tel. 501/660-4558, 8am-5pm Mon.-Fri., 8am-noon Sat.) offers all the popular mainland adventures. **Signature Belize Weddings** (tel. 501/610-4457, www.signaturebelizeweddings.com) can help with all your nuptial planning needs.

Caye Caulker

TOP EXPERIENCE

About 1,300 Hicaqueños (hee-ka-KEN-yos; derived from the island's Spanish name, Cayo Hicaco) reside on this island 21 miles northeast of Belize City, just south of Ambergris Caye and a mile west of the reef. It's five miles long from north to south, but the developed and inhabited part is only a mile long, from The Split to the airstrip.

It's true that there have been changes in recent years, including the arrival of boutique luxury condominium resorts as the island realizes its unique spot in Belize's growing tourism economy. Yet the authenticity of life in a small Caribbean fishing village remains—original clapboard houses dot the coastline and side streets, and the only rumble you'll hear is from the sound of the few golf carts and bicycles crushing the sand-only roads or the daily street chatter among residents. There's a happy, familial coexistence on Caye Caulker among expats and locals, and all are determined to conserve the island's history and surroundings through community education and involvement. In the end, Caye Caulker is more affordable than Ambergris, and it's as laid-back as its "Go Slow" motto indicates, but no less entertaining.

ORIENTATION

The best landmark to start with is Caye Caulker's **"Split"**—also the most popular swimming and snorkeling spot. The Split cuts Caye Caulker into two areas: the southern inhabited part of the island, or "the Village," and the northern mangrove swamps.

Heading south from the Split, the main path lining the shore is **Front Street,** where you'll find seafront hotels, eateries, and the water taxi terminal. The other two main streets that shoot off parallel to Front Street are the simply named **Middle Street** and **Back Street.** Each leads to sandy roads with more accommodations, restaurants, and residents' homes. The entire island can be quickly explored in a couple of hours yet is big enough that it can take weeks to delve into each corner.

There's a fuel pump on the western pier. Sailors exploring nearby cayes can anchor in the shallow protected waters offshore; the water here is open sea but is still often referred to as a "lagoon."

Front Street's south end comes to a dead end by the **cemetery,** and you have a choice: Follow the narrow beach path along the water, or turn right and then left, where you'll find another sandy avenue that leads to the airstrip at the back of the island.

Bordering the airstrip is a rapidly developing neighborhood called Bahia Puesta del Sol, which has a small grocery store and a high school. The land opposite the airstrip, called **South Point,** consists of mangrove swamps, with a narrow path cleared for golf cart or bicycle passage, for a coastal ride through an area rich in nature—trees, birds,

Caye Caulker

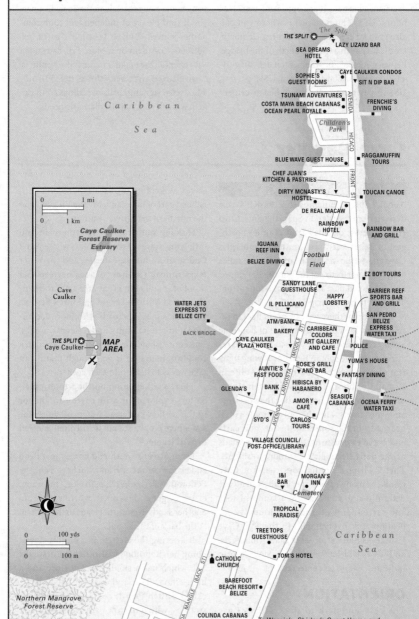

THE SPLIT

The Split

LAZY LIZARD BAR

SEA DREAMS HOTEL

SOPHIE'S GUEST ROOMS

CAYE CAULKER CONDOS

SIT N DIP BAR

TSUNAMI ADVENTURES
COSTA MAYA BEACH CABANAS
OCEAN PEARL ROYALE

FRENCHIE'S DIVING

Children's Park

AVENIDA HICACO

BLUE WAVE GUEST HOUSE

RAGGAMUFFIN TOURS

CHEF JUAN'S KITCHEN & PASTRIES

TOUCAN CANOE

DIRTY MCNASTY'S HOSTEL

DE REAL MACAW

RAINBOW HOTEL

(FRONT ST)

RAINBOW BAR AND GRILL

IGUANA REEF INN

Football Field

BELIZE DIVING

EZ BOY TOURS

SANDY LANE GUESTHOUSE

HAPPY LOBSTER

BARRIER REEF SPORTS BAR AND GRILL

IL PELLICANO

WATER JETS EXPRESS TO BELIZE CITY

SAN PEDRO BELIZE EXPRESS WATER TAXI

ATM/BANK

BAKERY

CARIBBEAN COLORS ART GALLERY AND CAFE

BACK BRIDGE

CAYE CAULKER PLAZA HOTEL

MIDDLE ST

POLICE

ROSE'S GRILL AND BAR

YUMA'S HOUSE

AUNTIE'S FAST FOOD

HIBISCA BY HABANERO

FANTASY DINING

BANK

GLENDA'S

AMOR Y CAFÉ

SEASIDE CABANAS

AVENIDA LANGOSTA

OCENA FERRY WATER TAXI

SYD'S

CARLOS TOURS

VILLAGE COUNCIL/ POST OFFICE/LIBRARY

I&I BAR

MORGAN'S INN

Cemetery

TROPICAL PARADISE

Caribbean Sea

TREE TOPS GUESTHOUSE

TOM'S HOTEL

AVENIDA MANGLE (BACK ST)

CATHOLIC CHURCH

BAREFOOT BEACH RESORT BELIZE

COLINDA CABANAS

To Weezie's, Shirley's Guest House and CCBTIA Mini-Reserve

Northern Mangrove Forest Reserve

To Airstrip

OASI

Caribbean Sea

---

0   1 mi

0   1 km

Caye Caulker Forest Reserve Estuary

Caye Caulker

THE SPLIT
Caye Caulker

MAP AREA

---

0   100 yds

0   100 m

© MOON.COM

and crocodiles—and lined with off-the-grid solar-powered homes and docks.

SIGHTS
★ The Split

Popular long before it appeared on the TV show *The Bachelor*, Caye Caulker's infamous "Split," or "cut," as it's still called by residents, is the favorite go-to swimming and sunset rendezvous spot on the island. It's no surprise, then, that so much interest centered on this plot of land when a change in management and renovation took place in 2015, with plans for an expanded beach, a rebuilt bar, and the addition of new kiosks for food and other services.

This "Split" corner of the island once resembled a perfect island movie set—not least for having the most decent stretch of sand, although it's narrow and flat. The story most people like to tell is that the Split came to be when Hurricane Hattie widened the channel in 1961 and "cut" the island in two, north and south. Boat captains and longtime residents will tell you that, in fact, the hurricane created only a tiny water passage that was later dug wider by anglers and politicians who wanted larger boats to pass. Eventually, daily sweeping tides made it as large as it is today. Either way, travelers and locals used to be found here at all hours of the day swimming, snorkeling, sunbathing on concrete slabs, sharing finger foods on picnic tables anchored in shallow water, or drowning in rum punch and music from the on-site bar.

Hurricane Earl hit the Split hard in August 2016. Though it was a Category 1 hurricane, the water surge was unexpected, and the Split narrowed considerably in size. It was fixed up quickly and reopened. A new, foreign-owned company took over the site and its Lazy Lizard Bar in 2014 and four years later, the Split is looking better than it ever has with new platforms for sunning, a nicely built seawall with steps to ease into the sea, and a relaxed atmosphere. Travelers still flock here for sun, rum, and a swim.

Caye Caulker Marine Reserve

The island's very own "local channel" off the reef is 0.5 mile from shore and just under 10 minutes by boat. Here, you can snorkel surrounded by dozens or more stingrays and nurse sharks in what's known as Caye Caulker's very own "shark ray alley," as well as explore beautiful coral gardens. The Caye Caulker Marine Reserve is often overlooked by those who head to Hol Chan, making for a less crowded experience, and visibility is just as excellent. Note that you must have a tour guide present, as these are protected waters. The tour can also be combined with other snorkel stops for a small additional fee. Let **EZ Boy Tours** (tel. 501/226-0349, www.ezboytoursbelize.com, US$35 pp) bring you here. Another option if it's booked up is **French Angel Expeditions** (tel. 501/226-0637, www.frenchangelexp.com, US$35 pp).

On the north end of this reserve is a channel that attracts manatees during their mating season (May-Sept.). Two or three manatees, sometimes more, can be spotted at the surface at any time. It's a spectacular sight; just remember to respect the reserve rules and not touch or swim with the marine animals. Any of the tour companies will bring you here.

Caye Caulker Forest Reserve Estuary

One of the best excursions from Caye Caulker takes you to the **estuary** (Front St., adjacent to Popeye's, tel. 501/633-8515, www.belizeestuary.com, US$35 pp), part of the North Forest Reserve just a 10-minute boat ride away. The hike lasts 1.5 hours and passes along untouched and protected landscape, where you'll spot birds, spiders, mangroves, and lagoons where a handful of crocodiles roam. A sturdy wooden bridge crosses red and black lagoons on a winding walk hugged by all sorts of mangroves and critters. You'll stop at various points to spot the crocodiles that roam here, who might come to greet you, including Scarface. The hike over part of these 50 acres also takes you past a variety of Belizean trees, and the occasional iguana

may appear. Look for the spot where crocodiles have been captured at night hatching their eggs during the June solstice and carrying them in their mouth to the lagoon. A wild and beautiful slice of Caye Caulker, it's a great educational day out for families and individuals.

★ Swallow Caye Wildlife Sanctuary

This protected area comprises nearly 9,000 acres of sea and mangrove at the north end of the Drowned Cayes, just a few miles east of Belize City. The sanctuary is comanaged by the **Belize Forest Department** and **Friends of Swallow Caye** (tel. 501/605-0280, www. swallowcayemanatees.org, outreachmanatee@ gmail.com). Check the website for more information, including membership, tours, and manatee facts. Trips are chartered and not daily, so you'll have to arrange in advance. A minimum of three to four persons is required (US$125-250).

Chocolate's Manatee Tours was the premier operator for Swallow Caye; unfortunately, Mr. Chocolate (a local legend on the island and in the ecotourism trade) died in April 2013. Mr. Chocolate was instrumental in the sanctuary's creation in July 2002. He earned environmental and tourism awards for providing quality trips to hundreds of tourists every season. Other guides are sure to uphold his legacy. Your best bet at the moment is the Manatee Watch Tour with **Caveman Snorkeling Tours** (Front St., near Split and Sponge Bob sign, tel. 501/604-0345, www.cavemansnorkelingtours.com, four persons minimum, including lunch and gear, US$90pp), combining a stop at Swallow Caye to spot manatees, followed by lunch on St. George's Caye and two snorkel stops at Caye Chapel Channel and local coral gardens.

From Belize City, this trip is combined with snorkeling on the barrier reef and looking for

Atlantic bottlenose dolphins. Park fees are US$5 per person.

South Point

Directly opposite the airstrip, away from town and tucked behind the abandoned Belize Odyssey Resort, is a narrow sandy path that leads to a little-visited side of the island. The trail winds through a maze of glorious landscape—mangroves, almond trees, coconut palms, and saltwater palmettos—with pockets of sea views on the left and off-the-grid solar- and wind-powered homes on the right. Keep straight on the path and follow its twists and turns until you reach a dead end, noting the last house on the right. After dousing yourself generously with mosquito repellent, hike through a small littoral forest to reach the last dock. There lies a breathtaking scene of open water, blue skies, and sailing birds at the southernmost reach of the island. This is South Point, the raw inhabited Caye Caulker, where electrical poles are nonexistent and selling seafront lots has yet to completely change the nature that fills this area.

Don't venture here in the rainy summer months without a golf cart— not least because the occasional crocodile could very well be crossing your path as you pass. The ground could also prove particularly muddy and treacherous during rains. Golf cart taxis can also bring you here; just ask around for a reliable driver.

SPORTS AND RECREATION

There's enough to do on this five-mile island with ideal calm waters and fewer crowds than San Pedro to keep you occupied for days if you so choose—pick from an exciting list of water activities above or below the sea, in addition to turf action such as biking, yoga, or indulging in healing spas.

Beaches

Beaches on most of Caye Caulker are of the thin, hard variety—don't expect to find a thick, soft, endless stretch of sand. Still, there's

1: Caye Caulker at sunset; 2: the Caye Caulker Marine Reserve

sand to feel under your toes, and the ratio of crowds versus beach space is favorable, such that finding your own sandy plot of the island is an easy feat. And if you can get past the first few inches of harmless seagrass and don't mind the lack of wave action due to the mile-distant barrier reef, you'll find the water is just as soothing and in the same jade color of Belize—all in all, a happy compromise.

The beachfront is a public area, and if you prefer to jump deeper into the sea to avoid the seagrass, docks are also a dime a dozen, unless marked "private." Just be mindful of boat activity and stay alert while snorkeling or swimming underwater.

The island is relatively small, so finding the beach merely requires going to the front or back areas of Caye Caulker. The best stretch for your towel are the docks or platforms of the Split area on the north end of the island. A newer option is to swim off the dock of **Sip N' Dip Beach Bar** (Front St., tel. 501/600-0080, 10am-6pm Tues.-Sun.). For those looking to read quietly, **Playa Asuncion** going along the front side of the caye from the arrival dock but going south (turning left) fits the bill. Along the back of the island are smaller stretches of beach, and swimming may be best off a dock, but the views are still lovely. Grab a frozen cocktail at Sea Dreams Hotel's upstairs Banyan Tree Bar or at Iguana Reef's new beach bar and sit by the water to watch the sunset.

Diving and Snorkeling

Like at Ambergris Caye, dive shops on Caye Caulker offer excursions to the most-visited dive and snorkeling sites along the Barrier Reef, including the Great Blue Hole and surrounding atolls. The most popular snorkel sites—prices vary only slightly—are Hol Chan Marine Reserve and Shark Ray Alley (from US$65-75), Caye Caulker Marine Reserve (half-day, from US$35-40), and Swallow Caye (US$90). A common snorkeling tour package combines Hol Chan with stops at Shark Ray Alley and the Coral Gardens, as well as San Pedro for lunch (not included).

The reef you see from Caulker's eastern shore provides fantastic snorkeling and diving opportunities right in your front yard. Snorkeling can be as simple and cheap as renting masks and fins for US$5 per day from one of the tour operators (or bringing your own) and using them off almost any dock. If renting, you may be required to leave your ID behind for the day as security. Note that several tour operators are hesitant to pass out equipment so as not to encourage snorkeling beyond the docks in the protected marine reserves without a guide.

You could check to see if you can snorkel off the island's most popular swimming spot: the Split—although the surrounding beach and land were under construction as of publication time. Avoid the heavily trafficked part and be aware that swimming here can be dangerous because of the pull of the current, which is strong enough to overpower children or weak swimmers. Your best bet is to go around the bend, only a few yards out of the Split, to avoid the dangerous boat traffic. Be mindful where you step or dive at the Split, as old construction materials have been dumped here for fill.

To snorkel the reef itself—just a mile away, leaving no excuse not to before your trip is over—it's necessary to sign up for a boat tour, and plenty are offered for beginner or advanced snorkelers and divers. Trips can go for half a day or a full day, depending on the excursion, and there are enough to fit all budget ranges. I recommend **EZ Boy Tours** (tel. 501/226-0349, www.ezboytoursbelize.com) for all the standard snorkel tours on its sailboat—whether at Hol Chan, Caye Caulker Marine Reserve, or Swallow Caye—as well as overnight camping trips to Placencia. Owner Hans and his guides know their home island and its surrounding waters like the back of their hands. EZ Boy's three-day sailing and camping trip (US$350) to Placencia stops along the Southern Coast of Belize, with overnights on St. George's Caye and Tobacco Caye, on its Belizean-built wooden sailboat *Inri*. You can also check the website ahead of time for departure dates; the trip requires a minimum of eight people.

Raggamuffin Tours (Front St., tel. 501/226-0348, www.raggamuffintours.com) is well known for its sailing trips on the *Ragga Gal*, *Ragga Prince*, *Ragga Queen*, or *Ragga King* boats. Raggamuffin regularly sails to Hol Chan (full-day trip US$50, includes lunch and rum punch on board), but its most popular journey is the overnight sail from Caye Caulker to Dangriga.

Belizean guide and dive master Shadrack Ash offers friendly, professional snorkeling, manatee-watching, fishing trips, and night dives through his company **French Angel Expeditions** (tel. 501/206-0637 or 501/670-7506, www.frenchangelexp.com), which gets rave reviews from past clients. Walk straight down the street from the water taxi on Calle del Sol.

Climb aboard the *Gypsy* with **Carlos Tours** (tel. 501/600-1654, carlosaya@gmail.com), which has an excellent reputation for personal attention and a focus on safety. Carlos is the only shop to offer a full-day snorkel tour to Hol Chan combined with a lunch stopover in San Pedro, where you get to eat and explore Ambergris Caye for 1.5 hours on your own (US$50 pp). Carlos loves underwater photography and will share and sell photo CDs immediately after a trip (US$15). His office is on Front Street next to Amor y Café.

Two local brothers run **Anwar Tours** (tel. 501/226-0327, www.anwartours.page.tl), and with 15 years of experience, they get positive reviews for both snorkel trips and inland tours, including **island tubing. Tsunami Adventures** (tel. 501/226-0462, www.tsunamiadventures.com) is near the Split and rents underwater cameras waterproof to 130 feet (US$10 per day), snorkeling gear (US$5 per day), and kayaks (US$47.50 for 2 days).

Belize Diving Services (Chapoose St., across from the soccer field, tel. 501/226-0143 or U.S. tel. 888/869-0233, www.belizedivingservices.com) has a solid reputation and an operation that is all computerized and offers both recreational and technical dives at the Miner's Gold and Treasure Hunt dive sites. It also offer weekly dives at the Great Blue Hole and the atolls thanks to a 46-foot custom Newton dive boat, equipped with showers and ideal for the long ride. Certification courses are available. **Frenchie's Diving Services** (tel. 501/226-0234, www.frenchiesdivingbelize.com) is a reliable dive shop with knowledgeable dive masters. It also offers half-day dive excursions to the nearby Caye Caulker Marine Reserve (US$90) and PADI courses.

LIGHTHOUSE REEF ATOLL, THE GREAT BLUE HOLE, AND TURNEFFE

Many visitors are willing to brave four hours (two hours each way) on a boat in mostly open sea to dive the Great Blue Hole, Lighthouse Reef Atoll, and Turneffe Atoll. There is no "number one" dive site, as every diver is looking for something different, but some are indeed renowned for their marine diversity; just be sure to discuss the options before booking the trip, and make sure you're comfortable with the boat, guides, group size, and gear. Consider whether gear is included in the price or not, and don't quickly jump on the cheapest package. Go with who feels right for you from one of the following.

The most recommended dive shops for excursions to the atolls are **Belize Diving Services** (Chapoose St., across from the soccer field, tel. 501/226-0143 or U.S. tel. 888/869-0233, www.belizedivingservices.com) and **Frenchie's Diving Services** (tel. 501/226-0234, www.frenchiesdivingbelize.com) with a 43-foot boat that has a small on-board changing room idea for long trips to the Great Blue Hole (US$310 three-tank dive, US$175 snorkel; includes park fees and lunch) and Turneffe (US$235). Frenchie's keeps a handy calendar on their website of set dive excursion dates; email them if you don't see one that fits. Most trips depart at 6am from the dive center's dock and you'll be asked to meet there at 5:30am prior to departure.

Snuba and Sea Trek

The new way of exploring Hol Chan is to snuba or sea trek with **Discovery Expeditions** (tel. 501/671-2881 or 501/671-2882, www.discoverybelize.com, US$68-74, includes hotel transfers but not the US$10 Hol Chan park fee) out of San Pedro. Catch the 8am water taxi over to San Pedro, where you will get picked up for your tour. The experience includes orientation before experiencing depths of 20-30 feet, enjoying marinelife and corals without needing a tank or worrying about being dive certified. Both activities are safe for anyone in good physical condition and older than age eight.

Boating and Sailing

Raggamuffin Tours (Front St., tel. 501/226-0348, www.raggamuffintours.com) offers sunset cruises and day sails. Its best-known adventure is the overnight sailing trip on the 50-foot Stonington Ketch *Ragga Queen* sailboat or on the *Ragga Empress* catamaran south to Dangriga (Tues. and Fri. departures), including an overnight on Ragga Caye and a final third-day drop-off in Dangriga to continue your travels; it's three days of sun and sea and two nights camping out on idyllic cayes. The trip costs US$400 per person, including all gear, delicious food prepared by the crew, including fresh catch, snorkeling, and fishing; expect a higher holiday rate during the last week of December. Check how many passengers are signed up on your trip if you prefer smaller crowds.

EZ Boy Tours (tel. 501/226-0349, www.ezboytoursbelize.com) has a sunset sail that is the most relaxing and longest-lasting I have been on: three hours (5pm-8pm) drifting all along the coast of Caye Caulker, with bottomless rum punch and Captain Ian's freshly made shrimp ceviche. Day sails to Hol Chan are popular, too. The local tour operator now runs a similar three-day sailing and camping trip to Placencia, with stops along the Southern Coast of Belize and overnight stops on St. George's Caye and Tobacco Caye, on its Belizean-built wooden sailboat *Inri*. You can check the website ahead of time for departure dates; the trip requires a minimum of eight people.

Fishing

Try to catch your dinner off one of the island's many piers. You can buy bait and rent fishing rods at the Badillos' house near the soccer field (look for a small porch sign). Or fish like a local with a hook, line, and weight. You can also take a walk toward the back of the island, where you'll find fishers cleaning their fish, working on lobster traps, or mending their nets in the morning. Many will be willing to take you out for a reasonable fee. The main trophies are grouper, barracuda, and snapper—all good eating. Small boats are available for rent by the hour.

For professional fishing tours, go to **Anglers Abroad** (tel. 501/226-0602, www.anglersabroad.com, half-day US$220, full-day US$330, includes lunch) near the Split. Owner and licensed guide Haywood Curry sells and rents a complete selection of fly and spin gear (US$20-30 per day), and he is happy to give advice to the novice or expert fisher. He offers lessons (US$100 for 4 hours) and DIY instruction by canoe or on foot and sets up half-day, full-day, and overnight adventure trips. Group tours, as well as private lessons, are available. The shop occasionally works with well-known, award-winning, and experienced reefs and flats fishing guides, including Parnel and Kenan Coc, the 2011, 2012, and 2014 Top Guide title winners in the prestigious annual Tres Pescados Slam Tournament. Anglers Abroad now also teaches a fly-fishing high school class at Ocean Academy.

Local fishing guide Esley Usher of **Esley Usher Fishing Tours** (tel. 501/624-6555, esleyusherfishingtours@live.com, half-day US$200, full-day US$300, includes lunch) is a safe bet for deep-sea and reef fishing.

Shadrack Ash, owner of **French Angel Expeditions** (tel. 501/226-0637, www.frenchangelexp.com, half- or full-day US$200-350), can take you catch-and-release fly-fishing, spin casting with an option to grill your catch for you, and lobster fishing (June 15-Feb. 15).

Kayaking

Toucan Canoe and Kayaks (Front St., across from De Real Macaw, tel. 501/663-8432, toucancanoe@yahoo.com) has the most comprehensive canoe and kayak tours and rentals on the island. Private and group lessons are offered by Canadian Belizean owner Allie Johnstone, who is a top-placing international canoe racer and licensed tour guide and naturalist. Her most popular excursion is the **Paddle the Mangrove Tour** (US$40 pp), which takes you on an informative kayak trip with Allie around the coast of Caye Caulker—25 percent of your tour fee also goes to the island's local high school. Ask about beach stargazing options and an herbal walk to learn about the various medicinal plants and other flora on the island.

Kayak for a Purpose with **SEaTIDe** (Hattie St., next to Sea Dreams Hotel, tel. 501/226-0321, www.oaseatide.com), the local high school's Center for Social Enterprise, Technology, Innovation and Development, to explore the island's wildlife and ecosystem with a group of trained student guides from the local high school. Along the way you'll discover places you wouldn't find on your own—where to spot seahorses, manatees, or even the entrance to an underwater cave. This innovative method of pairing visitors with the island's youth who have spent their whole lives playing in their marine backyard leads to a dynamic way of learning about the destination. What's more, the funds from your tour support the award-winning high school's numerous educational programs. You can also rent double kayaks from SEaTIDe (US$10 per hour) and explore on your own; that's another great way to give back.

Tsunami Adventures (tel. 501/226-0462, www.tsunamiadventures.com) also offers kayak and canoe rentals (US$7.50 per hour).

Wind Sports

Nondivers can rest assured: Caye Caulker is on the cutting edge of water sports, including the latest trend of stand-up paddleboarding, in part thanks to great bump-and-jump conditions—shallow crystal-clear waters protected by a nearby reef and the Caribbean trade winds.

For fun in the water and the wind, find **KiteXplorer** (Front St., toward the Split, tel. 501/635-4967, www.kitexplorer.com, 9am-6pm daily), offering beginner to advanced kite

sea kayaks for rent

KAYAK RENTALS

surfing, stand-up paddle surfing, and wind-surfing lessons (introduction to kite surfing US$180 for 2 hours) with three licensed instructors, or equipment rentals (stand-up paddleboard US$12 pp per hour, windsurfing board US$22 per hour). Note that these sports are seasonal and best from October through March. **Reef Watersports** (Ave. Hicaco/Front St., just before the Split, tel. 501/635-7219, www.reefwatersports.com) offers Jet Ski rentals (US$75 for 30 minutes) as well as wakeboarding and fly boarding (US$180 per hour for 2 people).

The best place to practice paddleboarding solo on the island is on the "lee side" of the island, as Hicaqueños call it—the calm, flat side starting behind the Split. Passionate water sports owners, trained dive masters, and surf enthusiasts run **Contour Ocean Ventures** (Front St., Playa Asuncion, tel. 501/615-8757, info@countourbelize.com, 9am-noon and 1pm-6pm daily) where you can find paddleboards for rent (US$15 per hour, US$60 per day, includes 15-minute lesson, full damage insurance optional) and innovative mangrove paddleboarding tours (US$90). They also offer surfing trips (US$49 half-day on surfboard, includes insurance) for those who have some experience, with surfing at a reef break just 2.5 miles off Caye Caulker. Other fun excursions include windsurfing (lessons are limited to 3 students per class, 3-day package US$300 or US$55 per hour).Windsurfing rentals are also available (US$70 for 2 hours).

Tubing

A popular activity as of late, tubing is a fun way to cool off, have a drink—yes, **Anda De Wata Tours** (Front St., across from Happy Lobster, tel. 501/666-7374, www.snorkeladw.com, US$35 pp) has a beer delivery system from the boat to your inner tube while you are towed along—and take in Caye Caulker's magnificent coast, birds, and even tarpons along the way. Up to seven tubes can enjoy the ride together.

Bicycling

An ideal way to explore the island and get a workout is by renting a bicycle and finding its nooks and crannies at your leisure. Most locals here are on bikes, even with their little ones in tow. The better spots to rent are **SEaTIDe** (Hattie St., next to Sea Dreams Hotel, tel. 501/226-0321, www.oaseatide.com, US$2.50 per hour, US$7.50 per day)—the local high school's social enterprise tour shop—where 100 percent of your rental fees go to support its students. The organization received a fleet of 40 bikes from the Planeterra Foundation as part of a grant.

Better yet, sign up for a **Bike for a Purpose Tour** (US$25 pp) to explore the island with a pair of seniors who will share tales from their childhood as they show you around Caye Caulker all the way to the back of the island and through the nature reserve. Along the way you'll also stop at the high school for a quick visit.

M&N Mel's Bike Rentals (Chapoose St., off Front St., tel. 501/226-0229, US$2 per hour, US$7 per day, US$25 per week) and the Friendship Convenience Store on Front Street rent bicycles. Many hotels also throw in complimentary bicycle use, so be sure to check beforehand.

Birding

More than 190 species of resident and migratory birds have been identified on Caye Caulker, some of which are rarely seen elsewhere. The white-crowned pigeon, rufous-necked wood-rail, and black catbird are commonly seen here. The northernmost part of the island, part of a protected forest and marine reserve system since 1998, is ideal for birding and made up of miles of reef, grass flats, lagoons, and mangroves. Guided ecotours can be arranged through the **BTIA Resource Center** (cayecaulkerbtia@gmail.com). Caye Caulker's South Point has plenty of birdlife; rent a golf cart and explore at your leisure.

Massage and Bodywork

You'll feel rejuvenated, make friends, and maybe pick up a Kriol phrase or two at the newly expanded, two-story **Purple Passion Beauty Studio** (Calle del Sol, tel. 501/633-4525, cell tel. 501/660-0046, www.purplepassionbeautystudio.com, 9am-noon and 1pm-6pm Mon.-Sat.), just a few steps from Rose's Grill. Inside the purple-colored cabin, talented Belizean sisters Stacy and Gina Badillo, with more than a decade in the industry, run a tight beauty ship, offering full salon and spa services, including body scrubs, facials, waxing, and hot-stone or other types of massages in one of two cozy treatment rooms upstairs, There's a couples massage room as well. The spa has a contemporary-chic feel, and it's a welcome respite from the outside rush of bicycles and pedestrians. Don't miss Gina's magical hands (US$60 per hour, hot stone US$75 per hour) or skillful nail art (get a Belizean flag on those tips) and Stacy's hair-coloring and makeup talent. This hardworking duo also gets hired for weddings on the island and around Belize.

Eva McFarlane's fragrant **Healing Touch Day Spa** (tel. 501/206-0380, www.healingtouchbelize.com) on Front Street is a second option, offering options from deep tissue and Swedish massage to Reiki, reflexology, aura cleansing, waxing, manicures, and facials, albeit at a higher price. All treatments are US$60 for an hour, US$85 for 90 minutes.

Namaste Café (tel. 501/637-4109, www.randomyoga.com) hosts donation-based outdoor yoga classes—you decide what to pay—Monday through Saturday at 9am on the café's beautiful rooftop terrace (across from Enjoy Hotel). No need to preregister, just show up.

ENTERTAINMENT AND EVENTS

For a small island, Caye Caulker offers just enough "liming" (socializing over food and drink) options, from watering holes to late-night dancing.

Nightlife

For drinks while watching the sunset, head to the lively **Lazy Lizard Bar** (Front St., tel. 501/226-0636, www.lazylizardbarandgrill.com, 10am-10pm daily) at the Split, and opt for a Caye Caulker iced tea (laced with liquor), margarita, or frozen concoction. Lazy Lizard also serves bar munchies, including chicken fingers, nachos, and burgers. Their full moon parties are quite popular, with fire and dance shows on the beach, as well as DJ club nights. The top deck has been transformed into a beach chic, relaxed lounge and tapas bar called **El Portal,** with cozy couch seating areas, ample dance floor space, top-shelf liquor, wine and cocktails, as well as bar foods. Wednesdays are for Latin and Ladies Night, and there are occasional live music performances.

Over time the **Barrier Reef Sports Bar and Grill** (Front St., tel. 501/226-0077, until midnight), directly on the beach and a few steps from the water taxi docks, has turned into the happy hour and party spot where locals and tourists gather for loud music and beers before moving on to the next spot. The Friday guitar jam (3pm-7pm) attracts a lively crowd of visitors and residents; feel free to get up there and sing your heart out or dance. Saturday nights are popular as well. Service can be slow at the busy bar, so go early. Tuesday nights are for free movies and popcorn, with matinees and evening screenings.

A free boat ride can take you north of the Split to **Koko King** (tel. 501/661-5656), the latest local favorite for cocktails and bites—happy hour is 4pm-6pm—and late-night DJ parties on the beach, particularly on full moon nights. The boat shuttle departs from the main back dock, right past Caye Caulker Plaza Hotel and Bowen & Bowen.

Do not dare leave the island without a drink and a glimpse of the three-story **I&I Reggae Bar** (Traveler's Palm St., 4pm-1am daily), one of the best in the Caribbean with its eye-catching interior decor of all things Rastafarian, swing bar chairs, and late-night ambience of reggae and dance beats. For more of a lounge vibe, head upstairs and people-watch on the deck. A small but nicely lit VIP room with its own bar adds a special touch, although the real party is still in the main room, where tipsy sun-kissed travelers and locals on the prowl converge on a disco-lit floor until closing.

Looking to extend sunset romance or just for something to do on a weekday night? Pick a futon and lay back while sipping on a fancy cocktail—mojitos to martinis—or snacking on delicious bar bites, including tacos and sushi, from the neon-lit **Bondi Bar** (Front St., tel. 501/226-0610, 1pm-midnight, Mon.-Sat.).

Sunday nights are for live music and fancy, pricey cocktails at the small **Il Barretto Wine Bar** (OASI Apartments, tel. 501/226-0384, www.oasi-holidaysbelize.com, 5pm-10pm Sat.-Sun., no cover)—relax to the sounds with a cacao martini, with cacao nibs on the rim, or go for the pitaya margarita.

Festivals and Events

With a claim to being the original host and creator of **Lobsterfest** in 1995—which is now held here annually in late June, as well as in neighboring San Pedro, and in the southern beach town of Placencia—Caye Caulker's lobster season launch celebration grows bigger and more original every year, attracting visitors from across Belize and earning its committee the 2018 Belize Tourism Board National Award for festival of the year. The three-day weekend event is filled with Belizean-style recreation, including a Miss Lobsterfest beauty pageant, dozens of food booths to sample the crustacean in all its forms—grilled, stewed, or in ceviche—and beach parties with live music, games, and a paint party. The fun continues on the Split for a big late outdoor party.

SHOPPING

All shops on the island are open daily. You'll find **Laca Laca Toucan,** the largest souvenir and beachwear store, and a sprinkling of small gift shops on and around Front Street selling T-shirts, hot sauce, hammocks, art,

sarongs, beach apparel, postcards, photo albums, and other Belizean souvenirs. Caye Caulker's sandy streets have several skilled artisanal vendors. On Front Street is a collection of numbered stalls called **Palapa Gardens.** Here you can find hand-carved ziricote and rosewood, hand-painted T-shirts, Guatemalan textiles and handicrafts, beautiful model sailboats complete with rigging, jewelry, and music CDs.

Jewelry is a popular craft on the island, often sold from tables set up in the street. **Calvin** sells his cool handmade island necklaces, anklets, and earrings at his table set up between Habaneros and Rose's Grill; he started 30 years ago, well before souvenir stores opened on the island. **Celi's Music** (Front St.) is where Mr. August can be found at a small table beside the shop, cutting and polishing conch shell pieces. There's a good selection of popular Belizean music and videos.

Who doesn't love sweet-smelling bath products? Don't miss Lisa Novelo's handcrafted, fragrant, and colorful soaps—so pretty they look like candy—including face and body lotions and scrubs. If there were a Belizean equivalent to Bath and Body Works, this would be it. **Lisa's Soap Delights and Body Products**—try the soap made with a dash of Belikin beer or the patchouli body lotion—are displayed and sold at **Village Treasures Boutique** (Front St., tel. 501/629-7508, lisanovelo@hotmail.com, 9am-5pm Mon.-Sat., closed at lunch) and make for great gifts or treats. The small boutique—quite possibly the best-smelling place on the island—also sells tasteful imported clothing, from bikinis to shorts and cocktail dresses. You can also find **reef-friendly mineral sunscreen** here, Lisa's latest creation (US$15).

At the Split, **Aria Kat Art** (Front St., tel. 501/226-0420, www.debbiecooper.artspan.com, 11am-5pm Mon.-Tues., 10am-8pm Wed.-Sun., US$10-220) sells colorful Caribbean art and posters, many in funky frames, big and small, hand-painted by Belizean artists, as well as hand-painted canvas totes; they make great gifts. The **Go Slow Art Gallery,** in Palapa Gardens stalls 6 and 7, encourages the Belizean art community and sells paintings of different styles, including acrylic on canvas, realism, and primitive works. Seek out pieces by well-known local artists Nelson Young and Marcos Manzanero. Also look out for **Jacob & Stevens,** a modest art and jewelry stall just before Palapa Gardens, with longtime island resident Jacob Cabral's colorful and unusual fish-motif paintings.

FOOD
Belizean

Hicaqueños love their breakfast snacks, baked goods, street food, and mobile vendors—who wouldn't want grab-and-go pieces of home-cooked goodness at super-cheap prices?

It all begins on Back Street—if you're early enough, you might luck out with sampling the morning delights at ★ **Glenda's** (tel. 501/226-0148, 7am-10am and 11:30am-1pm Mon.-Sat.), set up inside a home and offering inexpensive, delicious Belizean breakfast and lunch options. Getting up early for homemade cinnamon rolls and a large glass of fresh-squeezed orange juice (all for US$2) is well worth it; unfortunately Glenda's does run out quickly, so be sure to ask before taking a seat. For lunch, try the *garnaches* (crispy tortillas under a small mound of tomato, cabbage, cheese, and hot sauce) or burritos.

No breakfast in Belize is complete without sampling fry jacks—delicious fried dough that resembles a flat beignet, best accompanied by jam or as a side to your beans and eggs. Several eateries serve them, but the best I've tried are at **Tropical Paradise** (Front St., tel. 501/226-0124, 6:30am-9:30pm daily except Tues.) and ★ **Happy Lobster** (Front St., tel. 501/226-0064, 6am-9:30pm Wed.-Mon.), which has a solid breakfast menu. Along with local fare like fry jacks are more mainstream options such as pancakes and waffles, and there's morning coffee for US$1.50. It has outdoor seating and free Wi-Fi as long as you're eating. Happy Lobster also serves lunch (local dishes, surprisingly tasty pastas, and hot sandwiches)

and dinner. Prices are reasonable, and it's one of the few eateries open on Sunday.

Those in search of a cheap lunch snack should listen for (and will hear) the calls of the gregarious **Dukunu Man** (Mark Fitzgibbon) as he starts his rounds from the beachfront water taxi arrival dock area at 8:30am and continues along Back, Middle, and Front Streets all the way to the Split until he sells out of his US$0.50 delicious vegetarian or US$1.25 chicken-filled hot *dukunu*—a Creole version of a small tamale, made of corn and wrapped in a banana leaf. He occasionally sells tamales. At the very least, you should meet him!

★ **Auntie's Fast Food** (Calle del Sol, tel. 501/226-0478, 7am-9pm Fri.-Wed., 7am-3pm Thurs., US$3.50-6) is a local haunt and comes to the rescue when you crave a quick, plentiful takeout lunch midafternoon to assuage post-snorkeling hunger pains. The window-service establishment dishes out everything from chicken fingers to stew chicken and daily local Central American specialties, such as *escabeche* (onion soup), conch soup, or barracuda, along with rice and beans or slaw. Cheap options like the chicken burger, just US$2.50, attract plenty of backpackers. It's doing so well that Auntie rebuilt a new facility with bigger windows and more picnic tables to dine outdoors. Service can be erratic—don't be surprised if the wait is long at mealtimes or if you're skipped over for another patron.

Another breakfast or dinner highlight is at ★ **Chef Juan's Kitchen & Pastries** (Crocodile St., next to Bella's Backpackers, 7:30am-8:30pm daily except Fri., US$4-8), a humble roadside, picnic-table spot where Chef Juan Ical serves flavorful breakfasts—veggie wraps, Belizean breakfasts, and more—as well as fish curries, pulled pork sandwiches, chili bowls, and lobster (in season). His key lime merengue pie is delicious.

Sip N' Dip Beach Bar (Front St., tel. 501/600-0080, 10am-6pm Tues.-Sun., US$5-8) has daily lunch options ranging from ceviche to quesadillas and rice and beans—pick up from its window across the actual bar or have it served seaside.

A hole-in-the-wall that you might mistakenly ignore, tucked in a corner across from Auntie's, **Panda** (Calle del Sol, no phone, 11am-midnight daily, from US$4) serves up some of the tastiest Chinese food you'll find on the island, if not Belize. It's also very affordable. I've had many a tasty wonton and chicken soup here to treat my colds. Other favorites include the kung pao chicken and the lo mein dishes. If you come at night, you'll find a host of rowdy local men boozing the night away—drinks are cheap—so come earlier.

A little farther south off Back Street and up two flights of steep stairs is **Little Kitchen** (tel. 501/667-2178, 4pm-10pm daily, US$5-10), where you can get *salbutes* (a kind of hot, soggy taco dripping in oil), *garnaches* (crispy tortillas under a small mound of tomato, cabbage, cheese, and hot sauce), and *panades* (little meat pies, 3 for US$1), burritos, and home-cooked seafood dishes, all for very cheap. Seating is casual at outdoor picnic tables, with reggae music and a nice breeze. The area is a bit sketchy, so get a round-trip taxi ride.

International

Two blocks south of the dock, longtimer **Amor y Café** (6am-noon daily, US$4-6) is a laid-back spot for a morning coffee (no refills) and breakfast, with seating choice between an upper deck or street-level sandy-floored patio for early-bird people-watching. Omelets, waffles, grilled sandwiches, and other options are served in regular portions. It's a tad pricey for the island, but the yogurt-granola is welcome when you tire of starch and eggs.

Caribbean Colors Art Gallery and Café (Front St., tel. 501/605-7205, www.caribbeancolors.com, 6:30am-9pm Fri.-Wed., US$6-10), serves gourmet coffee as well as breakfast burritos, omelets, and brownies on its outdoor patio. The homemade lunch specials vary daily, and include lobster salad, Mexican tortilla soup, and fresh sushi rolls, among other delectable choices. Make sure to take a look at Ms. Lee's gorgeous local paintings for sale both inside and outdoors.

The Brooklyn-type, colorful **Namaste Café** (7:30am-4:30pm, from US$4), serves Belizean brews and French press coffee daily as well as teas, smoothies, salads, and sandwiches. Take a seat on the sandy ground floor or upper deck for views and a breeze. Breakfasts are about croissant French toasts, egg casseroles, or bagels.

Toward the Split, **Paradiso Café** (Front St., tel. 501/226-0511, 6:30am-6pm daily, US$10-22) is popular with those leaving on an early excursion—serving breakfasts, lunch sandwiches, salads, smoothies, and wine. The narrow outdoor veranda directly faces the sea, and there's plenty more casual indoor seating.

For lunch or dinner, Belizean-owned ★ **Rainbow Bar and Grill** (off Front St., tel. 501/226-0281, 10:30am-9pm Tues.-Sun., US$10-25) offers diners a lovely seaside ambience and view—the covered outdoor deck stretches over the water—and solid local seafood options as well as delicious sandwiches (try the club; it's huge). Day-trippers to the island often pick this restaurant for its ideal location a short walk from both the water taxi and the Split.

Fantasy Dining (Front St., tel. 501/607-2172, 8am-10pm daily, US$5-20) invites you to "wine and dine on island time" and is a great choice for reasonably priced and solid local and international fare, including American, Mexican, Italian, and seafood. The space is inviting, with outdoor seating on sand under *palapas* or indoors under mood lighting. Breakfasts and dinners are popular; try the veggie lasagna, burgers, or shrimp ceviche. The turkey meal I had here for Thanksgiving was a standout. The only catch is you'll likely have a long wait.

The beachfront **Barrier Reef Sports Bar and Grill** (Front St., tel. 501/226-0077, 9am-midnight daily, US$12-25) serves breakfast, lunch, dinner, and bar food. With options such as steaks, seafood, and pasta entrées and

1: Glenda's; **2:** the over-the-water Sip N' Dip Beach Bar

satellite television screens showing sports, it's an easy choice for those picky eaters seeking a taste of home.

Crêpes and Dreams (Front St., tel. 501/670-4870, 7am-1pm Thurs.-Mon., US$5-13) is the first *crêperie* on the island, dishing out authentic, fresh salty and sweet crepes—think banana and Nutella. Over time, it has expanded its menu to offer omelets, eggs Benedict, and waffles.

The tiny outdoor dining terrace at **Pasta Per Caso** (Front St., tel. 501/602-6670, armuzuma@ymail.com, from 6pm Mon.-Fri., from US$11) beckons with lanterns and soft music, despite its basic picnic-table seating. Run by an expat Italian couple from Verona, the menu invites you to taste "homemade pasta"—although it's not as tasty as I anticipated.

Fine Dining

Il Pellicano (49 Pasero St., tel. 501/226-0660, 5:30pm-9:30pm Tues.-Sun., US$15-35) is a delightfully decorated Italian fine dining restaurant tucked in a residential area, away from any street noise and surrounded with gardens for an alfresco experience. The Italian owners provide as authentic an Italian menu as you'll find in Belize—homemade gnocchi, spaghetti with meatballs, *porchetta,* and stuffed ravioli are among some of the tastiest options. Whether the prices are justified is debatable.

★ **Hibisca by Habanero** (Front St., tel. 501/626-4911, 5:30pm-10:30pm daily except Thurs., US$6-25) is the priciest restaurant and lounge by the island's standards, but its Central American cuisine is a notch above the others, with unique and absolutely delicious seafood options—from the seafood curry to coconut-encrusted snapper—and several other vegetarian and meat specialties. The raised porch is ideal for enjoying the lavishly presented meals and live music, and the indoor bar is tiny but has chic ambience. Make sure to try the frozen mojito, and the Creole voodoo cakes are to die for (watch out for the habanero pepper sauce). Reservations are strongly recommended; this popular restaurant only seats 36 and fills up as early as 7pm.

Next door, **Bondi Bar & Bistro** (Front St., tel. 501/226-0610, 1pm-midnight Mon.-Sat., US$9-16) serves up tasty tapas in a trendy, neon-lit alfresco lounge with platform futons, swank chairs, and electronic music. The food and drinks are some of the priciest you'll find on the island, but if you're up for a smaller crowd, fancy cocktails, and gourmet snacks (the Mediterranean platter and the miniburgers are good, or try the sushi), this is a decent pick.

Dessert

Got a sweet tooth or craving dessert? Several locals are skilled bakers. Look out for a sweet evening aroma as bicycle carts filled with delicious cakes and pies, homemade daily, roll through the sandy streets; try **Estella's** coconut pie or banana bread, if you're lucky enough to spot her.

Groceries

Chan's Mini Mart (Middle St., across from Caye Caulker Plaza Hotel, tel. 501/226-0165, 7am-9pm daily) is pretty much the heart of "downtown" Caulker—check the bulletin board for ads and events or go inside for a full-size supermarket minus the deli counter. **Chinatown Grocery** (Av. Langosta and Estrella St., tel. 501/226-0338, 7am-11pm daily) also has a good selection. If you're looking for basics, please first stop by **El Hicaqueño** (Av. Langosta, 9am-4pm Mon.-Fri.), the only other Belizean-owned grocery store left on Caye Caulker, aside from Chan's.

There are a few great fruit, vegetable, and juice stalls around town; look near the bakery and Atlantic Bank. A favorite is **Julia's Juice** (Front St., US$2.50), where she sells watermelon, orange, lime, soursop, and mixed-fruit juice in recycled plastic bottles—you can mix and match your juices. Another reliable stand is the newer **Seachoice Island Produce** (Pasero St., opposite Atlantic Bank, 6:30am-5pm Mon.-Thurs., 8am-noon Sun.). For fresh fish or lobsters, go to the **Lobstermen's**

Co-op Dock (Calle del Sol) on the back of the island; ask what time the fishing boats come in with their catch.

ACCOMMODATIONS

Prices given are for high-season double occupancy, but you can often get discounts year-round, especially if you're staying for five or more days. Be sure to check directly with the hotel or take note of social media pages for the latest specials. Reservations are recommended during the high season (late Dec.-Apr.), as rooms tend to fill quickly, particularly during national holidays such as Easter. The rest of the year, rooms are easy to find on the spot, and choices will be plentiful (except in October, when a few properties close for renovation).

Staying at a seafront property or by the hustle and bustle of Front Street and the Split is always lovely, but since everything is a short walk away, staying off the main drag and in the center or back of town won't hurt your vacation—particularly with the sandy streets all around. Be warned that you'll be spoiled for choice of affordable, cozy places to stay. Plenty of delightful hotels, condos, and B&B options with great sea views or relaxing gardens are spread around the island.

When arriving off the boat or plane, ignore any pushy taxi drivers or local "guides" who attempt to help with your bags and pressure you into staying at specific properties; often these individuals obtain commissions, or worse, you may end up at a hotel with low security, hence the aggressive tactics. Smile and head to your first choice of accommodations, or ask around for advice on the way to the island. Both airline and water taxi terminals often carry pamphlets and maps for visitors. My best advice, if you're completely unsure and traveling solo, is to head to Caye Caulker Plaza Hotel (Calle del Sol, across from Chan's), a short walk from the arrival dock and a place with 24-hour friendly front-desk staff.

Under US$25

There are many budget guest rooms along Front Street, or even Middle Street, that are easy to find.

Yuma's House (tel. 501/206-0019, yumahousebelize@gmail.com) is a small waterfront hostel to the right as you walk off the town arrival dock. It offers dorm-style rooms (US$13) plus a few private rooms (US$29-30) with shared baths and a kitchen. There's a dock peppered with hammocks, or you can chill in the garden while looking out at the sea. Just beware of the owner's strict rules: nonguests are not allowed past the front gate, not even if your fellow traveler friend is dying to use the restroom (ask me about that if you meet me), and no outside chatter is permitted after nightfall. A more laid-back, if more "party hostel" is **Bella's Backpackers** (Crocodile St., next to Chef Juan's, tel. 501/824-2248, www.bellasinbelize.com/bella-s-caye-caulker.html) with a range of six-person dorm rooms (US$12.50-17.50), with or without air-conditioning, and private cabins or rooms (US$32.50-45). Bella's has a sister hostel in San Ignacio.

In the heart of the village, across from the soccer field, are two great options for reasonable rooms and cabanas. Set in a private fenced yard is ★ **Sandy Lane Guesthouse and Cabanas** (corner of Chapoose St. and Av. Langosta, tel. 501/226-0117, www.belizeexplorer.com), offering hostel-type accommodations, with nine guest rooms (US$12.50 with shared outdoor bath, US$17 with private bath) and four basic cabanas with kitchenettes, TVs, and hard beds (US$30). There is a communal outdoor cooking area as well. Up the lane, closer to Front Street, is **M & N Hotel and Apartments** (Chapoose St., tel. 501/226-0229, www.aguallos.com/mandnhotel, US$15-30), which has eight basic and clean guest rooms with shared baths.

US$25-50

★ **Sophie's Guest Rooms** (Almond St., behind Sea Dreams Hotel, tel. 501/661-2715, besophiesguest@gmail.com, US$34.50) has grown hugely popular with budget travelers, and it makes sense—it has a dream location near the Split yet with enough distance to have its own sunset views. There are basic rooms—double beds, a standing fan, and a small mirror with sink—that are ideally located: under the shade of coconut trees and facing the sea. There's a dock for easy swimming, and the laid-back quiet island vibe on that street is hard to beat. But if you want more noise, it's also just a one-minute walk over to the Split and Lazy Lizard Bar. Baths are shared, with each room having a key to a shower with hot and cold water and a toilet cabin steps from the rooms. There's no air conditioning, but with the water this close, you won't need it much at night. Ask for Room 5 for a bonus microwave and fridge.

For a dose of "old Caye Caulker," check in to one of the rustic beachfront cabins at **Morgan's Inn** (tucked away in a cluster of palms near the old cemetery, tel. 501/226-0178, morgansinn@gmail.com, US$28-45); cabins are spacious and rustic. Kayaks and windsurfing are available.

Set in a private villa, **Ocean Pearl Royale** (tel. 501/226-0074, oceanpearl@btl.net, US$27.50-45) is on a side street before the Split. There are 10 guest rooms with a choice of fan or air-conditioning, single or double beds, and wireless Internet around a large communal living area and kitchen with a fridge, a microwave, and a coffeemaker. In the pretty garden is a delightful studio-size cabana with a full kitchen and a porch, for rent by the week (US$250) or month (US$500), without air-conditioning.

★ **Blue Wave Guest House** (Front. St., tel. 501/669-0114 or 501/206-0114, US$22-71) has clean, basic guest rooms with shared baths, TVs, an outdoor communal kitchen, wireless Internet, and a private dock. There are also private guest rooms (US$71), one of which is seafront, cozy, and clean, with a flat-screen TV; it's ideal for one or for a couple. It's a great deal for the location, just a few steps from the Split. There are also options for guest rooms with private baths.

US$50-100

De Real Macaw (Front St., tel. 501/226-0459, www.derealmacawbelize.com, US$30-70) is a small and rustic, pet-friendly, thatched-roof property whose 10 units have private baths, minikitchens, TVs, wireless Internet, and spacious private verandas with hammocks. A condo-apartment and a two-bedroom beach house (both US$150) are also available, and for the solo traveler seeking only a safe place to stay, the "little budget room" ($25) has a single bed, a private bath, and ceiling and floor fans.

Closer to the Split, off a side street, is **Sea N Sun Guesthouse** (Lind's Coral St., left on road across from Raggamuffin Tours, tel. 501/206-0610, www.seaandsunguesthouse.com), owned by a longtime Caye Caulker family. Seven colorfully painted cabana rooms hug a leafy courtyard. Rooms have a shared bathroom option ($35) or are more spacious with private bath and air-conditioning starting at $75. There's a communal kitchen, free kayaks, snorkel gear, and bikes for use.

When **Caulker Plaza Hotel** (Calle del Sol/Middle St., tel. 501/226-0780, www.cayecaulkerplazahotel.com, US$90-110) first came along with 32 guest rooms, traveling groups had finally found an option to stay under one roof, as the smaller hotels on the island lacked capacity. It remains a decent pick, located just a five-minute walk to the sea and with street-view balconies. Rooms include air-conditioning, Internet access, in-room safes, fresh coffee in the lobby daily from 6am, a top-floor terrace overlooking the island, and 24-hour front-desk presence. The newer **Enjoy Hotel** (tel. 501/226-0305, US$75) boasts a similar layout with 33 rooms, with king or double beds, but rooms are slightly less cozy or comfortable (watch the slippery floors). It does boasts a super balcony and rooftop with 180-degree views over Caye Caulker, but for the price you might want to find beachfront digs.

Barefoot Beach Resort Belize (southern end of Front St., tel. 501/226-0205, www.barefootbeachbelize.com, US$72-159), has cottages, studios, and rooms that are clustered on the beach; a few bigger suites are the size of a small apartment, each with an outdoor patio. The small, cheerful guest rooms have comfortable queen or king beds, ceiling fans, small fridges, private baths with hot showers, air-conditioning, plus their own deck or patio with seating and access to a dock. Complimentary use of one bike is provided per room, although walking to town is entirely feasible.

Just a few steps south is a quiet, postcard-perfect boutique property, secluded yet close to town, at **Colinda Cabanas** (tel. 501/226-0383, www.colindacabanas.com, US$69-149). The resort offers eight cabana rooms and a few more on the way. Standard guest rooms have fans, and the upstairs beachfront suites are spacious and tastefully decorated with Belizean paintings, with full kitchens, air-conditioning, and an amazing deck view of the barrier reef. A lovely *palapa* sunning and swimming dock is available, and all rooms have their own coffeemaker, porch, hammock, and wireless Internet access.

Quite possibly the most charming B&B on the island, ★ **Tree Tops Guesthouse** (tel. 501/226-0240, www.treetopsbelize.com, US$72-125) is tucked down a private side alley off the beach near Tom's Hotel. It's a luxurious little gem in a tall white building. Austrian native Doris has created a wonderful ambience with her colorful ceramics and thematically decorated guest rooms—including two sea-facing suites, the African Room and the Malaysian Room, which have private balconies, TVs, fridges, full baths, and memorable decor. Two cheaper guest rooms share a bath, and each has a TV, a fan, and a fridge. The two-level rooftop has 180-degree views of the island and hammocks to enjoy them.

US$100-150

In recent years, a host of boutique and "higher-end" accommodations have sprouted on the island—offering more luxurious surroundings but still at a reasonable price compared to neighboring San Pedro.

Close to the Split, the towering three-story suites at ★ **Costa Maya Beach Cabanas** (Front St., close to the Split, tel. 501/226-0432, www.costamayabelize.com, US$150) offer a dream location—on the main drag, set back enough from foot traffic yet a minute's flip-flop shuffle to the Split and Lazy Lizard corner of the island. There are six reasonably furnished self-catering suites and a top-floor penthouse. All have access to the rooftop terrace, with hammocks and the most stunning

Colinda Cabanas is a secluded and affordable beachfront resort.

panoramic view of the island, including part of the Split. The rooms are equipped with full kitchens, air-conditioning, and flat-screen TVs. The atmosphere is laid-back, and there used to be a private dock for taking in the sunrise until Hurricane Earl took it away in August 2016; whether it gets rebuilt remains to be seen.

Ideally tucked along the last side street before the Split, ★ **Sea Dreams Hotel and Guest Houses** (Hattie St., tel. 501/226-0602, www.seadreamsbelize.com, US$125-215) offers the private, thatched-roof, one-bedroom Orchid Cabana with a partial sea view, the gorgeous one-bedroom and full kitchen Bougainvillea Bungalow at the back of the property, as well as five single "courtyard" or ground-floor guest rooms and three beautiful two-bedroom apartments with full kitchens. Air-conditioning, wireless Internet, complimentary use of bicycles and snorkel gear, and a daily hot breakfast on the second floor with outdoor table seating are included. The private dock and *palapa* for impromptu swims or sunset viewing (even better than at the Split), a rooftop deck peppered with hammocks for yoga, naps, or massages (US$65 per hour), and cocktails from the Banyan Tree Bar make it as ideal a spot for lovers—a few have left here engaged—as it is for solo travelers. Owners Heidi and Haywood Curry and their friendly staff have transformed Sea Dreams into a perfect home away from home. Fees for kayak rentals and local tours also go directly to the island's high school, which Heidi Curry helped found.

Longtimer **OASI** (tel. 501/226-0384, www.oasi-holidaysbelize.com, US$100-110), outside the main buzz of town toward the airstrip, gets rave reviews from its previous guests. It's no surprise—there are four quiet, self-contained, beautifully kept and decorated apartments with patios, air-conditioning, and ceiling fans, hot and cold rainwater showers, equipped kitchens, TVs, and wireless Internet. The top-floor apartment in particular is simply lovely (I could live here). The entrance is a large tropical garden with a fountain, and there are two dogs on the property. There's a recreation area in the garden with a gorgeous, small swimming pool with wooden deck, a grill for guest use, and **Il Baretto** Wine Bar with fancy martini and margarita cocktails and weekend live music. Your warm host, Luciana Essenziale, can help plan your days; complimentary use of bikes makes the five-minute ride to town easy.

Nearby, newcomer ★ **Weezie's** (Airport Rd., U.S. tel. 970/376-2167, www.weeziescayecaulker.com, US$149-189) has colorful, sleek studios of varying size that remind you you're on a beach vacation, boasting all the amenities, from air-conditioning to full kitchens. Tucked away from the hustle and bustle on Back Street, yet a short ride to the heart of it, the hotel is a cluster of two buildings and rooms hugged by a lush, shaded yard. There's also a beachfront with a private dock just for guests (passcode protected), offering ample seating and steps into the sea. Otherwise, there's a delightful, though narrow swimming pool at the heart of the resort, under grape trees—it's often quiet during the day when guests are on tours or activities. Get the seafront building, with a higher floor and balcony views from your hammock. There's free Wi-Fi, coffee, and tea all day. And the cinnamon Creole bread vendor often passes down the alley around 4pm.

The bright, centrally located, and longtime family-run **Rainbow Hotel** (Front St., tel. 501/226-0123, rainbowhotel@btl.net, US$115) completed major guest-room upgrades in December 2011, giving them upscale decor throughout, with quality bedding, spacious baths with glass shower doors, flat-screen TVs with premium cable, wet bars with mini-fridges, coffeemakers, and microwaves. The popular waterfront Rainbow Bar and Grill is across the street, famous for its seafood.

At the foot of the town dock, **Seaside Cabanas** (Calle del Sol, tel. 501/226-0498, www.seasidecabanas.com, US$145-189) is a brightly painted 16-room miniresort. The smart guest rooms and cabanas are equipped with air-conditioning, cable TV, wireless Internet access, and cheerful decor surrounding a fine swimming pool and sporting lots of rooftop space. The **Uno Mas** bar is open daily until 10pm, and upstairs seating has ocean views.

Apartment-style accommodations are found at **Caye Caulker Condos** (tel. 501/226-0072, www.cayecaulkercondos.com, US$79-139), near the north end of the village by the Split; eight fully furnished suites, each facing the sea, have all the amenities, including a small pool. The balconies and rooftop hangout have nice views.

Pura Vida Inn (Front St., Playa Asuncion, www.puravidainn.com, US$135-175) is a good pick for couples or friends who want to stay seafront close to amenities but far enough from the noise and foot traffic of Front and Middle Streets. Past the small swimming pool at the front of the inn are four ground-floor efficiency units. Each has a queen bed, an en suite bath, a decent-size living room and a fully equipped kitchen, Wi-Fi, flat-screen TVs, and air-conditioning. Opt for the last unit, number 4, which has more windows. There's a rooftop lounge to enjoy the views, sit for a read, or grill food, as well as a private dock on the beach facing the hotel, with hammocks for those afternoon naps closer to shore. The single master suite on the second floor is ideal if you have no need for a full kitchen and can do with a minifridge. Bikes and kayaks are complimentary.

Over US$150

The **Iguana Reef Inn** (tel. 501/226-0213, www.iguanareefinn.com, from US$179) was one of the first to raise the bar with its 13 upscale rooms built around a well-kept complex on the west side of the island behind the soccer field. And it is continuously improving its looks with a greener yard and a clean wide beach. Its rooms are spacious with a beach feel, and all have comfortable touches like minifridges, porches, bathtubs, hot and cold water, and other modern conveniences. Continental breakfast is included. The bar, swimming pool, and clean beach area face the sunset and are more private and quiet than those on the island's windward side. There's also a penthouse (US$489) and, more importantly, a renovated waterfront deck for sunning and a ladder for easy entry into the sea.

CayeReef (Front St., tel. 501/226-0382, www.cayereef.com, US$183-219) has the most upscale boutique accommodations on the island: six spacious luxury apartments. Although the decor isn't mind-blowing, they have all the bells and whistles. Fully furnished sea-facing units have full kitchens and two bedrooms with en suite baths; a penthouse is on the third floor. There's a swimming pool with an infinity-like view from the apartments' top-floor balconies.

Vacation Homes

Caye Caulker Rentals (tel. 501/630-1008, www.cayecaulkerrentals.com) rents more than 20 holiday houses, cabanas, and cottages. The website sorts homes by price, location, and size and provides photos. Nightly rental rates range US$60-379, with one luxury villa that sleeps six going for US$379. A minimum number of nights is required, and monthly rentals are available.

Caye Caulker Accommodations (tel. 501/226-0382, www.cayecaulkeraccommodations.com) manages nine vacation properties and books suites for two upscale hotels. You can see photos and make reservations through the website.

INFORMATION AND SERVICES

There is plenty of online research you can do while planning your trip to the Northern Cayes. Check the official website of the **Caye Caulker Belize Tourism Industry Association** (CCBTIA, www.gocayecaulker.com). The most active website is probably www.ambergriscaye.com. The forum also has a Caye Caulker section that is easily searched and where you'll find a large community of knowledgeable folks who are generally quick to answer. There is no visitor information booth on the island; just walk off the dock and ask at your hotel or at the water taxi terminal.

Caye Caulker Ocean Academy

Ocean Academy

The story behind the 2008 opening of Caye Caulker's first high school, Ocean Academy (near the airstrip, tel. 501/226-0321, www.cayecaulkerschool.com), speaks to the island's strong community spirit. In 2007, Hicaqueños had no option but to send their children to the mainland once they completed primary school. Only the privileged few could afford daily or even weekly commute costs to Belize City, much less the school fees and uniforms. As a result, many children on the island stopped attending school at age 12, falling behind in the most basic of skills.

Enter Heidi Curry, an American expat who left the rat race to make a new life for herself and her family in Belize. While tutoring primary schoolchildren in her free time, she learned of the alarming gap in learning opportunities. It wasn't long before her passion for the island's children led her to the idea of opening a high school. After an initial phone inquiry to the Ministry of Education (as simple, she says, as asking "How does one open a high school?"), the community rallied behind her—including cofounder Joni Miller, parents, business owners, volunteers, and resident Dane Dingerson, who donated land and funded construction. Within eight months, a nonprofit high school was born. The first high school graduation ceremony took place in 2011.

In addition to core academic classes, subjects taught include marine biology, graphic design, tour guiding, fly-fishing, and scuba certification. Environmental education has a big place here, with projects such as mangrove restoration and composting. Students are offered annual apprenticeship placements on the island, giving them a role in Caye Caulker's growing tourism industry.

Travelers have many opportunities to get involved. The school hosts service-learning groups, volunteer teachers, and mentors year-round; needed volunteer skills and school supplies are listed online. Cash donations are welcome and can help sponsor the school year-round, particularly supporting the completion of a partially finished second floor of classrooms. Guided tours of the school campus (US$5 pp) are available.

Tsunami Adventures (tel. 501/226-0462, www.tsunamiadventures.com), up toward the Split, acts as a local travel agency. **Seaside Cabanas** (Calle del Sol, tel. 501/226-0498, www.seasidecabanas.com) also has reliable travel agents.

Banks

Atlantic Bank (Middle St., 8am-3pm Mon.-Fri., 8:30am-noon Sat.) is the only bank on the island. Atlantic's ATM accepts international cards. A Western Union office is located in the bank, and another is down the street inside Syd's (Middle St. at Av. Langosta). Be warned that the ATM tends to run out of cash by noon, but it is replenished again in the afternoon. Be sure to get enough cash if you're on the island just before a weekend.

Health and Emergencies

The free **health clinic** (south end of Front St., tel. 501/226-0190, 8am-7pm daily) will help you with meds, if it has the supplies; it is staffed by a Cuban doctor and a Belizean nurse. For any serious emergency, your best bet is an emergency flight to the mainland; all hotels keep a list of emergency boat captains and pilots. There is a pharmacy across from Chinatown Grocery.

Media and Communications

At the south end of Front Street is the Village Council office (upstairs in the community center) and community library, health clinic, and **post office** (8am-noon and 1pm-5pm Mon.-Thurs., 1pm-4:30pm Fri.). The mail goes out every morning. **FedEx** services are available at the **Tropic Air** cargo office at the airstrip.

The **BTL Office** (Back St., 8am-noon and 1pm-5pm Mon.-Fri.) sells DigiCell SIM cards for those with an unlocked phone; getting a local number requires an ID (passport or driver's license) for registration purposes.

Cayeboard Connection (Front St., tel. 501/206-0022, 10am-9pm daily, US$6 per hour) is a small Internet hub and bookstore with an extensive collection of used travel guidebooks and random romance novels, as well as Belize-related cultural books. Staff will burn CDs and print photos; scanning and copying services are also offered.

TRANSPORTATION
Getting There
AIR

Tropic Air (tel. 501/226-2012, U.S. tel. 800/422-3435, www.tropicair.com) and **Maya Island Air** (tel. 501/223-1140 or 501/223-1362, www.mayaislandair.com) make daily flights to Caye Caulker from Belize City's municipal and international airports as part of their San Pedro run. The airstrip on Caye Caulker is simple—you arrive just 15 minutes early and wait outside or on the veranda of the small building that serves all flights. Fares on Tropic Air, slightly higher than Maya Island Air, are US$54.50 one-way to Belize City's municipal airport (about 10 minutes) and US$89 one-way to the international airport (8 minutes). Tropic Air also flies between the Belize international airport and Cancún, Mexico, with connections to Caye Caulker and San Pedro—yet another option for flying into Belize.

BOAT

The short water taxi ride between Caye Caulker and either Belize City or San Pedro is the most common and affordable way to get to the island. The Belize City-Caye Caulker trip costs US$15 one-way on the San Pedro Belize Express. Many boats are partially open-air, with benches for seats, although San Pedro Belize Express has a fleet of forward-facing three- and four-seat rows and covered interiors, but with less legroom. A light cardigan or rain jacket is always handy for windy trips. If you're lucky, there's free Wi-Fi on board. The boats are often packed to the point of being overloaded and sometimes depart late, although some companies are guiltier of these offenses than others. The safest bet is often the San Pedro Belize Express.

Three competing water taxi companies have alternative schedules and similar fares. Tickets for the **San Pedro Belize Express**

(San Pedro tel. 501/226-3535, Caye Caulker tel. 501/226-0225, Belize City tel. 501/223-2225, www.belizewatertaxi.com) can be purchased from the ticket office on Caye Caulker's Front Street. Boats depart from the dock across from the police station. Express departures to Belize City run 6am-5pm daily and to San Pedro 8am-5:30pm daily. San Pedro Belize Express Water Taxi also offers service to the Muelle Fiscal in Chetumal, Mexico. The boat departs from Caye Caulker at 7am daily and San Pedro at 7:30am daily and returns from Chetumal at 3:30pm daily. Caye Caulker connections are available. The 1.5-hour one-way trip costs US$55.

Ocean Ferry (tel. 501/223-0033, www. oceanferrybelize.com) boats depart Caye Caulker from the main pier on the east side of the island; buy tickets at the office right on the dock before boarding the boat. Departures to Belize City run 6:30am-4:30pm daily and to San Pedro 8:45am-6:15pm daily.

Water Jets Express boats (San Pedro tel. 501/226-2194, Caye Caulker tel. 501/206-0234, Belize City tel. 501/207-1000, www. sanpedrowatertaxi.com) offers service to Chetumal in Mexico (US$55 one-way) that departs Caye Caulker at 7am daily and San Pedro at 8am daily and returns from Chetumal at 3pm daily. It also has a boat that

leaves San Pedro at 3pm daily for Corozal and Sarteneja, which returns at 7am daily.

Getting Around
BICYCLE
The navigable part of town—from the airstrip north to the Split—is one mile long and easily explored on foot. Still, a bicycle will make things easier, particularly on hot days and if you're staying in one of the more southern accommodations. Ask if your hotel provides one, or rent at **Friendship Center** on Front Street. **M&N Mel's Bike Rentals** (Chapoose St., just off Front St., tel. 501/226-0229, US$2 per hour, US$25 per week) is also a safe bet.

GOLF CART
If you're staying far south of the village, you might consider renting a golf cart from **Nando's Golf Cart Rental** (Av. Langosta, next to Chan's Mini Mart, tel. 501/629-6835) or **Buddy's Golf Cart Rentals** (Av. Langosta, tel. 501/628-8508, 8am-6pm daily).

A golf cart taxi ride is cheap and worth it when moving around the island with heavy luggage. A number of taxi guys are available, including **Reynaldo's Taxi** (tel. 501/653-4320), **Chano's** (tel. 501/633-5510), and **Peter's** (tel. 601/634-2105). One-way fares are US$2.50.

Diving Turneffe and the Great Blue Hole

Belize's atolls are a sight to behold—with some of the clearest turquoise waters as well as abundant marinelife. No trip to these easterly islands is ever wasted, whether to snorkel, dive, or swim, taking in Belize's breathtaking waters, not to mention some of the most beautiful beaches.

Getting There
Dive excursions to Belize's atolls depart mostly from Belize City, Ambergris Caye,

and Caye Caulker, although some dive shops also offer occasional long trips from Placencia. From the northern cayes, which are the most popular departure point because most tourists stay on the cayes, the trip takes at least two hours to Lighthouse Reef and the Great Blue Hole, and slightly more to Turneffe, which is actually closer to Belize City. You can't go wrong choosing between these atolls (you can't do both in one day); this is simply some of the best diving in Belize and you'll get plenty of satisfaction in terms of seeing marinelife, vibrant corals, and spectacular waters and beaches. Prices are similar on the northern cayes; look for comfortable, large boats for these long trips as well as a solid track record and PADI-certified dive shop recommendations listed in this book under Caye Caulker and San Pedro.

Most dives to the atolls are considered advanced diving, so you'll want to check in with the dive shop on any prerequisites, as well as check ahead for dates when you go on a trip (The Great Blue Hole in particular, requires advanced PADI certification plus one local dive beforehand). There are usually minimums required for them to go out to the atolls, but these numbers are easily reached in high season. Most dive trips to the atolls include at least two to three tank dives, split between morning and afternoon, lunch, nonalcoholic beverages, and the rum punch for the way back when all dives are completed and you're returning to the cayes.

If you're a major dive enthusiast and only interested in spending your time in and under the water exploring the Belize Barrier Reef, then a stay on one of the atolls would make complete sense and provide bang for your buck. Turneffe has a choice of higher-end accommodations, while Lighthouse Reef Atoll has as range of lodges as well as a camping adventure expedition outfitter every winter, Island Expeditions. Accommodations on both atolls offer all-inclusive packages, based on your interests.

TOP EXPERIENCE

TURNEFFE ISLANDS

A renowned diving and fishing destination about 30 miles east of Belize City, most of the Turneffe islands are small dots of sand, mangrove clusters, and swamp, home only to seabirds and wading birds, ospreys, manatees, and crocodiles. Only Blackbird Caye and Douglas Caye are of habitable size, supporting small populations of fishers and shellfish divers. In November 2012, Turneffe Atoll was officially declared a protected marine reserve.

Most visitors to Turneffe are day-tripping divers based in Ambergris Caye or Caye Caulker; a select few choose to book an island vacation package. There are a couple of upscale resorts and one research facility where visitors can stay.

Diving and Snorkeling
RENDEZVOUS POINT

This is a popular first dive for overnighters out of Ambergris Caye. It provides a great opportunity for divers who haven't been under in a while. The depth is about 40-50 feet and affords sufficient bottom time for you to get a good look at a wide variety of reef life. Angelfish, butterfly fish, parrotfish, yellowtails, and morays are well represented. This will whet appetites for the outstanding diving to come at the Elbow.

★ THE ELBOW

Most divers have heard of the Elbow (just 10 minutes from Turneffe Island Lodge), a point of coral that juts out into the ocean. This now-famous dive site offers a steep sloping drop-off covered with tube sponges and deepwater gorgonians, along with shoals of snappers (sometimes numbering in the hundreds) and other pelagic creatures. Predators such as bar jacks, wahoo, and permits cruise the reef, and the drop-off is impressive. Currents sweep the face of the wall most of the time, and they typically run from the north. However, occasionally they reverse or cease altogether.

LEFTY'S LEDGE

A short distance farther up the eastern side of the atoll from the Elbow is another dive to excite even those with a lot of bottom time under their weight belts. Lefty's Ledge features dramatic spur-and-groove formations that create a wealth of habitats. Correspondingly, divers will see a head-turning display of undersea life in both reef and pelagic species. Jacks, mackerels, permits, and groupers are present in impressive numbers. Wrasses, rays, parrotfish,

Turneffe Islands

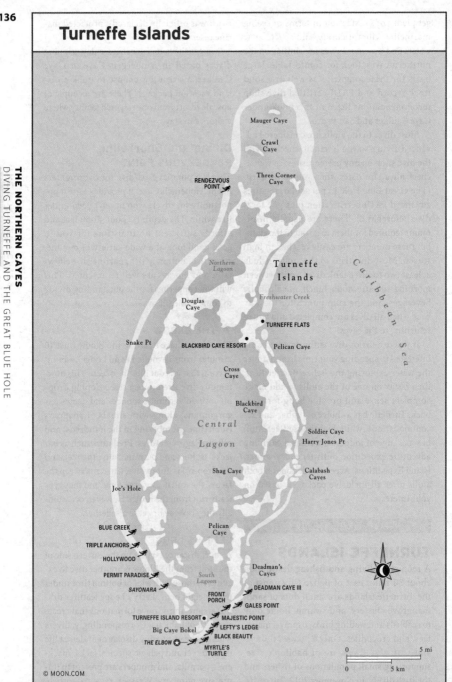

Mauger Caye

Crawl Caye

Three Corner Caye

RENDEZVOUS POINT

Northern Lagoon

Turneffe Islands

Freshwater Creek

Douglas Caye

TURNEFFE FLATS

Snake Pt

BLACKBIRD CAYE RESORT

Pelican Caye

Cross Caye

Blackbird Caye

Central Lagoon

Soldier Caye

Harry Jones Pt

Shag Caye

Calabash Cayes

Joe's Hole

Pelican Caye

BLUE CREEK

TRIPLE ANCHORS

HOLLYWOOD

PERMIT PARADISE

SAYONARA

South Lagoon

Deadman's Cayes

DEADMAN CAYE III

FRONT PORCH

GALES POINT

TURNEFFE ISLAND RESORT

MAJESTIC POINT

Big Cave Bokel

LEFTY'S LEDGE

BLACK BEAUTY

THE ELBOW

MYRTLE'S TURTLE

Caribbean Sea

0   5 mi

0   5 km

© MOON.COM

and butterfly fish are evident around the sandy canyons. Cleaning stations are also evident, where you'll see large predators allowing themselves to be groomed by small cleaner shrimp or fish. The dive begins at about 50 feet, and the bottom slopes to about 100 feet before dropping off into the blue.

GALES POINT
Gales Point is a "don't-miss" dive a short distance up the eastern side of the atoll from Lefty's Ledge. Here the reef juts out into the current at a depth of about 45 feet, sloping to about 100 feet before the drop-off. Along the wall and the slope just above it are numerous ledges and cave-like formations. Rays and groupers are especially common here—some say this may be a grouper breeding area. Corals and sponges are everywhere in numerous varieties.

SAYONARA
On the leeward, or western, side of the atoll, the wreck of the *Sayonara*, a tender sunk by Dave Bennett of Turneffe Island Lodge, lies in about 30 feet of water. Close by is a sloping ledge with interesting tunnels and spur-and-groove formations. Healthy numbers of reef fish play among the coral, and some barracuda tag along. Divers' bubbles often draw down large schools of permits.

HOLLYWOOD
A bit farther up the atoll from the *Sayonara*, Hollywood offers divers a relatively shallow dive (30-40 feet) with moderate visibility, unless the currents have reversed. Here you'll find lots of basket and tube sponges and lush coral growth. Many angelfish, parrotfish, grunts, and snappers swim here. Although not as dramatic as an eastern-side dive, Hollywood has plenty to see.

BLACK CORAL WALL
Along this wall north of Turneffe, you might spot the elusive whitespotted toadfish, as well as trunkfish, giant anemones, and healthy corals.

COCKROACH CAYE WALL
Northeast of Turneffe, Cockroach Caye Wall rewards with coral gardens and abundant reef fish, including angelfish and parrotfish against a backdrop of gorgonians. If you're lucky, you'll spot Belize's whitespotted toadfish.

Fishing
If you're looking to hook a bonefish or a permit, miles of crystal flats are alive with both hard-fighting species. Tarpon are abundant late March-June within the protected creeks and channels throughout the islands. Those who seek larger trophies will find a grand choice of marlin, sailfish, wahoo, groupers, blackfin tuna, and many more.

Accommodations
Turneffe Island Resort (tel. 501/532-2990, U.S. tel. 800/874-0118, www.turnefferesort.com, 3-night package US$1,490-2,290) is on **Little Caye Bokel,** 12 acres of beautiful palm-lined beachfront and mangroves. Book a seven-night dive or fishing package and stay in one of eight ground-floor deluxe guest rooms, four second-floor superior rooms, and eight stand-alone cabanas. It's a popular location for divers, anglers, and those who just want a hammock under the palms. At the southern tip of the atoll, the lodge is a short distance north of its larger relative, Big Caye Bokel. This strategic location offers enthusiasts a wide range of underwater experiences—it's within minutes of nearly 200 dive sites. Shallow areas are perfect for photography or snorkeling; you can see nurse sharks, rays, reef fish, and dolphins in the flats a few hundred yards from the dock. All the dives mentioned earlier and many more are within 15 minutes by boat. The dive operation is first-rate, and advanced instruction and equipment rentals are available. Anglers have a choice of fishing for snappers, permits, jacks, mackerels, and billfish from the drop-offs. They can stalk the near-record numbers of snook, bonefish, and tarpon in the flats and mangroves. The lodge's fishing

guide has an uncanny way of knowing where the fish will be.

On the eastern side of the Turneffe Islands, **Blackbird Caye Resort** (tel. 501/223-2772, U.S. tel. 866/909-7333, www.blackbirdresort. com) encompasses 166 acres of beach and rainforest, and promises "an adventure" and not just an average vacation. It can accommodate 36 guests (double occupancy) with hot-water showers, private baths, and double and queen beds, as well as a duplex and a triplex featuring private guest rooms and air-conditioning. Snorkeling, fishing, and diving packages are offered for about US$2,570-3,000 per week, depending on activities and accommodations, and can include three dives a day, all meals, lodging, and airport transfers.

Turneffe Flats (tel. 501/232-9022, U.S. tel. 800/512-8812, www.tflats.com, packages from US$1,690) is famous among international saltwater fly fishers who know the value of being able to sight fish in wadable flats for permits, bonefish, and tarpon. Or go for barracuda, snappers, jacks, or snook and eat your catch up at night. Guided fishing is in the lodge's 16-foot Super Skiff flats boats. Divers are welcome and will enjoy daily forays to scores of sites throughout Turneffe Atoll and Lighthouse Reef. Varied beach accommodations are comfortable and well appointed, and meals are eaten family-style.

TOP EXPERIENCE

LIGHTHOUSE REEF

The most easterly of Belize's three atolls, Lighthouse Reef lies 50 miles southeast of Belize City. The 30-mile-long, 8-mile-wide lagoon is the location of the Great Blue Hole, a dive spot made famous by Jacques Cousteau and a favorite destination of dive boats from Belize City, Ambergris Caye, and Caye Caulker. The best dive spots, however, are along the walls of Half Moon Caye and Long Caye, where the diving rivals any in the world.

Think of the atoll as a large spatula with a short handle and a long blade. At the northern tip of the spatula blade, **Sandbore Caye**

is home to a rusty lighthouse and a few fishing shacks. It is also the favorite anchorage of several of the dive boats that do overnight stops, including *Reef Roamer II*.

Big Northern Caye, across a narrow strait, has a landing strip that used to serve the now-closed resort here. There are long stretches of beach to walk, beautiful vistas, mangroves, and lagoons, home to snowy egrets and crocodiles.

Halfway down the spatula-shaped atoll, about where the blade meets the handle, lies the magnificent **Great Blue Hole,** a formation best appreciated from the air but also impressive from the bridge of a boat.

At the elbow of the handle is **Half Moon Caye,** a historical natural monument and protected area with its lighthouse, bird sanctuary, shipwrecks, and incredible diving offshore. Finally, on the handle, **Long Caye** is a lonely outpost with a small dock, large palms, and glassy water.

The Great Blue Hole

This circular underwater formation, with its magnificent blue-to-black hues surrounded by electric-blue water, is emblematic of Belize itself. The submerged shaft is a karst-eroded sinkhole with depths exceeding 400 feet. In the early 1970s, Jacques Cousteau and his crew explored the tunnels, caverns, and stalactites here, created by past earthquakes.

Most dive groups descend to a depth of about 135 feet. Technically, this is not a dive for novices or even intermediate divers, though many intermediate divers do it with a guide. It requires a rapid descent, a very short period at depth, and a careful ascent, requiring excellent buoyancy control. For a group of 10 or more, at least three dive masters should be present. The Great Blue Hole is everything it is hyped to be; my own personal experience there was extraordinary, and I gasped at the sight of the gigantic formations, the infinite depth, and the Caribbean reef sharks that circled nearby. It's akin to an out-of-body experience. The lip of the crater down to about 60-80 feet has the most life: fat midnight parrotfish,

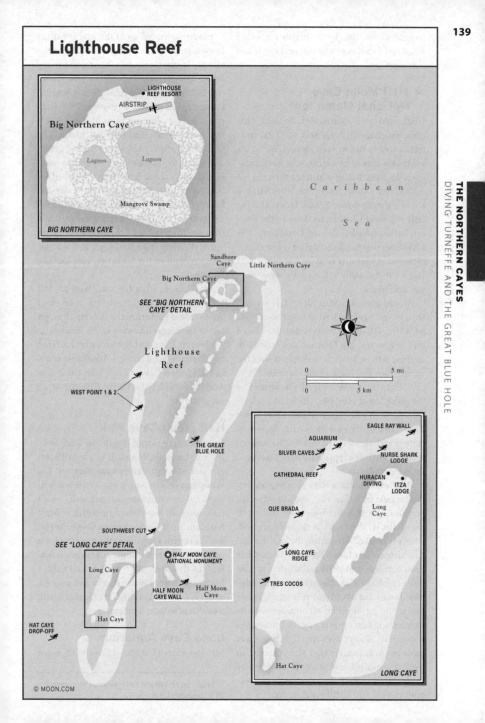

Lighthouse Reef

BIG NORTHERN CAYE

LIGHTHOUSE
REEF RESORT

AIRSTRIP

Big Northern Caye

Lagoon   Lagoon

Mangrove Swamp

Caribbean

Sea

Sandbore
Caye   Little Northern Caye

Big Northern Caye

**SEE "BIG NORTHERN
CAYE" DETAIL**

Lighthouse
Reef

WEST POINT 1 & 2

0   5 mi

0   5 km

THE GREAT
BLUE HOLE

SOUTHWEST CUT

SEE "LONG CAYE" DETAIL

Long Caye

Hat Caye

HAT CAYE
DROP-OFF

✛ HALF MOON CAYE
NATIONAL MONUMENT

HALF MOON
CAYE WALL   Half Moon
Caye

EAGLE RAY WALL

AQUARIUM

SILVER CAVES

NURSE SHARK
LODGE

CATHEDRAL REEF

HURACAN
DIVING   ITZA
LODGE

QUE BRADA

Long
Caye

LONG CAYE
RIDGE

TRES COCOS

Hat Caye

LONG CAYE

© MOON.COM

stingrays, angelfish, butterfly fish, and other small reef fish cluster around coral heads and outcroppings.

★ Half Moon Caye National Monument

Dedicated as a monument in 1982, this crescent-shaped island was the first protected area in Belize. Half Moon Caye, at the southeast corner of Lighthouse Reef, measures 45 acres, half of which is a thriving but endangered littoral forest; the other half is a stunning palm-dotted beach. This is also the only red-footed booby sanctuary in the western hemisphere besides the Galápagos. The US$40 per person admission fee is sometimes included in your dive boat fee, but sometimes you'll pay it directly to the park ranger when you disembark.

As you approach Half Moon Caye, you'll believe you have arrived at some South Sea paradise. Offshore, boaters use the rusted hull of a wreck, the *Elksund,* as a landmark in these waters. Its dark hulk looms over the surreal blue and black of the reef world. The caye, eight feet above sea level, was formed by the accretion of coral bits, shells, and calcareous algae. It's divided into two ecosystems: The section on the western side has dense vegetation with rich fertile soil, while the eastern section primarily supports coconut palms and little other vegetation.

Besides offshore waters that are among the clearest in Belize, the caye's beaches are gorgeous. Hawksbill, loggerhead, and green sea turtles lay their eggs on the southern end, which is marked off during the nesting and hatching season June-October—sometimes until November to prevent disturbance. You must climb the eight-foot-high central ridge that divides the island and gaze south before you see the striking half-moon beach with its unrelenting surf erupting against limestone rocks. Half Moon Caye's first lighthouse was built in 1820, modernized and enlarged in 1931, decommissioned in 1997, then felled by the elements in 2010. A newer lighthouse was built in 1998 and is still functioning.

Everyone should go to the **observation tower,** built by the Audubon Society in the ziricote forest; climb above the forest canopy for an unbelievable 180-degree view. Every tree is covered with perched booby birds in some stage of growth or mating. In March, you'll have a close-up view of nests where feathered parents tend their hatchlings. The air is filled with boobies coming and going, attempting to make their usually clumsy landings (those webbed feet weren't designed for landing in trees). Visitors also have a wonderful opportunity to see the other myriad inhabitants of the caye. Thieving magnificent frigates (the symbol of the Belize Audubon Society) swoop in to steal eggs, and iguanas crawl around in the branches, also looking for a snack.

It's 52 miles from the mainland to Half Moon Caye, a long boat trip over open ocean. Most visitors make the trip through one of the bigger dive shops, like Amigos on Ambergris Caye. Otherwise, only chartered or privately owned boats and seaplanes travel to Half Moon Caye. Check with the Belize Audubon Society in Belize City for other suggestions.

Half Moon Caye Wall

On the eastern side of Lighthouse Reef Atoll, the reef has a shallow shelf in about 15 feet of water where garden eels are plentiful. The sandy area broken with corals extends downward till you run into the reef wall, which rises some 20 feet toward the surface. Most boats anchor in the sandy area above the reef wall. Numerous fissures in the reef crest form canyons or tunnels leading out to the vertical face. In this area, sandy shelves and valleys frequently harbor nurse sharks and gigantic stingrays. Divers here are sure to return with a wealth of wonderful pictures.

Long Caye Aquarium

Minutes from Half Moon Caye Wall, often

1: beach on Half Moon Caye National Monument;
2: St. George's Caye

combined with a Blue Hole trip, is a spectacular dive site ideal for photos and with the most marinelife spotting—even more than at Half Moon Caye Wall. The electrifying deep-blue waters will stun you, as will the schools of bright colorful fish and the large eagle rays, sea turtles, stingrays, and nurse sharks.

Silver Caves

The shoals of silversides (small gleaming minnows) that gave this western atoll site its name are gone, but Silver Caves is still impressive and enjoyable. The coral formations are riddled with large crevices and caves that cut clear through the reef. As you enter the water above the sandy slope where most boats anchor, you'll be in about 30 feet of water and surrounded by friendly yellowtail snappers. Once again you'll see the downwardly sloping bottom, the rising reef crest, and the stomach-flipping drop into the blue.

Tres Cocos

On the western wall, "Three Coconuts" refers to trees on nearby Long Caye. The sandy bottom slopes from about 30 feet to about 40 feet deep before it plunges downward. Overhangs are common features here, and sponges and soft corals adorn the walls. Another fish lover's paradise, Tres Cocos does not have the outstanding coral formations you'll see at several other dives in the area, but who cares? There's a rainbow of marinelife all about. Turtles, morays, jacks, coral, shrimp, cowfish, rays, and angelfish are among the actors on this colorful stage.

West Point

Farther north and about even with the Great Blue Hole, West Point is well worth a dive. Visibility may be a bit more limited than down south, but it's still very acceptable. The reef face here is stepped. The first drop plunges from about 30 feet to well over 100 feet deep. Another coral and sand slope at that depth extends a short distance before dropping vertically into very deep water. The first shallow wall has pronounced overhangs and lush coral and sponge growth.

Accommodations

Stay overnight on **Long Caye** with **Huracan Diving** (U.S. tel. 954/802-5005, www. huracandiving.com), where you can choose from either a four- or seven-night all-inclusive dive package (US$990-1,490). The four guest rooms at Huracan's lodge have private baths, king beds, ceiling fans, and screened windows. Pickup and transfer from Belize City are included in your package. A second option on Long Caye is **Itza Lodge** (tel. 501/223-3228, U.S. tel. 305/600-2585, www.itzaresort. com, R&R 3-night package US$995-1,650, 7-night package US$1,395-2,795), a 20-room oceanfront resort offering diving, fishing, water sports such as kite surfing, and "R&R" packages.

For even more adventure and to fully embrace the stunning outdoors on this atoll, sign up for a three-day "Lighthouse Getaway" overnight on Half Moon Caye with **Island Expeditions** (U.S. tel. 800/667-1630, www. islandexpeditions.com, US$599 pp)—the only adventure-travel outfitter with a tent camp on the island. It's a well-run, professional operation with daily water sports of all kinds—for the novice and expert alike—and a great way to travel with a group. The tents are sturdy and have single or double beds and kerosene lamps, and they are well sheltered from the elements. This ecofriendly camp on Half Moon Caye provides shared composting toilets, cold-water showers (with outdoor warm-water hoses when the weather cooperates), and evening generator use until 9:30pm. Meals are communal.

ST. GEORGE'S CAYE

The most historically significant caye—a national landmark and the first capital of the British Settlement (1650-1784)—is a little-known getaway. Nine miles or a 20-minute water taxi hop from Belize City, this small caye is home to **St. George's Caye Mangrove Reserve,** established in 2005 and covering 12.5 acres on the southernmost point of the island. One luxury resort has a full-service dive shop that also offers other water sports: **St. George's Caye Resort** (U.S. tel. 800/813-8498, www.belizeislandparadise. com, US$129-159 pp, packages available). The rest of the island is lined with private villas and docks owned by affluent Belizeans who escape here on the weekends.

St. George's Caye Day is celebrated nationwide on September 10 to honor a 1798 British battle that took place here and prevented Spanish invasion. Today, the small cemetery gives evidence of St. George's heroic past and is Belize's smallest archaeological reserve.

The **St. George's Caye Research Station and Field School,** founded by ECOMAR in 2009, hosts a group of Texas State University professors and students who spend a month on the island to conduct research digs. It also conducts coral reef research and educational trips based here.

St. George's Caye Aquarium

Ever visited a professional aquarium created by a 10-year-old? Walk south of St. George's Caye Resort, past the renowned St. George's Caye cannon, where the British Baymen fought off an attempted Spanish invasion of Belize in 1798, to the **St. George's Caye Aquarium** (tel. 501/662-2170, karlbischof@ yahoo.com, 8am-5pm daily, US$3), clearly indicated at the entrance to a home. In 2011, at the age of 10, Karly Bischof opened and has since managed the only indoor marine display of this kind in Belize, home to over 100 species of fish. He shows visitors around, describing each of the creatures that are native to Belize, from seahorses to scorpionfish and even a toadfish, and providing details on Belize's

underwater life. Like his father, he hopes to become a marine biologist, and there's no better place to prepare for it than Belize. Karly's aquarium has even appeared in overseas publications and is a worthwhile stop if you find yourself visiting the caye.

DROWNED CAYES

Spanish Lookout Caye is a 187-acre mangrove island at the southern tip of the Drowned Cayes, only 10 miles east of Belize City. There's no resort operating here but you could snorkel here and kayak.

GOFF'S CAYE

Near English Caye, Goff's Caye is a favorite little island stop for picnics and day trips out of Caye Caulker and Belize City, thanks to a beautiful sandy beach and promising snorkeling areas. Sailboats often stop overnight; camping can be arranged from Caye Caulker by talking with any reputable guide. Bring your own tent and supplies. Goff's is a protected caye, so note the rules posted by the pier. Goff's has seen major impact from the cruise ship industry, which sometimes sends thousands of people per week to snorkel around and party on the tiny piece of sand, and a few reports have said that this is destroying the coral.

ENGLISH CAYE

Although this is just a small collection of palm trees, sand, and coral, an important lighthouse sits here at the entrance to the Belize City harbor from the Caribbean Sea. Large ships stop at English Caye to pick up one of the two pilots who navigate the 10 miles in and out of the busy harbor. Overnights are not allowed here, but it's a pleasant day-trip location.

Belmopan and Cayo

Tucked in the foothills of the Maya Mountains,

the Cayo District—home to a world of eco-adventures and archaeo-logical wonders—is Belize's largest and the most visited area after the Northern Cayes.

This westernmost district begins where the Western Highway—renamed the George Price Highway in 2012—leaves the outskirts of Belize City toward Belmopan, the nation's quiet and landlocked capital. From there, it spills onto part of the aptly named Hummingbird Highway and stretches west all the way to Guatemala, leading toward rivers, rainforests, swimming holes, national parks, Mayan temples, caves, Thousand Foot Falls—the largest waterfall in Central America—and Mennonite villages, all in the space of two hours.

Highlights

Look for ★ to find recommended sights, activities, dining, and lodging.

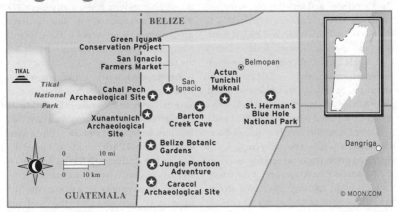

★ **St. Herman's Blue Hole National Park:** Get out the hiking boots and bathing suit! St. Herman's Cave offers fun for novice spelunkers, the park is teeming with local wildlife, and a swim in the Blue Hole should not be missed (page 160).

★ **Cahal Pech Archaeological Site:** The site is unique for both its archaeological intrigue and its location within the city limits of San Ignacio (page 163).

★ **San Ignacio Farmers Market:** Head to the most colorful and enjoyable farmers market in Belize (page 164).

★ **Green Iguana Conservation Project:** See exotic iguanas up close at this successful breeding and release project (page 166).

★ **Belize Botanic Gardens:** Hike the beautiful grounds to tour a variety of habitats; the Native Plant House is magical (page 166).

★ **Jungle Pontoon Waterfall Adventure:** A journey down the remote Vaca Dam Lake leads you to a number of stunning waterfalls, some of which are reached by wading through the lake and hiking through surrounding rainforest (page 166).

★ **Actun Tunichil Muknal:** The Cave of the Crystal Maiden is the wettest, dirtiest, most adventurous spelunking trip available (page 182).

★ **Xunantunich Archaeological Site:** This ancient city is easily one of the most gorgeous Mayan sites in Belize (page 188).

★ **Barton Creek Cave:** This cathedral-like cave is filled with giant stalactites, ancient Mayan ceramics—and plenty of mystery (page 192).

★ **Caracol Archaeological Site:** These remote ruins are rife with discovery and beauty. Enjoy long, peaceful views from atop the excavated temples (page 199).

Hike rainforest paths and medicinal trails that lead to ancient Mayan ceremonial caves. Canoe the Macal River on the way to the farmers market or ride a hand-cranked ferry across the Mopan River. Climb the boulders of the Río Frio in the Mountain Pine Ridge Reserve. Trek to the top of the Mayan archaeological site of Caracol, where scarlet macaws can be seen swooping across the valleys of green.

The district's true hub, San Ignacio, is a hilly, pedestrian-friendly town with a Latin pulse all its own. It's a favorite among Belizeans and expats, with outdoor cafés, authentic eateries, and arguably one of the best farmers markets in the country. Staying in town is an option, with several budget favorites, but a short drive away are the country's best jungle lodges, offering a variety of experiences—campsites, riverside cabins, and luxury tree houses. Recent developments have given San Ignacio a more modern look, with a cobblestoned main street (Burns Ave.) and a Welcome Center that once hosted food shacks and restaurants but is now oddly empty unless there's an event. For those seeking seclusion, the Mountain Pine Ridge, one of the remotest areas in the country, offers more accommodations options and plenty of outdoor exploration.

Once the heartland of the indigenous Maya, the Cayo District's countryside stretches to San José de Succotz and the border town of Benque Viejo del Carmen, revealing a diverse mix of mostly Creole, Chinese, Mayan, and Mennonite rural villages and towns alongside a mixed population of expats. Green pastures with mahogany and sapodilla trees—reminders of a colonial past—are peppered with orange orchards, chicken coops, and grazing cattle, signs of Cayo's main industry besides tourism. The region produces most of the livestock, poultry, and grain consumed in the country, earning it the nickname "breadbasket of Belize."

PLANNING YOUR TIME

Budget travelers will be pleased to see that their dollar goes farther in Cayo than in other parts of Belize. Most visitors find plenty to do, signing up for a new activity every day, but there's no rush, and you can easily travel around the area for weeks without getting weary. The beauty is that no two stays in Cayo are the same.

Belmopan is worth an overnight stop for its surrounding natural parks and attractions. Save half an hour for a hike in **Guanacaste National Park,** explore **Monkey Bay Wildlife Sanctuary,** and take a dip in **Blue Hole National Park**'s sinkhole. The world-famous **Ian Anderson's Caves Branch** offers easy accommodations near each.

Even if you've only got a day or two, **San Ignacio** is close enough to the coast and worth a trip; the forest runs right up to the city limits, where you'll find several trails and a fascinating archaeological site. San Ignacio also provides an excellent base for tours to **Actun Tunichil Muknal** or into **Tikal,** Guatemala. Jungle lodges line the Macal River and into the **Mountain Pine Ridge.**

Previous: hidden falls and pools in Cristo Rey Village; Blue Hole National Park's sinkhole; hand-cranked ferry to and from Xunantunich Archaeological Site.

Belmopan

After Hurricane Hattie destroyed government buildings and records in Belize City in 1961, the new capital of Belmopan was built far away from the coast to keep it safe from storm damage, with the expectation that large numbers of the population of Belize City would move with the government center. They didn't. Industry stayed behind, and so did most jobs. Today, while there is some growth in Belmopan, the masses are still in Belize City, which remains the cultural and commercial hub of the country. Some capital employees live in Belize City and commute 50 miles back and forth each day. Belmopan, however, was designed for growth and has continued to expand, with a population of around 20,000, plus a surge of several thousand commuters during weekdays. Today, Belmopan still isn't a destination for travelers; but it has several services, including a bus station and hub for going to other parts of the country, an excellent coffee shop nearby, and a couple of decent restaurants. You'll also find most foreign embassies and international organizations here as well as most important Belizean government services, including immigration. Other than that, it's a city—and the feel inside the city grid (within Ring Rd.), with rows of small cement homes and chain-link fencing, has been compared to a lower-middle-class Los Angeles suburb.

The majority of travelers, however, see only Belmopan's bus terminal and, if they have time, the small open-air market right next door. Some jog across the market to take a peek at the government buildings (only a few hundred yards away). Their intentionally Mayan-influenced arrangement—built around a central plaza—gives the scene just enough strange irony to make it worth the visit. Just beyond Belmopan, the Hummingbird Highway is one of the most beautiful roads in the region, snaking through densely forested hills that are riddled with trails, rivers, cenotes, and caves.

ORIENTATION

Belmopan is just east of the Hummingbird Highway and just south of the George Price Highway; it is usually accessed by Constitution Drive, which leads straight into the center from a traffic circle. Banks, buses, the market, and government buildings are tightly clustered within easy walking distance of one another. Turning right on Bliss Parade from Constitution Drive, you'll find the dilapidated Belmopan Hotel on your right and Novelo's bus station and the market on your left. Bliss Parade joins Ring Road, which loops around the central town district. Ring Road passes various government buildings and embassies on the left before meeting back up with Constitution Drive.

SIGHTS

George Price Centre for Peace and Development

This homage to the founding father of Belize, George Price, is an impressive and modern air-conditioned museum, library, and center for conflict resolution and peace. The **George Price Centre for Peace and Development** (Price Centre Rd., tel. 501/822-1054, www. gpcbelize.com, 8am-6pm Mon.-Fri., 9am-noon Sun., free) is just off the eastern part of the Loop Road, near the Catholic church. Set aside at least 30 minutes to tour the display, which now includes a setup of Price's modest living quarters while he was alive, and watch a worthwhile 23-minute documentary, *Man of Purpose and Vision,* in the media center, or admire the original flag that flew at Belize's independence ceremony in 1981. The website features a list of events and some fascinating information on George Price's legacy and Belizean history.

Born in 1919, Price died at the age of 92

Belmopan and Cayo

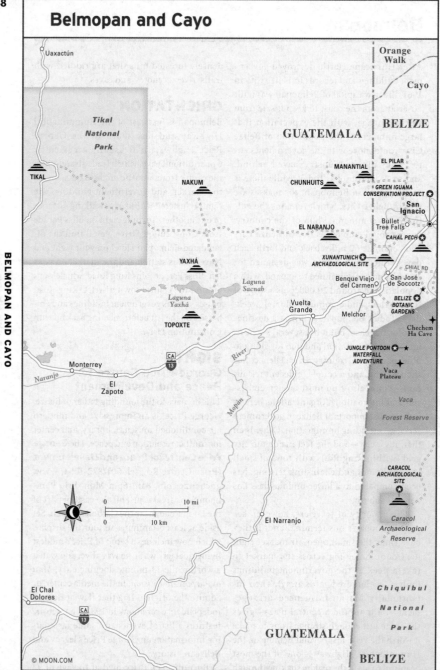

Uaxactún

Orange
Walk

Cayo

GUATEMALA

BELIZE

Tikal
National
Park

TIKAL

EL PILAR

MANANTIAL

CHUNHUITS

NAKUM

GREEN IGUANA
CONSERVATION PROJECT ✪

San
Ignacio

EL NARANJO

Bullet
Tree Falls

CAHAL PECH ✪

YAXHÁ

XUNANTUNICH ✪
ARCHAEOLOGICAL SITE

CHIAL RD

Laguna
Sacnab

Benque Viejo
del Carmen

San José
de Soccotz

Laguna
Yaxhá

Vuelta
Grande

BELIZE
BOTANIC
GARDENS

TOPOXTE

Melchor

Chechem
Ha Cave

River

JUNGLE PONTOON ✪ ★
WATERFALL
ADVENTURE

Vaca
Plateau

Monterrey

Naranjo

El
Zapote

CA
13

Mopán

Vaca

Forest Reserve

CARACOL ✪
ARCHAEOLOGICAL
SITE

El Narranjo

Caracol
Archaeological
Reserve

0   10 mi

0   10 km

Chiquibul

National

Park

El Chal
Dolores

CA
13

GUATEMALA

BELIZE

© MOON.COM

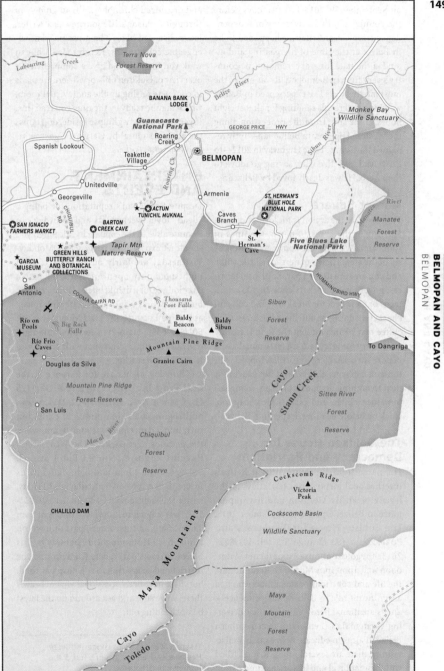

on September 19, 2011, just two days before the country's 30th anniversary of independence from Great Britain. I happened to be in Belize at the time of his passing and attended the state funeral ceremony, the country's very first, in Belmopan. It was one of the most moving days I've experienced in Belize, watching the crowds standing for almost eight hours in the sun, from the procession along the Western Highway in Belmopan—aptly renamed the George Price Highway in 2012—to the burial in Belize City, saying goodbye to their hero. He was dearly loved by Belizeans.

Market Square

This is where the action is for local shoppers. Starting at the crack of dawn, the lines of stalls are alive with the commerce and gossip of the area. Hang out here for a little while and you are sure to see a parade of local farmers, government workers chowing down on tacos or stew beef for breakfast, and colorful characters going about their business. The coffee may be instant, but the food is freshly made—try some fry jacks, a tasty tamale, or a plate of *garnaches* (crispy tortillas topped with tomato, cabbage, cheese, and hot sauce) for next to nothing. Bananas, oranges, mangoes, tomatoes, chiles, and carrots are cheap too; stock up before heading deeper into Belize.

The Goldson House for Democracy and Patriotism

His name figures prominently at Belize's international airport, but few know of the legacy of Philip Goldson and his importance to Belize. Opened in September 2015, **The Goldson House for Democracy and Patriotism** (82 Orange St., tel. 501/822-2613, thegoldsonhouse@gmail.com, 9am-noon and 1pm-3pm Mon.-Fri., free) honors the life and contributions of a man who had a significant role in Belize's independence—and is a national hero—in particular, defeating Guatemala's then-claim over southern Belize. It aims to educate Belizeans as well as visitors; there are several rooms to tour, filled with biographical and historical information

and organized chronologically to guide you through Goldson's life journey as a writer, journalist, and hero. The museum's knowledgeable coordinator, Kendra Griffith, can walk you through and give a comprehensive overview of Goldson's history. There are plans to complete setting up the audiovisual room, which may be ready by the time you read this. If you only quickly glimpse inside, don't miss the gorgeous mural by German Figueroa, titled *Founding Fathers*.

ENTERTAINMENT AND EVENTS

Despite Belmopan's reputation for being a "dead" town, weeknights and Saturday can be quite alive in the capital city, although you shouldn't expect a big party scene. Monday-Wednesday are fairly quiet; in fact, most nightspots only open midweek. There's a cozy lounge for a drink, bites—think ceviche, burgers, wings—and non-deafening music at **Desire Lounge** (37 Half Moon Ave., tel. 501/822-0356, 11am-2pm and 4pm-midnight daily, US$5-10), a clean spot with ample and tasteful futon seating.

Thursday nights are for karaoke at the **Bull Frog Inn's Restaurant & Bar** (25 Half Moon Ave., tel. 501/822-2111, www.bullfroginn.com, 8pm-midnight daily) but turn into a dance party around 11pm, when the place can get packed. The Wing Stop's **Puccini Lounge** (Nim Li Punit St., tel. 501/636-0048, 10pm-midnight daily) turns into a dance spot on Thursday and Friday, with a DJ. Nightspot **La Cabaña** (tel. 501/822-1577, www.aguallos.com/lacabana, 6pm-2am Thurs.-Sat.), in the western part of town on a hill above Hummingbird Highway by Las Flores, attracts partygoers from around the district and sells drinks and cheap bar food, but there have been occasional violent brawls there, so be sure and ask around on the latest before heading out.

1: sunset at Banana Bank Lodge and Belize Horseback Adventure; 2: Surf & Turf; 3: the Hummingbird Highway

On September 21, Belmopan celebrates **Independence Day** along with the rest of the country. The day begins with a morning official ceremony at the Court House Plaza (you may glimpse the prime minister of Belize from a distance making an address) and includes military parades. After the speeches comes the fun part of the day, with food and music all around the market area and town, and a citizens parade along Bliss Parade, complete with colorful floats and costumes. Line up around the Bliss Parade area or Constitution Drive near the market to catch the start of all the fanfare, and follow the crowds.

SHOPPING

Besides Market Square, you'll find a few handy stores in Belmopan. In the market area you'll find plenty of pharmacies, shops, and Internet spots. **Angelus Press** (Constitution Dr., tel. 501/822-3861, 7:30am-5:30pm Mon.-Fri., 9am-noon Sat.) has a good office supply store and bookstore in the building right across from the bus station. **The Art Box** (Mile 46, George Price Hwy., tel. 501/822-2233, www. artboxbz.com, 8am-6pm Mon.-Sat.) is on the George Price Highway and has an excellent selection of woodworking materials, watercolors, and picture frames in addition to standard gift-shop fare (as well as Christian books and CDs).

FOOD

Even if you're not staying in Belmopan, it is a common lunch stop for anyone traveling to or from Belize City. The cheapest meals, which are quite good, I might add, are at the market stalls and small restaurants that surround the bus terminal. Don't be surprised to see folks eating full meals at 8am, including stew beef and rice. But the restaurant scene in Belmopan has slowly evolved, and a few of these eateries are worth the stop.

Belizean

Miriam's Sunrise (across from First Caribbean Bank and Court House Plaza,

6am-3pm daily, US$2-5) is a delightful spot for breakfast and a good alternative to Market Square, serving up excellent, inexpensive local dishes—stews, soups, burgers, tacos, and more—from breakfast through lunch, as well as fresh-squeezed local fruit juices (try the *horchata,* very refreshing on a hot Belmopan day). Seating is casual on picnic tables and often shared, ideal for meeting locals or expats and asking about the town.

★ **Surf & Turf** (South Ring Rd., tel. 501/602-3194, 11am-10pm Wed.-Sun., US$5-10) sits behind the Shell station in downtown Belmopan, and you might otherwise miss it. But this small, cozy spot serves up some of the best ceviche and conch fritters in town, as well as curry shrimp. As its name suggests, the menu includes succulent *arrachera* and sirloin steaks, burgers, as well as pork ribs—ask for the daily specials, too. Note that the schedule might vary during the slow tourist season. They deliver in town or you can stay and enjoy your meal at the bar, indoors to fans, or out on a picnic table.

Caladium Restaurant (across from Market Square, tel. 501/822-2754, caladium@ btl.net, 7:30am-8pm Mon.-Fri., closes earlier Sat., US$5-14) is a longtime favorite, serving up solid local breakfasts, rice and bean dishes, and stews for lunch—ask for the day's special (the chile relleno looked amazing)—and an international menu of seafood, salads, steaks, burgers, and a lot more. The tiled dining room is cozy and air-conditioned, with a full bar.

International

Scotchies (7753 Hummingbird Hwy., tel. 501/832-2203, 11am-9pm Sun.-Wed., 10:30am-11pm Fri.-Sat., US$3.75-16), the popular Jamaican chain restaurant specializing in jerk cuisine, was a hit when it started in Belize. The setup is similar to its Jamaican counterparts: a gated yard with thatch huts and wooden benches, albeit a lot more polished. Outdoor cooking of pork, chicken, and sausage is on pimento logs covered in zinc sheets, the traditional jerk way. Ask for dipping sauces made from scotch bonnet peppers. Side options include breadfruit and the trusted Belizean rice and beans. There's ample seating—surprisingly large for a small town—and a bar serving mostly beers and soft drinks. A more popular stop and better pick for deliciously smoked meats is ★ **The Smoke Shack** (1534 Constitution Dr., tel. 501/627-5166, 11am-midnight Mon.-Fri., noon-9pm Sat., US$5-10), tucked away in its own yard, with a bar and an ample open-air dining terrace. Enjoy delicious burgers (the teriyaki burger is a hit), ribs, wings starting at US$0.50 each, hot dogs, imported steaks, and the best-smoked barbecue in Belmopan (the owner, a Belizean-LA transplant, even invented his own smoker that bakes, steams, and smokes at once). Friday nights are for karaoke until midnight, and happy hour specials run 5pm-7pm.

For a quick and healthy lunch, ★ **Angles Rotisserie** (tel. 501/615-2246, 11am-2pm and 4:30pm-7pm Mon.-Sat., US$4) is a welcome addition to town, offering roasted chicken (whole or in quarter/half) with sides like rice, tortillas, or steam veggies, panini, salads, desserts and ice cream. The restaurant is a dream turned reality for Belmopan native Jane Longsworth, a former accountant. Angles gets extra points for using biodegradable bags and containers. There's a small covered side veranda with about three tables if you want to enjoy on-site.

Pepper's Pizza (St. Martin Ave., across from Bull Frog Inn, tel. 501/822-4663, 11am-9pm Mon.-Sat., noon-9pm Sun., US$5-16) delivers free anywhere in town. **Pasquale's Pizzeria** (corner of Forest Dr. and Slim Ln., delivery tel. 501/822-4663, www.pasqualesbelize.com, 11am-9pm Mon.-Sat., noon-9pm Sun., US$8-15) is quite popular with those who can afford U.S. prices and offers large hand-tossed New York-style pizzas, pastas, wings, and burgers. **Wing Stop** (Hummingbird Ave. and Mountain View Blvd., tel. 501/636-0048, 11am-11:45pm daily, US$5-14) is where you can get—you guessed it—wings, from 6 pieces to a bucket of 24 or more, among other options.

The open-air restaurant and bar at the **Bull Frog Inn** (25 Half Moon Ave., tel. 501/822-2111, www.bullfroginn.com, 7am-10pm daily, US$10-40) has a long-standing reputation among the elite of Belmopan, and this is one of the most popular spots in town to dine. The fish fillet, chicken, and burgers are all good and moderately priced, and there's a daily local special. For an international menu prepared by a chef from England, and the prices to go with it, **Corkers Restaurant & Wine Bar** (top floor of Hibiscus Plaza, tel. 501/822-0400, www.corkersbelize.com, 11am-9pm Mon.-Sat., US$7-25) caters to the expat crowd and has salads like tuna niçoise as well as wraps, burgers, steaks, and pastas. There are trivia nights on Monday and a happy hour (4pm-10pm Thurs.-Sat.) with half-price cocktails.

Among the many Chinese restaurants, **Chon Saan Palace** (7069 George Price Blvd., tel. 501/822-3388, 10am-midnight daily, US$5-10) is the best.

Cafés

You can also grab coffee and get online across the street at **Formosa** (Nim Li Punit St., tel. 501/822-0888, 9am-7pm Mon.-Thurs., 10am-8pm Fri.-Sat.), a small but cozy café, with additional seating in an adjoining room. There's everything you'd need in one place—including Taiwanese bubble milk tea, breakfast food, burgers and soups, gourmet coffee, and desserts. The service is very friendly.

Moon Clusters Coffee House (E. Ring Rd., behind Brodies, tel. 501/602-1644, 11am-7pm Mon.-Sat.), the second of two Belizean-owned Moon Clusters in the country (the other is in Belize City), serves the most delicious frozen espresso drink I've had in a while: the Choli—a double shot of espresso topped with ice cream and cinnamon. It's to die for. There's a nice seating area and plenty of other hot and cold beverage options, including hot chocolate and smoothies. Owner Amilcar Aguilar takes pride in his coffeehouse, a place to "have a nice drink and good conversation"

Belmopan

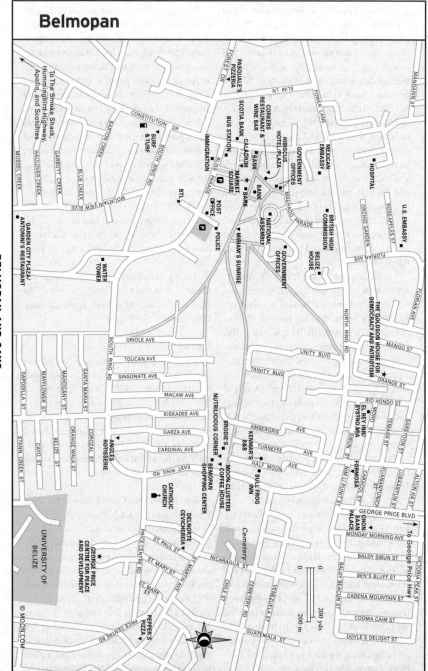

To The Smoke Shack, Hummingbird Highway, Apollo, and Scotchies

MANDARIN ST

CONSTITUTION DR

FOREST DR

PASQUALE'S PIZZERIA

N1 W1TS

POWER LANE

SLIM N1

CORKERS RESTAURANT & WINE BAR

SCOTIA BANK

CALADIUM

BANK

BUS STATION

BUSS PARADE ST

IMMIGRATION

MEXICAN EMBASSY

HIBISCUS HOTEL/PLAZA

GOVERNMENT OFFICES

MARKET SQUARE

BANK

MALHADO PARADE

HOSPITAL

ORCHID GARDEN

ROSEAPPLES ST

U.S. EMBASSY

BARTON CREEK

SOUTH RING RD

MOUNTAIN VIEW BLVD

BLUE CREEK

GARBUTT CREEK

HAULOVER CREEK

MUSSEL CREEK

SURF & TURF

BTL

POST OFFICE

POLICE

NATIONAL ASSEMBLY

MIRIAM'S SUNRISE

GOVERNMENT OFFICES

BRITISH HIGH COMMISSION

BELIZE HOUSE

FLORIAN AVE

GARDEN CITY PLAZA/ ANTONIN'S RESTAURANT

WATER TOWER

THE GOLDSON HOUSE FOR DEMOCRACY AND PATRIOTISM

NORTH RING RD

MANGO ST

ORIOLE AVE

SOUTH RING RD

TOUCAN AVE

SINSONATE AVE

UNITY BLVD

TRINITY BLVD

ORANGE ST

RÍO HONDO ST

FLORIAN AVE

MACAW AVE

KISKADEE AVE

GARZA AVE

CARDINAL AVE

NUTRILICIOUS CORNER

BRODIE'S

AMBERGRIS AVE

KENMAR'S B&B

TURNEFFE AVE

HALF MOON AVE

MOON CLUSTERS COFFEE HOUSE

BULLFROG INN

EL REY INN/ BYSTRO MIA

MOHO ST

SIBUN ST

NIM LI PUNIT ST

CARACOL ST

FORMOSA ST

XUANANTUNICH ST

LUBAANTUN ST

ALTUN HA ST

TERMASH ST

SARSTOON ST

ANGLES ROTISSERIE

ORANGE WALK ST

COROZAL ST

BELIZE ST

MAHOGANY ST

SANTA MARIA ST

MAYFLOWER ST

SAPODILLA ST

EAST RING RD

BELMOPAN SHOPPING CENTER

CATHOLIC CHURCH

DELNORTE CEVICHEREIA

CHON SAAN PALACE

GEORGE PRICE BLVD

MONDAY MORNING AVE

BALDY SIBUN ST

To George Price Hwy

VICTORIA PEAK ST

BALDY BEACON ST

UNIVERSITY OF BELIZE

GEORGE PRICE CENTRE FOR PEACE AND DEVELOPMENT

PRICE CENTRE RD

ST. PAUL ST

ST. MARY ST

ST. MARTIN AVE

ST. MARK ST

NICARAGUA ST

Cemetery

CHILE ST

CEMETERY RD

VENEZUELA ST

BEN'S BLUFF ST

CADENA MOUNTAIN ST

COOMA CAIM ST

DOYLE'S DELIGHT ST

PEPPER'S PIZZA

GUATEMALA ST

STANN CREEK ST

CAYO ST

0   200 m
0   200 yds

© MOON.COM

with no Internet to distract—now, there's a refreshing concept.

Vegetarian and Vegan
Nutrilicious Corner (E. Ring Rd., next to Paula's Salon, tel. 501/604-8125, 8am-6pm Mon.-Thurs., 8am-5:30pm Fri., US$5) is the current top pick for vegans and vegetarians alike. It's a daily takeout-only buffet, offering a variety of options, including lentil beans, curry rice, soy grind meat, veggie salads, soy burgers, callaloo, and veggie panades, among other dishes. Wash it all down with a fruit smoothie or juice.

ACCOMMODATIONS
If you're staying in downtown Belmopan, you're a businessperson, a diplomat, a development worker—or just overnighting.

US$50-100
★ **KenMar's Bed & Breakfast** (22-24 Half Moon Ave., on the side street behind the Bull Frog Inn, tel. 501/822-0118, www.kenmar.bz, US$85-125) is an adorable, spotless guesthouse, with 10 air-conditioned guest rooms in a large house, each with an en suite bath and plenty of amenities—cable TV, minifridges, coffeemakers, and more; there's also a luxury suite (US$140). Owner Marion Fuller (call her "Miss Mar") has thought of everything, including irons, shower gel bottles, purified water in the guest rooms, and free continental breakfast (if you're lucky, it will include her homemade cinnamon rolls), and she's a gem of a host. There is a very nice common area, a small pool at the back, full Internet access, and sometimes the smell of fresh baking from the kitchen.

Yoli's B&B (30 Haulover Creek, off Constitution Dr., tel. 501/822-2556, US$75) is your authentic homestay experience, where your gregarious Belizean host, Ms. Yoli, rents out three cozy rooms, with air-conditioning and TV, two of which have an en suite private bath. A daily breakfast is included; stay five days and get your laundry done free. There's a lovely garden and porch for some fresh air.

The **Hibiscus Hotel** (Hibiscus Plaza, Melhado Parade, below Corkers Restaurant, tel. 501/633-5323, www.hibiscusbelize.com, US$60) offers six decent-size guest rooms with king beds, flat-screen TVs, air-conditioning, Internet access, and simple baths. The location is convenient for those arriving by bus, just one street over from the hustle and bustle of the bus terminal and Market Square. Half of the profits go to the **Parrot Rescue and Rehabilitation Centre of Belize** (www.belizebirdrescue.com), a nonprofit created by Hibiscus owners and British expats Jerry Larder and Nikki Buxton. Note that there is no check-in possible on Sunday.

US$100-150
There are rave reviews for **The Inn at Twin Palms** (Mile 54, Hummingbird Hwy., tel. 501/822-0231, cell tel. 501/610-2831, tasmithbz@yahoo.com, US$115-125, includes breakfast), a six-room inn seemingly tucked away from the main road and city, yet a close ride to town. It has nicely landscaped grounds and a small swimming pool, with plenty of garden seating areas. The guest rooms, equipped with queen or double beds, are nicely furnished and include all the necessary amenities, including air-conditioning, minifridges, coffeemakers, irons, cable TV, and Wi-Fi. The guesthouse is directly behind a school, and you might occasionally hear the children playing in the yard all afternoon.

The **Bull Frog Inn** (25 Half Moon Ave., tel. 501/822-2111, www.bullfroginn.com, US$97.50 plus tax) has 28 guest rooms that could be mistaken for those of any basic roadside hotel in the United States. The inn reports that 80 percent of its guests are businesspeople doing work for the government or private businesses. The on-site restaurant is solid, and the bar turns into an all-night disco on Thursday.

Jungle Lodges
When they first arrived in Belize more than 30 years ago, Montana cowboy John Carr and his wife, Carolyn, ran ★ **Banana Bank**

Lodge and Belize Horseback Adventure (tel. 501/832-2020, www.bananabank.com, US$150) as a working cattle ranch. Today, most pastures have been converted to fields for growing corn and beans, and the ranch now hosts a lodge. Half of the 4,000-acre ranch is covered in lush rainforest, and within its borders guests will discover not only a wide variety of wildlife but also a small Mayan ruin.

There are five guest rooms in the main house (three share a bath) to accommodate guests, and five cabanas that sleep up to six people each. There's an old-school elegance to the guest rooms, suites, thatched-roof cabanas, dorm rooms, and chalets—no two are alike, and some have beautifully funky bathtubs and Carolyn Carr's stunning paintings of Belizean life, and all are a few steps away from the riverfront. Food is delicious, with breads and pastries baked in-house and served family-style; breakfast is included in the room rates, and lunch (US$10) and dinner (US$15) are available.

With 90 saddle horses in its stables and 25 miles of horse trails, Banana Bank is passionate about guests experiencing horseback riding. John Carr is known for using the horse-whisperer method, and horses are carefully matched to their riders. Ask about moonlight rides, often followed by a riverside bonfire.

Banana Bank is also a place for birdwatching, fishing, hiking, or taking a boat trip down the Belize River, with plenty of time left for a cooling swim in a gorgeous swimming pool. Look for Tikatoo, a beautiful jaguar the Carrs rescued as a cub and have cared for since (they are the only people in the country, besides the Belize Zoo, to have a license to do so). You can take a closer look at Tikatoo in her fenced-off jaguar enclosure right on the lodge grounds. Take photos— she's used to it.

The Carrs are wonderful hosts who will make you feel right at home. Artist and owner Carolyn Carr is considered one of the country's premier artists; be sure to visit her onsite **Galleria Carolina,** on the second floor of the building overlooking the swimming pool. There's also a fascinating museum next to the gallery, showcasing Mayan artifacts found at Banana Bank, among other items.

Next door to Banana Bank Lodge, the **Belize Jungle Dome Hotel Resort** (Mile 47, George Price Hwy., tel. 501/822-2124, www.belizejungledome.com, US$95-165, or US$1,195 4-night all-inclusive) has five guest rooms in a unique geodesic dome setting. The guest rooms are fully equipped with queen beds, air-conditioning, private baths, and wireless Internet, and there is a lovely pool and a separate four-bedroom villa. The Jungle Dome serves three meals daily and caters to all dietary requirements. The resort is a licensed tour operator and runs a full range of tours as well as airport transfers. The owner, Andy Hunt, is a retired British Premier League soccer player.

Banana Bank is located across the Belize River, about 10-15 minutes by car from the George Price Highway. Turn into Roaring Creek by taking the turn next to the big Westar gas station and hotel on the right. You'll come across the Calendar Hamilton Trust Bridge; continue straight to head to the entrance, and two miles in is the actual lodge.

INFORMATION AND SERVICES

For well-stocked supermarkets and drugstores, head to the Belmopan branch of **Brodies** (tel. 501/822-2010 or 501/822-3078, brodiesbmp@btl.net, 8am-7pm Mon.-Sat., 9am-1pm Sun.), or try **The Mall** (Hummingbird Hwy., tel. 501/822-3399, 8am-9pm daily), selling everything from groceries to hair extensions.

Some students and scientists come to Belmopan to do research in the **Belize Archives Department** (26-28 Unity Blvd., tel. 501/822-2097, archives@btl.net, 8am-5pm Mon.-Thurs., closes earlier Fri.), a closed-stacks library popular with both local students and foreign researchers.

Garden City Plaza (Mountain View Blvd., about US$2.50 by taxi from the city center) has a few shops, including **Antonini's Restaurant** (tel. 501/802-0263, 11:30am-8:30pm daily), offering decent fast food and sandwiches, an Internet café, a health food store, and an Atlantic Bank branch.

TRANSPORTATION

If you are traveling Belize by bus, it's nearly impossible *not* to visit Belmopan, as all buses traveling between Belize City and points west and south—even express buses—pull into the main Belmopan terminal for 5-30 minutes as they rustle up new passengers (and the driver takes a break for lunch or a smoke). If you need a local taxi driver while in Belmopan, they are usually parked by Market Square, outside the bus terminal, or standing by the station exit asking every exiting passenger if they need a ride.

Buses leave Belize City to Belmopan (US$2) every 15 minutes 4am-8:30pm daily. Buses from Belmopan to Benque at the Guatemalan border leave every 30 minutes 6:30am-7pm daily. Buses from Belmopan to points south such as Dangriga and Punta Gorda leave hourly 6:30am-7:30pm daily. Arrive at least 30 minutes prior to your departure to line up, if you don't want to risk the bus filling up before you have a chance to get on (it does happen).

For private transfers and vans that can comfortably take you and your group from Belmopan to other points in Belize, I recommend getting in touch with **Belize Transfers** (tel. 501/822-3272, www.belize-transfers.com). It has reliable, friendly drivers and an excellent range of vehicles.

VICINITY OF BELMOPAN

The Hummingbird Highway stretches south from Belmopan to St. Margaret's and farther on to Dangriga. The road was paved only recently and boasts some of the most scenic driving in Central America (in my humble opinion). The drive from Belmopan southeast toward Dangriga is an awesome reminder of just how green and wild Belize really is. Some of the canopy took a hit during Hurricane Richard's strange inland rampage in 2010, but the forest grows quickly in these parts, and it is still most impressive.

The highway passes through towering karst hills and long views of broadleaf rainforest as you cross the Caves Branch Bridge and enter the Valley of Caves. It climbs into the Maya Mountains and then descends toward the sea. The junction with the Southern Highway is 20 miles east of Over the Top Pass, and Dangriga is another five miles from there.

Guanacaste National Park

Located at the T-junction on the George Price Highway where the Hummingbird Highway begins, the 50-acre **Guanacaste National Park** (tel. 501/223-5004, 8am-4:30pm daily, US$2.50 pp) is probably one of the most overlooked small attractions in Belize. Comanaged by the **Belize Audubon Society** (tel. 501/223-4987 or 501/223-5004, www.belizeaudubon.org) and the government, this park gets its name from a massive 360-year-old guanacaste, or *tubroos,* tree that was once on the property. The original tree is no longer living (they had to cut the limbs off for safety), but the park is known for its ceibas, cohune palms, mammee apple, mahogany, quamwood, and other trees as well as wildlife like agoutis, armadillos, coatis, deer, iguanas, jaguarundis, kinkajous, and more than 100 species of birds. Among the rare finds here are resident blue-crowned motmots. The *amate* fig also grows profusely on the water's edge and provides an important part of the howler monkeys' diet. Unfortunately, the park was hit badly by Hurricane Earl in August 2016, losing its swimming deck as well as substantial canopy. Check back in to see if it's in shape again, because if it is, it makes for a great spot for a picnic and a dip—at the quiet spot in the Roaring River just before it enters the Belize River—on your way to or from Belize City.

Roaring River Golf Course

The only functioning golf course in all of Belize is the **Roaring River Golf Course** (Mile 50.5, George Price Hwy., tel. 501/820-2031, www.belizegolfcourses.com), an

Vicinity of Belmopan

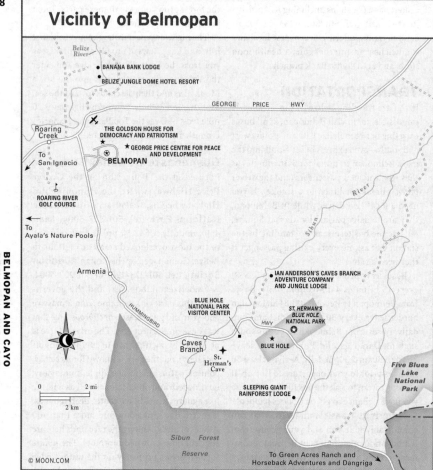

BANANA BANK LODGE

BELIZE JUNGLE DOME HOTEL RESORT

Belize River

GEORGE PRICE HWY

Roaring Creek

To San Ignacio

THE GOLDSON HOUSE FOR DEMOCRACY AND PATRIOTISM

GEORGE PRICE CENTRE FOR PEACE AND DEVELOPMENT

BELMOPAN

ROARING RIVER GOLF COURSE

To Ayala's Nature Pools

River

Armenia

Sibun River

HUMMINGBIRD

IAN ANDERSON'S CAVES BRANCH ADVENTURE COMPANY AND JUNGLE LODGE

BLUE HOLE NATIONAL PARK VISITOR CENTER

ST. HERMAN'S BLUE HOLE NATIONAL PARK

HWY

Caves Branch

St. Herman's Cave

BLUE HOLE

Five Blues Lake National Park

SLEEPING GIANT RAINFOREST LODGE

0   2 mi

0   2 km

Sibun Forest Reserve

To Green Acres Ranch and Horseback Adventures and Dangriga

© MOON.COM

unpretentious executive-type nine-holer (3,892 yards, par 64, slope rating 116). It's a short drive from Belmopan and a worthy activity for anyone staying in an area lodge or resort, whether you're a seasoned slugger or just golf curious (free lessons are offered for beginners). The feel of the course, clubhouse, and restaurant is tranquil, the staff are friendly, and the greens fees are reasonable (US$18 per round or US$25 all-you-can-play).

This is a unique rainforest-golf opportunity by any measure. More than 120 bird species have been identified on and around the property, there are crocodiles in the water hazards, and you'll hear the sound of the nearby river, which flows from Thousand Foot Falls in the Mountain Pine Ridge. After sweating out a round, take a dip in one of the cool, clean, shady pools of the river.

Roaring River Golf Course is well maintained with a level layout and interesting landscaping dividing the fairways; greens boast Bermuda grass, grown from seed. Paul, the South African owner, notes that his course uses chemicals very sparingly, almost not at all—"just a bit of spraying for the ants," he

Guanacaste National Park

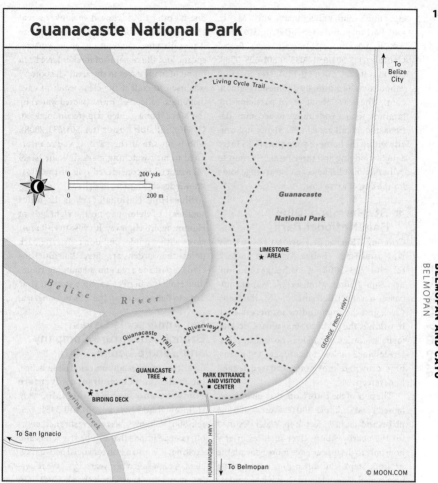

says. The property uses water from a natural spring flowing from within the mountain.

Plant your nongolfing family members in the river for the day while you hit those links. The restaurant **Meating Place** (11am-9pm daily, US$10-20) has earned several "best steak in Belize" comments from reviewers (Paul's wife, Jennie, who hails from South Carolina, cures and ages the meat herself); its top fillet goes for US$18. Make sure to make reservations ahead of time.

Guests can stay in one of four well-furnished **villas** with air-conditioning, Internet access, TVs, queen beds, fridges, coffeemakers, work counters, lounge suites, and stunning back porches over the river. Staying here is a perfect option for someone who really wants to get some early rounds in, or for anyone trapped by an assignment in Belmopan, which is only 10-15 minutes away.

Armenia

Bed-and-breakfast homestay options are sometimes available in several villages up and down the Hummingbird Highway, notably in Armenia. This is a quiet settlement, eight miles south of Belmopan, with a Mayan and Latino population offering **Rock of Excellence Homestays** (call Maria "Betty" Gonzalez, tel. 501/630-7033 or 501/625-0088, community tel. 501/660-1881, sreynosa18@ yahoo.com, hummingbirdhomestay@gmail. com). There are about seven participating families, with a wide range of accommodations, though all are simple, rustic, and usually within the home of your hosts (US$30 for a night's lodging and three meals); it's best to call a day ahead. They can also arrange tours for the day, at extra cost.

★ St. Herman's Blue Hole National Park

Covering 575 acres, **St. Herman's Blue Hole National Park** (Belize Audubon Society, tel. 501/223-5004, www.belizeaudubon. org, 8am-4:30pm Mon.-Fri., US$4) encompasses a water-filled sinkhole, St. Herman's Cave, and the surrounding rainforest. Rich in wildlife, the park harbors jaguars, ocelots, tapirs, peccaries, tamanduas, boa constrictors, fer-de-lance snakes, toucans, crested guans, blue-crowned motmots, and red-legged honeycreepers.

The pool of the **Blue Hole** is an oblong collapsed karst sinkhole, 300 feet across in some places and about 25 feet deep. Water destined for the nearby Sibun River surfaces briefly here only to disappear once more beneath the ground. Steps lead down to the swimming area, a pool 25 feet deep or so. It is a 45-minute hike from the visitors center, or you can cheat and park closer a little farther down the highway. You can also go tubing and caving here.

St. Herman's Cave requires a hike of a little more than 1.5 miles across rugged ground. A flashlight and sturdy, rubber-soled shoes are necessities (you can rent flashlights), and a light windbreaker or sweater is a wise choice in the winter. The trail begins near the changing room. The nearest cave entrance is actually a huge sinkhole measuring nearly 200 feet across, funneling down to about 65 feet at the cave's lip. Concrete steps (laid over the Mayan originals) aid descending explorers. The cave

doesn't offer the advanced spelunker a real challenge, but neophytes can safely explore it to a distance of about one mile. Pottery, spears, and the remains of torches have been found in many caves in the area. The pottery was used to collect the clear water of cave drippings, called *zuh uy ha* (sacred water) by the Maya. For a guided trip (recommended, US$40), call **Job Lopez** (tel. 501/633-7008), who is on-site at the park. If you're interested in bird-watching, park director Israel Manzanero is considered one of the most knowledgeable birders in Belize.

Blue Hole National Park is 12 miles southeast of Belmopan on the right side of Hummingbird Highway. It's wise to visit most caves with a guide, and don't visit the park unless the wardens are there. Amenities include a parking area and a changing room. Blue Hole is a perfect daytime stop on your drive to Belmopan, San Ignacio, or Dangriga.

Ian Anderson's Caves Branch Adventure Company and Jungle Lodge

One of the premier adventure lodges in Belize, **Ian Anderson's Caves Branch Adventure Company and Jungle Lodge** (Mile 41.5, Hummingbird Hwy., tel. 501/610-3451, U.S. tel. 866/357-2698, www.cavesbranch.com) offers expeditions that can be strenuous and exciting; it is also a hub for social active travelers. As Ian said a few years ago, "We're certainly not for everyone—thank God!" On the 58,000 acres of this private estate are 68 known caves, and Ian has discovered and explored them all, developing a variety of trips around many of them. The longest and deepest of these Mayan ceremonial caves extends seven miles. Pristine dry caves glisten with crystal formations. Some caves still have pottery shards, skeletal remains, and footprints coated with an icing of rock crystals. Ian offers **expeditions** (ranging 1-7 days), including tubing trips through river caves.

1: Belize's national flower; 2: view of Sibun River from Sleeping Giant Rainforest Lodge

All expedition guides have received intensive training in cave and wilderness rescue, evacuation, and first aid; they are, in my mind, some of the best guides in the country, in every sense of the term. Popular excursions include the Black Hole Drop—a grueling 1.5-hour hike, followed by an amazing 400-foot rainforest rappel landing at the entrance of an enormous cave—Waterfall Cave expedition, and best tubing in the district. Its honeymoon packages are particularly creative and adventurous.

The lodge offers its brand of "rustic luxury" in its 25 units, which include **rainforest cabanas and suites** (US$169-294), all the way up to spectacular 800-square-foot luxury **tree-house suites** (US$426-591) with views to write home about. The screened accommodations are open to the sights and sounds of the surrounding wildness. Lighting is still by the glow of kerosene lamps and the moon, but flush toilets and hot and cold water are available throughout (actually, the warm "jungle shower" is the highlight of many a guest's stay). The guest rooms have electricity for lights and wicker fans, but there are no outlets or appliances. Additions include a spa, wedding facilities, and a helipad. Guests dine together in the main open-air lodge, where they discuss the day's stories and the next day's plans over family-style meals (breakfast US$8, lunch US$12, dinner US$16, plus taxes).

Also on the property is an **orchid garden** (9am-4pm, free), which has one of the largest collections in the country of orchids native to Central America. Ella Anderson, who oversees the garden, received several of the plants from the older women in the nearby city of Belmopan who were no longer able to care for them. Once a month, these women come by the resort to enjoy the pool and visit the botanical garden to check on their favorite orchids. If you go during spring, you will get to examine the hundreds of blooming flowers here, all carefully labeled for an easy self-guided tour; grab a bench and enjoy the fragrant air. Guides are also available to show you around; stop by the lodge's front desk for more information.

An exciting addition to the lodge is the on-site **Cheese House,** where all of Ian Anderson's signature cheeses are made from scratch. A free tour and tasting takes place every day at 3pm for guests of the lodge. Make sure to peek inside the aging room.

Access to Ian Anderson's Caves Branch is on the Hummingbird Highway between the Blue Hole National Park visitors center and the parking lot for the Blue Hole; turn left (if you're headed south) and continue to the end of the mile-long dirt road. If you're traveling by bus, you'll have to hike in from here if you haven't arranged to be picked up by lodge staff.

Sleeping Giant Rainforest Lodge

What began 20 years ago as the home of David Haas, one of Belize's tourism pioneers, turned into one of the most beautiful rainforest lodges in the Cayo District in 2012. Set on a portion of a private 100,000 acres around the Sibun forest, along one of the cleanest and most picturesque rivers in Belize, ★ **Sleeping Giant Rainforest Lodge** (tel. 786/472-9664, www.vivabelize.com/sleeping-giant, US$299-549) offers a combination of mountain-view suites, riverside casitas, and new river-view units tucked amid lush, exquisitely manicured grounds. The five Mountain View Suites are the most coveted, booked months in advance and for good reason: The view from the outdoor terrace and infinity heated tub over the verdant mountains and "sleeping giant" figure over the Maya Mountains is breathtaking. The 10 Spanish Casitas are no less charming, each one facing a creek along its private veranda with hammocks—easily the perfect place to nap to the sound of streaming water; casita 8 in particular is lovely.

All units are decorated with Belizean hardwood and provide comfort amenities such as king beds, air-conditioning, glass showers, outdoor baths, espresso makers, irons, and minifridges.

Supportive of comfortable but active vacations, the lodge is a great base for hiking excursions—don't miss a sunrise hike to the gazebo for spectacular views of the river and citrus fields—mountain biking the grounds, kayaking the Sibun River solo or with a guide, heading out to nearby caves and Mayan sites for extreme adventures, or simply strolling the manicured grounds and relaxing in the beautiful fountain pool. An on-site restaurant serves excellent meals, from local to international dishes.

San Ignacio

The region from San Ignacio on is referred to as "Cayo" by the locals. Most visitors choose to stay in this area rather than Belmopan, mostly because of the allure of bustling San Ignacio. San Ignacio is a charming town in the heart of Belize's much-visited green and hilly western district—home of Mayan sites and caves amid a lush interior of mountains, rivers, pine forests, waterfalls, and citrus plants. One of Belize's crown jewels of tourism, San Ignacio is popular with locals and visitors alike for its hip, laid-back village feel, its picturesque landscape, a Latin vibe, cheap and authentic eateries, a wide variety of accommodations options—from camping to some of the most upscale jungle lodges in the country—and outdoor activities. The area around San Ignacio is ideal for travelers seeking an outdoors type of getaway and organized activities in Belize's lush rainforest interior. There is plenty to do here, from the mild to the extreme: canoeing the rivers, spelunking, rappelling, exploring archaeological sites and botanical gardens, or sampling authentic Belizean cuisine. Together with the neighboring sister town of Santa Elena, the population here is mostly mestizo—a mix of Mayan and Spanish—and there are sizable Mennonite, U.S., and Chinese expat communities. Spanish is spoken more frequently than Kriol, in addition to English.

ORIENTATION

Driving to San Ignacio from Belize City, you'll first pass through its sister town of Santa Elena, turning right at the Social Security building and continuing across the **Wooden** **Bridge** to the San Ignacio side of the Macal River, close to the open market grounds. From there, turning left will take you directly into "downtown" San Ignacio, marked by a five-road intersection that is nearly always abuzz with activity. **Burns Avenue** crossing here is the main drag for locals and travelers alike. Within two or three blocks in any direction of that intersection, you'll find most of San Ignacio's budget accommodations, restaurants, Internet cafés, and tour operators.

The town's three banks are on the block of Burns Avenue that runs east toward the river from the big intersection, and at the end of that block you'll find a tiny traffic circle in front of the police station, which guards the western abutment of the **Hawksworth** **Bridge.** Built in 1949, the Hawksworth is the only suspension bridge in Belize; it is also the starting line of the big canoe race in March. Normally, only eastbound traffic is allowed on the one-lane bridge from Santa Elena to San Ignacio, except when the lower bridge floods and traffic is diverted, as it was several times in 2008 during the highest recorded river levels since 1961. Any of the roads that lead uphill from downtown San Ignacio will eventually place you back on the George Price Highway heading toward Benque and the Guatemalan border.

SIGHTS
★ Cahal Pech
   Archaeological Site
A 10-minute walk uphill from downtown San Ignacio, **Cahal Pech** is a great tree-shaded destination filled with ancient

Cahal Pech Archaeological Site

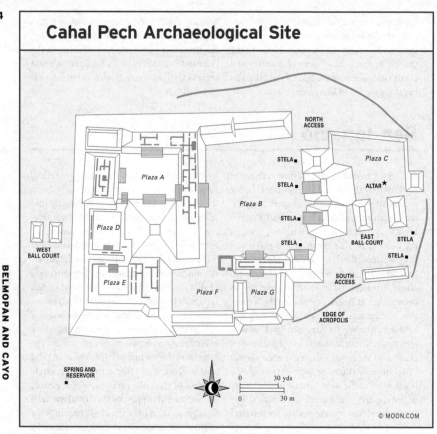

tales. The ruins of Cahal Pech (Place of the Ticks) features an excavated series of plazas and royal residences. The site was discovered in the early 1950s, but research did not begin until 1988, when a team from San Diego State University's anthropology department began work with local archaeology guru Jaime Awe. Thirty-four structures were built in a three-acre area. Excavation is ongoing, and visitors are welcome. It is well worth your trip and admission fee (US$5), paid at the Cahal Pech **visitors center** (tel. 501/824-4236, 8am-5pm daily). The visitors center also houses a small museum of artifacts found at the site, along with a skeleton from Xunantunich.

Nearby **Tipu** was a Christian Mayan town during the early years of colonization. Tipu was as far as the Spanish were able to penetrate in the 16th century.

★ San Ignacio Farmers Market

Every Saturday morning, from dawn through the afternoon, vendors from all of Cayo's villages descend on San Ignacio's market to sell locally grown fruits and vegetables, dairy, Guatemalan spices, meats, clothing, and more. Fresh mestizo food is cooked and sold on-site as well, and everyone comes out to shop and sit and enjoy a brunch of *pupusas*, tacos, empanadas, and tamales. **Pupusería Damaris** sits smack in the center, but there are now two permanent restaurants within the market. **El Fogon** (US$1/taco) is the top pick, with a girl rolling and making fresh

San Ignacio

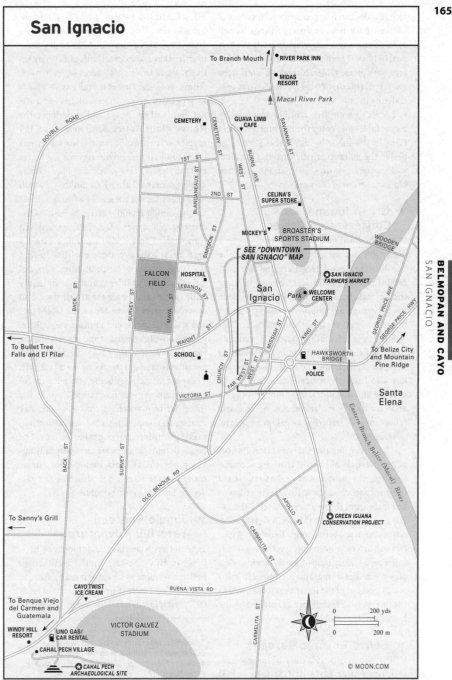

tacos outdoors while you order your choice of chicken, pork, beef, or shrimp fillings, as well as fresh juices and coffee. It's literally the best deal in town. There's a thatch-covered seating area with picnic tables. Next door, a few steps away, is **El rinconcito de Dona Blanca,** specializing in *pupusas.*

Locals sit with their families around long picnic tables and enjoy the live music. Others relax in the shade by the Macal River, just beside the market, or rifle through the tents looking for a new dress. It's San Ignacio's one big social event of the week.

★ Green Iguana Conservation Project

When the local iguana population was in a noticeable downward cycle, the folks at the San Ignacio Resort Hotel created this successful breeding and release project to bring the animals back and protect the riverside from further development. Groups go on hunts for eggs, capture the females, and hijack the eggs, which they raise in a predator-free, food-rich environment before releasing the iguanas back into the wild. The program has also trained former iguana hunters to become iguana guides, a far more profitable and sustainable endeavor, and hosts many school groups, featuring its Adopt an Iguana program.

The Green Iguana Conservation Project and a **medicinal jungle trail** are accessed through the **San Ignacio Resort Hotel** (perched above the Macal River, a short downhill walk from the town center, tel. 501/824-2034 or 501/824-2125, U.S. tel. 855/488-2624, www.sanignaciobelize.com). To date, 175 species of birds have been observed here, including a rare family pair of black hawk eagles, plus a number of mammals. Tours (30 minutes, US$7 pp) of the iguana project as well as the interpretive herbal trail are offered on the hour 7am-4pm daily.

★ Belize Botanic Gardens

Visiting the country's only botanical garden, the **Belize Botanic Gardens** (Chial Rd., tel. 501/834-4800 or 501/824-3101, www.belizebotanic.org, 7am-4pm daily, entrance US$7.50, guided tour US$15 for 1.5-hour tour), makes a wonderful half- or full-day activity. Walk through 45 acres of fruit trees, palms, tropical flowers, and native plants as you learn about the medicinal and ritual plants of the Maya and experience the **Native Plant House,** with more than 100 species of orchids. Botanists' work here has resulted in 20 new orchid records for Belize and one species new to science: *Pleurothallis duplooyii* (named after Ken duPlooy), which has a bloom about the size of a flea. Look out for the vanilla orchid—native to Belize—the original source of the famous flavor enjoyed worldwide. There is also a rainforest trail, a pine forest habitat complete with a 30-foot fire tower, plenty of bird-watching, a special guidebook for children, and a sustainably built visitors center for meetings, yoga, and other activities. There are picnic tables too, and you can easily spend a fun afternoon here, with an on-site restaurant and the river below for a freshwater swim. Call to find out about a shuttle from San Ignacio, or get a taxi ride. There are also classes being offered: a three-day ethnobotany course (US$50 pp/day), a three-day bird-watching course, or one-day courses in composting, plant identification, making fertilizers, among other options. The Belize Botanic Gardens are owned by Judy duPlooy, who sold the adjacent lodge she ran for many years to focus on the running the garden and making it sustainable.

★ Jungle Pontoon Waterfall Adventure

Take in Cayo's spectacular outdoors by hopping on this one-of-a-kind adventure in Belize, as remote as it gets, offered by **Jungle Splash Eco Tours** (Burns Ave., tel. 501/666-0935, www.junglesplashtours.com). Belizean owner Robert dreamed of showing off the

---

1: Belize Botanic Gardens; **2:** Burns Avenue in downtown San Ignacio; **3:** barbecue in Santa Elena; **4:** views of San Ignacio and the hills from Cahal Pech Village

spectacular scenery he grew up around in the Che Chem Ha area, deep in the Maya Mountains and near the Vaca Dam Lake, and he's done a great job. Your adventure begins with an hour-long ride from San Ignacio towards the Hydro Road, Che Chem Ha, and onto the banks of the Vaca Lake. Hop on a pontoon boat that feels like you're on an Indiana Jones adventure, and you'll begin to slowly glide along the water, floating between the Vaca River dam and the Mollejon river dam. The day includes stops at three waterfalls (depending on your physical shape)—one of which will require climbing, but I'll leave that as a surprise. The second and third waterfalls are stunning, including the 60-feet Río Frio and its deep pool. You'll swim in crispy cold waters to your heart's content; tubes are also provided. A barbecue lunch is prepared on board, which you can enjoy on the boat or on a sandbank near the third falls. It won't be long before you wish you weren't going back to civilization.

SPORTS AND RECREATION

Cayo District is home to a beautiful lattice of trails, from short nature walks and medicine trails to a range of hiking trips through the surrounding hills. Mountain biking the Cayo District is fun, beautiful, and a great way to burn off a few Belikins, but it can be dusty in the dry season. Equestrians will find horseback riding at a growing number of jungle lodge resorts and custom tour operators in and around San Ignacio.

Many Cayo resorts offer excellent guided cave trips of varying levels of difficulty, for everyone from the beginning spelunker to the professional speleologist; day and overnight trips are available. Ask about the varied experiences to be had in Actun Tunichil Muknal (worth every penny), Barton Creek Cave, Actun Chapat, Actun Halal (on private property), Chechem Ha Cave, or any of the most recently discovered ones that are as yet unnamed.

Canoeing, kayaking, and tubing are absolute musts and popular ways to enjoy the Macal and Mopan Rivers. One popular trip is to paddle up the Macal River from downtown San Ignacio, making your way to the Ix Chel Rainforest Medicine Trail or Belize Botanic Gardens.

Canoeing and Kayaking

Canoe five miles up the Macal River to Chaa Creek and the Belize Botanic Gardens; pick the vivacious **Andy Tut** (cell tel. 501/610-5593 or 501/634-5441, www.birdinginbelize.com, US$40 pp, includes pickup from San Ignacio) as an excellent canoeing guide stationed at the Crystal Paradise Resort and offering trips along the Macal River as well as river birding; he'll pick you up from San Ignacio.

Cave Tubing

Plop yourself in a tube and float along the stream passing through deep caves (weather and water levels permitting), while admiring the stunning scenery of limestone, pottery shards, and rainforest canopy; your best option is the seven-mile float along the **Caves Branch River.** The original creator of this signature Belize adventure activity is **Ian Anderson's Caves Branch Adventure Company and Jungle Lodge** (Mile 41.5, Hummingbird Hwy., tel. 501/610-3451, U.S. tel. 866/357-2698, www.cavesbranch.com, offered Mon., Wed., and Fri., US$95 pp, minimum 4 people).

Cave tubing inside the cave system at Jaguar Paw also gets great reviews—contact any of the Cayo tour operators to arrange or compare pricing.

Hiking

Right in town is San Ignacio Resort Hotel's **medicinal jungle trail,** easily explored in 30 minutes or for as long as you'd like to examine all the "bush medicine" surrounding you.

Just outside of town, visitors can head over to **The Lodge at Chaa Creek** (tel. 501/824-2037, US$10 pp) for a short riverside hike, highlighting the medicinal plants of the Maya and their uses. The site also boasts the **Blue**

Cayo Guides and Tour Operators

Cayo is famous for both the quantity and quality of its guides, naturalists, and tour operators. Signing up for a tour is as easy as contacting your hotel's front desk or walking up Burns Avenue, where most of Cayo's tour operator offices are located. It's often the same price to book a trip through your hotel as it is directly with the tour company, but if you'd like to handle it on your own, here are a few recommendations.

- **Belizean Sun Tours** (San José de Succotz, tel. 501/601-2630, www.belizeansun.com, US$95) is passionate about preserving Cayo's history and giving visitors an off-the-beaten-track experience. Operator Kenneth Dart is an excellent guide whose Actun Chapat and Actun Halal Caving Adventure begin with a rugged eight-mile Land Rover ride through the rainforest (quite the adventure!), then a hike to several sites, including Actun Chapat, a cave with 60-foot ceilings and huge formations. The Maya used this cave extensively for rituals and left behind altars, terraces, carved faces, and artifacts. These two caves are among the most unique in Belize. Since it's on private property, this is an exclusive trip, and you will be the only people here.

- **Cayo Adventure Tours** (tel. 501/824-3246, www.cayoadventure.com) offers all kinds of day trips in the area, including horseback riding and mountain biking (both US$75).

- **David's Adventure Tours** (tel. 501/804-3674, cell tel. 501/628-2837, davidstoursbz@gmail.com) is one of the old standbys, offering volumes of local knowledge and the full range of tours, including canoe trips (US$15-50 pp), birding (US$30 pp), and an overnight rainforest tour (US$75 pp).

- **Hun Chi'ik Tours** (tel. 501/670-0746 or 501/600-9192, www.hunchiik.com, US$85-90) has experienced guides and a creative range of trips. The company is conscious of the importance of "oral tradition and local knowledge" to enhance the educational value of its tours.

- **Pacz Tours** (30 Burns Ave., tel. 501/824-0536, www.pacztours.net, cave trip US$110 pp, Tikal US$150) is the number-one tour operator in town, offering the Actun Tunichil Muknal cave trip as well as overnight camping options with some combination of river running, a waterfall, ruins, rappelling, and caves—always with fun cultural stops along the way. It is also the only licensed guide to camp overnight at Caracol. Walk-in prices are a little less than online, but you risk not getting your preferred tour dates as Pacz sells out fast. When major U.S. film crews come to town—National Geographic, Discovery, Travel Channel—they call Pacz.

- **Paradise Expeditions' Tut brothers** (Crystal Paradise Resort, cell tel. 501/610-5593 or 501/634-5441, www.birdinginbelize.com, US$40 pp, includes pickup from San Ignacio) specializes in canoeing, horseback riding, and birding, for an off-the-beaten-track fun journey into the rainforest.

- **River Rat** (tel. 501/628-6033 or 501/661-4562, www.riverratexpeditions.com) specializes in Actun Tunichil Muknal, kayak expeditions, and overnight float trips.

- **Yute Expeditions** (Burns Ave., opposite Hotel Casa Blanca, tel. 501/824-4321, yuteexp@btl.net, www.inlandbelize.com, cave trip US$90 pp for 2, includes equipment, entrance fees, and lunch; half-day Xunantunich trip US$45 pp) is run by a very experienced Cayo family. It's especially good for families and groups and has a top-notch fleet of air-conditioned vehicles.

Morpho Butterfly Breeding Center and the **Chaa Creek Natural History Museum,** with exhibit areas that examine ecosystems, geology, and Mayan culture in the Cayo area.

Love exploring on foot? A nice walk is from San Ignacio town to the Hawksworth Bridge and crossing over into **Santa Elena,** with lovely views of the Macal River and everyday life as you go along.

Horseback Riding

Book your horseback riding trip with **Andy**

Bush Medicinal Trails

the "hot lips" medicinal plant

Belize's rainforests are home to hundreds of trees, plants, fruits, and vines that have traditionally been used for medicinal purposes. "Bush medicine" in Belize dates back to the days of the Maya, thousands of years ago, when they relied on nature both to survive and to cure their ailments. Sadly, the number of living bush doctors and practitioners has declined, particularly since the 1996 death of Cayo's great Elijio Panti, Belize's most respected Mayan healer.

Medicinal plants are everywhere today—in the rainforests and in gardens, even alongside the highway—though less abundantly. Belizeans continue to use the same plants for medicinal

Tut (cell tel. 501/610-5593 or 501/634-5441, half-day US$45 pp for 2 people)—a reliable local guide to have whether you're a novice or advanced rider; his energy and laughter are contagious. He'll pick you up from San Ignacio and you'll ride through the Cristo Rey Village, stopping at a waterfall to cool off.

Mountain Equestrian Trails (Mile 8, Chiquibul Rd., tel. 501/669-1124, www. metbelize.com, half-day and full-day rides US$61-90) is the area's premier riding center, with one of the biggest trail systems in the Pine Ridge.

Cayo Adventure Tours (tel. 501/824-3246, www.cayoadventure.com, US$75) also offers horseback riding trips.

Swimming

Who doesn't love a cool dip in fresh water,

along with a picnic on a sunny afternoon? On the weekends in particular, you'll spot local families and children splashing about along the banks of the **Macal River.** Some swing from a tree branch, and others sit on the grass to contemplate their beautiful district. Another wonderful river, safe and even cleaner to swim in, is the **Mopan River.**

Birding

The Cayo District has an abundance of bird-life, and it's almost impossible to go wrong wherever you choose to roam—over 300 species have been spotted within 10 miles of San Ignacio. But the best way to increase your sighting odds is to explore with the best guides in the area. Contact **Paradise Expeditions' Tut brothers** (Crystal Paradise Resort, cell tel. 501/610-5593 or 501/634-5441, www.

purposes, as many were raised learning of the benefits as well as the dangers of the rainforest. There are plants for ailments ranging from sunburn, cough, and toothache to male impotency.

Exploring the various medicinal trails in Cayo, you'll learn about the rainforest and various plant and tree uses. Knowing what's in your backyard can come in very handy when there's no pharmacy nearby. You'll also hear fascinating stories from your local guides and even children about their own healing experiences, passed on from their parents and grandparents, and some of the amusing names given to these plants.

- **Calico Jack's Village** (Mountain Pine Ridge, tel. 501/832-2478, www.calicojacksvillage.com) has a guided walk of its "Ancient Jungle Garden Trail," one of the most informative and entertaining tours around. Learn about the "tourist plant," or red gumbo-limbo (*Bursera simaruba*), whose tree bark looks just like peeling red skin and is used to treat sunburn.

- **The Lodge at Chaa Creek** (tel. 501/824-2037, 8am-4pm daily, guided tour US$10 pp, self-guided US$5) features many of the medicinal plants Elijio Panti used in his practice and offers a historical background on his achievements. Guided hour-long tours run every hour on the hour, or you can walk the trail on a self-guided tour.

- **Nu'uk Che'il Cottages and Hmen Herbal Center** (Maya Centre, near Cockscomb, tel. 501/533-7043, nuukcheil@yahoo.com, entrance US$2.50) is about a two-hour drive from Belmopan. Owned and operated by Aurora Garcia Saqui, niece of the late Elijio Panti, it features a four-acre botanical garden, a medicinal trail, herbs for sale, and seminars on herbal medicine.

- **San Ignacio Resort Hotel** (above the Macal River, downhill from the town center, tel. 501/824-2034, U.S. tel. 855/488-2624, www.sanignaciobelize.com, US$5) offers another great medicinal trail, where you can take a 30-minute guided tour (9am, noon, 1pm, and 4pm daily).

To learn more about bush medicine, pick up a copy of *Sastun: My Apprenticeship with a Maya Healer* by Rosita Arvigo, about her decadelong apprenticeship with Elijio Panti, or *Rainforest Remedies: 100 Healing Herbs of Belize* by Rosita Arvigo and Michael Balick.

birdinginbelize.com), who offer multiple bird-watching tours in the area for all levels of birders; ask them about birding at Aguacate Lagoon. You can also do it solo and head to the Botanic Gardens, rainforest trails, and expert on-site birding guides for advice.

Marie Sharp Culinary Class

Rest your bones from all the outdoor adventures and sign up for a Belizean cooking class. Hosted inside the **Marie Sharp Tourist Center** (Rainforest Haven Inn, rainforesthavens@gmail.com, 9am-noon and 4pm-7pm Mon.-Sat., US$50pp for three-hour class/minimum 2 people), owned by Ms. Sharp's granddaughter, this class will show you how to make some local specialties, from fry jacks to stew chicken, in a start-of-the-art kitchen. You'll get a complimentary bottle of

rum at the end of your class, as well as recipes and photos of you in action.

Massage and Bodywork

Right in San Ignacio, you can find reasonably priced massages, pedicures, manicures, facials, and body waxing at **Gretel's Salon and Spa** (Joseph Andrews Dr., above Western Dairies, tel. 501/824-4888 or 501/604-1126, gkuylen@yahoo.com, 8:30am-7pm Mon.-Fri., closes later Sat., 1-hour massage US$37.50, wash and blow dry US$17.50), a locally owned and oriented beauty salon.

Of course, there are full spa services at some of the upscale resorts in the area, notably **Hilltop Spa** (US$85-105) at the Lodge at Chaa Creek; combine a visit here with a trip to the nearby botanic gardens or a paddle on the river. **Ka'ana Resort and Spa** (Mile

69.25, George Price Hwy., tel. 501/824-3350, U.S. tel. 305/735-2553, www.kaanabelize.com, US$80-150) offers massages, facials, and body scrubs with homegrown brown sugar, cacao, and coffee; it also offers energy work with a Mayan healer.

ENTERTAINMENT AND EVENTS

Nightlife

In San Ignacio you can find somewhere to go for a drink after a long day exploring the countryside. It's a small town, so locating the buzz is not difficult; just follow the masses as they trek between bars, or ask around for the latest. Thursday-Saturday are the most popular nights. Start your evening with a happy-hour cocktail on Burns Avenue. For a more upscale bar scene, head to the **San Ignacio Resort Hotel** (above the Macal River, tel. 501/824-2034, www.sanignaciobelize.com, noon-midnight daily). Post-dinner, the bar at **D Catch** (corner Bullet Tree Rd. and Joseph Andrews Dr., tel. 501/653-0332, dcatchbelize@ gmail.com, 11am-midnight daily) has a nice atmosphere and cocktails, with tunes playing in the air-conditioned room.

On weekends, the **Cahal Pech Village** bar (tel. 501/824-3740, noon-midnight Thurs.-Sat.) is buzzing with locals and travelers hanging out poolside, with lovely views of the Cayo hills at night and a boom box playing all the latest tunes. Ask for bartender Oscar's signature Belizean Snow cocktail; he won the 2009 Best Bartender title at the annual Taste of Belize event.

For some dancing or late drinks, you can try the only real nightclub in San Ignacio, **Club Next** (inside Princess Casino, no phone, 9pm-2am Thurs.-Sat.), though it gets smoky inside. Across the street is the popular chain **Thirsty Thursdays** (Apollo St. and Buena Vista Rd., tel. 501/824-2727, www. thirstythursdaybelize.com, 5pm-midnight Wed.-Thurs. and Sun., 5pm-2am Fri.-Sat.,

1: tubing on a river; 2: rappelling into a rainforest in Cayo

US$4-14), set back in a lush garden with a *palapa* bar, with plenty of seating and a front wooden deck to dance to reggae and international beats played by a resident DJ. Avoid **Blue Angel's** in town (Post Office Rd., no phone, 10pm-2am Fri.-Sat.); it gets dicey late at night, and there have been stabbings and scuffles.

Festivals and Events

Belize's biggest sporting event is **La Ruta Maya Belize River Challenge** (www. larutamaya.bz), an exciting and convivial canoe race held during the first week of March and timed to coincide with National Heroes and Benefactors Day (formerly Baron Bliss Day) celebrations. If you are in San Ignacio for the start of the race, you'll watch 100 teams of paddlers mass together in the Macal River, then bolt downstream—racing five days down the 173-mile length of the Belize River all the way to Belize City. Crowds gather all around the river, and it makes for one lively event. Increasingly popular since its inception in 1998, La Ruta Maya has many divisions to compete in, including women's, mixed gender, amateur, dory, and pleasure craft, and it offers more than US$15,000 in prize money. The race is part athletic event, part tourism draw, and several parts fiesta.

Organized by the Belize Cycling Association (www.belizecycling.com), Belize's **Annual Holy Saturday Cross-Country Cycling Classic** takes place every year on the Saturday before Easter Sunday. Teams race from Belize City all the way to the hills of Cayo, passing through the twin towns of San Ignacio and Santa Elena, and back.

SHOPPING

There are small gift and supply shops along Burns Avenue in San Ignacio, but the best shopping in the area (some would say in all of Belize) is a few miles east of San Ignacio at **Orange Gifts & Gallery** (Mile 60, George Price Hwy., tel. 501/824-3296, www. orangegifts.com, 7:30am-5:30pm Mon.-Fri.). Orange Gifts (there's also a shop in San Pedro) has an enormous collection of original and imported arts and crafts, including the custom hardwood furniture and the art of proprietor Julian Sherrard. You'll also find jewelry, paintings, textiles, and practical items for travelers like laminated maps, books, postcards, and Gallon Jug Coffee. Orange has an excellent restaurant and bar.

Across the highway from Orange, **Hot Mama's Belize** (Mile 60, George Price Hwy., tel. 501/824-0444, www.hotmamasbelize.com, 9am-5pm daily) makes some fine and spicy condiments. Gift packages and other sundries, as well as tours, are available.

Gifts from Mayaland (tel. 501/661-1952, 11am-6pm daily) is tucked in a wooden shack across from the market and is well worth the find for its made-in-Cayo gifts from various local artists, including handmade bath soaps and Mayan crafts. Look for Linda's section of the store, **Riverbend Wines & Condiments,** and get a bottle of her tropical fruit wines—organic and made at her farm in Camalote village. Flavors are seasonal and include golden plum and blackberry wine, honey mead, and even a tangy mango liqueur she calls Mangoluah.

To sample Belizean music and take some home, **Venus Photos and Records** (6 Hudson St., across from the post office, tel. 501/824-2101, 8am-6pm Mon.-Sat., closed for lunch Mon.-Fri.) has a good selection.

FOOD
Belizean
Erva's (4 Far West St., tel. 501/824-2821, 8am-10pm Mon.-Sat., US$3-10) has dished out reasonably priced Belizean food for many ears. Dine inside or out on the patio and choose from breakfast, stew chicken, rice and beans, burritos, and a full menu of comfort dinners, including chicken cordon bleu. Prepare to wait, as everything is prepared from scratch.

A more popular pick, in my opinion, is ★ **Cenaida's Belizean Food** (West St., tel. 501/631-2526, 11am-4pm and 5:30pm-9pm daily, US$4), just steps away, with a lovely screened, immaculate, and red-colored

dining room where the service is friendly and the daily Belizean dishes delicious and cheap (they also make some of the best pico de gallo sauce I've tasted). Options vary, from fajitas to seafood. The plating is lovely too, in case presentation matters to you.

El Fogon (inside San Ignacio Market) has delicious, fresh-made and hand-rolled as you watch tacos, with a variety of fillings, as well as fresh juices. It's the best deal in town if you're looking to eat and go quickly or are on a tight budget.

Ko-Ox-Han-Nah (5 Burns Ave., tel. 501/824-3014, 6am-9pm daily, US$5-16), which means "let's go eat," is one of the most popular local restaurants, offering Belizean fare with daily specials, plus a large cosmopolitan menu that includes Asian, Indian, and vegetarian dishes along with an ample wine list, all prepared with organic ingredients and meat raised by the owner. Portions are sizable for the price, and the food is excellent.

★ **Pop's** (tel. 501/824-3266, 6:30am-1pm daily, US$3-6) may be the closest Belize comes to a small-town American-style diner, with booths, bottomless cups of coffee, and customers watching the news and talking religion and politics—except Pop's is owned by a 100 percent Belizean Hemingway look-alike; the delicious breakfast is the best in Cayo. It is so popular that the place expanded from its small, noisy diner size to a larger, more comfortable and modern diner-style space—but the breakfast remains unbeatable in San Ignacio.

Mestizo
San Ignacio has a higher-than-average number of cheap mestizo fast-food places—a mix of Mayan and Spanish dishes—and a few *pupuserías* serving El Salvadoran *pupusas:* fried tortillas stuffed with beans, cheese, and meat for good measure. Check out the row of shacks across from the Welcome Center. Saturday morning at the market, very early, is the best bet for cheap eats, as organic farmers, local cooks, and produce vendors congregate at the outdoor space. This is the best place to chow

Downtown San Ignacio

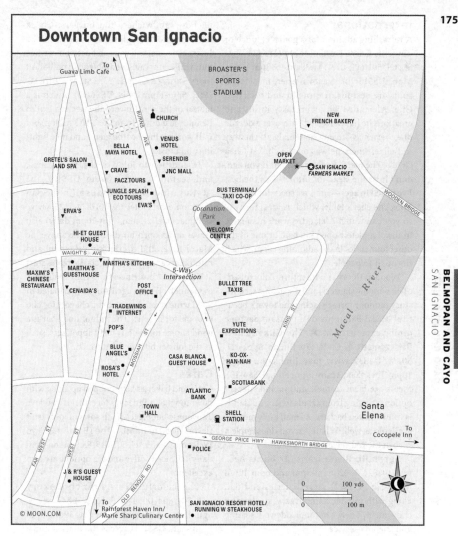

To
Guava Limb Cafe

BROASTER'S
SPORTS
STADIUM

BURNS AVE

CHURCH

VENUS
HOTEL

BELLA
MAYA HOTEL

SERENDIB

GRETEL'S SALON
AND SPA

CRAVE

JNC MALL

NEW
FRENCH BAKERY

OPEN
MARKET

SAN IGNACIO
FARMERS MARKET

WOODEN BRIDGE

PACZ TOURS

JUNGLE SPLASH
ECO TOURS

EVA'S

BUS TERMINAL/
TAXI CO-OP

ERVA'S

Coronation
Park

HI-ET GUEST
HOUSE

WELCOME
CENTER

WAIGHT'S   AVE

Macal   River

MAXIM'S
CHINESE
RESTAURANT

MARTHA'S
GUESTHOUSE

MARTHA'S KITCHEN

5-Way
Intersection

CENAIDA'S

POST
OFFICE

BULLET TREE
TAXIS

KING ST

TRADEWINDS
INTERNET

POP'S

YUTE
EXPEDITIONS

MOSSIAH ST

BLUE
ANGEL'S

CASA BLANCA
GUEST HOUSE

KO-OX-
HAN-NAH

ROSA'S
HOTEL

SCOTIABANK

ATLANTIC
BANK

Santa
Elena

TOWN
HALL

SHELL
STATION

To
Cocopele Inn

FAR WEST ST

WEST ST

GEORGE PRICE HWY   HAWKSWORTH BRIDGE

POLICE

J & R'S GUEST
HOUSE

OLD BENQUE RD

0   100 yds

0   100 m

To
Rainforest Haven Inn/
Marie Sharp Culinary Center

SAN IGNACIO RESORT HOTEL/
RUNNING W STEAKHOUSE

© MOON.COM

BELMOPAN AND CAYO
SAN IGNACIO

down on fresh eats before catching a bus to other regions or even before your next activity. Fresh *pupusas,* tacos, barbecued meats, and more are made on-site, and locals come here to eat all day long on shared picnic tables.

Mickey's (7 Burns Ave., no phone, 11am-9pm daily, from US$1), a small joint next door to Hannah's Restaurant, serves up excellent Creole dishes, made fresh and served quickly. The rice and beans are delicious, and

there's always a daily special. It gets crowded with locals at lunchtime, all the validation you need. Right next to Mickey's is a similar "fast-food" shack, **Mincho's** (Burns Ave., no phone, 11am-6pm daily), serving mestizo grub from *garnaches* to tacos and *panades* (3 for US$0.50) and the best fresh-squeezed juice (US$1) you'll find anywhere in town—choose among papaya, lime, watermelon, coconut water, and more.

International

A refreshing addition for a gourmet lunch or dinner is **Crave House of Flavors** (24 West St., tel. 501/602-0737, 11:30am-9:30pm Wed.-Mon., US$10-20), in a town where most lunch spots are best for running in and back out. Chef Alejandro whips up tasty meals and creations he has perfected with over a decade of experience—from Guatemala all the way to Belize, where he was once a chef at Chaa Creek. The menu varies daily, but if you can, don't miss the steak for dinner—it's the best I've tasted in ages—and save space for dessert. Book the chef's table, which is ideal for two, so you can watch Alejandro work his magic in the completely open kitchen, or one of the other four tables in the adjoining room, which fits up to 15 people.

Wooden floors and furniture, colorful art, open window shutters, and a spacious second-story outdoor terrace facing the town's beautiful Macal Park provide a pleasant daytime dining experience at ★ **The Guava Limb Restaurant & Café** (79 Burns Ave., tel. 501/824-4837, www.guavalimb.com, 11am-10pm Tues.-Sat., 11am-10pm Sun., US$4-13). Meals are farm-to-table and include decent options ranging from salads to jerk quesadillas and chicken baskets. A small kid's menu is available as well. Whatever you do, sample a slice of the red velvet cheesecake.

Serendib Restaurant (27 Burns Ave., tel. 501/824-2302, 6am-3pm and 6pm-10pm Mon.-Sat., US$12) serves curries and dal, along with reliable hamburgers, steaks, and chow mein. There's outdoor sidewalk seating and friendly service.

Martha's Kitchen (10 West St., tel. 501/804-3647, 7am-midnight daily, US$4-8) has some good pizza, plus a full menu that includes stir-fried vegetables, T-bone steak with gravy and fries, and a simple club sandwich.

Eva's (22 Burns Ave., tel. 501/804-2267, www.evasrestaurant.aguallos.com, 6:30am-10:30pm Wed.-Mon., US$5-12) is the hub of Burns Avenue—a place for sidewalk people-watching along with hearty breakfasts and, later in the day, Latin comfort dishes like

nachos, sandwiches, and burgers. Check out the patio through the back door; there's Internet access, and you can book tomorrow's tour while you wait. For ambience, you'll want to try **Sanny's Grill** (E. 23rd St., tel. 501/824-2988, 6pm-11pm daily, US$6-10), which is a bit out of the way (toward the western exit to Benque, just down from the UNO station) but well worth it for the fine menu and nice lighting and music.

In addition to juicy steaks, pork chops, and seafood entrées (from US$10), the ★ **Running W Steakhouse** (in the San Ignacio Resort Hotel, tel. 501/824-2125, www.sanignaciobelize.com, 7am-10pm daily) also serves up an open-air dining patio above the Macal River and overlooking the pool and rainforest canopy. Belizean classic plates start at US$5 and feature beef from the restaurant's own ranch. Try the aged Angus marinated in a red wine reduction, and the chayote (or cho cho) pie for dessert. The indoor hotel bar is a good choice for equally tasty appetizers, such as the lobster bites or fried conch.

Cafés

Cafés and bakeries have popped up along with downtown San Ignacio's face-lift. If you love Taiwanese bubble tea in all sorts of local fruit flavors, head to **Bambu Tee** (Booth #3, Cayo Welcome Center, tel. 501/615-8327, noon-9pm daily); the iced coffee and tea options are also excellent.

The colorful **New French Bakery** (tel. 501/804-0054 or 501/620-0841, www.aguallos.com/frenchbakery, 6:30am-6pm Mon.-Sat., US$1) is across the market and a stone's throw from the Welcome Center. It serves fresh-baked breads, all sorts of pastries—from tasty beef patties to doughnuts, cheese croissants, pizza slices, and apple turnovers—and has ample seating, both on an outdoor terrace and indoors. There's regular fresh coffee daily—good enough to wash down your snacks.

Barbecue

The best barbecue cooks set up in Santa Elena,

just over the Hawksworth Bridge. They cater especially to weekend party crowds, offering grilled mounds of meat, rice, and beans used by many customers to soak up all that beer sloshing around in their stomachs. Most swear by the chicken at **Boiton's Bar-B-Q and House of Pastries** (23 George Price Hwy., Santa Elena, tel. 501/804-0403, 10:30am-9pm Tues. and Thurs.-Sat., 5pm-close Wed. and Sun., US$8), just after the bridge entrance, and others are loyal to **Rodriguez** (no phone, 11am-5pm daily, US$2.50), just a couple of blocks farther up—a more casual experience where your crispy chicken is served on a piece of foil and bench tables are shared.

Chinese

Maxim's Chinese Restaurant (23 Far West St., lunch and dinner daily, US$10) is a family-run café with a good reputation among the locals. Prices are moderate; you won't pay much for the best meal in the house and a beer.

Dessert

For ice cream, there's longtimer **Cayo Twist** (near the western exit to town, nearly across from the UNO station, tel. 501/667-7717, 6pm-9:30pm Thurs.-Sun.), which has delicious soy ice cream. The **Ice Cream Shoppe** (24 West St., tel. 501/634-6160, icecreambelize@gmail.com, 11am-8:30pm Mon.-Fri., 11:00am-9:30pm Sat.-Sun.) is a favorite for creamier treats. A stone's throw from the market, the popular Mennonite-owned chain **Western Dairies** (tel. 501/223-2374, 9am-5pm Mon.-Sat.) sells locally made ice cream by the cone or by the tub; there's also thick pepperoni pizza available by the slice (US$2).

Groceries

Across from the Belize Tourism Industry Association, **Celina's Super Store** (43 Burns Ave., tel. 501/824-2247, cell tel. 501/669-1222, celinasbz@yahoo.com, 8am-noon and 1pm-6pm Mon.-Sat.) is the largest, best-equipped supermarket in town, but there are many other Chinese shops scattered around as well.

ACCOMMODATIONS

Choices abound for such a small town; there are many cheap, clean, converted family homes, most within a few blocks of one another. Cayo can get hot at times, but remember that it's generally cooler than the rest of the country, so air-conditioning may not be a big priority, especially October-February. Also, note that most (but not all) accommodations in Cayo quote prices with tax and service charges included; most also offer deep discounts in low season and for multiple nights. The rates quoted in this chapter, as in the rest of the book, are high-season double-occupancy rates only.

Under US$25

The **Hi-Et Guest House** (West St., tel. 501/824-2828, thehiet@yahoo.com, http:// hietguesthouse.aguallos.com/index.htm, US$12.50-25) is an excellent option built right into the owner's large home. The five guest rooms with shared baths and cold water are clean and comfortable and have hardwood floors. The five guest rooms with private baths in the next building are a big step up in quality and not much in price—they're well-kept and have tiled floors and balconies but no air-conditioning. There's a common area with a fridge and seating, and Wi-Fi access is included.

Find quiet, friendly lodging at **J & R's Guest House** (20 Far West St., tel. 501/626-3604, jrguesthouse@yahoo.com, US$10-23); there are four guest rooms, two with private baths, and breakfast is included, for now. It may be a bit tricky to find, but once you do, it's amazing how close it is to town—just a couple of minutes' walk downhill.

US$25-50

One of the best-value midrange hotels is the well-located **Casa Blanca Guest House** (10 Burns Ave., tel. 501/824-2080, www.casablancaguesthouse.com, US$30-50, with a/c US$50-70), where Ms. Betty keeps eight immaculate, cozy guest rooms with private baths, hot and cold water, and TVs as well as access to a beautiful common living room, kitchen, balcony, and rooftop deck. It's on Burns Avenue near the banks and across from Hannah's Restaurant.

Rosa's Hotel (65 Hudson St., tel. 501/804-2265, www.rosashotelbelize.com, rosashotel@yahoo.com, US$28-38, breakfast included) has a selection of guest rooms with private baths and fans or air-conditioning; guest rooms range from small and stuffy to high and airy—check out a few before deciding, and check the door locks: Some show wear and tear. A better pick, right over the bridge into Santa Elena and walking distance from town, is ★ **Cocopele Inn** (tel. 501/620-3055), an "inn with character," friendly service, and a variety of rooms that range from economy rooms (US$39.50) to standard and deluxe rooms (US$50). Some boast either air-conditioning or fan, and others include free laundry, Wi-Fi, cable TV, and a shared kitchen. All rooms have private baths.

A longtime standard is **Venus Hotel** (Burns Ave., tel. 501/824-3203, www.venushotelbelize.com, US$33-48), right in the middle of town with 32 decent guest rooms with private baths; take your pick of those overlooking the park or the street.

US$50-100

Martha's Guesthouse (10 West St., tel. 501/804-3647, www.marthasbelize.com, US$65-90) continues to offer a tasteful atmosphere in the center of San Ignacio town, with an abundance of common lounging areas for guests to mingle in. The 16 guest rooms have hardwood floors and furniture, private baths, fans, hot water, wireless Internet access, and cable TV. Laundry services are available. There's a decent restaurant downstairs that has outdoor patio seating, and the front desk can arrange tours. Martha's just expanded into a six-room annex, about a three-minute walk up Burns Avenue, with beautiful apartment-style options, several with kitchenettes and porches (US$50-65, weekly rates available).

A new fair deal in town is **Rainforest Haven Inn** (2 Victoria St., tel. 501/674-1984, www.rainforesthavens.com, US$58.50-74.50), offering five rooms with double beds, air-conditioning, TV, minifridge, Wi-Fi, iron, and phone. There's a shared lounge area, a large communal kitchen fully equipped, as well as a rooftop with views over San Ignacio. There's a culinary center and rum tasting bar on the ground floor.

If you love being in the middle of the action and street buzz, there's **Bella Maya Hotel** (36 Burns Ave., US$65-70, includes continental breakfast). it offers 16 simple and modern standard to deluxe rooms with air-conditioning, TV, and private baths. The third floor has a cozy rooftop, and a pool is on the way, as well as additional rooms.

★ **Clarissa Falls Resort** (tel. 501/833-3116, cell tel. 501/668-6979, http://clarissafallsresort.aguallos.com) is at the end of a mile-long dirt road, accessed on the right at Mile 70.5 on the George Price Highway. I fell in love with the grounds when I first visited. This is an intimate, laid-back, and affordable lodge. Whether you hang out by the outdoor dining area or swing in a hammock in the yard by your cabana, you can listen to and enjoy the view of the cascading water below. You can walk down just a few steps to the waterfall and the Mopan River for a swim, or tube down the stream. Guests can camp in their own tents (US$7.50 pp), stay in a cottage with private bath (US$38 pp), or choose a suite (US$175 per night). The shared toilet and shower building has hot and cold water and is cement-basic. Don't miss the nature trails and a hike (or horseback ride) to Xunantunich, the highest pyramid visible from the cottages. The dining room serves tasty food, including a few specialties such as black mole soup and great cheap Mexican-style tacos or stuffed squash (US$6-9). You'll get much bang for your buck at Clarissa Falls.

US$100-150

Only a two-minute drive from San Ignacio, **Cassia Hill Resort** (George Price Hwy., tel. 501/824-2017, www.cassiahillbelize.com,

US$99-129) sits on its own lovely rise, just above the George Price Highway. You'll find 25 well-appointed, clean, air-conditioned deluxe cottages and standard guest rooms with private baths, hot and cold water, ceiling fans, private verandas with hammocks, an infinity swimming pool, a fitness center, and a recreation room complete with a TV, a bar, table tennis, and darts. Cassia Hill specializes in tours and multiday packages with meal plans. Guests enjoy canoeing, caving, horseback riding, nature tours, and hiking trails. Meals are served in the casual thatched-roof Black Orchid Restaurant.

Talk about a vista! ★ **Cahal Pech Village** (Cahal Pech Hill, tel. 501/824-3740, www.cahalpech.com, US$116-163) offers a variety of guest rooms and cabanas spread out on a spacious hillside with stunning views of San Ignacio and the valley below. The 21 guest rooms have private baths and air-conditioning, or choose a thatch-and-wood cabana overlooking the hills, with a private bath, hot and cold water, and a screened porch with a hammock. There are third-level suites, from which the already amazing views of Cayo are now jaw-dropping, with a 180-degree wraparound balcony—you can see San Ignacio, Santa Elena, and even Spanish Lookout in the distance. Cahal Pech is ideal for groups, families, and retreats. A restaurant, a lively bar, and a creative swimming pool round out the resort, in addition to its quick access to the Cahal Pech ruins down the hill. The road leading up to Cahal Pech is just a little rough, but it's well worth it. The resort also sells water taxi tickets to the Cayes and has an on-site tour-operating company as well as an on-call masseuse, Flor (1-hour Swedish US$55).

US$200-300

The **San Ignacio Resort Hotel** (tel. 501/824-2034, U.S. tel. 855/488-2624, www.sanignaciobelize.com, US$240) is proud of having hosted Queen Elizabeth in 1994 and has never stopped improving the property toward the luxury side of things. From the grand marble lobby and reception hall to the bar lobby and the lap pool and range of services, this is definitely an excellent upscale option that is both in town and a tad remote-feeling. The hotel is perched above the Macal River and a short downhill walk to the town center (it feels longer walking back uphill). There are 24 deluxe air-conditioned guest rooms, some with their own secluded balconies; the guest rooms have private tiled baths, TVs, comfy furniture, and phones. There is also a honeymoon suite on the second floor. The hotel hosts the Running W Steakhouse & Restaurant, one of the best fine dining spots in town; a rainforest-view patio deck ideal for bird-watching; a tennis court; a disco; a casino (bring ID); and convention and wedding facilities. Bird-watching tours are available with the on-site guide, who can also show you the Green Iguana Conservation Project and medicinal jungle trail on the hotel's grounds (tours on the hour).

Ka'ana Resort and Spa (Mile 69.25, George Price Hwy., tel. 501/824-3350, U.S. tel. 305/735-2553, www.kaanabelize.com, US$315) opened in 2007, a few miles west of San Ignacio. Ka'ana is a small, full-service boutique resort with 15 guest rooms and 10 fully equipped casitas, luxurious one- and two-bedroom pool villas, around a larger swimming pool, spa, and lounge. The restaurant (7am-9pm daily, dinner entrées US$12-33) and bar offer an elite departure from the standard fare in San Ignacio; at the bar, try the sweet corn colada (cocktails US$5-12). There are tastings held at 7pm each evening in the well-stocked climate-controlled wine cellar. You can also sign up for a Mayan cooking class.

Camping

Smith's Family Farm (13 Branch Mouth Rd., tel. 501/604-2227, www.smithsfamilyfarm.com) is a peaceful 25-acre retreat up Branch Mouth Road with a shaded campground (US$5 per night) and a collection of cabins (US$25-40), all with private baths, hot and cold water, and simple furniture. Weekly rates are available, and the owner, Roy, sometimes lets you trade labor on his organic farm for a stay at the place. On the same road, just past the Midas Resort, **River Park Inn** (13 Branch Mouth Rd., tel. 501/824-2116, www.riverparkinnbelize.com, US$20) is a 15-minute walk from town and has pretty grounds, many big trees, and mowed lawns where you can pitch your tent or park your RV. It's on the Mopan River and has shared baths and showers, but it's somewhat isolated.

A couple of miles outside San Ignacio on the George Price Highway, **Inglewood Camping Grounds** (Mile 68.25, George Price Hwy., tel. 501/824-3555, www.inglewoodcampinggrounds.com, electricity metered at US$0.40 per kWh, tent camping US$20 for 2) offers full hookups for RVs (US$30). Following the same road, you'll find campgrounds at the lovely **Clarissa Falls Resort** (tel. 501/833-3116, US$7.50 pp).

Jungle Lodges

Set on 90 lush acres of rolling countryside on the banks of the Macal River is **Sweet Songs Jungle Lodge** (formerly duPlooy's, tel. 501/824-3101, www.sweetsongslodge.com, US$115 all inclusive/night). Guests have a number of choices, from double queen or king casitas to a tree house; amenities include bathtubs, full kitchens, and private decks; you'll get to your room via wooden catwalk, which gives you your own canopy tour on the steep riverbank. Meals, packed lunches, and a dining room provide top-notch, cow-free sustenance—vegetarians welcome. The lodge offers river canoeing and tubing, horse trails, and bird-watching tours. You can also set up a visit to the adjacent Botanic Gardens, an independent site that continues to be run by its founder and owner, Judy duPlooy.

The Lodge at Chaa Creek (Chaa Creek Rd., tel. 501/824-2037, www.chaacreek.com, from US$389-799, includes breakfast) is frequently rated as one of the best jungle lodges in Central America. Chaa Creek's 365 acres on the Macal River host the ever-evolving vision of owners Mick and Lucy Fleming, an American-British couple who came to Belize in the late 1970s, fell in love with the land, and stayed. Among the ever-updated accommodation options are luxury rainforest villas, spa villas some with plunge pools, river suites, and 23 *palapa*-roofed cottages with private verandas for viewing wildlife, furnished with fine fabrics and works of art from around the world, There are also "treetop" suites with jetted tubs perched on the riverbank, their wide

Black Rock Lodge, located high above the Macal River, is surrounded by stunning scenery.

porches boasting views of iguanas basking in the branches. Chaa Creek guests choose among on-site activities, included in the rates, such as daily birding walks, canoeing and swimming in the Macal River, a butterfly farm tour, and a medicinal trail walk. There is full concierge service and meals prepared with many local ingredients (packed lunch US$15, dinner US$36).

One of the best deals in the region is Chaa Creek's ★ **Macal River Camp** (www.macalrivercamp.com, US$65 pp), a 10-minute walk from the main lodge. Accommodations are in a screened, lantern-lit casita with a porch and access to all the main Chaa Creek facilities and activities. Dinner and breakfast are included. There are 10 units centered around a fire pit and eating area, all with access to a shared restroom and shower house. Homemade meals are excellent and eaten communally under a thatched roof, with a bar available as well.

Another couple of river bends later is ★ **Black Rock Lodge** (Mojellon Rd., tel. 501/834-4038, www.blackrocklodge.com, US$140-245, meals and taxes extra), easy to recommend for the sheer beauty of its location. The seven-mile drive to the lodge takes in grazing cattle, citrus orchards, coconut trees, and river views, and there's an incredible vista from the open-air dining pavilion. Guests stay in one of 14 units that include gorgeous River Suites, a stone's throw from the river below the main lodge, with marble floors, wooden decks, and French windows. Communal meals are served at long tables, and the menu includes four-course dinners (US$22) as well as breakfast and lunch (US$12 each). There are numerous hikes on the 242-acre property, 30 species of trees in a fruit orchard, a small organic garden, unique bird habitats, and plenty of wildlife in the area, as the lodge is across the river from Elijio Panti National Park. Yoga practitioners will enjoy the yoga *palapa;* inquire about occasional yoga retreats. Black Rock is off the grid and powered by a combination of solar and hydro technology, including solar hot-water heating.

INFORMATION AND SERVICES
Visitor Information
There is an official visitor information post at the **Cahal Pech Visitors Center** (8am-5pm daily). The **Belize Tourism Industry Association** has a stand near the Savannah Taxi Co-op downtown (tel. 501/824-2155), offering brochures for local resorts, taxi charters, and a town map. However, you'll find out much more by reading the posters and advertisements at the various restaurants around town. The most regularly updated website on Cayo's businesses and attractions is www.bestofcayo.com.

For travel arrangements, **Exodus International** (2 Burns Ave., tel. 501/824-4400 or 501/824-4401, exodusbze@yahoo.com) is at the beginning of Burns Avenue, near the bridge.

Banks
Atlantic Bank, Scotiabank, and **Belize Bank** are all on Burns Avenue, just past the Hawksworth Bridge as you come into town; all have 24-hour ATMs.

Media and Communications
The **post office** (Hudson St., 8am-4pm Mon.-Fri.) is in the center of town. **Tradewinds Internet** (Hudson St., next to the post office, tel. 501/824-2396, 7am-10pm Mon.-Sat., 10am-10pm Sun.) has fast machines, scanners, and printers. **Venus Photos and Records** (6 Hudson St., tel. 501/824-2101, 8am-6pm Mon.-Sat.), across from the post office, sells camera batteries, memory cards, and some camera equipment.

TRANSPORTATION
Getting There
AIR
All resorts can arrange for a transfer (US$125) from **Philip S. W. Goldson International Airport** (BZE, 10 miles west of Belize City, tel. 501/225-2045, www.pgiabelize.com); since December 2012, visitors have been able to fly direct from Belize City's international

airport to Cayo on **Tropic Air** (tel. 501/226-2626, www.tropicair.com, US$119.25 pp one-way), landing at the Maya Flats airstrip near Chaa Creek. **Belize San Ignacio Shuttle & Transfer** (tel. 501/620-3055, belizeshuttle@yahoo.com, www.williamshuttlebelize.com, US$95 for 2 people) can arrange rides anywhere, including both airports; the owner, William Hoffman, is accommodating and flexible.

BUS

Westbound buses from Belize City and Belmopan run through the middle of town, stopping at the Welcome Center (essentially the town square) as part of the daily runs to Benque. The street running along the Welcome Center is the bus station. Expect limited service on Sunday. Express buses take about two hours between Belize City and San Ignacio, including the quick stop in Belmopan. Regular buses leave every hour, and there are a handful of express buses 7am-7pm daily. Check the express departure times the day before your journey, as the bus schedules are constantly changing.

In addition to the main buses running back and forth on the George Price Highway, village buses come into the Welcome Center area from most surrounding towns, returning to the hills in the afternoon. To the south, buses only run as far as the village of San Antonio.

Getting Around

Downtown San Ignacio is tiny and entirely walkable, although there are a few steep hills, including the trek to Cahal Pech and the walk to San Ignacio Resort.

TAXI

Taxis anywhere within the city limits cost US$2.50-4 per person. Cheap *colectivo* taxis run from San Ignacio in all directions throughout the day, making it easy to get to towns and destinations in the immediate vicinity (including Bullet Tree, Succotz, and Benque). If you want your own driver, a safe bet is Mr. William from **William's**

Taxi Service (tel. 501/625-4365, williams_taxiservice@yahoo.com); he'll take you pretty much anywhere you want to go, whether around town or to sites and other parts of Belize. Don't hesitate to ask your guesthouse or resort for taxi recommendations—they often keep a couple of names handy.

CAR

Anyone wishing to travel independently to the Mountain Pine Ridge, Caracol, Hydro Road, or El Pilar might consider renting a car—either in Belize City or at one of the few places in San Ignacio and Santa Elena. Renting in Cayo (as low as US$60 per day) is cheaper than in Belize City, and it's a good way to go if you really want to explore this area.

At the top of the Old Benque Road at the western edge of San Ignacio, by the UNO gas station, you'll find **Cayo Rentals** (81 Benque Viejo Rd., tel. 501/824-2222, cell tel. 501/610-4779, www.cayoautorentals.com), with a handful of newish vehicles for rent in the UNO parking lot; US$45-75 for 24 hours *includes* insurance, which is cheaper than any place in Belize City. There's also **Matus Car Rentals** (18 Benque Viejo Rd., tel. 501/663-4702, www.matuscarrental.com, US$68-75 per day, US$315-367 per week), on the hill up from the town center, which offers decent weekly rates.

VICINITY OF SAN IGNACIO

On the George Price Highway toward San Ignacio, after passing the Hummingbird Highway junction, you are greeted with a jarring series of speed bumps at the roadside village of Teakettle. Turning left at the Pook's Hill sign carries you past cornfields grown atop ancient Mayan residential mounds.

TOP EXPERIENCE

★ Actun Tunichil Muknal

This is the acclaimed "Cave of the Crystal Maiden," one of the most spectacular natural and archaeological attractions in Central

America, and recently named the number-one cave by *National Geographic*. The trip to ATM, as the cave is also known, is for fit and active people who do not mind getting wet and muddy—and who are able to tread lightly around ancient artifacts.

Tours start in San Ignacio with a ride to Teakettle. After the initial 45-minute hike to the entrance (fording three rivers on foot) and a swim into the cave's innards, you will be asked to remove your shoes for climbing up the limestone into the main cathedral-like chambers. The rooms are littered with delicate Mayan pottery and the crystallized remains of 14 humans. There are no pathways, fences, glass, or other partitions separating the visitor from the artifacts, nor are there any installed lights. The only infrastructure is a rickety ladder that, toward the end of the journey, will lead you up to the chamber of the Crystal Maiden herself, a full female skeleton that sparkles with calcite under your headlamp's glare, more so during the drier months.

Be careful—the fact that visitors are allowed to walk here at all is as astonishing as the sights themselves. At the time of this writing, somebody had already trod on and broken one of the skulls, and in 2012 a visitor dropped a camera on a second ancient skull, prompting the current strict no-camera rule.

Only a few tour companies are licensed to take guests here: **Pacz Tours** (San Ignacio, tel. 501/604-6921 or 501/824-0536, www.pacztours.net, US$110) is the most popular provider. The Actun Tunichil Muknal cave is not for the out-of-shape—you need to be agile and in good health—nor recommended for small children or claustrophobics. In fact, children under the age of 8 (or 12, depending on whom you ask) are not permitted inside. Entrance to the site is US$25 per person.

POOK'S HILL LODGE
Arriving at the remote clearing that is **Pook's Hill Lodge** (tel. 501/832-2017, www.pookshilllodge.com, accommodations US$250), you'll have a hard time believing that you are only 12 miles from Belmopan and 21 miles from San Ignacio, so dense and peaceful is the forest around you. Towering hardwoods, flowering bromeliads, and exotic birds hem in the accommodations, which are built around a small Mayan residential ruin. Pook's Hill is a 300-acre private nature reserve, bordered by the Tapir Mountain Nature Reserve and the Roaring River, and offers active travelers 10 thatched-roof cabanas from which to base their Cayo explorations. The cottages have private baths, electricity, and comfortable furnishings. The lounge-bar area overlooks a grassy knoll that gently slopes toward the creek. The dining room is downstairs from the lounge, and filling meals are shared on lantern-lit dining tables, communal-style. Vegetarian or other food preferences can be accommodated with advance notice.

There are plenty of guided walks, including night walks (prepare to see all sorts of creepy crawlies—including the occasional snake—and listen as the rainforest comes alive), as well as birding and tubing opportunities, all included in the lodging rates for guests. Pook's Hill is the only lodge within walking distance of Actun Tunichil Muknal and offers early morning private tours before the crowds arrive.

To get there, look for the hand-painted sign at Teakettle (around Mile 52.5, George Price Hwy.); turn left and follow the signs to Pook's Hill for 5.5 miles (there are a couple of turns). The road can be rough, and a 4WD vehicle is recommended, as is calling ahead so they know to expect you.

TAPIR MOUNTAIN NATURE RESERVE
Covering 6,741 acres, the **Tapir Mountain Nature Reserve** (www.belizeaudubon.org, no public access) is one of the jewels in the country's crown of natural treasures. The deep, steamy rainforest is ripe with an abundance of plantlife. Every wild thing native to

the region roams its forests, from toucans to tapirs, coatis to kinkajous. At present, the reserve is off-limits to all but scientific expeditions, but you can see a piece of it by going on an Actun Tunichil Muknal trip.

Spanish Lookout

Turn off the George Price Highway at the Spanish Lookout sign and watch the landscape change from ragged forest to neat, rolling green countryside with green lawns and men riding John Deere lawn mowers. Spanish Lookout is one of Belize's largest Mennonite communities, with about 3,000 farmers and builders who supply a large part of the furniture, dairy, and poultry products for the country. Many Mennonites here have embraced organic living, and if you drive around, you'll find produce and items that cannot be had anywhere else in Belize. The discovery of oil in the area has added a modern twist to this unique scene (you'll pass a few pumps and the refinery on your way in).

Spanish Lookout has no accommodations, but it has a few excellent places to eat as well as shopping and services (Scotiabank has an ATM here, and there are three gas stations). Folks from all over Belize come to shop at places like Farmer's Trading Centre, Reimer's Feeds, the Computer Ranch, and Westrac (the best place for car parts, period). There's an average restaurant, **The Golden Corral** (Rte. 20 W., tel. 501/823-0421, www.spanishlookout. bz/goldencorral.htm, 10:30am-2:30pm Mon.-Wed., 10:30am-2:30pm and 5pm-8:30pm Thurs.-Sat.); it's about US$7.50 for the all-you-can-eat buffet and all-you-can-drink homemade iced tea. There are amazing meat pies and other goodies at **Midway Convenience** (Center Rd., tel. 501/823-0095, 7am-4:30pm Mon.-Sat.).

If you're in the area close to sunset, drive to the community's **Countryside Park,** and once at the gate, let the security guard know you'd just like to take some photos by the lake. There are no benches, but the views are beautiful. You might even spot an armadillo or two, aside from bird colonies.

Bullet Tree Falls

This sleepy old village of a few thousand people is less than three miles north of San Ignacio on the road to El Pilar. Bullet Tree's ultra-mellow riverbank mood, combined with cheap and easy access to the relative bustle of San Ignacio, makes it a pleasant midrange alternative to the usual Cayo fare of fancy jungle lodges and backpacker camps. On my first visit to Belize, I stayed in this village and still had access to the full range of Cayo-area activities, and San Ignacio was easily reached by *colectivo* taxi (US$2 pp) or private cab (US$5). Most people like to just sit by the river or float it in a tube. You can also arrange a hike with Beto Cocom, a Mayan shaman who offers medicinal-plant trail walks for donations; ask at any local hotel. Hotels can also arrange horseback expeditions to El Pilar and other sites.

FOOD AND ACCOMMODATIONS

If you're looking for a smaller, budget lodge experience, **Cohune Palms River Cabanas** (tel. 501/664-7508, www.cohunepalmsbelize. com, US$69) is a great pick, a brief 10-minute ride from San Ignacio with plenty of public transportation if you need. There are just four cabins—thatched roofs, with queen bed or double beds, and private baths, porch, and hot and cold water. There's an open air, part covered central dining area with Wi-Fi, as well as two spacious wooden decks overlooking the Mopan River. The property is dotted with cohune palms, while you might spot agouti scurrying about the grounds. There's a swimming platform with a rope swing if you dare. Cabins don't have air-conditioning but the fresh air from fans alone will cool you off. Meals can be had on-site; Margaret serves up fresh local breakfasts and dinners. Shared taxis usually drop off at main road but will take you to the door if you have a suitcase. Waking to birdsong right by the river is what this place memorable.

Also a short ride from San Ignacio, award-winning ★ **Vanilla Hills** (Vanilla Hills Rd., www.vanilla-hills.com, US$105-135) is

Mennonite Life in Belize

a Mennonite horse and buggy

Cayo is a cultural melting pot, home to at least five different cultural groups. Of these, you will no doubt notice the tall, blond, blue-eyed Mennonites, who also reside in various parts of the country, notably the west and the north.

The German-speaking Mennonites started emigrating to Belize in 1958, after a long nomadic journey that took them from Switzerland to the Netherlands, Russia, and Canada in the 1800s, and Mexico after World War I. They decided to remain in Belize after finding the land ideal for farming. The government agreed not to subject them to either property tax or military service and gave them freedom to practice their own religion, schools, and banking. In turn, they have brought valuable farming knowledge and enough capital to invest in the country, although they do not vote.

You'll notice Mennonites as you head to the Saturday market in San Ignacio, selling cheese, fruits, and desserts. The men grow long beards and often wear overalls and straw hats, while the women wear long plain dresses and head caps. Mennonites travel for trade within Cayo, but choose to live in their own communities, notably Barton Creek (traditional Mennonites)—where a traditional sawmill is powered by horses—and Spanish Lookout (progressive Mennonites).

Traditional Mennonites tend to stand out—they do not use any modern machinery or conveniences, traveling instead by horse and buggy. Most traditional Mennonite men work hard at farming, cutting wood, or selling produce at the markets or on the roadside; women tend to the home and children. Mennonite villages run their own churches and schools (most education consists of homeschooling) and, on Sunday, go to church and rest.

Visiting a traditional Mennonite community is a worthwhile experience, although you cannot disturb them on Sunday. Most Mennonites are friendly and will welcome your questions; be courteous and don't take photos without asking, even from a distance. Mennonite markets supply most of the country with poultry, dairy, and vegetables (plus they sell the sweetest-tasting watermelon I've ever had). Look for Mennonite supermarkets and market stands in and around San Ignacio, and for stands on the highway.

an exquisite boutique lodge at the entrance to Bullet Tree Falls. The sound of trickling fountain welcomes as you enter the gate and leads you on to the outdoor dining terrace with views of the green hills below. Appealing to young millennial couples as well as generational vacations, no detail is spared here as owner Claudia and her husband love to take care of their guests as well as this 45-acre property, with 1,500-foot river frontage. Solar power reigns, as well as a rainwater system, and there's a greenhouse on-site. The tree house, reached past a pond where ducks relax, is a dream cabin in the woods and feels tucked away from the rest of the lodge and guests; an outdoor deck, outdoor shower, and on-site coffeemaker and fridge complete the picture. Don't miss breakfast, featuring Claudia's baked breads, pastries, homemade jams, organic eggs and dairy, and other treats. A few steps away are six stand-alone guesthouses as well as two more tree houses. A pool is in the works for 2019-2020, and the lodge offers its own unique caving and horseback riding trips through local guides.

Rolling into town, you'll pass the soccer field on your right and then come to a fork in the road; this is the bus stop. Fork left to cross the bridge and reach the turnoff for El Pilar or right to reach **Parrot Nest Lodge** (tel. 501/669-6068 or 501/660-6336, www.parrot-nest.com, US$50-75), which is a rustic hideaway with immediate river access (and free use of inner tubes). The tropical gardens have remarkable on-site birding. There are seven simple, cozy cabins, including two tree houses on stilts under the limbs of a gigantic guanacaste tree. Each cabin has 24-hour electricity, a fan, linoleum flooring, and a simple single or double bed; four have private baths, and others share a bath. Meals are reasonably priced (breakfast US$4-6, dinner US$12).

El Pilar Archaeological Site

Seven miles north of Bullet Tree Falls, these rainforest-choked Mayan ruins are visited by only a handful of curious travelers each day; the rough approach road plus the lack of attention paid to the site by most tour operators help make El Pilar the uncrowded day trip that it is. Entrance is US$10. Two groupings of temple mounds, courtyards, and ball courts overlook a forested valley. Aqueducts and a causeway lead toward Guatemala, just 500 yards away. There have been some minor excavations here, including those by illegal looters, but the site is very overgrown, so the ruins retain an intriguing air of mystery. Many trees shade the site: allspice, gumbo-limbo, *ramón*, cohune palm, and locust. It's a beautiful hiking area and wildlife experience as well. Note that it's isolated out here, and there have been past incidents where guests and their guide were robbed; be vigilant and leave valuables at the hotel.

Even if you book your El Pilar trip in San Ignacio, be sure to start your quest with a visit to the **Amigos de El Pilar Visitors Center** (9am-5pm daily) and **Be Pukte Cultural Center** in Bullet Tree Falls. Here you'll find a scale model of the ruins, some helpful booklets and maps, and guide and taxi arrangements (it's about US$25 for a taxi to drive a group out and wait a few hours before bringing you back).

San José de Succotz

About 6.5 miles from San Ignacio, you'll find this hillside village on your left, above the Mopan River, right where the ferry to Xunantunich is located. In Succotz, the first language is Spanish, and the most colorful time to visit is during one of the fiestas: March 19 (feast day of St. Joseph) and May 3 (feast day of the Holy Cross).

A stroll through the rough village streets is enjoyable if you're into observing village life. **Magana's Art Center** (George Price Hwy., 1 block before the Xunantunich ferry) is the workshop of David Magana, who works with

---

1: view of Mopan River from Cohune Palms River Cabanas; 2: sunset in Spanish Lookout; 3: Xunantunich Archaeological Site

the youth of the area, encouraging them to continue the arts and crafts of their ancestors. You'll find the results inside in the form of local wood carvings, baskets, jewelry, and stone (slate) carvings unique to Belize.

FOOD AND ACCOMMODATIONS

There are a few taco stands in town, including the popular local eatery **Benny's Kitchen** (George Price Hwy., across from the Xunantunich ferry, tel. 501/823-2541, 7am-9pm Mon.-Fri., closes later Sat.-Sun., from US$5), where you can get a substantial breakfast, delicious lunch, and other tasty items such as smoothies for good prices. Cold draft Belikin is served in frosty mugs.

Just before entering San José de Succotz, look on your left for the ★ **Trek Stop** (Mile 71.5, George Price Hwy., tel. 501/823-2265, www.thetrekstop.com, US$24-28), a backpacker classic offering 10 cabins set in lush gardens on 22 acres of second-growth tropical forest. You can hear the highway, but you can also hear howler monkeys, birds, and the inspired conversation of your hosts and fellow travelers. There are camping facilities (US$7 pp) with access to composting toilets and solar showers, a patio restaurant with inexpensive Belizean dishes, and walking access to the Xunantunich ruins. Simple wood cabins have twin or double beds, electricity, porches, and a shared bath; a larger, more private cabin with a private bath is available.

Even if you're not spending the night here, come visit the Trek Stop's **Tropical Wings Nature Center** (9am-5pm daily, US$3 adults, US$1.50 under age 12), one of the best and most diverse butterfly ranches in the country. Be sure to leave time for a round on Belize's only disc golf course, a nine-basket Frisbee golf game through the rainforest; discs are available (US$5 pp). The course is a par 31 with narrow and challenging fairways that leave little room for error (wear long pants and closed footwear to retrieve those errant drives). There is a nice view and sometimes a breeze from the Mayan ruins atop hole 6.

★ Xunantunich Archaeological Site

One of Belize's most impressive Mayan ceremonial centers, **Xunantunich** rests atop a natural limestone ridge with a grand view of the entire Cayo District and the Guatemalan countryside. The local name for the site, Xunantunich (shoo-NAHN-ta-nitch), or Stone Lady, continues to be used, even after the ancients' own name for the site, Ka-at Witz, or Supernatural Mountain, was discovered, carved into a chunk of stone. In the summer of 2016, one of the largest tombs ever discovered in Belize was found at Xunantunich, lying 16-26 feet deep, and inside it were skeletal remains of a Maya leader, jade beads, vases, and other Mayan tools and artifacts.

Xunantunich is believed to have been built sometime around 400 BC and deserted around AD 1000; at its peak, some 7,000-10,000 Maya lived here. Though certainly not the biggest of Mayan structures, at 135 feet high **El Castillo** is the second-tallest pyramid in Belize, missing first place by just one foot. The eastern side of the structure displays an unusual stucco frieze (a reproduction), and you can see three carved stelae (stone monuments) in the plaza. Xunantunich contains three ceremonial plazas surrounded by house mounds. It was rediscovered in 1894 but not studied until 1938, by archaeologist J. Eric Thompson. As the first Mayan ruin to be opened in the country, it has attracted the attention and exploration of many other archaeologists over the years.

In 1950, the University of Pennsylvania, noted for its years of outstanding work across the Guatemala border in Tikal, built a facility in Xunantunich for more study. In 1954 visitors were invited to explore the site after a road was opened and a small ferry built. In 1959 archaeologist Evan Mackie made news in the Mayan world when he discovered evidence that part of Xunantunich had been destroyed

Xunantunich Archaeological Site

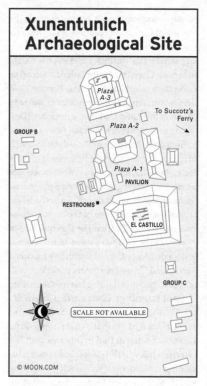

Plaza A-3

To Succotz's Ferry

Plaza A-2

GROUP B

Plaza A-1

PAVILION

RESTROOMS

EL CASTILLO

GROUP C

SCALE NOT AVAILABLE

© MOON.COM

by an earthquake in the Late Classic Period. Some believe it was then that the people began to lose faith in their leaders—they saw the earthquake as a sign from the gods. But for whatever reason, Xunantunich ceased to be a religious center long before the end of the Classic Period.

Located eight miles west of San Ignacio, the site is accessed by crossing the Mopan River on the Succotz ferry, easily found at the end of a line of craft vendors. Buses ($0.75) and taxis (US$10 private or US$1.75 *colectivo*) can take you from San Ignacio to the ferry entrance. The hand-cranked ferry shuttles you (and your vehicle, if you have one) across the river, after which you'll have a 30-minute, one-mile hike (or a 5-minute drive) up a steep hill to the site. The ferry, which operates 8am-3pm daily, is free, but tipping the operator is a much-appreciated gesture. Don't miss the 4pm return ferry with the park rangers, or

you'll be swimming. Be forewarned that during the rainy season the Mopan River can rise, run fast, and flood, canceling this service and closing access to Xunantunich until conditions improve.

Entrance to the site is US$10 per person; guides are available for US$20 per group and recommended if you have the time—both to learn about what you're seeing and to support sustainable tourism, as all guides are local and very knowledgeable. There's a **visitors center,** just past the ticket booth, with beautiful and informative displays of Mayan history, Belize's various archaeological sites, and the history of Xunantunich itself. It's worth a stop here before continuing on your hike to the temples.

BENQUE VIEJO DEL CARMEN

Benque Viejo del Carmen (www.benqueviejotown.com) is the last town in Belize (the Guatemalan border is about one mile farther), approximately eight miles west of San Ignacio. Located on the Mopan River, Benque Viejo has been greatly influenced by the Spanish, both from its historical past when Spain ruled Guatemala and later when Spanish-speaking *chicleros* and loggers worked the forest. At one time, Benque Viejo (Old Bank; riverside logging camps were referred to as "banks") was a logging camp. This was the gathering place for chicle workers, and logs were floated down the river from here for shipment to England. After this industry waned in the 1940s, many deserted the town, and the area never quite recovered from this decline.

Today, Benque remains a quiet village between the road and the river, with a handful of shops and Chinese restaurants, but it is slowly coming out of its lull: Efforts are under way to revive the community and use the area's historical and cultural significance to attract more visitors. Renovations have taken place, including George Street and the main drag; parks are being cleaned up; and a couple of banks have opened, including Belize Bank.

Sights

On one side of town, behind the central **Centennial Park,** a Mayan mound was discovered, and the National Institute of Culture and History's Archaeology Department is considering ways to excavate it in the future. Catch a glimpse of the beautiful **Our Lady of Mount Carmel Church,** and make sure you stop by the **Benque House of Culture** (64 St. Joseph St., tel. 501/823-2697, benquehoc@nichbelize.org, 9am-5pm Mon.-Fri., free), established in 2001 and now one of the most active in the country, for museum displays on mestizo culture, the latest exhibits, and more information on the town itself.

Besides cultural experiences, it's only right that folks should pass through this charming town, if only to get a slice of the old Cayo. Music aficionados will want to arrange a visit of the country's famous recording studio, **Stonetree Records** (35 Elizabeth St., tel. 501/823-2241, www.stonetreerecords.com). The country's sole and excellent publisher, **Cubola Books** (Elizabeth St.), is also based in Benque.

Entertainment and Events

Easter remains Benque's most vibrant and meaningful time of the year, when the village celebrates Holy Week, or Semana Santa—complete with a reenactment of the Passion of Christ and beautiful *alfombras* (colorful carpets of dyed sawdust) all over the village streets; this spiritual experience is a sight to behold. **Christmas** is the culmination of the celebration called **Las Posadas.** Benque Viejo del Carmen remains the only area of Belize to celebrate this Latin tradition, a nine-day (Dec. 16-24) reenactment of Joseph and Mary's biblical journey from Nazareth to Bethlehem in search of an inn. I experienced the first posada night in December 2012, and it was a unique experience worth the short night drive from San Ignacio. Summer sees Benque's second-liveliest celebration of the year, and one of the most popular ones in the Cayo District: The **Benque Fiesta** celebrates the village's patron saint, Nuestra Señora de Monte Carmelo, with live marimba bands, food, drink, amusement park rides, and, of course, plenty of dancing late into the night.

Cool Runnings Cevicheria (Church St., tel. 501/635-1429, 11am-11pm Wed.-Thurs., 11am-midnight Fri.-Sat., 10am-10pm Sun., US$4-5) is a dream find in this area with few eateries. Order fresh seafood and ceviche, including shrimp, octopus, conch (in season), and throw back a few beers on your way back from Benque explorations. Friday nights are for karaoke.

Our Lady of Mount Carmel Church in Benque Viejo del Carmen

Transportation

Buses from Belize City to Benque and the Guatemalan border run daily, starting at ungodly morning hours on both ends. Most bus service to and from San Ignacio also serves Benque and the border. The most efficient way to travel to the border from San Ignacio is by *colectivo* taxis, which run in a constant and steady flow roughly 6am-7pm daily; the ride should cost approximately US$2, but you take the chance of sharing your cab with as many people as your driver can fit. By private taxi, expect to pay about US$10 for the same trip.

THE HYDRO ROAD

Look for the left-hand turn in the middle of Benque Viejo, at the top of the hill. The Hydro Road leads south to a few unique attractions and accommodations, all well off the beaten path. The road is equipped with mile markers on small white posts. A few miles in, a right turn leads to the border village of Arenal, where a few *milpero* (corn farmer) families scrape a life from the soils of the Mopan River Valley. The road continues south for 11 miles, where it dead-ends at the Mollejon Dam.

Poustinia Land Art Park

This 60-acre reclaimed cattle ranch is now devoted to the nurturing of art and nature, where foreign and Belizean artists can stay and contribute to the ongoing project and visitors can come take a look and soak it all in. If you're looking for an out-of-the-ordinary sight, this would be it. The lush grounds are part of a 270-acre second-growth forest. Visiting the unique **Poustinia Land Art Park** (admission US$10) is by appointment only and can be arranged at the **Benque House of Culture** (tel. 501/823-2697).

Chechem Ha Cave and the Vaca Plateau

At Mile 8, you'll find a turnoff to the left for **Chechem Ha Farm** (tel. 501/660-4714), a

mile or so down a rutted road; it belongs to the Morales family. The place is designed to give nature-loving travelers the chance to enjoy the Chechem Ha Spring, Chechem Ha Falls (a 175-foot cascade with a treacherous trail down to its misty bottom), and **Chechem Ha Cave,** a dry cave except for the dripping water that has created all the formations over the years. The pottery inside is estimated to be as old as 2,000 years. You can climb and explore various ledges and passageways, but the highlight is a deep ceremonial chamber in the heart of the hill. In some places, you need a rope to help you get around. While those of average physical abilities can enjoy Chechem Ha Cave, take care when moving amid the pottery.

Stay at the farm in one of several simple **cabins** made of clay, rock, wood, and thatch; they are well constructed and comfy-looking. For US$41 per person, you get a night's stay and three meals. There's no electricity, and the toilets are outhouses. **Camping** is US$5 per person; bring your own tent. Individual meals are available (US$5-10), as is an inexpensive transfer from Benque.

Martz Farm

Less than a mile beyond the Chechem Ha road, another left turn will take you to **Martz Farm** (Mile 8.5, Hydro Rd., tel. 501/834-4646, http://martzfarm.com, US$78-88), a unique and relaxed homestead built and maintained by the hardworking Martinez family. A combination of an open-air tree house, a cabin, and garden rooms—ideal for families, with king and double beds and en suite baths—make up this rainforest escape. Garden rooms have balconies and living and dining areas. Family-style meals are made over a traditional fire hearth in a quaint kitchen, and farm animals wander the grounds with the guests. Home-cooked meal plans and free transfers from San Ignacio or Benque are available.

The Mountain Pine Ridge

Some of Belize's most breathtaking natural and archaeological treasures are found within this vast crinkle of mountains and wildlands, as are a few of the country's remotest and most charming accommodations. Despite bark beetle damage to vast tracts of pine trees in the Mountain Pine Ridge (MPR) Forest Reserve, the forests are rebounding, and MPR's waterfalls, swimming holes, and vistas are well worth enduring the rutted roads. My first drive through this area left me speechless, and it reminds me why I fell in love with Belize.

CHIQUIBUL (PINE RIDGE) ROAD

The Chiquibul Road begins at Georgeville (Mile 63, George Price Hwy.) and heads south over the Mountain Pine Ridge, terminating 30-some miles later at Caracol. You'll pass through tropical foothills, citrus farms, and cattle ranches before the terrain rises, gradually changing to sand, rocky soil, red clay, and finally groves of sweet-smelling pines. The road is notorious for becoming a slushy mud bed when it rains and a dusty backbreaker when it's dry. Once you start driving, there are few services besides those offered at the resorts, but if you need a drink, beer, a meal, supplies, or emergency gasoline, look for the Junction Store, a wooden building right where the San Antonio Road meets the Chiquibul Road.

TOP EXPERIENCE

★ Barton Creek Cave

This unique cathedral-like wet cave was once used for ceremonial purposes and human sacrifices by the Maya. A pair of Peace Corps volunteers stumbled on the cave in 1970 and found that it had been looted but still contained an enormous amount of pottery and artifacts. Archaeologists didn't study the cave until 1998; they found large ceramics on high ledges, plus evidence of 20 sets of human remains, including a necklace made of finger bones.

The tall, cavernous, and low ceilings of Barton Creek Cave are fascinating, and in my opinion it is one of the top two must-see caves in Belize. The experience is impressive and available to anybody physically able enough to step into a canoe—but a heads up: The ceiling is so low through many parts of the cave that you'll occasionally have to lean all the way back in the canoe to save your skull. Still, it's well worth the experience of gliding across, contemplating the quiet as your guide slowly paddles you deeper into the earth, the watery sound of the rowing echoing on the limestone. The cave is at least seven miles deep, but tours only go in about a mile or so before turning around.

Barton Creek is protected and managed by government archaeologists and accessed by turning off the Chiquibul Road around Mile 4, then driving 20-30 minutes on a bumpy road through orange groves and a beautiful small Mennonite settlement. You'll need to have someone with you who knows the way, as there are many roads and no signs. The visitors center charges US$10 per person, then you'll have to rent canoes (US$7.50), lights, and a guide, all available at Mike's Place (tel. 501/670-0441, www.bartoncreekcave. com), right at the cave's entrance. If you come as part of a prepaid tour, you won't need to worry about such details. And if you sign up to tour with Pacz Tours (San Ignacio, tel. 501/824-0536, cell tel. 501/604-6921, www. pacztours.net), you'll experience an awesome pit stop along the way at Karina's fruit tree-filled farm within the Mennonite community of Barton Creek.

Calico Jack's Village

On 365 acres in El Progreso (Mile 7), Calico Jack's Village (just off Chiquibul

Rd., El Progreso, tel. 501/832-2478, www.
calicojacksvillage.com, US$140) is a small,
customized, Belizean-owned authentic adventure resort. Calico Jack's top offerings include
an excellent medicinal hiking trail, caving experiences, and a fantastic (and safe) zip line,
one of the longest (2,700 feet) in Belize. Climb
and zip among 15 platforms high in the trees,
rock rappel, cable walk, and travel through
the rainforest in an impressive hydraulic lift,
designed by Chester Williams, the owner's
spouse and a former engineer. Tours range
from a 20-minute express experience to the
full two-hour *extremo* exploration (US$40-
85). Or try the massive *columpio*, a one-of-a-
kind rainforest swing, which will send you
200 feet in the air after you are hoisted above
the top of a re-created Mayan pyramid.

The two Jungle Villas have one- and two-
bedroom units, built in Mayan temple style,
with kitchenettes, living rooms, and air-
conditioning; all have access to a bar, a restaurant, and a pool.

Green Hills Butterfly Ranch and Botanical Collections

The beautiful **Green Hills Butterfly
Ranch and Botanical Collections** (Mile 8,
Chiquibul Rd., tel. 501/834-4017, www.green-
hills.net, 7am-4pm daily, last tour 3:30pm,
US$12.50 pp) is a butterfly breeding, educa-
tion, and interpretive center run by Dutch biologists Jan Meerman and Tineke Boomsma.
The standard tour of the center takes about
an hour. There's also a walk into the forest to
see Mayan artifacts and the impressive mahogany reforestation project. Your entrance
fee (family discounts available) grants you access to the 3,000-square-foot butterfly house,
blue morpho breeding facilities, botanical
garden (with over 100 labeled species), hummingbird observation spot, and a display on
the life cycle of a butterfly (egg-caterpillar-
pupa-butterfly). Between 25 and 30 different species are raised at the center, including
the tiny glass-winged butterfly, the banana
owl (the largest butterfly in Belize), and, of
course, the magnificent blue morpho. Arrive

early enough in the morning to watch a butterfly emerge from a pupa right before your
eyes. Or time your visit with "*Caligo* hour"—a
unique event that begins one hour before sunset (in December around 4:45pm; in summer
about 5:45pm) when the owl butterflies become very active and synchronize their flight;
owl butterflies can have wingspans of up to
seven inches, so it's quite impressive. Jan literally wrote the book on Belizean butterflies (*Lepidoptera of Belize*, Gainesville, FL:
ATL Books, 2000), and both he and Tineke
can be available to give lectures to student
groups. Green Hills is a worthwhile stop for
anyone traveling to and from other sites on
the Chiquibul Road, not least for the hummingbird garden, where you can watch an
amazingly active assortment of hummers
buzz in and out all day long. Picnic facilities
are available.

Slate Creek Preserve

A group of local landowners and lodge operators have set aside 3,000 acres as the private
Slate Creek Preserve. The purpose of the
preserve is to protect the watershed, plants,
and animals of a valley called the Vega, one
of several valleys in the area. The unique
limestone karst ecosystem, which borders
the Mountain Pine Ridge Forest Reserve,
teems with life. Mahogany, Santa Maria,
ceiba, cedar, and cohune palms tower above.
Orchids, ferns, and bromeliads are common.
Birds such as the aracari, emerald toucanet,
keel-billed toucan, keel-billed motmot, king
vulture, and various parrots and hummingbirds can be found here. Pumas, ocelots, coatis, pacas, and anteaters roam the forests.

Mountain Equestrian Trails

At **Mountain Equestrian Trails** (Mile 8,
Chiquibul Rd., tel. 501/669-1124, U.S. tel.
800/838-3918, www.metbelize.com, packages from US$1,381), the Bevis family keeps
27 sturdy steeds with Endurance saddles.
Visitors have a choice of gentle or spirited
horses to carry them over 60 miles of trails to
waterfalls, swimming holes, Mayan caves, and

The Mountain Pine Ridge

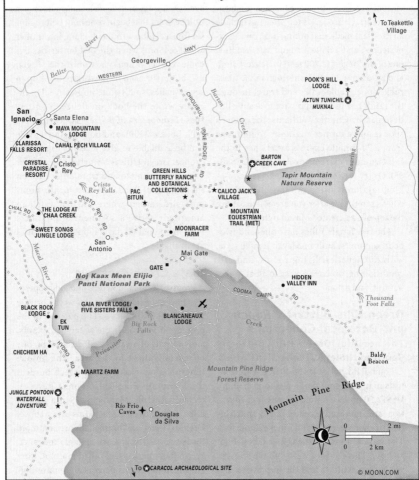

other sites. Beginners and experienced riders are welcome—children at least 10 years old with previous riding experience are welcome. Riders are required to sign a liability waiver.

Food and Accommodations

Accommodations at ★ **Mountain Equestrian Trails** (MET, Mile 8, Chiquibul Rd., tel. 501/669-1124, U.S. tel. 800/838-3918, www.metbelize.com) are in 10 "safari-style" cabanas of thatch and stucco with exotic wood interiors and private baths with hot and cold water (no electricity—kerosene lanterns used). Meals are served in the cozy cantina-restaurant, which offers excellent food (breakfast US$8, lunch US$11, dinner US$20, plus tax). Even though MET's small cantina is a 20-minute drive from San Ignacio, it still attracts visitors and locals from all around for drinks, dinner, and good conversation. All-inclusive, multiday packages are available; riding fees are extra.

CRISTO REY ROAD

Heading south from the George Price Highway at Santa Elena, this road winds through the villages of Cristo Rey and San Antonio before joining the Chiquibul Road and the Mountain Pine Ridge. It is usually better maintained than the alternative route along the Chiquibul Road, and there are a handful of interesting stops along the way. Village buses that travel the road leave the center of San Ignacio daily, and shared taxis should be available for reasonable rates as well. Most tour operators who travel this road will stop at any of the following places, depending on group size and desires.

Slate Carving Art Galleries

About six miles south on Cristo Rey Road, look for the **Sak Tunich Art Gallery** (9am-6pm daily), home of the Magana brothers, Jose and Javier. This indoor-outdoor display is built into the hillside on your left and worth a look for anyone interested in Mayan crafts. These industrious guys are re-creating a Mayan temple and cave by carving them into the limestone on the steep hillside next to the road and their home.

A couple of miles farther, you'll find more art at **The Garcia Sisters** (tel. 501/820-4023, artistmai1981@btl.net). These six siblings made a nationwide name for themselves in 1981, when they turned to their Mayan heritage and began re-creating slate carvings reminiscent of those done by their ancestors at Caracol. Their Mayan art gallery, shop, and museum are called the **Tanah Mayan Art Museum and Community Collection** (tel. 501/669-4023, 8am-6pm daily), located just north of San Antonio. The Tanah Museum is an echoey one-room affair with long shelves full of fascinating artifacts. The sisters, nieces of the famed healer Elijio Panti, are charming and determined ambassadors of San Antonio Village. They're also clever artists who make Belizean dolls, native jewelry, and hand-drawn art cards. Ask about the Itzamna Society, a community-based NGO of which Maria is the chairperson, which works

to protect the forest and community. They also sometimes offer language lessons in the Yucatec Maya language or cooking classes and can perform blessings, healings, and other ceremonies. The Garcias were instrumental in organizing a big December 21, 2012, Hawk Fire Ceremony, held at Caracol with elders from the various Mayan groups in Belize.

San Antonio Village

With a population of 3,500 descendants of the Maya, mostly milpa farmers and, increasingly, youth and employees of nearby lodges, San Antonio is approximately 10 miles from San Ignacio on the way to the Mountain Pine Ridge Reserve. It has the potential to serve as a low-key gateway to the surrounding wilderness, but as of yet, there are few visitor services in town (there is a gas station—better fill up before the drive to Caracol). There are horse and hiking trails nearby, as well as several caves, waterfalls, and ruins. You'll also notice plenty of farmland and men harvesting as you drive through, as San Antonio Village is one of the main sources of vegetables for all of Belize, producing carrots, sweet peppers, potatoes, peanuts, pumpkin seeds, corn, red beans, and more.

A *palapa*-roofed shop at the **Women's Center** (tel. 501/669-4023, mayanspirit7@ yahoo.com) just off the main road with some nice ceramics for sale. On the way out of town is a little-visited Mayan site called **Pac Bitun,** at the end of an unmarked side road, a mile or so before the T-junction.

Nearby is the well-hidden **Cristo Rey "showers"** (off Cristo Rey Rd., right past the Chai Garden Ashram), formerly called Monkey Falls, or a freshwater pool with mini-cascades, known mostly to locals but becoming increasingly popular. Come here during the week or in the early weekend mornings for a blissful swim in nature. You'll need to ask for directions and get here in a solid SUV.

Noj Kaax Meen Elijio Panti National Park

The 13,000-acre reserve of **Noj Kaax Meen**

Elijio Panti National Park (www.epnp. org) in the mountains surrounding the village of San Antonio is filled with trails, waterfalls, and peaks, but there is not much access or tourism development. Ask at the Tanah Museum (tel. 501/669-4023, 8am-6pm daily) or the Women's Center (tel. 501/669-4023, mayanspirit7@yahoo.com) if there are any licensed guides taking people into the park.

Food and Accommodations

Only one mile south of the George Price Highway, Maya Mountain Lodge (Mile 0.75, Cristo Rey Rd., tel. 501/824-2164, www. mayamountain.com, US$69-129) feels remote enough to warrant a listing outside of town; it's a US$5 taxi ride from San Ignacio. This is one of the most moderately priced rainforest hideaways. The property is 108 acres, and it's about a 20-minute walk to the river's edge. A meandering trail through the gardens has signs identifying plants, trees, and birds; there's a nice pool for after your hike. Accommodations range from six simple guest rooms in a raised wooden building to family cottages and a two-bedroom suite with tiled floors, air-conditioning, extra bunks, and wood furniture. The restaurant features theme nights, homemade bread, and buckets of freshly squeezed orange juice (their Baha'i faith prevents them from selling liquor for profit, but you are welcome to bring your own). Breakfast costs US$6-10, and dinner is US$20. Ask about workshops on biodiversity and multiculturalism. This is a great place for families, with discounted or free lodging and tours for children and teens.

Before the advent of tourism, the Tut family (Victor and Teresa and their 10 children) grew fruit and vegetables and then transported them by canoe to the town market in San Ignacio. Today, they are the proud owners and operators of ★ Crystal Paradise Resort (Cristo Rey, tel. 501/615-9361, www. crystalparadise.com, US$95-125, breakfast US$10 pp, dinner US$15 pp), a low-key lodge that attracts many satisfied repeat customers. The 21-acre property near Cristo Rey Village is a few hundred yards from the river, and it's an easy walk to a canoe. The Tuts' sons, who are avid bird-watchers and nature lovers, maintain the beautiful grounds and serve as your guides on a variety of tours, including hiking, biking, horseback riding, kayaking, and bird-watching. Find them at Paradise Expeditions (Cristo Rey, cell tel. 501/610-5593 or 501/634-5441, www.birdinginbelize. com), which is based at the resort. Teresa and her daughters keep the guest rooms clean and comfortable and also cook up the best in traditional Belizean and international cuisine. Near the property's wide, open dining *palapa*, the accommodations come in several styles; there are 17 units in all, including simple thatched cabanas with cement walls, tiled floors, hot and cold showers, and shaded verandas with hammocks for relaxing. Other units are clean and comfortable but more of a clapboard style; all offer ceiling fans and electricity. Additions include a pool and four canopy-level luxury guest rooms. The Tuts also offer bird-watching (ask about the birding platform), nature walks, and tours. There's an on-site medicinal trail.

Table Rock Jungle Lodge (tel. 501/672-4040, www.tablerockbelize.com, US$145-225, riverside camping US$30) is an ecofriendly touch of class on a 100-acre preserve. Five gorgeous cabanas (four-poster king and queen beds, private baths with hot water, ceiling fans, and private porches) are designed to stay cool the natural way, using adobe construction. There is a beautiful trail leading down a series of stone steps to the Macal River, where guests can go birding, canoeing, swimming, or tubing, all included in the room rates for guests. You can also tour the on-site fruit farm, growing all sorts of goodies from star fruit to craboo. The food is excellent, with unexpected dishes like pan-seared jack with chipotle papaya coconut sauce, cooked in cohune palm oil and served with couscous and okra. The palm-lined entrance through an orange grove is at Mile 5 on Cristo Rey Road.

At Mystic River Resort (tel. 501/834-4100, www.mysticriverbelize.com,

The Southern Pine Bark Beetle

Shortly after the creation of the Mountain Pine Ridge Forest Reserve, the Pine Ridge experienced a huge forest fire; combined with the cycles of logging, the forest was left with an unnaturally uniform population of trees, making it more susceptible to disease and insects. In the 1990s, a three-year drought helped establish a disastrous infestation of the southern pine bark beetle (*Dendroctonus frontalis*), which has wreaked havoc throughout Central and North America.

Today, the forest is coming back wonderfully—thanks both to naturally rich seed sets and a massive replanting campaign (24 million seedlings are required for reforestation of 70,000 acres over four years). It will be another 10-15 years before the new generation of pines fully matures, however. Check out www.reforestbelize.com for an update and to find out how you can help.

all-inclusive packages US$1,135-2,250 and up, includes transfers and tours), it's about being surrounded with nature and the river below. Guests like to hike or ride upstream, then float back to the lodge in a canoe or on a tube. The six units (so far) are spacious and well furnished, with local tile floors, nice verandas, and fireplaces for cool December nights. The place is a model of sustainable living. It has an on-site stable and an organic garden, and raises its own chickens; plans are under way to make cheese on-site as well. Tom is still cutting trails and discovering archaeological sites on his property, which you can explore—either by foot or on Tom's ATV. The lodge now has its very own **BushDog Adventures** tour company, offering off-the-beaten-track adventures in the area and accommodations packages tailored to your activity of preference, although room-only bookings are considered on request (US$250-275). Be sure to make it to Dancing Tree Lookout for sunset views of Guatemala. At the campsite atop this housing mound, you'll admire the same view that Mayan families saw 1,000 years ago. By car, Mystic River Resort is accessed at Mile 6 on the Cristo Rey Road.

Macaw Bank Jungle Lodge (tel. 501/665-7241, www.macawbankjunglelodge.com, US$135-145) occupies an isolated, peaceful clearing in the forest. There are five miles of nature trails on the 50-acre property and many birds and other wildlife, and you can go swimming at a sandy bend on the Macal River, a 5- to 10-minute walk away. The five

comfortable units have wooden bunks and furniture, private baths, hot and cold water, some solar power, and kerosene lanterns. There is a nice restaurant *palapa* with wireless Internet. Campers (US$12.50 pp) are welcome.

Moonracer Farm (Mile 9, Mountain Pine Ridge Rd., www.moonracerfarm.com, US$60-120) gets rave reviews, providing a pair of comfortable wooden cabins in the forest in one of the best deals in the Mountain Pine Ridge. The cabins are fairly large, with private screened porches. There's a Cohune Camping Casita cabin for two, with shared external shower for just US$35. Meals are available for US$30 per day and include the fresh homemade cooking of owners Marge and Tom. Hiking trails explore their 50 acres and connect to the Mountain Pine Ridge Forest Reserve and Elijio Panti National Park.

MOUNTAIN PINE RIDGE FOREST RESERVE

Prepare for a treat: This is one of Belize's most beautiful landscapes. After you steadily ascend along the Chiquibul (Pine Ridge) Road for 21 miles, a gate across the road marks your entrance to the **Mountain Pine Ridge Forest Reserve,** Belize's largest and oldest protected area, established in 1944. The 300-square-mile area features Caribbean pine and bracken ferns instead of the typical tropical vegetation found in the rest of Belize. It also features a massive granite uplifting; the exposed rocks are some of the oldest formations in the Americas, and they make for amazing swimming holes and waterfalls. In fact, some geologists think that the Mountain Pine Ridge, whose highest point is 3,336 feet above sea level at Baldy Beacon, was one of the few exposed islands when the rest of Central America was underwater.

Most San Ignacio tour operators offer day trips to the Pine Ridge's attractions, often combined with a trip to the Caracol ruins. There are way more sights than can fit into a day, but a number of lodges can put you right in the thick of it all.

Thousand Foot Falls

Occasionally referred to as Hidden Valley Falls, this torrent of Roaring Creek is probably a good deal taller than 1,000 feet and considered the highest waterfall in Central America. The turnoff to a viewpoint of the falls is a couple of miles beyond the forest reserve gate and well signed. It's quite a little drive to get all the way there, and though the view is magical, you don't get the reward of being able to jump in. From the turnoff, the road continues down for about four miles and brings you to **Thousand Foot Falls** (US$2 pp) and a picnic area. View the falls from across the gorge and through breaks in the mist. A small store (7am-5pm daily) and picnic tables can be found at the viewpoint.

Big Rock Falls

A hand-painted sign on the dirt road to Gaia Lodge is the only indicator to the trailhead for **Big Rock Falls.** You can park and hike down a trail with steps leading down to a series of spectacular jade pools, and to the left, a loud, gushing waterfall: Big Rock. The entire scene—from pine trees towering over the water to giant rocks and verdant forest—is worth the stop and a swim. Use the gray rocks to follow the path as close to the water as possible. There's no clear entry point, so step carefully until you reach the bigger pool by Big Rock Falls. Sneakers are a must. After a

refreshing dip, brace yourself for a steep hike back.

Río On Pools and Río Frio Cave

Most Caracol packages try to squeeze in an afternoon stopover at these lovely sites. Heading south on Chiquibul Road toward Augustine, you will cross the Río On Pools. It's well worth the climb over an assortment of worn boulders and rocks to waterfalls and several warm-water pools. There's a parking area just off the road. Turn right at Douglas de Silva ranger station (the western division of the Forestry Department) and continue for about five miles to reach Río Frio Cave. Follow the signs to the parking lot. From here, visitors have a choice of exploring nature trails and two small caves on the road or continuing to Río Frio Cave, with an enormous arched entryway into the 0.5-mile-long cave. Filtered light highlights ferns, mosses, stalactites, and geometric patterns of striations on rocks. Watch for sinkholes. At times, a military escort is necessary to Río Frio. Ask at the Douglas de Silva ranger station on Chiquibul Road.

Food and Accommodations

Situated on 7,200 acres of private property in the heart of the Mountain Pine Ridge Forest Reserve, **Hidden Valley Inn** (4 Cooma Cairn Rd., tel. 501/822-3320, www.hiddenvalleyinn. com, about US$335-445, meals not included, packages available) is a quiet paradise for hikers and bird-watchers, who have a blast exploring the resort's 90-plus miles of walking trails and old logging roads. Later, after dining under the stars, they cozy up in front of their cottage's fireplace. The property encompasses lush broadleaf forest and pine tree habitat, and two diverse ecosystems are divided by a geological fault line that marks the edge of a towering 1,000-foot escarpment. Birders, be prepared to check off orange-breasted falcons, king vultures, stygian owls, azure-crowned hummingbirds, green jays, and golden-hooded tanagers. Picnic lunches are provided for the myriad day trips available. The main house, built of local hardwoods, feels more like a ski lodge than a tropical resort, with several spacious common rooms, including a fireside lounge, a card room, a bar, a library, and the restaurant. The cottages have Saltillo tile floors, vaulted ceilings, cypress-paneled walls, fireplaces, ceiling fans, screened louvered windows, comfy beds, and private baths with hot and cold water, some with waterfall orchid showers in a private outdoor bath. Hidden Valley Inn is three miles in from the Mile 14 turnoff onto Cooma Cairn Road—just follow the signs.

Francis Ford Coppola first came to Belize just after the country gained independence in 1981; he tried and failed to persuade the new government to apply for a satellite license in order to become a hub of world communications. He did, however, succeed in finding an abandoned lodge on a pine-carpeted bluff overlooking the rocks and falls of Privassion Creek. It served as a private retreat for the film producer until 1993, when he "tricked it open" by flying a group of family and friends down for his 54th birthday. Today, **Blancaneaux Lodge** (tel. 501/824-4914, U.S. tel. 866/356-5881, www.blancaneaux. com, from US$250) remains one of Central America's premier resorts, featuring the design of Mexican architect Manolo Mestre. Splashes of color, dark hardwoods, Central American lines, and soaring thatched ceilings mark Blancaneaux's 20 guest rooms, consisting of luxurious cabanas and villas. There is a U-shaped hot pool above the river and a spa built in an Indonesian rice house with Thai massage therapists.

Blancaneaux's **Ristorante Montagna** offers an Italian-centric menu with a range of salads, pastas (US$14), seafood, sandwiches, pizzas (US$18), and, of course, a selection of wines from Coppola's Napa Valley vineyards—smooth and costly. Two honeymoon cabanas with their own private infinity pools and choice of two views (US$420) and the Enchanted Cottage kick things up a notch in luxury. The Enchanted Cottage is also available for a small group of friends

looking to celebrate a special event who can afford US$1,470 per night. An on-site hydroelectric dam powers the entire operation, and a 3.5-acre organic herb and vegetable garden supplies many of the restaurant's needs (and those of Turtle Inn). It has a stable with 29 healthy horses and a number of guided trail trips. The lodge is at Mile 14.5 and has its own airstrip, which many guests prefer to the 2.5-hour drive from Belize City.

Originally built in 1991, **Gaia River Lodge** (tel. 501/834-4024, www.gaiariverlodge.com, US$200-395) sits high atop the stunning Privassion Creek in the Pine Ridge, above the Five Sisters Falls. Cabanas are located on the top of the steep canyon; they include beautifully thatched garden-, mountain-, or waterfall-view cabanas—16 in all—as well as an exclusive riverside villa. The waterfall-view suite is ideal for honeymooners, with two levels, a living room with an open deck, mosquito netting, and complete privacy. Various activity packages are offered. Have a beer or a meal on the outdoor restaurant's deck, and enjoy the commanding view above the river and the constant, gushing sound of the falls. The hardy can walk the 300 steps down to the river and Five Sisters; if you're too tired after splashing around, not to worry—the hydro-powered rainforest tram will carry you back up the hill, at least between 8am and 5pm. Gaia is one of nine Green Globe-certified resorts in Belize and the sister resort to Matachica in San Pedro, equally upscale yet laid-back.

★ CARACOL ARCHAEOLOGICAL SITE

Archaeologists Diane and Arlen Chase believe that **Caracol** (www.caracol.org), one of the largest sites in Belize, is the Mayan city-state that toppled mighty Tikal, just to the northwest, effectively shutting it down for 130 years. Located within the Chiquibul Forest Reserve, Caracol is *out there,* offering both natural wonders and Mayan mystery. To date, only a small percentage of the 177

Caracol Archaeological Site

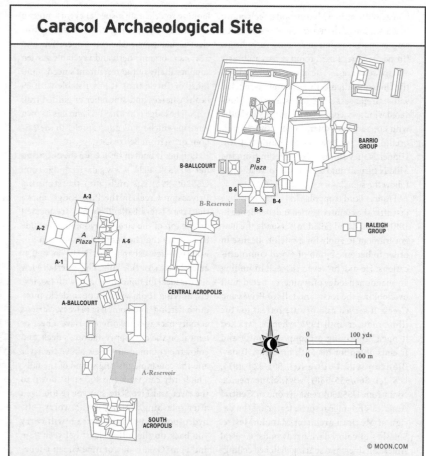

BARRIO GROUP

B-BALLCOURT

B Plaza

B-6

B-Reservoir

B-4

B-5

A-3

A-2

A Plaza

A-6

A-1

RALEIGH GROUP

A-BALLCOURT

CENTRAL ACROPOLIS

A-Reservoir

0   100 yds

0   100 m

SOUTH ACROPOLIS

© MOON.COM

square kilometers that make up the site has even been mapped, identifying only 5,000 of the estimated 36,000 structures lying beneath the forest canopy.

The centerpiece is no doubt the pyramid of Canaa, rising 136 feet above the plaza floor (about a foot taller than El Castillo at Xunantunich), one of the tallest structures—ancient or modern—in Belize. Canaa was only completely cleared of vegetation in 2005 by the Tourism Development Project (TDP), whose work has unveiled most of the structures you see. The vistas from the top of Canaa are extensive and memorable.

In addition to the aforementioned superlatives, Caracol, a Classic Period site, is noted for its large masks and giant date glyphs on circular stone altars. There is also a fine display of the Maya's engineering skills, with extensive reservoirs, agricultural terraces, and several mysterious ramps. Caracol has been studied for more than 20 years by the Chases and their assistants, student interns from Tulane University in New Orleans and the University of Central Florida. According to John Morris, an archaeologist with Belize's Institute of Archaeology, a lifetime of exploration remains to be done for 6-9 miles in every direction of the excavated part of Caracol. It's proving to have been a powerful site that controlled a very large area, possibly once home to over 100,000 inhabitants. The rainforest you see now would have been totally absent in those days, as the wood was cleared to provide fuel and agricultural land to support so many people.

Many carvings date from AD 500-800, and ceramic evidence indicates that Caracol was settled around AD 300 and continued to flourish when other Mayan sites were in decline. Carvings at the site also indicate that Caracol and Tikal engaged in ongoing conflicts, each defeating the other on various occasions. After the war in AD 562, Caracol flourished for more than a century in the mountains and valleys surrounding the site. A former archaeological commissioner named the site Caracol (snail in Spanish) because of the winding logging road to reach it, although some contend it was because of all the snail shells found during initial excavations.

Visiting the Site

Entrance to Caracol is US$15. The small visitors center presents a scale model and interesting information based mostly on the work of the Chases over the last two decades. A planned **Monument Museum** will allow visitors to view a range of artifacts and stelae from the site and will be based on the work of the Tourism Development Project. There are no official guides on-site, as most groups arrive with their own. However, the caretakers know Caracol well and will be glad to walk you through and explain the site for a few dollars. Most tours start with the Raleigh Group, move by the enormous ceiba trees, then circle through the archaeologists' camp, and end with a bang by climbing Canaa.

Transportation

Most tour operators offer Caracol day trips, often involving stops at various caves and swimming holes on the way back through the Mountain Pine Ridge. The ride should take 2-3 hours, depending on both the weather and the progress made by road improvement crews, who hopefully will not run out of money before you read this. If you're driving, a 4WD vehicle is a must; gas is not available along the 50-mile road, so carry ample fuel. Camping is not allowed in the area without permission from the Institute of Archaeology in Belmopan. The closest accommodations are those along the Pine Ridge Road.

At times, a military escort is necessary to visit Caracol. Be sure to ask at your lodge. Tour operators know to show up at 9:30am at the Augustine (Douglas de Silva) gate to convoy to the ruins.

Into Guatemala

The western *frontera* into Guatemala is only 11 miles from San Ignacio. Be prepared to pay a US$19 per person exit fee (exact change will be requested) on the Belizean side, which includes a Protected Areas Conservation Trust (PACT) fee; the rest of the money goes to the private Border Management company, a point of contention for local tour providers and would-be Guatemalan day-trippers. Expect the usual throng of money changers to greet you on both sides of the border—they're fine to use as long as you know what rate you should be getting—or you can use the official Casas de Cambio on either side.

Bus and Taxi

The trip from San Ignacio can be made for around US$3 per person in a *colectivo* taxi, less in a passing bus bound for Benque Viejo. A private taxi from San Ignacio should cost about US$15 total.

Car

If you're driving your own car, make sure you have all the necessary papers of ownership

and attendant photocopies of all your documents, including your driver's license and passport, which they *will* want to see. You are required by law to have your tires fumigated when entering/exiting Belize and Guatemala, which costs a dollar or two. If driving a private or rental vehicle into Guatemala, you will have to pay a toll to cross the bridge going over the Mopan into Melchor. If your car has Belizean tags, the fee can be as low as 5 quetzales (US$0.65). If your tags are from far away, like Canada or the United States, be prepared to pay 50 quetzales (US$6.50) and not one peso more. Save the receipt if you are returning to Belize, as it is good for a two-way crossing. In addition, based on some reports, travelers have to ensure that they have received a proper exit stamp when leaving Belize for both themselves and their vehicle. Double-check your passport before continuing on to Guatemala.

Melchor

After clearing Guatemalan immigration and shaking off the sometimes aggressive *taxistas,* you'll find yourself on the edge of the Mopan River, across which begins the town of Melchor de Mencos. Before crossing the bridge, you'll find the **Río Mopan Lodge** (tel. 502/7926-5196, US$20) on your left, a nice riverside hotel and restaurant whose proprietors (a Swiss-Spanish couple) are a wealth of information on remote ruins in the area. There are other places in Melchor if you get stranded in town for some reason or are embarking on your own rainforest expedition to unexplored ruins. Otherwise, head on toward the most popular place to visit in Guatemala from the western border of Belize: Tikal National Park.

TIKAL NATIONAL PARK

Guatemala's most-visited attraction opened to the public in 1955 and was declared a UNESCO World Heritage Site in 1979. One of the most magnificent of all Mayan sites, the 222-square-mile **Tikal National Park** is located in northern Guatemala, in the heart of El Petén, Guatemala's largest department. The park also belongs to the 21,000-square-mile Reserva de Biosfera Maya (Mayan Biosphere Reserve), considered the most biodiverse region in the country, with the largest area of tropical rainforest in Central America. Much of the reserve still consists of dense forests with more than 300 species of commercially useful trees, such as cedar, mahogany, and chicle, as well as abundant wildlife.

Amid El Petén's stunning canopy of green sit several Mayan archaeological sites, including Uaxactún and El Mirador. But the most unique of all is Tikal. No visitor forgets that first glance at Tikal's gigantic pyramids dominating the park's green skyline. Temple I and Temple IV, at commanding heights of over 100 to 200-plus feet, are sheer masterpieces. Visitors can climb up some of these temples, while others are considered too steep and remain closed.

Even more mind-boggling is that only about 15 percent of Tikal has been uncovered thus far. Under the auspices of the University of Pennsylvania, the site was excavated and studied over a period of 13 years (1956-1969). An estimated 4,000 structures were located, including temples, palaces, ball courts, a marketplace, and residential compounds. Restored areas include the Great Plaza, the North Acropolis, the Lost World, the Twin Pyramid complexes, and Temples I, II, IV, and V. Stelae, burials, ceramics, and other offerings were discovered during this time, and causeways connecting the various areas of Tikal were restored. Thousands more structures continue to lie buried under thick rainforest, covered up for the past thousands of years since the ancient Maya deserted this city around AD 900 for reasons that remain unknown.

Coupled with its natural and historical significance, and a host of affordable accommodations options in the nearby charming lakeside village of El Remate or the neighboring island town of Flores, capital of El Petén,

---

1: Barton Creek Cave; **2:** Big Rock Falls; **3:** view from Temple IV at Tikal National Park

Into Guatemala

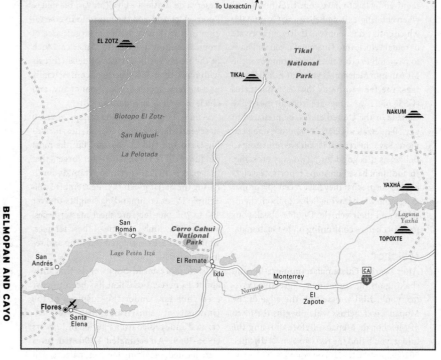

Tikal is a must-see if you have a day to spare during your stay in western Belize.

History

Tikal, commonly translated from Mayan as "City of Spiritual Voices," was first inhabited in 600 BC, although its first structures weren't erected until at least 100 years later, around 500 BC. The Pre-Classic Period saw the erection of several structures, including the North Acropolis's ceremonial buildings and the Pyramid at El Mundo Perdido.

By the Early Classic Period, circa AD 250, the Great Plaza began to emerge as Tikal became a key city, with its growing commerce, population, and culture. Its first ruler was King Yax Ehb' Xook, who established the Tikal lineage; Tikal's history and the evolution of its architecture are closely tied to its rulers—33 of them presided over 800 years, and the most important of them all was Ruler 26, Hasaw Chan K'awil, from the Late Classic Period (682-734).

There are signs that Tikal's history was linked to Teotihuacán, a non-Mayan city 630 miles away, northeast of Mexico City, which reached its peak AD 150-650. One example is that the designs at the Lost World Complex and other designs found on ceramics seem to replicate signs of the Teotihuacán, including its god Tlaloc. Moreover, in the fourth century AD, the Mexican city sent over one of its warriors to aid Tikal in a war against neighboring Uaxactún and helped elevate Tikal to where it dominated the Petén region for centuries to come.

Five hundred years later, as Teotihuacán's influence waned, Tikal faced the threat of

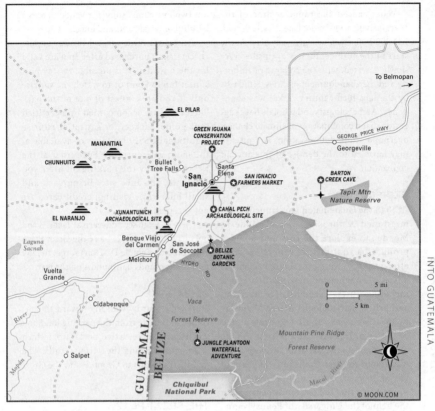

regional dominance by the powerful city of Calakmul, in northern Guatemala and present-day Mexico. Unfortunately for Tikal, Calakmul forged an alliance with Caracol, currently Belize's largest Mayan site. A preemptive strike on Caracol eventually backfired: Archaeologists believe that during one counterattack against Tikal in AD 562, Caracol toppled Tikal, shutting down the city for 130 years, during which time no monuments were erected or inscribed and many of Tikal's stelae were desecrated, although it was discovered recently that Temple V was built during this period.

HEIGHT AND DECLINE

Eventually rebounding, in AD 682 Tikal entered a golden period when Ruler Ah-Cacao (Hasaw Chan K'awil, or Lord Chocolate) took over and began the construction of Tikal's most impressive structures, erecting them at a dizzying pace. Other significant achievements of his reign, which lasted until 723, were his two successive and successful attacks against Calakmul, capturing and executing its two kings, first Jaguar Paw (Ich'ak K'ak) and, a year later, Split Earth, thus weakening any further alliance against Tikal and reclaiming its position as the greatest city in Petén.

Hasaw Chan K'awil thereby reinstated a powerful dynasty at Tikal. During this Classic Period, AD 250-900, a time recognized as the peak in Mayan art, architecture, and intellectual achievements across the Mundo Maya, Tikal's five main temples were built. At the city's height, an estimated 100,000 Maya lived in Tikal, covering an area of about 12 square miles.

What caused the rapid decline of the Mayan civilization in the Late Classic Period, AD 800-900, remains a great mystery. At the start of the 10th century, Mayan sites were slowly deserted, with the collapse of authority and the abandonment of cities. Similarly, by the late 10th century, Tikal was abandoned. Archaeologists and scholars have suggested that a combination of climate change, overpopulation, deforestation, and disease may have led to the demise of this ancient civilization.

REDISCOVERY

In 1848 the Guatemalan government commissioned Ambrosio Tut and Modesto Méndez to explore the site, and Méndez produced a first official report on Tikal after a week's visit. Several other scientists passed through after viewing this report, including Gustav Bernoulli of Switzerland and British archaeologist Alfred Maudslay in 1881, who was the first to draw a map of the area. He was also the first to take photographs of the site after the vegetation was removed after thousands of years of burial. It wasn't until an airstrip was built in the 1950s that the real study began, with the help of the University of Pennsylvania, which carried out excavations from 1956 to 1969.

The latest discoveries date to 1996, mainly including the inscriptions on Temple V that indicate that the site was built during the 130 years Tikal was previously believed to have shut down after a defeat by Caracol and Calakmul.

Visiting the Site

Tickets to **Tikal National Park** (www. tikalnationalpark.org, 6am-5pm daily, US$20 per day) are sold at the main entrance gate, and you can also purchase an official site map (US$10). From the gate, there's a 15- to 20-minute drive to the parking lot and **visitors center.** Be sure to purchase your entrance ticket at the first gate and not at the second. Once on-site, there's a large parking lot, two museums, souvenir vendors, and a handful of restaurants and lodges.

Tickets are valid only for the day of purchase; tickets purchased after 3pm are valid for the next day. It is possible to stay past sunset (up to 9pm) or to watch the sunrise only if you are a guest of one of the park lodges *and* are accompanied by a certified tour guide. Tickets for sunset or sunrise (additional US$10 fee) are not available at the main gate entrance but rather at the ticket booth by the parking lot after you reach the entrance site. Bring cash and small bills while visiting; credit cards are not accepted.

There's a lot to see and learn at Tikal. If you only have half a day, explore the Great Plaza and climb up Temple IV. Don't forget to look for monkeys and coatimundis on the way.

CEIBA TREE

Start your tour by walking toward the entrance of the site from the parking lot. Soon you'll see a giant ceiba tree, not far from which is a map indicating the various trails. The middle trail leads to Group F and the Great Plaza.

THE GREAT PLAZA

If you only have a couple of hours at Tikal, this is where you want to be. The central plaza of Tikal is most impressive architecturally, with four temples towering over the gigantic area. The Great Plaza buildings—North Acropolis, Temple I, Temple II, and the Central Acropolis—took more than 1,000 years to construct. The sheer city-like size of this courtyard—as well as the 70 stelae carved with images and hieroglyphs—is sure to impress.

TEMPLE I

Temple I is one of three temples towering around the Great Plaza, the heart of what was once the great city of Tikal. Temple I, known as the Big Jaguar, was built by Hasaw Chan K'awil (Lord Chocolate) in AD 700. His tomb was later found under the 151-foot-high

Tikal National Park

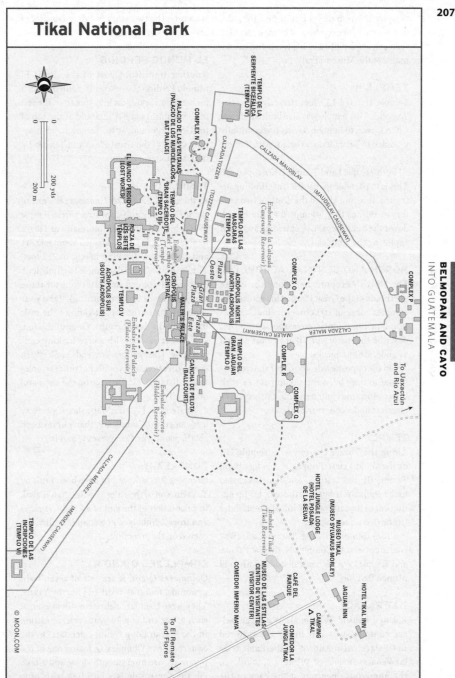

TEMPLO DE LA
SERPIENTE BICEFALICA
(TEMPLO IV)

COMPLEX N

PALACIO DE LAS VENTANAS
(PALACIO DE LOS MURCIÉLAGOS,
BAT PALACE)

CALZADA TOZZER

CALZADA MAUDSLAY
(MAUDSLAY CAUSEWAY)

EL MUNDO PERDIDO
(LOST WORLD)

TEMPLO DEL
GRAN SACERDOTE
(TEMPLO III)

(TOZZER CAUSEWAY)

TEMPLO DE LAS
MASCARAS
(TEMPLO II)

Embalse de la Calzada
(Causeway Reservoir)

COMPLEX O

COMPLEX P

PLAZA DE
LOS SIETE
TEMPLOS

Embalse
del Templo
(Temple
Reservoir)

Plaza
Oeste

ACRÓPOLIS
CENTRAL

ACRÓPOLIS NORTE
(NORTH ACROPOLIS)

Gran
Plaza

ACRÓPOLIS SUR
(SOUTH ACROPOLIS)

TEMPLO V

MALER'S PALACE

Plaza
Este

CALZADA MALER
(MALER CAUSEWAY)

COMPLEX R

Embalse del Palacio
(Palace Reservoir)

TEMPLO DEL
GRAN JAGUAR
(TEMPLO I)

COMPLEX Q

CANCHA DE PELOTA
(BALLCOURT)

Embalse Secreto
(Hidden Reservoir)

To Uaxactún
and Río Azul

CALZADA MÉNDEZ
(MÉNDEZ CAUSEWAY)

TEMPLO DE LAS
INSCRIPCIONES
(TEMPLO VI)

Embalse Tikal
(Tikal Reservoir)

HOTEL JUNGLE LODGE
(HOTEL POSADA
DE LA SELVA)

MUSEO TIKAL
(MUSEO SYLVANUS MORLEY)

HOTEL TIKAL INN

JAGUAR INN

CAFÉ DEL
PARQUE

MUSEO DE LAS ESTELAS,
CENTRO DE VISITANTES
(VISITOR CENTER)

CAMPING
TIKAL

COMEDOR LA
JUNGLA TIKAL

COMEDOR IMPERIO MAYA

To El Remate
and Flores

0
200 yds

0
200 m

© MOON.COM

temple, his remains surrounded by jade, pearls, and other symbols of human sacrifice (you can see a replica of his tomb and his remains at the Museo Tikal).

TEMPLE II

Temple II rises 125 feet directly opposite Temple I. This temple was also built by Hasaw Chan K'awil, to honor his wife. It was initially intended to be of identical height with Temple I.

Both Temple I and Temple II are roped off. This is in part due to insufficient climbing infrastructure, but also to the death of two visitors in 1992 as they attempted to climb back down the steep steps. Use extreme care when exploring the temples.

NORTH AND CENTRAL ACROPOLIS

The North Acropolis lies along the entire north side of the Great Plaza. This enormous, complex maze of structures includes a section housing smooth, engraved **stelae** that describe the history of Tikal's rulers as well as underground masks.

On the opposite side, the Central Acropolis is said to have been the site of palaces with interconnecting chambers and stairways centered around a courtyard.

TEMPLE III

Along the Tozzer Causeway is Temple III, or the Great Priest Temple, at 196 feet high. Temple III is unrestored and remains closed to the public. You can spot the temple's tip jutting out of the rainforest, while the remainder sits buried under foliage.

From Temple III, the Tozzer Causeway continues west to Complex N, the Bat Palace, and Temple IV. Another trail leads south to El Mundo Perdido.

BAT PALACE

Located behind Temple III is a large palace complex, which includes the restored Bat Palace. Also known as the Palacio de las Venatas (Palace of Windows), thanks to the numerous openings at the back of the

structure, the two-story building consists of several rows of rooms.

EL MUNDO PERDIDO

Another significant part of the site is El Mundo Perdido (Lost World), named as such for having a varying architecture from the rest of the buildings at Tikal. Stand at the top of the Great Pyramid, at 105 feet high, for stunning views of the Great Plaza and Temple IV in the distance.

TEMPLE IV

At the end of the Tozzer Causeway lies one of the site's most significant structures: Temple IV, the highest and most impressive of Tikal's temples. Temple IV was erected about AD 741 and stands at a dizzying height of 212 feet. This is the most popular temple to climb; look for parallel wooden staircases (one for those going up, another for returning). Take your time getting to the top, hold on to the railing, and take deep breaths. Once at the top, you'll be rewarded with a breathtaking canopy view: The rainforest extends endlessly in every direction, and you'll spot other temples in the distance. Find a place on the steps and take it all in.

At Temple IV, the Maudslay Causeway leads north to Complex P, then curves back south, passing by Complexes Q and R.

COMPLEX P

Complex P is believed to have been built by Yax Kin, son of the ruler Hasaw Chan K'awil, in celebration of the end of a *k'atun*. Jaguars and frogs, symbols of power and fertility, are carved on the structure.

COMPLEXES Q AND R

Complexes Q and R are sets of seven twin pyramids, found at Tikal and nearby Yaxhá. They were built to celebrate cyclical events, such as the end of a 20-year cycle, or *k'atun,* in the Mayan Long Count calendar. On the eastern side of Complex Q, facing one of the pyramids, are nine smooth stelae and altars. On the south side is a building with nine doorways, believed to have been a ceremonial palace. Of note here is **Stela 22,** portraying Yax Ain II in his full costume; he took the throne in AD 768.

Museums

There are two museums at Tikal, located at opposite ends. The open-air **Museo Lítico** (9am-noon and 1pm-4:30pm Mon.-Fri., closes earlier Sat.-Sun., free) is at the visitors center, set around a courtyard close to the entrance. Exhibits include a large-scale model of the site, showing the city as estimated around AD 800. There are also photographs of Tikal as it was first being excavated by a team from the University of Pennsylvania.

Save some time for a stop at the second museum, **Museo Tikal** (also called Museo Sylvanus G. Morley, 9am-5pm Mon.-Fri., closes earlier Sat.-Sun., US$5), just past the Jaguar Inn. The museum houses a replica burial chamber with the remains of Hasaw Chan K'awil (Lord Chocolate), whose skeleton was found beneath Temple I. Also on display are ceramics, bloodletting instruments, and incense burners, all found in burial sites. Another exhibit showcases jade necklaces, amulets, and elaborate incense burners found beneath Temple V as well as stelae found buried under the North Acropolis.

To get the most out of these museums, ask a guide to explain the significance of these artifacts (there isn't much labeled).

Birding and Wildlife-Watching

Tikal's surrounding rainforest makes it an ideal wildlife-watching destination. More than 50 species of mammals and 400 species of birds have been spotted here. Look for toucans, oropendolas, spider and howler monkeys, coatimundis, deer, and more. Jaguars, whose symbolic faces were carved into the stelae at Tikal, still inhabit the park. There are also crocodiles and reptiles, including a resident alligator, and poisonous snakes, although these are known to be nocturnal.

Arrange for special bird-watching tours with **La Casa de Don David** (El Remate, tel. 502/5306-2190, www.lacasadedondavid.com), which has excellent English-speaking birding guides that are knowledgeable about the park. Another excellent tour company is outfitter **Cayaya Birding** (tel. 502/5308-5160, www.cayaya-birding.com), based in Guatemala City.

Canopy Tour

Canopy Tikal Tours (tel. 502/4739-2587, www.tikalcanopy.com, 7am-5pm daily, US$30) offers a zip line across the park either before or after you tour the site (I recommend after). There are 11 platforms at heights of up to 80 feet above the forest canopy. A second, higher zip line is also available (if you dare). Pickups are free from within the park; you can also arrange to be picked up from Flores for an extra fee. Canopy Tikal Tours also offers horseback riding at Tikal.

Food

All the hotels inside Tikal National Park have restaurants, the most popular of which is the one at the Jungle Lodge. However, there are also independent restaurants (*comedores*) clustered near the entrance, offering Central American fare as well as burgers for about US$5-10. These include **Comedor Tikal** (the better one), and **Restaurant Imperio Maya.** All *comedores* open early for breakfast and serve food until 9pm daily.

For better menu options, don't hesitate to try the hotel restaurants. If you are a guest, your host may offer to-go lunch sandwiches for purchase.

Accommodations

There are three hotel options and a campground within Tikal National Park, all surrounded by lush tropical forest. Note that you're paying for the location and a unique experience at a World Heritage Site and perhaps not so much for comfort or service. This is a protected reserve, so conservation is a high priority: Electricity is available only during certain hours of the day (usually 2-3 hours at a time both in the morning and the evening), and none of the hotels have air-conditioning (you might consider bringing a small battery-operated fan, but the temperature is usually bearable). For more "comfort" with less "creature," stay in nearby Flores or El Remate, although you won't get the spectacular rainforest surroundings.

Originally built to house archaeologists working on Tikal, the guest rooms at **Jungle Lodge** (tel. 502/7861-0447, www.junglelodgetikal.com, US$40-84) are set around a lovely tropical garden and swimming pool. The hotel is close to the park entrance and offers bungalows and junior suites, as well as cheaper guest rooms with shared baths. There's a restaurant on-site (US$5-10) serving three meals a day; tour groups are often brought here at lunchtime. There's also Wi-Fi, although it's spotty.

The **Jaguar Inn** (tel. 502/7926-2411, www.jaguartikal.com, US$75-90) is close to the Tikal Museum and just a couple minutes from the site entrance. It has 13 comfy bungalows with private baths, hot and cold water, fans, and 24-hour electricity. There's an on-site restaurant serving decent meals daily. Transfers or tours can be arranged. Although unadvertised, camping (US$3.50) is available, as well as hammocks with netting (US$5)—just bring your bug spray and a flashlight.

Next door, **Tikal Inn** (tel. 502/7861-2444, www.tikalinn.com, US$50-85, includes dinner and breakfast) gets rave reviews for service, location, and value. Choose among spacious standard hotel rooms, poolside bungalows, and junior suites. Electricity runs 6am-8am and 6pm-9pm daily. Both Jaguar Inn and Tikal Inn are solid options if you plan to experience sunrise from the top of nearby Temple IV.

Looking to sleep even closer to nature? The Tikal **campground** area (US$4 pp) is opposite the visitors center and has shared shower and restroom facilities.

Transportation

If you're planning to visit Tikal on your own, have a strong dose of patience and be prepared. If traveling from the Belize border, bring your passport, exit tax (US$15), and the PACT conservation fee (US$3.75).

AIR

Tropic Air (tel. 501/226-2012, U.S. tel. 800/422-3435, www.tropicair.com) offers flights from Belize City's Philip S. W. Goldson International Airport (BZE, 10 miles west of Belize City, tel. 501/225-2045, www.pgiabelize.com) to Flores (US$304 roundtrip). Vehicles head to Tikal from the Flores airport, but be sure to reserve a reliable driver or tour operator ahead of time.

BUS

There are no direct buses to Tikal from Benque Viejo del Carmen on the Belize border. There are chicken buses that will pick up from the Guatemala side and head to Flores as well as taxis (US$20 pp, depending on the number of people). You'd then have to find your way to Tikal from Flores.

Another option is to catch the bus to Flores, get off at the crossroads in Ixlu, and then wait for another bus heading north to El Remate or all the way to Tikal. However, the wait could be long as the schedules are not published. It's also generally safer to arrange a ride with a recognized guide than going it alone.

It's possible to catch the bus all the way to the Cayo District, then all the way to Benque Viejo del Carmen and the border, and then wing it once you make it past immigration. But if you're not fluent in Spanish, or would rather play it safe (recommended), there are several tour companies with buses heading directly to Flores and Tikal from Belize City's Water Taxi Terminal (by the Swing Bridge), as well as by the San Pedro Belize Express terminal, a couple of blocks farther down.

First try **S&L Travel and Tours** (91 N. Front St., Belize City, tel. 501/227-7593 or 501/227-5145, www.sltravelbelize.com), a very reliable company, or contact **Atlanta Tour Express Bus Service** (inside the San Pedro Belize Express Water Taxi Terminal, Belize City), with direct service to Tikal and

Flores via the Guatemalan Línea Dorada buses (www.lineadorada.info). The journey to the border takes about 4.5 hours. If you're lucky, crossing the border will be smooth and painless, although lines can occasionally get long.

CAR

If you decide to rent a car, check out **Crystal Auto Rental** (Mile 5, Philip Goldson Hwy., Belize City, tel. 501/223-1600, www.crystal-belize.com, from US$65 per day), one of the only companies that will allow you to take a rental vehicle into Guatemala (be sure to inquire about insurance).

TOURS

Most tour guides in San Ignacio offer regular trips to Tikal, almost daily during the busy tourist season (Dec.-Apr.). If you opt for a tour, you won't have to worry about anything except bringing your passport, paying for the tour, and hopping in a van—the rest is taken care of, from border crossing to entrance fees. I highly recommend **Pacz Tours** (tel. 501/824-0536, cell tel. 501/604-6921, www.pacztours.net, full-day US$145, all-inclusive overnight US$400 with hotel, meals, guide, taxes, and fees), with its own resident Tikal expert.

EL REMATE

The lakeside village of El Remate is the closest town to Tikal National Park. Just 22 miles away, it is 0.5 mile north of "El Cruce," the main traffic circle with signs to Tikal. El Remate has become a favorite for overnight stays among travelers heading to the Mayan site who want to avoid the more distant Flores area and the expense of an overnight in the national park. There are plenty of transportation options in El Remate, making it easier to find shared rides with fellow travelers, and the lake is clean and safe to swim in. Hotels, restaurants, and recreation are also plentiful.

There's plenty to do in El Remate if Tikal isn't enough for you. Half- or full-day birding tours with local guides are available through

La Casa de Don David (tel. 502/5306-2190, www.lacasadedondavid.com, US$40-75). La Casa de Don David can also help arrange all kinds of other activities.

The best swimming is in front of the Biotopo Cerro Cahui Nature Reserve or at El Muelle Restaurant.

Food and Accommodations
UNDER US$25
A clean budget place that gets rave reviews is the **Sun Breeze Hotel** (Calle del Lago, tel. 502/7928-8044 or 502/5898-2665, US$10). The colorful double rooms have private baths, fans, porches, hammocks, and a working shower (the hot water is temperamental). For the price, you can't beat the quiet location within a minute's walk of the lake. The hotel can arrange for transportation to Tikal and even to Belize City.

US$25-50
Not far along on your route, ★ **La Casa de Don David** (off the main road, tel. 502/5306-2190, www.lacasadedondavid.com, US$23-28, includes either breakfast or dinner) is the preferred choice of many. This is a cozy, simple, and safe place to stay with standard or premium guest rooms set in a lush garden, with private baths, balconies, fans or air-conditioning, and hot water. There's an on-site restaurant serving home-cooked Guatemalan specialties as well as wireless Internet access. The hotel owners have a wealth of information on the area and can arrange for all kinds of tours.

The rustic and charming lakeside ★ **Posada del Cerro** (tel. 502/5376-8722 or 502/5305-1717, www.posadadelcerro.com, US$40-56) offers simple but charming accommodations, including cottages with thatched roofs, a patio, and a serene environment. Posada del Cerro is right next to the entrance of the Biotopo Cerro Cahui Reserve, hence the lovely lake views and freshwater swimming. There's an on-site restaurant and lounge area for guests to enjoy.

US$50-100

Right on the main road, the Western-inspired **Palomino Ranch Hotel** (tel. 502/7928-8419, www.hotelpalominoranch.com, US$50) offers eight double rooms, each equipped with air-conditioning, a TV, and hot water, in a large villa with a swimming pool. The hotel also offers horseback riding trips and gets rave reviews for its service.

US$150-200

Petén's ultimate in luxury is ★ **La Lancha** (tel. 502/7928-8331, U.S. tel. 855/670-4817, www.blancaneaux.com, US$160-240, breakfast included), Francis Ford Coppola's 10-room lodge in Guatemala. The lakeshore views may be its best feature, as its location in the village of Jobompiche is somewhat remoter than the other hotels. Choose from lake-view casitas or rainforest casitas, all tastefully decorated with Guatemalan fabrics, Balinese wood, and beautiful decks where you can laze in a hammock. The on-site restaurant serves Guatemalan specialties (lunch and dinner US$20 pp), and there's a lovely pool below the restaurant.

FLORES

Flores is a small island town located in Lake Petén Itzá, with cobblestone streets and lakeside bistros. It is connected to its twin town on the mainland, Santa Elena (although they are often collectively referred to as Flores) by a causeway. Santa Elena itself is a noisy commercial center, and few visitors choose to stay here. Flores, once a popular stopover, is now slowly being replaced by the up-and-coming El Remate, mostly because the accommodations there offer better value, the lake is clean and safe to swim in, and its location is closer to both Tikal National Park and Belize.

Still, a couple of sights worth checking out in Flores include the **Yaxhá-Nakum-Naranjo Natural Monument** (8am-5pm daily, US$10), home to several Mayan sites, the most prominent of which is Yaxhá, made even more famous when the TV show *Survivor Guatemala* was filmed here in 2005.

Food and Accommodations

Eco Lodge El Sombrero (tel. 502/4215-8777, www.ecolodgeelsombrero.com, US$20-35) offers basic guest rooms in thatched-roof lakefront bungalows. While there's a dock, it isn't safe to swim here, unless you want to be chased by crocodiles. There's an on-site restaurant with decent food. The upside is the location, right next to the Yaxhá site and surrounded by rainforest, lakes, and the occasional visiting howler monkey.

Southern Coast and Cayes

The Southern Coast has an Afro-Caribbean soul. It also boasts a beautiful coastline, lush rainforests, waterfalls, the world's only jaguar preserve, the country's highest point, and the longest stretch of beach.

The Stann Creek District is at the heart of the country's fascinating Garifuna culture, declared endangered by the United Nations in 2001 yet still thriving thanks to a concerted effort to preserve tradition. The seaside town of Dangriga, Garifuna hub and Belize's "culture capital," is home to a third of Stann Creek District's 36,000 inhabitants, and its economy is as varied as its culture and geography; tourism is only as important as the orange, banana, and shrimp industries. Unassuming and untouristed, Dangriga is more than just a pit stop

Highlights

Look for ★ to find recommended sights, activities, dining, and lodging.

Gulisi Garifuna Museum
Garifuna Settlement Day
Mayflower Bocawina National Park ★
★ Dangriga
Cockscomb Basin Wildlife Sanctuary ★
★ Hopkins
★ Tobacco Caye
Glover's Reef Atoll ★
Garifuna Culture Tour
★ South Water Caye Marine Reserve
Placencia Village ★
○ Placencia
Caribbean Sea
★ Laughing Bird Caye National Park
© MOON.COM
0   15 mi
0   15 km

★ **Gulisi Garifuna Museum:** Enjoy an interactive history lesson on the fascinating Garifuna culture (page 220).

★ **Garifuna Settlement Day:** November 19 celebrates the arrival of the ancestral Garinagu to Belize's shores. A colorful reenactment is followed by parades, processions, and a multitude of events from outdoor concerts to all-night drumming (page 225).

★ **South Water Caye Marine Reserve:** One of Belize's most beautiful offshore islands offers excellent snorkeling right off the beach and impressive dive sites within a marine reserve (page 231).

★ **Tobacco Caye:** Sitting right atop Belize's barrier reef, Tobacco Caye can be a social hot spot of world travelers or an isolated island experience, depending on the time of year (page 232).

★ **Glover's Reef Atoll:** Glover's spectacular snorkeling and diving are a short journey from the southern shore. The waters are ideal for all kinds of sports (page 236).

★ **Garifuna Culture Tour:** Dress up and immerse yourself in Garifuna history, spirituality, and culinary culture at the Palmento Grove Cultural & Fishing Lodge (page 240).

★ **Mayflower Bocawina National Park:** Rappel waterfalls, swim in jade pools, zip across 7,100 acres of forest canopy, and enjoy bird- and wildlife-watching (page 254).

★ **Cockscomb Basin Wildlife Sanctuary:** This extensive reserve is famous for its multitude of birds, jaguars, and other rainforest critters—and you can camp here overnight (page 256).

★ **Placencia Village:** Peppered with boutique hotels, restaurants, and bars, the village is as low-key or active as you'd like. It's a perfect jumping-off point to some of the best diving and snorkeling in Belize (page 263).

★ **Laughing Bird Caye National Park:** Palms, sand, and excellent snorkeling are found at this national park, part of a 10,000-acre protected marine area (page 280).

on the way to Placencia or the gateway to the Southern Cayes; independent travelers can get off the beaten path here and explore African-inspired art galleries, make their own drums, and perhaps enjoy a meal at a Garifuna home. That's when you're not off trekking in the nearby Cockscomb Basin Wildlife Sanctuary, waterfall rappelling at nearby Mayflower Bocawina National Park, or cooling off in Billy Barquedier's emerald streams. It's astounding how many activities are within reach.

More traveler-friendly yet still authentic, the nearby fishing village of Hopkins has uncrowded wide-open beaches, a host of lodging options to fit all budgets, drumming lessons, and authentic Garifuna cuisine.

Beachcombers and dive enthusiasts looking to add pulsating nightlife to their trip will be happy to continue on to the Placencia Peninsula, one of the most rapidly developing tourist areas of Belize. With the longest (and nicest) stretch of beach on the mainland, a mixed Garifuna and Creole vibe, and the oft-photographed Silk Cayes and a UNESCO World Heritage Site just a quick boat ride away, Placencia offers plenty to love.

PLANNING YOUR TIME

There's a lot to see and do on the Southern Coast. For a decent glimpse into this area, you'll need at least five or six days, with time saved for an offshore island-hop. Start with **Dangriga.** Walk along the **North Stann Creek Bridge** and **Commerce Boulevard,** and then head to Y-Not Island for some beachfront breezes and river views. Squeeze in a visit to the **Gulisi Garifuna Museum** and **Pen Cayetano Studio Gallery,** where you'll learn all about this Afro-Caribbean Garifuna culture. With an extra day, you can tour the Marie Sharp's Factory, where the most popular hot sauce in Belize is made and bottled.

Hopkins is just an hour away by bus from Dangriga. Stay right in the village at one of several budget beachfront guesthouses, bike around, sample Garifuna dishes, and take drumming lessons at **Lebeha Drumming Center.** The nearby Sittee River offers birding and wildlife-watching.

From Hopkins, trek to a waterfall in **Mayflower Bocawina National Park** and spend the night in **Maya Centre.** Shop for crafts, converse with herbal healers, and arrange an expedition within the **Cockscomb Basin Wildlife Sanctuary.**

Placencia is the "barefoot perfect" beach area of Belize, although sargassum issues have plagued it lately, but it's easily reached by bus from Hopkins and you can journey along the gorgeous southern reef and dive to your heart's content. Rent a cheap cabana on **Maya Beach** and barhop the night away, or make a day trip to **Laughing Bird Caye.**

If you choose to travel along the Southern Coast in this way, Hopkins is your best bet for a halfway base from which to explore.

Previous: view of the Placencia Village pier; Placencia Village beach; Tobacco Caye Paradise Cabins.

Southern Coast and Cayes

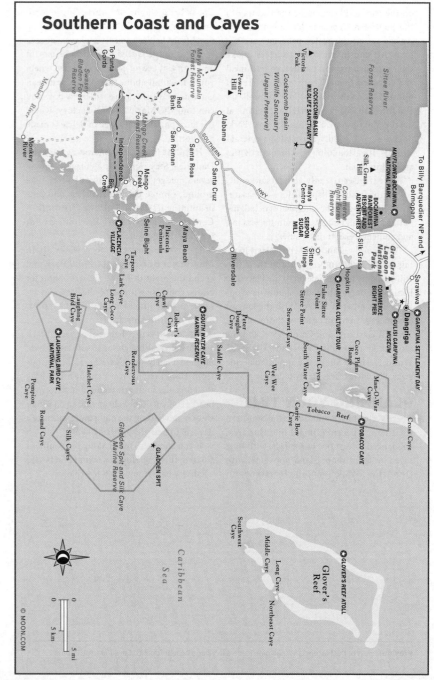

To Punta Gorda

Monkey River

Monkey River

Swasey Bladen Forest Reserve

Maya Mountain Forest Reserve

Victoria Peak

Powder Hill

Cockscomb Basin Wildlife Sanctuary (Jaguar Preserve)

COCKSCOMB BASIN WILDLIFE SANCTUARY

Sittee River

Sittee River Forest Reserve

To Billy Barquedier NP and Belmopan

MAYFLOWER BOCAWINA NATIONAL PARK

BOCAWINA RAINFOREST RESORT AND ADVENTURES

Silk Grass Hill

Commerce Bight Forest Reserve

Gra Gra Lagoon National Park

To Billy Barquedier NP and Belmopan

Saraawina

GARIFUNA SETTLEMENT DAY

Red Bank

Mango Creek Forest Reserve

Independence

Big Creek

Mango Creek

San Roman

Santa Rosa

Alabama

Santa Cruz

SOUTHERN HWY

Maya Centre

SERPON SUGAR MILL

Silk Grass

Sittee Village

COMMERCE BIGHT PIER

Hopkins

GARIFUNA CULTURE TOUR

GULISI GARIFUNA MUSEUM

Dangriga

GARIFUNA SETTLEMENT DAY

PLACENCIA VILLAGE

Seine Bight

Placencia Peninsula

Maya Beach

Placencia Bight

Riversdale

Tarpon Caye

Lark Caye

Long Coco Caye

Laughing Bird Caye

LAUGHING BIRD CAYE NATIONAL PARK

Hatchet Caye

Round Caye

Pompion Caye

Silk Cayes

Gladden Spit and Silk Caye Marine Reserve

GLADDEN SPIT

Crawl Caye

Robert's Caye

Rendezvous Caye

SOUTH WATER CAYE MARINE RESERVE

Peter Douglas Caye

Saddit Caye

Wee Wee Caye

South Water Caye

Stewart Caye

Sittee Point

False Sittee Point

Twin Cayes

Coco Plum Range

Man-O-War Caye

TOBACCO CAYE

Tobacco Reef

Carrie Bow Caye

Cross Caye

Caribbean Sea

Southwest Caye

Middle Caye

Long Caye

Northeast Caye

Glover's Reef

GLOVER'S REEF ATOLL

Glover's Reef Atoll

N

0   5 km
0   5 mi

© MOON.COM

Dangriga

"*Mabuiga!*" shouts the sign in Garifuna, welcoming you to this cultural hub and district capital. Built on the Caribbean shoreline and straddling North Stann Creek (also called Gumagarugu River), Dangriga's primary boast is its status as the Garinagu's original port of entry into Belize—and its modern-day cultural center. But although the majority of Dangriga's 12,500 or so inhabitants are Garifuna descendants of that much-celebrated 1823 landing, the remaining few are a typically rich mix of Chinese, Creoles, mestizos, and Maya, all of whom are out interacting on the town's main drag.

Aside from Dangriga's ideal location for accessing the surrounding mountains and seas—and the limited visitor services available to do so—its chief attraction may just be its total lack of pretense. Dangriga, formerly known as Stann Creek Town, does not outwardly cater to its foreign visitors the way Placencia or San Pedro does—there is simply too much else going on in this commercial center, including fishing, farming, and serving the influx of Stann Creek villagers who come weekly to stock up on supplies. Consequently, this area is still relatively undeveloped for tourism, which is either a shortcoming or an attraction, depending on what kind of traveler you are. It could be intimidating for the novice traveler, but the people here are welcoming. The area is slowly evolving, finding ways to showcase its wonders—from its drumming culture to nearby national parks—and the mayor has made great strides in improving roads and infrastructure as well as cleaning up beaches. Dangriga, by the way, means "sweet still waters" in Garifuna.

If poking around the casually bustling vibe of Dangriga sounds intriguing, you'd do well to stay a couple of nights. And if it's culture you're looking for, with the drumming "sheds," the daily local scenes, and one of the most picturesque seaside areas in Belize, you'll want to stay a bit longer.

ORIENTATION

As you pull into town, three massive ceremonial *dügü* drums of iron will greet you. This is the *Drums of Our Fathers* monument, erected in 2003 as a symbol of Garifuna pride—and as a "call to war" against the erosion of Garifuna culture. Turn right to reach the deep dock at Commerce Bight or go left (north) to enter Dangriga Town. Heading north from the drums on St. Vincent Street, the old bus terminal is on your left before the first bridge. Continuing, you'll find more shops and eateries, culminating in the center of town on either side of the North Stann Creek Bridge; across the bridge, St. Vincent Street turns into Commerce Street and offers an informal market often set up along the north bank of the river. Catch a boat to the cayes from one of several places here. The airstrip is a mile or so north of Stann Creek, where you'll also find Pelican Beach Resort, Dangriga's fanciest digs and restaurant.

SIGHTS

Dangriga does not offer many traditional sights per se. A better term would be *experiences,* because there is plenty going on—it's an explosion of culture, scenery, and people for any newcomer to this town. Moreover, Dangriga's central location—a detail often lost on travelers new to the area—makes it an excellent base for excursions around the region, much more so even than Placencia. You can browse the few crafts and music stores on St. Vincent Street and ask around for the drum-making workshops, one of which is set up at the Y-Not compound by the beach at Stann Creek. You might even walk away with an instrument of your own. Drums are often heard throughout the town to mark celebrations and funerals; sometimes it's simply

Dangriga

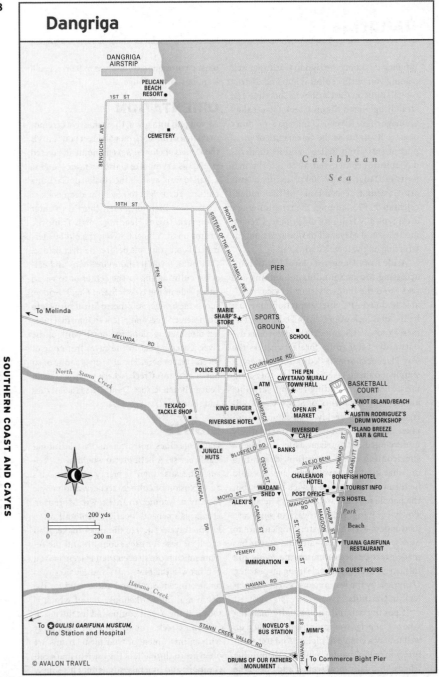

DANGRIGA AIRSTRIP

PELICAN BEACH RESORT

1ST ST

CEMETERY

BENGUCHE AVE

10TH ST

Caribbean Sea

SISTERS OF THE HOLY FAMILY AVE

FRONT ST

PIER

PEN RD

To Melinda

MELINDA RD

MARIE SHARP'S STORE

SPORTS GROUND

SCHOOL

North Stann Creek

POLICE STATION

COURTHOUSE RD

ATM

THE PEN CAYETANO MURAL/ TOWN HALL

BASKETBALL COURT

Y-NOT ISLAND/BEACH

TEXACO TACKLE SHOP

KING BURGER

OPEN AIR MARKET

AUSTIN RODRIGUEZ'S DRUM WORKSHOP

RIVERSIDE HOTEL

COMMERCE ST

RIVERSIDE CAFÉ

ISLAND BREEZE BAR & GRILL

JUNGLE HUTS

BLUEFIELD RD

BANKS

ST

HOWARD ST

GARBUTT LN

ALEJO BENI AVE

ECUMENICAL DR

CEDAR ST

CHALEANOR HOTEL

BONEFISH HOTEL

MOHO ST

WADANI SHED

POST OFFICE

TOURIST INFO

ALEXI'S

CANAL ST

MAHOGANY RD

D'S HOSTEL

Park

SHARP ST

MAGOON ST

Beach

0 200 yds
0 200 m

YEMERY RD

ST VINCENT ST

TUANA GARIFUNA RESTAURANT

IMMIGRATION

Havana Creek

HAVANA RD

PAL'S GUEST HOUSE

To ✪ *GULISI GARIFUNA MUSEUM,* Uno Station and Hospital

STANN CREEK VALLEY RD

NOVELO'S BUS STATION

HAVANA ST

MIMI'S

© AVALON TRAVEL

DRUMS OF OUR FATHERS MONUMENT

To Commerce Bight Pier

The Best of the Southern Coast

The southern part of Belize is less traveled than the Northern Cayes, but those who venture here will find much bang for their buck: the country's most beautiful coastline, from golden beaches to offshore islands; national parks, home to stunning waterfalls and wildlife; and plenty of culture, from Garifuna to Mayan, along the way. While it does require a few more days to fully take in the south, it's not impossible. Driving down the scenic Hummingbird Highway—with a stop for tamales at Miss Bertha's—will lead you to Dangriga, and from there, on to Hopkins and Placencia. You won't be able to see it all, but this initial itinerary will give you an appreciation for the unique offerings of the Stann Creek District.

- **Day 1:** Head to Dangriga, where you'll check in and lunch at Pelican Beach Resort before heading out to the heart of town. Stroll along the North Stann Creek Bridge and Commerce Boulevard, taking in the beautiful river-to-sea views and fishers selling their catch along the riverbanks. Catch a taxi to the Pen Cayetano Studio Gallery, where you'll learn all about the Garifuna culture, followed by a visit to the Gulisi Garifuna Museum. End the day with a dinner at Pelican Beach Resort's outdoor restaurant.

- **Day 2:** Hop on the bus or drive to Hopkins. Once there, drop your bags at your hotel—stay right in the village for ease of getting around—and grab a Garifuna lunch at Laruni Hati Beyabu Diner. Find a hammock on the beach and take an afternoon nap to the sound of gentle waves, or else treat yourself to a Garifuna experience at Palmento Grove Cultural & Fishing Lodge. End the day with a nice dinner at Chef Rob's Gourmet Cafe, with a seafood meal alfresco on the beach, or at the Coconut Husk on the beach.

- **Day 3:** Get an early morning ride to Bocawina Rainforest Resort, where you'll check into your waterfall suite, tucked inside the Mayflower Bocawina National Park. Begin your adventures with an afternoon hike and swim at Antelope Falls. Spend the evening soothing your muscles and filling your belly with seafood or steak specialties at the Wild Fig Restaurant.

- **Day 4:** Arrange a morning expedition to Cockscomb Basin Wildlife Sanctuary and bathe in one of several waterfalls—Tiger Fern is the most stunning and requires effort—and look for fresh jaguar tracks on the way. You could even spend the night here in one of the new cabanas.

- **Day 5:** It's beach time again: Hop on the bus or drive down to Placencia Village, where you can rent a cheap cabana and paint the beach red at night, hopping from Barefoot Beach Bar to Tipsy Tuna—with excellent happy-hour deals—to the Street Feet Lounge & Night Club.

- **Day 6:** Take a day trip to Laughing Bird Caye or Silk Cayes with Splash Dive Center and spend the day snorkeling at sea with colorful fish, or learning to dive.

- **Day 7:** Fly back to Belize City to catch your flight home.

a few people practicing the rhythms of their history. There's an abundance of artistic talent that can't be missed. Austin Rodriguez and his daughter are known for making authentic Garifuna drums, which end up in musicians' hands around the country. Other local artists of national prominence include painter Benjamin Nicholas and craftswoman Mercy Sabal, who makes colorful dolls sold all over the country. Beyond this, however, what makes Dangriga unique is the opportunity to experience authentic culture. Those with a keen eye will also notice how scenic Dangriga is—you will want to take photos of its bridges, rivers, pelicans, and anglers; it's quite the photographer's dream.

★ Gulisi Garifuna Museum

The **Gulisi Garifuna Museum** (George Price Dr., tel. 501/542-2700, gulisimuseum@ yahoo.com, 10am-5pm Mon.-Fri., 8am-noon Sat., US$5) is a mile west of town on the south side of the highway; you'll see it on your right when driving into Dangriga, next to the thrusting Chuluhadiwa Garifuna Monument (taxi from downtown US$2-3). The small two-room display is packed with a wealth of fascinating information on the Garinagu of Belize and a vast collection of artifacts, quotes, photos, and biographies of prominent Garifuna figures in Belize. The museum is named after the person thought to be the first Garifuna woman to arrive and settle in Dangriga. She had 13 sons, and many of Dangriga's modern residents believe they are descended from her. In 2008 the "language, dance, and music of the Garifuna" was inscribed on UNESCO's Representative List of the Intangible Cultural Heritage of Humanity, originally proclaimed in 2001.

Marie Sharp's Store and Factory

Be sure to save time to stop by **Marie Sharp's Store** (north of Stann Creek Bridge, tel. 501/522-2370, 8am-5pm Mon.-Fri.) to stock up on the area's famous hot sauce and other products; you can purchase hot sauce here for a tiny fraction of the normal retail price. Better yet, make the trip to **Marie Sharp's Factory** (Melinda Rd., Stann Creek Valley, tel. 501/532-2087, www.mariesharps-bz.com, 9am-4pm Mon.-Fri.), just a short ride from town, where you'll be offered a free tour of the farm and factory. The factory sits on a 400-acre estate. To reach it, drive west on the Hummingbird Highway from Dangriga about eight miles and turn right after you cross a bridge and see the White Swan on your left.

The Pen Cayetano Mural at Dangriga Town Hall

While in town, drop by the **Dangriga Town Hall** to view the impressive 2012 mural by Pen Cayetano, one of the country's foremost painters and musicians and creator of the popular Belizean music genre *punta* rock. The mural, *Hayawadina Wayúnagu* (Images of Our Ancestors), depicts the Garifuna culture, including the landing of the Garinagu (the collective term for the Garifuna people) in Dangriga, and pays homage to those who have documented and perpetuated the culture. The mural also shows the interaction of other Belizean ethnic groups—the Maya, Kriol, mestizo, Chinese, and Caucasian—with the Garinagu, a glimpse of how multiethnic Belize has become. It's a "cultural mural," as he describes it, intended to further educate the young but also resist the potential disappearance of a rich history. His own **artist's studio** (3 Aranda Crescent, tel. 501/628-6807, www. cayetano.de, 9am-5pm Mon.-Fri.) is worth a stop—if you're lucky, you'll get to see some of his stunning masterpiece oil paintings and find out the story behind each of them.

Mercy Sabal

Born and raised in Dangriga, with over 20 years of experience in her craft, **Mercy Sabal** (tel. 501/604-6731, US$25-35) is a well-recognized name in town thanks to her striking, handmade Garifuna folklore dolls, each telling a story through art. Some have reversible outfits, and some hold firewood or other symbolic tools. They make for unique souvenirs; you might also spot Mercy's dolls on sale at the airport gift shops. And if you're into learning more about the Garinagu, Mercy is your woman. You can ask to spend the day with her; she'll cook a Garifuna dish or two and share tales of Garifuna life.

Sabal Farm

Three miles outside Dangriga, you can visit the country's sole cassava-producing farm. **Sabal Farm** (US$20 pp, US$2.50 pp for groups of 8), not to be confused with Mercy Sabal, has operated for the past 25 years. Those with an interest in African culture and the Garinagu will be fascinated by this family-run operation, producing most of the cassava bread and other cassava-based products sold

Drums of Our Fathers: From Poem to Monument

"In our culture, songs aren't composed; they just come from inspiration," explained Garifuna National Council cofounder, author, and educator Roy Cayetano. Cayetano's famous poem "Drums of Our Fathers" was turned into a monument erected in 2003. The structure consists of three large, equal-size Garifuna *dügü*, or ceremonial drums. It stands high at the entrance of Dangriga, greeting every newcomer to the Garifuna hub and cultural capital.

Roy Cayetano wrote "Drums of Our Fathers" in 15 minutes. It was "a call to war" and the need to act to preserve the endangered Garifuna culture, language, and heritage. At the time he dedicated the poem to his grandmother, his wife, and his child to be, symbolizing the past, present, and future.

When Sylvia Flores, then a member of the House of Representatives for the Dangriga area, mentioned her desire to commission the construction of a Garifuna monument in Dangriga, one that represented the spiritual aspect of the culture, Cayetano knew just what to suggest. The placement of three ceremonial Garifuna drums of equal size would be symbolic: the top middle drum resting on the lower two would symbolize the Garinagu present resting on the past and the ancestors and yet looking to the future. The goal was to immortalize the culture's most significant symbol, the drum, representing a sound of the people that was never quieted by the colonial masters, a sound that must continue to be heard.

Artist Steve Okeke, of Nigerian origin and based in Belize City, completed the monument within two months after it was commissioned. The resulting artwork was so impressive that a more central place was given to *Drums of Our Fathers* at the entrance to town, a constant reminder that the Garifuna culture was never silenced, the beat of the drums goes on, and its people's voices will continue to echo.

all around the country. Cyril Sabal and his sister, Clotilda, run the impressive 30 acres, of which six are used for harvesting other crops, including citrus. Learn the process of making cassava, from peeling a cassava root all the way to baking and roasting it the old-fashioned organic way. Beyond the cassava, the farm is a symbol of cultural preservation at its finest.

Contact Brother David of **CD's Transfer** (1163 3rd St., tel. 501/502-3489, cell tel. 501/602-3077, breddadavid@gmail.com) to arrange a ride to and from the farm and to figure out the best day to visit.

Billy Barquedier National Park

Established as a protected area in 2001, **Billy Barquedier National Park** (Mile 16.5, Hummingbird Hwy., Steadfast, 9am-4:30pm daily, US$4) is an often overlooked and little-known attraction. The park is comanaged by the Steadfast Tourism and Conservation Association, a grassroots community

organization, and the Forestry Department. The approximately 1,500 acres of untouched rainforest are home to abundant wildlife, including howler monkeys, numerous bird species, and even the elusive tapir. The park has a separate entrance at Mile 17.5 for quick access to the **Billy Barquedier Waterfall,** its principal attraction. A 20-minute hike along a marked (albeit a bit rundown) trail and maneuvering across some tricky rocks will lead you to a beautiful stream with a refreshing emerald pool.

There are no accommodations in the park, but primitive **camping** (US$10 pp) is available at the Mile 16.5 entrance. Accommodations are a 10-minute ride away in Dangriga, easily accessible by bus along the Hummingbird Highway.

SPORTS AND RECREATION

Dangriga is ideally placed within a short drive of several of Belize's most stunning parks

Marie Sharp: The Spice Lady

Marie Sharp, the spice queen of Belize

She's a household name. Her bottles of hot sauce—ranging from Mild to Beware—are on almost every restaurant tabletop in the country and in every grocery store. Some Belizeans even carry her in their purses. You can't consume anything without an extra dash of Marie. It's the first thing to look for when served at a local eatery. And if it's not on the table or within immediate view, everyone asks "gat some Marie Sharp?"

You can visit her hot sauce factory—recently expanded; and if you're extremely fortunate, meet her in person—in Dangriga. It's a 10-minute ride outside town, down a gravel road and past some citrus orchards, to the 400-acre **Marie Sharp's farm and factory** (Melinda Rd., Stann Creek Valley, tel. 501/532-2087, www.mariesharps-bz.com, free). This humble Belizean entrepreneur, mother, and grandmother is nothing short of a legend in her country, and her story is one of adversity and success.

Marie started experimenting in her kitchen with a batch of leftover peppers she didn't want to throw out. Using a carrot base that became a hit with friends, she sold her sauce out of that kitchen for three years under the name Melinda's. The real kicker? She partnered with a U.S.-based distributor who conned her out of her product's name and tied her into an exclusivity contract, attempting to force her to give up the recipe. Years of hard work and a legal battle later, Marie decided not to give up. Instead, she started over from scratch using her original recipe, which she never revealed. Marie gave the sauce her name, so no one could steal it, and her name is now known throughout the country and Central America. "I was the chief cook and bottle washer up to five years ago," she said, smiling and pointing at the small room in her factory where she started over.

Marie's factory, run with the help of her spouse, sons, and grandson, is on the verge of a major expansion, already producing nine different types of pepper sauce (the most popular is the Fiery Hot) and nine types of jams and jellies (my favorite is the guava). For all her fame, Marie Sharp doesn't want anyone to recognize her when they visit her factory. But she's proud of her success, as she should be—her products are a symbol of Belizean cultural pride. Rare is the visitor who leaves without a bottle or two in their suitcase.

and wildlife reserves; it's just 20 miles from Cockscomb Basin and Maya Centre, 17 miles from both Billy Barquedier and Mayflower Bocawina National Parks, and 40 miles from Blue Hole National Park. This puts an incredible amount of activity at your fingertips, particularly for day trips, from birding to jaguar-track spotting, waterfall swimming or rappelling, and hiking numerous nature trails.

There are no tour operators based in Dangriga, but you can arrange for a simple transfer to and from sites with David Obi, or "Brother David," of **CD's Transfer** (1163 3rd St., tel. 501/502-3489, cell tel. 501/602-3077, breddadavid@gmail.com, 2-person Cockscomb tour US$140, Hopkins Village US$65 pp, 2-person Xunantunich tour US$190). Obi is an excellent and accommodating local guide who will take good care of getting you to and from your chosen site.

If you'd rather be with a tour guide and sign on for group tours, look into Hopkins as your base.

Beaches
The locals' favorite beach in Dangriga is at **Y-Not Island,** where the river meets the sea. Although erosion tends to push the beach back, it's still a lovely, picturesque stretch to take a dip, and the views of the pelicans and the anglers are reminders of Dangriga's peacefulness and authenticity. There are often events held here as well as fruit and food vendors throughout the week. Another ideal beach is at **Pelican Beach,** by the Pelican Beach Resort. If you're not staying there, treat yourself to lunch or drinks and bring your bathing suit to jump off the dock and enjoy the water.

Diving and Snorkeling
The most untouched parts of the Belize Barrier Reef, along with some of the most beautiful cayes and one of Belize's three atolls, are a few miles offshore, along the **South Water Caye Marine Reserve** and the **Port Honduras Marine Reserve** off the Punta Gorda coast. The Southern Coast is more than a mere gateway to these idyllic plots of land, and the islands have a lot more to offer than a day trip for those who love to fish, dive, or want a "castaway" experience.

ENTERTAINMENT AND EVENTS
Nightlife
There's no such thing as a dull evening in Dangriga. You won't find big shiny nightclubs, but there's plenty of entertainment, whether it's watching lively and intense dominoes tournaments at the sheds, dancing to in-club drumming and live *punta*, or barhopping across neighborhoods. "Griga" isn't as dead as they'll have you think. Be sure to have a ride to and from these venues late at night; don't walk the streets at night unless there's a festival taking place.

Dangriga is the birthplace and home of several nationally known *punta* bands: the Warribaggabagga Dancers, the Punta Rebels, the Punta Boys, the Turtle Shell Band, and the Griga Boyz. The music and dancing feature syncopated West African-style rhythms and interesting mixtures of various southern Belizean cultures. There is often live music or drumming on weekends; ask around for where the latest event is (taxi drivers are often the best source of information, or even your hosts).

Grab some drinks and settle in for some people-watching at the local "sheds" or traditional bars in town, where you'll find men slamming dominoes and throwing back Guinness under a thatched-roof hut. Try the **Wadani Recreation Centre** (St. Vincent St., 11:30am-midnight daily), known as "Wadani Shed." A local favorite in the laid-back Dangriga style, **Islands Breeze Bar & Grill** (S. Riverside Dr., tel. 501/502-3087, 5pm-midnight Wed.-Sun., US$5-8) is a colorful spot facing the river with good vibes for drinks and a chat. It also hosts live drumming nights and other special events. For weekly drumming and dancing on Thursday nights, head to the open deck and bar at **K's**

The Garifuna *Jankanu* Dance

The centuries-old tradition of *jankanu*, a West African masquerade dance, dates back to the days of slavery. *Jankanu* was a celebration by the enslaved of their few days of freedom at Christmastime, during which they would dance and mock the European masters by wearing pink flesh-colored masks, white clothes, and suspenders.

In the Garifuna *jankanu* dance, the performer dictates the beat to the drummer with his movements: feet together, knees bent, arms raised, palms facing the drummers, and hips rocking quickly side to side. There are costumes that include special touches, including cowrie shells strapped above the knee and feathers shooting up from the masks.

In 2010 an annual *jankanu* dance contest was launched in Dangriga to improve the quality of the dance and pass it on to younger generations. It hasn't been steady but when it takes place, in December, usually the day after Christmas, at Y-Not Island in Dangriga, the basketball court is transformed into a makeshift dance floor.

A *jankanu* dancer competes at an annual contest in Dangriga.

Cool Spot (Hummingbird Hwy. near corner Isla St., no phone, Thurs.-Sun. 10pm-2am, no cover) located on the left-hand side as you enter Dangriga town, right before you hit the roundabout; ask around for any other potential shows and drumming while you're in town.

For the occasional live music show or party, check the schedule at the beachfront, palm-fenced **Slaughter House Bar & Grill** (no phone, by Social Security Office), or stay for a cold one by the sea.

Festivals and Events

The month of December is a festive time in Dangriga. The days leading up to Christmas are celebrated with *jankanu* dancing in the streets and dancers performing from house to house. The Institute of Creative Arts, a branch of the **National Institute of Culture and History** (tel. 501/227-0518, www.nichbelize.org), occasionally sponsors an annual **Habinaha Wanaragua Jankanu Dance Contest** every December 26 (Boxing Day) at Y-Not Island. The festival has been sporadic, but it's good to keep an eye out for announcements; either way there are *junkanu* dances on the 26th around town as it's the tradition.

TOP EXPERIENCE

★ GARIFUNA SETTLEMENT DAY

Easily one of the most popular cultural events in Belize, **Garifuna Settlement Day** (Nov. 19) celebrates the arrival of the first Garinagu onto Belizean shores, and it's a national holiday. The biggest celebration in the country takes place in Dangriga, with a complete re-enactment of the first arrival of Garinagu on the coast of Belize in dugout canoes filled with cassava, plantains, and other staple foods. The town comes alive the entire week of November 19, with concerts, art exhibits, drumming, and more; a schedule is printed that month, or you can inquire with your guesthouse or host. Almost every night leading up to Settlement Day, there is dancing and drumming under the "sheds" in town, such as Wadani Shed, from 8pm until the wee hours of the morning.

1: cassava bread-making at the Sabal Farm; **2:** Y-Not Island's beach

On the morning of the 19th, the crowd heads over to the main bridge in town across the North Stann Creek River, lining up along the river starting at 7am, waiting for the boats to arrive and cheer them on. The merriment continues with a colorful, hair-raising procession to the church, and ends with an afternoon parade in town. Settlement Day in Dangriga is one of the best cultural experiences in all of Belize. Hotels book up months in advance, so make sure you make arrangements well ahead.

SHOPPING

Mercy Sabal's Garifuna dolls (tel. 501/604-6731, US$25-35) make for a unique gift; each is meticulously made by hand and depicts an aspect of the culture. Call ahead to view them, and she'll bring a selection to your hotel.

Pen Cayetano Studio Gallery (3 Aranda Crescent, tel. 501/628-6807, www.cayetano. de, 9am-5pm Mon.-Fri.) is a must-see. The master painter, musician, artist, and ambassador of the Garifuna culture keeps his oil canvas collection here in his artist studio—if you're lucky, he'll be there when you visit so you can get insight on his masterpieces—along with the unique textile art of his wife and fellow artist, Ingrid Cayetano. There's also a museum section to the gallery (entrance US$2.50), including CDs, drums, and souvenirs, as well as homemade fruit wines and jellies. The fruit tree-filled backyard—from soursop to bananas—has a nice stage for live performances as well as displays of Garifuna cooking tools and an outdoor hearth, which Cayetano still uses. The gallery often hosts groups for a day of Garifuna culture, in case you're interested.

Along a side street just up from Riverside Café, you'll find a nice assortment of made-in-Stann Creek drums, turtle shells, paintings, carvings, and more at the Garinagu Crafts & Art Gallery (46 Oak St., tel. 501/522-2596, grigaservices@yahoo.com, 9am-6pm Mon.-Fri.). Don't miss peeking into the adjoining museum, a room displaying traditional Garifuna tools and instruments. You can get an interpretive tour from passionate owner Francis Swaso, who patiently built and collected items for this gallery for more than a decade.

FOOD

The restaurant scene in Dangriga has evolved over the past two years, a happy development for a town that once lacked options for dining out.

★ Tuani Restaurant (Beachfront, just north of Alejo Beni Park, tel. 501/502-0287 or 501/672-0287, 7am-10pm daily, US$5-10) is one of the first, established sit-down Garifuna restaurants in town and the sea view as well as the interior, colorful art murals by Dangriga native Isaac Nicholas, depicting scenes of Garifuna culture, make it a delightful stop while in town. There's outdoor seating, best as the sun goes down the breeze blows, and indoor seating with fans. Daily Garifuna dishes are available—the *hudut* and *darasa* are excellent—as well as a variety of Belizean stews, fry chicken, quesadillas, and more. Wash it down with natural juices, or Garifuna *sahou* and *hiu* (cassava drinks). You can also call for preorders and delivery. Drumming is every Sunday night.

When you're in a rush for lunch, there's Alexie's (a block from Habet Hardware, tel. 501/522-2261, 7am-7pm Mon.-Sat., US$3-6), serving Creole options with a set daily special, including chicken stew, curry pork, burgers, burritos, fish, and local desserts. Take it to go or grab a seat in the nicely screened dining room You could go for dessert afterwards at Mimi's (Havana St., tel. 501/615-2922, noon-9pm daily) and cool off with your local fruit-flavored pick and some air-conditioning, just don't expect smiles with your order.

★ Pelican Beach Resort (tel. 501/522-2044, www.pelicanbeachbelize.com, 7am-10pm daily, US$5-15), on the north end of town, prepares and serves delicious food in its recently expanded beachfront dining terrace, the most moderately upscale setting you'll find. Daily lunch specials and occasional Garifuna dishes are offered, particularly on

Garifuna Eats

a plate of *hudut*

Dangriga is so authentic that you'll be hard-pressed to find public Garifuna eateries—most residents prepare and eat their traditional dishes at home. If you're lucky, you might be invited to break bread at a Grigan home. Otherwise, you can sample some of these dishes at the Pelican Beach Resort. Hopkins has more Garifuna restaurants than any other spot in the country. The following are the specialties to sample when in the land of the Garinagu. All have cassava, fish, banana, and coconut as common ingredients.

- **Cassava:** You're likely to find a soothing bowl of cassava porridge in Dangriga. On Settlement Day morning, it's common to see folks warming up with a few spoonfuls of this cassava flour and coconut milk mixture while waiting for the reenactment canoes to come in. Cassava bread has the consistency of a crispy cracker or flatbread and is made in Dangriga at the only cassava-producing farm in the country, then sold in other districts. It's the Garifuna staple, a snack that symbolizes the ancestors' survival on long boat journeys in search of freedom and preservation.

- **Darasa:** These banana tamales are a Garifuna snack, with the green banana steamed in coconut milk and wrapped in green banana leaves.

- **Hudut:** Pronounced "HOO-doot," this is fish—usually snapper—simmered in a coconut milk sauce spiced with garlic, black pepper, and thyme, then served with a mound of mashed plantain all in one bowl. Grab some of the mashed plantain with your fingers, pinch a bit of fish as well, dip it in the coconut sauce, and savor away. It takes almost three hours to prepare this dish from scratch, and it's the most labor-intensive of all Garifuna dishes, so when you find it, enjoy every bite.

- **Tahara:** I first tasted this in Hopkins at Tina's Kitchen, where I learned that there is such a thing as a Garifuna breakfast. Chunks of mashed green bananas are wrapped inside heated banana leaves, left in the oven, and eventually unwrapped. The final crunchy roasted pieces are served with fried fish, sprinkled with a tomato and onion sauce.

Sunday. The restaurant and its happy hour (5pm-9pm Thurs.-Fri.) are popular with local businesspeople who come here to relax and escape the hustle of town.

An additional perfect spot for cocktails and food by the sea, especially at sunset or after your day tours, is ★ **Island Breeze Bar & Grill** (South Riverside Dr., tel. 501/502-3087, 4pm-midnight Wed.-Sun., US$3-10). From quesadillas and nachos to seafood entrées, you'll find all your favorites. Expect some live music or drumming on the weekends.

Longtimer fast-food joints are also still around. **King Burger** (tel. 501/522-2476, 7am-3pm and 6pm-10pm Mon.-Sat., US$2-10), on the left as you cross the North Stann Creek Bridge from the south, offers breakfast, fresh juices, sandwiches, shakes, and simple comfort dinners, from fried chicken to burgers and fresh snapper dinners. Another standby is the **Riverside Café** (Corner S. Riverside and Oak St., tel. 501/669-1473, 6:30am-9pm daily). It's popular with travelers (boats to the cayes leave from right outside) and a gathering spot for local fishers. Grab a table or belly up to the bar and order a Guinness with your eggs and beans to fit in with the locals; it's US$4.50 for stew chicken, US$6 and up for fish and shrimp. For something different, try the cassava fries. Dinner is also available, with plenty of seafood options (US$9-13).

If you want cheaper food, walk back to the main drag and grab a fistful of street tacos for a few coins, or go to a number of Chinese fast-food restaurants for fry chicken to go.

On the road toward Dangriga, you can't miss the **Café Casita de Amor** (Little House of Love, Mile 16.5, Hummingbird Hwy., STACA/Steadfast Community bus stop, tel. 501/660-2879, 7:30am-5pm Tues.-Sun., US$4) on the Hummingbird Highway. This heart-shaped eatery serves both German and local dishes for breakfast and lunch—everything from milk shakes, gourmet coffee, and smoothies to burgers and sandwiches. Campers are welcome to pitch a tent, and the Billy Barquedier Waterfall is just down the road. Another popular pit stop is **Ms.**

Bertha's for delicious tamales, also on the Hummingbird Highway.

Groceries

Pick your own liquor or wine from the impressive imported selection at **Family City** (Ecumenical Dr., no phone, 8am-9pm daily); the large supermarket also has a well-stocked perfume and beauty products counter. Another well-stocked store is **Grigalizean Shopping Center** (Stann Creek Valley Rd., tel. 501/522-3668, 8am-9:30pm daily), on the highway less than a mile from the *Drums of Our Fathers* monument going out of town—the sign was taken down to correct the originally misspelled "Gregalizean," and it isn't back up yet and may never be.

ACCOMMODATIONS
Under US$25

Dangriga's main drag has a handful of low-budget options, including the **Riverside Hotel** (north end of the bridge on Commerce St., tel. 501/660-1041, US$15 pp). Pick one of the basic front guest rooms for a chance of a breeze; all have shared baths, wood floors, thin sheets, and fans. A better budget bet is ★ **D's Hostel** (tel. 501/502-3324, www.valsbackpackerhostel.com, US$12.50 pp), across from a pleasant park overlooking the ocean. Dana is a cheerful and friendly host who loves meeting her guests from around the world and putting them up in one of her cement bunk rooms; each bed has a fan and a massive locker to stash your gear (even a suitcase). The communal lounge area has a chess table, a book exchange, and a movie library. Amenities include wireless Internet, bikes for rent (US$5 per day), and laundry service. Val can help arrange a fishing trip, a transfer to Tobacco Caye, a night wildlife tour, or language and cultural exchange opportunities.

US$25-50

Pal's Guest House (868 Magoon St., tel. 501/522-2095, cell tel. 501/660-1282, palbz@btl.net, US$43, US$60 with a/c), around the corner from the bus station, has upgraded its

16 clean, modest cement guest rooms at the corner of North Havana Road and Magoon Street. Guest rooms all have private baths, cable TV, and optional air-conditioning. Seaside guest rooms are better, with lino-leum floors, ceiling fans, hot and cold private showers, TVs, and balconies at the ocean's edge; louvered windows on both ends of the rooms create good cross-ventilation. Wireless Internet is available for an extra cost. In the high season, the Raati Grill has breakfast, lunch, and dinner options for guests.

At the towering ★ **Chaleanor Hotel** (35 Magoon St., tel. 501/522-2587, chaleanor@ btl.net, US$27-78), friendly owners Chad, Eleanor, and their children offer a dated but homey atmosphere in a residential neigh-borhood. Economy guest rooms (US$21.50) are equipped with a bed and a fan; the rest-room and shower are shared. The well-used standard rooms have private baths with hot water, TVs, and fans (air-conditioning is op-tional at extra cost). Laundry service is avail-able. There's a gift counter in the lobby, and you can help yourself to coffee and bananas all day long.

US$50-100

The **Bonefish Hotel** (15 Mahogany St., tel. 501/522-2243, www.bluemarinlodge.com, US$95) is near the water with eight guest rooms, offering well-used private baths, air-conditioning, Wi-Fi, complimentary coffee, and a second-floor lobby and bar. It caters to active travelers who want to fish and dive. Most guests continue on to **Blue Marlin Lodge** on South Water Caye, which is allied with the Bonefish. Guest rooms at the Blue Marlin Lodge are clean and carpeted, with private hot- and cold-water baths, cable TV, wireless Internet, and air-conditioning.

US$100-150

Griga's high end is found at the north end of town at the end of Ecumenical Drive, right next to the airstrip: ★ **Pelican Beach Resort** (tel. 501/522-2044, www.

pelicanbeachbelize.com, from US$135-165, includes breakfast) rests comfortably on the Caribbean. Its 17 guest rooms are open and well lit with wood and tile floors, bathtubs, and porches facing the ocean, with gorgeous views of the beach and dock. At the time of my visit, eight new rooms were being built and are likely completed by the time you read this, including ground-floor rooms boasting senior and wheelchair accessible bathrooms, includ-ing showers with ramps. Various packages are available that include meal plans, excursions, and time spent at the Pelican's stunning sister resort on South Water Caye (easily the most beautiful caye in Belize, in this island lover's opinion). Pelican is a full-service resort with many amenities and plenty of history behind its owners. A swimming pool is also on the way.

INFORMATION AND SERVICES

Belize Bank (8am-3pm Mon.-Thurs., 8am-4:30pm Fri.) and **Scotiabank** (8am-2:30pm Mon.-Thurs., 8am-2:30pm Fri., 9am-11:30am every other Sat.) are on St. Vincent Street near the bridge; both have ATMs.

There is a BTIA **tourist info booth** (15 Mahogany St., tel. 501/522-2243, 9:30am-4pm Mon.-Fri.) directly across from Bonefish Hotel.

Southern Regional Hospital (tel. 501/522-3834) is just out of town and serves the entire population of Stann Creek District.

Mail your postcards at the **post office** (Mahogany St., across from D's Hostel, tel. 501/522-2035, 8am-11am and 1pm-5pm Mon.-Thurs., reduced hours Fri.).

Val's Laundry and Internet (tel. 501/502-3324, 7:30am-7pm Mon.-Sat., morn-ing on Sun., US$1 per pound) is on Sharp Street near the post office. Fast and friendly satellite Internet is available (US$2.50 per hour), as well as FedEx service, local infor-mation, and organic fresh-squeezed juices. You can also get online at the air-conditioned **DNK Internet Café** (15 St. Vincent St., across from Scotiabank, tel. 501/522-0383, U.S. tel.

646/522-7939, dnkInternetcafe@gmail.com,
US$2.50 per hour).

TRANSPORTATION

Dangriga is on the coast, only 36 miles south
of Belize City as the crow (or local airline)
flies. However, the land trip is much longer,
roughly 75 miles along the Manatee Road or
100 miles via the Hummingbird Highway.

Air

Maya Island Air (tel. 501/223-1140, U.S.
tel. 800/225-6732, www.mayaislandair.com)
and **Tropic Air** (tel. 501/226-2626, U.S. tel.
800/422-3435, www.tropicair.com) have a
number of daily 20-minute flights between
Belize City and Dangriga. It's also possible
to fly from Dangriga to Placencia and Punta
Gorda.

Boat

You can arrange boat service from Belize City,
but there is no scheduled run; they tried operating a regularly scheduled shuttle, but it
didn't make money. Ask around the docks
by the gas station, at your hotel, or at the
Belize Tourism Board. Expect to pay a fair
amount for this trip (probably US$100 each
way). Service to and from local cayes or other
coastal villages is also dependent on how
many people want to go. Only two passengers
are required to make the trip to Tobacco Caye
(US$35 pp); ask at the Riverside Café for the
latest information. You can also check with
Pelican Beach Resort as to whether you can
catch a ride with them (for an additional fee)
when they head to South Water Caye.

Bus

Bus service between Belize City and Dangriga
takes close to three hours, including a stop in
Belmopan, and costs US$5 each way; buses
run 5:15am-6:15pm daily. There are a few express buses during the day, but the schedule
changes regularly, so be sure to check at the
station.

James Bus Line (tel. 501/664-2185 or
501/631-1959, www.jamesbusline.com) operates several daily southbound buses to Punta
Gorda (from 7:30am until the day's only express at 5:30pm), a three hour trip. Buses
to Punta Gorda stop in Mango Creek; from
there you can make a connection to Placencia
on the water taxi. As of press time, four buses
go directly to Placencia (2.5 hours), thanks
to **Ritchie's Bus Service** (tel. 501/523-3806,
www.ritchiesbusservice.com): 11am daily,
2pm Mon.-Sat., 4:30pm daily, and 6pm daily.
These buses used to stop in Hopkins and
Sittee River, but that schedule is in question,
so ask around the station. Buses leave from
Dangriga to Hopkins at 10am daily; the first
pickup is by the riverside, next to Ricky's
Restaurant, where the bus will be parked
starting at 9am.

Car

From Belize City, take the George Price
Highway to either the Coastal (Manatee) Road
or Hummingbird Highway, which you follow
till it ends. Taking the Coastal Road may shave
20 minutes off the Hummingbird Highway
route, but the rutted, red-dirt surface may also
destroy your suspension and jar your fillings
loose. The unpaved Coastal Road is flat and
relatively straight and occasionally graded
into a passable highway, but you'd better have
a sturdy ride. Be prepared for lots of dust in
the dry season and boggy mud after a rain.
Numerous tiny bridges with no railings cross
creeks flowing out of the west, and the landscape of pine savanna and forested limestone
bluffs has nary a sign of human beings (except
for the crappy road, of course). About halfway to the junction with the Hummingbird
Highway, you'll find a pleasant place to stop
and take a dip at Soldier Creek; just look for
the biggest bridge of your trip and pull over.
Watch out for snakes in the bush, and once
you reach your destination, try not to spend
those hard-earned extra 20 minutes all in one
place.

Islands Near Dangriga

WATERFOOT CAYE

Stay on this one-acre island at **Yok Ha Resort** (tel. 501/610-2717, www.yokhabelizeresort.com, US$410-535; US$2,000 per day for groups), just 25 minutes by boat from Dangriga. Opened by a Belizean who returned home after a career overseas, the resort offers five cabins of approximately 400 square feet each, ideal for couples who wish to escape reality but remain close to the mainland. Cabins offer king beds or doubles, with Wi-Fi, air-conditioning, a sitting area, a private porch, and Mayan decor. An on-site restaurant and bar serves all-inclusive meals, and there's a guide and small dive shop here too. You can even take a cooking class and learn to make fry jacks or rice and beans. Other activities include kayaking or spearfishing using complimentary gear, yoga on the dock, or snorkeling around the island. If you're honeymooning, ask for the special cabana, fenced off from the resort and with its own private dock. Pickups are included.

★ SOUTH WATER CAYE MARINE RESERVE

Belize's largest protected marine area, included in the sweeping World Heritage Site designation of the Belize Barrier Reef System, the **South Water Caye Marine Reserve** (swcmr@yahoo.com, www.fisheries.gov.bz, park fee US$5, US$15 per week) covers 117,878 acres and is 15 miles southeast of Dangriga's coast, the closest jumping-off point. It stretches from the Tobacco Reef all the way south to just above Wippari Caye.

Few will disagree that this marine zone includes some of the healthiest and most abundant marine and coral life along the reef, hence some of the best snorkeling and diving in stunning royal-blue water. Home to sandy or mangrove cayes, in addition to littoral

forests and seagrass beds, the reserve is recognized as a vital area for several critically endangered species, including the hawksbill turtle, the loggerhead turtle, and the goliath grouper, in addition to important bird nesting colonies for the magnificent frigate and brown boobies.

With depths going only to 20 feet in some parts, the area is an ideal spot for beginning snorkelers and divers, particularly right off the beach at Pelican Resort on South Water Caye, where the reef is within a swim's reach. The shallow waters off Carrie Bow Caye, across South Water, are packed with bright corals.

It's no exaggeration to say that no island trip to southern Belize is complete without a jaunt to the South Water Caye Marine Reserve.

Because of the protected area's sheer size and reach, some of the islands on the northern end of this stretch are more easily reached (cost and distance-wise) from Dangriga or Hopkins—namely, Tobacco Caye, South Water Caye, and Glover's Reef Atoll.

Diving Bliss

This reserve, its surrounding islands, and numerous dive spots are also accessible to day-trippers from Placencia or Hopkins, who come here for some of the best wall dives in Belize. While it would require several trips to become familiar with this region alone, a couple of dive spots just off **South Water Caye** stand out above the rest. **Parrot Reef**'s 70-foot wall is home to nurse sharks, spotted rays, hawksbill turtles, gray and queen angelfish, lobsters, barracuda, yellowtail snapper, and schools of creole wrasse feeding on plankton, among other incredibly colorful sights of azure vase sponges and corals. You'll also see the invasive lionfish species, hovering above netted barrel sponges. **The Abyss** is a 40- to 130-foot wall that drops into an incredible

Islands Near Dangriga

YOK HA RESORT

Cross Caye

Dangriga

Reef

Man-O-War
Caye

TOBACCO CAYE PARADISE CABINS

Coco Plum
Caye

TOBACCO CAYE

COCO PLUM ISLAND RESORT

Thatch Caye

THATCH CAYE
RESORT

Tobacco

0   5 mi

0   5 km

GLOVER'S REEF ATOLL

Glover's
Reef

Twin Caye

PELICAN
BEACH

South Water Caye

Carrie Bow
Caye

Stewart Caye

Long Caye

Northeast
Caye

Middle Caye

Wee Wee
Caye

SOUTH WATER CAYE
MARINE RESERVE

ISLA MARISOL
RESORT

Peter
Douglas
Caye

Southwest
Caye

© MOON.COM

abyss of blues, where turtles, nurse sharks, eagle rays, and colorful reef fish roam at various depths.

★ TOBACCO CAYE

If your tropical island dream includes sharing a small, rustic island with a few dozen travelers, snorkelers, divers, backpackers, and adventurous souls from around the world, then **Tobacco Caye** is your place. This tiny island within South Water Caye Marine Reserve, has long been a popular backpacker and Belizean tourism destination, especially for divers. Tobacco Caye is just north of Tobacco Cut (a "cut" is a break in the reef through which boats can navigate).

Individual tour guides or resorts can arrange to whisk you each day to snorkeling within a few miles from the caye, fishing trips, or excursions to Man-O-War Caye and Tobacco Range to look for manatees. Glover's Reef, Blue Hole, and Turneffe trips are available (US$150-200); whale shark tours are usually running March-July. I recommend you book your trips with Tobacco Caye native and guide **Nolan Jackson** (tel. 501/671-3009 or

501/651-3009, njfishing3@gmail.com), who runs his own tours and knows the area like the back of his hand. He offers snorkeling trips (US$15 pp for 1 hour right off the caye), snorkeling with birding (US$35 pp), fly-fishing (US$250 half-day), live bait fishing (US$35 per hour), manatee-spotting, and transfers to Dangriga (US$20 pp for up to 3).

Food and Accommodations

Tobacco Caye's "resorts" offer similar packages but for a range of budgets. All accommodations are Belizean-run family affairs, each a bit different according to the owner's vision, and are comfortably crowded together on the five acres of sand. Apart from some basic differences in room quality, the more you pay, the better the food you'll be eating—a pretty important thing when checking into a guest room that also locks you into a meal plan. Some of the accommodations prices are per person per night and include three meals; always ask to be sure.

★ **Tobacco Caye Paradise Cabins** (tel. 501/532-2101, U.S. tel. 800/667-1630, http://tobaccocaye.com, US$80 all-inclusive with 3 meals per day) occupies the northern tip of the island, a short walk from the main bar, with six colorful, clean cabanas with porches right over the sea that will make you want to stay forever. The small, sandy compound is dotted with palm trees and hammocks and has the classic Tobacco Caye barefoot life vibe. Meals are communal, Wi-Fi is US$2.50 per day, and an activity booth doles out any snorkeling and kayaking gear you might need (at an additional hourly or daily rental fee).

Stepping things up a notch, find the renovated **Reef's End Lodge** (tel. 501/671-8363, www.reefsendlodge.com, US$315-510 for 3 days, includes 3 meals) on the southern shore; seven guest rooms and cabanas have private balconies—with romantic sunset views—fans, and private baths with hot and cold water. There is a bar and restaurant built over the water for those prepaid meals. Reef's End has the caye's only dive shop, which can be utilized by anyone on the island; this is an excellent location to begin a shore dive or snorkeling adventure. Dive packages are also available, ranging US$477-1,397 according to the number of days, and include meals, transfers, and two local dives daily.

Joe Jo's By The Reef (tel. 501/610-1647, U.S. tel. 954/249-5863, www.joejosbythereef.com, US$200-250, includes 3 meals) is owned by longtime resident Mr. Louis and raises the bar on the island with its six comfortable, private seafront ocean-view cabins with hardwood floors, hot water, and reef views from private decks. There are also three suites above the spacious restaurant, with double beds and baths, and a large veranda ideal for groups. All kayak and snorkeling gear are complimentary, and water excursions can be arranged to nearby cayes. The breeze doesn't reach this side as much during the day, but the lodgings make up for it, and like all accommodations on the island, nothing is too far away from the main island bar and snack shack.

Windward Lodge (formerly called Tobacco Caye Lodge, tel. 501/532-2033 or 501/223-6247, www.tclodgebelize.com, US$99 pp, includes 3 meals) occupies a middle strip of the island and offers six guest rooms in four colorful cabins facing the reef. You are summoned to meals by a dinner bell, to head to the newly renovated, screened dining room onsite. There's also a bar and snack shop, as well as hammocks on the beach. A few steps away, the **Tobacco Caye Marine Station** (tel. 501/620-9116, www.tcmsbelize.org) hosts visiting scientists, and you can ask to check out its reference materials on the area's habitats and species, rent snorkel gear (US$10 per day), or head out on a night snorkel (US$15 pp) with these experts. Note that they are closed during the slow tourist season.

Transportation

Water taxis to Tobacco Caye leave when the captain says there are enough passengers—but usually run 9am-1pm from the Riverside Café or the Tackle Stop farther upstream. **Captain Buck** (tel. 501/669-0869) is one option, or try Fermin, aka **Compa** (tel. 501/666-8699). The trip costs US$50 one-way or US$35 round-trip, with a return trip usually made midmorning. **Captain Nolan Jackson** (tel. 501/671-3009) also offers snorkel trips, so he's a solid pick. **Captain Doggie** (tel. 501/627-7443) is another charter option; he will take 1-3 people for US$70; groups of 4-12 can expect to pay US$17.50 per person. All the captains usually hang out by Riverside Café, either outside or inside.

By calling ahead to Reef's End Lodge or Tobacco Caye Lodge, you can arrange a pickup anytime from Dangriga and ensure a boat will still be there if you are arriving after midday. Be advised that if you need a boat after 3pm, you'll pay a lot more—seas get rough, and a private charter is necessary. Plan accordingly.

MAN-O-WAR CAYE

As recently as six years ago, **Man-O-War Caye** (Bird Isle) was a raucously chirping bird-choked, large plot of protected mangroves, and a crucial nesting site for frigates and brown boobies—one of only 10 in the Caribbean—amid beautiful turquoise

waters. Unfortunately, climate change effects have shrunk it in size, and many of its birds are gone. It's a sad update to what was once a magnificent stop on a snorkel trip to Tobacco and South Water Caye.

COCO PLUM CAYE

Coco Plum Island Resort (U.S. tel. 800/763-7360, www.cocoplumcay.com, 4 nights US$2,770-3,855 for 2 people, includes all water sports equipment) boasts 14 ocean-front, brightly colored cabanas on a 16-acre private island; it specializes in exclusive romantic packages and all-inclusive deals, attracting plenty of honeymooners as a result. A three-bedroom villa for eight also boasts its own swimming deck away from other guests. There's no swimming pool here yet, though one is in the plans, but the surrounding seawater is shallow enough that you don't need one. There's a new Serenity Spa at the end of the island, with a delightful outdoor deck; massages are available Tuesday, Wednesday, and Sunday. The on-site bar and restaurant gets rave reviews for its lively staff and Belizean-inspired menu. At the back of the island is a bare-behind beach—be warned. You can rent the entire island if you choose. They keep a copy of *Moon Belize* stacked at the bar.

TOP EXPERIENCE

SOUTH WATER CAYE

South Water Caye is a privately owned postcard-perfect island 14 miles off the shore of Dangriga and 35 miles southeast of Belize City. The reef crests just a stone's throw offshore, sitting atop a 1,000-foot coral wall awash in wildlife. The island stretches 0.75 mile from north to south and 0.25 mile at its widest point. This southern caye is what dream getaways are made of—it's easily one of the most beautiful cayes in southern Belize. And lucky you, overnight stays are possible.

1: Tobacco Caye Paradise Cabins; 2: a nesting site for frigates on Man-O-War Caye; 3: Isla Marisol Resort on Glover's Reef Atoll

Food and Accommodations

235

Once a convent for the Sisters of Mercy, the ★ **Pelican Beach Resort** (tel. 501/522-2044, www.pelicanbeachbelize.com, US$375-475, includes 3 meals) is what every dream island resort should look like: charming yet unpretentious. It occupies the entire southern end of the island—the best end, by far—with five second-story guest rooms, three duplex cottages, and two single-unit casitas, all decently spaced from one another, and all surrounded by dozens of coconut trees and fine, powdery white sand. The beach offers some of Belize's best and rare walk-in snorkeling sites—that's if you manage to get yourself out of the dozens of hammocks. The beach has eroded substantially in the past year, due to climate change, but it remains stunning. Power at the resort is now entirely from the sun, and private toilets use saltwater for flushing to help protect the fragile island ecology. The owners once had a strip of island next door that was home to Pelican's University, which hosted student research groups, but it shut down and the lumber was purposefully reused to build the two-story Brown Boobie Roost Cottage, tucked at the back along the dense mangroves, offering eight rooms ideal for groups. Each has its own bathroom, a queen bed and double, or a queen and twin. There's a long, shared private deck with sea views. There are also single rooms above the kitchen and expanded restaurant deck, with queen beds; the bonus is that the Wi-Fi from the communal area reaches here. End the day at the Heavenly Bliss Lounge sunset deck—also ideal for yoga—perched over the sea and beach, facing the resort.

Blue Marlin Lodge (tel. 501/532-2104, U.S. tel. 800/798-1558, www.bluemarlinlodge.com, from US$495, includes meals), sister resort of the Bonefish Hotel in Dangriga, is on the northern tip of the island, offering 17 guest rooms, air-conditioned "igloos," and five cabanas just steps away from the sea, as well as family cottages with air-conditioning, fan, minifridge. There's not much beach, and the sand is the hard, flat variety. The bar-dining room over the sea serves meals,

SOUTHERN COAST AND CAYES
ISLANDS NEAR DANGRIGA

snacks, and drinks. The Blue Marlin specializes in fishing trips and has a full dive shop, cable TV, and free Internet access. It's an easy and short walk along a coastal foot trail to the other parts of the island.

Transportation

South Water Caye is a 40-minute boat ride from Dangriga in good weather. You can either arrange for a pickup from Pelican Beach Resort, since it's the sister resort (US$68 pp, minimum 4 people for nonguests, but pricing varies according to space availability), or inquire with your resort on the island ahead of time.

CARRIE BOW CAYE

Just a few minutes' ride from South Water Caye, this dot of sand and palms, close to both the reef and mangrove systems and named after the original owner's spouse (Carrie Bowman), is home to the **Smithsonian Museum of Natural History's Caribbean Coral Reef Ecosystems Program** (http://ccre.si.edu), which has produced more than 800 published papers since 1972. The caye houses up to six international scientists at a time.

The public is welcome to stop by, but it's best to call ahead or arrange a visit through your resort host. Be sure to stop by the library to read and flip through the guest book, filled with fascinating observations and drawings from visitors over the years, most of whom are scientists and marine illustrators. On your way back, you can snorkel off the caye and admire coral in very shallow waters. The beach here also is a turtle-nesting site—over 100 turtles come to Carrie Bow Caye every year to nest at night, June-October.

WEE WEE CAYE

Wee Wee Caye, affiliated with the Possum Point Biological Station on the mainland near Sittee River, hosts a tropical field station, a marine lab, and an educational center, with a neat system of raised catwalks through the mangroves (it's beautiful, but there are lots of bugs). The caye also hosts a population of boa constrictors; contact **Paul and Mary Shave**

(tel. 501/523-7021, www.marineecology.com) about bringing your students here.

★ GLOVER'S REEF ATOLL

The southernmost of Belize's three atolls, **Glover's Reef Atoll** (named for a pirate, of course—John Glover) is an 80-square-mile, nearly continuous ring of brilliant coral, flanked on its southeastern curve by five tiny islands. A UNESCO World Heritage Site along with the Belize Barrier Reef, the atoll is 18 miles long and 6 miles across at its widest point; to the east the ocean bottom drops sharply and keeps on dropping, eventually to depths of 15,000 feet at the western end of the Caiman Trench, one of the deepest in the world.

The southern section of the atoll around the cayes serves as a protected marine reserve, with the largest no-take zone in Belize. Many travelers miss Glover's Reef in favor of the northern atolls, but Glover's is truly one of Belize's remaining underwater treasures.

Diving and Snorkeling

Divers and snorkelers will find a fabulous wall surrounding the Glover's Reef Atoll, plus more than 700 shallow coral patches within the rainbow-colored lagoon. There are wreck dives and an abundance of marinelife, especially turtles—loggerheads are abundant off **Middle Caye Wall**—manta rays, and all types of sharks, including reefs, hammerheads, and whale sharks. The names of the dive sites speak for themselves: **Shark Point, Grouper Flats, Emerald Forest Reef, Octopus Alley, Manta Reef, Dolphin Dance,** and **Turtle Tavern.** Other marinelife includes spotted stingrays; barracuda; queen, blue, and French angelfish; trunkfish; hogfish; butterfly fish; blue tangs; groupers; sergeant majors; and bluehead wrasses, among a host of other species.

Fishing

Anglers will have a chance at bonefish and

Glover's Reef Atoll

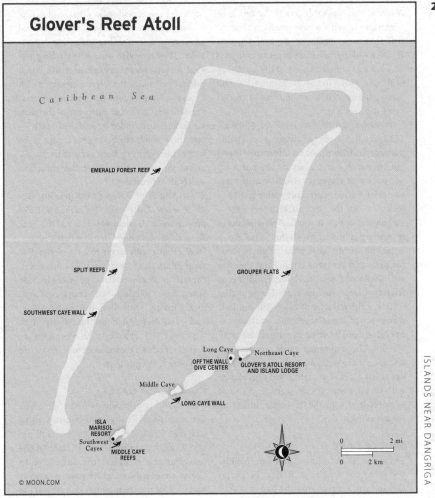

Caribbean Sea

EMERALD FOREST REEF

SPLIT REEFS

GROUPER FLATS

SOUTHWEST CAYE WALL

Long Cave
OFF THE WALL
DIVE CENTER
Northeast Caye
GLOVER'S ATOLL RESORT
AND ISLAND LODGE

Middle Cave

LONG CAVE WALL

ISLA
MARISOL
RESORT
Southwest
Cayes
MIDDLE CAYE
REEFS

0   2 mi
0   2 km

© MOON.COM

permits as well as the big trophy species, including sailfish, marlins, wahoos, snappers, and groupers.

There is also fantastic paddling, sailing, stand-up paddleboarding, and anything else you can dream up. Glover's is a special place indeed.

Accommodations
SOUTHWEST CAYE
The first bit of land you'll reach from the mainland is owned by the Usher family, which runs the high-end full-service **Isla Marisol Resort** (tel. 501/610-4204, www.islamarisolresort.com, 3-night all-inclusive scuba package US$1,290 pp) for avid divers, snorkelers, and sportfishers. There are rustic but comfortable cabanas with air-conditioning and porches, outfitted with composting toilets (no wood chips, thankfully); or stay in one of two reef houses with spectacular deck views of the reef, ideal for either families or honeymooners. Many all-inclusive packages are available for a three-night minimum.

A lively, cozy dockside bar is the center of nighttime activity, where guests get merry, fish, feed nurse sharks, or play board games. If you're looking for a place to get away from it all, soak up the Belizean island life, go diving or fishing, swing from your hammock as you please, and eat delicious home-cooked meals every day, this is it.

Island Expeditions (U.S. tel. 800/667-1630, www.islandexpeditions.com, 3-day package US$639 pp) is an adventure-travel outfitter with a tent camp on the north tip of Southwest Caye; it's a well-run professional operation with daily water sports of all kinds—for the novice and expert alike—and a great option if you like meeting other travelers and bonding with them on a group trip. The sturdy tents have single or double beds and kerosene lamps, and they are well sheltered from the elements. This eco-friendly camp provides shared composting toilets, cold-water showers (with outdoor warm-water hoses when the weather cooperates), and evening generator use until 9:30pm. The communal meals are excellent, and guests are welcome to head over to the bar at Isla Marisol at night. I had a great time with this dynamic group, learning a couple of water sports for the first time, including sea kayaking.

MIDDLE CAYE

There are no accommodations on Middle Caye, unless you're a Belize Fisheries Department ranger, a marine biologist with the Wildlife Conservation Society, or a PhD student with special permission. If staying on one of the surrounding cayes, ask your host about arranging a trip to see what's going on here.

LONG CAYE

The 13 acres of Long Caye form the gorgeous backdrop to the thatched-roof base camp of **Slickrock Adventures** (U.S. tel. 800/390-5715, www.slickrock.com, 5-night package US$1,675 pp); check out the website for a range of active Belizean adventures. Slickrock

has a veritable armada of kayaks, windsurfing boards, and other water toys; conditions and equipment will cover beginners and experts alike. They now also offer **kitesurfing** lessons. Guests stay in very private, rustic beach cabins overlooking the reef and equipped with kerosene lamps, foam-pad mattresses, and great views. Outhouse toilets are of the plein air variety, surrounded by palm leaf "walls"—offering possibly the best views from a toilet in the entire country. Book a trip to the island, or link the trip with wild inland adventures as well (call for a catalog).

Off the Wall Dive Center (tel. 501/532-2929, www.offthewallbelize.com, US$1,595 pp per week all-inclusive) is a PADI 5-Star Resort. Stay on Long Caye in a rustic oceanfront cabana with access to a top-notch dive shop, gift shop, and yoga deck. The maximum capacity is 10 guests. Package prices include seven days' lodging, boat transportation, meals, diving, snorkeling, fishing, kayaking, and stand-up paddleboarding. Whale shark trips and PADI scuba certification courses are popular; yachties are welcome to come ashore and browse the gift shop.

NORTHEAST CAYE

This island is privately owned and run as **Glover's Atoll Resort and Island Lodge** (tel. 501/532-2916, www.glovers.com.bz, US$40/night), a primitive island camp. A 68-foot catamaran takes you from Sittee River to Glover's remotest caye, where you can camp or shack up for the cheapest weekly rates on the atoll: US$109 per week of camping, US$164 to stay in the dorm, or US$274-328 for rustic thatched cabins perched over the water. Prices include transportation, a week of primitive lodging, use of the kitchen, and nothing else—not even water. Show up at the guesthouse in Sittee River at 7am Saturday and be prepared for the week. It's best to bring your own food, drinking water, and a few camping basics, or pay at least US$42 per day to be provided these amenities. A dive shop and kayak rentals are also available, and the snorkeling is out of this world.

Hopkins and Vicinity

Hopkins was built in 1942 after a hurricane washed away Newtown, just up the coast; it's a scenic coastal fishing village that has steered more and more toward tourism in the past decade. More beachfront condominium developments and luxury private villas continue to go up on either end of the village's beautiful long stretch of beach, one of the nicest in Belize, but for now nearly everything in between remains chill, spread out, and reasonably priced. There's really no place in Belize like Hopkins. Its 1,000 or so inhabitants are mostly Garinagu, making this one of the more exciting places to be to learn about their culture. Traditional village life is ever present here, and residents are holding on to it to make sure it isn't likely to disappear anytime soon. This is where you can experience culture on every corner simply by walking around or sitting on an outdoor patio. It's a much smaller area than Dangriga and less intimidating for newcomers; those with an open mind and a thirst for cultural immersion, coupled with a love for beaches, the outdoors, and nearby cayes, will leave happy. Hopkins is just as good of a base as Dangriga, a stone's throw away, for those seeking to island-hop to nearby South Water Caye and Tobacco Caye.

A newly paved road quickly leads into the village, a substantial improvement from the previous bumpy dirt path. With the advent of new resorts and time-share condos in Sittee, the continual trickle of backpackers that still show up in Hopkins Village, and visitors seeking a mix of beach and culture, there are a few decent crafts shops, way more Guatemalan souvenir shacks than usual, and cafés and restaurants along the main drag as well as on the southern end. There's also drumming once or twice a week, and karaoke nights are big at one or two local bars. Other than that, the sights are really just those that make up everyday village life, rarely seen elsewhere in Belize, along with, of course, the beach. On a weeknight,

this means drinking beer and bitters, playing drums and dominoes, and laughing away another hot, breezy day from a hammock. Of course, things pick up considerably on festival months or days, particularly Garifuna Settlement Day, Christmas, and Easter Week; expect accommodations to be in high demand during these times.

SIGHTS

The road that carries you into Hopkins from Dangriga splits the village into **Northside** (or "Baila" as the locals call it—pronounced BAY-la) and **Southside** (or "False Sittee"). Northside is a bit denser with local flavor, while Southside hosts most of the shops, restaurants, and accommodations.

TOP EXPERIENCE

Lebeha Drumming Center

You can't leave Hopkins without a Garifuna drumming lesson. Drums are a key part of the Garifuna culture, a symbolic connection to their African ancestors and a sound that is considered a metaphor for the collective voice that colonial masters were unable to silence. At the award-winning **Lebeha Drumming Center** (tel. 501/665-9305, www.lebeha.com, 9am-7pm daily), up on Northside (*lebeha* means "the end" in Garifuna), Garifuna drum master Jabbar Lambey offers both private (US$15 per hour) and group lessons (2 hours US$12.50 pp). He will ensure that you learn a couple of beats and have a grand time. You might even learn how to *punta* dance. Call or stop by to schedule a lesson.

Serpon Sugar Mill

If you're a history buff, head to Belize's first protected historical reserve. Sitting on 114 acres of rainforest, the **Serpon Sugar Mill** (www.nichbelize.org, 8am-5pm daily) houses remnants of Belize's colonial history—a semi-mechanized sugar mill's machinery and tools, including a boiler, a locomotive, a steam engine, and more. Once considered a technological breakthrough, these old life-size machines today are nothing short of surreal. The Serpon Sugar Mill was established in 1865 and operated until the early 20th century, when it was finally abandoned after sugar production became more profitable in the north of Belize. At its peak, it produced and shipped an estimated 1,700 pounds of sugar per month.

There's a small entrance fee (US$5) to this site protected by the National Institute of Culture and History, and a museum offers interesting manufacturing details and a historical timeline. The mill is about a mile along the Sittee River Village access road, off the Southern Highway, and can be toured in less than an hour.

★ Garifuna Culture Tour

A short bike ride to the very northern edge of Hopkins Village, followed by a kayak ride across the lagoon leads you to the historic 62-acre **Palmento Grove Cultural & Fishing Lodge** (Over Johnson Island Peninsula, Northend Hopkins Village, tel. 501/636-3247 or 501/661-6039, www.palmentogrovebelize.com, US$61 pp half day). It's a place that was much needed in this part of Belize, if not in the entire country: a one-stop shop to learn about Garifuna culture, beyond drumming, with hands-on activities. It's the vision and dream of Uhwanie Martínez, a former banking professional who quit the corporate life in Dangriga to live her passion of preserving her culture and uplifting her people. She transformed her three-generation family's compound into a cultural hub for visitors to experience Garifuna culture from history to spirituality to cooking. The setting is as authentic as it gets; you'll feel like you've stepped into a village within a village as soon as you arrive. Thatch huts are set up across the yard within view of the tranquil, mangrove-lined, freshwater Hopkins lagoon, each serving a specific purpose: a main welcome and dining area, museum, spiritual center, and cooking hut with traditional fire hearth. Uhwanie is also planting slowly to grow a sustainable farm, with cassava, coconut, yellow ginger, lime, moringa and other plants and fruit trees.

You'll start off the half-day immersion program by changing into a traditional outfit and beginning with a history introduction followed by lessons that include picking coconuts from a tree and making the dish *hudut* from scratch for your lunch. You can also go fishing for grouper or snapper or end the day

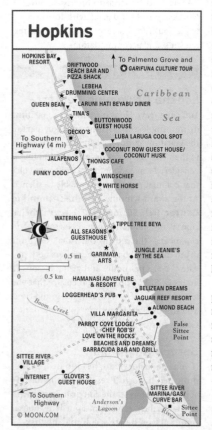

1: Palmento Grove Cultural & Fishing Lodge; **2:** the zipline course at Bocawina Adventures & Eco-Tours; **3:** Lebeha Drumming Center

kayaking along the lagoon or canal through mangrove tunnels that lead to an open, quiet end of Hopkins Beach. Uhwanie is an excellent guide and knows her culture inside out. Wear sneakers, long sleeves, and pants under your Garifuna outfit (for the ladies), and plenty of repellent, especially in the summer season.

Palmento Grove also offers a number of other unique experiences, including a Garifuna dancing class and a cassava farm tour. Ask about the new cabins if you're interested in overnighting—they were halfway completed at the time of my visit.

SPORTS AND RECREATION

There's plenty of inland exploration to keep you occupied near Hopkins, which is ideally located close to two of southern Belize's great parks, Cockscomb Basin Wildlife Sanctuary and Mayflower Bocawina National Park, offering plenty of hiking, rappelling, birding, and zip-lining.

For Mayflower Bocawina National Park, your best bet is to contact **Bocawina Adventures & Eco-Tours** (tel. 501/670-8019, U.S. tel. 844/894-2311, www.bocawinaadventures.com, single waterfall US$73 pp, zip-lining and waterfall rappelling expedition US$150 pp, lunch included), the only company to offer waterfall rappelling from the park's five stunning chutes, including an incredible 1.5-hour hike to the gorgeous 500-foot-high Antelope Falls, as well as birding and zooming across the canopy on the longest zip-line course in Central America, including night zip-lining. Don't miss hiking across the gorgeous Jesus Beatres Memorial Bridge—a suspension bridge through the rainforest, named after the former staff member who built it and sadly died soon after its completion from unrelated health issues. An even better way to experience the park is to stay overnight on-site at the Bocawina Rainforest Resort, tucked inside the lush park.

Charlton Castillo (tel. 501/543-7799, cell tel. 501/661-8199, charltoncastillo@yahoo. com, www.hopkinskulchatours.weebly. com) can guide you to the Cockscomb or to Mayflower Bocawina National Park. Charlton conducts night tours (6pm-11pm) in Cockscomb in case you want to try your luck with a jaguar encounter (US$60 pp for 2 people), daytime hiking and tubing on the South Stann Creek River (US$60 pp), and waterfall hikes at Bocawina (US$55 pp).

Beaches

Hopkins's beaches, all public, are some of the best in the country—I dare say even better than at Placencia Village. Stretching nearly five miles from Northside to Southside, they're wide, thick, never crowded, and have calmer waters. In the village you can take one very nice, very long beach walk, and you can lay your towel pretty much anywhere you please, except on chairs at private resorts.

If you're looking to mingle and eat on the beach, a great spot to hang out right in the village center, a block south from the village entrance and facing the sea, is **Luba Laruga Restaurant** (1 Hopkins Rd., tel. 501/661-3597, 8am-8pm daily, US$5-10). Get a beer or a plate of fresh grilled snapper or shrimp quesadillas, among other options, and go chill at the beachside picnic tables, or on the dock, steps away.

Up north, find a spot on the wide stretch by **Driftwood Pizza Shack** (tel. 501/667-4872 or 501/664-6611, www.driftwoodpizza. com, 11am-10pm Thurs.-Tues., US$8-23), where you can use Wi-Fi, eat, and hang out all day, or else you can lay your towel by **Laruni Hati Beyabu Diner** (Northside, tel. 501/661-5753, 10am-9pm daily), sitting on a gorgeous stretch. On the south end, there's no shortage of space either, although it tends to be quieter, if that's what you seek. In False Sittee, **Hamanasi Adventure and Resort** (tel. 501/533-7073, www.hamanasi.com) has a nice pool and beachfront, both of which you can use while having lunch at the restaurant.

Diving and Snorkeling

For diving or snorkeling, you can

hopefully make plans with **See More Dive and Adventure Shop** (tel. 501/602-4985 or 501/667-6626, https://seemoreadventures.com, $200/three-tank dive). After working with several of the area's dive shops, Elmar "Boo" Avila has been running his own dive center and crew and receiving rave reviews. Dive excursions take you along the south cayes, around South Water Caye Marine Reserve and Glover's Reef Atoll Marine Reserve, with over 20 sites to choose from. PADI dive certification classes are also available.

A long-standing dive center is **Hamanasi Adventure and Resort** (tel. 501/533-7073, www.hamanasi.com, 3-tank dive at Turneffe US$185, 2-tank dive at Southern Barrier Reef US$115). **Belize Underwater** (tel. 501/661-3401, www.belizeunderwater.com, US$175-400) also get rave reviews and offers PADI courses.

For snorkeling trips to the nearby cayes or fly-fishing, **Noawel Nuñez** (tel. 501/523-7219, cell tel. 501/662-3017, full-day snorkel trip US$175 for 2 people, half-day fishing US$238) is your man, operating out of his tour shack at the Watering Hole (his wife's restaurant).

Happie Go Luckie Tours (South Main St., tel. 501/635-0967, www.hgltours.com) can take you island-hopping and snorkeling (US$63 pp half-day), and their variety of boats allows for private chartered snorkel tours to the Barrier Reef (US$250/up to five persons, half-day) and water taxi service (to Dangriga, South Water, Tobacco). You can also go on a morning cruise along the Sittee River (US$35) or sign up for the Bioluminescent river tour (US$35).

You can rent snorkel gear and even goggles with an integrated camera and video camera (US$20 per day) from **Motorbike Rentals** (main road, just before Dong Lee's Supermarket, tel. 501/665-6292, www.alternateadventures.com, 8am-5pm daily).

Kayaking and Windsurfing

Most guesthouses in Hopkins rent kayaks and other small craft or provide them for guests to use. Hopkins's waters are calmer than the windier Northern Cayes, so kayaking is a safe bet, from the sea to the lagoon at the north end of the village.

Windschief Windsurfing School and Rental (on the beach toward the south, tel. 501/523-7249 or 501/668-6087, www.windschief.com, 1pm-midnight Mon.-Wed. and Fri.-Sat., US$10 per hour, private lessons US$30 per hour, group lessons US$20 pp) has a selection of slightly used windsurfing boards of various sizes for rent and offers lessons for mostly beginner levels, as wind conditions aren't consistently ideal to offer advanced sessions.

Biking

Many guesthouses and hotels either provide complimentary bicycles or rent them at a reasonable rate. It's really the best way to navigate Hopkins's sandy, rocky roads and explore its nooks and crannies. Bike rental shops in the village include **Fred's** (6am-7pm daily, US$2.50 per hour, US$10 per day), just behind Tina's, on the main drag.

Birding

Birding in Hopkins is as easy as walking out your front door. There are over 200 species of birds in the north and south parts of the village alone. You'll see grackles crossing the street, trotting along the beach, or, especially in November and December, mass-migrating across the village's trees at sunset. It's an incredible, intense sound I have yet to hear anywhere else. On the north end, beside Hopkins Bay Resort, you'll spot pelicans and dozens of other species at sunrise. Most of the tour companies offer birding tours to the nearby national parks, and while you can ask around for the best choice to fit your budget, first try the area's highly recommended birding expert, **Charlton Castillo** (tel. 501/543-7799, cell tel. 501/661-8199, charltoncastillo@yahoo.com, http://hopkinskulchatours.weebly.com, US$50 pp). Charlton also goes birding along the nearby Sittee River.

North of the village, **Fresh Water Creek Lagoon** offers plenty of birding; start early to spot beautiful herons and egrets, and navigate along the lagoon's lush mangroves. You can rent a kayak and explore solo, or take along a guide for better wildlife-spotting. Keep an eye out for the 35-foot lookout tower, then climb it and take in the views. The more adventurous could ask about guided night canoeing along Boom Creek, near Sittee River.

ENTERTAINMENT AND EVENTS
Nightlife

Tina's Kitchen (main road, left at the village entrance fork, tel. 501/650-3415, 7am-9:30pm daily, US$3-7) is always a safe bet for some beers, bites, and live drumming on Friday evening under a thatched roof. You'll find a nice crowd of locals here any day of the week.

From Friday onward, you may find other music or entertainment around Hopkins. As far as beach bars go, **Driftwood Beach Bar and Pizza Shack** (Northside, tel. 501/667-4872 or 501/664-6611, www.driftwoodpizza.com, 11am-10pm Thurs.-Tues., US$8-23) has a nice little operation going, with daily half-price happy hours and wood-fired pizza, and attracting plenty of travelers, expats, and a few locals. Monday is movie nights on the beach, but the most popular night is Tuesday, with live Garifuna drumming (the crowd picks up close to 9pm, so come earlier for seats).

The most local bar in town is the lively **Newtown Bar** (Back St., no phone, 8pm-midnight daily), a cool bamboo structure with sandy floors, drums hanging on the wall, dartboards at the back, and dimly lit Garifuna quotes, but where, to my own dismay, karaoke rules early in the evening Thursday-Saturday, followed by a DJ. The drinks are cheap, and the locals do come in droves.

A popular choice among expats is **Windschief Bar** (on the beach toward the south, tel. 501/523-7249, www.windschief.com, 1pm-midnight Mon.-Wed. and Fri.-Sat., US$4-10), particularly on Friday, when the small beachfront bar gets packed with expats

playing darts and table football and nibbling on the tasty small menu of the day.

Festivals and Events

Launched in 2011 and sponsored by the Belize Tourism Industry Association, the **Mango Festival** (May) celebrates all things mango. There are more than 15 varieties of mango in Belize, and villagers—from Garifuna locals to expat residents—offer up all sorts of dishes, including mango ceviche, mango salads, and mango pies.

The last weekend of July celebrates the existence of the Garifuna village of Hopkins with a big annual festival, **Hopkins Day,** held since 2000. The fun begins on Friday evening with cultural shows and food at the village basketball court. There are games, drumming, and dancing on Saturday lasting late into the night. Sunday is for family beach time. Check local listings for a detailed schedule.

As one of the main Garifuna areas in the country, Hopkins celebrates the arrival of the Garinagu in Belize with **Garifuna Settlement Day** (Nov. 19). A reenactment of the day the Garinagu arrived in the 19th century starts in the late morning of November 19 and is smaller in scale than Dangriga's full day of celebrations, but no less intense. There is plenty of drumming, singing, and chanting on the beach, including during the week leading up to the 19th. Plan for accommodations well in advance.

SHOPPING

While strolling through the village, you'll find several small shops, including **David's Woodcarving** and **Kulcha Gift Shop,** with Garifuna drums made in Hopkins and Dangriga, Marie Sharp's hot sauce, and plenty of local carvings. Both are on the main road in Hopkins Village.

Over the past couple of years, a handful of Guatemalans have set up shop in the village, but be aware that these are not Belizean-made products. A better bet would be to stop at **GariMaya Gift Shop** (south main road, no phone, 7:30am-8pm daily, US$3-10) at its

Hopkins Safety Tips

It may be that this is a worldwide phenomenon on the rise, but harassment and unsolicited attention toward female travelers has increased, and Belize is no exception—particularly in Hopkins Village. While it isn't anything to be alarmed about, and you should visit here to experience culture, here are some helpful tips:

- Stick to hiring licensed guides and visiting reputable establishments, as recommended in this guide.

- If approached, be polite but firm and do not answer any questions about traveling alone or where you are staying.

- Other than the folks who come recommended through your guesthouse, do not befriend complete strangers.

- Do not walk, bike, or wander solo at night—whether on the beach or roadside; hire a driver and stay in groups.

impressive location south of the village, with three rooms filled with Belizean handcrafts, textiles, art, and other classic souvenirs. I still think about the pair of woven Mayan pants I failed to purchase. Sometimes you'll catch an artist painting live outside. There's a smaller second location just north of the village entrance (take a second left after you reach the main entrance intersection). Owned by a Garifuna and Mayan couple, this is easily one of the best souvenir stores south of Belize City.

Save time for a bike ride just south of the village to pay a visit to **Sew Much Hemp** (S. Hopkins, tel. 501/668-6550, 11am-4pm Mon.-Sat.), where Barbara, a dreadlocked Oregonian, can teach you everything you need to know about the plant that can save the world. She sells excellent hemp products as well. If the sand flies are out, this is a great place to pick up some natural repellent.

FOOD

There are enough restaurants in Hopkins Village; most are very low-key small eateries serving either traditional Garifuna dishes or local Creole options. A couple of Western-style cafés and international or "fine cuisine" choices have popped up in the village in the past couple of years. Keep in mind that eating in Hopkins in itself is a cultural experience

unlike any other, and one you will create for yourself as you explore the village.

Garifuna

Several eateries are run by native Hopkins residents, the best way to experience authentic Garifuna cuisine. Most are casually set, with picnic tables under a thatched roof, but the meals are excellent. They require at least an hour's notice to have time to prepare, as Garifuna food is anything but the "fast" kind. The planning and wait, however, are well worth it. These dishes are also more likely to be ready on demand closer to the weekend (Fri.-Sat.). Most of these eateries also offer Belizean specialties, including stew chicken with rice and beans, or burritos, quesadillas, and other Central American fast foods.

My favorite breakfast is at ★ **Tina's Kitchen** (main road, left at the village entrance fork, look for signs, tel. 501/650-3415, 7am-9:30pm daily, US$3-7), where you will sample the tastiest Belizean meals—her fry jacks are to die for, as are her pancakes, and her stew chicken is equally flavorful. From Latin to Creole dishes and weekly Garifuna specialties, there's nothing Tina, a native of Hopkins, can't make. You can see her cook—sometimes in a traditional Garifuna dress—in her open kitchen as you wait to be served. There's weekly drumming on Friday evening.

Right on the village road going south is good but slow food at **Innie's** (main road, tel. 501/503-7333, 7am-9pm daily, US$8-17). Her *hudut* (fried fish in a coconut broth with mashed plantains) is delicious, although you may wait at your table for over an hour, and there are several other options for dinner, including *bundiga* (coconut fish soup with green banana dumplings), fish tea, and seafood dishes.

Still one of my favorites is Marva's ★ **Laruni Hati Beyabu Diner** (Northside, tel. 501/661-5753, 10am-9pm daily, US$4-6), a Garinagu-owned eatery and a favorite among longtime residents, serving the best of Belizean and Garifuna fare in the most ideal of settings—under a thatched roof and directly on a long stretch of beach. As long as you visit during high season, you can sample *hudut,* the traditional Garifuna dish of fried fish in a coconut broth with mashed plantains. Practice eating with your fingers, breeze blowing and toes buried in the sand. Note that to date, this is the only beachfront eatery run and owned by a Garifuna in Hopkins (*laru ni hati* means "clear blue sky" and *beyabu* means "seaside"). I sure hope she remains open, despite the rise in competing resorts and foreign restaurants—you can help by eating here.

Creole

Right in the village, **Siomara's** (South Rd., 6am-9pm daily, US$5) is a reliable fast pick for a casual lunch, from burritos to rice and beans. On the north side, beachfront ★ **Queen Bean** (no phone, 8am-3pm and 5pm-10pm Wed.-Mon., US$3-10) has tastier lunch plates that range from vegetarian quesadillas to shrimp pasta, fried chicken, and rice and beans dishes. You can also enjoy breakfast here, and there's drumming on Thursday nights.

T&C's Kitchen (main road, past the football field, no phone, 8am-4pm daily, US$3-6) is your best bet for delicious stews with rice and beans, among other local dishes, and has so many loyal customers that it sells out quickly. Get there early at mealtimes,

particularly lunch. T&C also bakes delicious desserts and cakes. The screened porch and outdoor courtyard seating options, now expanded with an outdoor bar, make it a good spot to sit and eat while watching the village go by or dominoes games.

The tiny kitchen at **Luba Laruga Cool Spot** (1 Hopkins Rd., tel. 501/661-3597, 8am-8pm daily, US$5-10) whips out decent-value seafood dishes, from freshly grilled coconut-crusted snapper to stuffed grouper and shrimp quesadillas. The beachfront picnic tables, dock, and music complete this casual, outdoor spot that tends to attract plenty of backpackers and locals.

Caribbean and International

The owners of Coconut Row filled a niche in the village when they opened the cozy, eight-table ★ **Coconut Husk** (Coconut Row, www.coconutrowbelize.com, 7:30am-8pm daily, US$4-8) next door, on their gorgeous piece of beachfront in the heart of Hopkins. The restaurant prides itself on using only unprocessed ingredients, but it's also a place to enjoy a meal quietly away from the village hustle and savor good food with great sea views. Grab breakfast on the open-air terrace in peace, and enjoy fresh-baked whole wheat coconut bread, organic free-range omelet, and all the Belizean breakfast specialties like fry jacks. Lunch and dinner options are also delicious with the likes of fish sandwiches, seafood platters, coconut curries, wraps, and tacos, among a myriad of options. Don't miss trying the cocktails, too.

A popular spot is the **Driftwood Beach Bar and Pizza Shack** (Beachfront northside, tel. 501/664-6611, www.driftwoodpizza.com, 11am-10pm Thurs.-Tues., US$8-23), where you can have decent-tasting wood-fired pizza, play beach volleyball, listen to live drumming, or just hang out at a lively spot. The bar is one of the most social in the village, crowded with expats, travelers, and a few locals. A second similar spot from the same owners, south of Hopkins, is **LoggerHeads Pub & Grill** (Sittee Point, near Jaguar Reef Lodge, tel. 501/650-2886, 11am-10pm Thurs.-Mon., US$8-23), serving grilled burgers in a variety of combinations in a relaxed open-deck atmosphere. On a matching social wavelength is the bar at **Windschief** (tel. 501/523-7249 or 501/668-6087, www.windschief.com, 1pm-midnight Mon.-Wed. and Fri.-Sat., 1pm-6pm Sun., US$5-7), with a daily casual dinner menu that includes fish-and-chips on Friday and gyros or burgers (that you can burn off while playing darts or table football).

Jalapeño's (main road, 10am-9pm Thurs.-Tues., from US$5) serves tasty burgers, fish, and pastas, conveniently located at the entrance to Hopkins. Nearby, **Gecko's** (north main road, tel. 501/629-5411, noon-9pm Mon. and Wed.-Sat., US$4-10) is a favorite among expats in an open-air spot with four tables and a Caribbean-influenced menu, as well as other surprises of the day (I like the jerk chicken). It's pricier than other local restaurants, but portions are large, with specials served with two sides.

Locally owned **Ella's Cool Spot** (main road, just before T&C's Kitchen, tel. 501/653-3055, noon-midnight Tues.-Sun., US$3-10) is a friendly, sandy-floored stop for a quick bite, including burritos, fry fish, wings, or a rice and beans plate of the day. The wait can be long, so be patient. The reggae or *punta* music is usually blasting while patrons throw back a few beers at the bar or one of the picnic tables.

For a quick coffee and snack, try **Thongs Café** (Main Rd., tel. 501/662-0110, www.thongscafe.com, 7am-3pm daily, US$8-12), with an outdoor roadside patio and light world music buzzing in the background. It's nice for people-watching and that first or second cup of morning coffee. The breakfast offerings range from cold sandwiches to cinnamon rolls.

Fine Dining

Have a unique experience at **Love on the Rocks Hot Rock Grill Restaurant** (at Parrot Cove Lodge, www.chefrobbelize.com, tel. 501/672-7272, 5pm-10pm daily, US$13-25), created by Chef Rob, where you can finish cooking your own entrée on 400-degree hot stones in the old way of the ancient Maya. Dishes include seafood, chicken, or steak with two sides—all of which are delicious. Have fun flipping your food over on the stone to your liking or warming up your sides at will. Those who don't want to "get stoned" can opt for pastas and other menu choices. The restaurant, consisting of an outdoor beachfront deck and bar, is immediately next door to the original Chef Rob's restaurant at Parrot Cove Lodge, another one not to miss.

★ **Chef Rob's Gourmet Cafe** (tel. 501/663-1812 or 501/670-1529, 5pm-9pm Mon.-Sat., 4-course meal US$28) is worth every penny and should be your top pick if you only have that one night in Hopkins and are looking for a special treat. Rob Pronk serves up his delectable, daily-created four-course dining experience with choices like coconut soup, rib-eye steak, Thai-style pork and shrimp, or Lobster Robert. The restaurant has expanded with a beachfront deck for dining alfresco. Reserve ahead.

Barracuda Bar and Grill (Beaches and Dreams, tel. 501/523-7259, 4pm-9pm or 10pm daily, dinner US$15-25, large lobster pizza US$25, cheese pizza US$12) is another solid pick for grilled meats, seafood, and homemade pastas. Set on a waterfront deck with mood lighting, it's a romantic dinner spot; reservations are recommended, as the restaurant can fill up quickly.

Groceries

There are five groceries and a produce stand in Hopkins, making it easier to stock up on nibbles and booze without breaking the bank. **Dong Lee's Supermarket** (Main Rd., 9am-midnight daily) has the largest selection of liquor. The Garifuna women's group sells johnnycakes, bread, and Creole buns; look out for the kids selling their mothers' baked goods, too.

ACCOMMODATIONS
Under US$25

On the Northside, next to Driftwood Pizza

Shack, budget travelers love the **Lebeha Drumming Center** (tel. 501/665-9305, www.lebeha.com), which has campsites (US$5), a dorm (US$7.50), and a couple of shared-bath stilted wooden guest rooms (US$25) set within the courtyard area; they are very simple (a ceiling fan, no hot water, a mosquito net, and a teakettle). There is wireless Internet.

Right in the village and hard to miss is the bright, eccentric ★ **Funky Dodo** (tel. 501/676-3636, www.funkydodo.bz, US$14), once a classic small backpacker hostel and upgraded into a hostel and guesthouse. There's a 16-bunk bed dormitory and shared baths as well as private guest rooms with outdoor baths or private baths. On the top floor are two private Tree Top rooms (US$54.45) that are among the best bang for your buck in all of Hopkins, with Wi-Fi and hot water. There's a sandy courtyard peppered with hammocks, Wi-Fi, and coffee daily. Owners Anna and Roy, Chicago expats, are friendly and have turned this hostel into a cozy, clean place to stay.

US$25-50

Continuing south along the beach, you'll come across two stilted seafront cabanas at **Windschief** (tel. 501/523-7249, www.windschief.com, US$25-40), right next to the Windschief bar and windsurfing school. They are sometimes on rent, other times not, so check ahead. Note that it gets noisy with music and bar patrons on weekends.

★ **Tipple Tree Beya** (tel. 501/615-7006, www.tippletreebelize.com, US$40-175) is a longtime favorite and remains constant. This well-maintained spot right on the beach offers basic guest rooms, en suite two-bedrooms, or a private cabin with a kitchenette. There is a shared porch with a hammock and beach chairs, and an outdoor cold-water shower if you stay in the budget room (US$40). Half-day or full-day kayak (US$15-20) and bicycle (US$5-9) rentals are available. Host Tricia is

able to direct you for inland tours and snorkeling trips. Directly adjacent to Tipple Tree are three more delightful one- and two-bedroom beachfront options (US$98-175), managed by Tipple Tree, at **AJ Palms.**

Lebeha Drumming Center (tel. 501/665-9305, www.hopkinscabanas.com, US$49) also has three cozy furnished cabanas set directly on a nice stretch of beach with kitchenettes, hot showers, and porches.

US$50-100

★ **White Horse** (tel. 501/651-7961, www.whitehorseguesthouse.com, US$50-100) has a clean, comfortable spot on the beach, steps from Ella's Cool Spot. The two stand-alone bungalows are perfect, a skip from the sea, equipped with queen bed, furnished kitchen and seating area (a/c is extra US$5/day), and private deck, and there are also rooms and a suite in the main house. There's no restaurant on-site but you're a stone's throw from a handful of options a short walk or bike ride away.

You'll also find good value at the **All Seasons Guesthouse** (tel. 501/523-7209, www.allseasonsbelize.com, US$55-75, includes tax and coffee). It's not right on the beach, but it's just a few steps away, and the guest rooms in the main compound are comfortable and nicely decorated by former owner Ingrid, a beloved longtime Hopkins resident who sadly passed away. Just next door are two fully furnished and delightful stand-alone, two-bedroom apartments (US$98, US$600 per week), making it a more ideal spot than ever for group stays.

A short distance after the pavement of Hopkins Village runs out, down the long dirt road, look for the left turn to **Jungle Jeanie's by the Sea** (tel. 501/533-8057, www.junglebythesea.com, US$60-120). This is a nice stretch of beach for guests staying in Jeanie's eight spacious rustic cabanas, three of which are beachfront. It's a bit remote from the rest of the village and you'll have to bike your way around. The more secluded cabins, along a small network of rainforest trails, have kitchenettes, private baths, hot

1: beachfront Laruni Hati Beyabu Diner; **2:** Coconut Husk

and cold showers, and verandas with a sea view; the Palmetto cabana, with three beds, is ideal for a family, and the tree-house cabana overlooks coco plum and sea grape trees. Camping (US$15 pp) is available, and in case you either fear or love dogs, there are three dutiful German shepherds on the property. The kitchen serves breakfast, and lunch and dinner on request, and there's a screened "jungle *palapa*" for thrice-weekly yoga sessions. Ask to see the beautiful marimba.

US$100-150

A welcome option right in the village is the colorful and immaculate ★ **Coconut Row Guest House** (Front St., tel. 501/675-3000, www.coconutrowbelize.com, US$110-180)— you can't miss the rainbow-colored beach chairs set on an idyllic stretch amid a garden of coconut trees, red hibiscus flowers, and plants. There are three beachfront single guest rooms on one side and two-bedroom apartments, fully furnished with a kitchenette, air-conditioning, and outdoor patios. Even cuter are the four stand-alone, colorful Palm Cove Cabins (US$125-135), which include a two-bedroom, right next to the main guesthouse, full of amenities, including air-conditioning and Wi-Fi. An inviting picnic area on the beach is available to guests, and the water is less than 10 steps away. There's an optional US$6 per person breakfast.

Buttonwood Guest House (Front St., tel. 501/670-3000, http://coconutrowbelize. com, US$130-145) is the ideal self-catering couples' or family hideaway right in the middle of the village yet down a quiet alley facing the beach. The two-story home offers luxurious ground-floor rooms, a studio, and a top-floor two-bedroom apartment with delightful views of the sea as well as a spacious deck. Air-conditioning is available at an extra cost. There are beach chairs and a thatched outdoor *palapa* for relaxation, as well as a rooftop with 360-degree panoramic views over the village and sea. Use of bicycles and Wi-Fi are complimentary. You can rent golf carts through Coconut Row Guest House, which manages the guesthouse. Book in advance to ensure you get your preferred travel dates.

Over US$200

On the northern tip of town, beside the lagoon, **Hopkins Bay Resort** (tel. 501/533-7804, www.hopkinsbayresort.com, US$130-512) has 19 one- and two-bedroom luxury villas that can be locked off, depending on your needs. No amenities are lacking in the homes, and there are two pools on-site, as well as a restaurant, daily housekeeping at the hour of your choosing, and complimentary use of kayaks and bikes. The resort also offers day trips to Thatch Caye, as well as cultural tours, including a "cook your catch" day and a Garifuna immersion experience, among the usual dive, snorkel, and inland tour options.

Fit for an episode of MTV's *Cribs,* on the south end of the village, **Villa Verano** (tel. 501/533-7016, U.S. tel. 877/646-2317, www.villaveranobelize.com, US$275-325) will have you gasping at every other step once you are inside the front door. Past the stunning open-ceiling Mediterranean courtyard are three floors, the second of which is rented as one unit (US$1,950); the remaining parts of the villa can either be locked off into separate units or rented as a whole. Some include rooms with bunk beds (with the plushest bunk mattresses I've seen) for families. With local paintings, wood carvings, granite tiling, French doors with stunning sea views, regally spacious baths with jetted tubs, library rooms fitted with gigantic plasma TVs, a 70-foot infinity pool, and a top-floor terrace "game room" complete with a pool, lounge seating, and a hot tub overlooking the Maya Mountains at the back, no luxurious detail has been spared. This is an ideal place for weddings, groups of friends looking for a treat, family retreats, or just a decadent getaway. Don't miss the view of the pool and the beach from the rooftop.

1: Buttonwood Guest House's beachfront; **2:** the beachfront shared by Jaguar Reef Lodge and Almond Beach resorts

INFORMATION AND SERVICES

The **Windschief Internet Café** and cocktail bar (on the beach toward the south, tel. 501/523-7249, www.windschief.com, 1pm-11pm Mon.-Wed. and Fri.-Sat., 6pm-11pm Sun., US$4-10) is where it's at, although most midrange hotels in Hopkins also offer computers and wireless service. **Hopkins Office Supply** (main road) also has a handful of desktops for Internet use—there's a two-hour minimum (US$2.50 per hour). Bring plenty of cash, as there's only one ATM in Hopkins (at the village entrance); the nearest ATMs beyond this are in Dangriga.

TRANSPORTATION

If you have your own transportation, getting to Hopkins is easy: Just follow the Southern Highway until you see the well-signed turnoff on your left; from there it's a four-mile straight stretch of dirt road (which can be under water during intense rains). Figure 30-40 minutes' total drive time from Dangriga.

Motorbike Rentals (main road, just before Dong Lee's Supermarket, tel. 501/665-6292, www.alternateadventures.com, 8am-5pm daily, starting at US$65 per day with all gear accessories) offers up a wide range of 150-200cc dirt- or cruiser-style motorcycles for rent. A rental, good for two, includes helmets, a map, a local cell phone, and help with designing a self-guided course to Cockscomb, Mayflower Bocawina, and other points of interest.

There are a few buses from Dangriga to Hopkins (8am and 5:15pm Mon.-Sat., US$2.50); buses return to Dangriga at 7am, 7:30am, and 2pm daily; confirm the schedule. Placencia buses used to go through Hopkins, but currently there are no buses taking that route. A popular alternative is to get off the bus at the Hopkins junction and hitch a ride to the village, or call for a taxi (contact **Mr. Abraham,** tel. 501/668-6166; **Mr. Mac,** tel. 501/665-0181; **Mr. Leroy,** tel. 501/664-5781; or **Mr. Rodriguez,** tel. 501/665-2445). Otherwise it's an expensive hotel shuttle or local taxi—which can cost up to US$50 from Dangriga. Once in Hopkins, you can rent a dirt motorcycle at Motorbike Rentals; some people do this to get to the Mayflower reserve or other nearby hiking spots. Bicycle rentals are also easy to find and useful for exploring the village.

FALSE SITTEE POINT

A few minutes' bicycle ride south from Hopkins Village brings you to a small oceanside strip of upscale resorts, restaurants, and condos facing a quiet, long stretch of beach. It has become an increasingly popular area to stay because of the quality of the hotels and guesthouses, as well as the location's direct access to many inland and offshore attractions and activities.

Food and Accommodations

A laid-back yet boutique-style option amid a stretch of larger resorts along False Sittee Point is **Beaches and Dreams Seafront Inn and Pub** (tel. 501/523-7259 or 501/662-6830, www.beachesanddreams.com, US$139-179), whose four ample guest rooms have tiled floors, porches, and private baths; ask about the tree house, which is great for families. Next door is a taller three-story building— the **Beaches and Dreams Hotel**—with six spacious, Belize-themed, tastefully decorated and colorful rooms (from US$195) that are pool and sea facing or with views of the Maya Mountains at the back. Don't miss the rooftop terrace; swing in the hammocks and marvel at the view of Victoria Peak ahead. Use of kayaks and bikes is complimentary, and there's a lovely *palapa* dock, ideal for relaxing and napping by the sea. On-site is a tour company offering packages, including culinary adventures.

Another decent midrange option is next door at the recently upgraded ★ **Parrot Cove Lodge** (tel. 501/523-7225, http://parrotcovelodge.com, US$189-300), with a handful of standard rooms and suites, plus five new ocean-view rooms. On-site are also a full PADI dive shop and two of the country's better restaurants: **Love on the Rocks** and the celebrated **Chef Rob's Gourmet Cafe.**

A more affordable option, across the street from the beach, is the boutique Mediterranean-style white-and-blue villa at **Cosmopolitan Guest House** (tel. 501/673-7373, www.cosmopolitanbelize.com, US$75-85), offering four small private ground-floor rooms with double beds that include air-conditioning, flat-screen TVs, minifridges, and veranda space, along with cozy poolside cabanas that are ideal for couples. Showers are solar heated, and amenities include bikes and Wi-Fi. Upstairs are the owners' quarters, where famous Chef Rob and his spouse reside. Though at this rate, you could also easily stay beachfront in Hopkins Village.

Awarded Hotel of the Year 2010 by the Belize Tourism Board, a solid pick for your buck is ★ **Jaguar Reef Lodge** (tel. 501/822-3851, U.S. tel. 646/503-1735, www.vivabelize.com/jaguar-reef, US$249-349), a full-service, intimately sized resort with 14 spacious furnished cabanas and four suites, sitting on a gorgeous stretch of Hopkins Beach. Each cottage welcomes you with a complimentary local rum and Coke package—hard not to love—and amenities aren't spared, including king beds, giant showers, Wi-Fi, air-conditioning, and a private porch. The Jaguar Reef end feels busier because of the beautiful on-site Paddle House, where Belizean Chef Rahim's delicious local and international creations are served for the resort as well as for its adjacent properties. Connecting next door and easily reached by walking on the beach side is charming sister resort **Almond Beach** (tel. 501/822-3851, U.S. tel. 866/624-1516, www.almondbeachbelize.com, US$299-599), offering a selection of even more luxurious stand-alone beachfront casitas and suites that fill up fairly quickly with couples. The outdoor shower is a treat. The cozy tiki swim-up bar has an infinity view of the sea, with happy hour starting at 2pm, and the water is delightfully warm in the evening. The two properties also share pools (including one for kiddies) and bars, along with bikes, kayaks, sand volleyball, and many activity-based

packages. The ultra-luxe "beachfront vista suite" on the Almond Beach side is an outrageously decadent five-bedroom penthouse (US$870) that includes a private chef. This is a popular spot for fancy weddings, especially with the addition of the **Butterflies Spa** (8am-7pm daily), offering a full range of treatments and salon care at about the same rates as back home. **Butterflies Coffee** next to it has grinds from all over Central America, roasted fresh daily, and cute patio seating. The third sister property, **Villa Margarita** (www.vivabelize.com/villa-margarita, US$349), a skip and a hop over, opened in January 2015 and raises the bar with six suites connected by a spiraling wooden staircase, including a top-floor penthouse with gorgeous panoramic views. No detail is spared, including Jacuzzis, giant plasma TVs, and local cell phones, while the villa's beachfront swimming pool is a treat.

Hamanasi Adventure and Resort (tel. 501/533-7073, www.hamanasi.com, from US$556) sits on 17 acres, including 400 feet of beautiful beachfront, and offers eight beachfront guest rooms, four suites (including a honeymoon option), and five deluxe tree houses tucked away in the littoral forest, all with views and tiled baths, air-conditioning, fans, and porches. Restaurant meals include pasta and, of course, fresh seafood; it's open to outside visitors as well (bring a towel). This place is ideal if you just want to laze and aren't into diving or inland adventures. There's a pool overlooking the beachfront as well as kayaks, bikes, and hammocks to use at your leisure. Hamanasi is popular among locals as much as visitors and has a high occupancy rate; make reservations ahead of time. There's a dive shop on-site.

Information and Services
Sittee River Marina (tel. 501/670-8525 or 501/520-7888, www.sitteerivermarina.com, 6am-5:30pm daily) has oil, gas, diesel, snacks, restroom and shower facilities, and cold beer. It also offers charters, and fuel at sea on request.

Transportation

Driving south on the road from Hopkins, you'll pass through False Sittee, a short drive east of the Southern Highway. There are usually two daily buses that pass through Sittee River and False Sittee Point, but the schedule varies; most accommodations will provide transfers from Dangriga.

SITTEE RIVER

Sittee River is a peaceful, riverine corner of the country with not a whole lot happening in it. It qualifies as a village only in the loosest sense, with a few houses and a couple of basic riverside places to stay. Sadly, businesses have become sparse in Sittee, and as of late it appears nearly abandoned, but its wildlife and natural setting remain; if you're not staying here—frankly, there are way better options in Hopkins Village—it's good for a drive through and perhaps a stop at the Curve Bar and the marina to soak in Belize's deepest and most beautiful river.

Sports and Recreation

On the road to False Sittee, past Jaguar Reef Lodge, you'll find **Diversity Café and Tours** (tel. 501/661-7444), offering help with tour planning, including snorkeling, fishing, and inland trips, which it outsources to local guides. There are also golf carts for rent (US$20 for 2 hours, US$50 per day).

Hopkins Stand Up Paddleboard (South Hopkins, behind Hamanasi Resort, tel. 501/650-9040, www.suphopkins.com) runs unique SUP and kayak tours, including a seven-mile SUP down Sittee River (US$70), or on a SUP tour to the southern Barrier Reef, with the boat ride departing from Sittee River Marina.

Food and Accommodations

The only decent option in Sittee at publication time is **River House Lodge** (tel. 501/543-7044, www.riverhouselodgebelize.com, US$70-85). It offers six cabanas with double beds, screened porches, and kitchenettes and is set along the Sittee River with a small

dock for gazing at the gorgeous view (but not for swimming—crocodiles live in the river). There's an on-site bar and restaurant and an indoor pool. Note that the lodge can be closed down during the slow season (Sept.-Oct.), so check ahead.

Have a sunset drink over the Sittee River under the thatched roof at the **Curve Bar** (Sittee River Marina, tel. 501/670-8525, 11am-9pm Sun.-Fri., check summer schedule, US$5-20)—enjoy lobster fritters, flatbread pizza, and Belizean snacks like ceviche. Be sure you have a ride arranged to and from the off-the-beaten path restaurant.

Transportation

The Sittee River area is about a 10-minute drive east of the Southern Highway through mostly orange orchards and riverside lots. There are usually two daily buses that run through Sittee River and False Sittee Point, but this schedule is always up in the air; your accommodations will provide some sort of transfer from Dangriga. Driving south on the road from Hopkins, you'll pass through False Sittee, followed by the village of Sittee River, occupying a few bends of the slow, flat river of the same name.

TOP EXPERIENCE

★ MAYFLOWER BOCAWINA NATIONAL PARK

Located 17 miles from Dangriga and 12 miles from Hopkins, **Mayflower Bocawina National Park** (entrance US$5 pp) comprises more than 7,100 acres of Maya Mountain wilderness set aside in 2001 to protect and showcase the area's five waterfalls and green-fringed Mayan ruins. A trail system offers excellent hiking, and it's an adventurous climb to Antelope Falls. A hike in Mayflower Bocawina can be combined with a day trip to Cockscomb (just to the south), or it can easily fill a whole day or more. Bocawina has been sponsoring Panthera Belize on their current monitoring of the park—a number of cameras have been installed around Bocawina to monitor jaguars and other resident wildlife.

Guides and Tours

Ramon Guzman (tel. 501/533-7136) is a long-time park warden, and he may even greet you at the entrance. Doreen Guzman is an officer in the **Friends of Mayflower Bocawina National Park** (mayflowerbocawina@yahoo.com), an organization that comanages the park with the government.

The licensed guides at **Bocawina Adventures & Eco-Tours** (tel. 501/670-8019, U.S. tel. 855/222-0555, www.bocawinaadventures.com) will pick you up wherever you are staying in the area. A day-long adventure (from US$50 pp, no minimum number of people) hiking to and rappelling from one or all five waterfalls inside the park—Antelope, Bocawina, Tears of the Jaguar, Peck Falls, and Big Drop Falls—is well worth it. When I rappelled the smaller 125-foot-high Bocawina Falls, the drive was just a little over 30 minutes, followed by a short hike of moderate difficulty but with an impressive view. The pool at the summit of **Antelope Falls** is absolutely breathtaking—that's if you can

manage the grueling, Indiana Jones-like hike of almost two hours uphill to get there, navigating with the use of steps and eventually just ropes! Well worth the adventure, but be sure you are reasonably fit to hike, and wear adequate shoes and clothing. Additional adventures include Belize's and Central America's longest single zip-line course, at 2,300 feet, and bird-watching.

To explore the park fully, you should overnight at **Bocawina Rainforest Resort and Adventures** (formerly Mama Noots Eco Resort, tel. 501/670-8019, www.bocawina.com, US$119-299, continental breakfast included), with duplex cabanas set on beautifully landscaped grounds right in the park, as well as suites with stunning panoramic views of the rainforest and the cascading Antelope Falls right from your king-size bed. Tours can be booked daily—if you're up for a real challenge don't miss this hike—and I can say with confidence that the guides here are some of the best I've experienced in Belize—ask for Julio or Tony, in particular. The on-site **Wild Fig Restaurant** has a full bar and serves excellent dishes, from burgers and quesadillas for lunch to lobster or steak dinners, courtesy of Chef Mo, Belize's youngest at just 19 years of age, trained under Chef Rob.

The exhilarating hike to the top of Antelope Falls ends at this jade pool.

While staying here, don't miss saying hello to the resident hicatee turtle, "Stinky"—from an endangered species but found on the grounds and now being cared for by the staff.

For birding or other inland tours from Hopkins, the best guide is **Charlton Castillo** (South Middle St., tel. 501/661-8199, charltoncastillo@yahoo.com, http://hopkinskulchatours.weebly.com, US$50 pp, minimum 2 people).

Transportation

The biggest challenge to enjoying Mayflower Bocawina is simply getting there; it lies 4.5 miles west of the Southern Highway with no public transportation of any kind making the trip. (The turnoff is just north of Silk Grass Village.) Sign in at the park office and interpretive center (7am-4pm daily) and pay the US$5 per person entrance fee. There is a **campground** (US$5) at the park entrance; bring your own gear.

RED BANK

Tucked away on a red-dirt road is the small Mayan village of Red Bank. Here, at the edge of the Maya Mountains, rare and impressive scarlet macaws gather to feed on the ripe fruits of pole-wood trees outside the village. This annual phenomenon was unknown to outsiders until 1997, when conservationists learned that 20 of the birds had been hunted for table fare; at that time it was thought Belize had a population of just 30-60 scarlet macaws. In response, Programme for Belize worked with the village council to form the Red Bank Scarlet Macaw Conservation Group, led by the village leader, Jeronimo Sho.

The small community-based ecotourism industry offers visitors accommodations, meals, crafts, and guide services. A reserve has been established about a mile from the village, and visitors must pay a small conservation fee; ask around for Mr. Sho. The best time to visit is mid-January-March, when the annatto fruit are ripe. As many as 100 scarlet macaws have been observed in the morning when the birds are feeding. Contact the **Scarlet Macaw Bed and Breakfast** (tel. 501/660-6320, https://scarletmacawbb.business.site, scarletmacawb3b@gmail.com, US$20; tour US$12.50 pp).

The Cockscomb Basin

The land rises gradually from the coastal plains to the Maya Mountains; driving south on the Southern Highway, you'll see the highlands to the west and flatlands to the left, mostly covered by orange and banana groves. The highway passes through a few villages and soon delivers you to the area's prime attraction: Maya Centre village and Cockscomb Basin Wildlife Sanctuary. Heavy rain along the peaks of the Maya range, as much as 160 inches per year, runs off into lush rainforest thick with trees, orchids, palms, ferns, abundant birds, and exotic animals, including peccaries, anteaters, armadillos, tapirs, and jaguars.

TOP EXPERIENCE

★ COCKSCOMB BASIN WILDLIFE SANCTUARY

Commonly called the "Jaguar Preserve," the **Cockscomb Basin Wildlife Sanctuary** is one of the most beautiful natural attractions in the country. A large tract of approximately 155 square miles of forest was declared a forest reserve in 1984, and in 1986 the government of Belize set the region aside as a preserve for the largest cat in the Americas, the jaguar. Since then it has become a primary breeding ground for jags, and counts about 80 of them in the park. The area is alive with wildlife, including margays, ocelots, pumas, jaguarundis, tapirs, deer, pacas, iguanas, kinkajous, and armadillos, to name just a few, along with hundreds of bird species and even howler monkeys. The park is also home to the red-eyed tree frog and the critically endangered Morelet's tree frog. And though you probably won't spot large cats roaming during the day (they hunt at night), it's exciting to see their prints and other signs—and to know that even if you don't see one, you'll probably be seen by one.

The sanctuary is managed by the **Belize Audubon Society** (www.belizeaudubon.org), which also conducts research and community outreach in support of conservation. The park is open 7:30am-4:30pm daily. Entrance is US$5 for non-Belizeans; pay at the Maya Centre Women's Group crafts shop at the head of the access road, immediately off the Southern Highway. Just past the entrance gate into the park is a gift shop and office, where you'll be asked to sign in. Visitor facilities include an interpretive center, a picnic area, and as of 2018, brand-new cabins with bunk beds—ideal to overnight in the park, whether you're a group of students or walk-in guests and avid birders.

Victoria Peak

The second-highest point in the country is the top of **Victoria Peak** (3,675 feet). Geologists believe the mountain is four million years old, the oldest geologic formation in Central America. Reportedly, area Mayan populations thought the peak was surrounded by a lake, unapproachable by people and occupied by a powerful spirit. The first people known to have reached the summit, a party led by Roger T. Goldsworth, governor of then-British Honduras, did so in 1888. Today it is a protected natural monument, managed by the Belize Audubon Society.

Summit trips can be arranged through the Audubon Society—they have trained guides to lead to Victoria Peak—in the dry season only (Feb.-May) and must include a permit

and a licensed guide (US$1,500 per group). The 30-mile round-trip trek takes three days; the up-and-down terrain is steep, and there are no switchbacks. A minimum of 10 people is required, plus two guides. For efficient and direct bookings as well as information, contact Ms. Delia Noble of the Belize Audubon Society (giftshop@belizeaudubon.org).

Contact the **Belize Audubon Society** (www.belizeaudubon.org) for trail and campsite details; entrance is US$5 per person plus camping fees.

There are also a few reputable mountain guides in the surrounding villages, including **Marcos Cucul** (tel. 501/600-3116, www.mayaguide.bz), who can take you rock climbing or on a backcountry trip to the top of Victoria Peak (US$500 pp).

Hiking

There are more than 20 miles of maintained hiking trails (or 17 trails), which range from an easy hour-long stroll along the river to a three- to four-day Victoria Peak expedition. An early morning hike on the **Wari Loop** offers the best chance to see wildlife and to admire the large buttress roots of the swamp kaway (*Pterocarpus officinalis*) trees. At the end of the **Tiger Fern Trail,** a rigorous hike, you'll find an impressive double waterfall. There are more waterfalls, including a less difficult fall with a pool, within a 30-minute hike. Check the front of the visitors center building for a detailed map. For more adventure, sign up for a night hike (US$60 pp).

If you climb **Ben's Bluff,** you're not just looking out over a park where jaguars live—you're at the entrance of a forest that goes all the way into the Guatemalan Petén, part of the largest contiguous block of protected forest in Central America. The bluff was named after Ben Nottingham, who monitored radio-collared jaguars with radiotelemetry. From here you can see Outlier Peak, a moderate one-day hike (about 8.5 miles round-trip) and great place to camp.

Bring your swimsuit when visiting, as you'll find cool natural waterfalls and pools for a refreshing plunge. You can also rent an inner tube (US$7.50) and float down South Stann Creek. All visitors are encouraged to bring sturdy shoes, a long-sleeved shirt, long pants, insect repellent, sunscreen, and plenty of water. Birding has also risen in popularity in Cockscomb; and there have been increased sightings of scarlet macaws over recent years. If you would like to hire a guide, there are several renowned wilderness guides who grew up in these forests and who can be found up the road in Maya Centre.

Food and Accommodations

The good news is that accommodation options have expanded at this popular national park. You can bring your own tent to stay at one of three well-maintained **campgrounds** (US$10 pp)—one is by the visitors center with outdoor showers and toilets, and the other two are on Tiger Fern Trail and Outlier Trail.

Cabins are available. The best options include a newly built **private cabin** (US$120) with screened veranda boasting gorgeous views, two bedrooms with double bed and bunk beds, private bath, living room, and kitchenette. There's also a five-bedroom, **dormitory** (US$20) that's a good bang for your buck or a **two-bedroom birdhouse cabin** (US$81.75). All accommodations are solar powered (flashlights are provided in case of outage), have hot water, and there's a shared communal kitchen.

Be prepared with food and supplies if you plan to stay a few days; the only food for sale in the visitors center is chips, cookies, candy bars, and soft drinks; future plans include an on-site cafeteria and cook. There are a couple of small shops in Maya Centre, so feel free to stock up there before catching a taxi into the park. You may also be able to arrange for meals to be cooked in Maya Centre and delivered to you. Otherwise, there is a communal kitchen with a refrigerator, gas stoves, and crockery and cooking utensils for rent. Again, visitors are required to bring their own food and water.

Transportation

Cockscomb Basin is about six miles west of the Southern Highway and the village of Maya Centre; from Dangriga, it's a total of 20 miles. The road can be rough after it rains. For public transportation, catch any bus traveling between Dangriga and Punta Gorda and hop off at Maya Centre. From there, it's an extremely long—at least an hour—and hilly walk; I strongly recommend a US$15-20 taxi ride.

MAYA CENTRE

This small village is at the turnoff to the famous Cockscomb Basin Wildlife Sanctuary. Many of the now 1,000 Mopan Maya who live here were relocated when their original home within the Cockscomb Basin was given protected status. Since then, they have had to change their lifestyle; instead of continuing to clear patches of rainforest for short-term agriculture, many men now work as guides and taxi drivers, while the women create and sell artwork. Still, the people of Maya Centre are struggling to support their town with tourism. Ever since they were prohibited from using the now-protected rainforest for subsistence farming and hunting, tourism has been their only hope, aside from working for slave wages at the nearby banana and citrus farms. The village has a few places to stay, eat, and experience village life, literally right down the road from the famous reserve.

At the very least, make sure that you—or the driver of your tour bus—stop at one of the three Mayan crafts stores, all on the road into the park. At the turnoff from the Southern Highway, you'll find the **Maya Centre Women's Group** (7:30am-4:30pm daily), which sells local crafts and collects the entrance fee for Cockscomb. The **Nu'uk Che'il Gift Shop** is 0.25 mile farther toward the park, offering fine jewelry, slate carvings, baskets, herbs, and other crafts.

Julio Saqui runs the store next to the women's co-op and offers satellite Internet access (US$4 per hour) and taxi service as well as meals to any overnight guests in the area who need it (US$7 pp per meal, including delivery).

Julio is a great guide and offers many services and tours, including to Victoria Peak; information is available on his website (www. cockscombmayatours.com).

Julio also runs the **Maya Centre Maya Museum** (tel. 501/660-3903, julio_saqui@ hotmail.com, mayamuseum@yahoo.com, 7am-6pm daily, US$7.50 pp), opened in 2010 and providing hands-on cultural activities; learn how to make corn tortillas or process coffee beans, and take home Mayan Coffee to share with friends while you tell of your adventures abroad. It also now sells its very own Che'il Mayan Chocolate bars, made from cacao beans farmed in Stann Creek.

Accommodations

There are two guesthouses in Maya Centre, owned by different families that each offer transportation in and out of the preserve, guides, meals, and other services.

★ **Nu'uk Che'il Cottages and Hmen Herbal Center** (tel. 501/670-7043 or 501/665-1313, nuukcheil@yahoo.com, www. nuukcheilcottages.com, US$20-80) offers tranquil accommodations more removed from the highway than the village's other guesthouse. Bunks with a shared bath are US$30 per person, and private guest rooms with hot showers available are US$80, tax not included. Camping is US$10 per person, Internet access US$2.50 per hour, and bike rental US$10 per day. The place is very well kept, with beautifully planted grounds; the guesthouse has experience hosting student groups and can arrange seminars on herbal medicine, cultural performances, and the like. Proprietress Aurora Garcia

Saqui's husband, Ernesto, was director of the Cockscomb Basin Wildlife Sanctuary until 2005 and is extremely knowledgeable about the area. Her late uncle, Elijio Panti, was a famous healer; she took over his work when he died in 1996. Aurora offers Mayan spiritual blessings, prayer healings, acupuncture, and massage (each for under US$15). Aurora also has a four-acre botanical garden and medicine trail (entrance US$2.50), offers herbs for sale, and can arrange homestays in the village for US$25 per person, which includes a one-night stay with a local family, one dinner, and one breakfast.

Another decent option is right on the highway, about 100 yards north of the entrance to Cockscomb: **Tutzil Nah Cottages** (tel. 501/636-4750, www.mayacenter.com, US$25-55) is owned and operated by the Chun family (who helped Alan Rabinowitz in his original jaguar studies and appear in his book *Jaguar*). There are four screened wooden guest rooms, all with private baths, all have queen beds, fans, ample space, nice furniture, and a raised deck. There's also a family house for additional rooms. Meals (US$6-12) are available, and camping (US$6-12) is possible on the grounds or in a separate campground about 0.25 mile into the bush. Inventive trips are available as an alternative to the standard fare, including kayak floats and night hikes.

Transportation

Maya Centre is accessed by hopping off any bus passing between Dangriga and Punta Gorda. Taxis will take you from the village to the Cockscomb Basin Wildlife Sanctuary for about US$15-20 per carload.

The Placencia Peninsula

Running parallel to Belize's Southern Coast, this stretch of beach and mangroves winds 16 miles southward from the coastal wetlands and shrimp farms near the village of Riverside all the way to Placencia Village, on the tip of the peninsula. The Belize Barrier Reef, surrounded by coral and mangrove islands, lies approximately 20 miles east off the coast of Placencia. Traveling to nearby cayes and inland attractions like the Cockscomb Basin Wildlife Sanctuary, Mayan villages, and ruins of Toledo District is possible from anywhere on the peninsula, although it's farther than from Dangriga or Hopkins. The area offers the full range of accommodations—whether you prefer to mingle with backpackers in Placencia Village or rub elbows with fellow guests at any of a number of beach resorts, from midrange to luxurious, each with its own personality. This is also the site of several enormous, ambitious, and controversial development projects, more of which are springing up all over the area. A municipal pier by the marina was completed in 2013, and recently renovated with fresh paint colors and bench seating, as well as snack-selling huts.

There are three main areas on the Placencia Peninsula: Maya Beach, Seine Bight, and Placencia Village, where most of the bars, restaurants, and shops are, along with the general buzz. Maya Beach and Seine Bight share a quiet, secluded vibe, with long stretches of beach, plenty of resorts sprawled along the shore, and a few restaurants. They are a bit distant from Placencia Village, so you'll have to either bicycle, if you're up for it, during the day or catch a taxi to go back and forth, which can be costly, so plan wisely. Staying in the village means being close to all the action, nightlife, and general noise, and also being near the beach, even if it's not as fine and pretty as in the other areas.

MAYA BEACH

About halfway down the peninsula, Maya Beach is a strip of simple, small, boutique accommodations. They're quite nice, in a relaxed, isolated way, offering more value for your money than nearly anything else in the area. In addition, the beach here is more beautiful than many places in Belize, including the rest of Placencia. You just have to be content with the relative lack of services in Maya Beach, since getting to and from Placencia Village can be an expensive endeavor, even though it's only seven miles away.

For all-American fun in the tropics, try bowling at **Jaguar Lanes and Jungle Bar** (tel. 501/601-4434, jaguarlanes@yahoo.com, 4pm-10pm Mon. and Wed.-Fri., US$3 per game, shoe rental US$1.25). There are four Brunswick bowling lanes as well as a snack bar (US$1.50-5.50) serving hot dogs, onion rings, nachos, and pizza. Outside the air-conditioned alley there's cold beer and mixed drinks. The venue holds various theme parties, including a "cosmic" bowling night (bowling with disco lights), and Wednesday is popular among the local women bowlers of Placencia.

You can grab a drink at the **Maya Breeze Inn** (5 Maya Beach Way, tel. 501/666-5238, cell tel. 501/628-4215, www.mayabreezeinnbelize.com, 11am-midnight daily), a casual beachfront bar offering cocktails and local favorites. Don't forget your swimsuit, and eat before you come here.

Food

Mango's Beach Bar and Restaurant (tel. 501/523-8102 or 501/610-2494, www.mangosbelize.com, noon-9pm Wed.-Sun., US$5-10) has a Belizean-Mexican menu and a breezy view to enjoy with your beer. It's popular with the handful of locals, offering darts and occasional live bands at night.

The ★ **Maya Beach Hotel Bistro** (tel.

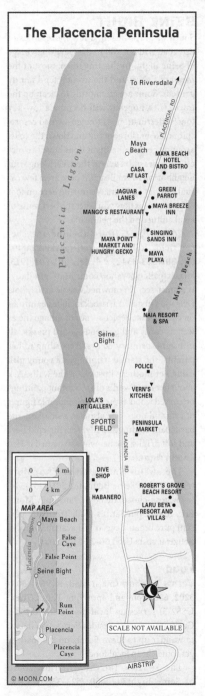

The Placencia Peninsula

To Riversdale

Placencia Lagoon

Maya Beach

MAYA BEACH HOTEL AND BISTRO

CASA AT LAST

JAGUAR LANES

GREEN PARROT

MANGO'S RESTAURANT

MAYA BREEZE INN

SINGING SANDS INN

MAYA POINT MARKET AND HUNGRY GECKO

MAYA PLAYA

Maya Beach

NAIA RESORT & SPA

Seine Bight

POLICE

VERN'S KITCHEN

LOLA'S ART GALLERY

SPORTS FIELD

PENINSULA MARKET

PLACENCIA RD

0   4 mi
0   4 km

DIVE SHOP

HABANERO

ROBERT'S GROVE BEACH RESORT

LARU BEYA RESORT AND VILLAS

MAP AREA

Placencia Lagoon

Maya Beach

False Caye

False Point

Seine Bight

Rum Point

Placencia

Placencia Caye

AIRSTRIP

SCALE NOT AVAILABLE

© MOON.COM

501/533-8040, 7am-9pm daily, US$16-28) is a breath of fresh air on the Belize culinary scene. Just reading the appetizer and meal choices will make your mouth water—few restaurants in the country have a menu this savory and creative. Australian chef John prepares dinner entrées like Sassy Shrimp Pot, Cacao Pork, and Mojo Roasted Chicken (with a jerk and honey glaze), not to mention fresh bread, an inspired bar food menu (honey-coconut ribs and roasted pumpkin-coconut green chile soup), a wine cellar, and a lovely assortment of breakfasts (US$6-11), including homemade bagels and imported lox (smoked salmon).

At the **Bonefish Grille** (at the Singing Sands Inn, tel. 501/533-3022, www.singingsands.com, 7am-9:30pm daily, US$10-23), everything is made from scratch: homemade pasta, ricotta cheese, breads, and the salad dressings, and there's no MSG. The menu features Asian and Italian cuisine, prepared with fresh ingredients. This place was Restaurant of the Year runner-up at the 2010 National Tourism Awards.

Accommodations

Maya Beach hotels are of the beach cabana variety, with a few furnished apartments, many with kitchenettes for cooking on your own. Most of these hotels also manage full houses and a few condos in the area; ask about weekly and monthly rates.

The first place you'll come to from the north is ★ **Maya Beach Hotel** (tel. 501/533-8040, www.mayabeachhotel.com, US$90-125), with five well-kept guest rooms, a few with waterfront decks, all with wireless Internet, private baths, hot showers, and a great stretch of sand—oh, and one of the best restaurants in Placencia, the Maya Beach Hotel Bistro. It has a small pool and one- and two-bedroom beach houses (US$100-180), all with fully equipped kitchens and amenities such as bicycles. A three-bedroom house (US$400), on a private beachfront parcel, has its own infinity pool.

Green Parrot Beach Houses

(Maya Beach, tel. 501/533-8188, www.greenparrot-belize.com, US$170 plus tax) has cozy thatched-roof A-frame cabanas with decks and loft bedrooms facing the ocean. Each sleeps four people and includes multiple beds, couches, a kitchen, and hammocks on the decks. There's a restaurant on-site, and continental breakfast is included. It's on a lovely, quiet stretch of beach, and use of bikes and kayaks is included.

Lovers of orchids and boutique luxury will enjoy the small but cozy **Singing Sands Inn** (tel. 501/533-3022, www.singingsands.com, US$110-275). The six thatched-roof seafront cabanas have front porches and wood floors, and the two standard guest rooms offer sea and garden views. All units have private baths, ceiling fans, and constant ocean breezes. Portable air-conditioning is available if desired. Breakfast is served in the open-air restaurant next to the pool; fresh lunches and dinners are served as well at the Bonefish Grille. Drinks and light fare can be enjoyed at Chez Albert's bar on the pier, 220 feet out into the Caribbean. Use of bikes and snorkel gear is complimentary, and golf carts, clear-bottomed kayaks, and sailboats are available for rent.

A real gem is ★ **Lost Reef Resort** (beachfront, www.lostreefresort.com, US$79-99), set far enough out of Placencia Village yet a short drive away, in Riversdale. There are four cabanas for rent, hugging a central swimming pool and a restaurant, with a cozy porch lounge and reggae music softly echoing out. This small resort has a true rootsy vibe that reminds me of the Belize I first fell in love with nine years ago, when it was still under the tourism radar. The resort offers its own snorkel tours that depart directly from their beach, onto Hideaway Caye and King Louis Caye, visible from shore. There's a monthly pig roast and music, ideally hosted on the wide beach. Cabins have air-conditioning, Wi-Fi, private bath, and include two sea kayaks and snorkeling gear—pick the one that is directly seafront for the breeze and added romance.

SEINE BIGHT

South of Maya Beach, a few more miles of dirt road will put you in the Garifuna village of Seine Bight. In this tiny town, most of the men are fishers and the women tend family gardens. Some are attempting to clean up the town, with hopes it will become a low-key tourist destination, as foreign-owned resorts sprout like mushrooms up and down the coast around them. Seine Bight does have the nicest stretches of **beach** in the area, along with neighboring Maya Beach. There are a few casual eateries and bars. Venturing here on foot or by bicycle is how you'll get the best sense of local culture on the peninsula.

Lola's Art Gallery (behind the soccer field, follow the well-marked signs, tel. 501/523-3342, cell tel. 501/601-1913, lolasartgallery@yahoo.com, 7am-7pm daily) is a must-see. A renowned Creole artist, Lola Delgado's inspired artwork includes paintings on canvas that depict scenes of village life as well as cards and gorgeous gourd masks, all in bright, primary colors. According to her parents, she started painting as a young girl, using her mother's lipstick on the walls. Ask about her latest works of art: vibrant paintings on carved wood, representing adorable figures of cats and dogs. She also has a small on-site bar (10am-midnight daily) serving cold beer and soft drinks; ask her why she named it **The Fallen Angel.**

The award-winning **Goss Chocolate** (north end of Seine Bight, tel. 501/523-3544, www.goss-chocolate.com, 9am-5pm Mon.-Fri., 10am-5pm Sat.) is made from 100 percent pure organic cacao and available only in Belize; it costs US$1.50-2.50 for a bar.

Food

Vern's Kitchen (main road, tel. 501/503-3202, 6am-2pm and 4pm-9pm Thurs.-Tues., US$2-5) serves up local dishes and often a Garifuna specialty. Besides Vern's, you'll have to wander up to Maya Beach, up the road, to get some cheap local food.

The **Seaside Restaurant** (just south of Seine Bight, tel. 501/523-3565, www.

robertsgrove.com, 7am-9pm daily, US$12-28) at Robert's Grove has an international menu: sandwiches, pizza, wings, and quesadillas for lunch; seafood appetizers and entrées, imported steaks, and à la carte options for dinner. The bar is open till midnight. **Habanero Mexican Café and Bar** (tel. 501/523-3565, noon-9pm daily, US$9-15) is an excellent lagoon-facing Mexican restaurant across the road from Robert's Grove resort.

If you need groceries, the locally owned **Publics** (Placencia-Seine Bight main road, no phone, 9am-10pm daily) has the widest selection.

Accommodations

The **Nautical Inn** (tel. 501/523-3595, www.nauticalinnbelize.com, US$135) offers various old-school but spacious beachfront accommodations surrounding a pool, and all guest rooms have air-conditioning, ceiling fans, and cable TV. Basic guest rooms have kitchenettes, and the two-bedroom suite has a full kitchen and a living room. Ask about special group rates.

One of the well-known resorts on the peninsula, **Robert's Grove Beach Resort** (just south of Seine Bight, tel. 501/523-3565, www.robertsgrove.com, from US$215) is a classic grand resort. It has various structures that are situated close together along a short stretch of decent beach, so it doesn't appear overwhelming. The various guest rooms, suites, and villas have high ceilings, king beds, and updated amenities. There are three pools, a tennis court, a spa, a gym, a trio of rooftop hot tubs, and an open-air restaurant. Robert's Grove has a dive shop on the lagoon side across the street (next to its Mexican restaurant, Habanero) and offers all kinds of underwater, offshore, and inland trips and packages, and at publication time, it was about to be run and operated by award-winning Splash Dive Center. Bikes, kayaks, and sailboats are available for your own explorations. The inn is popular with couples, families, and groups; ask about trips to the resort's private islands.

If you're going luxury, you might as well stay right next door: ★ **Laru Beya Resort and Villas** (tel. 501/523-3476, U.S. tel. 800/890-8010, www.larubeya.com, US$170-425) offers beautifully furnished beachfront accommodations and all the amenities (my favorite is the seafront balcony), with a touch of unpretentious luxury. The suites feel more like your own private condo than a resort. Penthouse suites have a ladder to a private rooftop jetted tub with a great view. It's a stone's throw from the beach, and you'll fall asleep to the sound of waves. The **Quarter Deck** restaurant and bar (7am-10pm daily) serves international cuisine and caters to destination weddings.

★ PLACENCIA VILLAGE

A fishing village since the time of the Maya and periodically flattened by hurricanes (most recently by Iris in 2001), Placencia continues rebuilding and redefining itself, in large part to accommodate the influx of foreigners. Placencia Village is still worlds away from the condo-dominated landscape of San Pedro on Ambergris Caye, and most locals claim it will never go that way, but time will tell. There are plenty of bulldozers, swaths of cut mangroves, and golf carts for rent, plus a pier and marina completed in 2013.

It's everyone's hope that despite area development, this town will remain the *tranquilo* ramshackle village it is today for years to come. Find a room, book some day tours, pencil in a massage before happy hour, and relax. Oh, yeah, and feel free to drink the tap water as you explore: Placencia's *agua* is piped in from an artesian well across the lagoon in Independence, reportedly the result of an unsuccessful attempt to drill for oil, and it's clean and pure.

Sights

There are few sights per se in this beach village. What you'll find, however, is plenty of sand, water sports, food, active bars and nightlife, and all the options you can think of to embody a fun beach vacation.

The north-south Placencia Road runs the

Placencia Village

Placencia Lagoon

AIRSTRIP

SPLASH DIVE CENTER

CHABIL MAR

TURTLE INN

PLACENCIA RD

To Independence

Mango Creek

CASA PALMA

CARIBBEAN BEACH CABANAS

ATLANTIC BANK

LYDIA'S GUESTHOUSE

MIRAMAR APARTMENTS

Caribbean Sea

CAPTAIN JAK'S

BREWED AWAKENINGS

SEA SPRAY HOTEL

THE ELLYSIAN

DE TATCH

GROCERY

SCOTIA BANK/ TOURISM OFFICE

RANGUANA LODGE

JULIA'S

POLICE

DEB AND DAVE'S LAST RESORT

BAREFOOT BEACH BAR

TIPSY TUNA

HOKEY POKEY DOCK

BACK RD

Placencia

The Sidewalk Strip

COZY CORNER

BTL

SECRET GARDEN RESTAURANT

PICKLED PARROT

MEDICAL CENTER

BELIZEAN NIRVANA

MR Q'S

WALLEN'S MARKET

OMAR'S

JOHN THE BAKERMAN

TRADEWINDS HOTEL

OMAR'S CREOLE GRUB

TUTTI FRUTTI GELATERIA

FISHERMAN'S CO-OP

THE SHAK BEACH CAFÉ

RUMFISH Y VINO

SOCCER FIELD

ATM

PLACENCIA BUS STOP

BJ'S RESTAURANT

WENDY'S

PHONE

SEA HORSE DIVE SHOP

SEA GLASS INN

Placencia Harbour

PARADISE VACATION HOTEL

YOLI'S

HARRY'S COZY CABANAS

Big Creek

SUNSET POINTE APARTMENTS

To Monkey River

0   0.25 mi
0   0.25 km

0   4 mi
0   4 km

Placencia Lagoon

Maya Beach

False Caye

False Point

Seine Bight

MAP AREA

Rum Point

Placencia

Placencia Caye

© MOON.COM

length of the peninsula, doglegs around the airstrip, continues along the lagoon, and then parallels the famous central sidewalk as it enters town. You'll see the soccer field on your right before the road curves slightly to the left, terminating at the Shell station and the main docks. If there is a "downtown" Placencia, it's probably here, in front of the gas station and dock. This is where buses come and go, taxis hang out, and most dive shops are based.

Aside from the beach, the main attraction in Placencia is the world-renowned **main-street sidewalk**, cited in the *Guinness Book of World Records* as "the world's most narrow street." It is 24 inches wide in spots and runs north-south through the sand for over a mile. Homes, hotels, Guatemalan goods shops, crafts makers, and tour guide offices line both sides. Several side paths connect it to the main road in the village. No bikes are allowed—pedestrians only.

Sports and Recreation

There's no shortage of guide services in Placencia, where most tour operators offer service to all nearby destinations: Cockscomb Basin Wildlife Sanctuary, Monkey River, snorkeling and fishing trips with lunch on a beautiful caye, the Mayan ruins of Lubaantun and Nim Li Punit, and a variety of paddling tours. For any of these trips, also refer to the dive shops and fishing guides listed in this chapter.

Many tour operators have their offices in shacks clustered in the village or by the main dock area in town, just past the gas station; most are subcontracted by the hotels that offer tours to their guests. If you're going it on your own, ask around and know that prices are often based on a minimum number of passengers, usually four. Prices vary little, but it's definitely worth comparing. Monkey River day trips, for example, range US$60-75 per person, depending on whether lunch is included and the size of the boat. Half-day snorkel trips are about US$35-75 per person, depending on group size. Most tours require

that you sign up the day before; reef tours typically leave around 9am, inland tours around 7am.

I highly recommend **Splash Dive Center** (across from Chabil Mar Resort, tel. 501/523-3080, cell tel. 501/610-0235, www.splashbelize.com) for snorkel and dive tours to the cayes—including PADI dive certification of all levels—whale shark experiences, and inland tours. The guides and drivers are professional and very friendly, their five boats well maintained, and no request is ever too much for owner Patty Ramirez, who loves to meet travelers and is absolutely top-notch—she goes above and beyond to make sure you're taken care of and happy. The good news is, they'll have a second location at Robert's Grove resort; it may be ready by the time you read this.

Locally run **Go Sea Tours** (tel. 501/523-3033, www.goseabelize.com) also offers PADI certification classes and whale shark experiences, while **Seahorse Dive Shop** (tel. 501/523-3166, www.belizescuba.com) is another reliable pick, offering local barrier reef dives as well as trips to Glover's Reef and the southern cayes. Locally owned **Ocean Motion** (sidewalk, near the pier, tel. 501/523-3363, www.oceanmotionplacencia.com) also gets great reviews and offers snorkeling and fishing tours to Ranguana and Silk Cayes (US$90 pp full day, lunch and equipment included; US$325 per boat for fishing 11-19 miles offshore). For tours of all sorts, try **Placencia Wildside Adventures** (tel. 501/672-3483, www.placenciasnorkeling.com).

For unique insight into Belizean culture, sign up for an excursion with Lyra Spang, a food anthropologist and organic farmer who owns **Taste Belize Food & Culture Tours** (tel. 501/664-8699, www.tastebelize.com, US$95-110). Options include chocolate trips to Punta Gorda, food tours to Mayan or Kriol villages, and tours of the famous Marie Sharp's Factory outside Dangriga, where the most popular hot sauce in the region is made and bottled.

BEACHES

Placencia Village offers a long uninterrupted stretch of thick golden sand, good for walks, jogs, and dips. The beach is public, so you can feel free to spread your towel anywhere, as long as it's unoccupied by a resort's lounge chairs. The water isn't perfect Caribbean turquoise-clear, but it's close. Popular stretches are just across from Tipsy Tuna, ideal for grabbing lunch, some sun, and even some beach volleyball. Another idyllic, quiet spot is the beach facing Mariposa Restaurant—grab some delicious lunch bites and dip in the pool or the ocean.

The prettiest beaches I have seen on the peninsula are in the Maya Beach area. You can pick any of the restaurants in that area—Robert's Grove, for instance—for lunch and swim off the beach for the day. A great unpretentious spot to chill for the day with a cocktail is the Maya Breeze Inn's beach bar; just bring a towel and your own snacks.

DIVING AND SNORKELING

Although the beach is usually fine for swimming and lounging, you won't see much with a mask and snorkel except sand, seagrass, a few fish, and other bathers. A short boat ride, however, will bring you to the barrier reef and the kind of underwater viewing you can write home about. Snorkel gear is available for rent (US$5 per day) everywhere, and trips to the cayes and reefs cost around US$50 per half day, depending on the distance.

The few dive shops have comparable prices, and you can either let your hotel arrange everything or do it yourself. **Splash Dive Center** (tel. 501/523-3080, cell tel. 501/610-0235, www.splashbelize.com, 2-tank dive US$120, snorkeling US$90 pp, lunch included) has two locations in Placencia: an appointment and **tour booking desk at Wendy's Creole Restaurant** and a topnotch dive center on the north end, across from Chabil Mar Resort. The dive center is

where Splash's six boats, including a 46-foot Newton, are docked, and from where trips depart. Splash has the most professional operation I've seen in Belize, from the way guides handle their gear to the attention they pay to their customers, first-timers or experienced. They take care of everything, from pickups to fittings to food. Owner Patty Ramirez—named a Sea Hero in 2012 by *Scuba Diving* magazine for her dive center's contributions to community building and marine environmental awareness—left a banking career 13 years ago to pursue her passion. Along with her partner, Ralph, they're a classic example of a passion turned into a success story. Splash is in the midst of launching a second location in Hopkins, at Jaguar Reef Lodge. They also offer inland tours across the Stann Creek, and can assist in finding suitable accommodations if needed.

Seahorse Dive Shop (near Municipal Pier, tel. 501/523-3166, www.belizescuba. com, whale shark dive US$265 pp, 2-tank local reef dive US$140 pp) is highly recommended. Its dive shop and dock were destroyed by Hurricane Earl in August 2016, but the company's back on its feet and operating from the main pier.

FISHING

Placencia has always been a fishing town for its sustenance, but with the advent of tourism, it has gained a worldwide reputation for sportfishing. Deepwater possibilities include wahoo, sailfish, marlin, kingfish, and dolphinfish; fly-fishing can hook you a grand slam—bonefish, tarpon, permit, and snook (all catch-and-release). Fortunately, serious angling means serious local guides, several of whom have been featured on ESPN and in multiple fishing magazines. Look up **Trip'N Travel Southern Guides Fly Fishing and Saltwater Adventures** (Placencia Office Supply Bldg., off Main St., tel. 501/523-3205, lgodfrey@btl.net). Most tour operators listed in this chapter offer fishing trips. Check www. placencia.com for more options.

1: Laru Beya Resort and Villas; **2:** Placencia Village beach; **3:** Splash Dive Center

KAYAKING AND PADDLEBOARDING

An unforgettable and underrated way to explore the nearshore cayes, mangroves, creeks, and rivers is by paddle. Plastic open kayaks are available to guests at most resorts, and many tour operators and dive shops have some for rent as well. Located behind the peninsula, the **Placencia Lagoon** is home to birds, saltwater crocodiles, manatees, and mangroves. While it's easily explored solo by kayak, I recommend going with a guide if you're not an experienced kayaker, in case of a surprise croc encounter. **Eric Foreman** (tel. 501/664-8121) offers guided lagoon kayak trips (half-day US$125 pp, US$160 for 2 people, includes kayaks) as well as sea kayak tours to the nearby inner-reef cayes (half-day US$225 pp, lunch not included); rentals are also available for US$40 per day.

BOATING AND SAILING

Opportunities abound for day trips, sunset cruises, snorkel voyages, and sail charters, all ideal for floating around the gorgeous Southern Cayes. A sure bet is Jeff Scott's **Daytripper Catamaran Charters** (Harbor Place North, Buba Wubba Grill dock, tel. 501/666-3117, www.daytripperbelize.com, US$75 pp with lunch). Jeff will take you on a fun, leisurely snorkel trip to the nearby cayes, under an hour away—including the Lark Range or Lighthouse Caye—where you'll spot stunning corals and marinelife. You'll likely be the only ones in the area.

Expensive, high-end **The Moorings** (tel. 501/523-3476, U.S. tel. 888/952-8420, www. moorings.com, US$500-1,700, minimum 3-day rental) has a dock for multiple catamaran adventures on its beautiful 40- to 46-foot cats, based on the lagoon side, just across from Laru Beya Resort. Bring your own crew or charter one with a crew and all the bells and whistles for a weeklong sail. Just across from town, **Placencia Yacht Club** (tel. 501/653-0569) is on Placencia Caye, featuring the Tranquilo Restaurant and Bar. The über-exclusive membership-based **Tradewinds Cruise Club** has headquarters here, in case you were wondering, at Robert's Grove Marina. Its 50-feet luxury cats will have you gawking.

MASSAGE AND BODYWORK

Sign up for a massage or other treatment at **The Secret Garden Massage and Day Spa** (behind Wallen's, tel. 501/523-3420, www. secretgardenplacencia.com), where a one-hour massage costs US$55 and a special four-hands treatment costs a bit more—there's a booking table where you can leave your name, number, and preferred appointment time. The **Turtle Inn** (1 mile north of the village, tel. 501/824-4914, U.S. tel. 866/356-5881, www. turtleinn.com) also has pampering services, as does **Siripohn's Thai Massage** (tel. 501/600-0375, www.thaimassagebelize.com, 10am-6pm Mon.-Sat., massage from US$75 per hour), right on the front street in Placencia Village, run by experienced Thais who offer seaweed treatments and papaya body polish.

If you're up for a workout, get in touch with **Evolution Beach Gym** (tel. 501-608-1643, rusterman.40@hotmail.com, 7am-7pm Mon.-Sat.) offering outdoor beach workout sessions, mornings and evenings at sunset.

Entertainment and Events
NIGHTLIFE

Placencia's bars, restaurants, and resorts do a decent job of coordination, so special events like beach barbecues, horseshoe tournaments, karaoke, and live music are offered through the entire week—especially during the high season. Your best bet is to check the *Placencia Breeze* (www.placenciabreeze.com) newspaper and look for current schedules, because bars, clubs, and parties come and go with the wind.

The **Barefoot Beach Bar** (Main Rd., tel. 501/523-3515, 11am-midnight daily) is the only constantly wildly popular venue in the high season. Flip-flop-clad revelers choose from hundreds of froufrou cocktails and bar food; there's live music (Fri.-Sun.) and happy hour (5pm-6pm daily) as well as never-ending theme parties. Another party constant is the beachfront **Tipsy Tuna** (now directly next door to Barefoot Beach Bar, tel. 501/523-3089, tipsytuna@hotmail.com, 11:30am-midnight daily), with Garifuna drumming on Wednesday nights and a general all-day-long party vibe. The happy hour (5pm-7pm daily) is excellent too, with US$0.50 wings and US$1.50 local rum drinks.

Another happening and locally popular bar and restaurant a bit farther down the harbor is **Yoli's,** with barbecue and ring toss starting at 3pm Sunday. Stop by the **Pickled Parrot** (between the sidewalk and the main road, just off the soccer field, tel. 501/636-7068, 11:30am-9:30pm daily), where you can have a Belizean "panty-ripper" via Jell-O shot or a three-rum Parrot Piss cocktail; maybe you'll have enough of those to graduate to its so-called secret VIP section.

The Street Feet Lounge & Night Club (Main St., tel. 501/523-3515, 10pm-2am daily), owned by the Barefoot Beach Bar crew, is the only indoor nightclub in Placencia as of publication time and conveniently located right in the village. The club hosts live DJs from around Belize, playing your favorite top dance and reggae tunes.

FESTIVALS AND EVENTS

The biggest party of the year happens the third week of June, during **Lobsterfest.** The whole south end of town closes down for lobster-catching tournaments, costumes, and dances, and there are food booths everywhere. **Easter weekend** is popular, as Placencia is a destination for many Belizeans as well as foreign visitors; rooms are typically booked months in advance, so be prepared for the crowds. Look for a Halloween celebration, complete with a parade and trick-or-treating for kids and adults alike.

Another annual gig, the **Mistletoe Ball,** wanders to a different hotel before Christmas every year and doubles as a fundraiser for the local Belize Tourism Industry Association chapter. **New Year's Eve** sometimes consists of one big outdoor party out on the soccer field, with all-inclusive drinks, hats, and more for just US$2.50 per person, or a no-cover beach party at **Barefoot Beach Bar** and **Tipsy Tuna.** The local humane society organizes various fundraising events as well; keep an eye out.

Shopping

Despite plenty of gift stores featuring Guatemalan crafts and clothes, there are a couple of talented Belizean artists and wood-carvers worth checking out and supporting. Stop by the father-and-son-operated shop **A Piece of Belize Wood Carvings** (sidewalk shortcut across from Omar's, tel. 501/621-1595 or 501/628-1279, apieceofbelize01@yahoo.com, 9am-6pm daily, US$15-50). Bob and Tyrone Lockwood make beautiful pieces using rosewood and ziricote wood, found only in Belize, including bowls, bracelets, and home decor pieces, even customized carved doors. Feel free to bargain with them. Just steps away, still on the sidewalk, is **Made in Belize** (tel. 501/205-5511, cell tel. 501/627-5125, 9am-5pm daily), where Leo has a shack filled with all sorts of creative carvings, including pieces made out of driftwood, mahogany, and ziricote.

Strike A Pose (main road, Placencia Village, 9am-7pm Tues.-Fri., 10am-6pm Sat., strikeapose.placencia@gmail.com) has a random selection of trendy clothes imported from Los Angeles, including plus-size options and evening dresses, in case you need a new outfit for a hot date.

Food

Placencia has a small number of restaurants, but there's enough variety to keep you stuffed during your visit: seafood cooked in coconut milk and local herbs, Creole stews and fry chicken, sandwiches, burritos, burgers, French, Italian, and adequate vegetarian options nearly everywhere you go.

BELIZEAN AND INTERNATIONAL
Omar's Creole Grub (Main Rd., tel. 501/523-4094, 7am-2:30pm and 6pm-9pm Sun.-Thurs., 6pm-9pm Sat.) will take care of you all day, with a lobster omelet, handmade

tortillas, and guava jelly (US$9) to start the morning off, then a burrito for lunch (US$4), and Creole-style barracuda steak (from US$7), pork chops, conch steak, or lobster for dinner. Chef Omar Jr. won the 2009 Lobsterfest Cook-Off with his stuffed lobster. Come for the seafood and stay for the conversation with the vivacious Omar and family, whose children all work at the restaurant. No alcohol is served.

Dawn's Grill n'Go (tel. 501/523-4079, grillngo@yahoo.com, 7am-3pm and 5:30pm-9pm Mon.-Sat., US$10-15) has finger-lickin'-good fried chicken—served on Friday—and a cozy spot on the main road where Miss Dawn loves to serve up her creative specials, whether local favorites or international dishes, including pastas, seafood, fajitas, and lobster burgers. There's nothing "fast" tasting about the food here. Be sure to sample her decadent banana bread pudding with One Barrel rum sauce—a bit pricey at US$3.50 for a small slice, but yum!

For grab and go, head to **Mr. Q** (Main Rd., across from Wallen's hardware, tel. 501/653-3568, US$5) for tasty barbecue meats and rotisserie chicken, with rice or beans, fries, as sides, at a great price.

★ **Wendy's Creole Restaurant and Bar** (Main Rd., tel. 501/523-3335, www.wendyscuisine.com, 7am-9:30pm daily, US$3-23) offers varied, consistently tasty Creole and international dishes at reasonable prices, the best outdoor people-watching veranda in the village, plus a glassed-in, air-conditioned seating area and a full bar. This is a great place to come to for Creole and Mexican cooking (it has the best stuffed fry jacks for breakfast, by the way), burgers (US$3-7.50), burritos (US$4.50-8), and fancier steaks and seafood items like Creole fish and curry lobster (US$13-23). There's no hit-or-miss at Wendy's no matter what you order—no wonder it won a tourism award in 2016.

If you're looking for a lunch spot where you can also dip in a swimming pool or beachcomb to your heart's content, then get a ride over to **Mariposa Restaurant** (Main St., tel. 501/523-4474, www.mariposabelizebeach.

com, 8am-9pm daily, call for free pickup, US$5-18), just on the way out of the village, where lunch offerings include meatball subs on baguettes and dinners means steak, pasta, and seafood options. Ask about the daily lunch special for good deals. The view from the top-floor dining terrace makes it worth a stop for a relaxing day away from everything.

BAKERIES AND CAFÉS

John the Bakerman (no phone, 7am-close daily) makes great breads, cinnamon buns, and coffee bread, available all day; he also sells his brother's meat pies. Look for his sign on the sidewalk and get it fresh out of the oven around 5pm.

You can get your latte or cappuccino fix at **Brewed Awakenings** (main road, Placencia Village, tel. 501/523-3312, 6:30am-5pm Mon.-Sat.), serving up Belizean coffee freshly roasted daily from a spacious outdoor shack with enough wooden picnic tables and benches, facing the street action. Flavor options to blend in your coffee range from Kahlúa to Nutty Irishman, and choices include iced cappuccino and other fancy coffee concoctions, as well as baked treats and fresh fruit smoothies.

In Placencia Village Square, ★ **Tutti Frutti Gelatería** (tel. 501/620-9916, tizi.lory@virgilio.it, 9am-9pm Thurs.-Tues.) serves up some of the best homemade gelato you'll have outside of Italy; it's made fresh daily with local fruits and traditional flavors. The fruit sorbets are dairy-free, and espresso drinks and iced coffees are served.

Up the road, just across from the town dock, look for **The Shak Beach Café** (tel. 501/523-3252, 7:30am-6pm Wed.-Mon.), which has 21 smoothie flavors, all made with fresh fruit, along with a healthy vegetarian menu, a view of the water from the dockside tables, and good breakfasts of banana pancakes or omelets with coffee or tea (US$5-6).

FINE DINING

The revamped ★ **Secret Garden Restaurant** (main road, Placencia Village, tel. 501/523-3617, www.secretgardenplacencia.com, 5pm-9pm Mon.-Wed. and Fri.-Sat., US$14-17) is a breath of fresh air, offering up tasty Caribbean, Latin, and Asian-fusion dishes, including delicious pasta, seafood gumbo, chicken Maya, and Argentinian steak, among others. There's a full bar and a wonderful ambience, with a garden patio or indoor seating. Don't miss the signature stacked ceviche or the Belizean lime tart, when available. The place fills up quickly, so be sure to make reservations.

Rumfish y Vino Wine and Gastro Bar (main road, Placencia Village, tel. 501/523-3293, www.rumfishyvino.com, 2pm-midnight daily, US$7-15) opened in 2008; the Solomons bought the place while honeymooning. The menu features a mix of international comfort food, from fish-and-chips to pastas and short ribs, as well as imported Italian and Californian wine.

Most of the resorts north of town have fine restaurants to brag about. Grab a fistful of dollars and a taxi and bon appétit. At the Turtle Inn's **Mare Restaurant** (main road, 1 mile north of the village, tel. 501/523-3244 or 501/523-3150, www.turtleinn.com, 9am-10pm daily, US$15-35), the chef prepares meals with greens from his own on-site organic herb garden, as well as those cultivated in its upland sister resort's extensive organic vegetable garden. In fact, this is the best place to come for a fresh green salad in Placencia—as well as seafood, pasta, and oven-baked gourmet pizza.

GROCERIES
Wallen's Market (8:30am-noon and 1:30pm-5:30pm Mon.-Sat.) is on the main road, close to the soccer field, and sells groceries, dry goods, and sundries. **Everyday Supermarket** (7am-9pm daily) is in the center of town.

Accommodations
All of Placencia's budget lodgings are found on or within shouting distance of the sidewalk, and most of the high-end resorts are strung along the beach north of town.

Remember, these are high-season double occupancy prices; expect significant discounts and negotiable rates May-November.

UNDER US$25
Right on the sidewalk, **Omar's** (tel. 501/634-4350, US$13 shared bath, US$22.50 private bath) is a wooden flophouse. If the office is closed, head to Omar's Creole Grub to inquire. Near the Anglican school, **Eloise Travel Lodge** (tel. 501/523-3299, US$20-25) has four guest rooms with private or shared baths and a communal kitchen. There is no reception office; ask for Miss Sonia Leslie.

If you're out of options, stop by **BJ's Restaurant** (the building on the corner of the soccer field, up the stairs, US$20-30) and ask Miss Betty about her two budget guest rooms—they're basic and nothing more than a place to crash but cheap. One has a double bed, fans, and a shared bath; the second has three single beds and a private bath, ideal for backpacking friends.

US$25-50
A good budget bet is ★ **Lydia's Guesthouse** (tel. 501/523-3117, lydias@btl.net, US$25), toward the north end of the sidewalk. Lydia's is a longtime favorite among backpackers. The eight clean, private guest rooms with a shared tile-floor bath also share a sociable two-story porch, a communal kitchen, fans, hammocks, and a 30-second walk to the beach. Miss Lydia will make you breakfast if you make arrangements the day before; she also makes fresh Creole bread and guava jam. **Harry's Cozy Cabanas** (Placencia sidewalk, tel. 501/523-3234, www.cozycabanas.com, US$30) has three simple cabanas with screened porches, which are another favorite budget pick.

As you enter Placencia, there is a gate by the Placencia Bazaar gift shop; **Deb & Dave's Last Resort** (tel. 501/523-3207, debanddave@btl.net, US$25) consists of four small, clean guest rooms surrounding a tidy sand courtyard and tropical garden favored by hummingbirds. The common screened-in porch space is excellent for meeting your neighbors and telling war stories from the day's paddling and snorkeling trips; there are clean shared baths for all, free Wi-Fi, and a coffeemaker.

Claiming to be the "first established hotel on the Placencia Peninsula" (since 1964), the **Sea Spray Hotel** (Placencia sidewalk, tel. 501/523-3148, www.seasprayhotel.com, US$33-85) is a decent choice, although staff friendliness can be hit-or-miss. It's 30 feet from the ocean and has 20 guest rooms with private baths, fridges, hot and cold water, and coffeepots. There are economy guest rooms and nicer units closer to the water, where guests can relax in hammocks and chairs under palm trees. **De Tatch** seafood restaurant, on the premises, is popular for breakfast and serves up lunch and dinner.

US$50-100

A good deal right on the beach is **Julia's** (tel. 501/503-3478, www.juliascabanas.com, US$69-109), with simple stand-alone cabanas complete with double beds, minifridges, wireless Internet, porches, and hammocks. The decor is a bit of a hodgepodge, but the price is right.

Well located within the village, right off the sidewalk, is **Sea View Suites Hotel** (tel. 501/523-3777, www.seaviewplacencia.com, US$85), which gets rave reviews and has nine immaculately clean tile-floor guest rooms with a beach ambience, double or king beds, coffeemakers, microwaves, beach towels, and cable TV.

At the extreme southern end of Placencia Village, look for the brightly painted **Tradewinds Hotel** (tel. 501/523-3122, trdewndpla@btl.net, US$85-95) on five acres near the sea, offering nine basic cabanas with spacious guest rooms, fans, refrigerators, coffeepots, and private yards just feet from the ocean. It's a bit dated but the interior is clean.

★ **Sea Glass Inn** (tel. 501/523-3098, US$79) is a lovely addition to the village, with six immaculate guest rooms with twin or double beds, air-conditioning, coffeemakers, fridges, ceiling fans, and verandas looking onto a nice quiet stretch of sand with a dock,

even if it's not quite a typical beach. Walk-ins are welcome, and the inn is well located, just a few steps from the sidewalk strip and the action in the village.

Paradise Vacation Hotel (tel. 501/523-3179, U.S. tel. 904/564-9400, www.belize123.com, US$89-159) has 12 air-conditioned guest rooms, each beautifully appointed, and an on-site seaside restaurant and bar, a spa, and a gift shop. Ask about room 12 if you want to live it up a little. There is complimentary use of bikes and kayaks as well as a rooftop hot tub with views of the Maya Mountains.

On the Placencia Village beachfront, the **Ranguana Lodge** (tel. 501/523-3112, www.ranguanabelize.com, US$89-94) has five private cabanas: three air-conditioned beach cabins and two cabins set back with garden views. All are spacious and have nice wood floors, walls, and ceilings. Be aware that you're close to the loud music at Barefoot Beach Bar, running late into the night.

US$100-150

★ **Miramar Apartments** (toward the north end of the sidewalk, tel. 501/523-3658, www.miramarbelize.com, US$110-200) is a favorite of mine and has now expanded into two buildings. The hot pink buildings, steps from De Tatch, boast beachfront studios, one-bedroom, and three-bedroom units. Each has a king bed, a full kitchen, air-conditioning, and cable TV. The new three-story building is even closer to the beach, offering one-bedroom studios equipped with full kitchens, a rooftop with panoramic views over Placencia Beach ideal for watching the sunrise, and a stunning swimming pool with a cascading fountain connecting both buildings. The location is great for a family getaway or solo traveler, and it still feels like a small, cozy boutique guesthouse run by the same wonderful manager and active community member, Ilsa Villanueva.

On the main strip and off the sidewalk, newcomer **Brisas del Oceano** (tel. 501/523-3259, www.brisaoceano.com, US$125-320) has 10 luxurious condos that are fully furnished, including a kitchen, and split into 24 individual rooms with private balconies. The colorful room decor is bright and beachy, from reds and blues to yellows and local woods. Kayaks and fishing and snorkeling gear are included. The location is just a skip from many of the village's restaurants and bars.

US$150-200

Featured on HGTV's *Beachfront Bargain Hunt,* the adults-only **Caribbean Beach Cabanas** (tel. 501/622-4142, www. carribbeanbeachcabanas.com, US$159-199) screams of beach escape with its cozy, tastefully decorated bamboo-and-wood seafront studio cabanas and thatched-roof one- and two- bedroom villas with private rooftops, facing a quiet stretch of Placencia Village's beach right off the sidewalk. Amenities include air-conditioning, Wi-Fi, and kitchenettes. There's a small pool on-site and beach toys for your use. A cozy two-bedroom and two-bath hacienda home is available as well, with full kitchen and private deck overlooking the pool, ideal for a group of friends.

US$200-300

★ **Belizean Nirvana** (tel. 501/523-3331, www.belizeannirvana.com, US$220-325) introduced boutique hotels to the village. Owned by a Belizean couple who returned from a life overseas, it's right in the heart of the action, with five one- and two-bedroom suites adorned with Belizean artwork, full kitchenettes, bathrobes, balconies with direct views of the beach, air-conditioning, and continental breakfasts delivered to your suite at your chosen hour of the morning. Amenities are plentiful, including use of bicycles, wireless Internet, a rooftop grill (don't miss the incredible view from up there), hammocks, a kitchen area, local cell phones you can buy minutes for during your stay, and a magicJack for calls overseas. The hotel can also book Tropic Air flights for you or pick you up from Belize City at additional cost.

Sunset Pointe Apartments (Placencia Lagoon, tel. 501/664-4740, U.S. tel. 904/471-3599, www.sunsetpointebelize.com, US$250-275) offers luxury two-bedroom condos for short- or long-term rental, often advertised online. They're back on the lagoon side, but they all have raised roof decks with a breeze. It's only a 10-minute walk to the beach from here, and there are many accessible restaurants and shops.

At the tip end of Maya Beach, **Belize Ocean Club** (tel. 501/671-4500, U.S. tel. 800/882-9282, www.belizeoceanclub.com, US$240-260) is a popular pick for families or groups seeking a medium-size beachfront resort escape with amenities in one place like a big pool with swim-up bar, on-site restaurant, dive shop, over-the-water spa, and water toys. There are 30 two-bedroom suites on the beach side and 30 across the road on the lagoon side, which is equally beautiful and more tranquil. Amenities include full kitchens, phones, flat-screen TVs, Wi-Fi, and bicycles. The resort also runs an island day trip to Ranguana Caye.

OVER US$300

★ **The Ellysian** (Placencia Sidewalk, tel. 501/523-4898 or 501/232-0018, www. theellysian.com, US$300-400) is the dream-come-true of Belize's first lady: turning her beachfront vacation home into a luxurious yet relaxed local oasis in the heart of the village. Ideally next to De Tatch, the popular breakfast spot, this luxury boutique hotel boasts 13 beachfront suites, with six overlooking the sea and infinity pool below from furnished private balconies, and six facing the Placencia Sidewalk. Beige and wood colors greet you at the entrance and continue on to immaculate, sophisticated rooms with king beds, curated art pieces, stocked minibar, and spacious bathrooms with a glass window wall for views into the room and the sea ahead when you want it. The standouts at The Ellysian are the personal touches like the welcome drink delivered to your suite by the bartender, and the turndown service with a surprise-handwritten note, a treat, and a candle. It's a hit with couples, and could easily be as perfect for discerning solo travelers who want to be close to the local action, but also enjoy a chic ambience back at their hotel.

Naïa Resort & Spa (Seine Bight, tel. 501/523-4600, U.S. tel. 888-439-5866, www.naiaresortandspa.com, US$375-425) is a destination spa resort, tucked down a leafy, winding stone driveway within the Cocoplum Community. The resort offers 35 beach houses—a variety of aqua and white studios and one-bedrooms, 10 with private plunge pool—that line a rustic beachfront dotted with trees and stretching across 19 acres. The units keep a simple beach feel: outdoor showers, sliding glass doors, wet bars, private verandas are among the amenities. The lobby welcomes with a view of the swimming pool and sea ahead, and three restaurants cater to guests—beachside, as well as finer dining at **1981.** A water sports shack has all the beach toys and activities. The highlight is undoubtedly the spa facility, reached across the resort on the lagoon side via a winding path through a verdant forest and across wooden footbridges. Named after a water nymph, Naïa's five individual and one couple spa treatment suites are cabanas perched over the lagoon (not for swimming), surrounded with nature and birds. There's a resting area outdoors, with a saltwater pool facing the lagoon. Within the spa compound you'll find a skin care and manicure-pedicure area, locker rooms, a state-of-the-art fitness center, a café, and the first aerial yoga studio in Belize, with an open view of the water. A shuttle takes guests to the village three times a day.

At **Chabil Mar** (tel. 501/523-3606, www.chabilmarvillas.com, from US$385), the privately owned luxury villas have richly decorated interiors and are furnished with all the modern conveniences one could ask for. On the beach less than a mile north of Placencia Village, the exclusive Café Mar provides butler service so you can dine where you please: poolside (there are two), on the pier or a private veranda, or in the comfort of your villa. It's a popular spot for small weddings.

Turtle Inn (U.S. tel. 866-356-5881, www.turtleinn.com) is one of the nation's premier luxe destinations, one of U.S. film producer Francis Ford Coppola's two Belizean properties. It is about one mile north of Placencia Village. Prices start at US$375 per night for the garden-view cottages and go up to US$1,850 per night for the master two-bedroom pavilion house with a private entrance, a pool, and a dining pavilion. Even if you're not staying here, swing by to treat yourself to a fine meal with beautifully framed views of the ocean. Turtle Inn has seven luxury villas and 18 cottages on offer. The guest rooms are designed along Indonesian and Belizean lines, with lots of natural materials and airy space. The high thatched ceilings absorb the heat, so there are fans only, no air-conditioning, but there are music players for your iPod as well as fancy shell phones. Amenities include two swimming pools, the über-mellow Laughing Fish Bar on the beach, and one of the peninsula's premier restaurants, the Mare Restaurant—now with an adjacent glass-encased wall-to-wall wine cellar holding over 1,200 bottles. There's also an on-site spa, dive shop, and more dining options; Auntie Luba's Belizean eatery and the Gauguin Grill are open for dinner 6pm-9pm daily.

Information and Services
VISITOR INFORMATION
The **Placencia Tourism Office** (back of the Scotiabank Bldg., 2nd fl., tel. 501/523-4045, www.placencia.com, 9am-5pm Mon.-Fri.) is in Placencia Village. After reading the various postings on the wall, pick up a copy of the latest *Placencia Breeze* (www.placenciabreeze.com), a monthly rag with many helpful schedules and listings, including happy hours and house rentals. The tourism office also sells books, maps, music CDs, and postcards, and it has a mail drop; the office will not recommend one business over another. Another solid bet to plan your stay or arrange any sort of transfer, tour, or accommodations is to contact award-winning **Splash Destination Management Company** (tel. 501/523-3080), which knows the area inside out and has contacts across the country.

BANKS

Belize Bank (8am-3pm Mon.-Thurs., 8am-4:30pm Fri.) is by the marina and has a 24-hour ATM. **Atlantic Bank** (8am-3pm Mon.-Thurs., 8am-4:30pm Fri.) has an ATM in town, across the road from Wendy's Creole Restaurant. **Scotiabank** (8am-2:30pm Mon.-Thurs., 8am-3:30pm Fri., 9am-11:30am Sat.) has an ATM just north of the BTL office.

HEALTH AND EMERGENCIES

The **Placencia Medical Center** (tel. 501/503-3326, 8:30am-4:30pm Mon.-Fri., or Dr. Kevin Guerra tel. 501/615-1571) is behind the school. For after-hour emergencies, **Dr. Alexis Caballero** (tel. 501/622-7648) makes house calls, should you have a severe shellfish reaction. The village of Independence, a short boat ride away, has the nearest 24-hour clinic to Placencia. If a medevac to Belize City is not possible, this is where a patient will be taken in an emergency. There is a **private clinic** (tel. 501/601-2769) on Water Side Street, a public hospital providing health care to the poor, and a **pharmacy** (above Wallen's Market, on the main road, close to the soccer field, tel. 501/523-3346).

For **police,** contact the Placencia police station (tel. 501/503-3142), the Seine Bight station (tel. 501/503-3148), or the **Tourism Police** (tel. 501/503-3181).

MEDIA AND COMMUNICATIONS

Placencia Office Supply (tel. 501/523-3205, U.S. fax 888/329-6302, plaofficesupply@gmail.com, 8am-5pm Mon.-Sat., closes at lunchtime), tucked off the main road in the town center, has a copy machine and Internet access and can send faxes; it will let you plug into its Ethernet or use the wireless Internet (US$4 per hour).

Transportation
GETTING THERE

There are a number of ways to travel the 100-plus miles between Placencia Village and Belize City. The tip of the long peninsula is not as isolated as it used to be, and various options

exist for continuing on to points south and west, including Guatemala and Honduras.

At last check, there were more than 20 **daily flights** in and out of Placencia's precarious little airstrip, to and from various destinations throughout Belize. Planes generally hop from either of Belize City's two airports to Dangriga, Placencia, and Punta Gorda (in that order, usually landing at all three), then turn around for the reverse trip north. For current schedules and fares, check directly with the two airlines: **Maya Island Air** (tel. 501/223-1403, www.mayaislandair.com) or **Tropic Air** (tel. 501/226-2626, U.S. tel. 800/422-3435, www.tropicair.com). There is sometimes air service between nearby Savannah Airport (near Independence Village) and San Pedro Sula in Honduras; there are three flights a week, and the cost runs about US$160.

The 21-mile road from Placencia Village to where the peninsula hits the mainland was a rutted, dusty nightmare for decades. Then, in July 2008, the highest officials in the land gathered at Robert's Grove Beach Resort and signed the papers to begin the paving project that was completed in 2010. And the people rejoiced. It's now about a three- or four-hour drive from Belize City. From Belize City, most people drive via the **Hummingbird** and **Southern Highways.** About half an hour after turning south before Dangriga, look for a left turn to Riverside, where you'll begin the peninsula road. The **gas station** (6am-7pm daily) is by M&M Hardware in the center of the village.

Placencia Village is served by three **daily bus departures and arrivals** (in high season, anyway; service is spotty the rest of the year). Buses come and go from the center of the village, right next to M&M Hardware, and current schedules are available at the Placencia Tourism Office and also published in the *Placencia Breeze*. Buses to Dangriga (Ritchie's Bus Service, tel. 501/523-3806) depart at 6:15am, 12:45pm, and 2:30pm Monday-Saturday, and 7am, 12:45pm, and 2:30pm Sunday. There's also a 6:15am express bus to Belize City (air-conditioned, US$13 pp).

Cruise Ship Tourism in Placencia

In 2013 the government of Belize signed a US$50 million contract with Norwegian Cruise Lines (NCL), authorizing NCL to develop Harvest Caye—a 75-acre untouched island of mangroves and beach, just under three miles off the coast of Placencia Village—into an "ecofriendly" cruise destination. This planned development has brought thousands of cruise ship passengers to the south, a once uncrowded, pristine part of Belize.

The project met fierce resistance from the start from Belize's top conservationists, local businesses, and industry stakeholders, who are against mass tourism and are striving to protect the Southern Coast, as well as the country's reputation as a leading ecofriendly destination in the region. But NCL has long arrived and the magnitude of the project leaves much to be desired: an island pier, a marina, a hub for mainland tours, a lagoon for water sports, and planned cultural entertainment using the various cultures of Belize. There's little doubt that dredging and development on this scale has harmed the surrounding coral habitat, mangroves, and the Placencia Lagoon—one of three main habitats for the endangered West Indian manatee.

The Belize Tourism Industry Association led a lawsuit against NCL to block the development, and while the Belize Supreme Court ruled in a significant decision that the environmental consultation process was short-circuited and must never happen in the future, the project went ahead. The 75-acre, resort-style cruise port was built, and the first cruise ship docked on November 17, 2016.

Otherwise, you'll need to change in Dangriga to reach Belize City. The fare is about US$5 or less for each leg of the journey. The more common—and quickest—bus route is via the boat to Mango Creek and Independence Village.

For those traveling to points south, like Punta Gorda or Guatemala, or for those who want to avoid the Placencia Road, a **boat-and-bus combo** will get you back to the mainland and on your way. **Hokey Pokey Water Taxi** (tel. 501/622-3213, 501/523-2776) provides regular service between the gas station dock behind M&M Hardware in the center of the village and the dilapidated landing at Mango Creek, charging US$5 one-way for the 15-minute trip through bird-filled mangrove lagoons. Boats leave Placencia at 6:45am, 7:45am, 10am, 12:30pm, 2:30pm, 4pm, and 5pm daily, and 6pm Monday-Saturday; the same boat turns around for the reverse trip: 6:30am, 7:30am, 8am, 10am, 11am, noon, 2:30pm, and 4:30pm. Hokey Pokey is a reliable family-run operation. Bus connections to all points are coordinated with the 10am and 4pm boats from Placencia, so the traveler need only worry about stepping onto the correct bus when the boat

lands in Independence after the quick taxi shuttle (US$0.50) to the bus depot by Rosa's Restaurant (5:30am-3pm daily). The last bus to Punta Gorda leaves at 8pm, sometimes later, and the last ride to Dangriga and Belize City is at 5:30pm daily. The earliest northbound bus from Punta Gorda arrives around 7am daily, and the James Bus express arrives at 9am daily.

TO HONDURAS AND GUATEMALA

The ship to **Puerto Cortés** (tel. 501/202-4506 or 501/603-7787, Honduras tel. 504/665-1200) leaves at 9am every Friday, returning at 2pm Monday afternoon. The trip costs US$60 and takes roughly four hours, stopping in Big Creek, Belize, for immigration purposes and carrying a maximum of 50 passengers. Buy tickets at the Placencia Tourism Office. Every now and then (sometimes as often as a couple of times a week), a boatload of passengers arrives in Placencia from Livingston, Guatemala, and seeks passengers to take with them back to Livingston (with an immigration stop in Punta Gorda). Inquire at **Caribbean Tours and Travels** (main road, tel. 501/523-3481, infor@ctbelize.com).

GETTING AROUND

Placencia Village itself is small enough to walk, and if you're commuting on the sidewalk, walking is your only option (riding a bike on the sidewalk can earn you a US$50 fine). Speaking of two-wheeled options, there are plenty of bicycle rentals in town. If you're bicycling north on the road, know that Seine Bight is 5 miles from Placencia and Maya Beach another 2.5 miles. The cheapest way (besides walking) to get up and down the peninsula is to hop on a bus as it travels to or from Dangriga.

There used to be a free shuttle service up and down the peninsula, but no longer. In the meantime, there are at least a dozen green-plated taxis hanging around the gas stations and the airstrip. Rides from town to the airstrip cost US$6 for one or two people, to the Seine Bight area one-way US$10, to Maya Beach US$20. Ask around the gas station and tourist office, and look for posted rate lists to know what you should be paying. The more trusted and long-standing taxi services include **Radiance Ritchie** (tel. 501/523-3321) and **Traveling Gecko** (tel. 501/523-4078). My own preferred driver is Noel of **Noel Taxi Service** (tel. 501/600-6047); he works late into the night, ideal for solo female travelers.

Rent a car for do-it-yourself land tours to the Cockscomb Basin Wildlife Sanctuary or Mayflower Bocawina National Park, or for trips to the ruins near Punta Gorda. Otherwise you'll pay US$50-100 per person to join a tour group. **Barefoot Rentals** (tel. 501/523-3066, cell tel. 501/629-9602, www. barefootservicesbelize.com) has a selection of cars (US$65-85 per day), golf carts (US$32-49 per day), and scooters (US$9 per hour). **Captain Jak's** (tel. 501/628-6447, www. captainjaks.com), right in the center of the village, rents golf carts.

MONKEY RIVER

An easy 35-minute boat ride from Placencia brings you to the mouth of the Monkey River and the village of the same name. Founded in 1891, Monkey River village was once a thriving town of several thousand loggers, *chicleros,* banana farmers, and anglers; that was then. Now, the very sleepy Kriol village of 30 families (about 150 people) makes its way with fishing and, you guessed it, tourism, though the latter has been slow of late as the village suffers from severe erosion and rising waters. Many villagers are trained and licensed tour guides who work with hotels in Placencia to provide unique wildlife-viewing experiences.

Ninety percent of the structures you see have been rebuilt since Hurricane Iris destroyed the town in 2001. The village is accessible by boat—most often through the mangroves from Placencia—but there is also an 11-mile road from the Southern Highway that ends across the river from the village.

If you're on a tour from Placencia, after negotiating the mangrove maze, your guide will take you into the river's mouth and dock up in town for a restroom break and a chance to place your lunch order for later in the day. Then you'll be off upstream, all eyes peeled for animals, from turtles to birds, crocodiles, and howler monkeys. You'll beach up at the trailhead to explore a piece of **Payne's Creek National Park,** a 31,000-acre reserve that is surrounded by even more protected area. You'll hike through the dense brush, now a regenerating broadleaf forest that will take decades to reach its pre-Iris glory. Then it's back down the river for lunch and a stroll through the village. Most head back to their guest rooms in Placencia, but you may wish to consider staying a night or two, either to experience village life or to get some serious fishing time in. Bring repellent.

Food and Accommodations

The formal guesthouse options in Monkey River have dwindled severely over the last couple of years; ask around for private room rentals and cabanas. Most on the Placencia Peninsula come out to explore on a day trip. You can also ask around for a place to eat. Most offer a set menu with a different entrée served each day. Reservations are required for meals, most of which offer rice and beans plates, and beers or juice.

Near the breezy part of the village by the mini-basketball court, **Alice's Restaurant** (tel. 501/543-3079, noon-3pm daily, US$7.50) offers meals served in a large dining room with a view of the sea; renting one of her airy wood guest rooms in a neighboring building costs US$23, with a fan and a shared bath with hot and cold water. There's a riverfront gift shop at the entrance of the village selling local arts and crafts.

Islands Near Placencia

From inner-reef cayes—a stone's throw from Placencia's coast—to larger, protected plots and World Heritage Sites such as Laughing Bird Caye or Silk Cayes, there's plenty to keep even the most avid island-hopper or diver busy in these parts. If anything, you'll want to have a separate budget just for these cayes while staying in Placencia. They're worth every penny and offer gorgeous marine and coral encounters, in addition to some of the most beautiful beaches in the country. While some islands are home to romantic resorts, others are ideal for day trips and marine exploration above and under water.

GLADDEN SPIT AND SILK CAYES MARINE RESERVE

Belize's famous seasonal whale shark site is the protected **Gladden Spit and Silk Cayes Marine Reserve** (tel. 501/523-3377, www.seabelize.org), 26 miles from the coast of Placencia. Gladden Spit, known as "the elbow" of the Silk Cayes Marine Reserve, is where whale sharks congregate once a month March-June to feed on spawning fish. Divers have the unique opportunity to swim alongside these giant creatures. For such a memorable experience, contact **Splash Dive Center** (tel. 501/523-3080, cell tel. 501/610-0235, www.splashbelize.com).

TOP EXPERIENCE

SILK CAYES

The **Silk Cayes,** also known as the **Queen Cayes,** are part of the Silk Cayes Marine Reserve: three tiny plots of land ranging from 0.5-4 acres one mile inside the barrier reef—and they seem to get tinier every year due to hurricanes and erosion. One plot is a protected birding area. They are easily the most photogenic islands of Belize, and what the Silk Cayes lack in size they make up for in diving bliss, with rich marinelife that includes stingrays, giant barracuda, and lobsters. Snorkeling is decent as well, with coral and reef fish to explore just steps off the islands' white-sand beaches.

Most dive shops offer full-day trips to the Silk Cayes, just under an hour away from Placencia, approximately 22 miles offshore. The main island, with restroom facilities and wooden picnic tables, is straight out of paradise, with frigates soaring above shallow turquoise and jade waters replete with coral. Across from this main island, you'll spot the second Silk Caye, this one a mere plot of sand and resident pelicans. Several tour company boats anchor here in high season—my advice is to come very early if you want some solo time before the crowds arrive or pick a weekday for your trip.

Snorkeling around these islands consists of colorful coral and small reef fish like sergeant majors and angelfish. The entry is easy and the water shallow, if rocky at first. It's an ideal spot for beginner snorkelers or divers, or for an all-around nice day of sun, swim, and beach. Compared to Laughing Bird

1: Monkey River; **2:** Silk Cayes; **3:** over-the-water cabanas on Thatch Caye; **4:** Laughing Bird Caye National Park

Caye, snorkeling at Silk is average—except for a unique snorkeling site now called **Shark, Ray, and Turtle Alley,** just a couple of minutes from the main island, where, thanks to lobster fishers cleaning their catch from a traditional wooden sailboat, you can see magnificent three-foot-long loggerhead turtles and impressive large southern stingrays as well as lemon and reef sharks. Observe from a healthy distance, as these creatures can get aggressive even among themselves while vying for the scraps being thrown into the sea. Splash Dive Center includes this snorkel stop on day trips to the Silk Cayes.

Diving at Silk Cayes is excellent, with a couple of walls to explore. The **North Wall** is one of the top sites in the reserve and in Belize, going down to 80 feet and offering a look at many of the Belize Barrier Reef's beautiful species in one place: hawksbill turtles, spotted eagle rays, moray eels, manta rays, black groupers, and the occasional reef shark. **White Hole** is a 30- to 70-foot dive that begins in a sandy area (resembling a white hole from the surface), where you'll spot yellowtail snappers, groupers, nurse sharks resting, passing spotted eagle rays, four-eyed butterfly fish traveling in pairs, angelfish, gorgonians, and walls of corals. Loggerhead and hawksbill turtles can also be spotted at the **Turtle Canyons** dive site, which goes to 60 feet, along with smaller species like spotted drums and arrow crabs.

RAY CAYE

A hit among couples and honeymooners, and recently upgraded, the 7.1-acre private resort **Ray Caye** (formerly Hatchet Caye, 18 miles offshore from Placencia Village, tel. 501/523-3337, www.raycaye.com, US$350-395) offers casitas with all the amenities, outdoor decks, and an on-site dive shop with complimentary sports gear—from kayaks to Hobie Cats, paddleboards, and fishing gear. There's also a new swimming pool and an on-site bar and restaurant (try the World Famous Lionfish Tacos). The caye has a bit more of an upscale vibe, and it gets rave reviews from vacationing

lovebirds. Its beach is decent, if flat in some parts. During the turtle-nesting season, hawksbill turtles come to lay their eggs on the beach. The island's location is ideal, a stone's throw from excellent snorkeling and diving sites off nearby Laughing Bird Caye and the Silk Cayes, which are visible from shore.

THATCH CAYE

Recently renovated and under new management, **Thatch Caye Resort** (tel. 501/532-2414, U.S. tel. 800/435-3145, www.thatchcayebelize.com, from US$349) is a 14-acre island complex nine miles from Dangriga, within the South Water Caye Marine Reserve and adjacent to Coco Plum Caye. The revamped caye offers five over-the-water bungalows on stilts, with glorious porch views, king or twin beds, air-conditioning, and en suite baths. There are also over-the-water villas with private rooftop decks, and island cabanas. There's a general lounge and dining *palapa*—serving communal meals on the beach—as well as plenty of hammocks and beach toys around the caye. The resort operates at 85 percent with solar power, and a backup generator is used at night. The evening happy-hour spot to be is the over-the-water bar at the back of the island, surrounded with great views. Various all-inclusive packages are offered according to your interest, including honeymoon deals.

★ LAUGHING BIRD CAYE NATIONAL PARK

Close to the Silk Cayes, **Laughing Bird Caye National Park** (entrance US$10) is an important protected area encompassing over 10,000 acres. With swaying palms, small beautiful beaches, an absence of biting bugs, shallow sandy swimming areas, roaming pelicans, and interesting snorkeling and diving, it's a popular day trip from Placencia, just 11 miles from shore or a mere 45-minute boat ride.

Laughing Bird Caye National Park was designated in December 1991 and gained World Heritage Site status along with the Belize Barrier Reef in 1996. It's managed by the nonprofit **Southern Environmental Association** (SEA Belize, office near Placencia town dock, tel. 501/523-3377, www.seabelize.org), also in charge of the Sapodilla Cayes, Placencia Lagoon, and Gladden Spit and Silk Cayes Marine Reserve, a famous whale shark site.

The reserve is visited regularly, mostly by researchers and travelers brought out by tour operators from Placencia for picnics, snorkeling, and diving. In high season, it's not unusual to see several tour groups on the island. Private yachts and sea kayaks also use the site regularly, and some mooring buoys have been installed to prevent anchor damage to the surrounding reef. There is one **trail** through the center of the caye. A park ranger remains on the caye at all times and greets daily visitors to give them a five-minute briefing on the park, including dos and don'ts in this no-take zone.

Named after laughing gulls that once inhabited the island, this particular kind of caye is referred to as a *faro;* the arms on each end make a kind of enclosure around a lagoon area on the leeward side. In this way, the island acts much like a mini-atoll. It's also a 100 percent no-take zone. All of this is good news for those wishing to **dive** or **snorkel** the front, or eastern, side of the island.

The snorkeling in particular is spectacular, and ideal for beginners. You'll find a lot of coral, sponges, and plentiful fish life. Starting in shallow waters, there are three designated snorkel entries. At the front side of the island, you'll spot sergeant majors, stoplight parrotfish, hogfish, porkfish, giant lobsters, sea cucumbers, and schools of blue-striped grunts hovering over corals. Ask to see the **elkhorn coral harvesting station,** where healthy elkhorn is planted and eventually used to replace dead coral in other parts of the reserve, which you can also see while you snorkel—proof of Belize's continued dedication in maintaining its reef's health. The leeward, or back, side of the island offers even more dazzling snorkeling—be sure not to forget a waterproof camera to capture large barracuda preying on smaller fish, healthy soft and hard corals, bonefish, blue tang, and even rays and nurse sharks, sergeant majors, trumpetfish, porkfish, schools of black jacks, princess parrotfish, and surrounding silversides.

Shutterbugs should stay at the back of the boat upon leaving the island, around midafternoon, to capture Laughing Bird Caye's gorgeous full-length view.

Both the Silk Cayes and Laughing Bird Caye can be enjoyed in a one-day trip (no overnights allowed) if you charter a boat, but a full day on each would be a much better plan.

RANGUANA CAYE

Located 18 miles away or about an hour from Placencia, **Ranguana Caye** (tel. 501/674-7264, www.ranguanacaye.com, day trip US$125 pp, 4-night all-inclusive US$2,399 per couple) is yet another paradisiacal plot. Perched atop the Belize Barrier Reef, this privately owned caye is a cozy two-acre island with a stunning white-sand beach at the front, swaying palms jutting out of its center, and all-around blissful scenery.

There's a casual restaurant and bar on-site. Four charming blue wooden cabanas on stilts are tucked at the back of the island under the shade of coconut trees. No phones, no Internet, no problem.

Swim and snorkel off the beach in shallow waters or get some sun with a cocktail in hand. Entry starts at the ankle level, and visibility is incredible at lower depths. Divers will find decent sites to explore just a couple of miles off Ranguana Caye, including the **Fox Hole,** a wall dive going to 100 feet, where hawksbill turtles, angelfish, nurse sharks, barracuda, ocean triggers, and queen triggerfish all roam in deep-blue waters. Splash Dive Center and several other tour operators offer a full-day excursion to Ranguana.

But you don't have to be a diver or snorkeler to enjoy this island. Rent a cabana, take in the turquoise views to the sound of birds and gentle waves, and walk the edge of the plot to feel as if you're walking on water. This island's glorious scenery encapsulates what Belize's cayes are all about.

Private Island Dreams

Where else in the Caribbean can you rent your own Caribbean island and live out your *Lost* fantasies? If you've got cash to spare or a big group to split the cost, you've got exclusive access to a handful of Belize's most stunning cayes.

- **Gladden Private Island** (U.S. tel. 888/666-4282, www.gladdenprivateisland.com, US$2,950): Co-owned by the executive producer and host of HGTV's *Island Hunters*, this newest five-star hideaway sits 20 miles off the coast of Placencia and is currently the most exclusive villa escape in Belize, 3,000 square feet fit for two to four guests. Surrounded by 360 degrees of Caribbean Sea and views of the reef, the Gladden Villa boasts all the bells and whistles including a gorgeous pool in the heart of the compound. You can hop on a 40-minute helicopter ride from the airport to the resort, or fly to Placencia and get a boat ride out.

- **The Enclave** (across The Point/Placencia Pier, US$2,400/week) is a stone's throw from the Placencia pier and under five-minute boat ride away. It was once a mangrove plot and is now a luxury island for rent to groups. There are seven cabanas or minihouses named after birds and beautifully furnished to accommodate up to 14 people. There's a nice, large, and open recreational area boasting a pool, pool table, a bar, and steps to the beachfront where hammocks await. A visit includes a private chef for those staying three to seven nights, and the short boat transfer to the mainland is included. The island runs on part solar, part generator (mangroves were cut down to make this hotel happen, so ask about their restoration efforts), and there's staff here 24/7.

- **Coco Plum Caye** (U.S. tel. 800/763-7360, www.cocoplumcay.com, 7-night package for 24 guests US$49,216): Via Coco Plum Island Resort, this gorgeous 16-acre island offers 14 cabanas for rent, for up to 28 people. The island rental package includes all meals, unlimited local beer and water, water sports gear, and up to five tours, two of which can be to the mainland. What folks rave most about here is the friendly staff.

- **Coral Caye** (www.thefamilycoppolahideaways.com/en/turtle-inn/dwellings/coral-caye, US$895-4,510): Formerly French Louie Caye, this tiny two-acre plot eight miles east of Placencia Village is owned by Francis Ford Coppola and now an upscale escape for 2-10 people. It has its own beach, coral reef—ideal for walk-in snorkeling—fishing dock, two rustic-chic cottages, and a Great House, or relaxation lounge, with full kitchen, bar, music, and games. An on-site caretaker cooks three meals a day, including the "catch and eat" type, and can organize any sailing or snorkeling trips you fancy. To upgrade the experience, you can request a private butler for an additional daily fee.

- **Ray Caye** (formerly Hatchet Caye, tel. 501/523-3337, www.raycaye.com, 3-night all-inclusive US$325): Located 17 miles east of Placencia, the island accommodates 26 guests for weddings, group retreats, and more. Features include a beautiful beach, a new swimming pool, gym, spa, and restaurant on-site, plus a full-service dive shop. All-inclusive rates are available.

- **Lime Caye** (tel. 501/722-0070, cell tel. 501/722-0070, www.garbuttsfishinglodge.com, 2-day package US$345, 4-day package US$700, includes cabin, all meals, snorkeling, transportation, and park fee): This island, off Belize's deep Southern Coast, within the Sapodilla Cayes Marine Reserve, is the site of turtle nesting. Garbutt's Marine and Fishing Lodge offers basic seafront huts (with outdoor showers and rustic baths), a pretty white-sand beach, and excellent snorkeling, where you're likely to be the only one exploring the reef. It doesn't get more distant or authentic than Lime Caye.

- **Ranguana Caye** (tel. 501/674-7264, www.ranguanacaye.com, day trip US$125 pp/day, all-inclusive): A private island two acres in size and 18 miles (90 minutes by boat) from the Placencia Peninsula, Ranguana is dreamy. Three cabanas on stilts have private baths, and there's a housekeeper. The surrounding scenery of turquoise and jade seas is breathtaking.

TARPON CAYE

Fifteen miles east of Placencia Village or a 45-minute boat ride away, the five-acre plot of Tarpon Caye is easily a fisher's dream: A tarpon lagoon surrounds the caye's entrance, while along its edges, permit glide by all day long. That was Charles Leslie Sr.'s goal when he opened **Tarpon Caye Lodge** (tel. 501/671-0286, www. tarponcaye.com, US$150, 3-day fishing package US$2,050 pp for 2) in 1996. Tarpon Caye continues to be family-owned and Belizean-operated and is one of the preferred getaways for avid anglers in search of a local experience.

Right off the three bright cabins on stilts, perched over the sea and equipped with a porch, a hammock, double beds, and solar power, is spectacular snorkeling, thanks to the Leslie family chasing off fishers and turning the surrounding waters into an unofficial marine reserve. The waterfront **Pesky Permit** restaurant is on-site, serving up excellent home-cooked Belizean meals and fresh catch. While the lodge caters primarily to anglers, it won't turn away couples seeking a no-frills Belizean island getaway. One thing's for sure: Evenings on this caye are anything but dull, from the starlit skies to the local jokes shared at the dinner table.

Punta Gorda and the Deep South

The Toledo District is "God's country," according to 15-year veteran adventure tour guide and Punta Gorda resident Bruno Kuppinger.

Because it's the farthest in distance from Belize City, few pick the Toledo District, or "PG"—as Belizeans affectionately call this area—over the more conveniently reached Cayo. But just an hour and a half on a regional flight from Belize City will land visitors in the real backcountry of Belize, where they'll find all that is authentically Belizean in one place: virgin rainforests, waterfalls, five Mayan archaeological sites, proximity to pristine cayes for snorkeling and sportfishing, and a population considered the most diverse in the country. Creoles, East Indians, Garinagu, and Maya all coexist here in a world where most

Highlights

Look for ★ to find recommended sights, activities, dining, and lodging.

★ **Drum Schools:** Two renowned drum masters keep Punta Gorda's African diaspora culture alive (page 289).

★ **Mayan Culture Tours:** Experience the traditional lifestyle of the Maya in their villages, cooking, making chocolate, or practicing crafts (page 292).

★ **Market Days:** Punta Gorda comes alive, with eateries, shopping, music, vendors, and goods from all the district's villages (page 296).

★ **Sapodilla Cayes Marine Reserve:** This distant yet alluring cluster of cayes offers abundant marinelife, giant corals, powdery beaches, and utter seclusion (page 307).

★ **Uxbenka Archaeological Site:** Visit southern Belize's oldest Mayan city dating back over 2,000 years, now open to visitors. Continue with an arranged Mayan lunch and experience in Santa Cruz village, still boasting 80 percent traditional Maya homes (page 317).

★ **Río Blanco National Park:** In addition to waterfalls, this beautiful national park offers diverse flora and fauna—including the possibility of jaguar sightings. Bring your camera (page 318)!

★ **Blue Creek Cave:** Swim up to 600 yards

inside this stunning cave—the source of the Río Blanco (page 318).

Punta Gorda and the Deep South

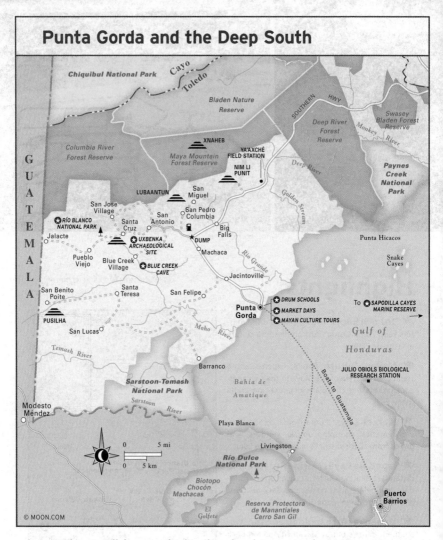

home cooking is still done on a fire hearth, and deer dances of the past are performed in the present.

The Toledo District has the lowest per capita income in Belize, yet it is also the most expensive in which to live. More than 10,000 Q'eqchi' and Mopan Maya are subsistence farmers in the Toledo countryside. This is chocolate country, home to organic cacao farms that supply all four of Belize's quality chocolate producers.

The district also encompasses the least visited islands, clustered around the very last tip of the Belize Barrier Reef. The Snake Cayes, resting inside the Port Honduras Marine Reserve, are a day-tripper's dream,

Previous: Uxbenka Archaeological Site; Río Blanco National Park; Central Park in Punta Gorda; Punta Gorda market.

with virtually no other boats and waters teeming with marinelife at shallow depths. The farthest, at just over an hour from shore, the Sapodilla Cayes—a designated UNESCO World Heritage Site along with other parts of the Belize Barrier Reef—beckon for a longer stay with two stunning islands and white-sand coral beaches at Lime Caye and Hunting Caye that are some of Belize's best stretches.

While tourism isn't yet booming in these parts, the mainland offerings continues to expand. More restaurants are sprouting, jungle lodges continue to thrive while new ones appear, and the Cacao Trail is growing. The cayes, easily accessible by boat from Punta Gorda, are slowly receiving more attention as the Northern Cayes and Southern Cayes become more popular. Rapid improvements to the Southern Highway and San Antonio Road, giving easier access to sights and villages, and daily air service to and from Punta Gorda are helping to put Toledo on the map. There's never-ending hope that visitors will realize this is the most untouched part of Belize.

PLANNING YOUR TIME

To best get a taste of the Toledo District before or during your getaway to the Snake or Sapodilla Cayes, you'll need to set aside at least 4-5 days. Spend your first half day exploring **Punta Gorda,** the urban heart of the deep south. Take a walk along **the waterfront,** join a Garifuna **drumming class,** and time your visit to coincide with one of Punta Gorda's **market days.** Spend the rest of the day on a scheduled **chocolate trail** tour to get a glimpse of a traditional Mayan village.

Make a day trip to **Port Honduras Marine Reserve** and its **Snake Cayes,** where you can snorkel and spot stunning coral and fish, dive, or simply soak in West Snake Caye's gin-clear natural swimming pool and relax on its coral white-sand beach.

Add on a visit to the inland **Uxbenka Archaeological Site,** a notable Mayan ruin now open to visitors. Another sure bet is **Río Blanco National Park,** a 45-minute drive from Punta Gorda, offering a spectacular waterfall, hiking trail, caves, and plenty of stunning scenery. See where the Río Blanco begins at stunning **Blue Creek Cave.**

If you have time to spare, add on a couple of days of relaxation and adventure in the **Sapodilla Cayes,** where you'll snorkel and dive amid shipwrecks before lazing on the prettiest of beaches at Lime Caye and catching the sunset over the reef from your porch.

Punta Gorda and Vicinity

Toledo District's county seat and biggest town, PG is simultaneously the lazy end of the road and an exciting jumping-off point to upland villages, offshore cayes, Guatemala, or Honduras. Punta Gorda's 5,000 or so inhabitants live their daily lives getting by from hurricane to hurricane.

Punta Gorda is a simple port, with no real beach but plenty of swimming spots, and its winding streets are framed by some old dilapidated wooden buildings and newer concrete ones. The majority of inhabitants are of Garifuna and East Indian descent, although there are representatives of most of the country's ethnic groups. Fishing was the main support of the local people for centuries; today many anglers work for a nearby high-tech shrimp farm. Local farmers grow rice, mangoes, bananas, sugarcane, and beans—mainly for themselves and the local market. Fair-trade-certified and organic cacao beans are an important export as well, used to make chocolate by the Green & Black's company in England.

ORIENTATION

Punta Gorda is a casual village with few street names. Arriving from the north, you'll cross a

Punta Gorda

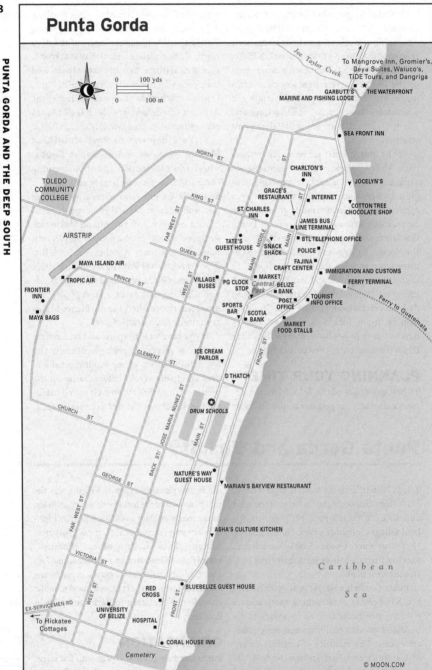

Joe Taylor Creek

To Mangrove Inn, Gromier's,
Beya Suites, Waluco's,
TIDE Tours, and Dangriga

GARBUTT'S
MARINE AND FISHING LODGE ★ THE WATERFRONT

SEA FRONT INN

NORTH ST.

CHARLTON'S
INN

JOCELYN'S

TOLEDO
COMMUNITY
COLLEGE

KING ST.

GRACE'S
RESTAURANT

INTERNET

COTTON TREE
CHOCOLATE SHOP

FAR WEST ST.

ST. CHARLES
INN

JAMES BUS
LINE TERMINAL

AIRSTRIP

QUEEN ST.

TATE'S
GUEST HOUSE

SNACK
SHACK

BTL TELEPHONE OFFICE

POLICE

MAYA ISLAND AIR

PRINCE ST.

WEST ST.

VILLAGE
BUSES

FAJINA
CRAFT CENTER

TROPIC AIR

PG CLOCK
STOP

MARKET

IMMIGRATION AND CUSTOMS

FRONTIER
INN

Central
Park

BELIZE
BANK

FERRY TERMINAL

MAYA BAGS

SPORTS
BAR

SCOTIA
BANK

POST
OFFICE

TOURIST
INFO OFFICE

Ferry to Guatemala

MARKET
FOOD STALLS

CLEMENT ST.

ICE CREAM
PARLOR

FRONT ST.

CHURCH ST.

D THATCH

BACK ST.

JOSE MARIA NUNEZ ST.

DRUM SCHOOLS

MAIN ST.

GEORGE ST.

FAR WEST ST.

NATURE'S WAY
GUEST HOUSE

MARIAN'S BAYVIEW RESTAURANT

ASHA'S CULTURE KITCHEN

VICTORIA ST.

C a r i b b e a n

WEST ST.

RED
CROSS

BLUEBELIZE GUEST HOUSE

S e a

EX-SERVICEMEN RD

FRONT ST.

UNIVERSITY
OF BELIZE

HOSPITAL

To Hickatee
Cottages

CORAL HOUSE INN

Cemetery

© MOON.COM

0   100 yds
0   100 m

bridge over Joe Taylor Creek—next to which is the famous Garbutt's Marine and Fishing Lodge operation—and then be greeted by the towering Sea Front Inn, with the Caribbean on your left. After the road splits at the Uno gas station, it forms North Park Street (a diagonal street one block long) on the right and Front Street on the left. Following Front Street will take you through town, past the boat taxi pier, the immigration office, the market, and several eating establishments; continue all the way south to Nature's Way Guest House at the bottom of Church Street and continue on to find a couple of seaside restaurants. The municipal dock and town plaza, just a couple of blocks in from the sea, form the town center.

If you arrive by bus or at the town dock from Guatemala, prepare to be greeted by a few local hustlers; feel free to shake them off by firmly refusing their services.

SIGHTS
The Waterfront
Even though there is no real lounging beach or developed waterfront, people go swimming and sunning off the dock just north of Joe Taylor Creek. The waterfront is rocky but quiet and tranquil, with small waves lapping the shoreline, and a walk along its length, especially at sunrise, is not to be missed. There's a new *palapa* over the water where you can relax and take the breeze in, right by the "I love Peini"—the town's Garifuna name—sign at the entrance to town.

Central Park
On a small triangle of soil roughly in the center of town, **Central Park** has an appropriately sleepy air to it, though plenty of activity swirls around it. At the north end is a raised stage dedicated to the "Pioneers of Belizean Independence." In the center of the park is a dry fountain, along with a few green cement benches, and a giant clock tower is on the south end. On market days, this is an especially pleasant spot to take a break, enjoy the blue sky, and watch the activities of the villagers who have come in to sell their produce.

★ Drum Schools
PG's diverse population provides a chance to learn drumming from two African-rooted cultures: Garifuna and Creole. For Garifuna drumming, Raymond "Ray" McDonald of the **Warasa Garifuna Drum School** (New Rd., tel. 501/632-7701, www.warasadrumschool. com, 4:30pm-8pm Mon.-Fri., 9am-8pm Sat.-Sun., US$12.50 per hour drum lessons, US$25 per hour drum making) is one of Belize's top drummers and a local star in Punta Gorda for his undeniable skills. He offers an introductory class on Garifuna drumming; learn about the various rhythms, how to produce the correct sound, and then start jamming. Ray also teaches drum making (ask to see his very own custom collection) and drumming at various lodges in town, particularly at Hickatee Cottages. The school's location in a Garifuna Reserve area on the edge of town is currently being upgraded with a large new thatched hut.

Continue your drumming tour of Belize's south with the **Maroon Creole Drum School** (tel. 501/632-7841 or 501/668-7733, methos_drums@hotmail.com, 7am-4pm daily, US$10 per hour), run by Belizean musician and drum master Emmeth Young and his partner Jill Burgess. Emmeth, originally from the Creole village of Gales Point, is a talented man whose drumming and efforts to preserve Belizean culture have been featured on the Travel Channel, among other media. Emmeth's *sambai* rhythms, which he learned as early as age eight, can be traced half a millennium back to the Ibo people of West Africa. He took a lifetime trip in 2018 to Guinea, West Africa, where he honed his drumming skills. Ask Emmeth about his "Drums not guns" initiative. Check ahead of time for scheduling.

SPORTS AND RECREATION
Caving
With the largest number of Mayan villages in Belize, it's not surprising that Punta Gorda has some of the country's most

Ranger for a Day with Ya'axché

Zip up your boots and play ranger for a day along the rivers and trails of the Golden Stream Corridor Preserve. Thanks to the Ya'axché Conservation Trust (pronounced ya-chay, 20A George Price St., tel. 501/722-0108, www.yaaxche.org), you can now experience a day in the life of a rainforest ranger in the deep south of Belize.

Established in 1997, the Ya'axché Conservation Trust works to maintain and manage the health of Belize's forests, rivers, and reefs in and around the "Maya Golden Landscape" of southern Belize, an area that includes the Golden Stream Corridor Preserve and the 100,000-acre Bladen Nature Reserve. To date, Ya'axché has some of the best-trained rangers in the country. In 2012 the organization's then-executive director Lisel Alamilla, who went on to become Belize's minister of forestry, fisheries, and sustainable development, was given the prestigious Whitley Fund for Nature Award for her leadership in conservation work at Ya'axché.

The day starts at the Golden Stream Field Station off the Southern Highway and easily accessible by bus. Sign up to join the day's patrol and hike alongside rangers, learning to detect illegal activities—like hunting—by logging bird and mammal species along the riverside trail. Other tasks include tracking jaguar and tapir tracks, learning to spot various birds, and, weather permitting, cooling off in the Golden Stream River.

While there's no set fee for this unique Ranger for a Day experience, a donation of US$30-45 is suggested. All contributions go toward the rangers' salaries—giving back to the community at large and helping sustain a fantastic organization. For more unique Ya'axché-led experiences, including day trips to Mayan communities, check out its EcoTourism Belize arm (20A George Price St., Punta Gorda, or Golden Stream Field Station, Southern Hwy., tel. 501/667-0864, www.ecotourismbelize.com).

off-the-beaten-path caving and hiking sites. **Toledo Cave and Adventure Tours** (tel. 501/604-2124, www.tcatours.com, US$95-115) offers trips to some of Belize's lesser-known attractions, including Yok Balum Cave, Tiger Cave, Gibnut Cave, and Oke'bal Ha. Owner Bruno Kuppinger, longtime resident of Punta Gorda, is an adventure junkie who loves to get deep in the bush. He also offers group pickups from Belize City and tours of his farm in Mafredi.

For some cave tubing fun, folks rave about **Big Falls Adventures** (Southern Hwy., Big Falls, tel. 501/634-6979, www.bigfallsextremeadventures.com, 8am-4pm daily, US$48-60, lunch US$10 extra), offering tubing along the Río Grande, followed by a dip in a local hot spring before getting back down into the river (I opted for the zip line across Big Falls).

Fishing, Diving, and Snorkeling

The waterways around Punta Gorda offer anglers the rare chance to bag a grand slam (permit, tarpon, bonefish, and snook). Fly-fishing is generally possible between November and May in shallow areas around the cayes, mangroves, and river mouths. Reel fishing is possible throughout the year, up the rivers or in the ocean; cast for snappers, groupers, jacks, barracuda, mackerels, or kingfish. Most guides help you bring your fish back and find someone to cook it up for you. Fishing trips can run upward of US$400-500 for four people.

Garbutt's Marine and Fishing Lodge (tel. 501/722-0070, cell tel. 501/604-3548, www.garbuttsfishinglodge.com), next to Joe Taylor Creek, at the entrance to Punta Gorda, is a top-notch operation run by the Garbutt brothers, who were raised in nearby Punta Negra and grew up exploring these waters. They offer the most reliable way to get out to the cayes for fly-fishing, diving, or snorkeling. Fishing charter packages for groups include

1: Punta Gorda's waterfront; 2: Emmeth Young, drummaster, teaches at his Maroon Creole Drum School. 3: Central Park

on-site seafront cabin lodging (7 nights US$2,865 pp, all-inclusive). They are also dive masters and offer PADI classes and certification as well as self-guided (US$5 per hour) or guided (US$12.50 half-day) kayak rentals.

TIDE Tours (Mile 1, San Antonio Rd., tel. 501/722-2274, www.tidetours.org, 7:30am-4:30pm Mon.-Fri., reduced hours Sat.) offers snorkeling (US$145 pp for 2 people) and diving (US$220 pp for up to 4 people) trips to the Sapodilla Cayes; kayak (US$12.50 pp half-day) and snorkel gear (US$5 pp per day) rentals are available. TIDE Tours is the customer service branch of the Toledo Institute for Development and Environment (TIDE), Belize's only "ridges to reef" NGO. TIDE does much of the guide training in the area, helping to teach people sustainable, often tourism-related, skills. TIDE staffers promote tours to protected areas and give presentations on their work in the Port Honduras Marine Reserve, in Payne's Creek National Park, and on the Private Lands Initiative. They also do tours to archaeological sites, caves, birding, and other inland cultural attractions. Revenue generated from TIDE Tours is used for education and outreach efforts.

Kayaking

TIDE Tours (Mile 1, San Antonio Rd., tel. 501/722-2274, www.tidetours.org, 7:30am-4:30pm Mon.-Fri., reduced hours Sat.) offers numerous inland and sea trips, including river kayaking (US$90 pp for 2 people). Kayak rentals (US$2.50 per hour) are also available. Many guesthouses also include complimentary kayak use. In town, you can explore Joe Taylor Creek, and if you're staying inland, the riverside lodges are ideal to launch your canoe.

Tours and Day Trips

Toledo offers more cultural tours than any other district, thanks to its diverse population, which includes East Indians, Maya, Garinagu, Creoles, and more. You can spend the morning in a Mayan community, or hop over to a Creole village by boat for lunch, and have the afternoon at a seaside Garifuna fishing village, observing entirely different worlds and lifestyles.

★ MAYAN CULTURE TOURS

One of the most unique immersion experiences in Toledo is a Mayan village homestay. You can arrange this with **Aguacate Belize Homestay Program** (tel. 501/633-9954, cucullouis@hotmail.com, www.aguacatebelize.com, US$9 pp per night, US$3.50 pp per meal, US$5 registration fee) or **San Jose Homestay Program** (contact Justino Pec, tel. 501/722-0109, cell tel. 501/668-7378, peck.justino@gmail.com).

I highly recommend **EcoTourism Belize** (20A George Price St., Punta Gorda, or Golden Stream Field Station, Southern Hwy., tel. 501/667-0864, www.ecotourismbelize.com, meal included), the sustainable tour-operating arm of the Ya'axché Conservation Trust, a leading conservation organization. By partnering with local women's cooperatives as well as farmers in the district, unique tours are available that take you to lesser-known areas. Spend a day in Indian Creek Village with the Maya Arts Women's Group learning to cook *caldo* by fire hearth, making chocolate, and watching traditional weaving and dancing (US$55 pp half-day); hike with a Toledo Mayan farmer and tour an organic, family-managed farm using ecofarm techniques (US$60 pp half-day); or take part in a spiritual healing ceremony led by one of a few remaining healers in southern Belize (US$95 pp half-day)—one week's notice is required to gather the herbs. Birding and snorkeling tours are also offered. Whichever activity you pick, 100 percent of profits from these tours go directly to support conservation programs in southern Belize—it doesn't get better than that.

The Living Maya Experience (Big Falls Village, tel. 501/627-7408, livingmayaexperience@gmail.com) offers visitors a day of immersion in Q'eqchi' Mayan culture. Set up on the Cal family's property, the day showcases what everyday village life involves—from touring a traditional Mayan home to learning about farming methods, basket weaving, and making tortillas over a fire hearth. You can contact them independently, let your resort know you'd like to set up a tour, or contact **TIDE Tours** (Mile 1, San Antonio Rd., tel. 501/722-2274, www.tidetours.org, 7:30am-4:30pm Mon.-Fri., reduced hours Sat., US$95pp for two) for the Mayan experience and zip-lining combo.

OTHER CULTURE TOURS

For a brief taste of another one of Belize's major cultural groups, stop by **LeeLa's Bistro** (6 Front St., tel. 501/668-7548, 10am-11pm daily), located at the front of renowned Creole recording artist Leela Vernon's home; the Queen of Brukdown music sadly passed away in 2017. Recognized as a national treasure, you used to be able to find her relaxing on her porch at the back of the bistro and singing a tune. Her home has now turned into a **Kriol Museum,** where you'll be able to see her musical instruments, her awards, and jewelry and costumes she used over the years; there's no fee and contributions are welcome. Go with an open mind to speak with her family members—her children run the café—hear her music and tales of the Kriol culture, and just take in the spontaneity that is life in PG.

TIDE Tours (Mile 1, San Antonio Rd., tel. 501/722-2274, www.tidetours.org, 7:30am-4:30pm Mon.-Fri., reduced hours Sat.), the tour-operating arm of PG's leading NGO, specializes in cultural visits, including half a day in **Barranco,** a traditional Garifuna village, where you'll get to tour, sample Garifuna food, and visit the museum and the sacred ceremonial temple (US$95 pp for 2 people). Another option is a day trip to **Punta Negra,** a Kriol peninsula with a beautiful golden beach and authentic Kriol food, or a craft lesson in the village of San Miguel, coupled with a visit to Lubaantun (US$65 pp for 2 people). TIDE offers several tour combos. They've also recently added new birding tours to their catalog, which take you into the beautiful Payne's Creek National Park as well as other protected areas managed by TIDE.

CHOCOLATE AND SPICE TOURS

Another solid option is a half-day trip to **Eladio Pop's Cacao Trail** in San Pedro Columbia. Eladio is a one-of a-kind individual, full of enthusiasm and knowledge of organic farming. He will walk you through his cacao orchards and land, showing you the

EcoTourism Belize runs unique culture tours.

cacao process from bean to chocolate. You'll end up at his home, where you'll get to watch cacao roasting and grind some yourself before tasting a delicious cup of hot chocolate the way the Maya used to have it. Tours are arranged through local lodges and operators, including **Toledo Cave and Adventure Tours** (tel. 501/604-2124, www.tcatours.com, US$90 pp).

The Cho family runs **Ixcacao Maya Belizean Chocolate** (formerly called Cyrila's Chocolate, tel. 501/742-4050, cell tel. 501/660-2840, www.ixcacaomayabelizeanchocolate.com, US$32.50 for 2 people) in the village of San Felipe. They offer a five-hour chocolate tour beginning with a visit to an organic cacao farm and continuing with lunch in Cyrila's home. She and her daughter then lead a chocolate-making session. They also offer shorter, two-hour chocolate-making lessons.

A popular excursion after chocolate is the **Belize Spice Farm & Botanical Garden** (tel. 501/732-4014, goldenstreamspicefarm@gmail.com, www.belizespicefarm.com, 7:30am-3:30pm, US$15 pp), the largest of its kind in Belize. Right off the highway, it's an easy stop before you head into Punta Gorda. You can show up solo in your own car or arrange a tour through your hotel or a local tour operator. For one hour, you'll tour the grounds filled with black pepper, vanilla, cardamom, cinnamon, nutmeg, and other exotic plants, as well as trees native to Belize. A restaurant is also available on-site for lunch.

For a more off-the-beaten track experience in this area, away from large tours, contact **Toledo Cave and Adventure Tours** (tel. 501/604-2124, www.tcatours.com, US$100 pp) and sign up for owner **Bruno's Farm and Jungle Adventure;** you'll visit his organic fruit farm in Mafredi, on the San Antonio Road, where you'll learn about Belize's exotic plants and trees, about organic farming and cooking, and taste along the way in a lush environment. Lunch is included. It's a great opportunity to learn about Belizean flora in an authentic setting.

ENTERTAINMENT AND EVENTS
Nightlife

There are a handful of small bars scattered around town, some with pool tables, all with plenty of booze. The nightlife in Punta Gorda is a bit scattered, and there's no one best hot spot. You pretty much have to hop from one spot to another to find the crowd, or ask around.

In the meantime, **Rainforest Reggae Bar** (Front St., tel. 501/627-7016, 3pm-midnight daily except Mon.) is a good spot to get a cocktail and snack—from fish to meatball sandwiches—before taking it up a notch. Sundays are for reggae on the deck.

Waluco's Bar & Grill (Mile 1, San Antonio Rd., tel. 501/702-2129, 7am-2pm and 5pm-10pm Mon.-Thurs., 7am-midnight Fri.-Sat., US$3.50-10) is right across from the sea, a short walk north of town, although at night a taxi or bicycle is best. The name means "son of the soil" in Garifuna. It's sometimes a happening spot, with live music, karaoke nights, or drumming on Friday and Sunday as well as during festival times. You'll find plenty of karaoke and some pool tables at **Seaside Heights** (tel. 501/722-2450 or 501/670-3672, 10:30am-3pm and 5pm-midnight Mon. and Wed., 4pm-midnight Tues., 10:30am-midnight Thurs.-Sun.), just a block from Waluco's. A little outside of town, you'll find a few more bars and nightclubs, open only on random weekends (no phone, 9pm-2am), including **Roots Rock Reggae** and **Embassy** on the Southern Highway.

Festivals and Events

Toledo's biggest event is the annual **Chocolate Festival** (Front St., www.chocolatefestivalofbelize.com, 3rd weekend in May) at the park. It's a weekend-long tribute to Belizean chocolate and the organic cacao farmers of the Toledo District. From a Wine and Chocolate Evening to open-air concerts with traditional Mayan and Garifuna music and chocolate tastings, Cacao for Kids storytelling and games, chocolate-flavored

Toledo's Chocolate Trail

The cacao tree (*Theobroma cacao*, "food of the gods") has gained renewed importance in the culture and economy of the Maya in southern Belize. Thousands of years ago, Mayan kings and priests worshipped the cacao (or *kakaw*) bean, using it as currency and drinking it in a sacred, spicy beverage. A revival of southern Belize's cacao industry has since led to choco-tourism. A few area lodges and families have found ways to connect ancient cacao farming with the modern craze for high-quality fair-trade food and products.

Today, farmers sell their cacao crop to the **Toledo Cacao Growers Association** (TCGA, Main St., a block north of Central Park, Punta Gorda, tel. 501/722-2992, www.tcgabelize.com), a nonprofit coalition of small farms that then sells the beans to acclaimed chocolatier Green & Black's, a Britain-based company specializing in fair-trade and organic-certified chocolate bars. Some beans remain in Belize, used by a few Mayan families and small-batch chocolate makers to produce chocolate for the domestic market.

Sustainable Harvest International (SHI, tel. 501/722-2010, U.S. tel. 207/669-8254, www.sustainableharvest.org) is a nonprofit organization working to alleviate poverty and deforestation throughout Central America. The organization works with more than 100 cacao-growing families, helping them develop multistory forest plots that mimic the natural forest; this provides a diversity of food and marketable produce for the families, plus a home for threatened plants and animals. Coffee, plantains, and other shade-loving crops are planted alongside the cacao trees, under a hardwood canopy. Sustainable Harvest Belize estimates that for every acre converted to multistory cacao forest, five acres are saved from destructive slash-and-burn practices. The organization offers sustainable chocolate tours and other voluntourism opportunities at work sites in southern Belize. Accommodations range from rustic homestays to the stilted cabins of Cotton Tree Lodge, where SHI maintains a demo garden.

cocktails, and an all-day food and crafts fair on Front Street, there are events from Friday evening through Sunday to entertain both children and adults, who come from all over Belize. Be sure to reserve accommodations ahead of time, and bring plenty of small change—there's no telling how much chocolate or art you'll be tempted to take home. The best part is that all the funds from the festival go to support community projects.

The **Deer Dance Festival** takes place over a week in August in the village of San Antonio. There are Mayan arts, crafts, music, and food showcased, but the highlight is the costume performance of the deer dance, an ancient ritual that reenacts the hunting of a deer, from chase to capture, accompanied by traditional Mayan harps and violins. This is one of the most off-the-beaten-path cultural events you could attend.

One of the largest Garifuna cultural events in the country, the **Battle of the Drums** (50 Main St., www.battleofthedrums.org) takes place in Punta Gorda, usually the weekend preceding November 19, Garifuna Settlement Day. While there are weekend-long events celebrating Garifuna culture through concerts and food fetes, the main event takes place on Saturday night, when drumming teams from all of Belize's Garifuna towns and villages, and from neighboring Honduras and Guatemala, compete for the title of best Garifuna drumming team. It's a spectacular display of music and dance and culture. Hotel rooms book up almost half a year in advance, so be prepared, and check the local papers for ticket prices, event times, and location details. You can also contact **Beya Suites** (tel. 501/722-2188 or 501/722-2956, www.beyasuites.com), the chief organizers of this event, for more information.

Going into its fourth year, the small **Yellow Ginger Festival** (between Aug. and Oct., varies) celebrates Toledo's East Indian heritage in Central Park with a feast of East Indian dishes, cooked with yellow ginger of course. Other activities include dance performances and live cooking demonstrations.

Mayan culture is celebrated in all its glory on **Maya Day** (Tumul K'in Center of Learning, Blue Creek, Mar.) in the village of Blue Creek. Folks descend from all over Belize to attend this event, which includes traditional dancing and performances, tortilla-baking competitions, firewood-splitting contests, plenty of *caldo* tastings, and other Mayan-inspired recreation. Get a copy of the latest *Toledo Howler* from the **BTIA Tourism Office** (46 Front St., tel. 501/722-2531, 8am-5pm Mon.-Fri.) or pick up a local newspaper for details.

SHOPPING

Next door to the airstrip, at **Maya Bags** (tel. 501/722-2175, U.S. tel. 917/697-2203, www.mayabags.org, 9am-6pm Mon.-Fri.) craft workshop, about 90 women from eight Mayan villages participate in this craft and export venture. The women make handwoven bags (US$50-140), embroidered yoga mats (US$43), beach bags, *jipijapa* purses, and other unique products. The bags are absolutely gorgeous, especially the clutches. If you have time, you can order a custom embroidered design; the craftsmanship is so good that the bags were featured in *Vogue* magazine in 2010 and sold in Barneys for several years. They also make home-decorating items from vases to throw pillows.

Tienda La Indita Maya (24 Main Middle St., no phone, 9am-5pm Mon.-Fri.) carries handmade jewelry, wooden bowls, pottery, and other handicrafts. The store lies just north of Central Park, at the end opposite the clock tower. Also check the **Fajina Women's Group Craft Center** (no phone, 7am-11am Mon.-Sat.) on Front Street near the ferry pier; it's a small co-op for quality Mayan crafts run by the Q'eqchi' and Mopan women. You'll find *jipijapa* baskets, *cuxtales* (bags), slate carvings, calabash carvings, jewelry, textiles, and embroidered clothes—when it's open, that is. If the door is closed, ask upstairs at the restaurant to get it opened up.

If you're a chocolate lover, don't miss the **Cotton Tree Chocolate Shop** (2 Front St., just south of the Uno station, tel. 501/621-8772, www.cottontreechocolate. com, 8am-noon and 1:30pm-5pm Mon.-Fri., 8:30am-noon Sat.). It makes milk, white, and dark chocolates; in addition to free chocolate samples, tours are available by appointment. A small gift shop sells chocolates, cocoa mix, cocoa butter, whole vanilla beans, and handmade chocolate soap by Dawn and Jo's Soap Company, which looks good enough to eat.

★ Market Days

Although there are four weekly market days, Wednesday and Saturday are the biggest. Monday and Friday are smaller but still interesting. Renovated in 2016, the market—once stretching across Front Street—sits across Central Park, where vendors have their own partially open concrete spaces to lay out their goods. Many Mayan vendors sell wild coriander, yellow or white corn, chili peppers of various hues, cassava, tamales wrapped in banana leaves, star fruit, mangoes, and much more. Many of the women and children bring handmade crafts as well. If you're inclined to snap a photo, ask permission first—and perhaps offer to buy something. Folks here are the most sensitive to photos that I've encountered in Belize. If you're refused, smile and put your lens cap back on. When you're done shopping—or before you do so—visit the breakfast and food stalls lining Front Street, where the market used to be.

FOOD

Punta Gorda offers mainly cheap local eats, with the added benefit of fresh seafood and a few excellent vegetarian options. Many restaurants are closed on Sunday and for a few hours between meals. The town has several good bakeries, and fruit and veggies are cheap and abundant on **market days** (Mon., Wed., Fri.-Sat.). Some of the best breakfast and lunch joints are also only open on these days; just walk along Front Street and you'll find a variety of shacks serving hot breakfasts. Notice which has the most crowds and place your order. Ask at any corner store for a sampling of the local Mennonite yogurt and bread, and be sure to try a seaweed shake, which you can buy fresh and cold at Johnson's Hardware Store, across from the market.

Belizean

For a true taste of a PG morning, head down to the old market location stretching along the water on Front Street, which is now lined with a row of breakfast casitas. Pick one of a couple of seats at the friendly **Addy's Kitchen** (Stall #4, no phone, 6:30am-2:30pm daily, US$3). Pick from stew chicken to fry jack and eggs, burritos, and other freshly made dishes for breakfast or lunch, along with instant coffee.

Hang out at the Central Park while having lunch at ★ **PG Clock Stop** (PG Central Park, tel. 501/626-5782, 4pm-9pm on Wed., 10am-9pm Thurs.-Sat., US$3-10). There are daily specials that include rice and beans plates, as well as other specialties like coconut curry conch, jalapeño burgers, jerk pork tacos, and even cohune cabbage—served out of a small kitchen set inside the PG clock tower! Enjoy on picnic tables. Desserts are also available, along with ice cream. There's free Wi-Fi in the park to boot.

Jocelyn's Cuisine & Catering (Front St., tel. 501/661-9267, 6am-9pm daily, US$2.50-4) is a cozy seaside deck across from the Uno gas station at the town entrance, serving delicious plates of local breakfast—freshly made johnnycakes, fry jacks, and even waffles—and a lunch of jerk chicken or Belizean stews and seafood. So popular is Jocelyn's that she expanded with more seating space and the same lovely breeze from the water.

Just steps away, continuing on Front Street into town is **LeeLa's Bistro** (6 Front St., tel. 501/668-7548, 8am-11pm daily, US$5-10), where national hero Leela Vernon's children cook and serve local dishes seafood, along with sides like callaloo, rice, and plantains. It's a little pricier than the average local joint, but it's worth it to spend time with a renowned Kriol family. The interior decor celebrates the Kriol culture, with drums and a large portrait of cultural icon Ms. Leela. There's drumming and live music on Friday and Saturday, occasionally featuring son Franz Vernon, and karaoke on Thursday. After your meal, ask to see the Kriol Museum at the back of the property, once Ms. Leela's home.

Grace's Restaurant (Main St., tel. 501/702-2414, 6:30am-10:30pm daily) is a long-standing joint with typical Belizean fare like stew chicken (US$4), tasty conch soup (US$9), and eggs and beans with fry jacks. It used to be popular, but the food quality has slightly declined over time. A better bet is **Miss Jessie's** (King St., no phone, 11am-4pm Mon.-Fri.) on the side street leading from the corner of Grace's and before Charlton's Inn, set in a small space with a glass counter. You might miss it as there is no outdoor sign, but the doors are usually left open. You'll find a fresh and delicious version of the day's rice-and-beans special, including curries, and homemade desserts, all at a reasonable price.

★ **Waluco's Bar & Grill** (Mile 1, San Antonio Rd., tel. 501/702-2129, 7am-2pm and 5pm-10pm Mon.-Thurs., 7am-midnight Fri.-Sun., US$3.50-10) is a favorite for its local meals and ambience, serving up tasty lunch specials, including stew chicken and fry fish, with the usual sides of rice and beans, callaloo (a leafy green vegetable), or coleslaw. The dinner menu is more varied, with pastas, burgers, and barbecue, and there may be music to go along with your meal if you come on a Friday or Sunday night.

An easy place to recommend for lunch or dinner is ★ **Marian's Bayview Restaurant** (72 Front St., tel. 501/722-0129, 11am-2pm and 6pm-10pm Mon.-Sat., noon-2pm and 7pm-9pm Sun., US$5), set on a rooftop over the water on the south edge of Punta Gorda, across from Nature's Way. Marian's serves East Indian cuisine, seafood, or a good ol' plate of rice and beans from her buffet—all with a view of Guatemala and Honduras across the sea.

Seaside Heights (off Southern Hwy., tel. 501/722-2450, 10:30am-3pm and

5pm-midnight Mon.-Wed., 10:30am-midnight Thurs.-Sun., US$4-10), serves Belizean, Central American, and East Indian options (call ahead to ensure they're open, as they tend to close in slow times). Entrées range from burritos to *tarkari* (East Indian curry), and there's a full bar and a huge top-deck seating area overlooking the waterfront. Add to that a pool table and plenty of karaoke nights.

On your way into or out of Punta Gorda, look out for a bright green building along the highway—that's **Loretta's** lunch spot (no phone, 11am-6pm daily, US$3-5), known mostly to bus drivers; you'll see the James buses parked at the back. There are daily specials, particularly East Indian specialties—get a curry chicken, or cohune cabbage on Friday. There's a screened porch with wooden tables to enjoy your plate, or you can order take out at the window. Fresh juices are also available.

If you don't have the time to visit the Mayan villages, stop by **Fajina Restaurant** (Front St., tel. 501/666-6141 or 501/666-6144, fajina.craft.center@gmail.com, 7am-8:30pm daily, US$3.50) for traditional Mayan fare, typically a delicious bowl of *caldo* (Mayan chicken soup served with corn tortillas). The small casual eatery is run by the same women's group that operates the craft shop downstairs. Occasionally you'll find callaloo (a leafy green vegetable), boiled plantains, or cohune cabbage on the daily menu.

A few Chinese restaurants offer reliable chop suey; some expats call **Hang Cheon** (Main St., tel. 501/722-2064, 10am-2pm and 5pm-midnight daily, US$3-10) the best Chinese in town.

Mexican

Palma's Tortilla Factory (Main St., no phone, 7am-1pm Mon.-Sat.) makes fresh tortillas every day and sells them for US$2.50 per pound; it also makes tacos (3 for US$0.50), *panades* (little meat pies), tamales, and the like.

1: PG Clock Stop; 2: Asha's Culture Kitchen; 3: LeeLa's Bistro

International

The **Snack Shack** (Front St., tel. 501/620-3499, 7am-3pm Mon.-Fri., 7am-noon Sat.) has been an expat favorite for breakfast, especially its giant US$3 egg burritos, a "gringo breakfast" option, fruit shakes, pancakes, fry jacks, and bagels. They recently moved into a smaller, two-story space with steep stairs that lead to the breakfast deck. For lunch, there's a "build your own" tortilla option (US$5), with flavored tortillas of your choice.

As you follow the highway north out of Punta Gorda, look for a driveway and sign on your left just as the road is about to turn away from the sea. Here you'll find ★ **Mangrove Inn and Restaurant** (tel. 501/623-0497, 5pm-10pm daily, US$6-10), a family affair with a charming dining balcony, complete with a bar, cozy lighting, and African decor. The cook, Iconie, has worked in fancy resorts across Belize but prefers working at home. Expect savory fish dishes, potpies, pasta, fresh salads, and rolls.

Perched over the water, steps from BlueBelize, is **Asha's Culture Kitchen** (74 Front St., tel. 501/722-2742, 4pm-10pm Fri.-Wed., US$5-13), a wooden casita with quite possibly the best outdoor deck and dinner setting in town. Asha's serves Creole seafood dishes made to order as well as curries and other entrées. A bright chalkboard menu with blue checks lists the day's availability, served up with two sides in generous portions (the garlic mashed potatoes are good). There is occasional live drumming here.

Vegetarian

★ **Gomier's Restaurant** (Hopeville 6, a block from Beya Suites, tel. 501/620-1719, 11am-2pm and 5pm-10pm Mon.-Sat., earlier close Fri. at 5pm, US$3-9) sits at the north entrance to town, next door to Beya Suites hotel. Expect a healthy haven of veggie, vegan, and fish options primarily. You can trust whatever Gomier recommends, as offers vary daily. The tiny restaurant cooks up tasty and creative daily specials, such as barbecued tofu served with baked beans, bread, and coleslaw,

Mayan Village Homestays

For the culturally curious traveler, the unique guesthouse and homestay programs in the Toledo District offer a threefold attraction: (1) firsthand observation of daily rural life in southern Belize; (2) a chance to interact with one of several proud distinct cultures while participating in a world-renowned model of ecotourism; and (3) a unique way to go deep into the lush natural world of the forests, rivers, caves, and waterfalls of southwestern Belize.

Simple guesthouse and family home networks in participating villages offer a range of conditions and privacy, but most are simple, primitive, and appreciated most by those with an open mind. Activities include tours of the villages and surrounding natural attractions. For nighttime entertainment, traditional dancing, singing, and music can usually be arranged; otherwise it's just stargazing and conversation.

These are poor villages, and the local brand of ecotourism provides an alternative to subsistence farming that entails slashing and burning the rainforest. Additionally, the community-controlled infrastructure helps ensure a more equitable distribution of tourism dollars than most tour operations (members rotate duties of guiding, preparing meals, and organizing activities).

Guests usually pay about US$11 for three meals. Breakfast in Mayan villages is generally eggs, homemade tortillas, and coffee or a cacao drink. All meals are indigenous fare, and lunch is the largest of the day; it is often chicken *caldo* (a soup cooked with Mayan herbs) or occasionally a local meat dish like iguana ("bush chicken") or gibnut (paca, a large rodent). Fresh tortillas round out the meal. Supper is the lightest meal of the day and generally includes "ground" food (a root vegetable such as potatoes) that the guide and visitors might harvest along the rainforest trail. The *comal* (tortilla grill) is always hot, and if you're invited, try your hand at making tortillas.

Families are located in the villages of Aguacate and San Jose:

- Contact Louis Cucul at the **Aguacate Belize Homestay Program** (Aguacate, tel. 501/633-9954, cucullouis@hotmail.com, www.aguacatebelize.com, US$9 pp per night, US$3.50 pp per meal, US$5 registration fee).

- Contact Justino Pec at the **San Jose Homestay Program** (San Jose, tel. 501/722-0109, cell tel. 501/668-7378, peck.justino@gmail.com).

---

plus a veggie grain casserole served with a salad (about US$5), a bulging soysage burger (US$3), delicious conch soup (in season), and tofu pizza. Other options include fresh local fruit juices (try the golden plum), soy milk, and soy ice cream. Ask Gomier about his vegan cooking classes.

Groceries

Check the **Supaul** store for local yogurt. Sophia Supaul's store on Alejandro Vernon Street (known locally as Green Supaul's, tel. 501/722-2089, 10am-7pm daily) carries imported cheeses (French brie in PG!), Mary's Yogurt (a must-try, in many flavors, including coconut), local jams and honey, a decent wine

selection, couscous, white chocolate, vegetables, and fruits.

ACCOMMODATIONS

Punta Gorda's few hotels and guesthouses occupy the blocks of Front Street near the main dock as well as a couple farther back; a good rule of thumb is not to book a room that is accessed via a smoky bar and pool hall. Quieter options are only a few blocks or a few minutes off the waterfront and an easy walk or bike ride away.

Under US$25

The solar-powered ★ **Ya'axché Field Station** (pronounced ya-chay, at Golden

Stream Field Station, Southern Hwy., tel. 501/722-0108 or 501/663-7128, www. ecotourismbelize.com/eco-bunkhouse-or-camp, US$20/bed, US$7.50/meal) now offers rustic accommodations on-site in a wooden house furnished with eight bunk beds—two of them are in a separate room within the larger space. Windows are screened, and outdoor baths and showers are available, including compost toilets. Lockers are available for valuables. You'll hear birds chirping in this verdant setting. Head out on one of two interpretive trails, relax in Ya'axché's main lounge area or shared kitchen, and mingle with expert conservationists, or set out for the day on one of the EcoTourism Belize experiences, all of which are close to the field station. Camping (US$5 per campsite) will likely be available by publication time (bring your own tent).

Nature's Way Guest House (65 Front St., tel. 501/702-2119, natureswayguesthouse@hotmail.com, US$19-24) is more akin to a hostel and has seen better days. Set at the back of a garden are six small, very basic fan-cooled guest rooms with bunk beds, all sharing baths. Three basic guest rooms have private baths and showers—don't expect too much. The place is run by Chet Schmidt, an American expat and Vietnam veteran who has been here for over four decades; he also spent 13 years teaching in the surrounding villages. He can help with information on Mayan and Garifuna village homestays.

US$25-50

St. Charles Inn (23 King St., tel. 501/722-2149, stcharlespg@btl.net, US$32.50, US$43.50 with a/c) is centrally located, with a dozen dated but generally clean guest rooms and a shady veranda that allows you to observe village life below. The guest rooms include springy mattresses, private baths, fans, and small TVs. Don't expect anything fancy, and it can get noisy at night—you get what you pay for.

As you leave the airport, you'll see the **Frontier Inn** (3 Airport St., tel. 501/722-2450, frontierinn@btl.net, US$35), a white two-story cement building. Twelve good-value, immaculate tile-floored guest rooms have TVs, wireless Internet, private baths, hot water, and colorful bedspreads and walls; there's even a standby generator. The place is owned by a local airplane pilot. It's a short two-minute bike ride from here to the center of town.

Tate's Guest House (34 Jose Maria Nunez St., tel. 501/722-0147, tatesguesthouse@yahoo.

Ya'axché Field Station

com, US$19-45) is set on the ground floor of a comfortable home with five double guest rooms in a quiet neighborhood setting—just be aware that the owner might give away your room to the first bidder even though you confirmed by email. Ask for room 4 or 5; they are spacious, with ceiling fans, TVs, sunrooms, louvered windows, and tile floors, and each has an additional entrance through the backyard. Internet access is available.

★ **Charlton's Inn** (9 Main St., 1 block from the Uno gas station, tel. 501/722-2197, www.charltonsinn.com, US$44) is a better option, close to everything in town, and there's a James Bus stop across the street. The 27 guest rooms are well kept, with hot and cold water, private baths, TVs, air-conditioning, wireless Internet, and fans; there are also nine furnished apartments available with monthly rates.

Located in a Mayan village just outside of town, and the best alternative for being surrounded by nature without shelling out on an expensive lodge, is **Big Falls Cottages** (Esperanza Rd., Big Falls Village, tel. 501/605-9985, www.bigfallscottages.com, US$47), which offers two cabins with beautiful garden views, set on a residential property. Amenities include kitchenettes, hot and cold showers, and porches.

US$50-100

One mile outside Punta Gorda, up Ex-Servicemen Road, award-winning ★ **Hickatee Cottages** (tel. 501/662-4475, www.hickatee.com, US$95-145) is a wonderful option near town yet on the edge of the rainforest. Your expatriate hosts Allison and Eduardo Gonzalez are simply wonderful and ready to show you their favorite part of Belize. The couple is passionate about immersing in cultural activities as well as running a green hotel with minimum environmental impact, from the food to maintaining a lush, pesticide-free rainforest environment that surrounds the cabins (you'll need mosquito repellent). The guesthouse also now runs off the grid, fully solar powered, with a backup

generator only for extreme cases. After you've settled into your well-appointed wooden cottage (there are six rooms, with private bath, hot water, hardwood furniture, ceiling fans, and veranda) or the honeymoon suite (more space, furnishings, and a kitchenette), take a walk through the beautiful grounds and nearly two miles of nature trails, followed by a dip in the plunge pool. You might even spot howler monkeys while having breakfast, like I did.

Hickatee Cottages is very popular with birders and naturalists; guests wander on a rainforest trail, participate in howler monkey research, watch orchid bees at work while having a cup of organic coffee, and observe the wild creatures of the night on the bug board. Bicycles are available to get to and from town. Ask about the included free visit to **Fallen Stones Butterfly Farm** (Wed. afternoon, advance reservations required, maximum 4 people)—an incredible opportunity for guests only. Also on-site, the Ex-Servicemen's Bar is where you can enjoy delicious home-cooked healthy meals made from the town's fresh produce (breakfast is continental and included, dinner US$20), including two-course table d'hôte dinners booked ahead (ask about their signature "Cacao three-ways" dessert) that rival the best farm-to-table restaurants. Pick up a book from the library in the main house, or enjoy the cultural nights, including a weekly Wednesday drumming show or lessons with Ray McDonald, a local Garifuna musician.

BlueBelize Guest House (tel. 501/722-2678, www.bluebelize.com, US$75-170 plus tax) offers five cozy suites—including one for honeymooners—that are large enough to feel like apartments and tastefully decorated, with one or two bedrooms, en suite baths, kitchenettes or full kitchens, hot and cold water, ceiling fans, lovely seating areas, and wireless Internet. The guest rooms open onto verandas or patios literally a stone's throw from the water's edge. Use of bikes is complimentary, as is continental breakfast, served on your veranda or in your suite. BlueBelize is popular with

PUNTA GORDA AND THE DEEP SOUTH
PUNTA GORDA AND VICINITY

visiting doctors, scientists, and volunteers, as well as travelers escaping cold dark winters up north.

US$100-150

Occupying a breezy, ocean-looking rise next to the hospital, Coral House Inn (151 Main St., tel. 501/722-2878, www.coralhouseinn. net, US$98-120) is an excellent seafront bed-and-breakfast with a small pool and bar and a quiet yard. It was opened after the owners drove to Belize from Idaho in their VW Microbus. The four guest rooms are pleasantly decorated with soft colors, local artwork, and comfortable beds; continental breakfast, use of bicycles, and wireless Internet are free for guests. This is where one of Belize's recent former prime ministers used to stay when in Punta Gorda. The living and dining rooms were being expanded as of publication time. Ask about the nearby Seaglass Cottage, a little one-bedroom, one-bath, small-kitchen option, pitched on a bluff above the ocean (US$125).

You can't miss the Sea Front Inn (4 Front St., tel. 501/722-2300, www.seafrontinn.com, US$119, includes continental breakfast) as you enter town: It comprises two towering stone buildings across the street from the sea. The 14 guest rooms and three apartments are also available for monthly rentals. Guests find comfortable, spacious guest rooms, no two alike, with TVs, fans, air-conditioning, private baths, and handmade furniture built with hardwoods. The third floor is the kitchen, dining room, and common area, overlooking the ocean.

Also on the waterfront, just before the bridge taking you into town, the Garinagu-owned Beya Suites (tel. 501/722-2188 or 501/722-2956, www.beyasuites.com, US$88-175) looks like a giant pink-and-white wedding cake. Inside you'll find cheery staff to show you to one of the comfortable, air-conditioned, tile-floored guest rooms with large baths and a sinus-clearing floral scent. There's a rooftop, a restaurant (breakfast only), a bar, a conference area, and fast Internet. Ask about apartments and weekly rates. Owner Darius Avila is the founder of the popular Battle of the Drums, an annual Garifuna cultural event held in Punta Gorda every November.

Over US$150

The area's sole rainforest-luxe property is Copal Tree Lodge (formerly Belcampo, Wilson Rd., tel. 501/722-0051, U.S. tel. 877/417-9478, www.copaltreelodge.com, US$179-359), atop a forested perch high above the Río Grande and a gorgeous expanse of rainforest, five miles north of PG. This is a unique spot targeting a unique market, and though it keeps changing hands, it remains relatively the same. The property encompasses 12,000 acres of rainforest and organic citrus, coffee, and cacao farms, including 4.5 miles of riverfront (reached by a rainforest elevator!) and Nicholas Caye, a pristine island in the Sapodilla Cayes. The sea is a 20-minute boat ride down the river, where you'll head for your sportfishing and snorkeling tours. Amenities include a pool, a farm-to-fork restaurant, use of kayaks and mountain bikes, a breakaway sitting room and veranda, and a spa as well as a screened rainforest veranda in your King or Queen Jungle tree house suite (there are 12); you may see a brightly colored toucan from your shower window or get a wakeup call from a howler monkey. The newer Signature Canopy Suites that are reached via tram offer respite from other guests, with a private infinity pool, and huge private terraces for incredible views from the rainforest to the Maya Mountains and the sea.

INFORMATION AND SERVICES
Visitor Information
Look for the Toledo Tourism Information Center (46 Front St., tel. 501/722-2531, btiatoledo@btl.net, 8:30am-4:30pm Mon.-Fri., 8:30am-noon Sat.), not far from the town dock and run by the Belize Tourism Industry Association. This is a concerted effort by local businesses to provide excellent and organized

information to visitors; staff will recommend accommodations, tour companies, transportation, and more. You can pick up a print copy of the *Toledo Howler,* a local magazine published by the BTIA, for upcoming events and updated transportation schedules, often including a recent map of the area.

Near the municipal dock, you'll find the **Immigration Office** (tel. 501/722-2247, 8am-close daily) for departures to and arrivals from Guatemala and Honduras. The departure tax is US$15 if you spent up to 24 hours in Belize, plus the US$4 PACT fee if you've been here longer.

Banks
The **Belize Bank** (tel. 501/722-2326, 8am-3pm Mon.-Thurs., 8am-4:30pm Fri.) is right across from the town square and has an ATM. Continue one block south for **Scotiabank** (8am-2:30pm Mon.-Thurs., 8am-4pm Fri., 9am-11:30am Sat.), which has a 24-hour international ATM. **Grace's Restaurant** (Main St., tel. 501/702-2414, 6:30am-10:30pm daily) is also a licensed *casa de cambio* (money changer) and can change dollars, Guatemalan quetzales, or traveler's checks. You may also find a freelance money changer hanging around the dock at boat time.

Health and Emergencies
Punta Gorda has a **police department** (tel. 501/722-2022), a **fire department** (tel. 501/722-2032), and a **hospital** (tel. 501/722-2026 or 501/722-2161) for emergencies. **NJV's Pharmacy** (Front St., tel. 501/722-2177, 8am-1pm and 4pm-8pm Mon.-Sat.) is a well-stocked drugstore, with everything from a pharmacy to books and office supplies.

Media and Communications
Opposite the Immigration Office are a couple of government buildings, including the **post office.** There are two Internet places just north of the park on Main Street, both with nice air-conditioning and decent machines: **Dreamlight Computer Center** (Main St. and North St., tel. 501/702-0113 or 501/607-0033, dreamlightpg@yahoo.com, 6:30am-8:30pm Mon.-Sat., 9am-1pm Sun., first hour US$1.50, US$2 per hour thereafter) and **V-Comp Technologies** (29 Main St., tel. 501/722-0093 or 501/601-0342, 8am-8:30pm daily, US$1.50 per hour), a nice operation with printing, copying, scanning, and even DVDs for sale.

TRANSPORTATION
If you're coming to the area by bus, plan on nearly a full day of travel on either end of your trip south (at least 5 or 6 hours from Belize City). Consider taking the quick flight from Belize City, Placencia, or Dangriga to Punta Gorda.

Getting There
AIR
Daily southbound flights from Belize City to Dangriga continue to Placencia and then to Punta Gorda. This is the quickest and most comfortable way to get to PG. For the return trip, **Tropic Air** (tel. 501/226-2626, U.S. tel. 800/422-3435, www.tropicair.com) and **Maya Island Air** (tel. 501/671-2190, www.mayaislandair.com) each offer flights to Placencia, Dangriga, and Belize City between 6:30am and 4pm daily.

CAR AND BUS
Punta Gorda is just under 200 miles from Belize City, a long haul by bus, even with the newly surfaced Southern Highway speeding things up. Count on 3-4 hours by car, 5-6 hours by express bus, or 7 hours on a non-express bus. **James Bus Lines** (tel. 501/722-2049, www.jamesbusline.com) has a centrally located terminal in Punta Gorda, at King and Main Streets, and runs up to 10 buses daily between Punta Gorda and Belize City, departing 3:50am-3:50pm Sunday-Friday, with one express at 6am. It now offers free on-board Wi-Fi with the express ride. The first departure from Belize City is a 5:30am express, and then service continues until 3:45pm; the only other express is this last bus of the day. The fare is US$11 one-way. The James Bus makes a

loop through PG before heading out of town. A few other bus lines make the trip, but much less regularly. Be sure to ask around about schedules the day before you leave.

Remember that you can get off in Independence and take a boat to Placencia, or you can get off at any other point, like Cockscomb Maya Centre (Cockscomb Basin Wildlife Sanctuary) or Dangriga.

Getting Around

Ask your hotel if it provides free use of a bicycle, or rent one at **Gomier's Restaurant** (5 Alejandro Vernon St., tel. 501/722-2929, 11am-2pm and 5pm-10pm Mon.-Sat.), near the entrance to Punta Gorda (US$10 per day). It's a great way to navigate the town, which can sometimes be a tad spread out on foot.

BUS

Every day has a different schedule, but buses go to the Mayan villages on Monday, Wednesday, Friday, and Saturday, generally around 11am, departing from Jose Maria Nunez Street (between Prince St. and Queen St.). From here it's possible to get to **Golden Stream, Silver Creek, San Pedro, San Miguel, Aguacate, Blue Creek, San Antonio,** and other villages. Some buses drop you off at the entrance road, leaving a walk of a mile or two. It's possible to make it a day trip and return later in the afternoon. Check the Toledo Tourism Information Center on Front Street for updated village bus schedules, or grab a copy of the latest *Toledo Howler* newspaper in town.

TAXI

Punta Gorda's taxis will take you anywhere within city limits for about US$3-4; look for their green license plates. It's US$10 to drive the six miles to Belcampo and US$12.50 to Jacintoville. Or you can call on **Jonathan Supaul** (tel. 501/669-4823 or 501/628-0460, 5am-10pm daily). Also try **Castro's Taxi** (tel. 501/602-3632).

Islands Near Punta Gorda

The Toledo District is the gateway to the least visited of Belize's offshore Caribbean islands—the Snake Cayes and the Sapodilla Cayes. For those who make the time and take the chance to venture this far south, the snorkeling and dive sites are rewarding, and with fewer boats (if any at all), you're likely to be one of the few out in the water. It's no exaggeration to say that you'll have the entire last end of the Belize Barrier Reef to yourself. Just be sure not to attempt the boat journey from Punta Gorda in rough weather. On a glorious day, this is as close as you can get to paradise.

Closest to Punta Gorda, a mere 30-minute boat ride away, are the **Snake Cayes,** part of the Port Honduras Marine Reserve. These are ideal for snorkeling, diving, and swimming, thanks to protected no-take zones. These islands, along with the remoter **Sapodilla Cayes,** are not one bit about luxury—it's about adventure and experiencing Belize's nature and barrier reef at its best, with simple accommodations on two cayes and plenty of neighboring plots to explore above or under the water. Relax in a phone- and Internet-free environment in your cabin or campsite at **Lime Caye,** and crash in basic rooms on **Hunting Caye,** home to one of Belize's most stunning beaches. You might not even use your room, it's that pretty outside. Try to stay at least two days in the Sapodilla Cayes area if you're heading that far. The Snake Cayes are an easy day trip from either Punta Gorda or the Sapodilla Cayes.

PORT HONDURAS MARINE RESERVE

The limits of the **Port Honduras Marine Reserve** (park fee US$5 pp) begin just three

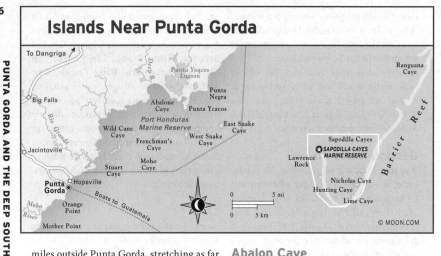

Islands Near Punta Gorda

To Dangriga
Big Falls
Jacintoville
Punta Gorda
Hopeville
Orange Point
Mother Point
Rio Grande
Moho River
Boats to Guatemala
Deep R.
Punta Yoqcos Lagoon
Abalone Caye
Port Honduras Marine Reserve
Wild Cane Caye
Frenchman's Caye
Stuart Caye
Moho Caye
West Snake Caye
Punta Negra
Punta Ycacos
East Snake Caye
Lawrence Rock
Sapodilla Cayes
SAPODILLA CAYES MARINE RESERVE
Ranguana Caye
Barrier Reef
Nicholas Caye
Hunting Caye
Lime Caye
0   5 mi
0   5 km
© MOON.COM

miles outside Punta Gorda, stretching as far as 160 square miles and encompassing mangrove forests and approximately 138 mangrove islands, plenty of fresh water from five rivers that flow into the reserve, and, in the distance, a seven-hill range with its peaks towering over the reserve. The **Snake Cayes** and a few other gorgeous islands are accessible for top-notch snorkeling and sportfishing—you'll likely notice private yachts on your way across the reserve, as top anglers head here for the best fly-fishing in the area, dubbed "the permit capital" of the world, not just Belize.

The Port Honduras Marine Reserve is comanaged and funded by the nonprofit **Toledo Institute for Development and Environment** (TIDE, tel. 501/722-2274, info@tidebelize.org), based in Punta Gorda. Its marine conservation efforts in the area are significant, the most notable of which has been the protection of, and increase in, the number of West Indian manatees. Seven years after gaining protected status, the reserve now boasts the second-largest population of these gentle sea cows. The park rangers play an important part in monitoring illegal fishing activity and removing gill nets, as well as protecting Middle Snake Caye, a strictly no-entry caye used for monitoring mangroves and marinelife research.

Abalon Caye

Your first stop in the Port Honduras Marine Reserve may be at **Abalon Caye,** in the center of the reserve. Abalon Caye is home to the ranger station and six full-time rangers. It's a great place to learn about the area, part of a World Heritage Site along with the Belize Barrier Reef. Whatever you do, don't miss climbing up the 60-foot-tall ranger station's **observation tower,** used to spot vessel activity. A steep, narrow wooden staircase leads to views of the reserve. The 180-degree panorama includes the Snake Cayes as well as neighboring Guatemala and even the Cockscomb range.

Snake Cayes

Shortly past Abalon Caye, you'll spot four plots in the distance, almost aligned from left to right. They are East Snake Caye, Middle Snake Caye, West Snake Caye, and South Snake Caye. Boa constrictors once lived here, hence the name.

The **Snake Cayes** make up the main area of the reserve used for daytime recreation purposes only—swimming, snorkeling, diving, and sportfishing—except for **Middle Snake Caye,** which is a strictly off-limits zone to everyone except researchers, with boats not being allowed to come 0.5 mile of the island.

The three accessible plots, ranging 1-2

acres, offer an incredible marine environment of healthy corals and reef fish on this end of the Belize Barrier Reef and are a worthwhile day trip from Punta Gorda. Snorkel stops include South Snake and East Snake, before ending at West Snake for swimming.

At two acres, **West Snake Caye** (also called Lagoon Snake Caye) has a beautiful white-sand beach—the only one among these islands—facing a turquoise stretch of water 250 feet wide and 3.5 feet deep for ideal swimming. Even if you're not snorkeling, it's great for all-around frolicking in a natural pool. There's a *palapa* on-site for barbecues, and not much else except glorious fine sand, making this one of the most romantic southern islands and fun daytime hangout spots.

South Snake Caye tops all for marinelife, with stunning schools of fish hovering amid bright corals. You'll need your underwater camera, as you'll likely gasp at the sight and abundance of fish in these parts, thriving in crystal-clear waters at relatively shallow depths. Giant barracuda, Caesar grunts, permits, schoolmasters, dog snappers, angelfish, porkfish, and porcupinefish are among the numerous species in these parts. **East Snake Caye,** home to a lighthouse, is popular for its stunning coral gardens.

When you get in or out of the boat on snorkel trips, keep your eyes peeled for spotted rays leaping up to one foot out of the water.

TOP EXPERIENCE

★ SAPODILLA CAYES MARINE RESERVE

One of the seven wonders of the Belize Barrier Reef Reserve System and the most southern of Belize's protected areas, the **Sapodilla Cayes Marine Reserve** (park fee US$10 pp, paid at Hunting Caye) is as remote as it gets. Few people make it out here from the mainland; most visitors venture over from neighboring Honduras and Guatemala, as well as a few locals from Placencia. Located 35 miles or 1.5 hours by boat from the shores of Punta Gorda—or an additional 45-minute ride from the Snake Cayes—it might seem like quite the trek (don't even attempt it on a cloudy, choppy day), but it's not that far to go for top-notch snorkeling and diving, gorgeous white-sand beaches on **Lime Caye** and **Hunting Caye**—the two available islands for overnight stays—and an overall stunning landscape of deep turquoise waters, flocking birds, and marinelife. These make it worth the extra journeying.

The reserve—comanaged by the Fisheries Department and the **Southern Environmental Association** (SEA, tel. 501/523-3377, www.seabelize.org)—covers approximately 80 square miles and is divided into a preservation zone, a conservation zone, a general use zone, and special management areas. It's also home to approximately 14 mangrove and sandy islands, many of which are privately owned, spread across its clear waters. The sandy islands are considered to be among the most beautiful of Belize's Southern Cayes, and I agree wholeheartedly.

This last edge and boundary of the Belize Barrier Reef forms a hook, or J-shaped curve, within which the Sapodilla Cayes are clustered. This is an area teeming with underwater life, where a ray jumping out of the sea or a loggerhead turtle swimming right up to the beach at sunset is no rare sight.

The reserve protects several endangered species, such as the West Indian manatee, three turtle species—with designated turtle-nesting beaches at Hunting and Lime Cayes—and over a dozen fish species. To add to its uniqueness, the Sapodilla Cayes Marine Reserve counts spawning aggregation sites, with whale shark sightings every year.

The rare scalloped hammerhead has been spotted here in the summer season.

Lime Caye

Owned and operated by the Garbutt family, who run the successful **Garbutt's Marine and Fishing Lodge** (tel. 501/722-0070, cell tel. 501/604-3548, www.garbuttsfishinglodge. com, 2-day package US$345, 4-day package US$700, includes cabin, all meals, snorkeling,

transportation, and park fee) based in Punta Gorda, this no frills gorgeous 3.5-acre island and hotel is your best bet for an overnight stay in these parts.

An often deserted soft white-sand beach—a designated turtle-nesting site—will greet you upon arrival, while the rest of the island is white sand shaded by grape trees and coconut trees.

Stays range 2-6 days in one of five no-frills wooden cabins painted in bright pastel colors. Two larger front cabins hold a mixture of bunk beds and a double bed for up to six people. The bathrooms are en suite, with clean and rustic shower tubs and toilets. Farther to the edge of the beach is a sea-facing wooden bunk-bed house, ideal for groups of 16—baths are of the shared outdoor variety.

For more privacy, opt for one of two stand-alone yet basic **reef-facing cabanas on stilts** at the very back of the island, ideal for couples or solo travelers. These are nothing more than a double bed, a nightstand, and shutters, but the atmosphere is cozy and the porch offers stunning views of the reef crest ahead, where the sun rises. Shared toilets and showers are a short walk away from the cabin. Bring sufficient towels as well as a rain jacket, as it can get cool in the mornings and evenings in high season. If you're up for it, you can get even closer to the elements by camping on the island (US$10 pp).

Haphazardly placed hammocks and iguanas shuffling in distant mangrove trees at the beach's end add to this remote, deserted island feel. Be sure to miss neither the sunset nor the sunrise, both of which are visible from the island—quite a rare treat.

Sanny's Kitchen, run by the lovely Sandra Garbutt, is on-site, serving delicious daily meals that are enjoyed family-style on outdoor picnic tables three times a day. They consist of fresh seafood and Belizean specialties as well as classic cocktails. You'll likely spend time reading prior guests' messages and

1: Sapodilla Cayes Marine Reserve; 2: a cabin on Lime Caye

signatures along the dining area's wood pillars and walls.

On Sunday, a local family or two might occasionally show up from Placencia for the day, unless a group reserves the caye in its entirety. Activities from Lime Caye—besides tanning, swimming, and strolling around the island—include diving, fly-fishing, and snorkeling.

Hunting Caye

Under five minutes from Lime Caye is **Hunting Caye,** known for having one of the most beautiful crescent-shaped white-sand beaches in Belize, accented by a lighthouse.

A turtle nesting site, the island serves as a base for staff from the Belize Coast Guard, Port Authority, Fisheries Department (rangers), a lighthouse keeper, and the University of Belize (UB). Because of this, the island has a fun local vibe. You'll hear *punta* music in the background and voices chatting in Kriol.

Luckily, UB does rent out its **basic double-bed rooms** to visitors (contact Victor Jacobs, tel. 501/602-4546, vrrjacobs@ yahoo.cm or vjacobs@ub.edu, US$40 pp). Camping (US$5 pp) is allowed with your own tent. There's a large kitchen for use onsite, if groups choose to cook for themselves. Otherwise, on-site meals are available with advance notice.

Hunting Caye feels a lot more spread out than Lime Caye, but it's equally laid-back and charming, with a small crowd of locals who live here. If you're staying on Lime Caye, ask for a ride to Hunting Caye for an hour or more of lounging on that gorgeous beach.

If you get the chance, meet the lighthouse keeper, Domingo Lewis, an interesting character who served 25 years in the British army and has interesting travel tales to share.

Diving and Snorkeling

There's little doubt that this deep southern area of Belize offers some of the best visibility for snorkeling and diving. Few make it this far, but those who do will have an entire reserve to themselves.

The Shipwreck is right off Lime Caye,

a 10- to 15-foot-deep dive site where you'll spot abundant marinelife—blue tangs, white grunts, angelfish, butterfly fish, lionfish, schoolmasters, and vibrant coral—surrounding a massive sunken ship. There are colorful schools of fish and amazing clarity, even in cloudy weather. The waters surrounding **Ragged Caye** offer decent snorkeling.

Lime Caye Wall is a top dive site, with plenty of big fish, such as groupers, snappers, giant spiny lobsters, and moray eels. Whale sharks also pass by here, in season.

Snorkelers will be equally amazed at the health and brilliance of the coral and the spectacular Caribbean waters, with those vibrant turquoise hues, similar to those surrounding Belize's atolls. They wash over lush coral gardens, densely packed and teeming with fish life. At **Vigilante Shoal,** right off Hunting Caye, you'll spot densely packed corals, many in giant form, at a depth of barely eight feet. Within a hand's breadth, you'll spot huge spiny lobsters, 15-pound dog snappers, blue hamlets, blue tangs, bluehead wrasses, rock beauty fish, and other Caribbean reef species, like the stoplight parrotfish, sergeant majors, and angelfish. Impossible to miss are the massive mountainous star corals, pillar corals, and grooved brain coral. No other boats showed up while my guide and I snorkeled at our leisure.

Garbutt's Marine and Fishing Lodge (tel. 501/722-0070, cell tel. 501/604-3548, www.garbuttsfishinglodge.com) offers a range of trips, from snorkeling to "Discover Scuba" courses and fishing.

REEF CONSERVATION INTERNATIONAL

If you're looking for a vacation that combines conservation education and recreation, **Reef Conservation International** (ReefCI, tel. 501/626-1429, www.reefci.com, divers US$1,330 per week, nondivers US$1,025 per week, all-inclusive) offers weekly and monthly dive trips to stay on **Tom Owens Caye,** a small one-acre private island in the Sapodilla Cayes with incredible snorkeling. The boat leaves Punta Gorda on Monday morning and returns on Friday afternoon. Reef Conservation offers scuba certification courses. It's worth stressing that not only will you be diving in the Sapodilla Cayes, but you'll also most likely be the only dive boat in the water (nondivers are also welcome). ReefCI offers various packages; there's often a discount for walk-in travelers and last-minute bookings. ReefCI customers have the opportunity to get involved in a number of projects, such as helping with the removal of the invasive lionfish and other preservation projects in the Sapodilla Cayes Marine Reserve. They also have the unique opportunity to get involved with the survey work, learn about the environment, and identify fish, coral, and invertebrates—and to combine this with recreational dives and other activities.

TRANSPORTATION

You'll find it more affordable to get to the Snake Cayes or the Sapodilla Cayes for a day trip when there's a group of at least four people heading out. Check your dates with **Garbutt's Marine and Fishing Lodge** (tel. 501/722-0070, cell tel. 501/604-3548, www.garbuttsfishinglodge.com) or with **TIDE** (tel. 501/722-2274, info@tidebelize.org), both solid transfer options; they can keep you posted on availability and tour dates. If you're staying on Lime Caye, the Garbutts will arrange for your transportation to and from the resort.

Maya Upcountry

The wild, unique, and stunning southwestern chunk of Belize is referred to as "upcountry" or simply "the villages." The Toledo District settlements to the west of Punta Gorda are home to Q'eqchi' or Mopan Maya, whose descendants fled to Belize to escape oppression and forced labor in their native Guatemala. Anthropologists now believe that the Mopan were probably the original inhabitants of Belize, but that they were forcibly removed by the Spanish in the late 17th century. The Q'eqchi' were close neighbors with the Mopan and the Manche Ch'ol, a Mayan group completely exterminated by the Spanish. The older folks continue to maintain longtime traditional farming methods, culture, and dress. Modern machinery is sparse—they use simple digging sticks and machetes to till the soil, and water is hand-carried to the fields during dry spells. It's not an easy life.

On the outskirts of each town, the dwellings are relatively primitive; they often have open doorways covered by a hanging cloth, hammocks, and dirt floors, and animals may wander throughout. People use primitive latrines or just take a walk into the rainforest. They bathe in the nearest creek or river, a routine that becomes a source of fun as much as cleanliness.

Within the towns, past the thatched homes on each side of the road, it becomes apparent that the effects of modern conveniences are only beginning to arrive. When a family can finally afford electricity, the first things that appear are a couple of lights and a refrigerator—the latter allows the family to earn a few dollars by selling chilled soft drinks and such. After that, it's a television set; you can see folks sitting in open doorways, their faces lit by the light inside.

SAN FELIPE AND JACINTOVILLE

Closest to Punta Gorda, Jacintoville is just seven miles out of town, traveling along the Southern Highway. From there, a side road heading south leads to the village of San Felipe. (This same road will also eventually get you to Barranco.)

Ixcacao Maya Belizean Chocolate (formerly Cyrila's Chocolate, tel. 501/742-4050, cell tel. 501/660-2840, www.ixcacaomayabelizeanchocolate.com, US$32.50 for 2 people) in the village of San Felipe offers a five-hour chocolate tour beginning with a visit to an organic cacao farm and continuing with lunch in Cyrila's home. She and her daughter then lead a chocolate-making session.

Tucked away on the San Felipe Road, about eight miles outside Punta Gorda, ★ **Chaab'il B'e Lodge & Casitas** (formerly Tranquility Lodge, Mile 9, Southern Hwy., tel. 501/665-9070, www.chaabilbe.com, US$110-125) offers well-appointed deluxe rooms and casitas popular with avid bird-watchers and orchid lovers; both have plenty to explore right here on 20 lush acres (only 5 of which are developed at the lodge area). There were 75 species of orchids at last count—both planted and volunteers—and more than 200 identified species of birds. Rates include breakfast; guest rooms have clean tile floors, private baths, air-conditioning, and fans. When there are no other guests, it's like having your own private lodge. Upstairs from the guest rooms is a beautiful screened-in (but very open) dining room, where you'll enjoy gourmet dinners (US$15-25). There's direct access to an excellent swimming hole on the Jacinto River, as well as a number of walking trails.

Cotton Tree Lodge (tel. 501/670-0557,

Mayan Upcountry

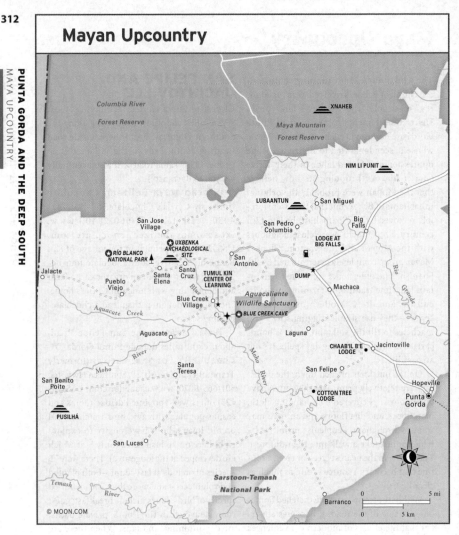

Columbia River
Forest Reserve

Maya Mountain
Forest Reserve

XNAHEB

NIM LI PUNIT

LUBAANTUN   San Miguel

San Jose
Village

San Pedro
Columbia   Big
Falls

UXBENKA
ARCHAEOLOGICAL
SITE

RÍO BLANCO
NATIONAL PARK

San
Antonio

LODGE AT
BIG FALLS

Jalacte

Pueblo
Viejo

Santa
Elena

Santa
Cruz

TUMUL KIN
CENTER OF
LEARNING

Blue

DUMP

Machaca

Río

Aguacaliente
Wildlife Sanctuary

Grande

Aguacate Creek

Blue Creek
Village

BLUE CREEK CAVE

Creek

Aguacate

Laguna

Moho   River

Santa
Teresa

Moho River

CHAAB'IL B'E
LODGE   Jacintoville

San Benito
Poite

San Felipe

Hopeville

PUSILHÁ

COTTON TREE
LODGE

Punta
Gorda

San Lucas

Temash   River

Sarstoon-Temash
National Park

Barranco

0   5 mi

0   5 km

© MOON.COM

U.S. tel. 212/529-8622, www.cottontreelodge. com, US$196-273, from US$419 pp all-inclusive) is 12 miles up the Moho River from PG, between Santa Ana and San Felipe Mayan villages. Its deluxe cabanas along the river's edge boast private balconies with stunning views. Cotton Tree produces the famous Cotton Tree chocolate, conducts voluntourism projects with Sustainable Harvest International, has developed a unique septic system using banana plants, and raises a good portion of the food it serves in its own organic garden. Available activities include the Cacao Trail, treks to Blue Creek Cave, mountain hikes, river and village trips, visits to ruins, spa treatments on-site, plus hands-on classes in subjects like chocolate making and Garifuna drumming. Sportfishing and fly-fishing trips are available as well. There is one honeymoon suite with a jetted tub and one cabin with wheelchair access.

The Unspoiled South: Toledo's Conservation Trail

Belize has the highest percentage of forest cover in Central America and the largest barrier reef system in the western hemisphere. These rich natural resources have survived relatively intact, primarily due to Belize having the lowest population density in the Central American region. This enviable status, however, is at risk, particularly in the south, where the country's most pristine environment—in the lush Toledo District—is faced with rapid population growth and immigration, combined with increasing deforestation and illegal fishing along marine and terrestrial borders.

Nonetheless, the Toledo District has managed to fight back and continues to rise as an example in protecting its fragile ecosystems. Since the late 20th century, conservation efforts in the heavily forested and biodiverse district have strengthened. As early as the 1990s, commercial interest from Malaysian logging was met with fierce resistance from local indigenous activists. The bulldozing of Toledo's forests had damaged drinking water supplies, leading to opposition from downstream communities. The late Mayan leader Julian Cho organized and led resistance to unsustainable logging on traditional Mayan land. The government of Belize responded by canceling these companies' licenses.

More recent conservation efforts owe successes to the implementation and use of a comanagement program, created by the Belizean government, whereby areas designated officially "protected"—such as the 100,000-acre no-public-access Bladen Nature Reserve—are monitored by nongovernmental organizations and residents of communities close to these protected areas, all working together and sharing in the financial burden of accomplishing the gigantic task. This comanagement system promotes both sustainable development and conservation, helping the local communities who depend on the health and sustainability of these resources.

Of note is former Minister of Forestry, Fisheries, and Sustainable Development Lisel Alamilla and her 2012 moratorium on the logging of rosewood from Toledo's forests. A few busts of illegal harvesting have since been made but efforts continue to prevent them.

Toledo has unique tropical forests and pristine coral reefs that provide livelihoods to the most culturally diverse population in Belize. If the protection of its resources continues in this vein, this district can be a globally recognized example of sustainable development.

Contributed by Lee McLoughlin, former manager of the Protected Areas Management Program at Ya'axché Conservation Trust

LAGUNA

Laguna is a small Q'eqchi' Mayan village of around 250 people living against a backdrop of limestone karst hills. The village is home to howler monkeys and many types of parrots, which can be seen flying over the village daily. Laguna is also home to a loosely organized women's crafts group that produces *cuxtales* (pronounced CUSH-ta-les, traditional woven Mayan bags), table mats, beading, baskets, embroidery, beaded necklaces, and earrings. There is a long, muddy farmers road that leads to the confluence of Blue Creek and the Moho River; this two- to three-hour hike is very beautiful but only recommended in the dry season (Mar.-May). There's also a super-cool

cave about a 20-minute hike away; it's really best to have a licensed guide with you. Inquire with Toleda Cave and Adventure Tours (tel. 501/604-2124, www.tcatours.com) or any tour company listed in this chapter.

To get to the village, take the Laguna bus directly to the village, or take any bus that can drop you at the Laguna junction (10 miles from Punta Gorda). It is only about three miles to the village from the highway.

BIG FALLS

Hugging a lush bend of the Río Grande as it sweeps near the roadside village of Big Falls, ★ **The Lodge at Big Falls** (tel. 501/732-4444 or 501/610-0126, www.

The Skull of Doom: Mystery Solved

In 1924, Anna Mitchell-Hedges, the daughter of explorer F. A. Mitchell-Hedges, allegedly found a perfectly formed quartz crystal skull at the Lubaantun archaeological site on her 17th birthday. The object has been the subject of much mystery and controversy over the years. Was it made by the Maya to conjure death? Atlanteans? Aliens? Did Mitchell-Hedges plant it for the pleasure of his daughter? Is the whole story a hoax?

The world got its answer in 2007 when the Smithsonian Institute put the Mitchell-Hedges skull under a scanning electron microscope. Researcher Jane MacLaren Walsh concluded, "This object was carved and polished using modern, high-speed, diamond-coated, rotary cutting and polishing tools of minute dimensions. This technology is certainly not pre-Columbian. I believe it is decidedly 20th century."

The skull currently resides in North America with the widower of Anna Mitchell-Hedges. Despite the Smithsonian's findings, some still warned of dire consequences if the skull was not returned to Lubaantun by December 21, 2012, but that also proved untrue.

thelodgeatbigfalls.com, US$206-229) is an elegant and quiet retreat in a peaceful, well-maintained green clearing. The nine cabanas are ideal for a nature-loving couple looking for a comfortable base from which to explore the surrounding country or just to laze in the pool and listen to the forest sounds. Special rates are offered for multiple nights and for families; it's a 20-minute drive to the town of Punta Gorda, and many day trips are available, as the Lodge at Big Falls is centrally located in the Toledo District.

Sun Creek Lodge (Mile 14, Southern Hwy., tel. 501/607-6363, www.suncreeklodge.de, US$60-120, includes full breakfast) offers three renovated octagonal cabanas and two villas with central posts and thatched roofs. Some have shared rainforest showers and toilets, a few have private baths, and the spacious Sun Creek Suite is for families or groups. Camping is available (US$5 tent/hammock per night). The lodge can help arrange for a myriad of tours in the area, from birding to caving. It also provides rental cars.

If you're driving through the area, make time for lunch (or any other meal) in Big Falls at **Coleman's Café** (tel. 501/630-4432 or 501/720-2017, 11am-4pm and 6pm-9pm daily, buffet US$7.50), just off the highway on the entrance road to Rice Mill. This is home-cooked Belizean food at its finest, and the restaurant is run by a friendly and accommodating family. Creole dishes, cohune cabbage, and East Indian curries are among the offerings. It even has free changing restrooms for those who need to get dry from their tours and grab a cold one.

NIM LI PUNIT ARCHAEOLOGICAL SITE

Near the village of Indian Creek, **Nim Li Punit** (Mile 75, Southern Hwy., tel. 501/665-5126, 8am-5pm daily, US$5) is atop a hill with expansive views of the surrounding forests and mountains. The site saw preliminary excavations in 1970 that documented a 30-foot-tall carved stela (stone monument), the tallest ever found in Belize—and among the tallest in the Mayan world. A total of about 25 stelae have been found on the site, most dated to AD 700-800. Although looters have damaged the site, excavations by archaeologist Richard Leventhal in 1986 and by the Belize Institute of Archaeology (NICH) in the late 1990s and early 2000s uncovered several new stelae and some notable tombs. The stelae and artifacts are displayed in the very nice visitors center built by the IOA.

Nim Li Punit is 25 miles north of Punta Gorda; it's about 0.5 mile west of the highway, along a narrow road marked by a small sign.

LUBAANTUN ARCHAEOLOGICAL SITE

On a ridge between two creeks, Lubaantun (Place of the Fallen Stones) consists of five layers of construction and is unique compared to other sites due to the absence of engraved stelae. The site was first reported in 1875 by American Civil War refugees from the southern United States and was first studied in 1915. It is believed that as many as 20,000 people lived in this former trading center.

Lubaantun was built and occupied during the Late Classic Period (AD 730-890). Eleven major structures are grouped around five main plazas—in total the site has 18 plazas and three ball courts. The tallest structure rises 50 feet above the plaza, and from it you can see the Caribbean Sea, 20 miles distant. Lubaantun's disparate architecture is completely different from Mayan construction in other parts of Latin America.

Most of the structures are terraced, and you'll notice that some corners are rounded—an uncommon feature throughout the Mundo Maya. Lubaantun has been studied and surveyed several times by Thomas Gann and, more recently, in 1970 by Norman Hammond. Distinctive clay whistle figurines (similar to those found in Mexico's Isla Jaina) illustrate lifestyles and occupations of the era. Other artifacts include the mysterious crystal skull, obsidian blades, grinding stones (much like those still used today to grind corn), beads, shells, turquoise, and shards of pottery. From all of this, archaeologists have determined that the city flourished until the 8th century AD. It was a farming community that traded with the highland areas of today's Guatemala, and the people worked the sea and maybe the cayes just offshore.

To reach Lubaantun from Punta Gorda, drive 1.5 miles west past the gas station to the Southern Highway, then take a right. Two miles farther, you'll come to the village of San Pedro. From here, go left around the church to the concrete bridge. Cross and drive almost one mile—the road is passable during the dry season. The entrance fee is US$5.

SAN PEDRO COLUMBIA

San Pedro is one of the biggest of the villages and is home to well-known Mayan musicians as well as Eladio Pop's Cacao Trail. A small Catholic church in town has an equally small cemetery; it sits on a hilltop surrounded by a few thatched dwellings.

Eladio Pop's Cacao Trail is a fantastic experience. Eladio is a one-of-a-kind Maya who will take you all over his farm and show you how the Maya once made chocolate, from the cacao tree all the way to his home, where his wife will roast, grind, and make hot chocolate the old-fashioned way. Contact **Toledo Cave and Adventure Tours** (tel. 501/604-2124, www.tcatours.com) to arrange a trip to Eladio's.

Two miles upriver from San Pedro Columbia you'll find **Maya Mountain Research Farm** (MMRF, tel. 501/630-4386, www.mmrfbz.org), a registered NGO and working demonstration farm situated on 70 acres. Maya Mountain promotes sustainable agriculture, renewable energy, appropriate technology, and food security using permaculture principles and applied biodiversity. The farm also operates on solar power and offers courses. The property has more than 500 species of plants (including lots of cacao), and the staff are working to establish an ethnobotanical garden of useful plants with their Q'eqchi' Mayan names and uses. Accommodations are simple rustic affairs, with solar lighting and Internet access.

From the turnoff for Punta Gorda at Mile 86 on the Southern Highway, take the road north. At about Mile 1.5, a turnoff on the right heads for San Pedro Columbia and other villages. The **Chun Bus** makes the run from Punta Gorda to nearby San Antonio (11:30am Mon.-Sat., about US$4 round-trip) but doesn't stop in San Pedro Columbia; instead you will have to get off the bus at the road and trek in several miles.

SAN MIGUEL

This friendly Q'eqchi' Mayan village has a village guesthouse, a nearby river, thatched

houses, and people in traditional dress carrying dishes and clothes (in buckets on their heads) from the swiftly flowing river. San Miguel is also experiencing intense change with recent access to electricity, water, better roads, and increased educational opportunities. During times when the villagers are harvesting coffee, you can witness the process of picking, shelling, drying, and grinding organic coffee. Tours of the village, cave, and milpa are also available. All activities are US$3.50 per hour. The Mayan site of Lubaantun, famous for the discovery of the "crystal skull" and unique architectural features, is about three miles from San Miguel. You can either walk to the site or charter a vehicle (US$7.50). The village does not have a restaurant, but meals are cooked and served at local homes (breakfast or dinner US$3.25, lunch US$4).

San Miguel buses leave Punta Gorda three times a day Monday-Saturday. You can catch the village bus on Jose Maria Nunez Street. The first bus leaves at 11:30am and is marked "Silver Creek." The bus has a 30-minute layover in Silver Creek before heading on to San Miguel. The other buses are also marked "Silver Creek" and leave the park at 4pm and 4:30pm. The bus ride is about 1.5 hours. Buses leave San Miguel for Punta Gorda at 6am, 12:30pm, and 1pm Monday-Saturday.

SAN ANTONIO TO SANTA CRUZ

The village of San Antonio is famous for its exquisite traditional Q'eqchi' embroidery. However, the younger generation is being whisked right along into 21st-century Belizean society, so who knows how much longer it will survive. Contact **Toledo Cave and Adventure Tours** (tel. 501/604-2124, www.tcatours.com, US$95-115) for a guided trip to Blue Creek Cave (bring a swimsuit) and advice about the area, as well as a swimming stop at the emerald waters of the **San Antonio waterfalls**—now complete with bench seating, changing room, and a small entrance fee (US$2). This is also great bird-watching country.

Transportation

To reach San Antonio, after leaving San Pedro, return to the main road and make a right turn. Soon you'll be in San Antonio, just down the road. From San Antonio the road is passable as far as Aguacate (another Q'eqchi' village). Uxbenka is west of San Antonio right at the entrance to the village of Santa Cruz and easy to get to via the trucks that haul supplies a couple of times a week. Known only by locals until 1984, Uxbenka is where six carved stelae were found, including one dating from the Early Classic Period. Numerous additional, uncarved stelae were found at the site.

The **Chun Bus** makes the run from Punta Gorda to San Antonio (11:30am Mon.-Sat., about US$4 round-trip). Note that this bus doesn't stop in San Pedro Columbia; instead you have to leave the bus at the road and trek in several miles. Catch the Chun Bus at Jose Maria Nunez Street in Punta Gorda to ensure getting a seat. Remember: No buses run on Sunday.

★ UXBENKA ARCHAEOLOGICAL SITE

The once difficult to access and largely unexcavated the small site of Uxbenka—a name adapted from the phrase "old place" in Mopan Maya (Uchben'kaj)given to the site by the people of Santa Cruz—was discovered in 1984 and has more than 20 stelae; it's also the oldest ancient city in Belize, in existence for over 2,000 years and continuously occupied for 1,000 years. The site is perched on a ridge overlooking the traditional Mayan village of Santa Cruz—the most authentic Maya village in Toledo, with 80 percent traditional homes, 129 families or 500 inhabitants—and provides a grand view of the foothills and valleys of the Maya Mountains. Here you'll see hillsides lined with cut stones; this construction

---

1: village of San Pedro Columbia; 2: village of Santa Cruz

method is unique to the Toledo District. In 2018, a new **visitors center** (9am-4pm; suggested donation US$5 pp) was opened, an initiative of Jose Mes, the village chairperson, who managed to reach an agreement for joint custody of the visitors center and the archaeological finds between the Santa Cruz community and the National Institute of Culture and History. All funds received go to maintaining the visitors center, the site, and surrounding caves. You can view the stelae there firsthand.

Uxbenka is just at the entrance to Santa Cruz, about three miles west of San Antonio Village. The most convenient way to see the site is with a rental car. Contact the **Uxbenka Kini'chahau Association** (UKKA, tel. 501/628-9535, ask for Jose Mes) for more information and to book local guides. Mr. Mes is also happy to arrange for a Mayan experience right after your tour of the archaeological site, taking you into his home and sharing stories of Mayan culture.

TOP EXPERIENCE

★ RÍO BLANCO NATIONAL PARK

Established in 1994 and comanaged by the government and the **Río Blanco Mayan Association** (the people of Santa Cruz, who volunteer their time as the park wardens, and chairperson Jose Mes), Río Blanco National Park is a favorite, providing stunning scenery and natural beauty for the visitor and an alternative income for members of neighboring villages. The park's 105 acres encompass a spectacular waterfall that is 20 feet high and ranges from a raging 100 feet wide during the rainy season to about 10 feet during the dry season. Locals say the turquoise pool under the waterfall is bottomless (one claims to have dived 60 feet and never touched bottom, although another says he touched it at 20 feet). The adventurous can jump off the surrounding rocks and fall 20 feet into crystal-clear water. There are also several pools to the back of the falls, plenty of space for a picnic, and two miles of nature trails, which

include the cave where the Río Blanco enters the mountain and a suspended cable bridge over the river.

Río Blanco National Park (tel. 501/628-9535, US$5) is a community-based effort, and 10 percent of entrance fees goes back into the surrounding villages, home to indigenous Maya. The park was recently upgraded, with a concrete walkway, a platform for jumps, and a footbridge over the water that makes for great photo ops. On-site, visit the **Craft & Snack Shop** (run by the Río Blanco Women's Association) for things like baskets, jewelry, and embroidery, plus the only cold beverages in the area.

Transportation

Río Blanco National Park is about 30 miles west of Punta Gorda, between the villages of Santa Cruz and Santa Elena on the road to Jalacte. From Punta Gorda, the park is a smooth one-hour drive or an easy hop off the bus. It's also an easy two-minute hike from the visitors center at the park entrance along a clear rainforest trail to reach the waterfall.

Two small bus companies serve the village of Jalacte, leaving from Jose Maria Nunez Street in Punta Gorda at 11:30am (Chun Bus, Mon.-Sat.) and 4pm (Bol Bus, Mon., Wed., and Fri.-Sat.); they return from the village on the same days at 3pm. Double-check the latest copy of the *Toledo Howler* to ensure the schedule hasn't changed, as it so frequently does around these parts.

BLUE CREEK VILLAGE

TOP EXPERIENCE

★ Blue Creek Cave

This village of some 275 Q'eqchi' and Mopan Maya was first settled in 1925. It is also called Ho'keb Ha ("the place where the water comes out"), describing the spot where the Río Blanco emerges from the side of a mountain and becomes Blue Creek, home to an extensive cave system. You'll need a guide who's familiar with these caves; ask at Punta Gorda or

Andy Palacio: Garifuna Legend

Barranco's pride and joy is Andy Palacio, whose pictures are still plastered around the village—clipped from old magazines, at the bar, inside homes, at the local museum, and on the village bulletin board. The talented artist, popular singer, and Garifuna activist was born in Barranco and buried in his home village far too soon; the star suffered a heart attack at the age of 47, and his death left behind a grieving nation.

Palacio's legacy is undisputed—anxious to preserve the Garifuna culture and language, he used music as his medium. The Afro-influenced rhythms of *punta* and *paranda* are accompanied by moving lyrics that carry socially conscious messages: "Our ancestors fought to remain Garifuna / Why must we be the ones to lose our culture?"

His last album, *Wátina*, was recorded with the Garifuna Collective, a group of Garifuna musicians from Belize, Honduras, and Guatemala. *Wátina* won worldwide acclaim and awards and put Garifuna music back in vogue, especially with the younger generation. (If you can, grab or download a copy; I still listen to it regularly.)

A year before his death, Andy Palacio was awarded the prestigious WOMEX Award and named UNESCO Artist for Peace. You can visit both his childhood home and his grave in Barranco.

at one of the nearby Mayan villages. Many of these folks know the nearby caves well. You can swim up to 600 yards into the cave; it's pretty stunning, with a small waterfall in the cave. Bring a flashlight and a swimsuit.

To get here, Kan's bus leaves Punta Gorda at 11:30am Monday-Saturday; Teck's bus leaves at noon on Monday, Wednesday, Friday, and Saturday. Check the latest bus listings in the local paper to be safe.

Tumul K'in Center of Learning

In the village of Blue Creek, the Tumul K'in Center of Learning (tel. 501/608-1070, www.tumulkinbelize.org) was established in 2002 to help preserve Mayan heritage, traditions, and practices. Most impressive is the center's Residential Academic Program. This Mayan high school of sorts takes in teenagers ages 13-16 for a four-year stint. In addition to regular academic classes, such as math and science, the students learn Q'eqchi' and Mopan, arts and crafts (pottery, sewing, basketry, and marimba playing), and specialize in one of four areas: agricultural science and production, agro-processing, eco-cultural tourism, and sustainable use of natural resources.

The center runs its own farm and sells various products to help sustain the school, including jams, honey, and bottled water. There

are also cultural tours and ecotours for visitors. You can visit several Mayan villages in a day, learn to dance to the marimba, or have a "Maya for a Day" experience, where you get to immerse yourself in a day in the life of a Mayan family—making tortillas, helping with household chores, and bathing in the river. Plenty of nature and adventure tours are also offered in the area. Maya Day, one of Toledo's biggest events, held in March, is organized by the center.

PUSILHÁ ARCHAEOLOGICAL SITE

Along the Moho River is a forgotten city, today mostly covered by corn and rainforest. Since its discovery in 1927, Pusilhá has received little attention due the remoteness of the ruins. Early investigations by the British Museum Expedition revealed stelae, extraordinary ceramics, eccentric flints, and the remains of a stone bridge. In 2001, shortly after a dirt track road connected the village to the rest of Belize, the Pusilhá Archaeology Project resumed investigations under the direction of Geoffrey Braswell. Recent analyses of ceramics suggest that Pusilhá was an important regional trading center.

Pusilhá is near San Benito Poite village, a few miles from the Guatemalan border.

Contact licensed tour guide **Manuel Cucul** (tel. 501/534-8659) or head there with **TIDE Tours** (Mile 1, San Antonio Rd., tel. 501/722-2274, www.tidetours.org, 7:30am-4:30pm Mon.-Fri., reduced hours Sat., US$95 pp for 2 people).

PUNTA NEGRA

One of the remaining traditional Kriol villages in Belize, Punta Negra has managed to stay so due to its relative remoteness from the mainland. Accessible only by boat from Punta Gorda, you can spend the day here with **TIDE Tours** (Mile 1, San Antonio Rd., tel. 501/722-2274, www.tidetours.org, 7:30am-4:30pm Mon.-Fri., reduced hours Sat.; call ahead for availability and pricing), while a much-awaited ferry remains a promise. This was a once thriving village, until fishing stocks declined and residents had to move to towns to find work and income. There are only five households today on Punta Negra. Ask about the annual Punta Negra beach bash around Easter, a great time to visit this unique corner of Belize.

Grab lunch at **Paula's** (tel. 501/628-6614; 11am-4pm daily; call ahead), a humble outdoor deck and kitchen directly facing a beautiful beach; savor catch of the day or chicken with rice and beans, and be sure to take home packaged boxes of Paula's famous coconut fudge. Also on sale is pure, delicious-smelling coconut oil. Go for a swim later or a beach stroll (bring body oil or repellent for sand flies).

BARRANCO

Barranco is an isolated, authentic Garifuna village, where activities include fishing along the river and traveling by dugout canoe up the river into the **Sarstoon-Temash National Park** to see howler monkeys, hicatees (river turtles), and iguanas. Many of Barranco's 600 inhabitants have traveled far from their village to become some of Belize's most renowned musicians, painters, and researchers; many have earned advanced degrees in their fields, giving Barranco one of the highest per capita number of PhDs in Central America.

Go on a tour of the village with **Alvin,** a local resident and tour guide who works with the Belize Tourism Board and will share Garifuna culture and history along the way. Visit a traditional Garifuna thatched-roof home—including the home of famous Garifuna artist Andy Palacio—and view the inside of the impressive *dügü,* or Garifuna

traditional homes in Barranco

temple, used for family reunions. Sample a Garifuna lunch of fried fish stewed in coconut broth, and visit the **Barranco House of Culture** for more on this fascinating Afro-Caribbean culture. Return for a refreshing glass of *hiu* (a spicy drink made of cassava and sweet potato) at the local bar and an evening of drumming.

You can get to Barranco by bus from the park in Punta Gorda, by boat from the Punta Gorda dock, or with your tour operator. **TIDE Tours** (Mile 1, San Antonio Rd., tel. 501/722-2274, www.tidetours.org, 7:30am-4:30pm Mon.-Fri., reduced hours Sat.) is your best bet for a trip to Barranco. If you can, arrange to return by boat—it's a lot faster and more pleasant than the 2.5-hour bumpy ride back to Punta Gorda.

Northern Belize

Northern Belize is home to the country's largest mestizo population (descendants of the Yucatec Maya and Spanish). Tourism is slowly emerging in these parts, as a closer look reveals more history and nature than meets the eye.

Agriculture remains the region's main economic base. But though most travelers only stop on the way to nearby sights, the Orange Walk and Corozal Districts are home to protected areas filled with rainforest and wildlife, including populations of jaguars, pumas, ocelots, jaguarundis, and even regionally endemic birds such as the ocellated turkey.

The Orange Walk District includes the archaeological site of Lamanai and its impressive rainforest trails, the Río Bravo

Highlights

Look for ★ to find recommended sights, activities, dining, and lodging.

★ **Banquitas House of Culture:** Located in Orange Walk Town, this exhibition hall features displays on history, industry, and culture (page 326).

★ **Lamanai Archaeological Site:** At one of the top attractions in all of Belize, a network of trails leads you through a partially excavated city on the shore of the beautiful New River Lagoon (page 335).

★ **Río Bravo Conservation Area:** Participate in a variety of research projects at field stations deep in the northwestern wilds (page 339).

★ **Sarteneja:** This remote village of fishers and boatbuilders is the perfect off-the-beaten-path destination (page 349).

★ **Shipstern Conservation and Management Area:** Spend the night amid unspoiled moist forest, savanna, and wetlands. Then, to experience nature at its best, enjoy unique cultural tours to Kriol and Mennonite villages nearby (page 352).

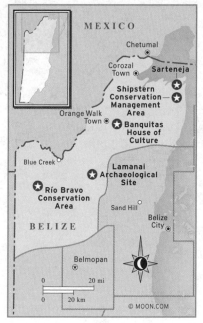

Northern Belize

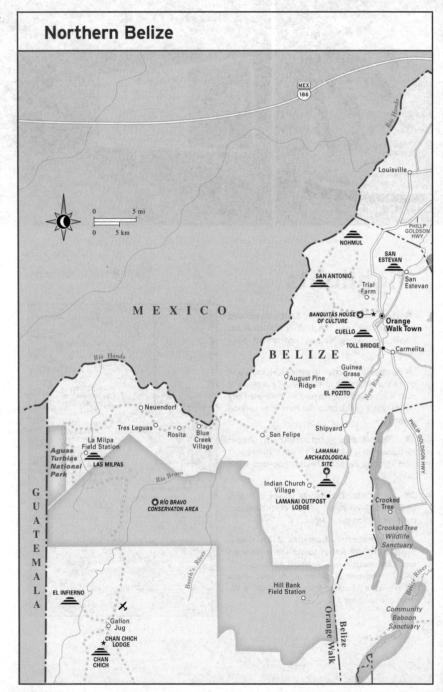

MEX
186

Louisville

PHILLIP
GOLDSON
HWY

0   5 mi
0   5 km

NOHMUL

SAN
ESTEVAN

San
Estevan

SAN ANTONIO

Trial
Farm

M E X I C O

BANQUITAS HOUSE
OF CULTURE

Orange
Walk Town

CUELLO

TOLL BRIDGE

Carmelita

B E L I Z E

Guinea
Grass

Río Hondo

August Pine
Ridge

EL POZITO

New River

Neuendorf

Tres Leguas

Rosita

Blue
Creek
Village

San Felipe

Shipyard

PHILIP GOLDSON HWY

La Milpa
Field Station

LAS MILPAS

Aguas
Turbias
National
Park

Río Bravo

LAMANAI
ARCHAEOLOGICAL
SITE

Indian Church
Village

Crooked
Tree

RÍO BRAVO
CONSERVATON AREA

LAMANAI OUTPOST
LODGE

Crooked Tree
Wildlife
Sanctuary

G
U
A
T
E
M
A
L
A

Booth's River

Hill Bank
Field Station

Belize River

EL INFIERNO

Gallon
Jug

CHAN CHICH
LODGE

CHAN
CHICH

Orange
Walk

Community
Baboon
Sanctuary

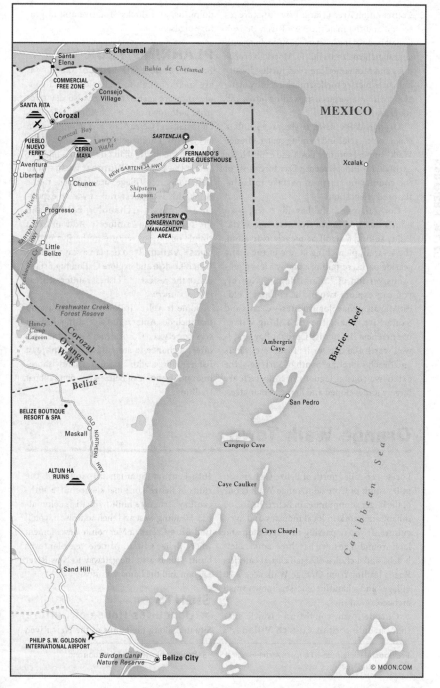

© MOON.COM

Conservation Area (a large private nature reserve), and the majestic New River, Belize's largest body of freshwater—28 miles long with abundant birds and wildlife. Morelet's crocodiles and Mesoamerican river turtles, locally known as hicatee turtles, inhabit these waters, along with numerous fish, wading birds, and waterfowl.

Orange Walk Town is the area's hub, a small commercial and farming center. Orange Walk's annual summer fiesta and a full-blown carnival on Independence Day lure most of the country up north to partake in Latin-flavored celebrations.

Corozal, a peaceful bayside town, is an hour's bus ride north from Orange Walk. Enjoy taking a stroll or bicycle ride along the seawall, picnicking at one of the many seaside parks, or taking a dip by a less glamorous version of "Miami Beach." Nearby, you can explore two of the country's oldest Mayan archaeological sites—Cerros and Santa Rita. The authentic fishing village of Sarteneja lies across Corozal Bay and is well worth the trip for its turquoise waters and beach shoreline. South of Sarteneja, the extensive coastal lagoons of Shipstern are largely undeveloped and home to manatees, dolphins, and flocks of native and migratory birds.

PLANNING YOUR TIME

Both **Orange Walk** and **Corozal** towns are small enough to be explored in a couple of hours each. There are also day trips from both towns to the Chetumal (Mexico), Lamanai, and Cerro Maya (commonly known as "Cerros") archaeological sites. To really dig into the north, plan on at least a night or two at the **Lamanai Outpost Lodge** or in Indian Church Village; situated close to the ruins, this is the best, fullest way to experience **Lamanai Archaeological Site** and the surrounding rainforest. Add an extra couple of days to venture to the **Río Bravo Conservation Area** or plan a stay at **Chan Chich Lodge** and explore Gallon Jug Estate, one of the vastest and lushest rainforest areas in the country.

Some travelers link Corozal into a loop that includes Ambergris Caye, using the boat service between Corozal and San Pedro. This offers a chance to stop off at **Sarteneja,** a fishing village with a beautiful sandy shoreline and the home of Belize's wooden sailboat tradition.

Orange Walk Town

Located 66 miles north of Belize City and 30 miles south of Corozal, Orange Walk is one of the larger communities in Belize. Its 16,700 inhabitants work in local industry and agriculture. If you're passing through, stop and look around. The town has three banks, a few hotels, and a choice of small casual eateries. Roads leading from Orange Walk access 20 villages and a handful of lesser-known small archaeological sites.

Outside town, you'll find historic sites that include **Indian Church Village,** a 16th-century Spanish mission, and the ruins of Belize's original sugar mill, a 19th-century structure built by British colonialists. Heading west and then southwest, you'll find **Blue Creek,** a Mennonite development where Belize's first hydroelectric plant was built. This is also the gateway to New River Lagoon and the Lamanai ruins.

SIGHTS
★ Banquitas House of Culture
Situated along the banks of the New River,

Previous: Mask Temple at Lamanai Archaeological Site; Sarteneja; Shipstern Conservation and Management Area.

Orange Walk Town

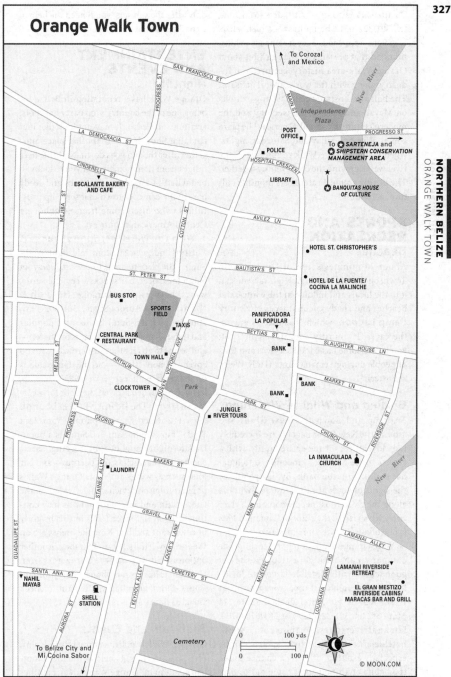

To Corozal
and Mexico

SAN FRANCISCO ST

PROGRESS ST

New River

Independence
Plaza

LA DEMOCRACIA ST

POST
OFFICE

PROGRESSO ST

POLICE

To ★ SARTENEJA and
★ SHIPSTERN CONSERVATION
MANAGEMENT AREA

CINDERELLA ST

HOSPITAL CRESCENT

ESCALANTE BAKERY
AND CAFE

LIBRARY

★ BANQUITAS HOUSE
OF CULTURE

MEJIBA ST

COTTON ST

AVILEZ LN

HOTEL ST. CHRISTOPHER'S

ST. PETER ST

BAUTISTA'S ST

HOTEL DE LA FUENTE/
COCINA LA MALINCHE

BUS STOP

SPORTS
FIELD

TAXIS

PANIFICADORA
LA POPULAR

CENTRAL PARK
RESTAURANT

BEYTIAS ST

QUEEN VICTORIA AVE

TOWN HALL

BANK

SLAUGHTER HOUSE LN

MEJIBA ST

ARTHUR ST

BANK

MARKET LN

CLOCK TOWER

Park

BANK

RIVERSIDE ST

PROGRESS ST

GEORGE ST

PARK ST

JUNGLE
RIVER TOURS

CHURCH ST

LA INMACULADA
CHURCH

New River

BAKERS ST

STAINES ALLEY

LAUNDRY

GRAVEL LN

MAIN ST

LOVER'S LANE

MUEFFEL ST

LAMANAI ALLEY

GUADALUPE ST

SANTA ANA ST

NAHIL
MAYAB

CEMETERY ST

KEYHOLE ALLEY

LOUISIANA FARM RD

LAMANAI RIVERSIDE
RETREAT

EL GRAN MESTIZO
RIVERSIDE CABINS/
MARACAS BAR AND GRILL

SHELL
STATION

AURORA ST

Cemetery

0   100 yds
0   100 m

To Belize City and
Mi Cocina Sabor

© MOON.COM

Banquitas House of Culture (Main St., tel. 501/322-0517, banquitashoc@nichbelize. org, 9am-6pm Mon.-Fri., free) is an exhibition hall that presents a broad exhibit about Orange Walk-area history, culture, and industry, along with the work of local artisans. The hall also hosts special traveling exhibits on Mayan and African archaeology and the modern culture of Central America. The plaza comes alive on Friday and Saturday nights, when young Orange Walk couples stroll the river walk enjoying the cool evening together. The nearby amphitheater hosts monthly cultural activities.

SPORTS AND RECREATION
Beaches

About 20 minutes south of Orange Walk Town, on the Old Northern Highway, you can join the locals and indulge in the white-sand beaches and shady coconut trees of **Honey Camp Lagoon,** which is as nice as any on the cayes. It's mostly a locals' picnic spot; you'll find some basic food services and tons of people during Semana Santa (Holy Week, at Easter).

Birding and Wildlife-Watching

Trips up and down the **New River** and around the New River Lagoon are incredibly rich adventures for the entire family, with a chance to see Morelet's crocodiles and iguanas sunning on the bank. By day you'll see the sights of verdant rainforest and wildlife along the river. Most people combine a river trip with a visit to the ruins of Lamanai. This is one of my favorite tours in Belize.

Your Orange Walk hotel or a local guide company can arrange a trip up the lagoon; check with Hotel de la Fuente for its local guide, Ignacio Lino, from **Lamanai River Tours** (at Hotel de la Fuente, 14 Main St., tel. 501/322-2290 or 501/670-0700, lamanairivertours1@yahoo.com, www. hoteldelafuente.com). Night safaris can be especially exciting, offering a chance to see the habits of animals that come out to play only after the sun sets; you'll need the help of a good guide and a spotlight.

ENTERTAINMENT AND EVENTS
Nightlife

Orange Walk has a reputation in Belize for being one of the country's top party hot spots, rivaling San Pedro. It may not look like it at first, but Shugah City is another place altogether after the sun goes down. Nightlife here ranges from house parties—if you're lucky to be invited—to modern nightclubs and seedy bars in the center of town that serve up prostitutes (who often come from neighboring Central American countries).

Wish You Were Beer Sports Lounge & Patio (Cinderella St., 4pm-midnight Wed.-Sun.) is the place to hang, under a *palapa*-roof patio, for a beer, bar snacks—ceviche verde, wings, burgers—and karaoke. **Hi5 Pub & Night Club** (8 Aurora St., tel. 501/602-1981, 7pm-5am Thurs.-Sun.) is the most popular and trendy hangout; the lounge is on the left—and seems to attract the most crowds, with no cover and pool tables—and the dance club is on the right, with a cover of US$5. Dress up, lest you be turned away at the door for wearing sneakers. The **Infinity Pub & Lounge** (San Francisco St., no phone, 5pm-2am Wed.-Thurs., 3pm-2am Fri.-Sun.) is a popular late-night hangout spot, serving classic cocktails—margaritas and beeritas—and bar food such as wings as well as Orange Walk's popular *salpicón* ceviche. Music videos of the latest Latin and international hits play continuously on flat-screen TVs in this brightly lit restaurant and bar. Karaoke nights are on Wednesday, Thursday, and Sunday. Another option is **Tijuana Sports Bar** (across from La Popular bakery, no phone, 7pm-midnight Thurs.-Sun.), although you'll want to check ahead as hours are erratic.

Festivals and Events

Orange Walk's main summertime event, **Fiestarama** (July) is held at the main football stadium in Orange Walk Town. Families and friends indulge in games, amusement park rides, mestizo foods, rum tastings, and live concerts well into the night. The highlight for me was witnessing the town's talented and lively marching bands performing along Queen Victoria Avenue to promote the start of the event on Saturday afternoon and later at the stadium. The weekend usually ends with a live concert. While the fun officially begins at 3pm, the crowds don't arrive until 8pm.

Started in 2011, the annual **Orange Walk Taco Festival** (Nov.) is growing in popularity. Held on the outdoor grounds of the Banquitas House of Culture, the event celebrates Shugah City's beloved snack all day long—chicken, sausage, pork, beef, and other creative concoctions—with live cooking and tastings from various vendors.

TOP EXPERIENCE

SEPTEMBER CELEBRATIONS
The most colorful time of the year in Orange Walk is during the **Orange Walk Carnival** (Sept. 21), with a full-blown Latin- and mestizo-inspired carnival sponsored by the local rum companies. The parade takes place all along the Philip Goldson Highway, starting in the heart of the town, close to D'Victoria Hotel. It's well worth the two-hour drive north from Belize City to watch the extravagant parade, with young marching bands and women in beautiful traditional mestizo outfits, and to indulge in some of the best street food in the country.

FOOD
Panificadora La Popular (1 Beytias Ln., tel. 501/322-3472, 6:30am-8pm Mon.-Sat., 7:30am-12:30pm and 3pm-6pm Sun.) is regarded as the best bakery in town and quite possibly in the country. There is a huge selection of breads and pastries—grab a tray at the entrance and make your rounds, picking up what strikes your fancy. Get pizza by the slice starting at 3pm, or have a whole pizza ready in 15 minutes (tel. 501/322-3229 to place an order). **Escalante Bakery and Café** (8

Cinderella St., no phone, 2:30pm-8pm Mon.-Sat.) serves espresso drinks and freshly baked goods, including sweet breads, cinnamon rolls, muffins, and brownies.

For a sit-down breakfast in Orange Walk—a rare treat—★ **Cocina La Malinche** (at Hotel de la Fuente, 14 Main St., tel. 501/322-2290, www.hoteldelafuente.com, 6:30am-10am daily, US$5-10) comes to the rescue—a casual café and lounge area beside the hotel's reception area, open to the public, and where a full breakfast menu is offered. Choices include "The Belizean" for a taste of Belize's fry jacks, as well as pancakes, French toast, and healthier fruit options.

Central Park Restaurant (New Market, near the village bus terminal, aka "Fort Cairns," no phone, 7am-5pm daily) is actually a collection of six restaurants styled after the old-school open market located next door. It serves everything a hungry traveler could want: burgers, tacos, empanadas, pizza, hot dogs, bacon and eggs breakfasts, rice and beans for lunch, sweet cakes, waffles, and the usual assortment of beverages, all for a couple of bucks.

For Orange Walk's famous tacos—there's a constant war on which taco stand is the best—you won't go wrong with **Mercy's Taco Stand** (across from the fire station, no phone, 6am-10pm daily), also serving up burritos. Tacos are just three for US$0.25. Wash it down with fresh orange juice or *horchata*.

Lamanai Riverside Retreat (Lamanai Alley, tel. 501/302-3955, lamanairiverside@hotmail.com, US$5-15) is open daily for breakfast, lunch, and dinner. It's a nice setting to relax after a long day of traveling and sightseeing. Its midrange dinner menu includes burgers, fajitas, burritos, and seafood dishes; fresh fruit juices and a full bar are also available. Karaoke nights (Fri., sometimes Sun.) attract a local crowd, and occasionally there is live music.

★ **Nahil Mayab** (corner of Guadalupe St. and Santa Ana St., tel. 501/322-0831, www.nahilmayab.com, 10am-3pm Mon., 10am-10pm Tues.-Thurs., 10am-11:30pm Fri.-Sat.,

Mestizo Eats: *Chimole* to *Tamalitos*

Northern Belize has a reputation for serving the best mestizo food in the country, a mix of Spanish and Mayan cuisine. Mestizo food is most often sold from a shack or eatery window on the roadside and also happens to be some of the cheapest and tastiest food around—the "three for a dollah" tacos are filling enough to send any budget traveler away happy. But there's a lot more to sample. Most of these mestizo dishes have corn as their common ingredient.

- *Chimole,* or "black dinner" as the locals call it, is a dark-colored and seasoned chicken soup, cooked with onions, tomatoes, potatoes, squash, black *recado* (a Belizean curry paste), and boiled eggs. Freshly made tortillas accompany this meal.

- *Escabeche* is a white-colored onion soup, served with a handful of tortillas. It's said to be excellent for a hangover. Other ingredients include garlic, white vinegar, cinnamon, and jalapeño peppers. Some also serve it with a slice of roasted chicken on the side.

- *Garnaches* are my favorite—small deep-fried corn tortillas topped with refried beans, grated cheese, chopped onions and peppers, thinly sliced tomatoes, and cilantro soaked in lime juice. These crispy treats are seriously addictive.

- *Tamalitos* are a Belizean take on the Mexican-style tamale, made with Mayan masa corn flour and wrapped in plantain or banana leaves.

US$5-15) is still the local Belizean favorite, or all-around favorite, offering the best dining atmosphere in Orange Walk; the outdoor patio is set in a beautiful tropical garden, and the air-conditioned restaurant has an attractive Mayan theme. The food is excellent; the menu includes Mayan and mestizo specialties (the tacos *arracheras* are popular), including seafood, steaks, and pastas, with happy hour 5:30pm-7pm daily. It also has a kids menu with finger foods and sandwiches. Nahil Mayab means "House of the Maya."

A few steps below Nahil Mayab is a more casual affair, **Juanita's Restaurant** (tel. 501/302-2677, 6am-3pm and 6pm-9:30pm Mon.-Sat., US$3-5), serving rice and beans and all the other Creole dishes in a classic Belizean atmosphere.

★ **Mi Cocina Sabor** (across from L&R Liquor, South Belize Corozal Rd., tel. 501/322-3482, 11am-10pm Wed.-Mon., US$5-13) has a menu that perfectly blends mestizo and Latin specialties, including mouthwatering appetizers like jalapeño poppers. The bar offers a myriad of cocktail options, and my favorite dish here is the Fisherman's Soup—a rich coconut broth with big seafood chunks, reminiscent of the Garifuna *hudut* dish, but served with a side of white rice and hot peppers as garnish. There's a screened porch as well as a spacious air-conditioned interior.

Maracas Bar and Grill (2 Naranjal St., tel. 501/322-1800, www.elgranmestizo.com, 11:30am-10pm Wed.-Sun., US$5-12) offers one of the best dining environments in Orange Walk—a beautifully lit restaurant with tables facing the New River, including a private table for two, with flowing drapes, set on a platform inches from the water. You can always go indoors if you prefer, but why miss that view and breeze? The menu, consisting mostly of Belizean mestizo specialties, doesn't disappoint. Opt for the Rum Fish, or try the Mayan empanadas or enchiladas Maracas.

For the best ceviche in Orange Walk Town, a cold beer, and an ultra-local vibe—no tourists here—head to **Cevichería La Enramada** (5 Cristock St., tel. 501/302-2868, 10am-10pm Mon.-Thurs., closes later Fri.-Sun., US$1.25-3.75). Set in a residential area, it's a lively spot on Friday and weekends, where you'll see the northern culture of Belize in full display—from the mestizo crowd to the juke-box blasting the latest Latin ballads and pop music.

Set in a residential neighborhood with a mestizo-style setting, just a couple of blocks from the center strip in Orange Walk, is a nice green respite from the heat—**Tan's Pizza Paradiso** (47 Castillo Alley, Riverside area, tel. 501/322-2669, louzal6@yahoo.com, 11am-10pm Wed.-Sat., US$5-10). You'll find delicious homemade pizza, local snacks like *salpicón*, local desserts, and a full bar. Tan's was expanding with a second seating area that should be ready by publication time.

Orange Walk may have the highest per capita number of Chinese restaurants in all of Central America, but be warned, the food is greasy and sometimes unclean or dated (food poisoning victim, here). But if you're on a meager budget, there's the established **Lee's Chinese Restaurant** (San Antonio Rd., near the fire station, 9am-midnight daily, US$3-12). I still recommend going for tacos instead, unless you're vegetarian.

For a cold treat or some fast food—burg-ers, nachos, hot dogs, pizza slices—head to the local favorite, **IceBreak** (5 Park St., tel. 501/322-0602, 8am-7:30pm Mon.-Thurs., 8am-10pm Fri.-Sat., 5pm-10pm Sun., US$2.50-10). The outdoor veranda is ideal for people-watching.

El Establo (tel. 501/322-0094, http://aguallos.com/elestablo, 11am-9pm Tues.-Wed., 11am-10pm Thurs., 11am-11pm Fri.-Sat.,11am-5pm Sun., US$5-20), outside of town, serves Belizean food as well as bar snacks in an upscale setting. Ask any taxi driver to take you there.

ACCOMMODATIONS

Orange Walk has a combination of well-equipped business-oriented hotels and a few old budget standards.

US$25-50

Named after the patron saint of travelers, the family-run **Hotel St. Christopher's** (Main St., tel. 501/302-1064 or 501/322-2420, stchristophershotel@btl.net) is popular with large groups; it has 22 colorful, tradi-tional Spanish-feeling guest rooms with tiled floors and private baths for US$35 with fan, US$54.50 with air-conditioning. Amenities include wireless Internet, laundry service, private parking, and complimentary coffee in the lobby. A conference room that seats 70 is available for meetings or catered meals. On the riverfront, the hotel has plenty of space for recreation: kayak and paddle rentals, a vol-leyball court, picnic tables, and greenery to attract birds and other wildlife. A few of the guest rooms have shared balconies with a view of the river.

You'll find solid value at the family-owned, boutique ★ **Hotel de la Fuente** (14 Main St., tel. 501/322-2290, www.hoteldelafuente.com, US$40-85), where 22 nonsmoking, air-conditioned guest rooms offer a range of ame-nities, including fully equipped apartments and free wireless Internet; it's great for busi-ness travelers who want to stay in the heart of town. Every year, the hotel upgrades its look and comfort. The lobby features a relax-ing seating area, and at the back is Cocina La Malinche café serving a full breakfast menu open to residents and guests, as well as all-day coffee and tea (self-service outside of open-ing hours), or a cold beer after hours. New rooms have been added with a walkway that connects directly to the café. Owners Orlando and Cindy de la Fuente are a wealth of infor-mation; be sure to say hello if you have time. The hotel also helps arrange tours, particu-larly to Lamanai—through reputable guide Ignacio Lino from Lamanai River Tours. Ten additional guest rooms are set at the back, away from the street noise, and connected to the main hotel via a bridge.

Lamanai Riverside Retreat (Lamanai Alley, tel. 501/302-3955, lamanairiverside@hotmail.com, US$45) is a small family-run business located on the New River. It has three basic guest rooms with fans (air-conditioning is also available), cable TV, and private baths. The Pelayos can take care of all your needs with a decent open-air riverside bar and

restaurant on-site and a variety of tour offerings. This place is unique in Orange Walk. Grab a drink, take a seat just a few steps from the river, and watch the occasional crocodile gliding by.

Another excellent value, if you're not keen on staying right in town and are driving, are the 12 hotel rooms at **La Enramada's Cabanas** (5 Cristock St., tel. 501/302-2868, US$25), set on ground level at the back of the popular restaurant. You'll find them immaculate, with the basics, including either double or single bed, private bath, air-conditioning, and TV.

US$50-100

Also facing the beautiful New River and a stone's throw away are luxurious cabanas at ★ **El Gran Mestizo Riverside Cabins** (Naranjal St., tel. 501/322-2290, www.elgranmestizo.com, US$80-130), for an intimate, quiet escape in nature and away from the dusty streets and bustle of Orange Walk. The cabins range from standard to premium—with a full kitchen and a living area. The single cabin for two is cozy, with an open space design (no bathroom door, but there is sufficient privacy). Wi-Fi is available throughout the property. The on-site waterfront restaurant—the **Maracas Bar and Grill**—is also popular with locals on the weekends and a nice spot for a relaxing meal. There are 11 new rooms as well set across a two-story building tucked toward the back, with double beds, minifridges, air-conditioning, and garden views, as well as loft apartments with full kitchens. Ask about the new backpacker dorm if you're on a budget—there are six bunk beds, sharing a flat-screen TV, minifridge, and en suite bath.

INFORMATION AND SERVICES

Orange Walk Town is the commercial center of the district, so there are many small

1: Tan's Pizza Paradiso; **2:** El Gran Mestizo Riverside Cabins

shops selling all kinds of merchandise, including agricultural supplies, local cookware (such as a cast-iron *comal* or a tortilla press, both heavy but useful souvenirs), and many used American-clothing shops. There are three major **banks** on Main Street and basic services for travelers, including laundry and cheap food. For an Internet café, try **FarWorld Tech** (65 Cinderella St., tel. 501/322-0716, 8am-6pm Mon.-Fri., 9am-1pm Sat., US$2 per hour).

TRANSPORTATION

During the cane harvest, the one-lane highway is a parade of trucks stacked high with sugarcane and waiting in long lines at the side of the road to get into the Tower Hill sugar mill. Night drivers beware: The trucks aren't new and often have no lights.

Bus

There is no main bus station, but the buses traveling between Corozal and Belize City all stop to idle next to **Fort Cairns** (the site is supposedly temporary, but nobody knows where the bus station is moving to) for a few minutes before lumbering on—they pass about every hour until 6pm daily. Buses passing through town after 6pm usually briefly stop by Town Hall. The last bus to Belize City passes around 6:45pm daily, and service to Corozal continues hourly until about 9pm daily. Some of the buses are express, but it's hard to tell which ones, unless they are the comfy, air-conditioned charter buses. Sunday service is about every two hours. Buses to Indian Church Village (near Lamanai) leave only on Friday, returning Monday. There are hourly buses to San Felipe to the west and Sarteneja to the east. Buses to Sarteneja can be found across the street from Banquitas House of Culture by the Zeta Ice Factory.

Boat

Traveling by boat is a pleasant way to get anywhere, especially up the New River to Lamanai. Enjoy nature's best along the shore of the river and the labyrinthine passageways through the wetlands. You never know what you'll see next—long-legged birds, orchids in tall trees, hummingbirds, crocs—it's like a treasure hunt. Bring your binoculars. Ask anywhere for directions to the boat dock. Some boat operators depart from the New Hill Toll Bridge south of town.

Taxi

There are a few taxi stands (tel. 501/322-2050 or 501/322-2560) on Queen Victoria Avenue, next to the sports field and across from the park. **Elido Vasquez** (tel. 501/651-1718) is a reliable taxi driver. Fares around the central part of Orange Walk Town run US$2.50, US$7.50 to the toll bridge, and US$10 to the airstrip.

CUELLO RUINS

On the property of a Caribbean rum warehouse are the minor **Cuello Ruins** (4 miles west of Orange Walk on Yo Creek, free). Check in at the gate office (tel. 501/322-2141, 8:30am-4:30pm daily), then investigate these relatively undisturbed ruins, consisting of a large plaza with seven structures in a long horizontal mound. There are three temples; see if you can find the uncovered ones. These structures (as at Cahal Pech) have a different look than most Mayan sites. They are covered with a layer of white stucco, as they were in the days of the Maya.

The ruins of Cuello were studied in the 1970s by a Cambridge University archaeology team led by Norman Hammond. A small ceremonial center, a proto-Classic temple, has been excavated. Lying directly in front is a large excavation trench, partially backfilled, where the archaeologists gathered the historical information that revolutionized previous concepts about the ancient Maya. Artifacts indicate that the Maya traded with people hundreds of miles away. Among the archaeologists' out-of-the-ordinary findings were bits of wood that proved, after carbon testing, that Cuello had been occupied as early as 2600 BC, much earlier than ever believed. Archaeologists now find, however, that these tests may have been incorrect, and the site's age is in dispute.

Also found was an unusual style of pottery—apparently in some burials, clay urns were placed over the heads of the deceased. It's also speculated that it was here, over a long period, that the primitive strain of corn seen in early years was refined and developed into the higher-producing plant of the Classic Period. Continuous occupation for approximately 4,000 years has been surmised, with repeated layers of structures all the way into the Classic Period.

Lamanai

Set on the edge of a forested broad lagoon are the temples of Lamanai. One of the largest and longest-inhabited ceremonial centers in Belize, Lamanai is believed to have served as an imperial port city encompassing ball courts, pyramids, and several more exotic Mayan features. Hundreds of buildings have been identified in the two-square-mile area. Archaeologist David Pendergast headed a team from the Royal Ontario Museum that, after finding a number of children's bones buried under a stela, presumed that human sacrifice was a part of the residents' religion. Large masks that depict a ruler wearing a crocodile headdress were found in several locations, hence the name Lamanai (Submerged Crocodile). The Institute of Archaeology has done a great deal of work at this site, and the main temples are impressive even to those not well versed in Mayan history. The High Temple can be climbed to yield a 360-degree view of the surrounding rainforest and lagoon.

With the advent of midday cruise ship

tours, the site boasts a dock, a visitors center, craft shops, and a museum. Lamanai is also a popular site for day-trippers from Ambergris Caye and can be quite crowded in the middle of the day, especially during the week. For a more solitary experience, go early in the morning or late in the afternoon, as cruise ship crowds arrive at noon and disappear in less than two hours.

★ LAMANAI ARCHAEOLOGICAL SITE

The **Lamanai Archaeological Site** (8am-5pm daily, US$10 pp) comprises four large temples, a residential complex, and a reproduction stela of a Mayan elite, Lord Smoking Shell. Excavations reveal continuous occupation and a high standard of living into the Post-Classic Period, unlike at other ancient Mayan sites in the region. Lamanai is believed to have been occupied from 1500 BC to the 19th century—Spanish occupation is also apparent, with the remains of two Christian churches and a sugar mill that was built by British colonialists.

The landscape at most of Lamanai is forest, and trees and thick vines grow from the tops of buildings. The only sounds are birdcalls and howler monkey voices echoing off the stone temples. These are some of the notable sites:

Two significant tombs were found at the **Mask Temple** (structure N9-56), built around AD 450. There are also two Early Classic stone masks; the second mask on the temple was exposed in late 2010.

At 100 feet high, the **High Temple** (structure N10-43) is the tallest securely dated Pre-Classic structure in the Mayan world. Among many findings was a dish containing the skeleton of a bird and Pre-Classic vessels dating to 100 BC. The view above the canopy is marvelous, and on a clear day you can see the hills of Quintana Roo in Mexico.

The game played in the **Ball Court** held

great ritual significance for the Maya, although because of the small size of Lamanai's court, some think it was just symbolic. In 1980, archaeologists raised the huge stone disc marking the center of the court and found lidded vessels on top of a puddle of mercury; miniature vessels inside contained small jade and shell objects.

The **Royal Complex** was the residence of up to two dozen elite Lamanai citizens; you can see their beds, doorways, and the like. It was excavated in 2005.

Dating to the 6th century AD, the **Jaguar Temple** (structure N10-9) underwent structural modifications in the 8th and 13th centuries. Jade jewelry and a jade mask were discovered here, as was an animal motif dish. Based on the animal remains and other evidence, archaeologists now believe that this was the site of an enormous party and feast to celebrate the end of a drought in AD 950.

In 1983 archaeologists began an investigation of **Stela Temple** (structure N10-27), where they discovered a large stone monument, designated Stela 9. The elaborately carved stela depicts Lord Smoking Shell in ceremonial dress. Hieroglyphic text on Stela 9, while incomplete, indicates that this monument was erected to commemorate the accession of Smoking Shell, the Lord of Lamanai. Further excavations near the base of the monument revealed a cache of human remains and artifacts, believed to be associated with a dedication ritual. Today, a replica stands at the stela temple; the original can be viewed in the museum at Lamanai.

Birding and Wildlife-Watching

The trip to the site, up the New River Lagoon, is its own safari; once you're at the ruins, you'll see numbered trees that correspond to an informational pamphlet available from the caretakers at the entrance of Lamanai Reserve.

Birders, look around the **Mask Temple** and **High Temple** for Montezuma oropendolas and their drooping nests. Black vultures are often spotted slowly gliding over the entire area. A woodpecker with a distinct double-tap rhythm and a red cap is the male pale-billed woodpecker.

Near the High Temple, small flocks of collared aracaris, related to the larger toucan, forage the canopy for fruits and insects. The black-headed trogon is more spectacular than its name implies, with a yellow chest, a black-and-white tail, and an iridescent blue-green back. Although it looks as if the northern jacana is walking on water, it's the delicate floating vegetation that holds the long-toed bird above the water as it searches along the edge for edible delicacies. Other fauna spotted by those who live here are jaguarundis, agoutis, armadillos, Central American river turtles, and roaring howler monkeys.

Transportation

All regional tour operators in Orange Walk, Corozal, and Belize City offer water tours to Lamanai. It is the most impressive way to approach the site, and a time-saver as well compared to going by land. Bob the crocodile and a group of spider monkeys have become regular tour stops, as they are accustomed to feeding routines. (Some boats invite spider monkeys on board to eat bananas, which should be discouraged; they can become aggressive toward people and cause serious injury.) Ask about night safaris, bird-watching tours, and sunrise trips up and down the New River.

Most hotels can arrange tours with licensed guides. Tours include the entrance fee, drinks, and usually a catered lunch as part of the deal; prices range US$40-70 per person. I highly recommend **Lamanai River Tours** (at Hotel de la Fuente, tel. 501/302-1600 or 501/670-0700, lamanairivertours1@yahoo.com, www.hoteldelafuente.com, US$50 pp for 4 people, private tour US$230 for 3 people)—ask for guide Ignacio Lino, who knows the area inside out. Another option is **Jungle River Tours** (20 Lovers Ln., tel. 501/670-3035 or 501/629-3069, US$40 pp for a group of 4), with boats leaving from a landing near the historic **La Inmaculada Catholic Church.** **Errol Cadle's Lamanai Eco Tours** (tel.

501/610-1753, errolcadle1@yahoo.com, US$50 pp for up to 10 people, includes lunch) caters to travelers who want a less frenetic pace, often from cruise ships.

Most visitors use one of the tour companies based in Orange Walk or the transfer services of their accommodations, but it is possible to do it yourself as well. A two-person boat transfer from Orange Walk should cost about US$125, less if you can get in with a bigger group. You can drive the San Felipe road in about 1.5 hours, depending on road conditions.

INDIAN CHURCH VILLAGE

The ruins of Lamanai huddle to one side of New River Lagoon and sprawl westward through the forest and under the village of Indian Church, which was relocated by the government from one part of the site to another in 1992. It is reachable by boat from Orange Walk or by road from San Felipe.

Contribute directly to the local economy by shopping at the **Indian Church Village Artisans Center,** a community-based organization founded in 2000 with the assistance of professional archaeologists, artisans, and architects working at the nearby Lamanai site. The center provides workspace, tools, materials, craft training, English classes, and a computer center to interested villagers. The center has a small shop at the Lamanai site, or you can check out the artisans' wares at their workshop in the village. Artisans produce silver and bronze jewelry, hand-sewn purses, bags, embroidered pillowcases, slate carvings, and fired clay statues. Most of the artwork emulates artifacts found at the Lamanai site, including silver pendants of the Lord Smoking Shell stela. Stop by the village workshop yourself or ask your guide to take you by the shop at the Lamanai site.

Food

In Indian Church Village, you'll find cheap local food at the **Grupo de Mujeres Las Orquideas Restaurant** (no phone,

11am-5pm daily, about US$5 per meal). This is a communal effort of nine women from nine families who are adept at dealing with both groups and individuals. You can also ask about Mayan cooking lessons and try your hand at making tortillas.

Accommodations

The Indian Church villagers have been hosting groups of foreign archaeologists, anthropologists, and biologists (and the odd gringo volunteer) for decades. In addition to the places listed, there are a few informal homestay options available. Find out the latest developments in the village's foray into tourism by calling the **community phone** (tel. 501/245-2015), or just wander into town and see what you find. Note that Indian Church is off the electricity and telephone grid, and solar panels and gasoline generators provide power. All budget options provide meals and cultural activities and can hook you up with local guides for the ruins and wildlife tours.

Olivia and David Gonzalez (tel. 501/667-3232 or 501/668-8593, from US$20 s, US$30 d) have a row of modern cement guest rooms with private baths and basic amenities, including a few hours of electricity each evening. **Doña Blanca's Guest House** (tel. 501/665-0044, US$40 with 3 meals, room only US$25) has 15 guest rooms with private baths, solar power, and hot and cold showers. Also available are very basic cabanas, ideal for the backpacker, with private baths (US$8). Call ahead to give them time to prepare your room.

About 0.5 mile up the bank of the lagoon from the Lamanai Archaeological Site, ★ **Lamanai Outpost Lodge** (tel. 501/670-3578, U.S. tel. 954/636-1107, www.lamanai.com) is one of Belize's premier rainforest retreats. Lamanai Outpost offers a low-key, escape-to-nature kind of setting, perfect for the bird-watcher, Mayaphile, naturalist, or traveler who wants to get away from the tourist trail for a while. The area is rich in animal life, including close to 400 species of birds as well as crocodiles, margays, jaguarundis,

anteaters, tayras, arboreal porcupines, and the fishing bulldog bat.

From the moment the staff greet you at the dock, you know you're in capable, welcoming hands. The lodge boasts 17 elegantly rustic thatched-roof, rough-hewn wood cabanas detailed with converted brass oil lamps and other amenities that contribute to an old-fashioned feel (although a couple of guest rooms add plasma-screen TVs, air-conditioning, and wireless Internet access to the old-timey mix). Outside, lush, landscaped grounds of orchids, ceiba trees, and palmettos provide cooling shade as you walk the gravel paths. Below the resort's lodge and dining room (which are the only parts of the complex visible from the river) lies the shore of the lagoon, where you'll find a dock, a swimming area, canoes, boats of various types, and an assortment of deck chairs. The dock is particularly peaceful at sunset. Activities keep you busy, from predawn hikes and canoe trips to nighttime "spotlight cruises." All-inclusive packages start at US$676; there's a two-night minimum stay, and rates include transfer to and from Belize City, meals, and two guided adventure activities per night booked. See the website for summer specials and individual pricing options.

The owners of Lamanai Outpost are involved in several scientific research projects that also allow nature-study opportunities for guests. Study topics include local bats, archaeology, howler monkeys, Morelet's crocodiles, and ornithology. Guests with some group programs can participate in the work.

Transportation

You can take the village bus to Indian Church, which leaves Orange Walk at 5pm-6pm on Friday and Monday. The same buses depart Indian Church at 5am-5:30am on the same days, so you'll have to make a weekend out of it—or more. On the opposite end of the time, comfort, and price spectrum, you can charter a 15-minute flight from Belize City to Lamanai Outpost Lodge's airstrip with one of Belize's private charter services.

Blue Creek and the Río Bravo

As the road meanders west from Orange Walk and Cuello, numerous small villages dot the border region. Occasionally you see a soft-drink sign attached to a building, but there's not much in the way of facilities between Orange Walk and Blue Creek. Heading west from San Felipe, you soon find flat, open farmland, with Mennonite accoutrements, dominating the landscape. Low, open paddy fields provide great bird-watching opportunities as well as placid scenery. In the foothills of the Maya highlands is Blue Creek village. Climbing up into the foothills you can see the flatlands of the Río Hondo and New River drainages to the east. The small village to the right is La Union, on the other side of the Mexican border. This part of northern Belize is much hillier and has an increasingly wild feel to it.

BLUE CREEK VILLAGE

In the village of Blue Creek, **The Hillside Bed & Breakfast** (about 30 miles west of Orange Walk, tel. 501/323-0155, bchillsideb_b@ yahoo.com, US$50) is a unique and peaceful place to stay. Guests experience Belizean Mennonite hospitality and life on a working farm. (As far as I know, this is the only lodging offered in a Mennonite community in Belize.) Guest rooms feature all the basic amenities, including air-conditioning, and rates include breakfast in the kitchen. Companies visiting the area have occasionally booked the entire place for a few months at a time, so call first before heading there.

At the top of the hill are the Linda Vista Credit Union and a **gas station**-general store. Fill up the tank if you're driving on to Río Bravo or Chan Chich, as this is the last gas station until you come back this way.

1: view of La Inmaculada Catholic Church from the New River; 2: Chan Chich Lodge

★ RÍO BRAVO CONSERVATION AREA

At the dramatic boundary of Programme for Belize's **Río Bravo Conservation Area** (RBCMA), the cleared pastureland runs into a wall of rainforest. There is a gate at the border, and if you aren't expected, the guard won't let you pass. Once inside the gate, you've entered the Río Bravo Conservation Area.

Programme for Belize (1 Eyre St., Belize City, tel. 501/227-5616 or 501/227-1020, www. pfbelize.org, US$82-88) is a Belizean nonprofit established in 1988 to promote the conservation of the natural heritage of Belize and wise use of its natural resources, centering on the RBCMA, a 260,000-acre chunk of Belize where Programme for Belize demonstrates the practical application of its principles (the land was originally slated for clearing). The RBCMA represents approximately 4 percent of Belize's total land area and is home to a rich sample of biodiversity, which includes 392 species of birds, 200 species of trees, 70 species of mammals, 30 species of freshwater fish, and 27 species of conservation concern.

Within the conservation area, the research station is housed in a cluster of small thatched-roof buildings. Programme for Belize is dedicated to scientific research, agricultural experimentation, and protecting indigenous wildlife and the area's Mayan archaeological sites—all this while creating self-sufficiency through development of ecotourism and sustainable rainforest agriculture, such as chicle production. A scientific study continues to determine the best management plan for the reserve and its forests.

Ongoing projects include archaeological research at the La Milpa Maya Site and other sites on the RBCMA in conjunction with Boston University and the University of Texas; timber and pine savanna research programs aimed at identifying the most optimal approach to sustainable timber extraction; a carbon sequestration pilot program, the first of seven globally approved projects to start on-the-ground research on how forest conservation could combat global warming; ecological research and monitoring of migratory and resident avifauna, such as the yellow-headed parrot; a freshwater management program, which looks at the New River Lagoon, its tributaries, and the New River; and the biological connectivity program, which looks at the RBCMA and the critical links it forms with other protected areas in northern Belize.

La Milpa Field Station

Programme for Belize's **La Milpa Field Station** lies nestled deep in the forests of northwestern Belize. This station is only three miles from the third-largest archaeological site in the country, the La Milpa archaeological site, which is just one of at least 60 archaeological sites found on the Río Bravo. Hiking nature trails, rainforest trekking, and birding are the order of the day at La Milpa. Spend a day in the nearby mestizo and Mennonite villages for a taste of Belizean culture or tour breathtaking and majestic ancient Mayan sites. Birders can compile a list of more than 150 species during a three-day trip to La Milpa.

ACCOMMODATIONS

For accommodations, guests can choose between charmingly rustic thatched-roof cabanas (US$82-88 pp) with private baths or a comfortable and tastefully decorated dormitory (US$41 pp) featuring state-of-the-art "green" technology with shared baths. The La Milpa venue has meeting facilities, telephones, and dining facilities and is family oriented, with 24-hour electricity and hot and cold water. All-inclusive packages start at US$180 per person, which includes accommodations, three buffet-style meals, and two guided tours on the property. Contact **Programme for Belize** (tel. 501/227-5616 or 501/227-1020, www.pfbelize.org) for details.

Hill Bank Field Station

On the banks of the New River Lagoon, the **Hill Bank Field Station** serves as a research base for sustainable forest management and specialized tourism, which incorporates research activities into the visitors' forest experience. Hill Bank, an important site in Belize's colonial history, acted as a center of intensive timber extraction for more than 150 years, commencing in the 17th century. The Hill Bank experience brings to life the architecture and artifacts of colonial land use, such as the quaint wooden buildings of logging camps, antique steam engines, and railroad tracks.

Explore the wilds of Hill Bank by canoeing, crocodile-spotting, hiking nature trails, birding, and rainforest trekking. The scenic boat ride, replete with wildlife sightings along the New River Lagoon, is a great experience in itself.

ACCOMMODATIONS

For accommodations, guests stay in Hill Bank's cabanas with private bath and verandas (US$87.50) or dormitories (US$68.75), with fans, no-flush composting toilets, and a rainwater collection system, with shared baths. Contact **Programme for Belize** (tel. 501/227-5616 or 501/227-1020, www.pfbelize. org) for details.

CHAN CHICH RUINS

As recently as 1986, the only way in to the Mayan site of Chan Chich (Kaxil Uinich) was with a machete in hand and a canoe to cross the swiftly flowing rivers. Most people making the trip were loggers, pot farmers, or grave robbers. Then, in the northwestern corner of Belize in Orange Walk District, near the Guatemalan border, an old overgrown road, originally blazed by the Belize Estate and Produce Company for logging, was reopened, and consequently the site of Chan Chich was rediscovered.

When found, three of the temples showed obvious signs of looting, with vertical slit trenches just as the looters had left them. No one will ever know what valuable artifacts were removed and sold to private collectors. The large main temple on the upper plaza had been violated to the heart of what appears to be one or more burial chambers. A painted frieze runs around the low ceiling. Today, the only temple inhabitants greeting outsiders are armies of small bats and spider monkeys.

The ruins provide opportunity for discovery and exploration, and the population and diversity of wildlife here are probably greater than anywhere else in Belize. The nine miles of hiking trails wind through the verdant rainforest and provide ample opportunities to see wildlife, including big cats.

This is not a public archaeological site, and the ruins are unexcavated. Chan Chich Lodge looks after the site.

Gallon Jug Village and Estate

Originally the hub of the British Belize Estate and Produce Company's mahogany logging operation, this land was purchased by Barry Bowen. **Gallon Jug Village and Estate** (tel. 501/227-7031, www.gallonjug.com) is now a diverse and privately owned working farm, ranch, and community, with an airstrip, a post office, a coffee-roasting facility, and a school. The scientific research conducted here, led by Bruce and Carolyn Miller, has focused on jaguars and neotropical bats.

Chan Chich Lodge

Chan Chich Lodge (Gallon Jug Estate, tel. 501/223-4419, U.S. tel. 877/279-5726, www.chanchich.com, from US$375, includes breakfast) was the country's very first rainforest eco-lodge. This elegant yet unpretentious retreat is surrounded on all sides by unexcavated pyramids and the second-largest tropical forest in the Americas. The landscaped grounds, subtly lit pool and jetted tub, and sunset views from the tops of the mounds complement the spacious cabanas, which rest inside an actual Mayan plaza and feature modern amenities like water coolers, fridges, huge tiled baths, and natural insulation and ventilation. Though decried by some archaeologists when it was built in 1988, the presence of Chan Chich Lodge serves as a deterrent to temple looters and marijuana traffickers, both of which used to thrive in northern Belize.

Guests spend their days birding (more than 80 percent of visitors are avid birders from North America), exploring the ruins and hiking trails, canoeing at the nearby Laguna Verde, or horseback riding from the Gallon Jug stables. Birding opportunities include seeing trogons, ocellated turkeys, toucans, and hundreds of other birds. All five species of Belizean cat, including jaguars, pumas, and jaguarundis, live in the surrounding forest and are spotted regularly on the property. If you're one of the lucky ones, you might get to write your sighting on the lodge's daily log board. Tours of the coffee plantation and experimental farm at Gallon Jug provide the opportunity to learn all the steps in the coffee-making process as well as other sustainable agricultural initiatives taking place here. And the day doesn't end at the peaceful dining veranda, where the best steak in the country is served, among other Belizean cuisine options. If you're not signed up for the night safari, then you can finish off at the Looter's Trench Bar. Ask about a nighttime canoe ride along Laguna Seca to spot crocodiles and absorb the sheer magnitude of life in the rainforest at night. Chan Chich is 130 miles from Belize City, an all-day drive from the international airport or a (much easier) 30-minute charter flight to Gallon Jug. In addition to accommodations, add about US$70 per day for meals, plus tours, guides, and taxes.

Corozal Bay

Corozal Town's 9,000 or so inhabitants casually get by while the Corozal Bay washes against the seawall running the length of town. While English is the official language, Spanish is just as common, since many residents are descendants of early-day Mayan and mestizo refugees from neighboring Mexico. Historically, Corozal was the scene of attacks by the Maya during the Caste War. What remains of Fort Barlee can be found in the center of town, west of Central Park.

The town was almost entirely wiped out during Hurricane Janet in 1955 and has since been rebuilt. As you stroll the quiet streets, you'll find a library, a museum, the town hall, government administrative offices, a Catholic church, two secondary schools, five elementary schools, one gas station, a government hospital, a clinic, a few small hotels, a couple of bars, and several restaurants. There's not a whole lot of activity here, unless you happen to be in town during the Mexican-style "Spanish" fiestas of Christmas, Carnival, and Columbus Day; there are also a few local events in mid-September and a monthly art festival. Nevertheless, Corozal has a calming aura; you'll see families, lovers, and friends along Corozal Bay's various parks, running, playing, watching the sunset, or frolicking in the water.

While there are no major attractions per se for visitors in Corozal Town, just a couple of historical sights, it's an unassuming base for fishing trips, nature excursions, and tours of a few nearby ruins and waterways.

Day-trip options include the Shipstern Wildlife Nature Reserve, Sarteneja village, and the Mayan sites of Cerro Maya and Santa Rita. Visitors enter Corozal from the north (from Mexico), from the south on the Philip Goldson Highway, or from Ambergris Caye to the east by boat or plane. Getting oriented to Corozal is easy, since it's laid out on a grid system with avenues running north and south

(parallel to the seawall) and streets running east and west. Corozal's two primary avenues are 4th and 5th, which run the length of town. The majority of restaurants and stores of interest to travelers are on, or adjacent to, these streets. Wander through the town square, stroll the waterfront and the Market Square in town, and strike up a conversation with the locals or expats who've come to love the laid-back lifestyle. Many of the seaside parks, especially the one called Miami Beach, are popular hangouts on the weekend and holidays.

COROZAL TOWN
Sights

In the **Town Hall** (across from Central Park, 8am-4:30pm Mon.-Fri.), you'll find a dramatic historical mural painted by Manuel Villamour. The bright painting depicts the history of Corozal, including the drama of the downtrodden Maya, the explosive revolt called the Caste War, and the inequities of colonial rule. It's well worth stopping in for a look.

The **Corozal House of Culture** (1st Ave., tel. 501/422-0071, 8am-5pm Mon.-Fri., US$5) opened in February 2012 in a refurbished historic building that was once a municipal market, built in 1886. It is slowly being stocked with historical displays on Corozal's past and biographies on Corozaleños of note. Stop in to view the current month's exhibit, such as a fascinating look into the lives of indentured East Indians brought to Corozal in the 19th century to work the sugar plantations.

Dubbed "Window to the Past" by its founder and curator Lydia Ramcharan Pollard, the **East Indian Museum** (129 South End, tel. 501/402-3314, 9am-11:30am and 2pm-4:30pm Mon.-Fri., 9am-11:30am Sat., free) is the first museum in the Caribbean—and the only one in Belize—dedicated to East Indian history, heritage, and culture. The museum was established in 2001, and

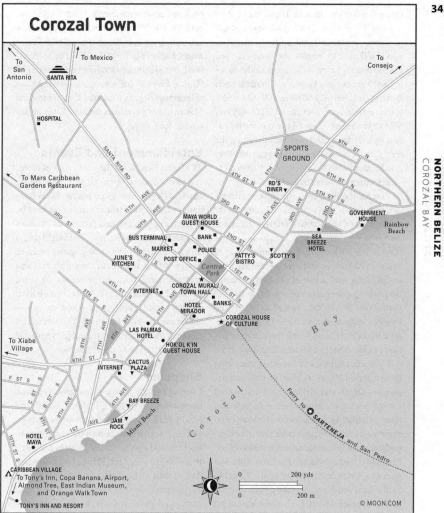

Corozal Town

Map labels: To San Antonio · To Mexico · To Consejo · SANTA RITA · HOSPITAL · SANTA RITA RD · 3RD ST S · To Mars Caribbean Gardens Restaurant · 11TH AVE · 10TH AVE · SPORTS GROUND · 9TH ST N · RD'S DINER · 4TH ST N · 5TH AVE · 6TH ST N · 5TH ST N · 2ND AVE · GOVERNMENT HOUSE · Rainbow Beach · MAYA WORLD GUEST HOUSE · 3RD ST N · 4TH AVE · 3RD AVE · BUS TERMINAL · MARKET · BANK · 2ND ST N · SEA BREEZE HOTEL · 2ND AVE · POLICE · PATTY'S BISTRO · SCOTTY'S · JUNE'S KITCHEN · POST OFFICE · Central Park · 1ST ST N · INTERNET · COROZAL MURAL / TOWN HALL · 1ST ST S · BANKS · 4TH ST S · 5TH ST S · HOTEL MIRADOR · COROZAL HOUSE OF CULTURE · Bay · To Xiabe Village · LAS PALMAS HOTEL · HOK'OL K'IN GUEST HOUSE · 6TH ST S · 7TH AVE · 8TH AVE · INTERNET · CACTUS PLAZA · Corozal Bay · BAY BREEZE · Miami Beach · 4TH AVE · Ferry to SARTENEJA and San Pedro · JAM ROCK · 1ST AVE · 9TH ST S · HOTEL MAYA · 10TH ST S · CARIBBEAN VILLAGE · To Tony's Inn, Copa Banana, Airport, Almond Tree, East Indian Museum, and Orange Walk Town · TONY'S INN AND RESORT · 0 200 yds · 0 200 m · © MOON.COM

its collections, gathered by Pollard through various means, include cooking utensils, musical instruments, and more. It is located on the Philip Goldson Highway, where Corozal Town meets Ranchito village.

Commonly referred to as "Cerros," the **Cerro Maya** (Maya Hill) archaeological site lords over both sea and rainforest on a peninsula across from Corozal called Lowry's Bight. Cerros was an important coastal trading center during the Late Pre-Classic Period

(350 BC-AD 250) and was occupied as late as 1300. Magnificent frescoes and stone heads were uncovered by archaeologist David Friedel, signifying that elite rule was firmly fixed by the end of the Pre-Classic Period. The tallest of Cerros's temples rises to 70 feet, and because of the rise in sea level, the onetime stone residences of the elite Maya are partially flooded. Be prepared for vicious mosquitoes here, especially if there's no breeze. You can reach the site by boat in minutes—hire one

through your guesthouse. If you travel during the dry season (Jan.-Apr.), you can get to Cerros by car; it takes up to 45 minutes, and you'll have to employ the hand-cranked Pueblo Nuevo Ferry. Admission to the ruins is US$10 per person. Guests at **Cerros Beach Resort** (tel. 501/623-9763 or 501/623-9530, www.cerrosbeachresort.com, US$40-60) can bike to the ruins; keep an eye out for jaguarundis, gray foxes, and coatimundis along the way. Cerros Beach Resort is a quiet, off-the-grid location with four screened-in thatch cabanas with private baths and hot water.

The **Santa Rita** site, one mile northeast of Corozal, was still a populated community of Maya when the Spanish arrived. The largest Santa Rita structure was explored at the turn of the 20th century by Thomas Gann. Sculptured friezes and stucco murals were found along with a burial site that indicates flourishing occupation in the Early Classic Period (about AD 300), as well as during the Late Post-Classic Period (1350-1530). Two significant burials were found from distant periods in the history of Santa Rita: One from AD 300 was a female and the other was a king from a period 200 years later. In 1985 archaeologists Diane and Arlen Chase discovered a tomb with a skeleton covered in jade and mica ornaments. It has been excavated and somewhat reconstructed under the Chases' jurisdiction; only one structure is accessible to the public. Some believe that Santa Rita was part of a series of coastal lookouts. To get to Santa Rita, you'll need to take a taxi. Corozal is a small place, and all taxis know how to get there.

Sports and Recreation

Corozal has beautiful, well-maintained stretches of green all along its seaside— **Mothers' Park, Children's Park,** and **Miami Beach Park.** Some parks include playgrounds, while others step into the bay, where children splash around or lovers cuddle up on concrete platforms, gazing at the sky. Spending a stolen morning hour at the park or sunset with friends is a favorite local activity. For fishing or boat activity while in Corozal, your best bet is **Our Island Tours and Charters** (tel. 501/633-9372 or 501/633-0081, ourislandtours@yahoo.com, full day of fishing US$400 for 4 people), offering boat rides across the bay to nearby Cerros for some Mayan history or across the New River or Río Hondo for fishing.

Entertainment and Events

At Miami Beach, on the south end of town, are two popular open-air bars: Swing by **Jam Rock** (1st Ave. S., no phone, 11am-8pm daily) while the bartender mixes a michelada, or have a cold drink and *botanas* at **Primo's Casita Bar** (no phone, noon-midnight daily) across the street. The most popular event in town is **Art in the Park,** a monthly arts and crafts festival held on the second or third weekend in Central Park. More than 30 local artists—from painters to wood-carvers—showcase the best of Corozal's talent. You can snag unique local crafts and gifts here and enjoy mestizo food and live music.

Shopping

Corozal has lots of little shops, grocery stores, bookstores, and a few gift shops. You'll find locally made jewelry, pottery, wood carvings, clothing, textiles, and a host of other mementos here and there, but the place is not overrun with gift shops yet. **White Sapphire** (7th Ave., south of the UNO station, no phone, 10am-6pm daily) has a large selection of local crafts and jewelry. Gifts, books, postcards, and other supplies can be obtained at **A&R** (4th Ave., no phone, 9am-5pm daily), near Patty's Bistro.

Food

The town market has a selection of cheap eats and is your best bet early in the morning if you have to eat and run to catch a bus just up the street.

1: Corozal is a small town that hugs the bay.
2: Scotty's Crocodile Cove

BELIZEAN

Head straight to ★ **Mars Caribbean Gardens Corozal** (Off College Rd., Corner of Corozo and Mahogany St., tel. 501/402-0108, 7am-9pm daily, from US$4), newly opened near the heart of town and serving authentic Belizean cuisine in all of its diverse forms, from Mayan to Garifuna, East Indian and Kriol, as well as local desserts and juices. Breakfast is also served all day. This sister restaurant to the popular Mars Caribbean in Los Angeles, owned and operated by talented culinary talent Ms. Marie, is equally tantalizing. Originally from Corozal, Ms. Marie dreamed of opening a business in her hometown, and she's certainly done it.

Patty's Bistro (2nd St. N., tel. 501/402-0174, 11am-9pm Mon.-Sat., US$5-9) is a long-time option as well for Belizean lunches and dinners. The conch soup has a unique hint of coconut, as does the curry shrimp entrée (US$7.50). There are fajitas and chicken dishes for less, and the burgers are excellent. Meals are served in an air-conditioned dining room.

Try the home-cooked daily specials at **June's Kitchen** (3rd St. S., tel. 501/422-2559, www.corozal.com/junes, breakfast and lunch daily, dinner by reservation only, US$4), where you're basically eating in Miss June's living room or on her porch. The breakfast plates are famous and huge, or stick to rice and beans with stewed chicken.

Scotty's Crocodile Cove (41 1st Ave., tel. 501/422-0005, http://scottysbarandgrill.com, noon-11pm Thurs.-Tues., US$5-12) is another good bet when passing through Corozal for some local and international bites before your boat ride—from burgers to pizza and sandwiches or just a cocktail. With a waterfront bar and second-story seating, it's also popular with expat residents.

Corozo Blues (Philip Goldson Hwy., tel. 501/422-0090, 10am-2am daily, US$10-18), found just before the turnoff to Tony's Inn, has a lovely setting and average food. But if you're looking to relax by the water in cozy cushioned seats or in your own gazebo set in a lush garden, it may be worthwhile. Serving international food and one local dish, dining options include wood-fired brick-oven pizzas, burgers, salads, and steaks.

INTERNATIONAL

Bay Breeze (1st Ave., tel. 501/402-3333, noon-11pm Tues.-Sun., US$5-10), across from Miami Beach, is a relaxed spot near the town's hotels, and the menu offers a range of pastas, grilled meats, and seafood. There's outdoor seating or indoor, open dining space.

GROCERIES

D's Superstore (College Rd., no phone, 9am-10pm daily) is the largest grocery in town. **Family Supermarket** (near Fort Barlee, no phone, 8am-midnight daily) is another option that is more centrally located.

Accommodations
UNDER US$25

Maya World Guest House (1st Ave., tel. 501/666-3577 or 501/627-2511, byronchuster@gmail.com, US$22.50-30) has clean rooms surrounding a cheery well-kept garden and cheery owners. It features a massive communal kitchen, cozy common areas, and a top-floor veranda with plenty of chairs and hammocks. The central location and conveniences such as bike rental and laundry service attract backpackers. **Caribbean Village RV Park and Campground** (Corozal Bay, tel. 501/422-2725, menziestours@btl.net, http://belizetransfers.com/caribbeanvillage) offers full RV hookups (US$20) and camping (US$5 pp).

US$25-50

Sea Breeze Hotel (23 1st Ave., tel. 501/402-3052, US$25 s, $30 d) offers budget waterfront accommodations in Corozal. Guest rooms have cable TV, fans (air-conditioning for additional cost), hot water, and wireless Internet. The seaside location of this hotel offers a cooling breeze in the evening, and it's a short walk from the water taxi pier.

Just two blocks south of the town center and right across from the water, the

Hok'ol K'in Guest House (89 4th Ave., tel. 501/422-3329, maya@btl.net, www.corozal. net, US$21-65) was begun by a former Peace Corps volunteer with the intention of supporting local Mayan community endeavors. In Yucatec Maya, Hok'ol K'in means "Coming of the Rising Sun," a sight you'll see from your window if you're up early enough. Follow your sun salutations with an excellent breakfast (and real coffee!) on the patio downstairs. Hok'ol K'in's 10 guest rooms have private baths, verandas, cable TV, and fans; free wireless Internet is available. Ask about available trips and homestays (or visits) with local families; the staff are very helpful in arranging things to do. This is one of the few lodgings in Belize equipped to handle a wheelchair (one room only, so be sure to specify if it's needed). There's a bar, and the restaurant (7am-7pm daily) serves a variety of good meals.

★ **Hotel Mirador** (tel. 501/422-0189, www.mirador.bz, US$35-75) is a 24-room lodging across from the main dock and seawall; the rooftop boasts the best views in town. The guest rooms are spotless, with private baths and hot and cold water, and the hallways are cavernous. There's cable TV and wireless Internet. Deluxe guest rooms with air-conditioning start at US$50. The bay-facing guest rooms have wonderful light and views.

On the road leading into town from the south, the **Hotel Maya and Apartments** (South End, tel. 501/422-2082 or 501/422-2874, www.hotelmaya.net, US$35-50) offers 20 guest rooms with air-conditioning, TVs, and private baths; the restaurant serves breakfast only. Furnished two-bedroom apartments with air-conditioning start at US$400 per month.

US$100-150
At ★ **Tony's Inn and Beach Resort** (South End, tel. 501/422-2055 or 501/677-5368, tonys@btl.net, www.tonysinn.com, from US$95-125), "beach" may be stretching it a bit, and the 24 guest rooms are set up more like a Motel 6 than a resort. Still, the large guest rooms have air-conditioning, private baths, and hot and cold water. The renovated Cielo restaurant is in a nice setting on the water, and the hotel has its own marina and runs a variety of local trips.

Information and Services
Corozal's main web portal (www.corozal. com) is a fount of information for travelers. Corozal also has several ATMs and branches of **Belize Bank, Scotiabank,** and **Atlantic Bank** (8am-2pm Mon.-Thurs., 8:30am-4:30pm Fri.). For emergencies, contact the **fire department** (tel. 501/422-2105), **police** (tel. 501/422-2022), or the **hospital** (tel. 501/422-2076). For Internet access, try the **Hotel Mirador** (across from the main dock and seawall, tel. 501/422-0189, www.mirador.bz) or **M.E. Computer Systems** (3rd St. S., 9am-9pm Mon.-Sat.). You can also find a couple of desktops at **Stellar Link** (39A 4th Ave., tel. 501/402-2043, 9am-5pm Mon.-Fri., 9am-1pm Sat.). There are a few other Internet places around the Central Park.

Transportation
AIR
There are five inexpensive daily flights on each of these airlines between Corozal and San Pedro. Contact **Tropic Air** (tel. 501/226-2626, U.S. tel. 800/422-3435, www.tropicair. com) or **Maya Island Air** (tel. 501/223-1140, www.mayaislandair.com) for schedules.

BUS
Check the ever-changing schedule at Corozal's Northern Transport Bus Station before departure. Northbound buses from Belize City alternate final destinations between Corozal and Chetumal, taking three hours to Corozal (US$6) and leaving Belize City frequently 5:30am-7:30pm daily. Southbound buses from Corozal leave regularly between 3:45am and 7pm daily, all of them originating 15 minutes or so earlier in Santa Elena. If you have connections to make in Chetumal, be aware that, unlike Belize, Mexico uses daylight saving time.

BOAT

The *Thunderbolt* (tel. 501/631-3400 or 501/422-0026, www.ambergriscaye.com/thunderbolt, US$22.50 pp) departs for San Pedro at 7am daily. Special promotions are often run during peak holiday times, so call ahead. From San Pedro, the boat leaves the Westside dock at 3pm daily; the trip takes about 90 minutes, and stops in Sarteneja are possible on request.

TAXI

There are a few taxi stands in town: **Los Toucanes Taxi Union** (tel. 501/402-2070) is by the market, a few steps away from the bus station; **Corozal Central Park Taxi Union** (tel. 501/422-2035) is by the Central Park. You can get around town for US$2.50, to the airstrip for US$5, to the border for US$10, or to Chetumal and Cerros for US$30—all convenient ways to go if you have a few people to split the costs. You can also contact **Belize VIP Service** (tel. 501/422-2725, www.belizevipautorental.com) for car rentals as well as transfers.

TOURS

One of the best independent guides around is **Vital Nature and Mayan Tours** (tel. 501/602-8975, www.cavetubing.bz), also known as Vitalino Reyes, whose years of experience qualify him to teach and certify many of Corozal's other guides. Vital runs night safaris as well as tours to local ruins, the caves at Jaguar Paw, the Belize Zoo, or anywhere else you want to go. **Belize VIP Transfer Services** (tel. 501/422-2725, www.belizetransfers.com) is your best bet for charter transportation, with vehicles that are great for groups. Belize VIP specializes in local tours (including a day tour of Corozal and Cerros), trips to Lamanai, Chetumal transfers (and other Mexican attractions), and Tikal or Flores trips to Guatemala. **George & Esther Moralez Travel Service** (tel. 501/422-2485, www.gettransfers.com) offers transfer services and tours and will also help you with hotel and local flight bookings (dial 00 before the phone number when calling from Mexico to Belize). **Hok'ol K'in Guest House** (89 4th Ave., tel. 501/422-3329, maya@btl.net, www.corozal.net) handles all such trips as well, especially to local villages.

CONSEJO VILLAGE

Nine miles north of Corozal, the tiny fishing village of Consejo is home to a beach hideaway, an upscale hotel, a nine-hole golf course,

The *Thunderbolt* has daily service between Corozal and Ambergris Caye.

and a retirement community of some 400 North Americans called **Consejo Shores** (www.consejoshores.com).

Rent one of three bayside units at **Smuggler's Den** (2 miles northwest of Consejo, tel. 501/600-9723, http://smugglersdenbelize.tripod.com, US$35-60), which are nicely furnished and have hot and cold water; they are quite a bargain if you're looking for isolation. Two units have private baths and kitchenettes, but the unit without a kitchen is cheaper. Discounts are sometimes available on request. Smuggler's is locally famous for its Sunday afternoon roast beef dinners; reserve in advance.

The **New Millennium Restaurant** (no phone, 11am-9pm Wed.-Mon., US$2-10), in the heart of Consejo village, is a friendly watering hole and eatery serving up daily specials at great prices.

★ SARTENEJA

From the Mayan *Tzaten-a-ha* ("give me the water"), Sarteneja was named after the 13 Mayan wells found in the area, carved into limestone bedrock and providing potable water. In addition to being a picturesque fishing village, Sarteneja is the only place on mainland Belize where you can watch the sun set over the water. The spot was first settled by the Maya as an important trading area. It is thought to have been occupied from 600 BC to AD 1200, and period gold, copper, and shells continue to turn up in the area. Mexican refugees from the Yucatán Caste War settled here in the mid-19th century, again attracted by the availability of drinking water. The village took a pounding from Hurricane Janet in 1955 but rebounded and became known for its boatbuilders and free-diving lobster and conch fishers.

Today, 80 percent of Sarteneja's households remain reliant on the resources of the Belize Barrier Reef. Tourism is creeping in, and Sarteneja offers one of the more off-the-beaten-path experiences in the country. Located on Corozal Bay, it is a well-kept secret in Belize, and few travelers have heard about its breathtaking sunsets, sportfishing, turquoise swimming waters, and importance as a protected area for manatees and bird-nesting colonies in the Corozal Bay Wildlife Sanctuary. This is slowly changing, as more travelers now stop here on their way to the Northern Cayes. Bring your swimwear—the water is beautiful, and a stop here feels like an island getaway.

Wooden Boats

Sarteneja is known for the annual **Easter Regatta,** during which newly painted sailboats of the artisanal fishing fleet, crewed by local anglers, race against each other in a tradition that has continued since 1950. The regatta, on Easter weekend, includes live music, food, and fun local "catch the greasy pig" games. Master boatbuilders Juan Guerrero and Jacobo Verde handcraft traditional wooden vessels at their workshops in Sarteneja—the wooden boatbuilding tradition is unique in Belize and also in all of Central America. During fishing season, these boats dock in Belize City by the Swing Bridge. If you're interested in culture and boats, ask around for the **Mitzi-Ba Wooden Boat Building** workshop to see master builder Guerrero at work. If you're lucky, you'll witness one being designed from scratch.

Sports and Recreation

Sarteneja's location is ideal for fishing, kayaking, sailing, or exploring the nearby reserves. You can rent kayaks from the office of the **Tour Guide Association** (Front St., US$5 per hour double kayak, up to 5 hours max.), or ask about its Manatee Day tour to go manatee-spotting (US$20 pp). The **beach** on the long, pretty coastline offers swimming and relaxing. The farther east you go, the prettier and more isolated the swimming areas get. Rent a bicycle from **Brisis Bike Rental** (Front St., no phone, 10am-4pm daily) if your guesthouse doesn't provide one. Other options include hiking in the Shipstern Nature Reserve, exploring the Bacalar Chico National Park and Marine Reserve on the northern tip of

Ambergris Caye, or fishing along Corozal Bay (US$30 pp for 2 people) with Ritchie Cruz of **Ritchie's Place** (Front St., tel. 501/668-1531).

With access to nearby Mayan sites and ties to the barrier reef at Bacalar Chico, Sarteneja has a lot to offer the adventurous traveler in search of the real Belize. The community is aware of its resources, and groups have joined forces to form the **Sarteneja Alliance for Conservation and Development** (N. Front St., sacdsarteneja@gmail.com), which comanages Corozal Bay Wildlife Sanctuary. Local anglers, now trained as guides, offer a number of guided tours, both marine and inland. Contact Evanier Cruz, the president of the **Sarteneja Tour Guide Association** (tel. 501/635-1655). The office is on the seafront; take a left from the arrival dock. It can also help visitors find a licensed local tour guide.

Sarteneja is also the location of the **Manatee Rehabilitation Centre,** run by Wildtracks, a local NGO that takes in and rehabilitates orphan manatee calves as part of a national program to protect this threatened species. The center is not open to visitors.

Food

Sarteneja Inn Restaurant (Tza ten a ha St., tel. 501/628-7541, 8am-8pm daily, US$3-5) has a spacious dining room serving tasty quesadillas, burgers, pasta, fish fingers, and rice and beans, as well as fresh squeezed natural juices. It's a good stop if you're in between waiting for the ferry and need Wi-Fi to boot. If you're lucky, you're in town when **Martineja** (N. Front St., tel. 501/423-2021, 8am-10pm Fri.-Mon., later close on weekend) is open—the best addition to Sarteneja, bringing gourmet waterfront dining to a small village that is slowly expanding. Choose from their large pizza menu, imported rib steaks and other grilled meats, teriyaki bowls, or popular Sunday brunch. All food is locally sourced and fresh. Also on the main drag, **Crabby Restaurant & Bar** (N. Front St., tel. 501/620-8358, US$3-5) is good for drinks and Belizean dishes and steps away from the arrival dock.

Accommodations

Most accommodations, eateries, and bars can be found along Front Street, abutting the sea and dock.

Experience local culture through the **Sarteneja Homestay Program** (tel. 501/634-8032, 501/661-8395, or 501/664-5490, sartenejahomestay@gmail.com, US$25 pp, includes meals). There are 13 families participating in the program, providing a unique village opportunity. Stay for a night or a week in a safe, comfortable, private room with shared indoor toilet. Enjoy three home-cooked meals, learn how to make tortillas, and practice your Spanish. The program gets rave reviews; don't hesitate to call a day ahead or ask on short notice.

★ **Fernando's Seaside Guesthouse** (tel. 501/423-2085, www.fernandoseaside.com, US$50 plus tax) was the first to open its doors in Sarteneja. Its guest rooms offer private baths, air-conditioning, cable TV, wireless Internet, and a nice veranda with hammocks and a waterfront view (a discount is available without air-conditioning). Like most men in Sarteneja, the owner Fernando Alamilla was once a full-time fisher who used to sail and fish for up to 10 days at a time; he passed away two years ago and his son Fernando Jr. helps run the guesthouse and can help arrange tours and transportation (including Tropic Air flights to the cayes) or pick you up from Chetumal for a fee.

Backpackers Paradise (Bandera Rd., tel. 501/423-2016) is about a 15-minute brisk walk north from the arrival dock. Accommodations at this funky, laid-back, rustic, and friendly hangout range from camping (US$3.50 pp) to guest rooms with shared baths and a few private cabanas (US$17-45). **Nathalie's Restaurant** (8am-2pm and 6pm-8pm daily), also on-site, serves up wonderful and affordable dishes, including crepes made by the French Vietnamese proprietress. Free wireless Internet is available, bicycles (US$10) and horses (US$35) can be rented for the day, and guided day trips are on offer as well. Guests can use the communal kitchen to prepare meals (Sarteneja has a few grocery shops and *tortillerias*) and relax in the shared screened reading room peppered with hammocks. If you choose, ask to be picked up from the dock by Nathalie in her horse and buggy.

Information and Services

You can get online at **Backpackers Paradise** (Bandera Rd., tel. 501/423-2016) for US$2.50 per hour. Laundry service is also available (US$5 per load). Be forewarned: There are no ATMs or banks in Sarteneja, only a local credit union for Belizeans, so bring enough cash to last your stay.

Transportation

Sarteneja has been linked to the rest of Belize by land for less than 40 years—roads are rugged and dusty and, during rainy season, often flooded and rutted. The road from Corozal to Sarteneja was recently upgraded through a European Union-funded project; although the route remains unpaved, it was a significant improvement. Still, expect a few rough spots after a heavy rain.

BOAT

Most visitors get to Sarteneja by boat from Corozal or San Pedro. The water taxi *Thunderbolt* (tel. 501/422-0026, cell tel. 501/610-4475, captain's cell 501/631-3400, www.ambergriscaye.com/thunderbolt), a well-run and locally owned operation, will stop in Sarteneja on its once-daily Corozal-San Pedro run. It departs Corozal at 7am, arriving in Sarteneja 40 minutes later before heading on to San Pedro. The San Pedro-Corozal boat (about 90 minutes) departs at 3pm from San Pedro, stopping at Sarteneja at approximately 4:30pm. Note that Sarteneja is an on-request-only stop on the way back, so let the captain and crew know as you board if you're heading to Sarteneja only on a day trip from Corozal to be sure to get picked up in Sarteneja on the 4:30pm return boat (Corozal-Sarteneja US$12.50 one-way, US$25 round-trip, San Pedro-Sarteneja US$22.50 one-way, US$42.50 round-trip). The *Thunderbolt* runs

every day of the year except Christmas and Good Friday.

AIR

Tropic Air (tel. 501/226-2012, U.S. tel. 800/422-3435, www.tropicair.com) has two flights a day that will stop at Sarteneja's tiny airstrip on request. Flights leave San Pedro at 7am and 4:45pm daily, arriving in Sarteneja 10 minutes later, as part of the San Pedro-Corozal schedule. Flights will stop later in the day if there is more than one passenger requesting to be dropped off or picked up in Sarteneja.

BUS

The bus from Belize City is often full of returning anglers and the most exciting way to get here. The distinctive light-blue Sarteneja buses leave Belize City from a riverside lot next to the Supreme Court building. Four buses make the three-hour ride (US$5 one-way), the first at noon and the last at 5pm Monday-Saturday. All buses stop just before the bridge at the Zeta Ice Factory in Orange Walk to pick up more passengers. Buses depart Sarteneja for Belize City (via Orange Walk) between 4am and 6:30am. There is a direct bus from Chetumal, via Corozal and Orange Walk, which runs every day, including Sunday, leaving Chetumal at noon or 1pm (depending on whether or not Mexico is on daylight saving time). The return bus departs for Corozal and Chetumal at 6am daily. Check with your host for any changes. There is also local traffic going to Sarteneja from Orange Walk via San Estevan.

CAR

From Corozal, head south and turn left at the sign for Tony's Inn. Follow this road, veering right until you come to a stone wall; then go left. Follow this road until you reach the first ferry across the New River, an experience in itself and free of charge. Sometimes there are lineups on Friday and Monday, so anticipate a bit of a wait. After crossing, continue on the unsurfaced road until you reach a T-junction. Turn left toward Copper Bank, Cerros, and the ferry to Chunox. On entering Copper Bank, keep driving until you see the signs for Donna's Place (an excellent eatery) and the Cerros ruins. If you're not stopping to eat or visit the ruins, turn left at the ruins sign and proceed until you see the sign for the ferry crossing. After crossing, continue until you reach another T-junction. Turn left for Sarteneja, or right for Chunox and the grinding drive through Little Belize back to Orange Walk.

★ SHIPSTERN CONSERVATION AND MANAGEMENT AREA

In Corozal District, Shipstern is in the northeastern corner on the Belize coast. Thirty-two square miles of moist forest, savanna, and wetlands have been set aside to preserve as-yet-unspoiled habitats of well-known insect, bird, and mammal species associated with the tropics. The reserve is home to about 300 species of birds, 70 species of reptiles and amphibians, and more than 270 species of butterflies (the reserve began the production of live butterfly pupae through intensive breeding). The reserve also encompasses the shallow **Shipstern Lagoon,** dotted with mangrove islands, which creates wonderful habitat for many wading birds.

The International Tropical Conservation Foundation has been extremely generous in supporting Shipstern. As at most reserves, the objective is to manage and protect habitats and wildlife, as well as to develop an education program that entails teaching the local community and introducing children to the concept of wildlife conservation in their area. Shipstern, however, goes a step further by conducting an investigation of how tropical countries such as Belize can develop self-supporting conservation areas through the controlled, intensive production of natural commodities found within such wildlife settlements. Developing facilities for the scientific study of the reserve

area and its wildlife is part of this important program.

Visitors Center

Start at the **visitors center** (3 miles outside of Sarteneja, tours 9am-noon and 1pm-3pm daily except Christmas, New Year's Day, and Easter, US$5). The admission fee includes a guided tour of the center, butterfly garden, botanical trail, and observation tower. The forest is alive with nature's critters and fascinating flora. Before starting your 20- to 30-minute walk, pick up a book with detailed descriptions of the trail and the trees at the visitors center. The lovely **Botanical Trail** starts at the parking lot by the entrance and meanders through the forest. Visitors have the opportunity to see three types of hardwood forests with 100 species of trees, many of which are labeled with their Latin and Yucatec Maya names. Go up the tower for a spectacular view of Sarteneja and the reserve.

Lodging and Tours

Shipstern now offers multiple overnight options for those who want to take in this conservation area fully. There are two dorm rooms with seven bunk beds each (US$20) and shared baths inside the hallway. For more comfort, two lodge cabins boast four rooms each. Common features include a screened porch, single beds or double, ceiling fans, air-conditioning, spacious private baths, and tub showers. There's Wi-Fi access on the property, and a communal dining room, which may have air-conditioning by the time you read this.

The cultural tours offered here are unique in kind, including a visit to Fire Burn, a Kriol settlement in the middle of a forest across Shipstern Lagoon, or to the Mennonite village of Blue Creek, as well as birding hikes in Xopol, 10 miles west of the reserve.

Transportation

It is easiest to take a boat from Corozal or to hire a local tour guide to arrange travel.

From Corozal and Orange Walk, figure a little more than an hour to drive here. The road takes you through **San Estevan** and then to **Progresso.** Turn right just before entering Progresso to **Little Belize** (a Mennonite community). Continue on to **Chunox. Sarteneja** is three miles beyond Shipstern. Don't forget a long-sleeved shirt, pants, mosquito repellent, binoculars, and a camera for your exploration of the reserve.

Sarteneja Adventure Tours (tel. 501/633-0067, www.sartenejatours.com) provides standard tours and overnight camping trips, with opportunities to explore Shipstern's trails by day or night and visit local caves, Mayan ruins, and nesting bird colonies. While accommodations are available by special request, visitors are encouraged to stay overnight in Sarteneja village.

Chetumal, Mexico

An exciting dose of culture shock is an easy 15 miles from Corozal. Chetumal, capital of the Mexican state of Quintana Roo, is a relatively modern, midsize city of more than 200,000—nearly as many people as in the entire country of Belize! If you don't come for the culture (wonderful museums, a few parks, a zoo, and a delicious seafront), then you must be here to shop in the new American-style mall or see a first-run film in Chet's brand-new air-conditioned Cineplex, inside the Plaza de las Américas mall.

Chetumal can be visited as a day trip from Corozal or used as a base from which to visit the many Yucatecan archaeological sites—including Tulum, just up the coast. It's also a gateway to Mexico's well-known Caribbean resort areas: Cancún, Cozumel, Playa del Carmen, and Akumal. Chetumal presents the businesslike atmosphere of a growing metropolis without the bikini-clad tourist crowds of the north. A 10-minute walk takes you to the waterfront from the marketplace and most of the hotels. Modern, sculpted monuments stand along a breezy promenade that skirts the broad crescent of the bay. Explore the backstreets, where worn, wooden buildings still have a Central American-Caribbean look. The largest building in town—white, three stories, close to the waterfront—houses most of the government offices. Wide tree-lined avenues and sidewalks front dozens of small variety shops.

SIGHTS

Do not miss the **Museo de la Cultura Maya** (Avenida Héroes, tel. 983/832-6838, 9am-7pm Tues.-Thurs. and Sun., 9am-8pm Fri.-Sat., US$5), located at the market; it is an impressive and creative experience by any standard. The **Museo de la Ciudad** (Av. de los Héroes 108, no phone, 9am-6pm Tues.-Sat., 9am-2pm Sun., US$12) is excellent as well, with a great deal of contemporary Mexican art.

On Avenida Héroes, five miles north of the city, is **Calderitas Bay,** a breezy area for picnicking, dining, camping, and RVing. Tiny **Isla Tamalcas,** 1.5 miles off the shore of Calderitas, is the home of the primitive capybara, the largest of all rodents. Twenty-one miles north of Chetumal on Highway 307 is **Cenote Azul,** a circular cenote over 200 feet deep and 600 feet across and filled with brilliant blue water. This is a spectacular place to stop for a swim, lunch at the outdoor restaurant, or just to have a cold drink.

FOOD AND ACCOMMODATIONS

Chetumal has quite a few hotels in all price categories (including a Holiday Inn near the market), although quite a few are lacking

Chetumal

Map labels:
To Main Bus Terminal and Mercado Nuevo Bus Terminal
MINIBUS TERMINAL
CRISTÓBAL   COLON
SUPER BODEGÓN
FARMACIA SIMILARES
SECOND-CLASS BUS STATION
MUSEO DE LA CULTURA MAYA/EDUCAL
COMBIS TO CALDERITAS
BULE BUZZ
AV. MAHATMA GANDHI
MONUMENTO AL MESTIZO
HOTEL UCÚM
To Chetumal Airport
Mercado Ignacio Manuel Altamirano
LAVANDERÍA INDUSTRIAL
EFRAIN   AGUILAR
HOTEL BRASILIA
200 yds
200 m
AV. JOSE MARIA MORELOS   MADERO
MUSEO MUNICIPAL
INTERNET CAFÉS
MUSEO DE LA CIUDAD
COMBIS TO BACALAR
HOTEL VILLA FONTANA
HEROES DE   CHAPULTEPEC
To San Pedro (Belize) Ferry
HOTEL LOS COCOS
EUROPCAR
LAZARO   CARDENAS
AV. 5 DE MAYO
© MOON.COM

in service, as well as many fine cafés specializing in fresh seafood. A convenient location and budget hotel in Chetumal is **Hotel Villa Fontana** (tel. 52/983-129-2003, US$20), with air-conditioning, TVs, and Wi-Fi. The hotel is on Avenida Héroes, the main street, which is home to most of the city's other hotels and the Museo de la Cultura Maya.

TRANSPORTATION

Corozal-based **Belize VIP Transfer Services** (tel. 501/422-2725, www.belizetransfers.com) and **George & Esther Moralez Travel Service** (tel. 501/422-2485, www.gettransfers.com) will arrange Chetumal transfers (and other Mexican attractions) and trips to local ruins.

Bus

Buses from Belize City to Corozal and Chetumal travel throughout the day all the way through the border (you'll need to get off twice to pass through immigration controls and pay a US$19 exit fee) to the Nuevo Mercado Lázaro Cárdenas in Chetumal. A local Chetumal bus from Corozal costs US$1.25; a taxi to the border costs US$10. If it's running, the express bus to Chetumal from Belize City takes about four hours and

costs US$11. Also check with the various kiosks and travel agents in and near the Ocean Ferry Water Taxi Terminal by the Swing Bridge in Belize City for direct bus service to Chetumal.

If you're traveling by bus from Belize, you will pass the main ADO bus terminal on Avenida Insurgentes; ask the driver to stop at the Pemex gas station on the corner of Avenidas Insurgentes and Héroes. Bus travel is a versatile and inexpensive way to traverse the Quintana Roo coast—there are frequent trips to Playa del Carmen and Cancún, and a fleet of luxury express buses is a treat after Belize's school bus system. Chetumal is part of the loop between Campeche, Cancún, and Mérida. Fares and schedules change regularly; currently the fare to Cancún is about US$30. It's about a 22-hour bus ride from Chetumal to Mexico City.

Boat

Chetumal can also be reached by water taxi on the **San Pedro Belize Express** (tel. 501/226-3535, www.belizewatertaxi.com, US$45 one-way from San Pedro), which departs for Chetumal at 7:30am daily (or 7am from Caye Caulker) and returns at 3pm. **San Pedro Water Jets Express** (tel.

501/226-2194, www.sanpedrowatertaxi.com, US$55 one-way) leaves San Pedro at 8am daily and returns from Chetumal at 3pm.

Car

A good paved road connects Chetumal with Mérida, Campeche, Villahermosa, and Francisco Escárcega. Highway 307 links all of Quintana Roo's coastal cities. Expect little traffic, and you'll find that gas stations are well spaced if you top off at each one. Car rentals are scarce in Chetumal; go to the **Hotel Los Cocos** for **Avis** (Av. de los Héroes, tel. 52/983-835-0430, 9am-5pm daily). Chetumal is an economical place to rent a car (if one is available), since the tax is only 6 percent. If you're driving, watch out for No Left Turn signs in Chetumal.

Background

The Landscape

GEOGRAPHY

Belize lies on the northeast coast of Central America, above the corner where the Honduran coast takes off to the east. Belize's 8,866 square miles of territory are bordered on the north by Mexico, on the west and south by Guatemala, and on the east by the Caribbean Sea and the Belize Barrier Reef. From the northern Río Hondo border with Mexico to the southern border with Guatemala, Belize's mainland measures 180 miles long, and it is 68 miles across at its widest point. Offshore, Belize has more than 200 cayes, or islands. Both the coastal

region and the northern half of the mainland are flat, but the land rises in the south and west to over 3,000 feet above sea level. The Maya Mountains and Cockscomb range form the country's backbone and include Belize's highest point, **Doyle's Delight** (3,688 feet). Mangrove swamps cover much of the humid coastal plain.

In the west, the Cayo District contains the **Mountain Pine Ridge Reserve.** At one time a magnificent Caribbean pine forest, it has, over the decades, been reduced by lumber removal, fires, and the pine bark beetle. Despite vast beetle damage, the upper regions of Mountain Pine Ridge still provide spectacular scenery, with sections of thick forest surrounding the **Macal River** as it tumbles over huge granite boulders (except where the river was dammed at Chalillo). **Thousand Foot Falls** plunges 1,600 feet to the valley below and is the highest waterfall in Central America. The **Río Frio** cave system offers massive stalactites and stalagmites to the avid spelunker. The diverse landscape includes limestone-fringed granite boulders.

Over thousands of years, what was once a sea in the northern half of Belize has become a combination of scrub vegetation and rich tropical hardwood forest. Near the Mexican border, much of the land has been cleared, and it's here that the majority of sugar crops are raised, along with family plots of corn and beans. Most of the northern coast is swampy, with a variety of grasses and mangroves that attract waterfowl and wading birds. Rainfall in the north averages 60 inches annually, though it's generally dry November-May.

Belize has had a contentious territorial dispute with Guatemala for nearly two centuries, with Guatemala claiming that over 50 percent of Belizean territory—particularly its southern half below the Sibun River—is indeed part of Guatemala and disputing the 1859 Treaty they signed with Great Britain, claiming it was not a border treaty agreement. Tensions have

flared on and off since at the border between the two countries. In 2008, Guatemala and Belize finally signed an accord that they would hold a referendum whereby each population would vote on whether or not to send the matter to the International Court of Justice. Guatemala voted "yes" in their national referendum held April 2018. In March 2019, before this edition is published, Belizeans will head to the polls to vote either "yes" or "no" to submit this long-standing dispute before the ICJ for final resolution. Opinions are as divided as you can imagine, with die-hard patriots saying to vote "no" while the current government is pushing for a "yes" so that this is permanently settled and convinced that strict legal interpretation by the ICJ (which would take at least several years in court) will only lead to Belize keeping its whole territory.

Cayes and Atolls

More than 200 cayes (pronounced "keys" and derived from the Spanish *cayo* for "key" or "islet") dot the blue waters off Belize's eastern coast. They range in size from barren patches that are submerged at high tide to the largest two, Ambergris Caye—25 miles long and nearly 4.5 miles across at its widest point—and Caye Caulker, five miles long. Some cayes are inhabited by people, others only by wildlife. The majority are lush patches of mangrove that challenge the geographer's definition of what makes an island (that's why you'll never see a precise figure of how many there are).

Most of the cayes lie within the protection of the 180-mile-long Belize Barrier Reef, which parallels the mainland. Without the protection of the reef—in essence a breakwater—the islands would be washed away. Within the reef, the sea is relatively calm and shallow. Beyond the reef are three of the Caribbean's four atolls: **Glover's Reef, Turneffe Islands,** and **Lighthouse Reef.** An atoll is a ring-shaped coral island surrounding a lagoon, always beautiful and almost exclusively found in the South Pacific.

The three types of cayes are **wet cayes,** which are submerged part of the time and can support only mangrove swamps; **bare coral outcroppings** that are equally uninhabitable; and **sandy islands** with littoral forest, which is the most endangered habitat in Belize due to development pressure. The more inhabited cayes lie in the northern part of the reef and include Caye Caulker, Ambergris Caye, St. George's Caye, and Caye Chapel.

Reefs

The polyps of reef-building corals deposit calcium carbonate around themselves to form a cup-like skeleton or corallite. As these small creatures continue to reproduce and die, their sturdy skeletons accumulate. Over eons, broken bits of coral, animal waste, and granules of soil contribute to the strong foundation for a reef that will slowly rise toward the surface. In a healthy environment, one can grow 1-2 inches a year.

Reefs are divided into three types: atoll, fringing, and barrier. An **atoll** can be formed around the crater of a submerged volcano. The polyps begin building their colonies on the round edge of the crater, forming a circular coral island with a lagoon in the center. Thousands of atolls occupy the world's tropical waters. Only four are in the Caribbean Sea; three of those are in Belize's waters.

A **fringing reef** is coral living on a shallow shelf that extends outward from shore into the sea. A **barrier reef** runs parallel to the coast, with water separating it from the land. Sometimes it's actually a series of reefs with channels of water in between. This is the case with some of the larger barrier reefs in the Pacific and Indian Oceans.

The Belize Barrier Reef is part of the greater Mesoamerican Barrier Reef, which extends from Mexico's Isla Mujeres to the Bay Islands of Honduras. The Belizean portion of the reef begins at Bacalar Chico in the north and ends with the Sapodilla Cayes in the south. At 180 miles long, it is the longest reef in the western and northern hemispheres.

CORAL

Corals are formed by millions of tiny carnivorous polyps that feed on minute organisms and live in large colonies of individual species. Coral polyps have cylinder-shaped bodies, generally less than half an inch long. One end is attached to a hard surface (the bottom of the sea, the rim of a submerged volcano, or the reef itself). The mouth at the other end is encircled with tiny tentacles that capture the polyp's minute prey with a deadly sting. At night, coral reefs really come to life as polyps emerge to feed. Related to the jellyfish and sea anemone, polyps need sunlight and clear saltwater not colder than 70°F to survive. Symbiotic algal cells, called zooxanthellae, live within coral tissues and provide the polyps with much of their energy requirements and coloration.

Estuaries

The marshy areas and bays at the mouths of rivers where saltwater and freshwater mix are called estuaries. Here, nutrients from inland are carried out to sea by currents and tides to nourish reefs, seagrass beds, and the open ocean. Many plants and animals feed, live, or mate in these waters. Conchs, crabs, shrimp, and other shellfish thrive here, and several types of jellyfish and other invertebrates call this home. Seabirds, shorebirds, and waterfowl of all types frequent estuaries to feed, nest, and mate. Crocodiles, dolphins, and manatees are regular visitors. Rays, sharks, and tarpon hunt and mate here. During the wet season, the estuaries of Belize pump a tremendous amount of nutrients into the sea.

Mangroves

The doctor on Christopher Columbus's ship reported in 1494 that mangroves in the Caribbean were "so thick that a rabbit could scarcely walk through." Mangroves live on the edge between land and sea, forming dense thickets that act as a protective border against the forces of wind and waves. Four species grow along many low-lying coastal areas on the mainland and along island lagoons and fringes. Of these, the red mangrove and the black mangrove are most prolific. Red mangroves in excess of 30 feet tall are found in tidal areas, inland lagoons, and rivermouths, but always close to the sea. Their signature is arching prop roots, which provide critical habitat and nursery grounds for many reef fish. The black mangrove grows to almost double that height. Its roots are slender upright projectiles that grow to about 12 inches, protruding all around the mother tree. Both types of roots provide air to the tree.

MANGROVE SUCCESSION
Red mangroves (*Rhizophora mangle*) specialize in creating land—the seedpods fall into the water and take root on the sandy bottom of a shallow shoal. The roots, which can survive in seawater, then collect sediments from the water and the tree's own dropping leaves to create soil. Once the red mangrove forest has created land, it makes way for the next mangrove in the succession process. The black mangrove (*Avicennia germinans*) can actually outcompete the red mangrove at this stage, because of its ability to live in anoxic soil (without oxygen). In this way, the red mangrove appears to do itself in by creating an anoxic environment. But while the black mangrove is taking over the upland of the community, the red mangrove continues to dominate the perimeter, as it continuously creates more land from the sea. One way to identify a black mangrove forest is by the thousands of dense pneumatophores (tiny air roots) covering the ground under the trees.

Soon, burrowing organisms such as insects and crabs begin to inhabit the floor of the black mangrove forest, and the first ground covers, *Salicornia* and saltwort (*Batis maritima*) take hold—thereby aerating the soil and enabling the third and fourth mangrove species in succession to move in: the white mangrove (*Laguncularia racemosa*) and the gray mangrove (*Conocarpus erectus*), also known as buttonwood.

DESALINIZERS
Each of the three primary mangrove species lives in a very salty environment, and each has its own special way of eliminating salt. The red mangrove concentrates the salt taken up with seawater into individual leaves, which turn bright yellow and fall into the prop roots, thereby adding organic matter to the system. The black mangrove eliminates salt from the underside of each leaf. If you pick a black mangrove leaf and lick the back, it will taste very salty. The white mangrove eliminates salt through two tiny salt pores located on the petiole (the stem that connects the leaf to the branch). If you sleep in a hammock under a white mangrove tree, you will feel drops of salty water as the tree "cries" on you. The buttonwood also has tiny salt pores on each petiole.

IMPORTANCE OF MANGROVES
Mangrove islands and coastal forests play an essential role in protecting Belize's coastline from destruction during natural events such as hurricanes and tropical storms. Along with the seagrass beds, they also protect the Belize Barrier Reef by filtering sediment from river runoff before it reaches and smothers the delicate coral polyps. However, dense mangrove forests are also home to mosquitoes and biting flies. The mud and peat beneath mangrove thickets is often malodorous with decaying plant matter and hydrogen sulfide-producing bacteria. Many developers would like nothing better than to eliminate mangroves and replace them with sandy beaches surrounded by seawalls. But such modification to the coastline causes accelerated erosion and destruction of seaside properties, especially during severe storms.

Birds of many species use the mangrove branches for roosting and nesting sites, including swallows, redstarts, warblers, grackles, herons, egrets, ospreys, kingfishers, pelicans, and roseate spoonbills. Along the

Belize Coral Watch

Belize's world-class reefs are impacted by overfishing, coastal development, sewage, sedimentation, coral bleaching, and inappropriate or uninformed marine tourism practices. Linda Searle, Belize Coral Watch Program coordinator and founder of ECOMAR, says that when you touch coral, you are destroying the thin layer of living tissue that keeps the coral healthy. It's like when people get a cut on their skin, she explains; the area becomes more susceptible to invasion by bacteria and disease. When a "cut" on a coral does not heal, this space can become invaded by a disease that can spread to the rest of the coral head, killing the entire colony. Divers and snorkelers can be strong and effective advocates for coral reef conservation. Experienced divers know the best way to enjoy a reef is to slow down, relax, and watch, leaving the reefs undisturbed. Follow these guidelines developed by the **Coral Reef Alliance** (CORAL, www.coral.org) to be a coral-friendly diver.

CHOOSE A CORAL-FRIENDLY DIVE OPERATOR

Coral-friendly dive operators practice reef conservation by:

· Giving diver orientations and briefings.

· Holding buoyancy-control workshops.

· Actively supporting local marine protected areas.

· Using available moorings (anchors and chains destroy fragile corals and seagrass beds).

· Using available wastewater pump-out facilities.

· Making sure garbage is well stowed, especially light plastic items.

· Taking away everything brought on board, such as packaging and used batteries.

BE MINDFUL IN THE WATER

· Never touch corals; even slight contact can harm them, and some corals can sting or cut you.

· Carefully select points of entry and exit to avoid walking on corals.

· Make sure all of your equipment is well secured.

---

seaside edge of red mangrove forests, prop roots extend into the water, creating tangled thickets unparalleled as nurseries of the sea. Juveniles of commercial species, such as snapper, hogfish, and lobster, find a safe haven here. The flats around mangrove islands are famous for recreational fisheries such as bonefish and tarpon.

The three-dimensional labyrinth created by expanding red mangroves, seagrass beds, and bogues (channels of seawater flowing through the mangroves) provides the home and nursery habitat for nurse sharks, American crocodiles, dolphins, and manatees.

Snorkeling among the red mangrove prop roots is a unique experience where you can witness the abundant marinelife that grow on prop roots and live between the roots. It is within the algae, plants, corals, and sponges that grow on the roots that juvenile spiny lobsters and seahorses can be found.

Destruction of mangroves is illegal in most of Belize; cutting and removal of mangroves requires a special permit and mitigation (although unfortunately, the latter hasn't been applied to many developers).

Seagrass

Standing along the coast of Belize and looking seaward, many visitors are surprised to see

- Make sure you are neutrally buoyant at all times.

- Maintain a comfortable distance from the reef, so that you're certain to avoid contact.

- Learn to swim without using your arms.

- Move slowly and deliberately in the water.

- Practice good finning and body control to avoid accidental contact with the reef or stirring up the sediment.

- Know where your fins are at all times, and don't kick up sand.

- Stay off the bottom, and never stand or rest on corals.

- Avoid using gloves and kneepads in coral environments.

- Take nothing living or dead out of the water, except recent garbage.

- Do not chase, harass, or try to ride marinelife.

- Do not touch or handle marinelife except under expert guidance and following established guidelines.

- Never feed marinelife.

- Use photographic and video equipment only if you are an advanced diver or snorkeler; cameras are cumbersome and affect a diver's buoyancy and mobility.

BECOME AN ECOMAR VOLUNTEER

As a Belize Coral Watch Volunteer, you'll learn how to identify coral species, coral reef ecology, coral disease, and coral bleaching. After attending a training session, you will be equipped with the knowledge needed to help identify resilient reefs in Belize. Divers and snorkelers are asked to monitor sites and submit reports online. Look for a dive or snorkel center or resort that participates in "Adopt a Reef" with ECOMAR, and help it complete surveys. For more information, contact **ECOMAR** (www.ecomarbelize.org).

something dark in the shallow water just off-shore. They expect the sandy bottom typical of many Caribbean islands. However, it is this "dark stuff" that eventually will make their day's snorkeling, fishing, or dining experience more enjoyable. What they are noticing is sea-grass, another of the ocean's great nurseries.

Seagrasses are plants with elongated ribbon-like leaves. Just like the land plants they evolved from, seagrasses flower and have extensive root systems. They live in sandy areas around estuaries, mangroves, reefs, and open coastal waters. Turtle grass has broader, tape-like leaves and is common down to about 60 feet. Manatee grass, found

to depths of around 40 feet, has thinner, more cylindrical leaves. Both cover large areas of seafloor and intermix in some areas, harboring an amazing variety of marine plants and animals. Barnacles, conchs, crabs, and many other shellfish proliferate in the fields of sea-grass. Anemones, seahorses, sponges, and starfish live here. Grunts, filefish, flounder, jacks, rays, and wrasses feed here. Sea turtles and manatees often graze in these lush marine pastures.

These beds and flats are being threatened in some areas by unscrupulous developers who are dredging sand for cement and land-fill material (especially on Ambergris Caye).

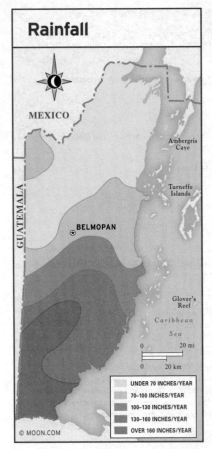

Rainfall

MEXICO

Ambergris Caye

Turneffe Islands

GUATEMALA

BELMOPAN ⊛

Glover's Reef

Caribbean Sea

0   20 mi

0   20 km

UNDER 70 INCHES/YEAR
70–100 INCHES/YEAR
100–130 INCHES/YEAR
130–160 INCHES/YEAR
OVER 160 INCHES/YEAR

© MOON.COM

CLIMATE

The climate in Belize is subtropical, with a mean annual temperature of 79°F, so you can expect a variance between 50°F and 95°F. The dry season generally lasts from December-ish through May, and the wet season June through November, although it has been known to rain sporadically all the way into February.

Rainfall varies widely between the north and south of Belize. Corozal in the north receives 40-60 inches a year, while Punta Gorda averages 160-190 inches, with an average humidity of 85 percent. Occasionally during the winter, "Joe North" (aka cold fronts) sweeps down from North America across the Gulf of Mexico, bringing rainfall, strong winds, and cooling temperatures. Usually lasting only a couple of days, the cold fronts often interrupt fishing and influence the activity of lobsters and other fish. Fishers invariably report increases in their catches several days before a norther.

The "mauger" season, when the air is still and the sea is calm, generally comes in August; it can last for a week or more. All activity halts while locals stay indoors as much as possible to avoid the onslaught of mosquitoes and other insects.

Hurricanes

Since record keeping began in 1787, scores of hurricanes have made landfall in Belize. In an unnamed storm in 1931, 2,000 people were killed and almost all of Belize City was destroyed. The water rose nine feet in some areas, even onto Belize City's Swing Bridge. Though forewarned by Pan American Airlines that the hurricane was heading their way, most of the townsfolk were unconcerned, believing that their protective reef would keep massive waves away from their shores. They were wrong.

The next devastation came with Hurricane Hattie in 1961. Winds reached a velocity of 150 mph, with gusts of 200 mph; 262 people drowned. It was after Hurricane Hattie that the capital of the country was moved from Belize City (just 18 inches above sea level) to Belmopan. Then, in 1978, Hurricane Greta took a heavy toll in dollar damage, although no lives were lost. More recent serious hurricanes affecting Belize include Mitch in 1998, Keith in 2000, Iris in 2001, Dean in 2007, and Earl in summer 2016, which was devastating to Belize City's outlying neighborhoods and inland areas from San Ignacio to the south Cockscomb region. There have also been a number of less serious "northers."

ENVIRONMENTAL ISSUES

Because of the country's impressive network of protected areas and relatively low population

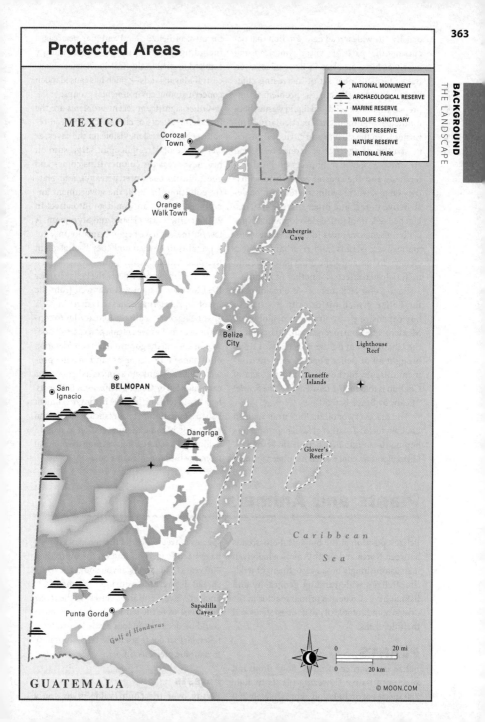

Protected Areas

MEXICO

Corozal Town

Orange Walk Town

Ambergris Caye

Belize City

Lighthouse Reef

Turneffe Islands

San Ignacio

BELMOPAN

Dangriga

Glover's Reef

Caribbean

Sea

Punta Gorda

Sapodilla Cayes

Gulf of Honduras

GUATEMALA

Legend:
- NATIONAL MONUMENT
- ARCHAEOLOGICAL RESERVE
- MARINE RESERVE
- WILDLIFE SANCTUARY
- FOREST RESERVE
- NATURE RESERVE
- NATIONAL PARK

0   20 mi
0   20 km

© MOON.COM

density, the widespread deforestation that occurs in other parts of Central America is not nearly as big a problem in Belize. However, Belize faces its own set of increasing challenges. Perhaps the biggest problem is improper disposal of solid and liquid wastes, both municipal and industrial, particularly agrowastes from the shrimp and citrus industries.

Mining of aggregates from rivers and streams has negative impacts on local watersheds and the coastal zones into which they empty, where sedimentation can be destructive to reef and other marine systems. Unchecked, unplanned development, especially in sensitive areas like barrier beaches, mangroves, islands, and riverbanks where changes to the landscape often have wide and unanticipated effects, is another problem.

Energy—or lack thereof—is a major issue for Belize, which historically has had to buy expensive electricity from neighboring Mexico. The controversial construction of the Chalillo Dam on the upper Macal River brought all of Belize's energy and environmental issues to the forefront (the saga of Chalillo is told in *The Last Flight of the Scarlet Macaw* by Bruce Barcott).

The discovery of oil in 2005 near Spanish Lookout fueled a market of foreign prospectors hoping to tap into new petroleum resources. Oil exploration concessions have been granted for most of Belize's land and marine areas—including, recently, to US Capital Energy Limited to drill in the Toledo District on ancestral Mayan lands—which has caused much concern among environmental groups.

Other significant recent problems are the increasing effects of climate change and resulting beach erosion, visible on the cayes, as well as the massive pileup of sargassum on beaches across the country (this comes and goes, but it's been pretty heavy), and plastic pollution. In 2018, the government announced that a ban would go into effect in 2019 on single-use plastics and Styrofoam. A few businesses have begun transitioning, but it remains to be seen how they'll implement this on a national scale.

Meanwhile, in good news, the Belize Barrier Reef Reserve System was removed from the list of World Heritage Sites in Danger in 2018, after being on it for almost 10 years due to concerns over mangrove cutting and excessive development and the government's consideration of offshore oil drilling around marine protected areas. Thanks to a concerted grassroots campaign led by Oceana Belize, and Belizeans' tenacity in refusing to allow it, the government issued a moratorium on any such activities and effectively became the first nation to ban oil drilling off its shores, thus earning it a removal from the in-danger list, for now.

Plants and Animals

Belize's position at the biological crossroads between North and South America has given it an astonishingly broad assortment of wildlife. Belize's wide-ranging geography and habitat have also been a primary factor in the diversity and complexity of its ecosystems and their denizens.

PLANTS

Belize is a Garden of Eden. Four thousand species of native flowering plants include 250 species of orchids and approximately 700 species of trees. Most of the country's forests have been logged off and on for more than 300 years (2,000 years, if you count the widespread deforestation during the time of the ancient Maya). The areas closest to the rivers and coast were the hardest hit because boats could be docked and logs easily loaded to be taken farther out to sea to the large ships used to haul the precious timber.

Forests

Flying over the countryside gives you a

view of the patchwork landscape of cleared areas and secondary growth. Belize consists of four distinct forest communities: **pine-oak, mixed broadleaf, cohune palm,** and **riverine** forests. Pine-oak forests are found in sandy dry soils. In the same areas, large numbers of mango, cashew, and coconut palm trees are grown near homes and villages. The mixed broadleaf forest is a transition area between the sandy pine soils and the clay soils found along the river. Often the mixed broadleaf forest is broken up here and there and doesn't reach great height; it's species-rich but not as diverse as the cohune forest. The cohune forest area is characterized by the cohune palm, which is found in fertile clay soil where a moderate amount of rain falls throughout the year. The cohune nut was an important part of the Mayan diet. Archaeologists say that where they see a cohune forest, they know they'll find evidence of the Maya.

The cohune forest gives way to the riverine forest near waterways, where vast amounts of water are found year-round from excessive rain and from the flooding rivers. About 50-60 tree varieties and hundreds of species of vines, epiphytes, and shrubs grow here. Logwood, mahogany, cedar, and pine are difficult to find along the easily accessible rivers because of extensive logging. The forest is in different stages of growth and age. To find virgin forest, it's necessary to go high into the mountains that divide Belize. Because of the rugged terrain and distance from the rivers, these areas were left almost untouched. Even today, few roads exist. If left undisturbed for many, many years, the forest will eventually regenerate itself.

Among the plantlife of Belize, look for **mangroves, bamboo,** and **swamp cypresses** as well as ferns, bromeliads, vines, and flowers creeping from tree to tree, creating dense growth. On the topmost limbs, orchids and air ferns reach for the sun. As you go farther south, you'll find the classic tropical rainforest, including tall mahoganies, *campeche, sapote,* and ceiba, thick with vines.

Orchids

In remote areas of Belize, one of the more exotic blooms, the orchid, is often found on the highest limbs of tall trees. Of all the orchid species reported in Belize, 20 percent are terrestrial (growing in the ground) and 80 percent are epiphytic (attached to a host plant—in this case trees—and deriving moisture and nutrients from the air and rain). Both types grow in many sizes and shapes: tiny buttons, spanning the length of a long branch; large-petaled blossoms with ruffled edges; or intense, tiger-striped miniatures. The lovely flowers come in a wide variety of colors, some subtle, some brilliant. The black orchid is Belize's national flower. All orchids are protected by strict laws, so look but don't pick.

ANIMALS

A walk through the rainforest brings you close to myriad animal and bird species, many of which are critically endangered in other Central American countries—and the world. Bring your binoculars and a camera, and be *vewy, vewy* quiet.

Birds

If you're a serious birder, you know all about Belize. Scores of species can be seen while sitting on the deck of your jungle lodge: big and small, rare and common, resident and migratory—and with local guides aplenty to help find them in all the vegetation. The **keel-billed toucan** is the national bird of Belize and often seen perched on a bare limb in the early morning.

Belize's hundred-plus cayes are teeming with seabirds, adding to the overall beauty of the scenery. According to the Belize Audubon Society, of the estimated 157 recorded species, 50 are residents, 42 of which breed in this offshore area. Many more are migrant birds. The cayes are important breeding grounds. The most impressive sighting is the **red-footed booby** colony on Lighthouse Reef's Half Moon Caye—a protected breeding site—home to a bird population of approximately 4,000.

Man-O-War Caye, near the coast of

Keeping Wildlife Wild

You are guaranteed to see wildlife in Belize, whether in the wild or in captivity. However, in Belize some poached birds and wildlife are often sold on the international market, while others end up in Belizean homes or in businesses that want to add "color" to attract tourists. **Belize Bird Rescue** (www.belizebirdrescue.com), a nonprofit organization, reports that 65 percent of all wild-caught captive birds die before they reach sale. Of those that make it, most are sold to people who have no idea how to raise a baby bird.

This is particularly a big deal for the yellow-headed Amazon parrot (*Amazona oratrix*), a gorgeous species under serious threat of worldwide extinction. Its numbers have plummeted from 70,000 to 7,000 in the last two decades. Human encroachment on their habitat fuels nest-robbing for the illegal pet trade.

In order to discourage the illegal trade in parrots and other animals:

- **Don't** have your photograph taken with captive indigenous wildlife. By encouraging the keepers of the wildlife, more will be taken from the wild.

- **Don't** patronize establishments with captive wildlife on display unless they are government sanctioned as a breeding or educational facility such as a zoo. There is no educational value to a single monkey or bird in a restaurant.

- **Don't** believe anyone who tells you that they "rescued" an orphan animal or bird, unless they run a licensed rescue facility. The vast majority of these animals were captured from the wild or bought from dealers. If people really want to rescue a bird or animal, they will turn it over to a proper rescue or rehab facility.

- **Don't** buy goods made from animal hides, skins, teeth or claws, or exoskeletons such as bugs and corals. Some leather goods are okay, but exotic ones (crocodile, snake, etc.) normally are not. Jewelry made from jaguar teeth has also appeared on the streets being offered to tourists. Buying them contributes to the decline of the remaining jaguar population. In Belize it is also prohibited to sell any products made out of sea turtles.

- **Do** contact the **Belize Forest Department** (tel. 501/822-2079, www.forestdepartment. gov.bz) if you observe any conditions where endangered terrestrial animals are being held in captivity or offered for sale. If you observe the sale of turtle meat or jewelry, report the location and date immediately to the **Belize Fisheries Department** (tel. 501/224-4552, www. agriculture.gov.bz).

Dangriga, is one of the largest nesting colonies in the Caribbean region for the **magnificent frigatebird** and also the sole nesting site in Belize for the **brown booby.** You can also spot these species in the deep south, around the numerous plots that make up the Port Honduras Marine Reserve and the Sapodilla Cayes Marine Reserve.

Pelicans and **royal terns** are a common sight, hovering around the Southern Cayes and coast, while **egrets** and **herons** can be spotted on the Northern Cayes.

Cats

Seven species of felines are found in North America, five of them in Belize. For years, rich adventurers came to Belize on safari to hunt the jaguar for its beautiful skin. Likewise, hunting margay, puma, ocelots, and jaguarundis was a popular sport in the rainforest. Today, hunting endangered cats (and other species) in Belize is illegal, and there are many protected areas to help safeguard their wide-ranging habitats.

The **jaguar** is heavy-chested with sturdy muscled forelegs, a relatively short tail, and small rounded ears. Its tawny coat is uniformly spotted and the spots form rosettes: large circles with smaller spots in the center. The jaguar's belly is white with black spots.

The male can weigh 145-255 pounds, females 125-165 pounds. Largest of the cats in Central America and the third-largest cat in the world, the jaguar is about the same size as a leopard. It is nocturnal, spending most daylight hours snoozing in the sun. The male marks an area of about 65 square miles and spends its nights stalking deer, peccaries, agoutis, tapirs, monkeys, and birds. If hunting is poor and times are tough, the jaguar will go into rivers and scoop fish with its large paws. The river is also a favorite spot for the jaguar to hunt the large tapir when it comes to drink. Females begin breeding at about three years old and generally produce twin cubs.

The smallest of the Belizean cats is the **margay,** weighing in at about 11 pounds and marked by a velvety coat with exotic designs in yellow and black and a tail that's half the length of its body. The bright eyeshine indicates it has exceptional night vision. A shy animal, it is seldom seen in open country, preferring the protection of the dense forest. The "tiger cat," as it is called by locals, hunts mainly in the trees, satisfied with birds, monkeys, and insects as well as lizards and figs.

Larger and not nearly as catlike as the margay, the black or brown **jaguarundi** has a small flattened head, rounded ears, short legs, and a long tail. It hunts by day for birds and small mammals in the rainforests of Central America. The **ocelot** has a striped and spotted coat and an average weight of about 35 pounds. A good climber, the cat hunts in trees as well as on the ground. Its prey include birds, monkeys, snakes, rabbits, young deer, and fish. Ocelots usually have litters of two kittens but can have as many as four. The **puma** is also known as the cougar or mountain lion. The adult male measures about six feet in length and weighs up to 198 pounds. It thrives in any environment that supports deer, porcupines, or rabbits. The puma hunts day or night.

You're not likely to spot a cat on the cayes, although as recently as December 2013, a jaguar was seen roaming loose on Ambergris Caye, as authorities spent weeks searching for it to ensure the safety of the animal and the population. Chances of catching sight of one on the mainland are equally slim—but not impossible, particularly if in the lush area surrounding Chan Chich Lodge in northern Belize.

Primates

In Kriol, the **black howler monkey** (*Alouatta caraya*) is referred to as a "baboon" (in Spanish, *saraguate*), though it is not closely related to the African species with that name. Because the howler prefers low-lying tropical rainforests (under 1,000 feet elevation), Belize is a perfect habitat. The monkeys are commonly found near the riverine forests, especially on the Belize River and its major branches. The adult howler monkey is entirely black and weighs 15-25 pounds. Its most distinctive trait is a roar that can be heard up to a mile away. A bone in the throat acts as an amplifier; the cry sounds much like that of a jaguar. The howler's unforgettable bark is said by some to be used to warn other monkey troops away from its territory. Locals, on the other hand, say the howlers roar when it's about to rain, to greet the sun, to say good night, or when they're feeding. The **Community Baboon Sanctuary** is the best place to see howler monkeys in the wild in Belize, though they are very common in the forests around many jungle lodges throughout the country.

Spider monkeys (*Ateles geoffroyi*) are smaller than black howlers and live in troops of a dozen or more, feeding on leaves, fruits, and flowers high in the rainforest canopy. Slender limbs and elongated prehensile tails assist them as they climb and swing from tree to tree. Though not as numerous in Belize as howler monkeys because of disease and habitat loss, they remain an important part of the country's natural legacy.

Rodents

A relative of the rabbit, the **agouti,** or "Indian rabbit," has coarse gray-brown fur and a hopping gait. It is most often encountered scampering along a forest trail or clearing. Not the brightest of creatures, it makes up for this lack of wit with typical rodent libido and fecundity. Though it inhabits the same areas as the paca, these two seldom meet, as the agouti minds its business during the day and the paca prefers nighttime pursuits. The agouti is less delectable than the paca. Nonetheless, it is taken by animal and human hunters and is a staple food of jaguars.

The **paca,** or **gibnut,** is a quick, brownish rodent about the size of a small dog, with white spots along its back. Nocturnal by habit and highly prized as a food item by many Belizeans, the gibnut is more apt to be seen by the visitor on an occasional restaurant menu than in the wild.

A member of the raccoon family, the **coatimundi**—or "quash"—has a long, ringed tail, a masked face, and a lengthy snout. Sharp claws aid the coati in climbing trees and digging up insects and other small prey. Omnivorous, the quash also relishes rainforest fruits. Usually seen in small troops of females and young, coatis have an amusing, jaunty appearance as they cross a rainforest path, tails at attention.

Tapirs

The national animal of Belize, the **Baird's tapir** (*Tapirus bairdii*) is found from the southern part of Mexico through northern Colombia. It is stout-bodied (91-136 pounds), with short legs, a short tail, small eyes, and rounded ears. Its nose and upper lip extend into a short but very mobile proboscis. Totally herbivorous, tapirs usually live near streams or rivers in the forest. They bathe daily and also use the water as an escape when hunted either by humans or by their prime predator, the jaguar. Shy, nonaggressive animals, they are nocturnal with a definite home range, wearing a path between the rainforest and their feeding area.

Reptiles

IGUANAS

Found all over Central America, lizards of the family *Iguanidae* include various large plant-eaters, in many sizes and typically dark in color with slight variations. The young iguana is bright emerald green. The common lizard grows to three feet long and has a blunt head and long flat tail. Bands of black and gray circle its body, and a serrated column reaches down the middle of its back, almost to its tail. During mating season, it's common to see brilliant orange males on sunny branches near the river. This reptile is not aggressive, but if cornered, it will bite and use its tail in self-defense.

Though hawks prey on young iguanas and their eggs, humans still remain its most dangerous predator. It is not unusual to see locals along dirt paths carrying sturdy specimens by the tail to put in the cook pot. Iguana stew is believed to cure or relieve various human ailments, such as impotence. Another reason for their popularity at the market is their delicate white flesh, which tastes so much like chicken that locals refer to iguana meat as "bamboo chicken."

CROCODILES

Though they're often referred to as alligators, Belize has only crocodiles, the **American** (*Crocodylus acutus,* up to 20 feet) and the **Morelet's** (*Crocodylus moreletii,* up to 8 feet). Crocodiles have a well-earned bad reputation in Africa, Australia, and New Guinea for feeding on humans, especially the larger saltwater varieties. Their American cousins are fussier about their cuisine, preferring fish, dogs, and other small mammals to people. But when humans feed crocs, either intentionally or by tossing food waste into the water, the animals can acquire a taste for pets, making them extremely dangerous. When apex predators become fearless of people, they are more prone to attack, especially small children. The territories of both croc species overlap in estuaries and brackish coastal waters. They are most abundant in the rivers, swamps, and lagoons of the Belize City and Orange Walk Districts. Able to filter excess salt from its system, only the American crocodile ventures to the more distant cayes, including Turneffe Islands.

Endangered throughout their ranges, both crocs are protected by international law and should not be disturbed. Often seen floating near the edges of lagoons or canals during midday, they are best observed at night with the help of a flashlight. When caught in the beam, their eyes glow red (LED flashlights make white eyeshine).

SNAKES
Of the 59 species of snakes that have been identified in Belize, at least nine are venomous, notably the infamous **fer-de-lance** (locally called a "Tommy Goff"), the most poisonous snake in Central America, and the coral snake.

Marinelife
Belize is world-famous for the diversity of its rich underwater wildlife, primarily due to its unique geology, the barrier reef lagoon system, and a government that actively works to protect marine habitat. There is also a great deal of marine research in Belize, often with opportunities for visitors to get involved. While all the standard Caribbean species are found in Belizean waters, there are a few animals in particular worth noting.

MANATEES
These "gentle giants of the sea" can reach 600-1,200 pounds, and move ever so gracefully in the water, rising to the surface in intervals to breathe.

Belize is considered the last stronghold of the **West Indian manatee** (*Trichechus manatus*) in Central America and the Caribbean; as recently as 2012, aerial surveys of Turneffe Atoll and Belize's coastline revealed 507 manatees. It's estimated that the global population of this species is less than 2,500. The **Antillean subspecies** (*T. m. manatus*) of West Indian manatee found in Belize's waters has been protected by local laws since the 1930s and is listed as endangered by the Wildlife Protection Act of 1981 and also red-listed by the International Union for Conservation of Nature (IUCN) as endangered, in continuing decline, with severely fragmented populations.

The country has designated several wildlife sanctuaries and protected areas for the benefit of manatees and other marinelife, including Swallow Caye Wildlife Sanctuary, Bacalar Chico National Park and Marine Reserve, South Water Caye Marine Reserve, and Port Honduras Marine Reserve.

SHARKS
Various shark species are present along Belize's coastline. Hard as it may be at first, put aside the Hollywood *Jaws* myth that all sharks are out to attack humans; you will end up surprised when a Caribbean reef shark passes by and ignores your presence.

Docile **nurse sharks** are bottom dwellers that are used to divers and snorkelers for the most part; you'll see them at Hol Chan Marine Reserve. Just remember: *Don't touch.* They feed on crustaceans, mollusks, and other fish, and can grow up to 14 feet in length and weigh over 700 pounds. Aside from nurse sharks, **reef sharks** are the most commonly encountered in Belize. They can reach up to 10 feet in length, have long and narrow fins, and are impressive-looking, reminding you of those Hollywood sharks. But not to worry; they feed primarily on reef fishes and are generally harmless to humans. They can get aggressive where there is bait, however, so beware if you're out spearfishing.

The impressive, migratory **whale shark** (*Rhincodon typus*) is a primary attraction in Belize, in season. Like all sharks it has a cartilaginous skeleton and visible gill slits, yet it feeds on zooplankton like a whale. It is the largest fish in the sea (up to 66 feet in length and weighing over 15 tons). Whale sharks bear live young (up to 300 have been found in one female), are believed to be long-lived—living more than 60 years—and may require up to 30 years to mature.

Other species less commonly spotted include **bull sharks, blacktip sharks, lemon sharks, great hammerheads, and scalloped hammerheads**. Divers occasionally spot great hammerheads on trips to the atolls, particularly Lighthouse Reef, home to the infamous Blue Hole.

RAYS

Rays are in abundance in Belize. They inhabit the reef from north to south and are particularly plentiful in marine reserves. When entering the water from the beach, particularly off the cayes, be sure to do the "stingray shuffle"; slowly rub the sandy bottom with your feet as you enter, in order not to startle any rays that may be resting on the seafloor, where they usually sit when not swimming.

The **southern stingray** can reach up to five feet across, with a long, thin tail outfitted with venomous barbs ranging 4-8 inches in length. Get a close glimpse of southern stingrays on a trip to Hol Chan Marine Reserve. **Manta rays** have a wingspan reaching up to 20 feet and are often seen leaping in and out of the water—up to 10 feet high! Elusive **spotted eagle rays** are mesmerizing with their glorious wing-like appendages that allow them to move quickly and give them the appearance of flying through the sea. The sight is made more dramatic thanks to their numerous white spots contrasting against the seawall's clear and deep blues. The spotted eagle ray's tail is equipped with up to five barbed spines, and its wingspan can reach up to five feet. They are considered near threatened by the IUCN, and often hunted by a wide variety of sharks.

SEA TURTLES

Belize is home to five species of sea turtles. Sea turtles have enjoyed protected status since 2002, resulting in more sightings for happy snorkelers and divers.

The **loggerhead turtle** (*Caretta caretta*) is the most endangered of the three species commonly found in Belize. It can weigh up to 400 pounds, and the reddish-brown shell or carapace can reach four feet in length. They can live up to 150 years, and they roam in shallow, coastal waters, lagoons, and occasionally open seas. You'll see them gliding along in search of crustaceans, mollusks, jellyfish, and seagrass.

While endangered, **green sea turtles** (*Chelonia mydas*)—named after the color of their skin and not their shell—are the most commonly spotted species and the second largest. They can weigh up to 500 pounds. To identify them, note the single pair of prefrontal scales—between the eyes—and the white lines on their bodies or shells.

The **hawksbill turtle** (*Eretmochelys imbricata*) is my favorite. These gorgeous tortoise-shelled creatures have a beak resembling a hawk's and can weigh up to 200 pounds. Their shells were once valuable and used by European colonial powers to make eyeglass frames, combs, and even jewelry, leading to overharvesting of the hawksbill and their inevitable decline. In 1993, the Belize Fisheries Department banned the capture of these turtles. Today, their numbers are highest of all sea turtles found in Belize—as confirmed by the Belize Sea Turtle Census. Hawksbill turtles love coral reefs, where they can feed on sponges.

The **leatherback turtle** and **Kemp's ridley turtle** are an extremely rare sighting.

You can help conserve turtles while you're out exploring—ECOMAR's Belize Turtle Watch Program (www.ecomarbelize.org) welcomes online submissions of your sightings and photos. Launched in 2011 by ECOMAR (www.ecomar.org), in partnership with the government's Fisheries Program and with support from various conservation organizations, the program provides training, monitoring, and in-water surveys, among other activities.

History

Early recorded comments following Columbus's fourth voyage to the Americas led the Spaniards to hastily conclude that the swampy shoreline of what is now Belize was unfit for human habitation. Someone should have told that to the Maya, who had been enjoying the area for quite some time. The pre-Columbian history of Belize is closely associated with that of its nearby neighbors: Mexico, Guatemala, and Honduras. The Maya were the first people to inhabit the land. They planted milpas (cornfields), built ceremonial centers, and established villages with large numbers of people throughout the region.

ANCIENT CIVILIZATION

Around 1000 BC, the Olmec culture, believed to be the earliest in the area and the predecessors to the Maya, began to spread throughout Mesoamerica. Large-scale ceremonial centers grew along Gulf Coast lands, and much of Mesoamerica was influenced by the Olmec religion of worshipping jaguar-like gods. The Olmec also developed the western hemisphere's first calendar and an early system of writing.

The Classic Period

The Classic Period, beginning about AD 250, is now hailed as the peak of cultural development among the Maya. For the next 600 years, until AD 900, the Maya made phenomenal progress in the development of artistic, architectural, and astronomical skills. They constructed impressive buildings during this period and wrote codices (folded bark books) filled with hieroglyphic symbols that detailed complicated mathematical calculations of days, months, and years. Only the priests and the privileged held this knowledge and continued to learn and develop it until, for some unexplained reason, the growth suddenly halted. A new militaristic society was born,

built around a blend of ceremonialism, civic and social organization, and conquest.

Maya Society Collapses

All evidence points to an abrupt work stoppage. After about AD 900, no buildings were constructed, and no stelae, which carefully detailed names and dates to inform future generations of their roots, were erected. What happened to the priests and nobles, the guardians of religion, science, and the arts, who conducted their ritual ceremonies and studies in the large stone pyramids? Why were the centers abandoned? What happened to the knowledge of the intelligentsia? Theories abound. Some speculate about a social revolution—the people were tired of subservience and were no longer willing to farm the land to provide food, clothing, and support for the priests and nobles. Other theories include population pressure on local resources, that there just wasn't enough land to provide food and necessities for the large population. Others believe drought, famine, or epidemics were responsible.

Whatever happened, it's clear that the special knowledge concerning astronomy, hieroglyphics, and architecture was not passed on to Mayan descendants. Why did the masses disperse, leaving once-sacred stone cities unused and ignored?

COLONIALISM

In 1530, the conquistador Francisco de Montejo y Álvarez attacked the Nachankan and Belize Maya, but his attempt to conquer them failed. This introduction of Spanish influence did not have the impact on Belize that it did in the northern part of the Caribbean coast until the Caste War.

Hernán Cortés

After Columbus's arrival in the Americas, other adventurers traveling the same seas

Maya Archaeological Sites

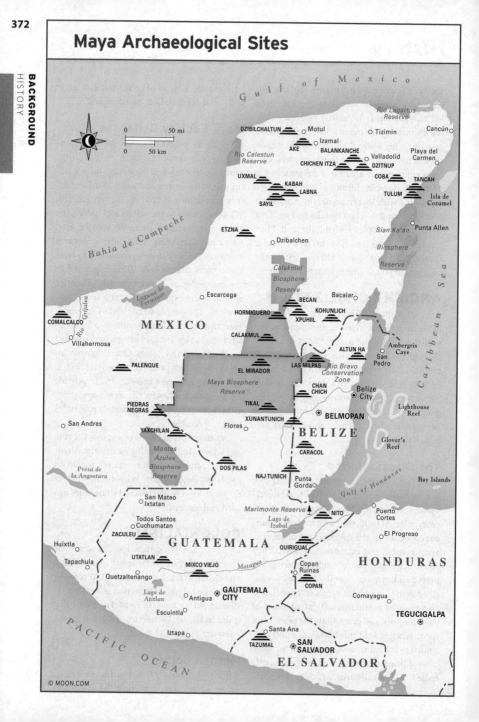

© MOON.COM

Cave Archaeology and the Maya

Large populations of Maya were concentrated in the limestone foothills, where water supplies and clay deposits were plentiful. Caves were a source of freshwater, especially during dry periods. Clay pots of grain were safely stored for long periods of time in the cool air and, thousands of years later, can be seen today. Looting of caves has been a problem for decades, and as a result, all caves in Belize are considered archaeological sites.

The Maya used caves for utilitarian as well as religious and ceremonial purposes. The ancient Maya believed that upon entering a cave, one entered the underworld, or Xibalba, the place of beginnings and of fright. They believed there were nine layers of the underworld, and as much as death and disease and rot were represented by the underworld, so was the beginning of life. Caves were a source of water—a source of life—for the Maya. Water that dripped from stalactites was used as holy water for ceremonial purposes. The underworld was also an area where souls had hopes of defeating death and becoming ancestors. As a result, rituals, ceremonies, and even sacrifices were performed in caves, evidenced today by many pots, shards, implements, and burial sites.

Caves were important burial chambers for the ancient Maya, and more than 200 skeletons have been found in more than 20 caves. One chamber in Caves Branch was the final earthly resting spot for 25 individuals. Many of these burial chambers are found deep in the caves, leading to speculation that death came by sacrificing the living, as opposed to carrying in the dead. Some burial sites show possible evidence of commoners being sacrificed to accompany the journey of an elite who had died—but who really knows?

The first written accounts related to cave archaeology began in the late 1800s. A British medical officer by the name of Thomas Gann wrote of his extensive exploration of caves throughout the country. In the late 1920s, he was also part of the first formal study of some ruins and caves in the Toledo District, and his papers provide insight no one else can give to modern-day archaeologists.

Little else was done until 1955, when the Institute of Archaeology was created by the government of Belize. Starting in 1957, excavations were organized throughout the years under various archaeologists. Excavations in the 1970s led to many important discoveries, including pots, vessels, and altars. In the 1980s, a series of expeditions was undertaken to survey the Chiquibul cave system. Other finds during this period include a burial chamber and one cave with over 60 complete vessels and other ceremonial implements.

Today, projects are underway in many caves around the country. The Institute of Archaeology does not have a museum—yet. They've been talking about one for years. In the meantime, you may have to get a little wet and dirty to go visit some of these artifacts yourself. Start by calling up a cave tour guide in Cayo, like **Pacz Tours** (tel. 501/604-6921 or 501/824-0536, www.pacztours.net).

soon found the Yucatán Peninsula. Thirty-four-year-old Cortés sailed from Cuba in 1519 against the will of the Spanish governor. With 11 ships, 120 sailors, and 550 soldiers, he set out to search for slaves, a lucrative business with or without the approval of the government. His search began on the Yucatán coast and eventually encompassed most of Mexico. However, he hadn't counted on the resistance and cunning of the Maya. The fighting was destined to continue for many years—a time of bloodshed and death for many of his men and for the Maya. Anthropologists and historians estimate that as many as 90 percent of Maya were killed by diseases such as smallpox after the arrival of the Spaniards.

Roman Catholicism

Over the years, the majority of the Maya were baptized into the Roman Catholic faith. Most priests did their best to educate the people, teach them to read and write, and protect them from the growing number of Spanish settlers who used them as slaves. The Maya practiced Catholicism in their own manner, combining their ancient beliefs handed down throughout the centuries with Christian doctrine. These mystic yet Christian ceremonies are still performed in baptisms, courtship, marriages, illness, farming, house building, and fiestas.

Pirates and the Baymen

While all of Mesoamerica dealt with the problems of economic colonialism, the Yucatán Peninsula had an additional headache: harassment by vicious pirates who made life in the coastal areas unstable. In other parts of the Yucatán Peninsula, the passive indigenous people were ground down, their lands taken away, and their numbers greatly reduced by the European settlers' epidemics and mistreatment.

British buccaneers sailed the coast, attacking the Spanish fleet at every opportunity. These ships were known to carry unimaginable riches of gold and silver from the Americas back to the king of Spain. The Belizean coast became a convenient place for pirates to hole up during bad weather or for a good drinking bout. And although no one planned it as a permanent layover, by 1650 the coast had the beginnings of a British pirate lair and settlement. As pirating slacked off on the high seas, British buccaneers discovered they could use their ships to carry logwood back to a ready market in England (logwood is a low-growing tree that provided rich dyes for Europe's growing textile industry until artificial dyes were developed). These early settlers were nicknamed the Baymen.

For 300 years the Baymen of Belize cut the logwood, and then, when the demand for logwood ceased, they starting felling mahogany trees from the vast forests. For three centuries the local economy depended on exported logs and imported food.

Agreement with Spain

In the meantime, the Spanish desperately tried to maintain control of their vast territories across the ocean. But it was a difficult task, and brutal conflicts continually flared between the Spanish and either the British

inhabitants or the Maya. The British Baymen were continually run out but always returned. Treaties were signed and then rescinded. The British meanwhile made inroads into the country, importing enslaved Africans (beginning in the 1720s) to cut and move the trees.

Politically, Belize (or, more to the point, its timber) was up for grabs, and a series of treaties did little to calm the ping-pong effect between the British and the Spanish over the years. One such agreement, the Treaty of Paris, did little to control the Baymen—or the Spanish.

In 1763, Spain "officially" agreed to let the British cut logwood. The decree allowed roads (along the then-designated frontiers) to be built in the future, though definite boundaries were to be agreed on later. For nearly 150 years the only "roads" built were narrow tracks to the rivers, which became Belize's major highways. Boats were common transportation along the coast, and somehow road building was postponed, leaving boundaries vaguely defined and people on both sides of the border unsure. This was the important bit of history that later encouraged the Spanish-influenced Guatemalans to believe that Belize had failed to carry out the 1763 agreement by building roads, which meant the land reverted back to Spain. Even after Spain vacated Guatemala, Guatemala tried throughout the 20th century to claim Belizean territory.

The Battle of St. George's Caye

The Baymen held on with only limited rights to the area until the final skirmish on St. George, a small caye just off Belize City. The Baymen, with the help of an armed sloop and three companies of a West Indian regiment, won the Battle of St. George's Caye on September 10, 1798, ending the Spanish claim to Belize once and for all. After that battle, the British crown ruled Belize until independence was gained in 1981.

Land Rights

In 1807 slavery was "officially" abolished in

History in a Nutshell

The peaceful country of Belize is a sovereign democratic state of Central America located on the Caribbean. The government is patterned on the system of parliamentary democracy and experiences no more political turmoil than any other similar government, such as that of Great Britain or the United States.

IMPORTANT DATES

- 1798: Battle of St. George's Caye
- 1862: Became a British colony
- 1954: Attained universal adult suffrage
- 1964: Began self-government
- 1973: Name of the territory changed from British Honduras to Belize
- 1981: Attained full independence

Belize by England. This was not agreeable to the powerful British landowners, however, and in many quarters it continued to flourish. Changes were then made to accommodate the will of the powerful. The local government no longer "gave" land to settlers as it had for years (British law now permitted the formerly enslaved and other "coloureds" to hold title). The easiest way to keep them from possessing land was to charge for it—essentially barring the majority in the country from landownership. So, in essence, slavery continued.

Caste War

It was inevitable that the Maya would eventually revolt in a furious attack. This bloody uprising in the Yucatán Peninsula in the 1840s was called the Caste War. Although the Maya were farmers and for the most part not soldiers, in this savage war they took revenge on European men, women, and children by rape and murder. When the winds of war reversed and the Maya were on the losing side, the vengeance wreaked on them was merciless.

Some settlers immediately killed any Maya on sight, regardless of that person's beliefs. Some Maya were taken prisoner and sold to Cuba as slaves; others left their villages and hid in the rainforest, in some cases for decades. Between 1846 and 1850, the population of the Yucatán Peninsula was reduced from 500,000 to 300,000. Guerrilla warfare ensued, with the escaped Maya making repeated sneak attacks on the European settlers. Quintana Roo, adjacent to Belize along the Caribbean coast, was considered a dangerous no-man's-land for more than 100 years until, in 1974, with the promise of tourism, the territory was admitted to the United Mexican States. The "war" didn't really end on the peninsula until the Chan Santa Cruz people finally made peace with the Mexican federal government in 1935, more than 400 years after it had begun.

Restored Mayan Pride

Many of the Maya who escaped slaughter during the Caste War fled to the isolated rainforests of Quintana Roo and Belize. The Maya revived the religion of the "talking cross," a pre-Columbian oracle representing gods of the four cardinal directions. This was a religious-political fusion. Three determined survivors of the Caste War and all wise leaders—a priest, a master spy, and a ventriloquist—knew their people's desperate need for divine leadership. As a result of their leadership and advice from the talking cross, the shattered people came together in large numbers and began to organize. The community guarded the location of the cross, and its advice made the Maya strong once again.

They called themselves Chan Santa Cruz (People of the Little Holy Cross). As their confidence developed, so did the growth and power of their communities. Living very close to the Belize (then British Honduras) border, they found they had something their neighbors wanted. The Chan Santa Cruz Maya began selling timber to the British and in return received arms, giving the Maya even more power. Between 1847 and 1850, in the years of strife during the Caste War in neighboring Yucatán, thousands of Mayan, mestizo, and Mexican refugees who were fleeing the Spaniards entered Belize. The Yucatecans introduced the Latin culture, the Roman Catholic religion, and agriculture. This was the beginning of the Mexican tradition in northern Belize, locally referred to as "Spanish tradition." The food is typically Mexican, with tortillas, black beans, tamales, squash, and plantains. For many years, these mestizos kept to themselves and were independent of Belize City.

They settled mostly in the northern sections of the country, which is apparent by the Spanish names of the cities: Corozal, San Estevan, San Pedro, and Punta Consejo. By 1857 the immigrants were growing enough sugar to supply Belize, with enough left over to export the surplus (along with rum) to Britain. After their success proved to the tree barons that sugarcane could be lucrative, the big landowners became involved. Even in today's world of low-priced sugar, the industry is still important to Belize's economy.

INDEPENDENCE

In 1862 the territory of British Honduras was officially created, even though the area had been ruled by the British crown since 1798. The average Belizean had few rights and a very low living standard. Political unrest grew in a stifled atmosphere. Even when a contingent of Belizean soldiers traveled to Europe to fight for the British in World War I, they were scorned for their dark skin. But when these men returned from abroad, the pot of change began to boil. Over the next 50 years the country struggled through power plays, another world war, and economic crises, but

What's in a Name?

No one knows for sure where the name Belize originated or what it means. The country was called Belize long before the British took the country over and renamed it British Honduras. In 1973 the locals changed it back to the original Belize as a first step on the road to independence. There are several well-known theories about its meaning. Some say it's a corruption of the name Wallis (wahl-EEZ), from the pirate (Peter Wallace) who roamed the high seas centuries ago and visited Belize. Others suggest that it's a distortion of the Mayan word *belix*, which means "muddy river." Still others say it could be a further distortion of the Mayan word *belikin*, the modern name of the local beer.

always the seed was there—the desire to be independent. The colonial system had been falling apart around the world, and when India gained its freedom in 1947, the pattern was set. Many small undeveloped countries began to gain independence and started to rely on their own ingenuity to build an economy that would benefit their people.

Even though Belize was self-governing by 1964, it was still dominated by outside influences until September 1981, when it gained its independence from the British crown. In September 1981 the Belizean flag was raised for the first time—the birth of a new country. Belize joined the United Nations, the Commonwealth of Nations, and the Non-Aligned Movement. The infant country's first parliamentary elections were held in 1984. You can see the original Belizean flag at the George Price Centre in Belmopan.

Government and Economy

GOVERNMENT

The **Government of Belize** (www.belize.gov.bz), or "GOB," as you'll see it referred to in the newspapers, is directed by an elected prime minister. The bicameral legislature, the National Assembly, comprises an appointed senate and an elected house of representatives. Belize has two main political parties, the People's United Party (PUP) and United Democratic Party (UDP). As in most democracies, the political rhetoric can get very animated, but political-based violence is unheard of.

The current prime minister, Dean Barrow of the UDP, took the post from longtime PUP leader Said Musa in 2008. The country's constitution, judicial code, and other legal documents are explained and can be downloaded from the **Ministry of the Attorney General** (www.belizelaw.org).

ECONOMY

The economy of Belize was traditionally based on the export of logwood, mahogany, and chicle (the base for chewing gum, from the chicle tree). Today, tourism, agriculture, fisheries, aquaculture (shrimp farming), and small manufactured goods give the country an important economic boost, but it is still dependent on imported goods to get by. The main exports are sugar, citrus, bananas, lobster, and timber. Overall, domestic industry is severely constrained by relatively high labor and energy costs, a very small domestic market, and the "brain drain" of Belize's most qualified managers, health professionals, and academics to the United States and Europe.

In general, and despite books by PUP economists declaring that all is well, Belize's economy is a mess, and the GOB has been on the verge of bankruptcy for years. In 2004, the government was rocked by a scandal over the use of millions of dollars of pension funds to pay the foreign debts of bankrupt companies controlled by government insiders. This led to the collapse of the overextended Development Finance Corporation (DFC), the effects of which are still being felt and evaluated today.

Thanks to tax concessions given to foreign investors, Belize has attracted new manufacturing industries, including plywood, veneer, matches, beer, rum, soft drinks, furniture, boatbuilding, and battery assembly.

Tourism

Belize is now a common destination for North American and European travelers. Tourism is one of the most critical economies in the country, responsible for about one in seven jobs and 22 percent of the country's GDP. The **Belize Tourism Board** (tel. 501/227-2420, U.S. tel. 800/624-0686, www.travelbelize.org) has gotten the word "Belize" buzzing on the lips of millions of potential visitors who, only a few years ago, had never even heard of the tiny country. Today, roughly 250,000 overnight visitors come to Belize each year; the majority (about 150,000) are from the United States.

In 2011 there were 716 registered hotels providing jobs to nearly 5,000 Belizeans, and that's not counting restaurant employees, guides, and transportation services. Tourism has encouraged the preservation of vast tracts of forests and reefs; it has helped the Institute of Archaeology enhance and develop Belize's archaeological sites as destinations, making possible astounding excavations and discoveries at the Caracol, Xunantunich, Lamanai, Altun Ha, and Cahal Pech ruins.

Of course, tourism can be a double-edged sword, and Belize's founding father, George Price, warned against it; Price said tourism would make Belizeans indentured servants to rich foreigners.

The Legacy of George Price

George Price was Belize's first prime minister upon independence in 1981, then served in the position again 1989-1993. Born in 1919, Price entered politics in 1944 and never looked back. He did not step down from the leadership of the People's United Party, which he founded in 1950, until 1996 when he retired in Belize City. Price also served as the mayor of Belize City several times. He was the most respected and loved individual in Belize, and you'd be hard-pressed to find anyone who didn't admire him. Price died on September 19, 2011, just two days shy of the country's 30th anniversary of independence. Belize held its very first state funeral that year, which I had the privilege of attending, and I witnessed the most spectacular display of love and unity all across the country. Belizeans were lined up for hours in the hot sun along the highways and streets of Belize City and Belmopan, waving flags, banners, and personal thank-you messages to their national hero. The **George Price Centre for Peace and Development** (www.gpcbelize.com) in Belmopan is a must-see to learn more about Price's central role in Belizean history.

CRUISE SHIPS

The image of numerous hulking cruise ships on the watery eastern horizon of Belize City is striking. The arrival of the cruise industry to Belize's shores in the 1990s was both a much-hailed and highly contentious event, and is still debated to this date. It happened quickly, and Belize soon recorded the highest growth in cruise ship arrivals in the entire Caribbean region: Annual cruise visitor arrivals grew from 14,183 in 1998 to a peak of more than 851,000 in 2004. Numbers have fluctuated over the years, but the cruise ship industry remains alive and well here.

The Belize Tourism Board officially promotes visits by cruise ships. There are approximately 2,000 people in Belize City who rely on cruise ships for their livelihoods, most of whom work in Tourism Village shops and restaurants. The board acknowledges the need to balance cruise ship tourism with overnight tourism, making sure that one does not take over from the other.

In Belize City, cruise ship arrival days are boom days for taxi drivers, tour operators, and shopkeepers. But critics say that's not enough. Stewart Krohn, a former Belizean journalist and now hotelier, writes that inviting cruise ship tourism is the equivalent of selling Belize cheaply. In one editorial, he wrote, "Tourism, at its heart, is a cultural encounter. Long, relaxed, unhurried stays by visitors who have time to meet, interact with, and understand Belizeans and Belize not only means more money in our pockets for beds, food, drinks, and tours; it produces the kind of relationships that small countries in a highly competitive world find increasingly necessary." Such meaningful encounters are impossible with hurried busloads of day-trippers, he argues. "Cruise tourism at best produces a few pennies for a few people; at worst a negative impression born of an impersonal encounter."

Other critics cite the impact on Belize's tiny, fragile infrastructure—damage to roads by cruise bus traffic, maxed-out septic systems, trash on the trails and in the caves. Passengers don't spend much onshore, and few of their dollars trickle very far from the pockets of those who own Tourism Village.

One thing is certain: Bring up cruise tourism at a Belizean barbecue, and you'll hear some fiery opinions (especially if you mention the expansion of cruise ships into Placencia and southern Belize). Despite resistance from Placencians, including many small business owners, the go-ahead was given, and it's a done deal. Many fear this upcoming cruise ship tourism will destroy the responsible tourism Placencia has worked so hard to build, as well as the natural resources surrounding the area. If anything, it's only causing more foot traffic and less income from cruise ship crowds who come to shore and barely spend a dollar.

Keeping the "Eco" in Tourism

The word *ecotourism* was created in the 1980s with the best of intentions—ostensibly, to describe anything having to do with environmentally sound and culturally sustainable tourism. It was the "business" of preventing tourism from spoiling the environment and using tourism as an economic alternative to spoiling the environment for some other reason.

The success of the concept—and its marketing value—led to a worldwide surge in the usage of that prefix we know so well, even if its actual practice may sometimes fall short of original intentions. Indeed, *eco* has been used and abused all over the world, and Belize is no exception. Some word-savvy tourism marketers have tried to freshen things up by using "alternative" or "adventure" tourism; when trying to describe an operation that practices the original definition of ecotourism, better terms are "sustainable," "responsible," "ethical," or even "fair-trade" tourism.

Belize is generally acknowledged as one of the world's most successful models of ecotourism. In 2009 Belize hosted the **Third Annual World Conference for Responsible Tourism,** featuring experts from around the world speaking on local economic development through tourism, the impact of mass tourism on local communities, and climate change.

The **Belize Audubon Society** (BAS, www.belizeaudubon.org) is the main organization concerned with keeping the "eco" in tourism—and in keeping pressure on the government of Belize to do the same.

People and Culture

The extraordinary diversity of Belize's tiny population (about 320,000) allows Belizeans to be doubly proud of their heritage—once for their family's background (Maya, Creole, Garifuna, Mennonite, and more) and again for their country. The mestizo (mixed Spanish and indigenous descent) population has risen to about 50 percent of the country's total, with Creoles making up about 21 percent, Maya 10 percent, Garinagu 4.5 percent, and others 9 percent (in the 2010 census). Here's a bit of background about Belize's diverse demography, but keep in mind that every one of these groups continues to mingle with the others, at least to some extent.

CREOLES

Creoles are a mix of two distinctive ethnic backgrounds: African and European, and they use the local English-Kriol dialect. Many Creoles are also descended from other groups of immigrants. The center of Creole territory and culture is Belize City. Half of Belize's

ethnic Creoles live here, and they make up more than three-quarters of the city's population. Rural Creoles live along the highway between Belmopan and San Ignacio, in isolated clusters in northern Belize District, and in a few coastal spots to the south—Gales Point, Mullins River, Mango Creek, Placencia, and Monkey River.

Cheap labor was needed to do the grueling timber work in thick, tall rainforests. The British failed to force it on the maverick Maya, so they brought Africans whom they enslaved, indentured laborers from India, and Caribs from distant Caribbean islands, as was common in the early 16th and 17th centuries. "Creolization" started when the first waves of British and Scottish began to intermingle with the imported enslaved population.

MESTIZOS

Also referred to as "Ladinos" or just "Spanish," mestizos make up the quickest-growing demographic group in Belize and encompass all Spanish-speaking Belizeans, descended from some mix of Maya and Europeans. These immigrants to Belize hail from the nearby countries of Guatemala, El Salvador, Honduras, and Mexico. Once the predominant population (after immigration from the Yucatecan Caste War), mestizos are now the second-most-populous ethnic group of Belize. They occupy the old "Mexican-mestizo corridor," which runs along the New River between Corozal and Orange Walk. In west-central Belize—Benque Viejo and San Ignacio—indigenous people from Guatemala have recently joined the earlier Spanish-speaking immigrants from Yucatán.

THE MAYA

Small villages of Maya—Mopan, Yucatec, and Q'eqchi'—still practicing some form of their ancient culture dot the landscape and comprise roughly 10-12 percent of Belize's population. After the Europeans arrived and settled in Belize, many of the Maya moved away from the coast to escape hostile Spanish and British intruders arriving by ship to search for slaves. Many Mayan communities continue to live much as their ancestors did and are still the most politically marginalized people in Belize, although certain villages are becoming increasingly empowered and developed, thanks in part to tourism (although some would argue at a cultural cost). Most modern Maya practice some form of Christian religion integrated with ancient beliefs. But ancient Mayan ceremonies are still quietly practiced in secluded pockets of the country, especially in southern Belize.

THE GARINAGU

The culture of the Garifuna people, collectively the Garinagu, developed on the Lesser Antillean island of San Vicente, which in the 1700s had become a refuge for escaped slaves from the sugar plantations of the Caribbean and Jamaica. These displaced Africans were accepted by the native Carib islanders, with whom they freely intermingled. The new island community members vehemently denied their African origins and proclaimed themselves Native Americans. As the French and English began to settle the island, the Garinagu (as they had become known) established a worldwide reputation as expert canoe navigators and fierce warriors, resisting European control. The English finally got the upper hand in the conflict after tricking and killing the Garifuna leader, and in 1797 they forcefully evacuated the population from San Vicente to the Honduran Bay island of Roatán. From there, a large proportion of the Garinagu migrated to mainland Central America, all along the Mosquito Coast.

On November 19, 1823, so the story goes, the first Garifuna boats landed on the beaches of what is now Dangriga, one of the chief cultural capitals of the Garinagu. They came ashore in Belize under the leadership of Alejo Beni, and a small Garifuna settlement grew in Stann Creek, where they fished and farmed. They began bringing fresh produce to Belize City but were not welcome to stay for more than 48 hours without getting a special permit—the Baymen wanted the produce but feared that these free blacks would help the enslaved escape, causing a loss of the Baymen's tight control.

The Garifuna language is a mixture of Amerindian, African, Arawak, and Carib dialects, dating from the 1700s. The Garinagu continued to practice what was still familiar from their ancient West African traditions—cooking with a mortar and pestle, dancing, and especially music, which consisted of complex rhythms with a call-and-response pattern that was an important part of their social and religious celebrations. An eminent person in the village is still the drum maker, who carries on the old traditions, along with making other instruments used in these singing and dancing ceremonies that often last all night.

Old dances and drum rhythms are still used for a variety of occasions, especially around Christmas and New Year's. If you are visiting Dangriga, Hopkins, Seine Bight,

The Gulisi Primary School

The Garinagu in Belize have been struggling to keep their culture alive, particularly with the younger generation. English and Kriol dominate the language scene, and with a diverse population, as well as a young population influenced by mainstream American pop culture and media, a significant number of Garifuna youth are not learning their native tongue, which isn't taught in most schools.

Enter the Gulisi Primary School. Established in 2007 adjacent to the Gulisi Garifuna Museum in Dangriga, it's unique in its genre: In addition to a regular primary school academic curriculum, it has a mandatory trilingual system, which requires students to take Garifuna language classes, along with English, the main language of instruction, and Spanish. The goal is to keep Garifuna children rooted in their culture and thus preserve their heritage, but not at the expense of a good education.

Teachers are required to speak fluent Garifuna (government-assisted funding covers their salaries), and the 185 students wear uniforms bearing the colors of the Garifuna flag. The school accepts children up to the 8th grade, including those from other cultures who are willing to learn Garifuna alongside everyone else. So successful is the school that it now faces overcrowding. Occasionally, classes are held in part of the museum next door.

For more information, contact Phyllis Cayetano (pcayetano@gmail.com), the school's founder and general manager.

Punta Gorda, or Barranco during these times (or on Settlement Day, November 19), expect to see, and possibly partake in, some drumming. Feel free to taste the typical foods and drinks. If you consume too much "local dynamite" (rum and coconut milk) or bitters, have a cup of strong chicory coffee, said by Garinagu to *"mek we not have goma"* (prevent a hangover).

EAST INDIANS

From 1844 to 1917, under British colonialism, 41,600 East Indians were brought to British colonies in the Caribbean as indentured workers. They agreed to work for a given length of time for one "master." Then they could either return to India or stay on and work freely. Unfortunately, the time spent in Belize was not as lucrative as they were led to believe it would be. In some cases, they owed so much money to the company store (where they received half their wages in trade and not nearly enough to live on) that they were forced to "reenlist" for a longer period. Most of them worked on sugar plantations in the Toledo and Corozal Districts, and many of the East Indian men were assigned to work as local police in Belize City. In a town aptly named Calcutta, south of Corozal Town, many of the population today are descendants of the original indentured East Indians. Forest Home near Punta Gorda also has a large settlement. About 47 percent of the ethnic group lives in these two locations. The East Indians usually have large families and live on small farms with orchards adjacent to their homes. A few trade in pigs and dry goods in mom-and-pop businesses. Descendants of earlier East Indian immigrants speak Kriol and Spanish. A few communities of Hindi-speaking East Indian merchants live in Belize City, Belmopan, and Orange Walk.

MENNONITES

Making up more than 3 percent of the population of Belize, German-speaking Mennonites are the most recent group to enter Belize on a large scale. These Protestant settlers from the Swiss Alps wandered over the years to northern Germany, southern Russia, Pennsylvania, and Canada in the early 1800s, and to northern Mexico after World War I. The quiet, staid

Mennonites and their isolated agrarian lifestyle conflicted with local governments in these countries, leading to a more nomadic existence.

Most of Belize's Mennonites first migrated from Mexico between 1958 and 1962. A few came from Peace River in Canada. In contrast to other areas where they lived, in Belize the Mennonites bought large blocks of land (about 148,000 acres) and began to farm. Shipyard (in Orange Walk District) was settled by a conservative wing; Spanish Lookout (in Cayo District) and Blue Creek (in Orange Walk District) were settled by more progressive members. In hopes of averting future problems with the government, Mennonites made agreements with Belize officials that guarantee them freedom to practice their religion, use their language in locally controlled schools, organize their own financial institutions, and be exempt from military service.

Over the years that Mennonites have been in Belize, they have slowly merged into Belizean activities. Although they practice complete separation of church and state (and do not vote), their innovations in agricultural production and marketing have advanced the entire country. Mennonite farmers are probably the most productive in Belize; they commonly pool their resources to make large purchases such as equipment, machinery (in those communities that use machinery), and supplies. Their fine dairy industry is the best in the country, and they supply the domestic market with eggs, poultry, fresh milk, cheese, and vegetables.

LANGUAGE

More than eight languages are commonly spoken in Belize. English is the official language, although Belizean Kriol serves as the main spoken tongue among and between groups. The number of Spanish speakers in Belize is increasing, as Central American immigrants continue to arrive. Spanish is the primary language of many native Belizean families, especially among descendants of Yucatecan immigrants who inhabit the Northern Cayes as well as the Orange Walk and Corozal Districts. There are only a few areas of Belize, mainly rural outposts in northern and western Belize, where knowing Spanish is essential to communicate. The Garinagu speak Garifuna, and the various Mennonite communities speak different dialects of Old German. Then there are Mopan, Yucatec, and Q'eqchi' Mayan tongues. Still other immigrant groups, like Chinese and Lebanese, also often speak their own languages among themselves.

The Arts

Belize has a fairly rich arts scene for such a small country. Several painters and visual artists from Belize have made a name for themselves internationally. Start your research by looking up the work of Gilvano Swasey, Pen Cayetano, Michael Gordon, Benjamin Nicholas, Carolyn Carr, Chris Emmanuel, and Yasser Musa, to name only a few. The government ministry responsible for the arts is the **National Institute for Culture and History** (NICH, www.nichbelize.org), which comprises four organizations: The Institute of Creative Arts (in Belize City), Museum of Belize and Houses of Culture (locations in Belize City, Orange Walk, Benque Viejo del Carmen, and San Ignacio), the Institute of Archaeology (in Belmopan), and the Institute for Social and Cultural Research (in Belmopan).

ARTS AND CRAFTS

You'll have a selection of Belizean and Guatemalan crafts to choose from when visiting any archaeological site, as vendors typically set up rows of stalls with similar gifts, crafts, textiles, and basketwork. You'll also see slate carvings, a recently resurrected skill of the Maya. Among the leading slate carvers are the **Garcia sisters, Lesley Glaspie,** and the **Magana family.** Their work can be found in several Cayo shops as well as elsewhere in the country. The Garcia sisters helped revive the slate craze, and their quality has always been high. **Mennonite furniture pieces** like hardwood chairs and small tables make possible take-home items.

MUSIC

The music of Belize is heavily influenced by the syncopated beats of Africa as they combine with modern sounds from throughout Latin America, the Caribbean, and North America. The most popular Belizean music is *punta,* a fusion of traditional Garifuna rhythms and modern electric instruments. The "Ambassador of Punta Rock" was Andy Palacio, a prolific musician from the southern village of Barranco, who died in 2008 and was honored as a national hero. While Palacio revived interest in *paranda* and *punta,* the creator of the *punta* rock genre was actually Pen Cayetano, another renowned Garifuna musician, artist, and advocate. The newer form of *punta* is characterized by driving, repetitive dance rhythms and has its acoustic roots in a type of music called *paranda.* A PBS special described *paranda* as "nostalgic ballads coupling acoustic guitar with Latin melodies and raw, gritty vocals . . . which can feature traditional Garifuna percussion like wood blocks, turtle shells, forks, bottles, and nails." A few of the original *paranda* masters, like Paul Nabor in Punta Gorda, can still be found in their hometowns throughout Belize. Several excellent compilation albums of Belizean and Honduran *punta* and *paranda* music are available from Stonetree Records.

Brokdong began in the timber camps of the 1800s, when the workers, isolated from civilization for months at a time, would let off steam by drinking a full bottle of rum and then beating on the empty bottle—or the jawbone of an ass, a coconut shell, or a wooden block—anything that made a sound. Add to that a harmonica, guitar, and banjo, and you've got the unique sound of *brokdong.* This is a traditional Creole rhythm kept alive by the legendary Mr. Peters and his **Boom and Chime** band until Mr. Peters died in 2010 at the age of 79.

Dub-poetry has emerged as an important format for musical expression in Belize. The most popular artist of this is **Leroy "The Grandmaster" Young,** whose album *Just Like That* is a wonderful listening experience and has been acclaimed by numerous international reviewers.

In the southern part of Belize, you'll likely hear the strains of ancient Mayan melodies played on homemade wooden instruments, including Q'eqchi' harps, violins, and guitars. In Cayo District in the west, listen for the resonant sounds of marimbas and wooden xylophones—from the Latin influence across the Guatemala border. In the Corozal and Orange Walk Districts in the north, Mexican *ranchera* and *romantica* music is extremely popular. Of course reggae is popular throughout the country, especially on the islands (Bob Marley is king in Belize).

Stonetree Records (www.stonetreerecords.com) has the most complete catalog of truly Belizean music, covering a wide range of musical genres and styles. This author's favorites include *Wátina,* a soulful album featuring traditional *paranda* music by the renowned late Andy Palacio and the Garifuna Collective, and *Belize City Boil-Up,* a funky collection of remastered vintage Belizean soul tracks from the 1950s, 1960s, and 1970s, featuring The Lord Rhaburn Combo, Jesus Acosta and the Professionals, The Web, Harmonettes, Nadia Cattouse, and Soul Creations.

In addition to recording and marketing dozens of albums, Stonetree, based in the town of Benque Viejo in Cayo, western Belize, is also very active in encouraging new Belizean musicians to experiment and develop their individual sounds. Buy albums online, or pick up a couple of CDs at any gift shop or music store during your visit.

FESTIVALS AND EVENTS

When a public holiday falls on Sunday, it is celebrated on the following Monday. If you plan to visit during holiday time, make advance hotel reservations—especially if you plan to spend time in Dangriga around Settlement Day on November 19 (the area has limited accommodations). Note: On Sunday and a few holidays (Easter and Christmas), most businesses close for the day, and some close the day after Christmas (Boxing Day); on Good Friday most buses do not run. Check ahead of time.

National Heroes and Benefactors Day

On March 9, this holiday is celebrated with various activities, mostly water sports. English sportsman Baron Henry Edward Ernest Victor Bliss, who remembered Belize with a generous legacy when he died, designated a day of sailing and fishing in his will. A formal ceremony is held at his tomb below the lighthouse in the Belize Harbor, where he died on his boat. Fishing and sailing regattas begin after the ceremony.

Carnaval

Carnaval, one week before Lent, is a popular holiday in San Pedro on Ambergris Caye. The locals walk in a procession through the streets to the church, celebrating the last hurrah (for devout Catholics) before Easter. Included are lots of good dance competitions.

Easter

Easter weekend is big in Belize: There are concerts, parties, and plenty of dancing and libation flowing all weekend from Belize City to the Northern Cayes and Southern Coast. The most popular events, including concerts and beach bashes, are in San Pedro and Caye Caulker, where most Belizean families head for a break by the sea. If you're not interested in being around large crowds, avoid the Northern Cayes on this long weekend.

But the most unique cultural celebration in the country takes place in the devoutly Roman Catholic historic western town of Benque Viejo del Carmen. It celebrates Semana Santa (Holy Week) with events starting on Palm Sunday and ending on Good Friday with a reenactment of the Passion of Christ (crucifixion). The weeklong events include *alfombras,* a 12-year tradition of creating colorful sawdust carpets on the streets in town to mark the route of the Santo Entierro procession, which represents carrying the body of the crucified Christ to the tomb.

Lobsterfest

Lobsterfest is now one of Belize's most popular festivals. The celebration of the lobster season is held in June in San Pedro, Caye Caulker, and Placencia. The celebration in San Pedro is the longest, with a weeklong series of events including a bar crawl and a Saturday outdoor food feast with top restaurants serving the crustacean prepared in a myriad of ways.

Maya Dances

If you're traveling in the latter part of September in San Antonio Village in the Toledo District, you have a good chance of seeing the **deer dance** performed by the Q'eqchi' Maya villagers. Dancing and celebrating begins around the middle of August, but the biggest celebration begins with a novena, nine days before the feast day of San Luis.

Actually, this festival was only recently revived. The costumes were burned in an accidental fire some years back at a time when (coincidentally) the locals had begun to lose interest in the ancient traditions. Thanks to the formation of the **Toledo Maya Cultural Council,** the Maya are once again realizing the importance of recapturing their past. Some dances are now performed during an annual Cacao Festival in the Toledo District during the last weekend in May.

San Pedro Day

If you're wandering around Belize near June 26-29, hop a boat or plane to San Pedro on Ambergris Caye and join the locals in a festival they have celebrated for decades, **El Día de San Pedro,** in honor of the town's namesake, Saint Peter. This is good fun; hotel reservations are suggested.

September Celebrations

September is Belize's golden month. With the country's Independence Day back-to-back with celebrations of the Battle of St. George's Caye and the Belize City Carnival, Belize enjoys weeks of riotous, cacophonous partying, known nationwide as the September Celebrations. Along the highways, you'll spot massive billboards listing events in districts countrywide leading up to Independence Day.

ST. GEORGE'S CAYE DAY

On September 10, 1798, at St. George's Caye off the coast of Belize, British buccaneers fought and defeated the Spaniards over the territory of Belize. The tradition of celebrating this victory is still carried on each year, followed by a weeklong calendar of events from religious services to carnivals. During this week, Belize City feels like a carnival, with parties everywhere. On the morning of September 10, the whole city parades through the streets and enjoys local cooking, spirits, and music with an upbeat atmosphere that continues well into the beginning of Independence Day on September 21.

CARNIVAL

Belize City also celebrates its very own **Carnival,** usually held in mid-September, following St. George's Caye Day. It consists of a full-blown Caribbean-style costume parade and dancing in the streets and along Central American Boulevard, with hundreds of themed floats blasting soca or *punta* music.

NATIONAL INDEPENDENCE DAY

On September 21, 1981, Belize gained independence from Great Britain. Each year, Belizeans celebrate with carnivals on the main streets of downtown Belize City and in all the district towns, as well as on Ambergris Caye and Caye Caulker. Like giant county fairs, they include displays of local arts, crafts, and cultural activities, while happy Belizeans dance to a variety of exotic *punta,* soca, and reggae rhythms. Again, don't miss the chance to sample local dishes from every ethnic group in the country.

Garifuna Settlement Day

On November 19, Belize recognizes the 1823 arrival and settlement of the first Garifuna people in the southern districts of Belize. Belizeans from all over the country gather in Dangriga, Hopkins, Punta Gorda, and Belize City to celebrate with the Garinagu. The day begins with the **reenactment** of the arrival of the settlers and continues with all-night dancing to the local Garifuna drums and live *punta* bands. Traditional food—and copious amounts of rum, beer, and bitters—is available at street stands and local cafés. November 19 in Dangriga is one of the most memorable celebrations I've experienced in Belize, and anywhere in the Caribbean, for that matter.

Christmas and New Year's

Christmas is celebrated around the country,

shops stay open late pre-Christmas Day, and there is a surge in visitors until just after Christmas, with hotels booked weeks ahead. Belizeans celebrate the eve, day of, and day after Christmas (Boxing Day). Prepare for two full days when stores are closed and everyone is home with family. New Year's is more festive, with various options for parties, concerts, and indoor parties across the country. San Pedro, Caye Caulker, and Placencia Village are known to have the liveliest New Year's bashes. In Belize City, the Radisson Fort George often puts on a New Year's Eve Gala with live music, food, and drinks.

Essentials

Transportation

GETTING THERE

Air

Dozens of daily international flights fly in and out of the country, served by a growing number of major carriers. In general, airfares to Belize are more expensive than your average Central American destination, but rates have certainly dipped slightly more over the past two years.

Most travelers to Belize arrive at **Philip S. W. Goldson International Airport** (BZE, tel. 501/225-2045, www.pgiabelize.

com), 10 miles west of Belize City, outside the community of Ladyville. The airport is named after Philip Stanley Wilberforce Goldson (1923-2001), a respected newspaper editor, activist, and politician. The midsize airport offers gift shops, currency exchange, and two restaurants; Internet access is available in the Sun Garden Restaurant upstairs from the American terminal. Check out the "waving deck" upstairs by the other bar-restaurant for exciting farewell and hello energy. The airport's ongoing runway and apron expansion is hoping to attract new carriers from farther away, particularly from Europe.

When it's time to leave, don't forget to carry enough U.S. dollars for your US$36 departure fee (although it's often already included in your ticket).

AIRPORT TRANSPORTATION

After clearing customs, you'll be besieged by taxi drivers offering rides into town for a fixed US$25; split the cost with fellow travelers if you can. If you are not being picked up by a resort or tour company and you choose to rent a car, look for the 11 rental car offices, all together on the same little strip, across the parking lot from the arrival area.

CONNECTIONS WITHIN BELIZE

To continue to the cayes, you can fly directly to Caye Caulker or San Pedro via the domestic airlines **Tropic Air** (tel. 501/226-2012, U.S. tel. 800/422-3435, www.tropicair.com) or **Maya Island Air** (tel. 501/223-1140 or 501/223-1362, www.mayaislandair.com). You could also take a taxi into town and get on a boat for about half the price and just a few hours longer. If it's your first time in Belize, flying is worth it, with gorgeous aerial views of the water, surrounding cayes, and Belize Barrier Reef.

To reach a resort on a south caye, you can fly via Tropic Air or Maya Island Air to the nearest jumping-off point—say, Dangriga, Placencia, or Punta Gorda—and from there

catch a boat taxi or the resort's arranged pickup. If you're merely going on day trips to the Southern Cayes, then the only connection you'll need is to your chosen mainland jumping-off point by either bus or local flight.

FROM MEXICO

Because airfares to Belize are so high, a few travelers choose to fly into the Mexican state of Quintana Roo on the Yucatán Peninsula, especially to Cancún, where discounted airfares are common. Getting by bus from Mexico to Belize is a cinch; many daily buses travel from the main terminal in Chetumal all the way to Belize City and back. You'll have to get out to wait in various customs and immigration lines, and it's a longer journey, but just follow the crowd and you'll be fine. There are also several Mexican bus lines that run daily between Chetumal, Belize City, Cayo (Benque), and Guatemala. Belize's **Tropic Air** (tel. 501/226-2012, U.S. tel. 800/422-3435, www.tropicair.com) offers direct service (Mon.-Fri., US$155 each way) between Cancún and Belize City's international airport. Moreover, Aeromexico offers direct flights between Mexico City and Belize City.

Boat

Boats travel back and forth daily to Punta Gorda from Puerto Barrios, Guatemala. There are two boat services to Puerto Cortés, Honduras (one leaves from Placencia, the other from Dangriga). Vessels traveling to the area must have permission from the Belizean Embassy in Washington DC.

Bus
FROM MEXICO

After passing through customs at the Cancún airport, you will find service desks for shuttle transportation and the ADO bus ticket agent. You want to go to Playa del Carmen, an hour south, where you will make a connection to Chetumal. It costs about US$23 for a shared shuttle to Playa del Carmen; private shuttle service is US$70-80, depending on group size. Visit the airport's website (www.cancun-airport.com) to search for rates and reserve shuttle transportation. The airport personnel are very helpful in directing you where you need to go and ensuring you have transportation from the airport; shuttle vans are immediately outside, and buses are to the right.

A bus to Playa del Carmen (about US$10) is the most economical route. Riviera buses are comfortable and air-conditioned; if you're the type of person who packs a sweater for your tropical vacation, it may be useful. After arriving at the station, a few blocks from an amazing beach, you have two options: continue immediately to Chetumal near the Belize border or overnight in Playa del Carmen. Playa del Carmen has two bus stations: Terminal Alterna on Calle 20 and Terminal Turística (also called Terminal Riviera, 5th Ave. and Ave. Juárez); you can buy tickets for any destination at either station, so always double-check where your bus departs from when you buy a ticket.

If you continue directly to Chetumal, check the bus schedule; you may need to take a taxi (US$2.50) to Terminal Turística. Buses to Chetumal (US$13.50-20) depart every hour until 5:15pm; the trip takes 5-6 hours and has a few stops in between if you need to grab a snack or use the restroom. Chances are you'll arrive in Chetumal later in the evening, and public transportation options to Belize may not be available.

If you'd rather linger in Playa del Carmen, you won't be sorry; find a hotel, head to the beach, or stroll along 5th Avenue. You can book a morning bus to Chetumal, and most likely, it will be departing from Terminal Turística.

The main ADO bus terminal in Chetumal is not too far from the Nuevo Mercado, where local buses to Belize depart. Outside the station you can find a taxi or continue walking across the plaza to Avenida Insurgentes. Continue left toward the Pemex gas station on the corner and turn right onto Avenida de los Héroes. Continue two blocks to Calle Segundo Circuito Periférico and turn left. You'll see the repainted school buses waiting at Nuevo Mercado Lázaro Cárdenas, in a parking lot on the right side of the street.

Car
FROM THE UNITED STATES
The road from Brownsville, Texas, to the border of Belize is just under 1,400 miles. You can make the drive in three days, especially now that there is a toll-road bypass around Veracruz and the Tuxtla mountains. The all-weather roads are paved, and the shortest route through Mexico is by way of Tampico, Veracruz, Villahermosa, Escárcega, and Chetumal. There is often construction on Mexican Highways 180 and 186. Lodging is available throughout the drive, although it is most concentrated in the cities and on the Costa Esmeralda, a beautiful strip of mostly deserted beach near Nautla (prices start at around US$20 for a very simple double). If attempting this trip, be sure you have a valid credit card, Mexican liability insurance, a passport, and a driver's license—all original documents and one set of photocopies.

One very important detail when entering Mexico from the United States is to request a *doble entrada* on your passport to avoid steep fees. This should only cost about US$10, if it's available. Returning to Mexico from Belize, you'll pay a US$19 per person Belizean exit tax.

FROM MEXICO
It is possible to rent a car in Cancún and continue south on a Belizean adventure, but it'll cost you both money and patience. Still, with the money you save with the cheaper airfare into Cancún, the mobility may be worth it. Cancún is 229 miles from the border at Santa Elena, roughly 4.5 hours in a car on Highway 307. Corporate international rental companies will not let you take their vehicles across the border, so you'll have to find a more accommodating Mexican company, like **J. L. Vegas,**

with one office near the airport and another in the Crystal Hotel. Next, you'll need to "make the papers," as the car guy will surely remind you. Another company that says they'll let you drive into Belize is **Caribbean Rent A Car** (U.S. tel. 866/577-1342, Mexico tel. 52/998-253-6112, www.cancunrentacar.com).

The most crucial part of driving into Belize from Mexico is having a letter of permission from the car's owner; customs will scrutinize this document. Next, to avoid being turned back at the border, be sure to get the vehicle sprayed with insecticide (US$5) from one of the roadside sprayers near the border—it's tough to pick them out, but look for a little white shack past the bridge after leaving Mexico and keep your receipt for when you reach customs and immigration. After passing through Mexican immigration (have your passport stamped and hand in your tourist card), you will cross a bridge welcoming you to Belize. On the right-hand side, you will see two unsigned buildings where you must purchase insurance. The tire fumigation is near the fork in the road before the free zone. You will likely be greeted when you first pull over by men offering to help you through the stations, but their services are unnecessary. Still, it can be wise to befriend these touts, as many of them are related to the officers at the border. Give a small tip and ask them to clean your windows while you are getting insurance at the Atlantic house (you must have insurance before you enter immigration).

Although in Mexico proof of registration suffices as proof of ownership, in Belize you may be asked to show a title. You will not need a Temporary Vehicle Importation permit if entering for one month or less; for more time, you may need to post a bond on your vehicle (in greenbacks, to be refunded in Belizean dollars later).

GETTING AROUND
Air

It is very reasonable and common to get around the country in puddle-jumper planes. Belizean airstrips are paved, a range of official

to semiofficial looking, and entirely safe. Because such small planes are used, you not only watch the pilot handling the craft, you may also get to sit next to him or her if the flight is full (which is easy in a 12-seater). Best of all, flying low and slow in these aircraft allows you to get a panoramic view of the Belize Barrier Reef, cayes, coast, and rainforest (keep your camera handy).

Two airlines offer regularly scheduled flights to all districts in Belize, from both the international and municipal airports: **Tropic Air** (tel. 501/226-2012, U.S. tel. 800/422-3435, reservations@tropicair.com, www.tropicair.com) and **Maya Island Air** (tel. 501/223-1140 or 501/223-1362, mayair@btl.net, www.mayaislandair.com). Daily flights are available from Belize City to Caye Caulker, San Pedro, Dangriga, Placencia, Punta Gorda, and a handful of other tiny strips around the country. Flights also link San Pedro to the Cayo District. The Maya Island Air and Tropic Air flights usually combine several destinations in one route, so if you're traveling to Punta Gorda, you may have to land and take off in Dangriga and Placencia first. Ditto for Caulker and San Pedro, which are linked together. There are also regular flights to Flores, Guatemala, and you can fly between Corozal and San Pedro. If your scheduled flight is full, another will taxi up shortly and off you go.

Several charter flight companies will arrange trips to remote or upscale resorts. **Javier's Flying Service** (municipal airport, tel. 501/824-0460 or cell 501/610-0446, www.javiersflyingservice.com) is one such charter, offering local and international flights, air ambulance, and day tours.

HELICOPTER

Charter a chopper for a transfer, adventure tour, filming or photography assignment, aerial property survey, search and rescue mission, or medical evacuation with **Astrum Helicopters** (Mile 3.5, George Price Hwy., near Belize City, tel. 501/222-5100, U.S. tel. 888/278-7864, www.astrumhelicopters.com); expect to pay around US$1,000 per hour (US$250 pp for most sightseeing tours). Astrum Helicopters also takes guests to Azul, Isla Marisol Resort, and Cayo Espanto, among other destinations. Astrum is a modern, professional outfit with new aircraft and a very skilled father-son pilot team.

Bus

Save money, meet Belizeans, and see the countryside on an unrushed trip between towns (if you can take the discomfort of school-size buses). The motley fleet that serves the entire country ranges from your typical run-down recycled yellow school bus to plush, air-conditioned luxury affairs. Belize buses are relatively reliable, on time, and less chaotic than the chicken-bus experience in other parts of Central America and Mexico. Even so, buses make many extra stops, including a requisite break in Belmopan for anywhere from 5 to 30 minutes for all buses traveling between Belize City and points west and south; it's a good restroom and taco break.

Your best up-to-date resource for all Belize bus schedules and information is www.belizebus.wordpress.com, an independent website that pays impressive attention to travel details. Another website with bus schedules is www.guidetobelize.info. Travel time from Belize City to Corozal or San Ignacio is about 2 hours, to Dangriga 2-3 hours, and to Punta Gorda 5-6 hours. Fares average US$2-4 to most destinations, US$7-12 for the longer routes.

In Belize City, nearly all buses still begin and end at the **Novelo's Terminal** (W. Collett Canal St., tel. 501/207-4924, 501/207-3929, or 501/227-7146); it's still called that even though the company no longer exists. Reach it by walking west on King Street, across Collett Canal, and into the terminal—definitely use a taxi when departing or arriving at night. Another walking route from the downtown area and water taxi is to go west along Orange Street, a busy shopping area, cross over the canal, then turn left and continue a short distance to the terminal.

James Bus runs the most reliable daily Punta Gorda service, using the block in front of the Shell station on Vernon Street (two blocks north of Novelo's) as its terminal.

There are at least a dozen booths to buy a ticket on the various international express bus services **to Guatemala and Mexico.** All are located inside or in front of the Ocean Ferry Water Taxi Terminal and Swing Bridge. Boat-bus connections are convenient and easy to make, but it all happens in the middle of one of Belize's busiest intersections.

Car

Driving Belize's handful of highways gives you the most independence when traveling throughout the country, but it is also the most expensive way to go. Rental fees were running US$75-125 per day and gasoline was approaching US$6 per gallon at press time. You'll also have to be adept at avoiding careless drivers and obstacles like pedestrians, farm animals, cyclists, iguanas, and the occasional moped-riding cruise ship passenger.

In some areas, like the Mountain Pine Ridge and other hinterlands, there is no public transportation, and a sturdy rental car is a good way to go if you're into traveling on your own schedule.

RENTAL CARS

One of the first things you'll see on walking out of the arrival lounge at the international airport is a strip of about a dozen car rental offices offering small, midsize, and 4WD vehicles. Vans and passenger cars are also available, some with air-conditioning. Insurance is mandatory but (like taxes) not always included in the quoted rates. If you know exactly when you want the car, it's helpful and often cheaper to make reservations. Note the hour you pick up the car and try to return it before that time: A few minutes over could cost you another full day's rental fee. Also take the vehicle inspection seriously to make sure you don't get charged for someone else's dings. And don't forget to fill the tank up before giving it back.

Crystal Auto Rental (Goldson

Driving Tips

- Drive defensively! Expect everyone out there to make sudden passes and unexpected turns—it's your job to stay out of their way.

- Valid U.S. or other foreign driver's licenses and international driving permits are accepted in Belize for a period of three months after entering the country.

- Try not to drive at night if you can avoid it. Besides the additional hazards of night driving in general, some Belizean drivers overuse their high beams, and many vehicles have no taillights.

- Watch out for unmarked speed bumps. No matter how slow you drive, on some you may bottom out.

- Driving rules are U.S.-style with one very strange exception: Sometimes a vehicle making a left-hand turn is expected to pull over to the right, let traffic behind pass, and then execute the turn.

- Tires frequently pop, so make sure you have a good spare to get you to the nearest used-tire dealer. New tires may be hard to come by, but Belizeans are geniuses with a patch kit. A decent used spare can be had for around US$30, a patch job about US$5.

- If you're going to the cayes and leaving a vehicle on the mainland, be sure to seek out a secure pay parking lot in your city of departure, especially if it's Belize City (the municipal airport is probably the best choice).

- If you plan on traveling during the rainy season or without a 4WD vehicle, make sure you are prepared in the event you get stuck in the mud.

- In general, road conditions may dictate where you can and cannot go, and it is always best to ask around town if you plan to go off the beaten path. Watch out for speed bumps, even on the highways.

- Expect police checkpoints anywhere around the country: Police will check your seat belt, car papers, and driver's license, and, courtesy of the U.S. Drug Enforcement Agency, dogs will sniff the vehicle for any drugs.

International Airport/Mile 5, Philip Goldson Hwy., tel. 501/223-1600, www.crystal-belize.com) has a large, reliable fleet of cars in Belize. It is also the only company that will allow you to drive across the border into Guatemala or Mexico, but you won't be insured. **AQ Belize Rental** (Mile 5.5 Philip Goldson Hwy., tel. 501/222-5122 or 501/635-6200 24-hr, www.aqbelizecarrental.com, from US$37 per day) has a location just outside the airport, as well as in the city and in Placencia. It guarantees the lowest prices on its fleet—from sedans to SUVs—including free pickups and drop-offs within Belize City limits. **Jabiru Auto Rental** (tel. 501/224-4680, www.jabiruautorental.bz) is also reliable and has low Internet rates. **Budget Rent a Car** (tel.

501/223-2435, www.budget-belize.com) offers new cars that are well maintained. You'll find a few other international brands with local Belizean branches, including **Avis.**

If you plan on traveling in the Cayo region, it's cheaper to use one of the San Ignacio-based car rental options. Start with **Cayo Rentals** (at the UNO station at the top of the hill, 81 Benque Viejo Rd., tel. 501/824-2222, www.cayoautorentals.com); US$75 per 24 hours *includes* taxes and insurance. Also in Cayo, **Matus Car Rentals** (18 Benque Viejo Rd., tel. 501/824-2005, www.matuscarrental.com) is another option with a handful of sturdy cars, and there is a Land Rover rental place in Central Farm, just east of San Ignacio, if you're really planning on going off-road.

Distances from Belize City

Belmopan	55 miles
Benque Viejo	81 miles
Corozal Town	96 miles
Dangriga	105 miles
Orange Walk Town	58 miles
Punta Gorda	210 miles
San Ignacio	72 miles

Travel Specialists and Tour Companies

BELIZE TRAVEL SPECIALISTS

More than travel agents but not quite tour operators, Belize country specialists are small, independent operations that work directly with their clients to arrange all kinds of niche, group, and solo travel within Belize. There is usually no charge for their services, so you really can't go wrong by letting them handle some of the planning and booking.

Barb's Belize (U.S. tel. 888/321-2272, www.barbsbelize.com) is one small operation that offers custom itineraries for any budget, from backpacker to decadent. Barb's specializes in unique interests such as traditional herbal medicine, rainforest survival, and extreme adventure expeditions. She does charge US$50 for her planning services and advice, which she credits to your invoice if you book through her.

Splash Destination Management Company (tel. 501/523-3080, www.splashbelize.com/category/splash-destination-management-company) can help arrange active itineraries across Belize, from hotels to activities, with contacts that stretch around the country, as well as in their Placencia Peninsula base.

ADVENTURE TRAVEL

Dangriga- and Vancouver-based **Island Expeditions** (U.S. tel. 800/667-1630, www. islandexpeditions.com) has been leading exciting sea kayaking, rafting, ruins, nature, and snorkeling adventures in Belize since 1987. It's a very experienced and professional outfit, and has stunning island camps in Glover's Reef and Lighthouse Reef Atolls with canvas-wall platform tents. It also offers popular lodge-to-lodge sea kayaking and paddleboarding trips, as well as inland river adventures, and can help you outfit your own kayak expedition.

Slickrock Adventures (U.S. tel. 800/390-5715, www.slickrock.com), based at its primitively plush camp on a private island in Glover's Reef Atoll, offers paddling trips of various lengths and specializes in sea kayaking, windsurfing, and inland activities like mountain biking.

With decades of experience as a premier land operator in Belize, **International Expeditions** (U.S. tel. 800/633-4734, belize@ietravel.com, www.ietravel.com) has a full-time office in Belize City. It offers group and independent nature travel in sturdy, comfortable vehicles and is staffed by travel and airline specialists, naturalists, and an archaeologist. Trips run 7-14 days with 2- and 3-day add-ons available.

You'll also find an interesting menu of tours offered by **Intrepid Travel** (U.S. tel. 800/970-7299, http://intrepidtravel.com), an Australian company that runs trips around the world and has a dozen trips that include Belize, some Maya-themed.

TOUR OPERATORS

For those interested in letting someone else do the driving (and planning, booking, etc.), various tour operators are reliable. In Belize City, Sarita and Lascelle Tillet of **S&L Travel and Tours** (91 N. Front St., tel. 501/227-7593 or 501/227-5145, www.sltravelbelize.com) operate as a Belizean husband-and-wife team. They drive air-conditioned sedans or vans and travel throughout the country, with airport pickup available. The Tillets have designed several great special-interest vacations and will custom-design to your interests, whether they be the Mayan archaeological zones (including Tikal), the cayes, or the caves and the countryside.

InnerQuest Adventures (U.S. tel. 800/990-4376, www.innerquest.com) has over 14 years of experience leading wildlife-viewing trips with local guides around the country. It's been featured in dozens of magazines. Minnesota-based **Magnum Belize Tours** (U.S. tel. 800/446-2735, www. magnumbelize.com) is one of the biggest, longest-standing tour operators, with an extensive network of resorts across the country; the staff is very experienced and can customize every aspect of your trip.

Sea & Explore (U.S. tel. 800/345-9786, www.seaexplore.com) is run by owners Sue and Tony Castillo, native Belizeans who take pleasure and pride in sharing their country with visitors by means of customized trips. They know every out-of-the-way destination and make every effort to match clients with the right areas of the country to suit their interests. Susan worked with the Belize Tourism Board before coming to the United States.

Jaguar Adventures Tours and Travel (4 Fort St., tel. 501/223-6025, www.jaguarbelize. com) is located in Belize City and offering night walks at the Belize Zoo, cave tubing trips, visits to Mayan ruins, snorkeling the reef, and diving the atolls, to name a few adventures.

The Mayan Traveler (U.S. tel. 888/843-6292, www.themayantraveler.com) can satisfy even the most serious temple junkie, going to some of the most spectacular sites in the region.

Visas and Officialdom

PASSPORTS

U.S. citizens must have a passport valid for the duration of their visit to Belize; citizens of the United States, British Commonwealth countries, Belgium, Denmark, Finland, Greece, Iceland, Italy, Liechtenstein, Luxembourg, Mexico, Spain, Switzerland, Tunisia, Turkey, and Uruguay do not need a visa. They are automatically granted a 30-day tourist pass and technically must have onward or return air tickets and proof of sufficient money (though I've never heard of anyone checking this). Visitors for purposes other than tourism, or who want to stay longer than 30 days, need to visit an immigration office of the government of Belize.

If you are planning on staying more than 30 days, you can ask for a new stamp at any immigration office in the country—there's one in every district, including in San Pedro, Belize City, and Dangriga—or you can cross the border and return, but this technique is no guarantee of readmission, particularly if you're gone only for a few days. The fee to extend for a month is US$25.

Make a photocopy of the pages in your passport that have your photo and information. When you get the passport stamped at the airport, it's a good idea to make a photocopy of that page as well, and store the copies somewhere other than with your passport. This will facilitate things if your passport ever gets lost or stolen. Also consider taking a small address book, credit cards, a travel insurance policy, and an international phone card for calling home. A separate passport pouch can be used for documents, but make sure it's waterproof so it won't get soggy when you sweat.

FOREIGN EMBASSIES

Only a handful of countries have embassies in Belize. The **U.S. Embassy** (4 Floral Park Rd., Belmopan, tel. 501/822-4011, fax 501/822-4012, belmopanpa@state.gov, https:// bz.usembassy.gov) is open for U.S. citizen services 8am-noon and 1pm-5pm Monday-Friday in its brand-new US$50 million fortified building. The after-hours emergency number for American citizens is tel. 501/610-5030. For inquiries pertaining to American citizens, email ACSBelize@state.gov.

U.S. citizens are strongly encouraged by the **U.S. State Department** (www.travel.state.gov) to register their trip online, no matter how short, so that the local embassy has emergency contact information on file.

The **British High Commission** (Melhado Parade, North Ring Rd., Belmopan, tel. 501/822-2146, brithicom@btl.net, www.ukinbelize.fco.gov.uk/en) is open 8am-noon and 1pm-4pm Monday-Thursday and 8am-2pm Friday. El Salvador and India also have embassies in Belmopan.

Countries with consulates in Belize City include Canada, China, Cuba, Mexico, Colombia, Holland, Sweden, and Taiwan.

Food

Belizean cuisine reflects its diverse population, and the very idea of a national cuisine is quite recent. Since the times of the Baymen, Belize has been an import economy, surviving mostly on canned meats like "bully beef" and imported grains and packaged goods. With independence, however, came renewed national pride, and with the arrival of travelers seeking "local" food, the word "Belizean" was increasingly applied to the varied diet of so many cultures. Anthropologist Richard Wilk wrote about the process in his book *Home Cooking in the Global Village: Caribbean Food from Buccaneers to Ecotourists.* A more recent book on Belizean cuisine made its appearance in 2012—*Flavors of Belize,* highlighting major cultural groups' staple dishes and Belize's top chefs.

The common denominator of Belizean food is **rice and beans,** a starchy staple pronounced as one word with a heavy accent on the first syllable: *"RICE-'n'-beans!"* Belizeans speak of the dish with pride, as if they invented the combination, and you can expect a massive mound of it with most midday meals. Actually, Belizean rice and beans *is* closer to the Caribbean version than the Latin: They use red beans, black pepper, and grated coconut, instead of the black beans and cilantro common in neighboring Latin countries. The rest of your plate will be occupied by something like **stew beef or stew chicken, fry chicken,** or a piece of fish, plus a small mound of either potato or cabbage salad. Be sure to take advantage of so much fresh fruit: oranges, watermelon, star fruit, soursop, mangoes, and papaya, to name a few.

For breakfast, you should try some **fry jacks** (fluffy fried-dough crescents) or **johnnycakes** (flattened biscuits) with your eggs, beans, and bacon.

One of the cheapest and quickest meal options, found nearly everywhere in Belize, is Mexican "fast-food" snacks, especially **taco stands,** which are everywhere you look, serving as many as five or six soft-shell chicken tacos for US$1. Also widely available are *salbutes,* a kind of hot, soggy taco dripping in oil; *panades,* little meat pies; and *garnaches,* which are crispy tortillas under a small mound of tomato, cabbage, cheese, and hot sauce.

Speaking of hot sauce, you'll definitely want to try to take home **Marie Sharp's** famous habanero sauces, jams, and other creative products. Marie Sharp is an independent Belizean success story, and many travelers visit her factory and store just outside Dangriga. (Her products are available on every single restaurant table and in every gift shop in the country.) Her sauce is good on pretty much everything. She's also opened a culinary center and store in San Ignacio.

Then, of course, there's the international cuisine, in the form of many excellent foreign-themed restaurants. San Pedro, Hopkins, and Placencia, in particular, have fine dining scenes.

Responsible Seafood

Many ocean waters are overfished, due in large part to increasing demand from tourists. These helpful tips will ensure you eat seafood responsibly.

- Don't order seafood out of season. The once-prolific lobster (season closed Feb. 15-June 15) is becoming scarce in Belizean waters, and conch (season closed July 1-Sept. 30) is not nearly as easy to find as it once was. Most reputable restaurateurs follow the law and don't buy undersize or out-of-season seafood; however, a few have no scruples.

- Small snappers are great fish to eat. Not only are they delicious, but they are one of the most sustainably caught fish in Belize (often caught locally with a hook and line).

- When dining out, check whether the restaurant is "Eat Right, Fish Right" certified, an initiative launched in partnership with Oceana Belize (www.fishrighteatright.com). If not, encourage them to sign up.

- Don't patronize any restaurant offering shark fin soup or *panades* made with shark meat. Not only are sharks critical to a functional marine ecosystem, but the meat is high in methyl mercury, so it's bad for you too.

- Avoid any restaurant that displays endangered reef fish, like the Nassau grouper or goliath grouper, in tanks as meal choices. In fact, stay away from grouper in general, especially goliath grouper (*Epinephelus itajara*), a critically endangered species that is also high in methyl mercury.

- Lastly, don't buy marine curios such as shark teeth or jaws, starfish, or coral.

Many restaurants in Belize have flexible hours of operation, and often close for a few hours between lunch and dinner. The omnipresent Chinese restaurants provide authentic Chinese cuisine of varying quality. Most Chinese places sell cheap "fry chicken" takeout.

SEAFOOD

One of the favorite Belize specialties is fresh fish, especially along the coast and on the islands, but even inland Belize is never more than 60 miles from the ocean. There's lobster, shrimp, red snapper, sea bass, halibut, barracuda, conch, and lots more prepared in a variety of ways. Be sure to know the in-seasons for legal consumption.

Conch has been a staple in the diet of the Mayan and Central American communities along the Caribbean coast for centuries. There are conch fritters, conch steak, and conch stew; it's also often used in ceviche— uncooked seafood marinated in lime juice with onions, peppers, tomatoes, and a host of spices. In another favorite, conch is pounded,

dipped in egg and cracker crumbs, and sautéed quickly (like abalone steak in California) with a squirt of fresh lime. Caution: If it's cooked too long, it becomes tough and rubbery. Conch fritters are minced pieces of conch mixed into a flour batter and fried— delicious. On many boat trips, the crew will catch a fish and some conch and prepare them for lunch, either as ceviche, cooked over an open beach fire, or in a "boil-up" seasoned with onions, peppers, and achiote, a fragrant red spice grown locally since the time of the early Maya.

DRINKS
Beer

Perhaps the most important legacy left by nearly three centuries of British imperialism is a national affinity for dark beer. Nowhere else in Central America will you find ale as hearty and dark as you do in any bar, restaurant, or corner store in Belize, where beer is often advertised separately from stout, a good sign indeed for those who prefer more bite and body to their brew.

At the top of the heap are the slender, undersize 280-milliliter (9.5-ounce) bottles of **Guinness Foreign Extra Stout,** known affectionately by Belizeans as "short, dark, and lovelies." Yes, Guinness—brewed in Belize under license from behind the famous St. James's Gate in Dublin, Ireland, and packing a pleasant 7.5 percent punch of alcohol. No, this is not the same sweet nectar you'll find flowing from your favorite Irish pub's draft handle at home, but you're in Central America. Enjoy.

Asking for a "beer" will get you a basic **Belikin,** which, when served cold, is no better or worse than any other regional draft. Brewed in Belize since 1971 by Bowen & Bowen Limited, it's the only beer in the Caribbean and Central America that uses a high percentage of malt, very close to Germany's 100 percent. **Belikin Stout** weighs in with a slightly larger 342-milliliter (11.5-ounce) bottle that is distinguishable from a regular beer bottle by its blue bottle cap. Stouts run 6.5 percent alcohol and are a bit less bitter than Guinness, but still a delicious, meaty meal that goes down much quicker than its caloric equivalent of a loaf of bread. **Belikin Premium** (4.8 percent alcohol) boasts a well-balanced body and is brewed with four different types of foreign hops; demand often exceeds supply in many establishments, so order early.

Lastly, the tiny green bottles belong to **Lighthouse Lager,** a healthy alternative to the heavies, but packing a lot less bang for the buck with only 4.2 percent alcohol and several ounces less beer (often for the same price).

All beer is brewed and distributed by the same company, Bowen and Bowen, in Ladyville, just north of Belize City; they also have the soft-drink market cornered. Most Belizeans vigorously wipe the open bottle mouths with the napkin that comes wrapped around the top—you'd be smart to do the same. Beers in Belize cost US$1.50-3 a bottle, depending on where you are.

Rum

Of all the national rums, **One Barrel** stands proudly above the rest. Smooth enough to enjoy on the rocks (add a bit of Coca-Cola for coloring if you need to), One Barrel has a sweet, butterscotchy aftertaste and costs about US$12 for a one-liter bottle, or US$3 per shot (or rum drink). The cheaper option is **Caribbean Rum,** which is fine if you're mixing it with punch, cola, or better yet, coconut water in the coconut. Everything else is standard white-rum rotgut.

The **"panty-ripper"** is Belize's unofficial national cocktail—a perfect blend of coconut rum and a splash of pineapple juice. Don't underestimate it as a girly drink; a couple of well-made "panty-rippers" can get you very tipsy.

Bitters

Bitters are made by soaking herbs like *palo del hombre* (man-root) and jackass bitters in 80-proof white rum or gin. They are available under the counter of many a bar and corner store and are known in Garifuna as *gífit.* Bitters are a cure-all used to treat everything from the common cold to cancer, sometimes taken as a daily shot to keep your system clean.

Belizean Garifuna expats used to bring bitters back to the United States by the gallon. The most famous bitters maker in the country was Doctor Mac (also known as "Big Mac"), a formidable man who used to make a "fertility" version of bitters for women, with the bottles labeled either "boy" or "gal." The latest bitters-making wonder is "Kid B," a spry 76-year-old from Silk Grass Village, who spent 36 years as a welterweight prizefighter in Chicago.

In addition to curing what ails you, however, bitters can get you quite wasted. Be careful with any usage—both for your liver's sake and because some say the ingredients carry trace amounts of arsenic. Talk about a hangover.

Nonalcoholic Beverages

There are wonderful natural fruit drinks to be had throughout Belize. Take advantage of fresh lime, papaya, watermelon, orange, and other healthy juices during your travels—they are usually made with purified water, at least in most tourist destinations.

Accommodations

HOTELS AND HOMESTAYS

Of the over 800 licensed hotels in Belize, the vast majority are small or medium-size. Large foreign-owned hotel chains are, however, increasing slowly in Belize, particularly on Ambergris Caye, Placencia, and very soon, Belize's first Four Seasons coming to Caye Chapel.

The **Belize Hotel Association** (BHA, 13 Cork St., Belize City, tel. 501/223-0669, www.belizehotels.org) is a nonprofit industry organization of some of the country's most respected resorts and lodges. It works with the Belize Tourism Board and handles much of the global marketing for Belize; it also has a helpful listing of accommodations on its website.

Budget accommodations are ample in Belize, if not as ample as next door in Mexico or Guatemala, with nightly rates under US$30. In Belize, US$25-30 is often the bottom line for low-cost lodging. Guesthouses and budget hotels sometimes offer a cheaper shared dormitory or bunk room, often with shared baths and cold water.

Some villages around the country try to emulate the guesthouse and homestay networks available in the southern Toledo villages. Such options are usually primitive accommodations, sometimes lacking electricity, running water, and flush toilets.

Hotel Rates

Exact hotel rates are an elusive thing in Belize; seasonal pricing fluctuations are compounded by various hotel taxes and service charges, sometimes as much as 25-30 percent above the quoted rate. Using a credit card can add another 3-5 percent. Universal standards for presenting prices are absent in Belize's hotel industry. Always make sure the rate you are quoted is actually the same amount you will be asked to pay.

High season is loosely considered to be mid-December through the end of April and marked by a rise in both the number of visitors and the price of most accommodations. Some places kick their rates up even higher during Christmas, New Year's, and Easter, calling these "holiday" or "peak" rates. A minority of hotels keep their rates the same year-round, but it's rarely that simple.

Great deals are abundant in the **low season** (May-Nov.), when room rates plummet across the board, and walk-in specials can save you as much as 50 percent off normal winter (high-season) rates.

Health and Safety

For up-to-date health recommendations and advice, consult the Belize "Mexico and Central America" page of the **U.S. Centers for Disease Control and Prevention** (CDC, wwwnc.cdc.gov/travel) or call their International Travelers Hotline (U.S. tel. 877/394-8747). You can also call the Belizean embassy in your country for up-to-date information about outbreaks or other health problems.

STAYING HEALTHY

Ultimately, your health is dependent on the choices you make, and chief among these is what you decide to put in your mouth. Expect your digestive system to take some time getting accustomed to the new food and microorganisms in the Belizean diet. During this time (and after), use common sense: Wash your hands with soap often; alcohol-based hand sanitizers are less effective at removing germs from your hands. Eat food that is well cooked and still hot when served. Be wary of uncooked foods, including shellfish and salads. Most importantly, be aware of flies, the single worst transmitter of food-borne illnesses. Prevent flies from landing on your food, glass, or table setting. You'll notice Belizeans are meticulous about this, and you should be too. If you have to leave the table, cover your food with a napkin or have someone else wave a hand over it slowly.

Drinking the Water

Even though most municipal water systems are well treated and probably safe, there is not much reason to take the chance, especially when purified bottled water is so widely available and relatively cheap. Canned and bottled drinks, including beer, are usually safe, but should never be used as a substitute for water when trying to stay hydrated, especially during a bout of traveler's diarrhea or when out in the sun.

If you plan on staying awhile in a rural area of Belize, check out camping catalogs for water filters that remove chemical as well as biological contamination. Alternatively, six drops of liquid iodine (or three of bleach) will kill everything that needs to be killed in a liter of water—good in a pinch (or on a backcountry camping trip), but not something you'll find yourself practicing on a daily basis. Also, bringing any water to a full boil is 100 percent effective in killing bacteria.

Oral Rehydration Salts

Probably the single most effective preventative and curative medicine you can carry is packets of powdered salt and sugar, which, when mixed with a liter of water (drink in small sips), is the best immediate treatment for dehydration due to diarrhea, sun exposure, fever, infection, or hangover. Particularly in the case of diarrhea, rehydration salts are essential to your recovery. They replace the salts and minerals your body has lost due to liquid evacuation (be it from sweating, vomiting, or urinating), and they're essential to your

body's most basic cellular transfer functions. Whether or not you like the taste (odds are you won't), consuming enough rehydration packets and water is very often the difference between being just a little sick and feeling really, really awful.

Sports drinks like Gatorade are super-concentrated mixtures and should be diluted with water to make the most of the active ingredients. If you don't, you'll pee out the majority of the electrolytes. Rehydration packets are available from any drugstore or health clinic. They can also be improvised according to the following recipe: Mix a half teaspoon of salt, a half teaspoon of baking soda, and four tablespoons of sugar in one quart of boiled or carbonated water. Drink a full glass of the stuff after each time you use the bathroom. Add a few drops of lemon juice to make it more palatable.

Sun Exposure

Belize is located a scant 13 to 18 degrees of latitude from the equator, so the sun's rays strike the earth's surface at a more direct angle than in northern countries. The result is that you will burn faster and sweat up to twice as much as you are used to. Did we mention that you should drink lots of water?

Ideally, do like the majority of the locals do, and stay out of the sun between 10am and 2pm. It's a great time to take a nap anyway. Use sunscreen of at least SPF 30, and wear a hat and pants. Should you overdo it in the sun, make sure to drink lots of fluids—that means water, not beer (or at least water and beer). Treat sunburns with aloe gel, or better yet, find a fresh aloe plant to break open and rub over your skin.

DISEASES AND COMMON AILMENTS

There is a moderate incidence of hepatitis B in Belize. Avoid contact with bodily fluids or bodily waste. Get vaccinated if you anticipate close contact with nature or plan to reside in Central America for an extended period of time. Get a rabies vaccination if you intend to spend a long time in Belize. Should you be bitten by an infected dog, rodent, or bat, immediately cleanse the wound with lots of soap and get prompt medical attention.

Tuberculosis is spread by sneezing or coughing, and the infected person may not know he or she is a carrier. If you are planning to spend more than four weeks in Belize (or plan on spending time in the Belize jail), consider having a tuberculin skin test performed before and after visiting. Tuberculosis is a serious and possibly fatal disease but can be treated with several medications. No cases of cholera have been reported in Belize since 2000.

Ciguatera

This is a toxin occasionally found in large reef fish. It is not a common circumstance, but it is possible for groupers, snappers, and barracuda to carry this toxin. If, after eating these fish, you experience diarrhea, nausea, numbness, or heart arrhythmia, see a doctor immediately. The toxin is found in certain algae on reefs in all the tropical areas of the world. Fish do nibble on the coral, and if they happen to find this algae, over a period of time the toxin accumulates in their systems. The longer they live and the larger they get, the more probable it is they will carry the toxin, which is not destroyed when cooked.

Dengue Fever

Dengue, or "bone-breaking fever," is a flulike, mosquito-carried illness that will put a stop to your fun in Central America like a baseball bat to the head. Dengue's occurrence is extremely low in Belize, but a few dozen cases are still reported each year. There is no vaccine, but dengue's effects can be successfully minimized with plenty of rest, acetaminophen (for the fever and aches), and as much water and hydration salts as you can manage. Dengue itself is undetectable in a blood test, but a low platelet count indicates its presence. If you believe you have dengue, you should get a blood test as soon as possible, to make sure it's not the hemorrhagic variety, which can be fatal if untreated.

Diarrhea and Dysentery

Generally, simple cases of diarrhea in the absence of other symptoms are nothing more serious than "traveler's diarrhea." If you do get a good case, your best bet is to let it pass naturally. Diarrhea is your body's way of flushing out the bad stuff, so constipating medicines like Imodium A-D (loperamide) are not recommended, as they keep the bacteria (or whatever is causing your intestinal distress) within your system. Save the Imodium (or any other liquid glue) for emergency situations like long bus rides or a hot date. Most importantly, drink lots of water! Not replacing the fluids and electrolytes you are losing will make you feel much worse than you need to. If the diarrhea persists for more than 48 hours, is bloody, or is accompanied by a fever, see a health professional immediately. That said, know that all bodies react differently to the changes in diet, schedule, and stress that go along with traveling, and many visitors to Belize stay entirely regular and solid throughout their trips.

Pay attention to your symptoms: Diarrhea can also be a sign of amoebic (parasitic) or bacillary (bacterial) dysentery, both caused by some form of fecal-oral contamination. Often accompanied by nausea, vomiting, and a mild fever, dysentery is easily confused with other diseases, so don't try to self-diagnose. Stool-sample examinations are cheap, can be performed at most clinics and hospitals, and are your first step to getting better. Bacillary dysentery is treatable with antibiotics; amoebic dysentery is treated with one of a variety of drugs that kill off all the flora in your intestinal tract. Of these, Flagyl (metronidazole) is the best known, but other non-FDA-approved treatments like tinidazole are commonly available, cheap, and effective. Do not drink alcohol with these drugs, and eat something like yogurt or acidophilus pills to repopulate your tummy.

Malaria

By all official accounts, malaria is present in Belize, although you'll be hard-pressed to find anybody—Belizean or expat—who has actually experienced or even heard of a case of it. Still, many travelers choose to take a weekly prophylaxis of chloroquine or its equivalent. The CDC specifically recommends travelers to Belize use brand-name Aralen pills (500 mg for adults), although you should ask your doctor for the latest drug on the market. A small percentage of people have negative reactions to chloroquine, including nightmares, rashes, or hair loss. Alternative treatments are available, but the best method of all is to not get bitten by mosquitoes, which transmit the disease.

BITES AND STINGS

Thousands of people dive in Belize's Caribbean and hike its forests every day of the year without incident. The information on possible bites and stings is only to let you know what's out there, not to scare you into remaining in your resort. Know what you're getting into and be sure your guide does as well, and then get into it.

Botfly

Also known as *torsalo,* screw-worm, or *Dermatobia hominis,* this insect looks like the common household fly. The big difference is that the botfly deposits its eggs on mosquitoes, which then implant them in an unsuspecting warm-blooded host. Burrowing quickly under the skin, the maggot sets up housekeeping. To breathe, it sticks a tiny tube through the skin, and there it stays until one of two things happen: You kill it, or it graduates and leaves home (to witness this, Google "botfly removal" and get ready for an eyeful).

A botfly bite starts out looking like a mosquito bite, but if the bite gets red and tender instead of healing, get it checked out. Though uncomfortable and distasteful, it's not a serious health problem if it doesn't get infected. A tiny glob of petroleum jelly or tobacco over the air hole often works to draw out or

suffocate the creature; just make sure you squeeze all of it out.

Mosquitoes and Sand Flies

Mosquitoes are most active during the rainy season (June-Nov.) and in areas with stagnant water, like marshes, puddles, and rice fields. They are more common in the lower, flatter regions of Belize than they are in the hills, though even in the highlands, old tires, cans, and roadside puddles can provide the habitat necessary to produce swarms of mosquitoes. The mosquito that carries malaria is active during the evening and at night, while the dengue fever courier is active during the day, from dawn to dusk. They are both relatively simple to combat, and ensuring you don't get bitten is the best prophylaxis for preventing the diseases.

First and foremost, limit the amount of skin you expose—long sleeves, pants, and socks will do more to prevent bites than the strongest chemical repellent. Choose accommodations with good screens, and if this is not possible, use a fan to blow airborne insects away from your body as you sleep. Avoid being outside or unprotected in the hour before sunset, when mosquito activity is heaviest, and use a mosquito net tucked underneath your mattress when you sleep. Consider purchasing a lightweight backpackers' net, either freestanding or to hang from the ceiling, before you come south—mosquito nets are more expensive in Belize than at home. Some accommodations provide nets; others are truly free of biting bugs and don't need them. If you know where you're staying, ask before you arrive whether you'll need a net. Once in Belize, you can purchase mosquito coils, which burn slowly, releasing a mosquito-repelling smoke; they're cheap and convenient, but try to place them so you're not breathing the toxic smoke yourself.

Sand flies don't carry any diseases that we know about, but, man, do they *suck!* Actually, these tiny midges, or no-see-ums, bite. Hard. They breed in wet, sandy areas and are only fought by the wind (or a well-screened room).

Don't scratch those bites! If you do, you'll not only have massive red bumps on your skin, but it will itch for days, even in the middle of the night, and you risk infection. For prevention, any thick oil is usually enough of a barrier—most people like baby oil or hempseed oil, and some swear that a hint of lavender scent in the oil keeps sand flies away too.

Scorpions, Spiders, and Snakes

Scorpions are common in Belize, especially in dark corners, at beaches, and in piles of wood. Belizean scorpions look nasty—black and big—but their stings are no more harmful than that of a bee and are described by some as what a cigarette burn feels like. Your lips and tongue may feel a little numb, but the venom is nothing compared to that of their smaller, translucent cousins in Mexico. Needless to say, to people who are prone to anaphylactic shock, it can be a more serious or life-threatening experience. Everyone has heard that when in a rainforest, never put on your shoes without checking the insides—good advice—and always give your clothes a good visual going-over and a vigorous shake before putting them on. Scorpions occasionally drop out of thatched ceilings.

Don't worry; despite the prevalence of all kinds of arachnids, including big, hairy tarantulas, spiders do not aggressively seek out people to bite and do way more good than harm by eating things like Chagas bugs. If you'd rather the spiders didn't share your personal space, shake out your bedclothes before going to sleep and check your shoes before putting your feet in them.

Of the 59 species of snakes that have been identified in Belize, at least nine are venomous, most notably the fer-de-lance (locally called a "Tommy Goff"), considered the most dangerous snake in Central America, and the coral snake. The chances of the average visitor being bitten are slim. Reportedly, most snakebite victims are children. However, if you plan on extensive rainforest exploration, check with your doctor before you leave home. Antivenin is available, doesn't require refrigeration, and keeps indefinitely. It's also wise to be prepared for an allergic reaction to the antivenin—bring an antihistamine and epinephrine. The most important thing to remember if bitten: *Don't panic and don't run.* Physical exertion and panic cause the venom to travel through your body much faster. Lie down and stay calm; have someone carry you to a doctor. Do not cut the wound, use a tourniquet, or ingest alcoholic beverages.

Marine Hazards

Anemones and sea urchins live in Belize waters. Some can be dangerous if touched or stepped on, so always look where you are placing your foot when entering shallow water. The long-spined black sea urchin can inflict great pain, and its poison can cause an uncomfortable infection. Don't think that you're safe in a wetsuit, booties, and gloves. The spines easily slip through the rubber, and the urchin is encountered at all depths. If you should run into one of the spines, remove it quickly and carefully, disinfect the wound, and apply antibiotic cream. If you have difficulty removing the spine, or if it breaks, see a doctor—pronto! Local remedies include urinating on the wound if nothing else is available.

Tiny brown gel-encased globules called *pica-pica* produce a horrible rash; look for clouds of these guys around any coral patch before getting in. Avoid the bottom side of a moon jellyfish, as well as the Portuguese man-of-war (usually only in March). Sea wasps are tiny four-tentacled menaces that deliver a sting. In addition, many varieties of fire coral will make you wish you hadn't. Cuts from coral, even if just a scratch, will often become infected. If you should get a deep cut, or if bits of coral are left in the wound, see a doctor.

MEDICAL CARE

Although there are hospitals and health clinics in most urban areas and towns, care is extremely limited compared with more developed countries. Serious injuries or illness may require evacuation to another country, and you should consider picking up cheap travel insurance that covers such a need—otherwise, you're looking at US$12,000 just for the medevac transportation.

Many Belizean doctors and hospitals require immediate cash payment for health services, sometimes prior to providing treatment. Uninsured travelers or travelers whose insurance does not provide coverage in Belize may face extreme difficulties if serious medical treatment is needed. **International Medical Group** (www.imglobal.com) is one reliable provider that offers short-term insurance specifically for overseas travelers and expats for very reasonable rates. Another is **World Nomads** (www.worldnomads.com).

Belize Medical Associates (5791 St. Thomas St., tel. 501/223-0302, www.belizemedical.com) is the only private hospital in Belize City. They provide 24-hour assistance and a wide range of specialties. Look under "Hospitals" in the BTL yellow pages for an updated listing of other options. In Santa Elena, **La Loma Luz Hospital** (tel. 501/824-2087 or 501/804-2985, www.lalomaluz.org) offers primary care as well as 24-hour emergency services and is one of the best private hospitals in the country.

First-Aid Kit

At the very minimum, consider the following items for your first-aid kit: rehydration salts, sterile bandages or gauze, moleskin for blister prevention, antiseptic cream, strong sunblock (SPF 30), aloe gel, some kind of general antibiotic for intestinal trouble, acetaminophen (Tylenol) for pain and fevers, eye drops (for dust), and antifungal cream (clotrimazole).

Medications and Prescriptions

Many medications are available in pharmacies in Belize. Definitely plan on the conservative side: Bring adequate supplies of all your prescribed medications in their original containers, clearly labeled and in date; in addition, carry a signed, dated letter from your physician describing all medical conditions and listing your medications, including their generic names. If carrying syringes or needles, carry a physician's letter documenting their medical necessity. Pack all medications in your carry-on bag and, if possible, put a duplicate supply in the checked luggage. If you wear glasses or contacts, bring an extra pair. If you have significant allergies or chronic medical problems, wear a medical alert bracelet.

Female travelers taking contraceptives should know the generic name for the drug they use. Condoms are cheap and easy to find, but be sure to buy the highest quality you can find. Any corner pharmacy will have them, even in small towns of just a few thousand people.

CRIME

Most of the crime in Belize (besides drug possession and trafficking) is petty theft and burglary, although gang-related violence and robberies at gunpoint in Belize City and parts of Ambergris Caye are a worsening problem. It's best not to wear expensive jewelry when traveling. And don't carry large amounts of money, your passport, or your plane tickets if not necessary; if you must carry these things, wear a money belt under your clothes. Most hotels have safe-deposit boxes. Don't flaunt cameras and video equipment or leave them in sight in cars when sightseeing, especially in some parts of Belize City. This is a poor country, and theft is its number-one crime.

It is not wise at all to wander around alone on foot late at night in Belize City or anywhere. Go out with others if possible, and take a taxi. Most Belizeans are friendly, decent people; however, as in every community, there are a small percentage of unscrupulous thieves who will steal anything given the opportunity. To many Belizeans, foreigners come off as "rich," whether they are or not. Local hustlers are quite creative when it comes to conning you out of some cash. Keep your wits about you, pull out of conversations that appear headed in that direction, and don't give out your hotel name or room number or mention them where they can be overheard by strangers. If you're riding a bike at night, don't put your bag in the basket in plain sight or hide your cash and valuables on your person.

In emergencies, dial **911** or **90** for police assistance. The number for fire and ambulance is also 90.

Police

If you are the victim of a crime while overseas, in addition to reporting it to local police, contact your embassy or consulate as soon as possible. The embassy or consulate staff can assist you in finding appropriate medical care and contacting family members or friends, and will explain how funds can be transferred to you. Although the investigation and prosecution of the crime is solely the responsibility of local authorities, consular officers can help you to understand the local criminal justice process and to find an attorney if needed. Belize police detectives and tourism police respond quickly and take these matters—even near misses—seriously.

Belizean police can hold somebody for 48 hours with no charges (one U.S. embassy warden called prison conditions in Belize "medieval," though this situation is improving). Some police officers have been arrested for rape and routinely beat and torture detainees (usually Belizeans). On the whole, though, most officers are good folks, making the best of a poorly paid job with very few resources. Don't try to bribe them if you're in trouble—you'll only contribute to a more corrupt system that does not need any encouragement.

Drugs

Belize's modern history began with lawbreaking pirates hiding out among the hundreds of cayes, lagoons, and uninhabited coastlines of the territory. The same natural features have made Belize a fueling stopover for Colombian cocaine traffickers. The drug runners' practice of paying off their Belizean helpers with product (in addition to sums of cash) has created a national market for cocaine and crack with devastating effects, especially in Orange Walk Town and numerous coastal communities.

The U.S. Drug Enforcement Agency (DEA) is active in Belize—as it is throughout Central America—to battle the flow of cocaine and other illegal drugs; the agency provides boat patrols, overflights, drug war technology and herbicides, and sniffing dogs at roadside checkpoints.

Cannabis sativa grows naturally in the soils and climate of Belize, although the country is no longer the major producer it once was. In the early 1980s, the DEA put an end to that with chemical-spraying programs, seizing and destroying 800 tons of marijuana in one year. Today, small-scale production continues, primarily for the domestic market. Some argue that the job vacuum created by marijuana suppression led directly to Belize's role in the trafficking of cocaine and the subsequent entrance of crack into Belizean communities.

Foreign travelers will most likely be offered pot (locally known as "ta-boom-boom") at some point during a visit. Legally, marijuana prohibition is alive and well in Belize, despite widespread use throughout the population. The policy allows harsh penalties for possession of even tiny quantities for both nationals and visitors alike.

Prostitution

Although illegal in Belize, prostitution is alive and well at a handful of brothels throughout the country (usually on the highways outside major towns). Prostitutes are rarely Belizean and are often indentured sex slaves unwittingly recruited from Honduras, Guatemala, or El Salvador with false promises of legitimate employment.

Travel Tips

CONDUCT AND CUSTOMS

Cameras can be a help or hindrance when trying to get to know the locals. When traveling in the backcountry, you'll run into folks who don't want their pictures taken. Keep your camera put away until the right moment. *Always* ask permission first, and if someone doesn't want his or her picture taken, accept the refusal with a gracious smile and move on. Especially sensitive to this are Mennonites and Maya, who often specifically request that you not take their photos. Many Internet cafés have readers for your digital camera card, so you can make backups as you go. To be safe, travel with extra cards, readers, and cables.

WHAT TO PACK

Pack for hot weather (80-95°F, both humid and dry), as well as the occasional cool fronts (60-80°F), which have become more frequent. At least one pair of pants and a light shell jacket are recommended, as the rainy season can push all the way into February, and it's guaranteed to be damp June through November. Long sleeves are helpful for avoiding mosquito bites and sunburn. Cayo and the Mountain Pine Ridge can drop to sweater weather in any part of the wet season and even in December. Bring a small first-aid kit, a flashlight or headlamp, and waterproof plastic bags for protection during rain or boat travel.

MONEY

The currency unit is the Belize dollar (BZD), which has been steady at BZD$2 to US$1 for some years. While prices are given in U.S. dollars in this book, travelers should be prepared to pay in Belizean currency on the street, aboard boats, in cafés, and at other smaller establishments. Everyone else accepts U.S. dollars.

When you buy or sell currency at a bank, be sure to retain proof of sale. The following places are authorized to buy or sell foreign currency: Atlantic Bank, Scotiabank, Barclays Bank, Belize Bank of Commerce and Industry, and Belize Global Travel Services. All are close together near the plaza in Belize City and in other cities. Most banks are open until 1pm Monday-Friday. You can also change money, sometimes at a rate a bit better than 2:1, at *casas de cambio.* But because *casas de cambio* must charge the official rate, many people still go to the black market, which gives a better rate.

At the Mexico-Belize border, you'll be approached by money changers (and you can bet they don't represent the banks). Many travelers buy just enough Belizean dollars to get themselves into the city and to the banks. Depending on your mode of transportation and destination, these money changers can be helpful. Strictly speaking, though, this is illegal—so suit yourself. The exchange rate is the same, but you'll have no receipt of sale. If selling a large quantity of Belizean dollars back to the bank, you might be asked for that proof.

Banks

Many banks are only open until 1pm or 2pm Monday-Thursday (staying open a bit later on Friday) and are often closed for lunch. Banks are always closed Saturday afternoon and Sunday. Automated teller machines (ATMs) are available in nearly all major Belizean towns, but they may operate on different card networks (Plus, Cirrus, etc.). You may have to try a few to get your card to work; it's best to check before traveling. They're also often out of cash, particularly close to the weekends or major holidays.

Costs

Make no mistake: Belize vies with Costa Rica for being the most expensive country in Central America, and backpackers entering Belize from Mexico, Guatemala, and

Honduras can expect some serious sticker shock after crossing the border. This was true even before the advent of tourism because of the import-reliant economy and whatever other invisible market hands guide such things. Shoestring travelers squeaking by on US$25-50 per person per day in Belize are most likely stone sober and eating street tacos three times a day; they are not paying for tours or taxis, and they are surely not diving in the Blue Hole. They can still have a grand old time, though, camped out in the bush (or in a US$10 room), doing lots of self-guided hiking, paddling, and cultural exploring. It's possible to travel on this little—but it depends on your comfort zone and definition of a good time.

If you've only got a seven-day vacation, figure at least US$100 per person per day if you want to pay for day trips and don't want to share a bath; serious divers or anglers should add a bit more. Weeklong packages at many dive and rainforest resorts run US$1,000-1,600 and go up from there.

There are usually low-budget, decent-quality exceptions to the rule across Belize, and I've tried to point all of those out in each region. In general, though, prices are high and getting higher. Many mid- and upscale accommodations have raised their rates by as much as 20 percent—and not all have increased the quality of their service to match. Alcohol is always a good indicator: A bottle of One Barrel Rum is peaking at US$12 in most stores; a six-pack of Belikin beer can go for US$16.

Be prepared for some additional taxes and service charges on your bill, which sometimes are and sometimes are not included in quoted rates:

- General sales tax (GST): 10 percent
- Hotel tax: 9 percent
- Service charge (often placed on bill): 10-15 percent
- Airport departure tax: US$20

If you use your credit card, it will cost you a little more at most businesses, sometimes an extra 3-5 percent of the bill.

Tipping

Most restaurants and hotels include a 10-15 percent service charge on the bill; if they don't, you should pay this amount yourself. It is not customary to tip taxi drivers unless they help you with your luggage. Always tip your tour guide 10-15 percent if he or she has made your trip an enjoyable one.

COMMUNICATIONS
Shipping and Postal Service

Posting a letter or postcard is easy and cheap, costing well under US$1, and the stamps are gorgeous. If you visit the outlying cities or cayes, bring your mail to Belize City to post—it's more apt to get to its destination quickly. Post offices are located in the center of (or nearby) all villages and cities in Belize, although they usually don't look too post-officey from the outside. You can receive mail in any town without getting a P.O. box—just have the mail addressed to your name, care of "General Delivery," followed by the town, district, and "Belize."

FedEx, DHL, and other international couriers are widely available, and the **Mailboxes, Etc.** in Belize City (on Front St., just up from the Ocean Ferry Water Taxi Terminal) can take care of most of your mailing and package needs. Sending mail within Belize, you can either use the post office system or hand your package to a bus driver or go through the bus station office.

Cell Phones

Some car rental companies offer a free cell phone; always ask. If not, they'll rent you one. Otherwise, **DigiCell** (www.digicell.bz) offers prepaid temporary service to travelers. Get it at BTL's Airport Service Center, or bring your own GSM 1900 MHz handset and purchase a SIM pack from any DigiCell distributor nationwide. There are several local cellular services, both analog and digital, and coverage along roadways and in major towns is decent but still improving. You'll need your passport or ID with you when visiting a BTL store to purchase a SIM card—by law all cell numbers must now be registered.

Smart Phones (Mile 2.5, Philip Goldson Hwy., Belize City, tel. 501/678-1010, www.smart-bz.com) is more user-friendly and cheaper than BTL and the rest, offering roaming service on your CDMA 800 MHz phone from home (including Verizon and Sprint). The activation fee is US$20, then you use prepaid cards available throughout the country.

International Calls

To call out of Belize, find a phone with international direct dialing service, then dial the international access code **00,** followed by your country code, and then the city or area code and the number. The country code for Canada and the United States is 1, Britain is 44, and Australia is 61. BTL's telephone directory has a complete listing of country codes. An (often cheaper) alternative is to dial 10-10-199 instead of 00, followed by the country code, etc. Although they are not toll-free from Belize, 800 numbers are dialed as they are written, preceded by the 00.

Belize's country code is **501.** To receive a call in Belize from the United States, for example, tell the caller to dial 011 to tap into the international network, followed by 501 and your seven digit number. To call collect to Belize from other countries, dial the MCI operator at U.S. tel. 800/265-5328.

Public Telephones

Buy a prepaid phone card from **Belize Telecommunications Limited** (BTL, www.btl.net) and punch in the card's numbers every time you borrow a phone or use a pay phone. All towns also have a local BTL office, usually identified by a giant red-and-white radio tower somewhere very nearby; they can place calls anywhere in the country or the world for you and will assign you to a semiprivate booth after they've dialed the number. They can also connect you to your homeland phone carrier. Note: According to one BTL employee,

credit-card calls made through hotel phones are expensive because the touch-tone "international operator" charges US$16 per minute.

VoIP Services

Skype and VoIP (voice over Internet protocol) are finally available in Belize, unrestricted and—believe it or not—only a recent development. Free VoIP services (like Skype) offer dirt-cheap rates on international calls and are getting better to use by the day. Prior to 2013, BTL blocked full and open access to VoIP-based services and applications. You can now use Skype freely wherever you get free Wi-Fi access and save on international calls.

Internet Access

Web access is widely available throughout the country and is improving all the time. Crappy dial-up connections are now the exception rather than the norm, and broadband (DSL, cable, and satellite) is springing up everywhere. If you're in town for a while, many Internet businesses have monthly memberships that include unlimited access. You are welcome to sign up for a BTL account if you don't have your own ISP (Internet service provider), but that may lead to more headaches than you need, and there are many other options.

Wireless Internet (Wi-Fi) access is increasingly available in Belize's accommodations, bars, and restaurants. I won't go so far as to tell you to expect wireless access yet—particularly on the cayes, where service can be sporadic at best—but if it's a concern, definitely inquire whether your hotel has it or not. Most of these connections are free—with the exception of BTL Hotspots, which are US$16 per 24-hour period (plus tax!), and it's your only option at a handful of upscale hotels, including the Radisson and the Inn at Robert's Grove.

Newspapers and Magazines

Four weekly, highly politicized Belizean newspapers come out on Friday, with occasional midweek editions, and you'll find many a

Belizean conducting the weekly ritual of reading his or her favorite over a cup of instant coffee, and then going to happy hour to yap away about the latest scandal. *Amandala* and the *Reporter* seem to be the most objective and respected of these rags. The other two are the *Belize Times* and the *Guardian*. There are also publications in San Pedro and Placencia.

The **Image Factory** (91 N. Front St., tel. 501/223-4093, imagefactory95@gmail.com, www.imagefactorybelize.com, 9am-5pm Mon.-Fri., 9am-noon Sat.) in Belize City is a good place for books and periodicals, and there are only a couple of other bookshops in the country. In most hotel gift shops, you'll find at least a few colorful Belizean history and picture books put out by Cubola Productions, a local publisher specializing in all things Belize, including maps, atlases, short stories, novels, and poems written by Belizeans. Cubola's publications give great insight into the country.

You will not find the *International Herald Tribune* on every newsstand like in other destinations. In fact, you probably won't find it at all. Check with the Radisson Hotel or Fort Street Guest House in Belize City, where you can sometimes find the *Miami Herald,* a relatively recent *Newsweek,* or if you're lucky, the *New York Times* or the *Times* of London. **Brodie's** (Albert St.) and **The Book Center** (North Front St.) also carry American magazines.

WEIGHTS AND MEASURES

The local time is Greenwich Mean Time minus six hours year-round, the same as U.S. central standard time; Belize does not use daylight saving time. Electricity is the U.S. standard 110 volts, 60 cycles, and uses U.S. two-prong plugs. Most distances are measured in inches, feet, yards, and miles, although there is some limited use of the metric system.

Time

As in many other Central American and Caribbean cultures, "Belizean time" is not as rigidly precise as it is in other parts of the world. "Nine o'clock a.m." is not necessarily a moment in time that occurs once a morning, as it is a general guideline that could extend an hour or two in either direction (usually later). Creoles say, "Time longa den da roop, mon" ("time is longer than the rope"), which means the same as the Spanish "*Hay mas tiempo que vida*" ("there is more time than there is life")—both of which boil down to the unofficial motto of Caye Caulker: "Go slow!"

A great deal of patience is required of the traveler who wishes to adapt to this looser concept of time. Buses generally leave when they are scheduled, but may stop for frustratingly long breaks during the journey. Don't use Belizean time as an excuse to be late for your tour bus pickup, and don't get angry when your taxi driver or server stops to briefly chat and laugh with a friend.

OPPORTUNITIES FOR STUDY AND EMPLOYMENT

There are many opportunities for volun-tourists to get their feet wet in the world of international development and resource conservation work throughout Belize. Some of the regional chapters listed throughout this book offer local volunteer opportunities or ways to help the community. For those interested in spending some time lending a hand, sharing their expertise, or supporting community efforts, there's plenty to choose from. Some of these programs cost money and some don't; be sure you know exactly what you're getting into when you sign up. Also, be clear on what kind of work your position will entail, as well as your host organization's expectations and Belizean legal requirements. Speaking of which, Belizean immigration officially requires long-term volunteers to apply for special visas, a process that takes months and is not cheap. Some NGOs get around this (for short-term assignments, anyway) by calling their volunteers "interns."

The **Belize Audubon Society** (BAS, 16

N. Park St., Belize City, tel. 501/223-5004, www.belizeaudubon.org) accepts qualified volunteers and interns for a variety of land and marine projects, with a three-month minimum (less for marine projects). Past skilled BAS volunteers have worked in community education; helped create trail signs, brochures, and management guidelines for protected areas and wardens; and analyzed the effectiveness of BAS gift shops. **Habitat for Humanity Belize** (tel. 501/223-2929), a world leader in providing low-income housing, operates in Belize City and beyond and accepts qualified volunteers and church groups to help erect home projects.

The **Belize Botanic Gardens** (tel. 501/671-3322, www.belizebotanic.org) sponsors a program where volunteers pay US$550 for room and board while working on various garden projects.

The **Cornerstone Foundation** (tel. 501/667-0210, www.cornerstone foundationbelize.org) is a humanitarian NGO, based in the Cayo District, whose volunteer opportunities include HIV/AIDS education and awareness, special education, adult literacy, working with youth or women, and teaching business skills.

Field Research and Educational Travel

Belize shines in this category. There are many opportunities to learn, teach, and volunteer at **The Belize Zoo and Tropical Education Center** (tel. 501/822-8000, www.belizezoo. org). The **Oceanic Society** (U.S. tel. 800/326-7491, www.oceanic-society.org), a nonprofit conservation organization, maintains a field station in the Turneffe Islands Atoll and invites curious travelers to participate in educational marine ecotourism activities, such as snorkel and kayak programs to learn about coral reef ecology and whale shark research projects (about US$2,000 includes everything for eight-day trips). The family program includes interaction with Belizean and American researchers.

Belize's nonprofit **TIDE** offers a conservation expeditions program called **Ridge to Reef Expeditions** (tel. 501/722-2129, www.fromridgetoreef.com, US$1,390 for a week for individual placement), whereby paying volunteers receive training and experience in real-world conservation on land and sea. Team expeditions (eight weeks) or individual placements of a week or more are available. Activities include scuba diving surveys of coral reef health, patrolling turtle-nesting beaches, teaching at children's summer camps, and hunting invasive lionfish.

Get involved with **ACES/American Crocodile Education Sanctuary** (tel. 501/623-7920, www.american crocodilesanctuary.org), a nonprofit conservation organization licensed by the Belize Forest Department to protect Belize's critical habitats and protected species, especially crocodilians, through scientific research and education. Anyone wishing to learn, observe, or help biologist Cherie Chenot-Rose collect data and conduct research is welcome, including students; 100 percent of their donations and proceeds go to croc care, croc rescues, research, and education.

Volunteer opportunities are also available at **Wildtracks** (www.wildtracksbelize. org), which hosts both Belize's Manatee Rehabilitation Centre and Primate Rehabilitation Centre, in partnership with the Belize Forest Department. Volunteer placements are normally for one month or more, and volunteers need to apply in advance through Global Nomadic or Global Vision International.

The St. George's Caye Research Station and Field School was founded in 2009 by **ECOMAR** (tel. 501/223-3022, www.ecomarbelize.org), which hosts archaeology students and also high school teachers and university professors interested in bringing their students to study marine ecosystems in the area. Other groups stay on St. George's Caye to participate in the Coral Watch Program and learn how to identify coral bleaching.

In the Toledo District, the **Belize**

Foundation for Research and Environmental Education (BFREE, tel. 501/671-1299, www.bfreebz.org) offers student programs from one week to a whole semester, with lots of activities and cultural immersion programs available. BFREE has spearheaded amphibian research and monitoring in the Maya Mountains as a participant in the Maya Forest Anuran Monitoring Project, among other things.

There is a huge array of research and educational programs at **Monkey Bay Wildlife Sanctuary** (tel. 501/820-3032, www.monkeybaybelize.com), which specializes in groups and classes.

Programme for Belize (1 Eyre St., Belize City, tel. 501/227-5616 or 501/227-1020, www.pfbelize.org) is the group that manages the 260,000-acre Río Bravo Conservation Area and has a full menu of ecology and rainforest workshops.

Two miles upriver from the village of San Pedro Columbia, in southern Belize, the **Maya Mountain Research Farm** (www.mmrfbz.org) is a registered NGO and working demonstration farm that promotes sustainable agriculture, appropriate technology, and food security using permacultural principles and applied biodiversity, and it offers hands-on coursework in all of the above.

Maya Study and Archaeological Field Work

For Mayaphiles and archaeology students, the **Belize Valley Archaeology Reconnaissance Project** (BVAR, bvararchaeology@gmail.com, www.bvar.org) conducts research and offers field schools at several sites in western Belize. The **Maya Research Program** (U.S. tel. 817/831-9011, www.mayaresearchprogram.org) has been running every summer from June to August since 1992 and offers two-week-long archaeological fieldwork—including lab techniques. Its Blue Creek project is open to all ages, both students and nonstudents, regardless of experience.

U.S. Peace Corps

The **Peace Corps** (www.peacecorps.gov) is a U.S. government program created by John F. Kennedy in 1961 whose original goal was to improve the image of the United States in the developing world by sending volunteers deep into the countryside of these countries. Fifty years later, some 8,000 volunteers are serving in more than 70 countries around the world. Accepted participants serve a two-year tour preceded by three months of intensive language and cultural training in the host country; they receive a bare-bones living allowance and earn a nominal "readjustment allowance" at the completion of their service.

The first group of Peace Corps volunteers arrived in Belize in 1962. Since that time, more than 1,700 volunteers have worked in Belize in a variety of projects. Currently, there are about 70 volunteers providing assistance in education, youth development, rural community development, environmental education, and HIV/AIDS prevention. Pre-service training is conducted in rural Creole and mestizo villages and includes Spanish, Q'eqchi', and Garifuna language classes, depending on where the volunteer is being sent. Volunteers are placed throughout the country's six districts to work with government agencies and NGOs.

Galen University

Galen University (tel. 501/824-3226, www.galen.edu.bz), based in the Cayo District, offers a Semester Study Abroad program (tuition, room, board, transportation, and field-trip fees US$10,065) of 15 credit hours, accredited through the University of Indianapolis. Students get to immerse in Belizean life and engage in community service, field trips, and regular classes of their choice, taught by local and international faculty members. Summer Abroad courses are also available from June through July, with options such as animal science, land-ocean interface, protected areas practicum, and forensic anthropology.

Gettin' Hitched and Honeymoonin'

Belize's reputation for romance is growing, and an increasing number of resorts cater to exotic weddings and honeymoon packages, including ceremonies conducted underwater, atop Mayan pyramids, or in caves. (Actually, I don't think anyone's been married in a cave yet, but someone's bound to do it.) Most couples, however, are quite content with a barefoot beach ceremony.

For a US$50 marriage license, the couple must arrive in Belize three business days before submitting marriage paperwork to the Registrar General's office on the fourth business day. A rush job costs US$250 and allows you to obtain your marriage license before arriving in Belize, in which case you can get married on your first day in country, if you so wish. For this service, you'll need a travel agent or wedding planner to act on your behalf in Belize.

The **Registrar General of Belize** (tel. 501/227-2053, www.belizelaw.org) handles marriage licenses. You'll need to show proof of your citizenship (i.e., a valid passport), proof that you're over 18, and, where applicable, a certified copy of a divorce certificate or death decree to annul a previous marriage. Forms can be obtained at two locations: the General Registry, Supreme Court Building, Belize City, and the Solicitor General's Office, East Block Building, Belmopan. No blood test is required.

A few select Belize wedding specialists can help you facilitate the paperwork, find ministers, and handle your party's flowers, accommodations, receptions, and everything else. Contact **Belize Weddings** (www.belizeweddings.com) in San Pedro or **Lee Nyhus** (www.secretgardenplacencia.com) in Placencia.

ACCESS FOR TRAVELERS WITH DISABILITIES

There are probably about as many wheelchair ramps in all of Belize as there are traffic lights (less than 10); disabled travelers will generally be treated with respect, but expect logistics to be challenging in places. **Pelican Beach Resort** (tel. 501/522-2044, www.pelicanbeachbelize.com) in Dangriga has built new ground-floor suites with ramp access, including to the shower. **Hok'ol K'in Guest House** (in Corozal, tel. 501/422-3329, www.corozal.net) has nice wheelchair-accessible suites and facilities. For more help, consult the Belize travel specialists listed earlier in this chapter.

TRAVELING WITH CHILDREN

Children love Belize, and Belizeans love children: It's very much a family-oriented society. While a select few romantic resorts do not allow children, most do. Any place offering a special "family package" is a place to start your research. Always check in advance and tell the staff the ages of your children. You'll find most resorts are quite experienced at dealing with all ages.

For babies, be prepared with your own travel kit, but don't stress it too much if you forget something. There is a modern selection of jarred food, diapers, bottles, formula, and the like at Brodie's supermarkets in Belize City. If you're short on jars, or if baby wants more than breast milk, you'll find enough fresh fruit and fish to keep your baby growing the whole time you're in Belize. A few resorts can provide a crib in your room if you want one, but make sure you verify this in advance; otherwise bring your own fold-up contraption, which can be great for the beach too, especially since you can easily drape a mosquito net over the top.

Once in Belize, a visit to the zoo is a must. There are a few kid-friendly cave trips, and, of course, scrambling on the pyramids at any of the archaeological sites is heaven for young explorers. Just be extra careful about covering them up with loose, long clothing against the sun and mosquitoes, and make sure they stay hydrated while they rage through the rainforest. Also, during the rainy season, it's best to steer clear of river activities like cave tubing, since rivers can be unpredictable when they swell with rain.

WOMEN TRAVELING ALONE

For the independent woman, Belize is a great place for group or solo travel. Its size makes it easy to get around, English is spoken everywhere, and if you so desire, you won't be lacking for a temporary travel partner in any part of the country. You'll meet many fellow travelers at the small inexpensive inns and guesthouses. Belizeans are used to seeing all combinations of travelers; solo women are no exception.

That said, sexual harassment of females traveling alone or in small groups can be a problem, although most incidents are limited to no more than a few catcalls. Just keep on walking; I've found that usually, some minor acknowledgment that you have heard them will shut harassers up more quickly than totally ignoring them. If they persist and follow to talk to you, tell them you're "on a mission" (i.e., rushing to your next stop); don't feel obligated to stop and respond. Although violent sexual assault is not a common occurrence, it does happen (like anywhere in the world). Several American travelers were the victims of sexual assaults in recent years. At least one of these rapes occurred after the victim accepted a ride from a new acquaintance, while another occurred during an armed robbery at an isolated resort. Never give the name of your hotel or your room number to someone you don't know.

Wearing revealing clothes *will* attract lots of gawking attention, possibly more than you want. Most of the small towns and villages are safe even at night, with the exception of Belize City—don't walk anywhere there at night, even with friends.

Useful Numbers

- Belize Coast Guard: 501/222-5262
- Belize Port Authority: 501/232-9440
- Belize Tourism Police Unit: 501/227-1440
- Date, Time, and Temperature: 121
- Directory Assistance: 113 or 115
- Diver's Alert Network: 001-919/490-2011
- Hyperbaric Chambers: 501/226-2851 or 501/226-3195, and 501/226-2660 (Ambergris Hope Clinic)
- Operator Assistance: 114 or 115
- Police, Fire, Ambulance: 90 or 911
- To Report Child Abuse: 0/800-776-8328
- To Report Crimes: 0/800-922-8477

SENIOR TRAVELERS

Active seniors enjoy Belize. Some like the tranquility of the cayes, others the birdwatching in the Mayan ruins. Many come to learn about the rainforest and its creatures or about archaeology. **Road Scholar** (formerly Elderhostel, U.S. tel. 800/454-5768, www.roadscholar.org) has a number of tours to Belize, including dolphin and reef ecology projects.

GAY AND LESBIAN TRAVELERS

Although there are plenty of out-and-about gay Belizean men (in Kriol, "batty-men" is a pejorative term), particularly in San Pedro, there is no established community or any gay clubs, per se. The foreign gay travelers we've seen were totally accepted by both their fellow lodge guests and Belizean hosts. Still, the act of "sodomy" (between men) is officially illegal in Belize, so a bit of discretion is advised.

Tourist Information

TOURIST OFFICES

The **Belize Tourism Board** (BTB, 64 Regent St., tel. 501/227-2420, U.S. tel. 800/624-0686, info@travelbelize.org, www.travelbelize.org) has a central office in Belize City, near the Mopan Hotel. The **Belize Tourism Industry Association** (10 N. Park St., Belize City, tel. 501/227-1144, www.btia.org) can also answer many of your questions and give you lodging suggestions. The **Belize Hotel Association** (BHA, 13 Cork St., Belize City, tel. 501/223-0669, www.belizehotels.org) is a nonprofit industry organization of some of the country's most respected resorts and lodges. The BHA can help you decide where to stay.

You'll find more information at the **Embassy of Belize** (2535 Massachusetts Ave. NW, Washington DC 20008, U.S. tel. 202/332-9636, www.embassyofbelize.org) in the United States and also the **Caribbean Tourism Association** (80 Broad St., Ste. 3302, New York, NY 10004, U.S. tel. 212/635-9530, www.onecaribbean.org).

MAPS

The most readily available and up-to-date map of Belize is published by International Travel Maps, whose 1:250,000 map of Belize makes a useful addition to any guidebook (or wall). The best and biggest country map to hang on your wall at home, or in your classroom (it's way too big to use as a travel guide), is a physical-political 1:265,000 scale, distributed by Cubola Productions and available at Angelus Press in Belize City for US$40. All of Belize's most heavily touristed areas create updated town maps, found most often at visitor information booths and car (or golf cart) rental places.

The **Government of Belize Land Department** in Belmopan has detailed topographic maps for the entire country—spendy at US$40 per quad, but vital if you're doing any serious backcountry travel. The British army and United Kingdom Ordinance Survey have created a number of map series of various scales, but tracking them down will be a challenge.

Resources

Phrasebook

KRIOL

I was once told that you're only a true Belizean if you speak Kriol. It's the first thing you'll hear when you arrive in Belize—the accent, the intonation, and the sentences that chop away at articles and verbs. Kriol, or Creole, is the lingua franca here. Like most patois tongues in the Caribbean, it has its roots in the days when the enslaved workers in mahogany camps were exposed to English and mixed it with their own West African dialects, hence the choppy grammar and the borrowed English words. Over time, efforts were made to ensure that Kriol was properly studied, written, and recorded as a language, thanks to the National Kriol Council, created in 1995 to promote all aspects of the Creole culture. Keeping this language going has been their goal, as a way of instilling a sense of identity and cultural pride in its people. It's now spoken and understood by almost all Belizeans, even non-Creoles, and knowing a couple of phrases is a great way to immerse and break the ice.

Basic Phrases

Gud maanin! Good morning!
Weh gaan an? What's up?
Aarite. All right.
Cho! What on earth!
Weh yuh naym? What's your name?
You da Belize? Are you from Belize?
Weh gaan ahn gyal? What's up, girl?
Da weh time? What time is it?
Mi naym da . . . My name is . . .
Lata! See you later.
Ah tayad/mi tayad. I'm tired.
Weh/weh-paat . . . Where is . . . ?
Evryting gud/aarite. Everything's fine.
Haul your rass! Get the hell out of here!
Fu chroo? Really? (Is that right?)
Mi love Bileez! I love Belize!

Sayings

Wahnti wahnti kyah geti an geti geti nuh wahnti. You always want what you can't have.
Dah no so, dah naily so. Where there's smoke, there's fire.
Wait bruk down bridge. Don't make me wait too long.
Sleep wit' yo' own eye. Only rely on what you know, not what others tell you.
One one craboo fill barrel. Every little bit counts (craboo is a Belizean fruit).
Ah wah know who seh Kriol noh gat no kulcha? Who said the Creole don't have any culture? (A phrase coined by renowned Belizean Creole artist and performer Leela Vernon).

GARIFUNA

A mix of Arawak, Carib, traces of West African dialects, French, and Spanish, the Garifuna language is being spoken less and less by the younger generation and isn't taught in Belize's school system. But it's hard to believe that this is a dying tongue after spending time in the south and hearing Garinagu addressing each other in their language every day. When I took the bus from Hopkins to Dangriga, and even walking around the village and town, there was no Kriol and no English exchanged, just Garifuna. If you're feeling brave, you too can practice and use these phrases to break the ice.

Basic Phrases
Mabuiga! Welcome!
Buiti binafi. Good morning.
Buiti rabounweyu. Good afternoon.
Buiti guñoun. Good night.
Ida bian? How are you?
Magadientina. I'm fine.
Seremein. Thank you.
Ka biri? What is your name?
...niri bai My name is...
Uwati megeiti. You are welcome.
Ka fidu ínwirúbei? What's up?

Q'EQCHI' MAYAN
Most of southern Belize's people of indigenous descent speak Q'eqchi' Mayan—though some communities speak the Mopan language instead, which is more closely related to Yucatec Mayan or Itzá Mayan.

In Belize, you may see the word *Q'eqchi'* spelled different ways. "Kekchi" is how Protestant missionaries labeled the Maya of southern Belize, and British colonial officials wrote "Ketchi." Today, in neighboring Guatemala, the indigenous leaders of the Guatemalan Academy of Maya Languages (ALMG) have developed a standard Mayan transliteration that the Q'eqchi' leaders in Belize have begun to use as well.

Making even a small attempt to speak and learn the language of your Mayan hosts will deepen your experience. Never mind the laughs your funny accent will attract—your noble attempts are an amusing novelty, and no one means any harm. Persist, and you will be rewarded in ways you would never have expected—indeed, learning another language in such an immersive setting is one of the most humbling and empowering experiences a traveler can have.

Should you want to learn more than the few words presented here, track down the grammar book and cassette tapes by Q'eqchi' linguist Rigoberto Baq, available in Guatemala City at the Academia de Lenguas Mayas (www.almg.org.gt) or at their regional offices in Coban, Alta Verapaz (in the municipal palace), or Poptán, Petén.

Greetings
All Q'eqchi' words are stressed on the last syllable. One of the first things you will probably be asked is, *"B'ar xat chalk chaq?"* (bar shaht chalk chok), to which you can respond, *"Xin chalk chaq sa' New York"* (sheen chalk chok sah New York, or wherever you are from).

In Q'eqchi', there are no words for "good morning," "good afternoon," or "good evening." You simply use the standard greeting, *"Ma sa sa' laa ch'ool"* (mah sah sah lah ch'ohl), literally, "Is there happiness in your heart?" (In Q'eqchi', however, you wouldn't use a question mark because the "Ma" indicates a question.) A proper response would be *"Sa in ch'ool"* (sah een ch'ohl), "Yes, my heart is happy."

Although it is falling out of custom with the younger generation, if you are speaking with an older woman or man, she or he would be delighted to be greeted with the terms of respect for the elderly: *Nachin* (nah cheen) for an elder woman, and *Wachin* (kwah cheen) for an elder man.

If you decide to go swimming in one of Toledo's beautiful rivers, you might want to first ask, *Ma wan li ahin sa' li nima* (mah kwan lee aheen sa le neemah), which means "Are there crocodiles in the river?"

"Ani laa kab'a?" (anee lah kabah) means "What's your name?" You can respond: *"Ix [woman's name] in kab'a"* (eesh ... een kabah) or *"Laj [man's name] in kab'a"* (lahj ... een kabah).

Basic Phrases
Chan xaawil? (chan shaa kwil) What's up?
Jo xaqa'in (hoe shakaeen) Not much; just fine.

B'an usilal **(ban ooseelal)** Please.

B'antiox **(ban teeosh)** or *T'ho-kre* **(ta HOH cree)** Thank you.

Us **(oos)** Good.

Yib'i ru **(yeeb ee rue)** Bad; ugly.

Hehe **(eheh)** Yes.

Ink'a **(eenk'ah)** No.

K'aru? **(kaieeroo)** What?

B'ar? **(bar)** Where?

Joq'e? **(hoekay)** When?

Jarub?' **(hahrueb)** How many?

Jonimal tzaq? **(hoeneemahl ssahq)** How much does it cost?

Chaawil aawib **(chah kwil aakweeb)** Take care of yourself [a good way to say good-bye].

Jowan chik **(hoek wan cheek)** See you later.

wi chik **(kwee cheek)** again

wa **(kwah)** tortilla

kenq **(kenk)** beans

molb' **(mohlb)** eggs

kaxlan wa **(kashlan kwah)** bread

tib' **(cheeb)** meat

tzilan **(sseeelan)** chicken

kuy **(kue-ee)** pork, pig

kar **(car)** fish

chin **(cheen)** orange

kakaw **(cacao)** chocolate

ha' **(hah)** water

woqxinb'il ha' **(kwohk sheen bill hah)** boiled water

cape **(kahpay)** coffee

sulul **(suelul)** mud

ab' **(ahb)** hammock

chaat **(chaht)** bed

nima' **(neemah)** river

kokal **(kohkahl)** children

chaab'il **(chahbill)** good

kaw **(kauw)** hard

najt **(nahjt)** far

nach **(nahch)** close

Special thanks to Clark University anthropologist Liza Grandia, who spent four years among the Maya.

Suggested Reading

Start with Belizean writers, particularly the novels of Zee Edgell, and then continue with the catalog of **Cubola Productions** (www.cubola.com), a publishing company whose Belizean writers series includes six anthologies of short stories, poetry, drama, folktales, and works by women writers. Cubola also publishes sociology, anthropology, and education texts; seek them out at any bookstore or gift shop in Belize, or order a few titles before your trip. **Angelus Press** is the other main publisher of Belizean writers. There is a large Angelus Press store in Belize City, as well as in other districts. You'll also want to read a book—or six—by **Emory King;** King arrived in Belize in 1953 when his yacht crashed on the reef at English Caye and has been talking and writing about his adopted country ever since.

ARCHAEOLOGY AND MAYAN CULTURE

Carrasco, David. *Religions of Mesoamerica: Cosmovision and Ceremonial Centers.* San Francisco: Waveland Press, 1998. Carrasco details the dynamics of two important cultures—the Aztec and the Maya—and discusses the impact of the Spanish conquest and the continuity of native traditions.

Coe, Michael D. *The Maya,* 8th ed. New York: Thames and Hudson, 2011. This updated classic, which has been in print for nearly 50 years, attempts to understand the "most intellectually sophisticated and aesthetically refined pre-Columbian culture." This edition has information on new discoveries, including the polychrome murals of Calakmul and evidence of Pre-Classic sophistication.

Coe, an archaeologist, anthropologist, epigrapher, and author, is a forefather of Mayan studies. This book is mandatory reading for both amateur Mayanists and pros.

De Landa, Friar Diego. *Yucatán: Before and After the Conquest*. New York: Dover Publications, 1978 (translation of original manuscript written in 1566). The same man who provided some of the best, most lasting descriptions of the ancient Maya also single-handedly destroyed the most Mayan artifacts and writings of anyone in history.

González, Gaspar Pedro. *13 B'aktun: Mayan Visions of 2012 and Beyond*. Berkeley, CA: North Atlantic Books, 2010. González is a Q'anjobal Mayan novelist, philosopher, and scholar from Guatemala. This book, translated to English by Dr. Robert Sitler, is unlike any other you'll read on the subject. It is written as a deep, lyrical dialogue—not just about 2012, but about all of creation, blending "past and present thought into a persuasive plan for moving into the new era."

Jenkins, John Major. *The 2012 Story: The Myths, Fallacies, and Truth Behind the Most Intriguing Date in History*. New York: Jeremy P. Tarcher, 2009. Jenkins is one of the most prolific, passionate 2012-ologists out there. *The 2012 Story* is his most all-encompassing book yet, covering the entire story—from the ancients' forward-reaching stone inscriptions to the modern-day 2012 meme and a summary of his and others' work on the subject.

Sitler, Robert. *The Living Maya: Ancient Wisdom in the Era of 2012*. Berkeley, CA: North Atlantic Books, 2010. This book begins with the Yucatec Maya greeting *"Bix a bel?,"* which means, "How is your road?" And that's right where the author puts us—on the road in the Guatemalan highlands and southern Mexico. Robert Sitler is a professor at Stetson University in DeLand, Florida. In

The Living Maya, he draws lessons from his four decades studying Mayan culture and traveling in the Mundo Maya. The most important messages we can take from the Maya, he writes, are: "Cherish our babies, connect with our communities, revere the natural world that sustains us, seek the wisdom of humanity's elders, and immerse ourselves in direct experience of this divine world."

Stephens, John L. *Incidents of Travel in Central America, Chiapas and Yucatán*. New York: Dover Publications, 1969 (originally New York: Harper & Bros., 1841). In this classic 19th-century travelogue, Stephens's writing is wonderfully pompous, amusing, and incredibly astute—with historical and archaeological observations that still stand today. If you can, find a copy with the original set of illustrations by Stephens's expedition partner.

FICTION

Edgell, Zee. *Beka Lamb*. Portsmouth, NH: Heinemann, 1982. The first internationally recognized Belizean novel, this story of a girl named Beka who is growing up with her country is required reading for all Belizean high schoolers and offers an excellent view of Belizean family life, history, and politics.

Lukowiak, Ken. *Marijuana Time*. London: Orion, 2000. Follow the author's experiences on a six-month "hardship posting" to Belize in 1983 with the British military: "The long days are palliated by a constant and increasingly compulsive supply of drugs and japes, until he starts using his position in the army post-room to send improbably large bundles of the stuff home—to his army flat in Aldershot."

Miller, Carlos Ledson. *Belize: A Novel*. Bloomington, IN: Xlibris, 1999. This history-laden piece of fiction offers an impressively thorough snapshot of Belize over the last 40 years.

Westlake, Donald. *High Adventure*. New York: Mysterious Press, 1986. Another marijuana-smuggling action thriller: "You are in the jungles of Belize. You pick your way carefully along the overgrown trail until you come to the clearing. There, above you, rest the ruins of a Mayan pyramid. Is that a stone whistle at your feet? An idol of the bat-god? Riches surround you and Kirby Galway will be more than happy to smuggle your finds to the United States in a bale of marijuana. Aren't you glad you met Kirby?"

HEALTH

Arvigo, Rosita. *Sastun: One Woman's Apprenticeship with a Maya Healer and Their Efforts to Save the Vani*. San Francisco: Harper, 1995. One of the better-known books about Belize, this tells the story of the American-born author's training with Elijio Panti, the best-known Mayan medicine man in Central America. It takes place in the remote, roadless expanse of the Cayo District in western Belize.

Bezruchka, Stephen. *The Pocket Doctor: A Passport to Healthy Travel*. Seattle: Mountaineers Books, 1999.

Schroeder, Dirk G. *Staying Healthy in Asia, Africa, and Latin America*. Emeryville, CA: Avalon Travel, 2000. Although out of print, if you can find it this is an excellent resource that fits in your pocket for easy reference.

Werner, David. *Where There Is No Doctor*. Berkeley, CA: Hesperian Foundation, 1992. A standard in the field.

HISTORY

Shoman, Assad. *13 Chapters of a History of Belize*. Belize City: Angelus Press, 1994. A no-nonsense history of Belize from a Belizean perspective.

Sutherland, Anne. *The Making of Belize: Globalization in the Margins*. London: Bergin & Garvey, 1998. This book deserves to be read by any visitor to Belize, whether arriving as a tourist or as a volunteer with one of the many international conservation organizations now operating there.

Wilk, Richard. *Home Cooking in the Global Village: Caribbean Food from Buccaneers to Ecotourists*. New York: Palgrave Macmillan, 2006. Using food to describe Belize's longtime struggle within "the great paradox of globalization," Wilk raises questions like "How can you stay local and relish your own home cooking, while tasting the delights of the global marketplace?" Includes menus, recipes, and "bad colonial poetry."

NATURE AND FIELD GUIDES

As Belize is one of the most exhaustively studied tropical countries in the world, there are innumerable references that span every conceivable niche of flora, fauna, and geology. They come in massive coffee-table sizes with color plates as well as in pocket-size field guides: *Tarantulas of Belize, Hummingbirds of Belize, Orchids of Belize*, and so on. Following are a few titles that make up the tip of the iceberg for this category.

Arvigo, Rosita, and Michael Balick (foreword by Mickey Hart). *Rainforest Remedies: 100 Healing Herbs of Belize*. Twin Lakes, WI: Lotus Press, 1998. A reliable and respected guide to medicinal plants found in Belize and herbal remedies of Mayan healers.

Beletsky, Les. *Belize and Northern Guatemala: The Ecotravellers' Wildlife Guide*. San Diego, CA: Academic Press, 1999. One of the best reasonably sized general nature guides to the area, with abundant color plates for all types of fauna.

Chalif, Edward L., and Roger Tory Peterson. *Peterson Field Guide to Mexican Birds*. New York: Houghton Mifflin Harcourt, 1999.

This is one of the best birder bibles for this region.

Dunn, Jon L., and Jonathan Alderfer. *National Geographic Field Guide to the Birds of North America*. Washington, DC: National Geographic, 2006. A gorgeous field guide worth lugging into the rainforest.

Jones, H. Lee, and Dana Gardner, illustrator. *Birds of Belize*. Austin: University of Texas Press, 2003. This is the long-awaited, much-acclaimed bible of Belize birding (say *that* three times fast); it's a big book (445 pages, 56 color plates, 28 figures, 234 maps), prompting some birders I met to cut out all the plates and travel with those only.

Sayers, Brendan, and Brett Adams. *Guide to the Orchids of Belize*. Benque Viejo del Carmen, Belize: Cubola Productions, 2009. This is an excellent field guide to the many orchids found throughout Belize.

Stevens, Katie. *Jungle Walk: Birds and Beasts of Belize, Central America*. Belize City: Angelus Press, 1991. Order through International Expeditions, U.S. tel. 800/633-4734.

PHOTOGRAPHY

Jovaisa, Marius. *Heavenly Belize*. Lithuania: Unseen Pictures, 2009 (www.heavenlybelize.com). This is a magnificent coffee-table tome of aerial photography. The Lithuanian author is an ultralight aircraft pilot who wanted to share the extraordinary vistas he had discovered. If you don't pick it up in Belize, download the iPad version from iTunes, with more multimedia features than just the book.

Rath, Tony. *Images of Belize*. Belize: Cubola Productions, 2015. This minibook by Belize's most renowned photographer makes for a great take-home gift or souvenir, filled with stunning images showcasing the beauty of the country's great outdoors and its diverse people. Rath shares key facts about the country throughout the book to "unveil the special relationship between people and their environment." Rath just released a second book in the series with images of Ambergris Caye.

TRAVEL AND MEMOIR

Barcott, Bruce. *The Last Flight of the Scarlet Macaw: One Woman's Fight to Save the World's Most Beautiful Bird*. New York: Random House, 2008. Fantastic nonfiction narrative about the Chalillo Dam in western Belize, a highly contentious construction project on the upper Macal River in Cayo. The author skillfully lays out the story and characters around the dam business, while providing a sweeping panoramic snapshot of a unique country as it makes its debut in the new global economy.

Bolland, O. Nigel. *Belize: A New Nation in Central America*. Boulder, CO: Westview, 1986. This book is one of many sociopolitical analyses by this prolific author.

Duffy, Rosaleen. *A Trip Too Far: Ecotourism, Politics and Exploitation*. Sterling, VA: Earthscan, 2002. A critical look at the impacts of ecotourism, using Belize as a case study.

Fry, Joan. *How to Cook a Tapir: A Memoir of Belize*. Lincoln, NE: University of Nebraska Press, 2009. The story of a young teacher's year abroad, living among the Maya in southern Belize in 1962. The author offers an intimate glimpse at Mayan village life in this heartfelt, oftentimes funny story of how she "painstakingly baked and boiled her way up the food chain" to gain acceptance among her neighbors and students.

Pattullo, Polly. *Last Resorts: The Cost of Tourism in the Caribbean,* 2nd edition. London: Latin America Bureau, 2005. Pattullo provides an interesting breakdown of how the Caribbean tourism industry is structured, as well as a hard-hitting commentary on who benefits and how, providing numerous examples from Belize.

Rabinowitz, Alan. *Jaguar: One Man's Struggle to Establish the World's First Jaguar Preserve.* Washington, DC: Island Press/ Shearwater Books, 2000 (originally 1986). If you've only got time to read one book on Belize, I recommend this excellent eco-memoir. In addition to telling the true story of his jaguar work in Belize, Rabinowitz gives an alluring glance at Belize's wild postindependence, pre-tourism phase.

Suggested Films

There are many excellent short films on Belize, on both the natural world and cultural issues. Look up Richard and Carol Foster's *Path of the Rain Gods* and Channel 5's *The Sea of Belize* and *The Land of Belize.* Then tune in to www.trphoto.blip.tv, which has some gorgeous educational shorts on Belize; these would be excellent for families to watch together before or after their trip to Belize.

Curse of the Xtabai, by Make-Belize Films (www.makebelizefilms.com). If you're into drama and fiction, check out U.S. producer Matthiew Klinck's first feature film. The story revolves around an evil spirit, Xtabai, unleashed onto the population of a Mayan village after an oil company blows open a sealed Mayan cave in San Antonio. What ensues is an attempt to save the villagers from an epidemic of deadly fevers, through sacred tasks as dictated by a Mayan elder.

Punta Soul, produced and directed by Nyasha Laing (www.parandamedia.com). This 2008 documentary film by a Belizean tells the story of Garifuna music as it evolved with the Garinagu's journey from the Caribbean islands to Central America. Laing addresses how the rhythms continue to influence the cultural revival of the ethnic communities in Belize. Buy the DVD at the Image Factory in Belize City.

Three Kings of Belize, by Katia Paradis. This 2007 film is a beautiful, poignant tribute to Belizean musicians Paul Nabor, Wilfred Peters, and Florencio Mess, who represent Garifuna, Creole, and Mayan music traditions, respectively. Though their music is internationally recognized, they live humble lives in Belizean villages. The film moves at the slow, relaxed pace of Belize itself. To find a copy, go to the Image Factory in Belize City or contact Stonetree Records (www.stonetreerecords.com).

Internet Resources

Ambergris Today
www.ambergristoday.com
Ambergris Caye's online news and travel publication, run by a dynamic Belizean team, with reviews on the latest and greatest hotels, restaurants, and activities across the island.

Belize Audubon Society
www.belizeaudubon.org
Belize Audubon manages a number of national parks and protected areas throughout the country and is the place to go for basic info

on visiting them. It also has background information on birding and checklists.

The Belize Forums
www.belizeforum.com/belize
This is one of the more popular forums, frequented by many prolific and colorful Belize-aholics.

Belize Search
www.belizesearch.com
The premier search engine for all things Belize, with access to 250,000 Belizean web pages and documents (and growing).

Belize Tourism Board
www.travelbelize.org
The official BTB website is helpful for quick background information, for anyone planning a trip.

Caye Caulker Vacation
www.cayecaulkervacation.com
The official site of the Belize Tourism Industry Association's Caye Caulker chapter is filled with information on where to stay and how to best spend your time on the island with the best sunsets in Belize, just a 20-minute boat ride from San Pedro.

Destination Belize
www.destinationbelize.com
The online version of the print magazine, *Destination Belize,* provides a summary on each main tourist destination in the country and a shortlist of things to do and see.

Government of Belize
www.belize.gov.bz
The official page of the federal government, an informative portal to the country.

San Pedro Sun
www.sanpedrosun.com
Belizean news and links from this island newspaper.

United States Embassy in Belize
https://bz.usembassy.gov
Official site of the U.S. Embassy in Belize.

Index

List of Maps

Acknowledgments

I want to express my sincere gratitude to all the wonderful friends and contacts in Belize who continue to offer their support and assistance with my work for *Moon Belize*. Your willingness to share expert insights on the country, whether in tourism, fishing, diving, culture, wildlife, or conservation, among other areas, is beyond appreciated. It continues to make me a better Belize writer, traveler, and person.

These wonderful folks include Eve Acevedo in Belize City, Stacy and Gina Badillo on Caye Caulker, Patricia Ramirez and Ralph Capeling in Placencia, Therese and Tony Rath in Dangriga, and all who have taught me about Garifuna culture, including the Cayetano and Sabal families, among others. Orange Walk wouldn't be the same without the insider tips from residents Orlando and Cindy de la Fuente, Talia Tillett, John Burgos and Senator Osmany Salas.

I am grateful to the hard-working business owners, guides, and conservationists who make Belize's tourism industry what it is, and are ready and willing to assist me at any time—Bruno Kuppinger, Leisa Caceres-Carr, Amanda Burgos-Acosta, Wendy Casasola, Ana Pereiro Ico, Tanya Silva, Dennis Garbutt, and Claudia Koe, among many others.

I would be remiss not to mention some of the wonderful folks who reached out to me ahead of my trip with some excellent suggestions, including Yoshinori Wakabayashi who was stationed in Crooked Tree Village with the Japan International Cooperation Agency, and Stephanie Patterson, one of my avid *Moon Belize* readers who fell in love with Belize on her first visit.

Last but not least, a huge thanks to my better half for supporting me when I'm away from home researching, and to my awesome team at Avalon Travel—Grace Fujimoto, Kimberly Ehart, Kristi Mitsuda, Darren Alessi, Kat Bennett, and the rest of the team.

Moon Travel Guides to
the Caribbean

ARUBA

BAHAMAS

BERMUDA

CUBA
CHRISTOPHER P. BAKER

DOMINICAN
REPUBLIC

JAMAICA

Central & South America Travel Guides

BELIZE

CARTAGENA
& COLOMBIA'S
CARIBBEAN COAST

COSTA RICA

ECUADOR
& THE GALÁPAGOS ISLANDS

TRIP OF A LIFETIME
GALÁPAGOS
ISLANDS

TRIP OF A LIFETIME
MACHU
PICCHU

TRIP OF A LIFETIME
PATAGONIA

PERU
RYAN DUBE

MAP SYMBOLS

▬▬▬	Expressway	✪	Highlight	✈	Airport	⛳	Golf Course
▭▭▭	Primary Road	○	City/Town	✈	Airfield	🅿	Parking Area
▭▭▭	Secondary Road	◉	State Capital	▲	Mountain	⛩	Archaeological Site
┄┄┄	Unpaved Road	⊛	National Capital	✦	Unique Natural Feature	⛪	Church
------	Trail	★	Point of Interest			⛽	Gas Station
············	Ferry	•	Accommodation	⇲	Waterfall	🐟	Dive Site
✕✕✕✕	Railroad	▼	Restaurant/Bar	▲	Park	🗺	Mangrove
▬▬▬	Pedestrian Walkway	■	Other Location	☐	Trailhead	🗺	Reef
▥▥▥	Stairs	Λ	Campground	☗	Lighthouse	🗺	Swamp

CONVERSION TABLES

°C = (°F - 32) / 1.8
°F = (°C x 1.8) + 32
1 inch = 2.54 centimeters (cm)
1 foot = 0.304 meters (m)
1 yard = 0.914 meters
1 mile = 1.6093 kilometers (km)
1 km = 0.6214 miles
1 fathom = 1.8288 m
1 chain = 20.1168 m
1 furlong = 201.168 m
1 acre = 0.4047 hectares
1 sq km = 100 hectares
1 sq mile = 2.59 square km
1 ounce = 28.35 grams
1 pound = 0.4536 kilograms
1 short ton = 0.90718 metric ton
1 short ton = 2,000 pounds
1 long ton = 1.016 metric tons
1 long ton = 2,240 pounds
1 metric ton = 1,000 kilograms
1 quart = 0.94635 liters
1 US gallon = 3.7854 liters
1 Imperial gallon = 4.5459 liters
1 nautical mile = 1.852 km

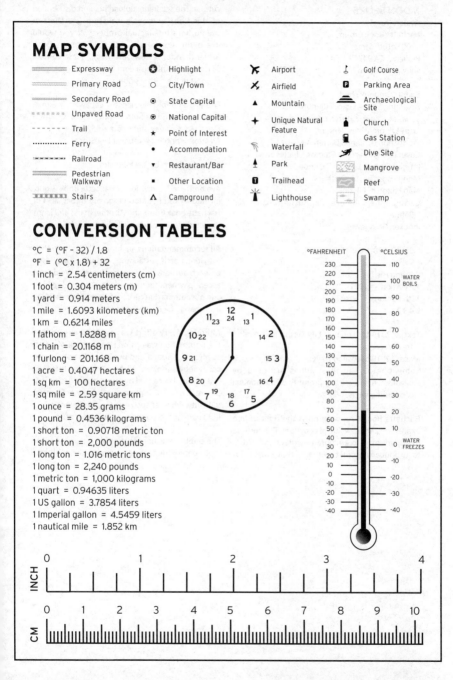

MOON BELIZE

Avalon Travel
Hachette Book Group
1700 Fourth Street
Berkeley, CA 94710, USA
www.moon.com

Editor: Kimberly Ehart
Acquiring Editor: Grace Fujimoto
Series Manager: Kathryn Ettinger
Copy Editor: Ashley Benning
Production Designer: Darren Alessi
Cover Design: Faceout Studios, Charles Brock
Interior Design: Domini Dragoone
Moon Logo: Tim McGrath
Map Editor: Kat Bennett
Cartographers: Karin Dahl, Austin Erhardt, Kat Bennett
Indexer: Greg Jewett

ISBN-13: 978-1-64049-042-0

Printing History
1st Edition — 1991
13th Edition — October 2019
5 4 3 2 1

Front cover photo: Rio Blanco © Lebawit Lily Girma
Back cover photo: South Water Caye © Simon Dannhauer | Dreamstime.com
All interior photos: © Lebawit Lily Girma

Printed in China by RR Donnelley

Avalon Travel is a division of Hachette Book Group, Inc. Moon and the Moon logo are trademarks of Hachette Book Group, Inc. All other marks and logos depicted are the property of the original owners.